Macworld® AppleWorks® 6 Bible

Steven A. Schwartz and Dennis R. Cohen

IDG
BOOKS
WORLDWIDE

IDG Books Worldwide, Inc.
An International Data Group Company

Foster City, CA ✦ Chicago, IL ✦ Indianapolis, IN ✦ New York, NY

Macworld® AppleWorks® 6 Bible

Published by
IDG Books Worldwide, Inc.
An International Data Group Company
919 E. Hillsdale Blvd., Suite 400
Foster City, CA 94404
www.idgbooks.com (IDG Books Worldwide Web site)

ISBN: 0-7645-3434-3

Printed in the United States of America

10 9 8 7 6 5 4 3 2 1

1B/RS/QZ/QQ/FC

Distributed in the United States by IDG Books Worldwide, Inc.

Distributed by CDG Books Canada Inc. for Canada; by Transworld Publishers Limited in the United Kingdom; by IDG Norge Books for Norway; by IDG Sweden Books for Sweden; by IDG Books Australia Publishing Corporation Pty. Ltd. for Australia and New Zealand; by TransQuest Publishers Pte Ltd. for Singapore, Malaysia, Thailand, Indonesia, and Hong Kong; by Gotop Information Inc. for Taiwan; by ICG Muse, Inc. for Japan; by Intersoft for South Africa; by Eyrolles for France; by International Thomson Publishing for Germany, Austria, and Switzerland; by Distribuidora Cuspide for Argentina; by LR International for Brazil; by Galileo Libros for Chile; by Ediciones ZETA S.C.R. Ltda. for Peru; by WS Computer Publishing Corporation, Inc., for the Philippines; by Contemporanea de Ediciones for Venezuela; by Express Computer Distributors for the Caribbean and West Indies; by Micronesia Media Distributor, Inc. for Micronesia; by Chips Computadoras S.A. de C.V. for Mexico; by Editorial Norma de Panama S.A. for Panama; by American Bookshops for Finland.

For general information on IDG Books Worldwide's books in the U.S., please call our Consumer Customer Service department at 800-762-2974. For reseller information, including discounts and premium sales, please call our Reseller Customer Service department at 800-434-3422.

For information on where to purchase IDG Books Worldwide's books outside the U.S., please contact our International Sales department at 317-572-3993 or fax 317-572-4002.

For consumer information on foreign language translations, please contact our Customer Service department at 800-434-3422, fax 317-572-4002, or e-mail rights@idgbooks.com.

For information on licensing foreign or domestic rights, please phone +1-650-653-7098.

For sales inquiries and special prices for bulk quantities, please contact our Order Services department at 800-434-3422 or write to the address above.

For information on using IDG Books Worldwide's books in the classroom or for ordering examination copies, please contact our Educational Sales department at 800-434-2086 or fax 317-572-4005.

For press review copies, author interviews, or other publicity information, please contact our Public Relations department at 650-653-7000 or fax 650-653-7500.

For authorization to photocopy items for corporate, personal, or educational use, please contact Copyright Clearance Center, 222 Rosewood Drive, Danvers, MA 01923, or fax 978-750-4470.

Library of Congress Cataloging-in-Publication Data

Schwartz, Steven A.
   Macworld AppleWorks 6 bible / Steven A. Schwartz and Dennis R. Cohen.
      p. cm
   ISBN 0-7645-3434-3 (alk. paper)
   1. Apple computer--Programming. 2. AppleWorks.
I. Cohen, Dennis R. II. Title.
QA76.8.A66 S45   2000
005.265--dc21   00-059736

ABOUT IDG BOOKS WORLDWIDE

Welcome to the world of IDG Books Worldwide.

IDG Books Worldwide, Inc., is a subsidiary of International Data Group, the world's largest publisher of computer-related information and the leading global provider of information services on information technology. IDG was founded more than 30 years ago by Patrick J. McGovern and now employs more than 9,000 people worldwide. IDG publishes more than 290 computer publications in over 75 countries. More than 90 million people read one or more IDG publications each month.

Launched in 1990, IDG Books Worldwide is today the #1 publisher of best-selling computer books in the United States. We are proud to have received eight awards from the Computer Press Association in recognition of editorial excellence and three from Computer Currents' First Annual Readers' Choice Awards. Our best-selling *...For Dummies®* series has more than 50 million copies in print with translations in 31 languages. IDG Books Worldwide, through a joint venture with IDG's Hi-Tech Beijing, became the first U.S. publisher to publish a computer book in the People's Republic of China. In record time, IDG Books Worldwide has become the first choice for millions of readers around the world who want to learn how to better manage their businesses.

Our mission is simple: Every one of our books is designed to bring extra value and skill-building instructions to the reader. Our books are written by experts who understand and care about our readers. The knowledge base of our editorial staff comes from years of experience in publishing, education, and journalism — experience we use to produce books to carry us into the new millennium. In short, we care about books, so we attract the best people. We devote special attention to details such as audience, interior design, use of icons, and illustrations. And because we use an efficient process of authoring, editing, and desktop publishing our books electronically, we can spend more time ensuring superior content and less time on the technicalities of making books.

You can count on our commitment to deliver high-quality books at competitive prices on topics you want to read about. At IDG Books Worldwide, we continue in the IDG tradition of delivering quality for more than 30 years. You'll find no better book on a subject than one from IDG Books Worldwide.

John J. Kilcullen
John Kilcullen
Chairman and CEO
IDG Books Worldwide, Inc.

Eighth Annual
Computer Press
Awards ≥1992

Ninth Annual
Computer Press
Awards ≥1993

Tenth Annual
Computer Press
Awards ≥1994

Eleventh Annual
Computer Press
Awards ≥1995

Credits

Acquisitions Editor
Michael Roney

Project Editor
Colleen Dowling

Technical Editors
Sally Neuman
Eileen Steele

Copy Editors
Sally Neuman
Michael D. Welch

Proof Editor
Patsy Owens

Project Coordinators
Danette Nurse
Joe Shines

Graphics and Production Specialists
Robert Bihlmayer
Darren Cutlip
Jude Levinson
Michael Lewis
Victor Pérez-Varela
Ramses Ramirez

Quality Control Technician
Dina F Quan

Book Designer
Drew R. Moore

Illustrators
Brian Drumm
Gabriele McCann

Proofreading and Indexing
York Production Services

Cover Illustration
Murder by Design

About the Authors

Dr. Steven A. Schwartz has been a computer-industry writer for 20 years and has written more than 40 books about popular business software, the Internet, and games. Formerly a technical support director and magazine editor, Steven is an expert at explaining computer techniques in a simple, straightforward manner. He currently writes for *Macworld* magazine and *PC World Online*.

Dennis R. Cohen has been a software developer, technical editor, and computer industry writer since the mid-70s. During his tenure at Claris, he worked on many of the company's products at various times, including both the U.S. and Japanese versions of ClarisWorks (now known as AppleWorks). He also coauthored *AppleWorks 6 For Dummies*.

To the dedicated AppleWorks users of the world.

—Steven A. Schwartz

To my family, friends, and especially my Boston Terrier—Spenser—who give me the support and encouragement to keep active.

—Dennis R. Cohen

Preface

The *Macworld AppleWorks 6 Bible* is a different kind of computer book. First, it's not a manual. Many people don't like computer manuals — perhaps because they feel obligated to read a manual from cover to cover, or perhaps because manuals are designed to explain how features work rather than how to make a program work for you. The *Macworld AppleWorks 6 Bible* is not a book you have to read. It's a book you'll *want* to read — because it provides easy-to-find, easy-to-understand explanations of many common tasks for which you bought AppleWorks in the first place. When you want to know how to use a particular program feature, you can use the table of contents or the index to identify the section of the book you need to read.

Second, unlike many computer books, this one is task-oriented. Most people don't buy computer books because they want to become experts with a particular piece of software. Instead, most people have a task they want to accomplish. In addition to the step-by-step explanations of normal AppleWorks procedures, the book also provides many worked-through task examples. Rather than spend your time reinventing the wheel, you can simply follow the numbered steps to accomplish many common business- and home-computing tasks.

Finally, the philosophy of this book — as well as the other books in the Macworld Bible series — is that you don't want or need a handful of books on a computer program; one should suffice. The *Macworld AppleWorks 6 Bible* is an all-in-one book. Rarely will you be referred to your manual or AppleWorks Help. You can find almost anything you want to know about AppleWorks in this book.

What Is AppleWorks?

AppleWorks belongs to a class of programs known as integrated software. The idea behind integrated software is that, within a single box, you acquire a core set of programs that fulfill all your basic computing needs. The typical program components, or *modules*, are word processing, spreadsheet, database, and various types of graphics. And the modules function together as a cohesive unit — more or less. We say "more or less" because the early integrated software packages (as well as most of the current ones) were often only a collection of programs. The programs frequently had little in common beyond being in the same box. Often you had no way to share data among the modules, or the command structures in the different modules had significant differences. As a result, learning how to use one module may have taught you nothing about using the other modules.

As a class of software, integrated software was viewed with disdain by computing purists for several reasons. The modules were often stripped down to bare-bones programs in order to squeeze the entire package into a reasonable amount of memory or disk space. Big-time features — such as a spelling checker, thesaurus, character and paragraph styles, and advanced searching and sorting — were routinely missing. Thus, many users felt (rightfully so) that the integrated modules couldn't hold a candle to full-featured, standalone programs.

Microsoft Works was the first major integrated package for the Macintosh. The Mac's native support for cutting and pasting made it relatively easy to merge data from different types of documents, enabling you to paste a graphic into a word processing file, for example. Although integration was considerably better than in the early programs, each Works module was essentially a standalone tool. To create a new spreadsheet for an annual report, you had to work in both the spreadsheet and word processor modules and then cut and paste the spreadsheet into the final document.

Why Choose AppleWorks?

AppleWorks has carried the integration concept forward to the next logical step. AppleWorks has separate components, but you can use features of the different components no matter what type of document you're currently working on. For example, although a word processing document is primarily composed of words, you can add a spreadsheet section to the document simply by selecting the spreadsheet tool and then drawing a frame, as shown in Figure 1.

While you are working in the spreadsheet frame, the menu bar, menu commands, and Button Bar change and become relevant to spreadsheets. If you click any part of the word processing text, the menus and Button Bar become appropriate for word processing. This tight integration among components makes AppleWorks significantly easier and more convenient to use than its competitors. In fact, Apple prefers that the AppleWorks components be referred to as *environments* — rather than modules — to emphasize the high level of integration among the different parts of the program.

AppleWorks has also made great strides toward including the "power features" that have traditionally been absent from integrated programs. For example:

+ The **word processor** includes a spelling checker, thesaurus, and outliner, as well as support for custom text and paragraph styles.

+ The **paint environment** offers gradients, and the **draw environment** has advanced drawing tools.

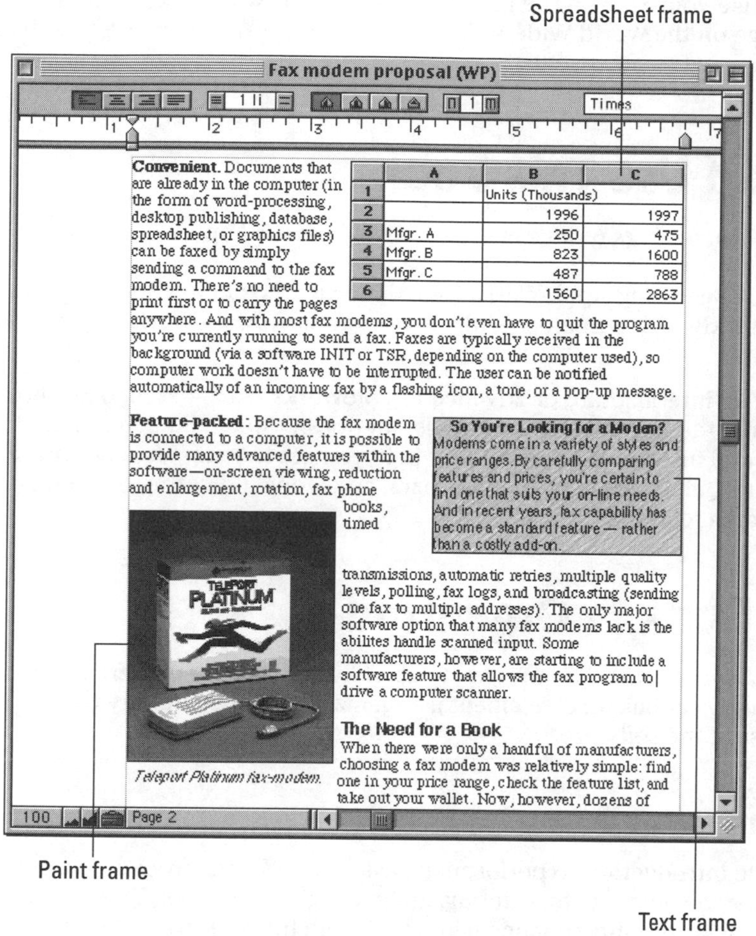

Spreadsheet frame

Fax modem proposal (WP)

Times

Convenient. Documents that are already in the computer (in the form of word-processing, desktop publishing, database, spreadsheet, or graphics files) can be faxed by simply sending a command to the fax modem. There's no need to print first or to carry the pages

	A	B	C
1		Units (Thousands)	
2		1996	1997
3	Mfgr. A	250	475
4	Mfgr. B	823	1600
5	Mfgr. C	487	788
6		1560	2863

anywhere. And with most fax modems, you don't even have to quit the program you're currently running to send a fax. Faxes are typically received in the background (via a software INIT or TSR, depending on the computer used), so computer work doesn't have to be interrupted. The user can be notified automatically of an incoming fax by a flashing icon, a tone, or a pop-up message.

Feature-packed: Because the fax modem is connected to a computer, it is possible to provide many advanced features within the software—on-screen viewing, reduction and enlargement, rotation, fax phone books, timed

So You're Looking for a Modem? Modems come in a variety of styles and price ranges. By carefully comparing features and prices, you're certain to find one that suits your on-line needs. And in recent years, fax capability has become a standard feature — rather than a costly add-on.

transmissions, automatic retries, multiple quality levels, polling, fax logs, and broadcasting (sending one fax to multiple addresses). The only major software option that many fax modems lack is the abilites handle scanned input. Some manufacturers, however, are starting to include a software feature that allows the fax program to drive a computer scanner.

The Need for a Book
When there were only a handful of manufacturers, choosing a fax modem was relatively simple: find one in your price range, check the feature list, and take out your wallet. Now, however, dozens of

Teleport Platinum fax-modem.

100   Page 2

Paint frame

Text frame

Figure 1: A spreadsheet frame within a word processing document

+ The **spreadsheet** includes charts, text wrap within cells, cell shading, and variable row heights and column widths, and it supports multiple fonts per worksheet.

+ The **database** offers calculation, pop-up menu, value list, checkbox, radio button, and multimedia fields. It also enables you to create multiple custom layouts for each database file.

+ The **presentations environment** provides transitions and organizational tools to create professional presentations.

+ The built-in **macro recorder** enables you to automate common or repetitive tasks with ease.

Finally, if you use your Mac on the Internet and have (or would like to have) your own home page on the World Wide Web, you'll find AppleWorks' new and enhanced Internet features extremely useful.

Who Should Use This Book

The *Macworld AppleWorks 6 Bible* is for anyone who uses AppleWorks 6:

✦ If you're a beginning AppleWorks user, detailed steps help you get up to speed quickly with common (and not-so-common) AppleWorks features and procedures.

✦ If you're an intermediate or advanced AppleWorks user — someone who wants only the AppleWorks essentials but doesn't need much hand-holding — the tips and insights in each chapter help you get the most from AppleWorks. You'll find Quick Tips sections, sidebars, and icons indicating the newest AppleWorks features.

How This Book Is Organized

The *Macworld AppleWorks 6 Bible* is made up of five parts, and numerous chapters, appendixes, and sections. Each element is organized in a specific way to help you make the most of the software.

Part I: The Basics

This is a gentle introduction to performing basic AppleWorks procedures, such as opening and saving documents, printing, and managing windows. This part also lists the major features and enhancements that were introduced in the various releases of ClarisWorks and AppleWorks. (ClarisWorks was the product's name until mid-1998.)

Part II: Using the AppleWorks Environments

This part explains the workings of each of the six major AppleWorks components (word processing, spreadsheet, database, draw, paint, and presentations).

Part III: Integrating the AppleWorks Environments

This part offers suggestions and examples for using elements of two or more environments in the same document (generating a mail merge and using spreadsheet frames to create word processing tables, for example).

Part IV: Mastering AppleWorks

This part covers material that helps you make more productive use of AppleWorks. It isn't essential to learn about these features immediately, but you will want to tackle them after you're comfortable with the AppleWorks basics.

Part V: AppleWorks and the Internet

This part discusses using AppleWorks and its Internet integration. Whether you want to create links from your documents to Web sites, develop your own Web pages, or publish your AppleWorks documents on the Web, we cover it here.

Appendixes

This part includes two appendixes to aid you in your work. Appendix A lists the many keyboard shortcuts in AppleWorks. If you're new to using a mouse or don't want to take your hands off the keyboard, you'll want to check out this appendix. Appendix B is a complete reference to the spreadsheet and database functions provided in AppleWorks 6.

Chapter Organization

We've organized each chapter of this book around a major task you're likely to perform in AppleWorks, such as working with the word processor, setting preferences, recording macros, and so on. When you need to perform a particular AppleWorks task, scan the table of contents to locate the chapter that addresses your need.

Each chapter usually contains the following sections:

✦ **In This Chapter** provides a list of topics covered in the chapter.

✦ **Steps** appear throughout each chapter. Each Steps section spells out the specific instructions necessary to accomplish a particular task.

✦ **Quick Tips** give useful tips about additional tasks you can perform in the AppleWorks environment or the subject being discussed. You can also turn to this section for ideas on how to use the features or the environment better.

✦ **Moving On Up** provides you with information on upgrading from an AppleWorks environment to a more advanced program.

✦ The **Summary** lists the main points covered in the chapter. You can turn to the Summary section of any chapter to see whether it contains the information you need at the moment.

Icons Used in This Book

This book uses four icons to highlight important information, new features, and ancillary material that may interest you:

 The New Feature icon marks discussions of features that are found only in AppleWorks 6 and not in earlier versions of the program (ClarisWorks 1.0–5.0/ AppleWorks 5).

 The Note icon identifies information and issues regarding a feature or topic that might be of interest to you.

 The Tip icon offers an insight into the feature or task being discussed, in many cases suggesting better or easier ways to accomplish it.

 The Caution icon warns you about potentially dangerous situations — particularly those in which data may be lost.

How to Use This Book

We won't tell you how to read this book. Reading and learning styles are very personal. When we get a new computer program, we frequently read the manual from cover to cover before even installing the software. Of course, we'd be flattered if you read the *Macworld AppleWorks 6 Bible* the same way, but we'd be surprised.

This book is written as a reference to "all things AppleWorks." When you want to learn about the database environment, there's a specific chapter to which you can turn. If you just need to know how to use the spelling checker, you can flip to the table of contents or the index and find the pages where we discuss the spelling checker. Most procedures are explained in a step-by-step fashion, so you can quickly accomplish even the most complex tasks. You can read this book as you would a Stephen King or Robert Parker novel (with fewer surprises, and less snappy dialog and violence), read just the chapters that interest you, or use the book as a quick reference for when you need to learn about a particular feature or procedure.

For those who prefer a little more direction than "whatever works for you," we've included some guidelines in the following sections — arranged according to your level of AppleWorks experience.

We do have one general suggestion: If at all possible, read this book with AppleWorks onscreen. Sure, you can read about editing a user dictionary for the spelling checker while relaxing in the tub, but — unless you have exceptional recall — what you read will be more meaningful if you're sitting in front of the computer, trying out the task at hand. We want you to get your hands dirty. *Then* you can go sit in the tub.

For the New AppleWorks User

Chapter 1 is a must-read for every AppleWorks user. Many AppleWorks tasks, such as arranging windows and printing, are not specific to any single environment. Rather than discuss them again in each of the environment chapters, we have included these procedures and features only in Chapter 1. In addition, Apple has completely revised the appearance of the product and adjusted the user interface to be ready for the forthcoming MacOS X, resulting in many changes in the way you now accomplish tasks.

From that point on, you should pick an AppleWorks environment — the word processor is a good place to start — and, with book in hand, work through the appropriate chapter in Part II. Each chapter in Part II explains the fundamentals for a single AppleWorks environment. The really advanced stuff is in Part III and Part IV. Although you'll eventually want to check out the material in those parts, too, you'll note that we've purposely separated the advanced matters from the basics to keep new users from being overwhelmed.

Although this book discusses many of the basic concepts and procedures necessary for the beginning user to start working productively with AppleWorks, it is not a substitute for the documentation that came with your Mac. As you work on the desktop and begin experimenting with AppleWorks, you're bound to encounter additional Mac issues. When that happens — and it will — it's time to drag out the manuals for your Macintosh, peripherals (printers, modems, and so on), and system software, and see what you've missed. After you fill in the gaps in your Mac education, you'll feel more confident and comfortable tackling AppleWorks and any other programs you eventually purchase. Apple did not include a user manual with AppleWorks 6, so this book will be a fine resource when the online help just doesn't tell you enough.

For Those Who Have Upgraded from a Previous Version of ClarisWorks or AppleWorks

If you're an experienced ClarisWorks 2.0, 2.1, 3.0, 4.0 or ClarisWorks/AppleWorks 5.0 user, the best place for you to start is Chapter 2. This chapter is a quick guide to the new features you need to learn in AppleWorks 6, and it directs you to the chapters in which the features are discussed.

Before you jump ahead, however, be sure to read through Chapter 1. Some of the basics of using the program have changed drastically, and you need to be familiar with these new procedures and options.

About System Software Versions

AppleWorks 6 is the first version of the product that hasn't made a strong attempt to be usable over a broad range of OS releases and hardware; it requires a PowerPC-based Mac and at least MacOS 8.1 (8.6 or 9.0 are strongly recommended for full functionality).

The majority of the screen shots in this book were created on a Mac running system software 9.0.4. If you are running an older version of system software, your screen may look somewhat different. You should also note that a few features and operations work differently in the different supported OS releases. Where relevant, these differences are described in the text.

Acknowledgments

I am grateful to the many people at IDG Books who worked so hard and offered their support for this new edition of the book. In particular, though, I'd like to thank Dennis Cohen. After years of employing him as a technical editor, I think this promotion to coauthor is *long* overdue. Thanks, Dennis!

—*Steven A. Schwartz*

I would like to thank Steve for requesting I work on this edition. In addition, my thanks go to the very supportive folks at IDG Books with whom I worked on this book—Colleen Dowling, Michael Welch, Mike Roney, and the talented production crew. Also, Sally Neuman and Eileen Steele for their work as technical editors (my job on the previous edition).

—*Dennis R. Cohen*

Contents at a Glance

Contents

Chapter 6: The Draw and Paint Environments 259

Part IV: Mastering AppleWorks   365

The Basics

AppleWorks Essentials

Before you leap into AppleWorks, you need to get some basics under your belt. If you're new to the Mac, you'll find this chapter particularly helpful. Many of the procedures it describes — such as starting the program, opening and saving documents, and printing — are applicable to almost any Mac program. Even if you consider yourself an experienced Mac user, you can benefit from at least skimming through this chapter. You may pick up a time-saving tip or two that improves your productivity with AppleWorks.

Note AppleWorks 6 requires MacOS 8.1 or later to operate and Apple (as well as your authors) strongly recommends MacOS 9 or later. All screen shots and discussion in this book are based on the assumption that you are running MacOS 9. We will, however, note where a MacOS 9 feature of AppleWorks is not available to users of MacOS 8.x (8.1, 8.5.x, or 8.6).

Launching AppleWorks

As with most Macintosh programs, you can launch AppleWorks in several ways. From the desktop (shown in Figure 1-1), you have many methods from which to choose:

✦ Double-click the AppleWorks 6 program icon.

✦ Click the AppleWorks 6 program icon to select it and then choose File ➪ Open (or press ⌘+O).

✦ Drag a document onto the AppleWorks 6 program icon.

✦ Double-click an AppleWorks document.

✦ Single-click an AppleWorks document and select File ➪ Open (or press ⌘+O).

✦ If you have opened AppleWorks recently, choose ✎ ➪ Recent Applications ➪ AppleWorks 6 or the documents in question from the ✎ ➪ Recent Documents submenu. (Note that you must have the Apple Menu Options control panel enabled for this method to work.)

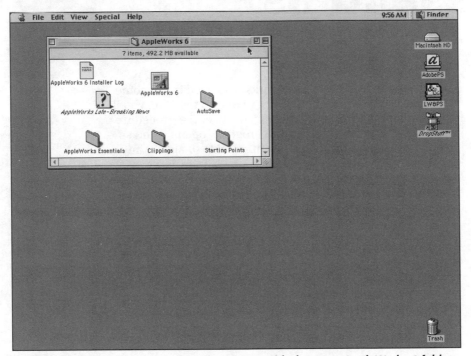

Figure 1-1: The Macintosh desktop for MacOS with the open AppleWorks 6 folder

The desktop shows icons for all mounted disks (both hard disks and floppy disks), the Trash, windows for open drives and folders, and icons for folders, programs, and data files.

Whether you open documents from the desktop or load them from within AppleWorks, you can open as many documents as memory allows.

Tip   You have a number of ways to make AppleWorks available in your Apple menu. The first is to select the AppleWorks 6 program (not folder) icon and choose ✎ ➪ Automated Tasks ➪ Add Alias to Apple Menu (if you have the Automated Tasks folder of AppleScripts in your Apple Menu Items folder). Another method is to add AppleWorks to your Favorites folder. You can accomplish this by selecting the AppleWorks 6 program icon and choosing File ➪ Add to Favorites, or by control-clicking the AppleWorks 6 program icon and choosing Add to Favorites from the contextual menu that appears.

Introducing the AppleWorks Desktop

AppleWorks provides many visual tools that enable you to use thumbnails and other pictures to invoke the multitude of commands in its six components. Figure 1-2 shows the desktop that greets you the first time you open a new document.

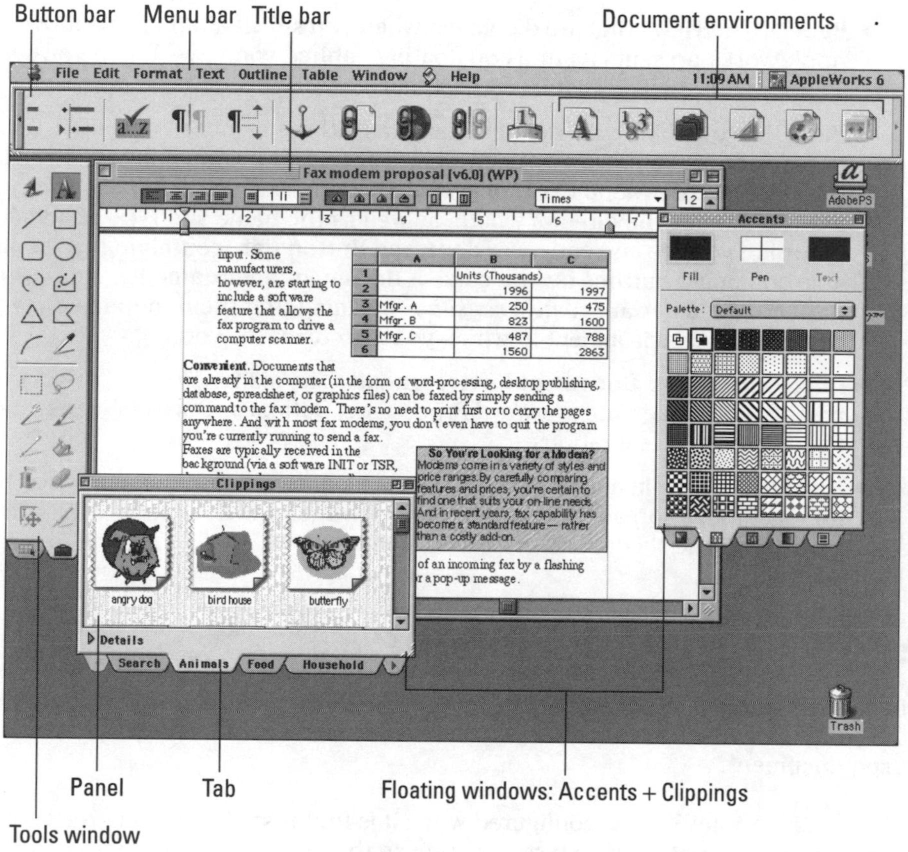

Figure 1-2: The AppleWorks 6 desktop

New definitions and terminology explained

AppleWorks 6 introduces some new terminology for its components that may be confusing when first encountered. Each of the following components is identified in Figure 1-2.

✦ **Floating Windows.** The floating palettes or small *windoids* (labeled Tools, Clippings, Accents, Controls, Links, and Styles) that are used by AppleWorks to provide tools for painting, drawing, table creation, formatting, and the use of clip art. The Button Bar (discussed later) also can be displayed as a floating window.

✦ **Tabs.** The small tags on a floating window that identify the various types of tool panels within the window.

✦ **Panels.** The views that are displayed when you select a tab in a window. AppleWorks presents its tools on floating, tabbed windows. When you select a tab, a set of tools is displayed on a panel.

✦ **Bars.** Every AppleWorks document contains three standard areas where information about the document—as well as access to commands—is stored. Three bars exist: Menu Bar (containing the menus used by AppleWorks), Title Bar (containing the directory path, as well as the name and type of document on which you are currently working), and Button Bar (containing customizable command buttons for the current document environment). The Button Bar and Menu Bar are *context-sensitive*, meaning that their contents change based on the environment in which you are currently working.

✦ **Environments or Document Environments.** The six types of AppleWorks documents you can create are Word Processing, Database, Spreadsheet, Drawing, Painting, and Presentations.

✦ **Frames.** An area in a document containing a different document environment; for example, a spreadsheet within a word processing document. This is the way to link the six document environments.

Creating a New Document

Each time you launch AppleWorks, the program loads, and the Starting Points window automatically opens so that you can create a new document or open a recently used document.

This is how AppleWorks is configured when it is first installed. If you prefer, you can change the AppleWorks start-up action so that it displays the Starting Points window, the Open dialog box (so you can open an existing file), or nothing at all. (To change the AppleWorks start-up action, see Chapter 11.)

STEPS: Creating a New Document at Start-Up

1. Launch AppleWorks. The Starting Points window (shown in Figure 1-3) appears. By default, the Basic panel's tab is selected the first time you launch AppleWorks. After that, you will be presented with the panel you last had displayed.

Figure 1-3: The Basic panel on the Starting Points window

If you have changed the "At Startup, Show" setting in the Preferences dialog box, you might see the Starting Points window, the Open dialog box, or nothing at all. In those cases, you must choose File ⇨ Show Starting Points (⌘+1) to make the Starting Points window appear, choose a document type from the File ⇨ New submenu, or click the document type you want on the Button Bar.

2. To start with a blank document from any of the six AppleWorks environments, click a document type icon from the Basic panel.

New documents also can be based on stationery files (called templates in Apple-Works 6), or they can be created for you by the AppleWorks Assistants. Templates are boilerplate documents that, when opened, present you with an untitled copy of themselves upon which to work. Apple ships a large selection of templates with AppleWorks 6 and makes many more available from the AppleWorks Web site at www.apple.com/appleworks. (See Chapter 11 for more information on templates.)

STEPS: Creating a New Document Using a Template or an Assistant

1. Select the Assistants tab (Figure 1-4) or the Templates tab (Figure 1-5).

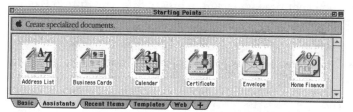

Figure 1-4: Selecting an AppleWorks Assistant

2. Click the Assistant or Template thumbnail you want to use.

If you choose an Assistant, you will be led through a series of dialog boxes asking you for the parameters needed to create your customized document. In some other applications, these Assistants are called *wizards*. If you click a template, you will be presented with your boilerplate document based on that template.

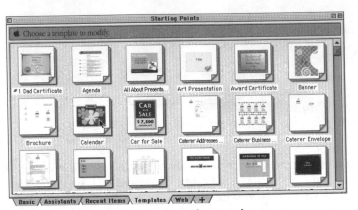

Figure 1-5: Selecting an AppleWorks Template

Note

If you have created a *default template* for an environment (see "Using Templates to Set New Environment Defaults" in Chapter 11), you see two different documents listed for that environment on the Basic panel. For example, a default word processing stationery document is simply listed as Word Processing. On the other hand, the AppleWorks standard document for that environment is listed as Standard Word Processing. (In ClarisWorks 3.0 and earlier versions, default stationery documents were known as *options stationery documents*.)

If you want to open an existing document instead of creating a new one, choose File ➪ Open and select the document (following the steps described in "Opening Existing Documents," later in this chapter) or, if you've opened it recently, click the Recent Items tab and select the document's thumbnail from that panel.

If you want to create a new document after the program has been running a while, you can either choose a document type from the File ➪ New submenu, or click the button for the document type you want to create from the Button Bar.

Memory Versus Disk Space (Storage Capacity)

New users often confuse a Mac's storage capacity with the amount of memory in the machine. *Storage capacity* refers to a Mac's total disk space, calculated by adding the capacity of all attached hard disks. The Mac's *memory* (also called *RAM* or Random Access Memory) is used to run programs and desk accessories and to manipulate data. Unlike disk storage, the contents of RAM disappears whenever you quit a program or shut down the Mac. Memory is for temporary storage; disks are for long-term storage. Thus, although you may have free disk space, this has no bearing on the amount of memory available for you to run programs such as AppleWorks (unless you allocate some of it to the MacOS's virtual memory).

You can create new documents or open existing documents at any time during an AppleWorks session. The only limitation on the number of documents you can have open at the same time is the amount of memory available to AppleWorks. See "Quick Tips" at the end of this chapter for help with changing the memory allocation for AppleWorks.

New documents are assigned a temporary name that consists of the word *untitled*, a number that represents the number of documents created thus far in the session, and a pair of letters in parentheses that represents the document type. For example, *untitled 4 (PT)* indicates that the document is a new Paint document and is the fourth new document created during the current AppleWorks session.

Remember that new documents are not automatically saved to disk. If you neglect to save a new document (see "Saving Documents," later in this chapter), it disappears forever after you click its close box or quit the program. If a document is important to you, be sure to save early and save often. Note that if you attempt to close a new document without saving, AppleWorks presents an alert dialog box that offers an option for you to save the document.

Opening Existing Documents

As mentioned earlier in this chapter, you can open existing AppleWorks documents from the desktop by double-clicking their icons. Doing so simultaneously launches AppleWorks and opens the selected document. After the program is running, you can open other AppleWorks documents, as well as documents created in many other programs.

Opening AppleWorks documents from within the program

To open an AppleWorks document while the program is running, choose File ➪ Open (or press ⌘+O). You will then see an Open dialog box like the one shown in Figure 1-6. Using the mouse or the arrow keys, select the particular file you want to open, and then either click the Open button or double-click the file name.

The AppleWorks Open dialog box has a special pair of pop-up menus at the bottom. You use the Document Type pop-up menu on the left to restrict the documents that appear in the file list to a particular type, such as database files. If you have a large number of files in a particular folder, using the Document Type pop-up menu can make it simpler to find the file you want.

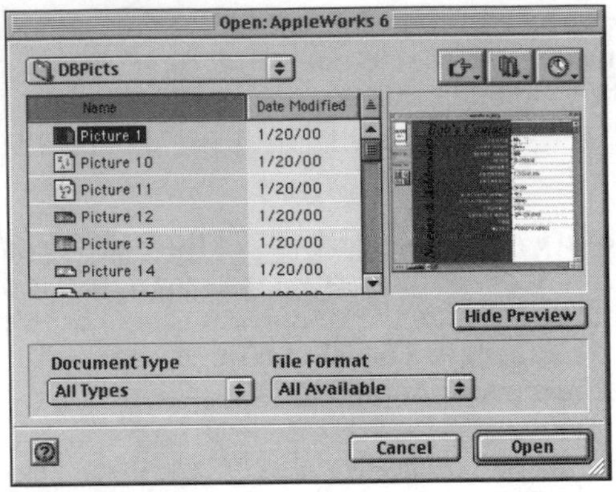

Figure 1-6: The Open dialog box

You use the File Format pop-up menu on the right to restrict the file list to only particular types of documents. You can specify whether you want to see regular AppleWorks documents (AppleWorks), AppleWorks template documents (AppleWorks Templates), or all document types for which you have translators (All Available). If you want to restrict the file list to just those documents in a particular program, such as Rich Text Format (RTF), you can select that document type in the File Type pop-up menu.

Note In previous versions of AppleWorks and ClarisWorks, Claris XTND translators for a wide range of document formats were included with the program. These translators are not recognized by AppleWorks 6. However, the DataViz translators (MacLink Plus 9 CW) accompanying ClarisWorks and AppleWorks 5 will work, as will the much larger collection of translators found in the commercial release of MacLink Plus (www.dataviz.com). These translators enable you to convert, for example, Microsoft Word for Windows documents into AppleWorks 5 documents, which AppleWorks 6 can read and convert. AppleWorks 6 ships only with translators for Text, EPSF, HTML, and ASCII text. The 6.0.3 and later updates (available free from the AppleWorks Web site at www.apple.com/appleworks) include the RTF translator.

The Open dialog box (shown previously in Figure 1-6) has a Show Preview option that enables you to see a thumbnail representation of many graphic documents selected in the file list or any AppleWorks document for which a preview was created (this is a preference setting). The Show Preview option will function only if Apple's QuickTime system software extension is currently loaded and the file has a preview resource. QuickTime is installed with AppleWorks unless you customize your installation to omit it, and it is also required to read and write many graphics file formats, as well as to include multimedia such as movies and sounds in your documents.

Note

Preview resources are scaled-down representations of an image stored with the file itself. Usually, you will see this for files whose icons are miniature representations of the contained image.

By clicking the Show Preview button, you instruct AppleWorks to show a preview image for any graphic or movie file for which a preview has been saved. (Note that previews are available for some text files, too.)

Opening non-AppleWorks documents

As described earlier, previous versions of ClarisWorks and AppleWorks used the Claris XTND extensions to read from and write to files in formats such as Microsoft Word, Microsoft Excel, or RTF. With ClarisWorks and AppleWorks 5, this was supplemented by a version of MacLink Plus, which enabled still more file translation possibilities. The XTND translators do not work with AppleWorks 6; however, the MacLink Plus translators do.

STEPS: Opening a Non-AppleWorks Document from Within AppleWorks

1. Choose File ⇨ Open (or press ⌘+O).

2. *Optional:* In the Open dialog box, click the Document Type pop-up menu and choose the type of file that you want to open (Word Processing, Drawing, Painting, Spreadsheet, Database, or Presentation). Similarly, if you want to restrict the file list to a certain type of document (just GIF or RTF files, for example), you can choose a program or file type from the File Type pop-up menu.

3. Navigate to the disk and folder where the document files are stored, and select the file you want to open. If the file you want does not appear in the file list, you do not have the translator that is needed to open the file.

4. Click the Open button or double-click the file name to load the file and convert it to AppleWorks format.

After you select the file, the Converting File dialog box appears. A progress bar shows the progress of the conversion. You can click the Cancel button at any time during the conversion if you change your mind about loading the file. Otherwise, after the conversion has finished, AppleWorks opens the document for you. (You should note that on today's fast processors and hard disks, this process will often be so quick that if you blink, you'll miss the progress meter.) The file is given a temporary name that consists of its original file name and a pair of letters in parentheses to indicate the document type (such as DB for a database document or WP for word processing document).

Caution

The conversion process does nothing to the original file; AppleWorks simply reads the file and opens a converted copy of it. The file that AppleWorks creates is not automatically stored on your disk. If you neglect to save the converted file, it disappears when you terminate your current session.

When you save a converted file, you have two options:

✦ **Save it with a different name from that of the original file.** This option leaves the original file intact and creates a second file in AppleWorks 6 format. (Note that if you have the Remember Translator preference enabled and an export translator exists for the original file format, the saved file will be in the same format as the original file.)

✦ **Save it with the same name as that of the original file.** This option replaces the original file with the new AppleWorks-formatted file (except, as noted previously, if you have Remember Translator enabled, it probably won't be in AppleWorks format). Use this option only if you have no further use for the original document.

You also can use *drag-and-drop* to cause AppleWorks to simultaneously open some non-AppleWorks documents. To use drag-and-drop to open a foreign file from the Finder, click once to select the icon for the non-AppleWorks document you want to open. Then, drag the icon onto the AppleWorks program icon or its alias. This drag-and-drop procedure can be used with several files at once, even if the files were created using different programs.

If AppleWorks is capable of interpreting the document you've selected, the AppleWorks icon darkens, and the program then launches and attempts to convert the document — just as it does when you open a foreign document from within AppleWorks. If the document is not one of the types AppleWorks can read, the AppleWorks icon does not darken, and the program fails to launch.

If you have MacLink Plus installed, however, the icon will invariably darken and you might get a message from inside AppleWorks that the conversion could not be completed. Depending on which version of MacLink Plus you're using, failure to open the file could be a prelude to an AppleWorks crash. Be sure that you limit this usage to document types that the translators can understand.

Note　If you are running MacOS 8.x and the foreign files are from a PC, you might need to disable the Translate Text Files setting for Macintosh Easy Open, thereby avoiding launching MacLink Plus before the file gets passed to AppleWorks. In MacOS 9, you will need to disable the "Translate Files Automatically" setting under the File Translation tab in Apple File Exchange.

Opening documents created with an earlier version of AppleWorks

One other type of conversion that many users are curious about is the manner in which AppleWorks 6 handles documents created by earlier versions of ClarisWorks and AppleWorks. You don't need to worry: When you open a file created with

ClarisWorks 1.0 through 5.0, a dialog box appears that states: "This document was created by a previous version of AppleWorks. A copy will be opened and '[v6.0]' will be added to the file name." (The [v6.0] Suffix option can be disabled in Preferences, if you like.) Note that this message says that a *copy* will be opened. As with translations of other foreign files, the original document is merely read into memory—it is not replaced on disk. If you want to save a permanent copy of the document in the current version's format, you need to use the Save or Save As command to save a new copy of the file.

Tip

AppleWorks 6 documents cannot be read by earlier versions of AppleWorks or ClarisWorks. If some of your colleagues use previous versions of ClarisWorks or AppleWorks, you'll be able to read their documents, but they will not be able to read yours. For now, the best solution is to use the Save As command to translate the file to a format their version of AppleWorks or ClarisWorks can read. AppleWorks 6 will save in ClarisWorks 4, ClarisWorks 5, and AppleWorks 5 format, as well as ClarisWorks for Kids (a variation of the ClarisWorks 4 format). A second approach is to save a copy of your word processing documents in Text format. All versions of ClarisWorks and AppleWorks can read text documents, but you will lose any formatting and style information when you save in Text format.

Inserting files and graphics

The Insert command (from the File menu) enables you to place the entire contents of a file into an AppleWorks document.

Tip

If you need to use only a portion of a file (such as a single paragraph or a graphic), it may be faster to simply open the second file, copy the portion you need, and then paste it into your document.

To insert a file or graphic into a document or frame:

1. Position the cursor where you want to place the inserted item.

2. Choose File ➪ Insert. A standard Open dialog box appears.

3. If you want to restrict your choices to a particular file type, choose the type from the File Format pop-up menu.

4. Navigate to the drive and folder containing the file.

Note

Only those file types that are supported for the current frame or document environment will appear in the File Format pop-up menu.

5. Select the file you want to insert by clicking it and clicking the Insert button, or by double-clicking the name of the file.

Note You also can use Insert as a method of inserting an AppleWorks file of one type into a document of another type. For example, you can insert a database document into a spreadsheet or a spreadsheet frame.

In addition to opening graphic files directly as Draw or Paint documents, you can use the Clippings window to insert or drag any of the graphics, text items, or spreadsheet cells from AppleWorks Clippings files into existing documents. (See Chapter 14 for details about the Clippings feature.)

Saving Documents

To save an AppleWorks document to disk, you use either File ⇨ Save or File ⇨ Save As. For new Mac owners, determining which command is the correct one to use is often a major source of confusion. This section clears up the confusion once and for all.

New Feature AppleWorks 6 includes a new *Autosave* feature that saves a copy of your open documents at set intervals as you work. You can change the interval — or disable this safety feature entirely — in AppleWorks Preferences. AppleWorks even places an alias of your working copy in your System Folder's Startup Items Folder so that, should your Mac crash, AppleWorks automatically launches and opens your documents when you restart your computer.

Saving existing files

You use the Save command (⌘+S) to save existing files. If the file is already on disk, the Save command merely replaces the old copy of the file with the new copy. No dialog box will appear.

Because the Save command automatically replaces the previous copy of the file, at times you might prefer to use the Save As command to save an existing file. The Save As command enables you to assign a new name to the file, as well as to specify a different format or a different location on disk in which to store the file. You can use the Save As command when you want to keep multiple versions of a file instead of just replacing the old version, or when you want to save a document in a different format.

STEPS: Using the Save As Command to Save an Existing File

1. Choose File ⇨ Save As. The standard Open dialog box appears.

2. Navigate to the disk drive and folder in which you want to save the file. If you want to create a new folder in which to store the file, click the New (Folder) button and type a name for the new folder.

3. Type a name for the file. If you want to save the file as something other than a standard AppleWorks file, choose a file type from the File Format pop-up menu.

4. Click a radio button to choose Document or Template. Choose Template if you want to save the document as a reusable template; otherwise, choose Document.

5. Click the Save button (or press the Return key). If you change your mind and decide not to save the file, click the Cancel button (or press Esc or ⌘+. [period]).

If you are saving a file that already exists on disk and you don't change the name from the suggested name, the MacOS will ask if you want to replace the existing file. Click the Replace button if you want to replace the old file with the new file, or click the Cancel button if you don't want to replace the old file. You can then specify a new name or location (a different disk or folder), or you can cancel the save process altogether. (The Replace dialog box appears whenever you choose the Save As command and try to save a file under its original name or under any other file name that's already in use.)

Tip

If you frequently keep or track multiple revisions of important documents, you may find Aladdin Flashback (a utility program from Aladdin Systems at www.aladdinsys.com) helpful.

Saving new files

You can save new files by using either the Save or the Save As command. After you select either command from the File menu, a standard Open dialog box appears and gives you the opportunity to name the new file and specify a location on the disk in which to store it. To avoid overwriting any files that are already on the disk, be sure to choose a name that is different from any existing file names.

Note

If the file you want to save has never been saved before (that is, it's a new file) and the file is empty, AppleWorks *grays out* the Save command (makes it unselectable). Until at least one character has been typed into the document, the only save option presented is Save As.

AppleWorks 6 enables you to save identifying information with any file by choosing File ➪ Properties. You can use the Properties dialog box to do the following:

✦ Provide a more elaborate title for a document

✦ Identify the author

✦ Specify a version number (to distinguish multiple revisions of a file, for example)

✦ Assign keywords that can be used to help identify the file's contents

✦ Specify a category and add descriptive text

An example of a Properties dialog box is shown in Figure 1-7. Because this information is primarily for your benefit, you can type as much or as little information as you like. If you later want to change some of the entries, choose the Properties command again, make your desired changes, and then save the document again. (Properties information is also discussed in Chapter 10.) This dialog box is also what you will use to assign a password to a document, as described later in this chapter.

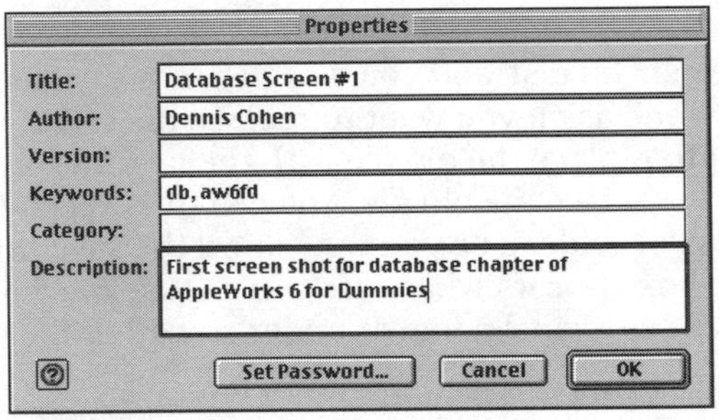

Figure 1-7: The Properties dialog box

Note   In previous versions of ClarisWorks and AppleWorks, the Properties dialog box and menu item were named Document Summary.

Note   For all practical purposes, the Keywords, Categories, and Description sections of the Properties dialog box are useless except as reminders to you, or to people to whom you give your documents, about what the document is for. In ClarisWorks and AppleWorks 5, there was a Find ClarisWorks/AppleWorks Documents Assistant; however, even it would not search the keyword field. This Assistant is not included with AppleWorks 6.

Using Save As options

When you use the Save As command to save a file, a Save dialog box appears, as shown in Figure 1-8. It looks a little different from the Save dialog box used by other programs. Using the radio buttons and the pop-up menu at the lower edge of the dialog box, you can do one of the following:

✦ Select from several file formats by clicking the File Format pop-up menu

✦ Save the file as a document or template file by clicking the appropriate radio button

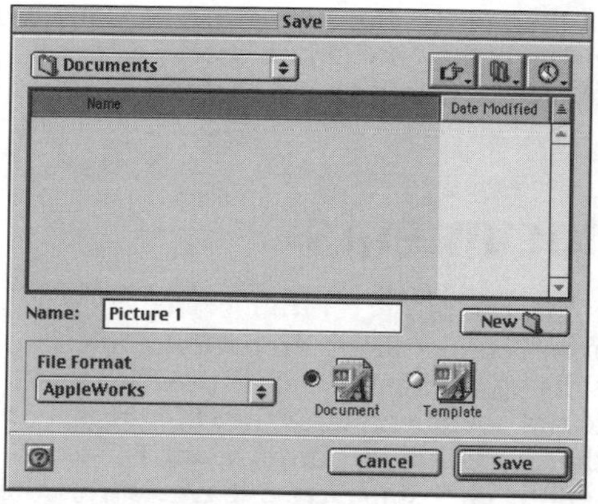

Figure 1-8: The AppleWorks 6 Save As dialog box

In most cases, you can leave the File Format pop-up menu alone. The default setting is AppleWorks, which means the file will be saved as a standard AppleWorks file. You can, however, tell AppleWorks to remember the translator used in your Preferences, in which case the setting will be the file format of the original document (when a matching export translator exists).

Depending on the file translators that are installed, the File Format pop-up menu may have options for saving the document as a non-AppleWorks file. You might want to save a spreadsheet in Microsoft Excel format, for example, if you plan to give it to a friend who uses Excel rather than AppleWorks. Or, you might want to save Draw graphic files in PICT format so they can be opened by any drawing program. Note that the file format options presented will vary, depending on the AppleWorks environment you're in when you choose Save As. For example, if you're saving a spreadsheet, the File Format pop-up menu lists only spreadsheet formats.

Tip

When saving a document in a non-AppleWorks format, it's a smart idea to save a copy of the file in AppleWorks format, too, so that if you ever use the document in AppleWorks again, you can work on the original rather than the translated copy of the file. Import and Export translators do not always support identical features. For example, the HTML translator will convert an AppleWorks table or spreadsheet frame to an HTML table, but it will not import an HTML table as either a table or a spreadsheet frame.

The radio buttons in the lower-right corner of the dialog box enable you to save the file as a normal document or as a template. A template is a piece of stationery for frequently used documents, such as fax forms and memos. If you click the Template radio button, AppleWorks automatically navigates to the Templates folder within the Starting Points folder (inside the AppleWorks 6 folder). You can later open any template saved in this folder by clicking the Template tab in the Starting Points window and then clicking the icon for the template you want to use.

Note The File Format pop-up menu and the radio buttons work together. You must select a file format from the File Format pop-up menu *and* choose a file type by clicking the Document or Template radio button if you do not want to use the default choices.

Password-Protecting Documents

You can assign a password to any document to protect it from prying eyes. To add a password to a new or existing document, choose File ⇨ Properties and click the Set Password button in the Properties dialog box that appears (see Figure 1-9). Type a password you want to assign to the document, click the OK button, confirm the password by typing it again, and then click the OK button again. Finally, to record the password, save the document by choosing Save or Save As from the File menu. (Note that if you assign a password to a template, you will have to type the password each time you create a new document based on that template.)

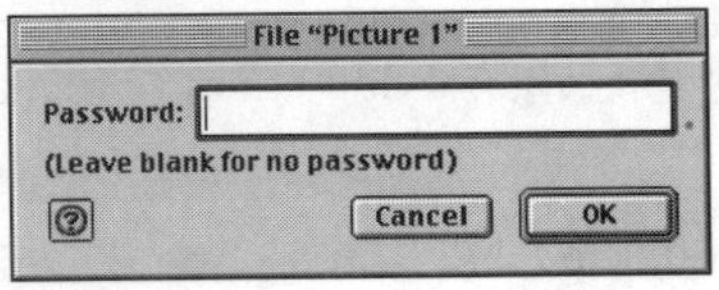

Figure 1-9: Assigning a password to a document

If you later want to change the password for a document, open the document and repeat this procedure. You will be asked to type the old password before you are allowed to create a new password. To remove an existing password (restoring the document to a "no password" state), leave the password field blank when you are asked to type and confirm the new password.

Caution Assigning a password to a document does not *encrypt* (scramble) it. Although a password will slow down casual snoopers, password-protected documents can easily be opened and viewed by many Macintosh utility programs. If you want real protection, you have to purchase a security or encryption program such as FolderBolt Pro (from Citadel at www.citadel.com), FileGuard (from Highware at http://euro.highware.com/fileguard/fg.html), Private File (from Aladdin Systems at www.aladdinsys.com), or PGP (from Pretty Good Privacy at www.pgp.com) — or use the encryption tools available in MacOS 9.

Closing Document Windows

Saving a document or file copies its contents to a file on disk. It does not close the document window. After you finish using a document, you can close its window by clicking the close box in the upper-left corner of the window, as shown in Figure 1-10, choosing File ➪ Close, or by pressing ⌘+W. If the file has been saved, the window immediately closes. If changes have been made to the file, you are given a chance to save the file before AppleWorks closes it.

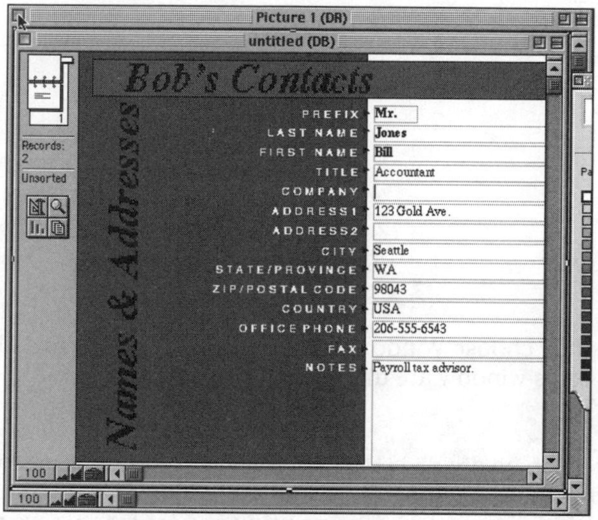

Figure 1-10: Click the close box to close a window.

You can close all the document windows at one time by holding down the Option key and either clicking the close box of an open document window, or by choosing File ➪ Close (⌘+Option+W). Choosing File ➪ Quit (or by pressing ⌘+Q) will close all open windows (asking if you want to save changes to modified documents), and then quit AppleWorks.

Selecting and Using Tools

One of AppleWorks' many floating windows is the Tools window. Within this window, you will find two tabs: one containing frame tools, and another containing graphics and table tools. The frame tools enable you to create new frames (such as adding paint graphics, a table, or a spreadsheet to a word processing document). The Tool panel lets you select drawing, painting, and table-editing tools. The Tool panel is indicated by a small red toolbox on its tab, while the Frame panel tab shows a small grid with an arrow and a dotted red outline (see Figure 1-2, earlier in this chapter, and Figure 1-11).

Note   In previous versions of ClarisWorks and AppleWorks, the frame, drawing, and painting tools were in a tool panel within the document window.

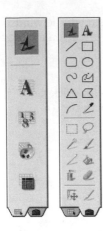

Figure 1-11: The Frame and Tool panels

If the Tools window isn't visible, choose Window ➪ Show Tools (⌘+Shift+T). Other ways to show and hide the Tools window are discussed later in this chapter in "Hiding and Showing Tools."

The objects in the Tool panel can be divided into the following categories, according to their functions: drawing tools, painting tools, and table tools. The two panels of the Tools window are shown in Figure 1-11. The painting and table tools are disabled (grayed out) when you are not working in an appropriate frame or document.

To create a new frame in the current document, click a frame tool: click the A for a word processing frame, the 1,8,3 grid for creating a spreadsheet frame, the paint palette for a paint frame, or the blue/green grid for a table. To add a Draw object to the document, switch to the Tool panel, click any of the draw icons you want to use, and then draw in your document.

Applying Graphic Accents

In previous versions of AppleWorks and ClarisWorks, you used pop-up palettes to set graphic attributes for the objects in your documents. Many users found this process confusing.

New Feature The Accents window shown in Figure 1-12 is another floating window. You use the tools in this window to set the graphic Fill (interior), the Pen (border), and the Text attributes for your AppleWorks objects. If the Accents window isn't visible, choose Window ➪ Show Accents (⌘+K).

The Accents window's five tabs are color, pattern, wallpaper, gradient, and line styles. The Accents window is covered in more detail in Chapter 6.

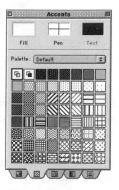

Figure 1-12: The Pattern panel of the Accents window

> **Tip**
>
> Option-clicking the close box for any palette simultaneously closes all open palettes. Similarly, Option-clicking in the grow/shrink box in the upper-right corner of a palette causes all palettes to grow or shrink.

AppleWorks 6 makes extensive use of floating windows. For instance, stylesheets are also presented as floating windows with their own miniature title bars, close boxes, and grow/shrink boxes. In other Macintosh programs, such windows are commonly referred to as *windoids*. In this book, the terms *palette*, *floater*, and *windoid* are used interchangeably because every AppleWorks palette is presented in a windoid, which is often referred to as a floating window or a floater.

> **Note**
>
> The Button Bar (discussed next) and the Tools window are special floating windows or floaters. They also can be "docked" against any edge of the screen. When they are docked, their Title Bars are hidden, as are the close and windowshade boxes that appear in a floater's Title Bar. (To dock a window, drag it to the edge of the screen where you want it to be located. When its appearance changes, release the mouse button.)

Using the Button Bar

To save you the effort of needlessly having to pulling down menus to choose commands or to memorize Command-key equivalents, AppleWorks 6 provides a Button Bar (which is also a floater) that normally appears just below the Menu Bar (see Figure 1-13), but which you can optionally reposition along the side or bottom of the screen. You can issue many common commands by simply clicking a button on the Button Bar. To make the Button Bar appear, choose Window ➪ Show Button Bar (or press Shift-⌘+X).

Figure 1-13: This Button Bar appears when you work in a spreadsheet or a spreadsheet frame.

The contents of the Button Bar change to match the environment or frame in which you are working. When you are working in a spreadsheet frame, for example, buttons relevant to spreadsheet operations are added to the default Button Bar.

Note
In ClarisWorks 4 and earlier, the Shortcuts palette served the same function as the Button Bar. ClarisWorks and AppleWorks 5 gave you multiple button bars with which to work. Although the Button Bar in AppleWorks 6 is easier to work with for most people, much flexibility and power was lost.

You can customize a Button Bar by adding and removing buttons or assigning macros (user-created AppleWorks scripts) or AppleScripts to buttons. (Chapter 12 discusses customizing Button Bars.)

Tip
⌘+Shift+X is a toggle to hide/show the Button Bar.

Creating and Using Frames

To integrate information from the various AppleWorks environments, you use frames. A *frame* is a rectangular area within a document that is—in most cases—a different environment than that of the underlying document. For example, Figure 1-14 shows a spreadsheet frame within a word processing document. The four types of frames correspond to the three environments: text, paint, and spreadsheet, plus the new tables.

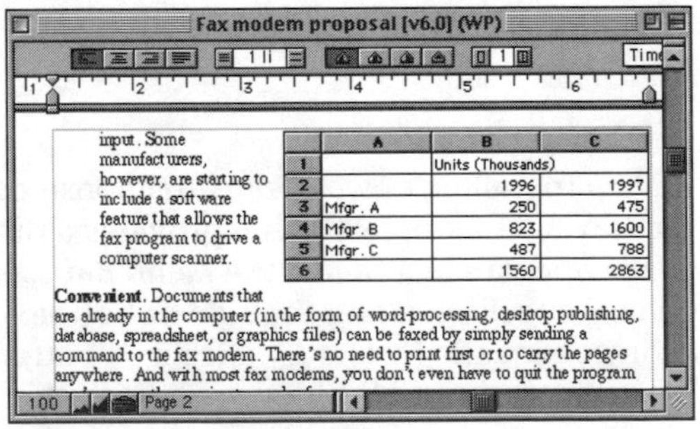

Figure 1-14: A spreadsheet frame in a word processing document

Note AppleWorks does not have a separate frame type for drawn objects. You can add a Draw object to most documents by selecting a draw tool from the Tool panel and then drawing. To create a frame, select one of the frame tools (text, spreadsheet, paint, or table) from the Tools window's frames panel. Click the mouse button over the spot where you want to position one of the frame's corners. Drag until the frame is the size and shape you desire, and then release the mouse button. You also can drag the frame tool onto the surface of your document to create a default-sized frame.

If you've never created a frame before, you might want to try it now. As an example, create a new word processing document or open an existing one, choose Window ⇨ Show Tools (if the Tools windoid is hidden), select the spreadsheet tool, and then click and drag in the document window. When you release the mouse button, the spreadsheet frame appears.

Note You can place additional word processing frames into a word processing document, or spreadsheet frames into a spreadsheet document, by pressing the Option key as you draw the frame.

After you create a frame, you can immediately begin working in it: entering data in spreadsheet frames, typing in text frames, typing or inserting graphics in a table, and creating bitmapped graphics in paint frames. You might discover, however, that a particular frame is incorrectly positioned, is the wrong size, or is no longer needed. If you need to move, resize, or delete a frame, here's how to do so:

✦ To move a frame, select the pointer from the Tool or Frames panel. Click the frame to select it. A set of black dots called *handles* appears around the frame to show that it is selected. Click anywhere within the frame and, while holding down the mouse button, drag the frame to the new position.

✦ To resize a frame, select the pointer from the Tool or Frames panel. Click the frame to select it. A set of handles appears around the frame to show that it is selected. Using the pointer tool, select one of the frame handles, and then drag it to change the size of the frame.

✦ To delete a frame, select the pointer from the Tool panel. Click the frame to select it. A set of handles appears around the frame to show that it is selected. Press the Delete or Clear key.

See Chapter 14 for additional information about frames.

Using Drag-and-Drop

AppleWorks 6 makes extensive use of a Macintosh system feature called *drag-and-drop*. In addition to using drag-and-drop to open foreign files in AppleWorks (as explained in "Opening non-AppleWorks documents," earlier in this chapter), drag-and-drop can be used to move text and objects from one AppleWorks document to another, to the desktop (as clipping files), or between other drag-and-drop-enabled programs (such as Adobe Photoshop).

To copy text or an object (such as a graphic or a spreadsheet frame) between AppleWorks documents, open both documents, select the text or graphic, and then drag it to the second document. Use the same procedure to copy text or objects between AppleWorks and any other drag-and-drop-enabled program.

To create a text or graphic clipping file, drag the text or object to your desktop.

Changing the Display

In AppleWorks, you can control what you see onscreen in several ways. For example, you can do any of the following:

✦ Move, collapse, or hide the Tools palette or any other floater to see more of a partially hidden or wide document

✦ Switch magnification levels to focus in on important areas or to get a bird's-eye view of the document

✦ Stack or tile windows to make it more convenient to work with several documents at the same time

✦ Zoom document windows to switch between two window sizes with a single mouse click

✦ Split the screen to see two, four, six, or nine parts of a document at the same time

✦ Create new views of a document to work with two or more copies of the same document at the same time

Hiding and showing tools

Although you usually want to keep the Tools windoid handy, sometimes you might want to make it disappear. If you have a small screen or are working on a very wide document, for example, hiding Tools enables you to see more of the document. You can hide or show Tools in one of two ways:

✦ Choose Show Tools or Hide Tools from the Window menu. (The wording for this command changes, depending on whether the Tools windoid is presently visible or hidden.) You also can issue this command by pressing ⌘+Shift+T.

✦ Click the Show/Hide Tools control at the lower edge of the document (see Figure 1-15).

Figure 1-15: Use the Show/Hide Tools control to view or hide the Tool panel.

Each time you issue the Show/Hide Tools command or click the control, the state of the Tools window switches. If the Tools window is currently hidden, it becomes visible. If it is currently visible, it becomes hidden.

Setting the magnification level

Occasionally, you might want to change a document's magnification level. Although this feature is extremely helpful in the paint environment (because it enables you to zoom in to touch up tiny areas), it is also available in the other environments. You can zoom out to get a thumbnail view of the layout for a word processing document without being distracted by the text, for example. You change the magnification with the Zoom Percentage box, the Zoom-Out control, or the Zoom-In control, all of which are located in the lower-left corner of every document window (see Figure 1-16).

Figure 1-16: Use the Zoom controls to change a document's magnification.

You can change the magnification in two ways:

✦ Click the Zoom Percentage box and drag to select a new percentage. If you select Other, a dialog box appears in which you can type a specific percentage, including percentages that are not listed in the menu.

✦ Click the Zoom-Out or Zoom-In control. Each click reduces or increases the magnification by one step.

Resizing windows

Resizable windows, such as AppleWorks document windows, contain three special boxes: the windowshade box, the size box, and the zoom box, as shown in Figure 1-17. To change the size of a window, click in the size box and drag until the window is the desired size. The windowshade box collapses a window to just its Title Bar so that you can easily see what is behind the window. Click it again to expand it back to its previous size. Each time you click a window's zoom box, it switches between a window that is large enough to show as much of the document in either direction as possible and the size and position that you last set for the window. (These aren't specifically AppleWorks features — they work with any Macintosh window that contains zoom and size boxes.)

Figure 1-17: Use the zoom, size, and windowshade boxes to change the size of a window.

Arranging windows

AppleWorks enables you to open and work with as many documents as available memory permits. Two commands in the Window menu — Tile Windows and Stack Windows — make it easy to juggle several open files.

The Tile Windows command arranges document windows in a vertical stack, one above the other. Documents are full width, but their height is reduced, as shown in Figure 1-18. Unfortunately, for those of you with large (or high-resolution) monitors, you have to manually set the horizontal tiling to get two documents side-by-side. You can make any document active by simply clicking it.

Tip   If you don't need to refer constantly to any of the other open documents, you can expand the current document so that it takes up as much of the screen as necessary by clicking its zoom box (the second button from the right in the document's Title Bar). When you're ready to switch to a different document window, click the current window's zoom box again to make it shrink to its original, tiled position.

The Stack Windows command arranges documents so that they cascade from the upper-left corner to the lower-right corner of the screen. Because a small portion of each document always shows, you can easily switch between documents by clicking the edge of the document you want to bring to the front.

Note   Regardless of how you have your windows arranged, you can bring any window forward and make it active by clicking in that window or by choosing its name from the Window menu. (All open documents are listed at the bottom of the Window menu, sorted alphabetically.)

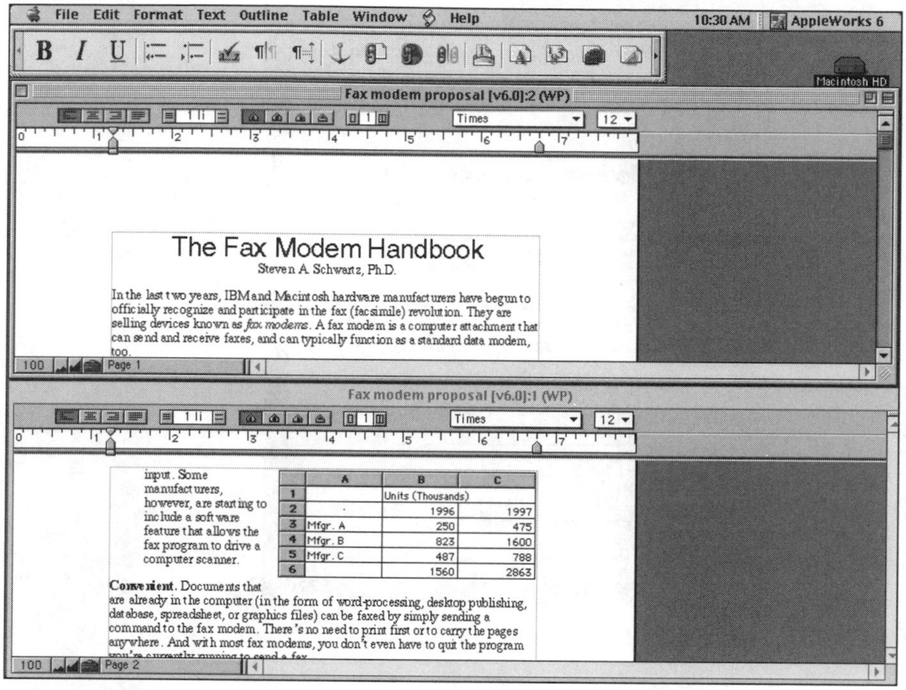

Figure 1-18: Tiled windows

Splitting the screen

AppleWorks enables you to split any document horizontally and/or vertically into two, four, six, or nine panes (see Figure 1-19). In each pane, you can examine or edit a different portion of the document. Each pane scrolls independently of the other panes, so working on one part of the document while viewing another part is easy to do. Changes you make in any pane are simultaneously recorded in all panes.

To split the screen, click the vertical or horizontal pane control and drag it to the spot where you want to divide the document. Then release the mouse button. A pair of dividing lines marks the edges of each pane.

To remove a split pane, double-click the dividing line, or click the dividing line and drag it back to the edge of the document window.

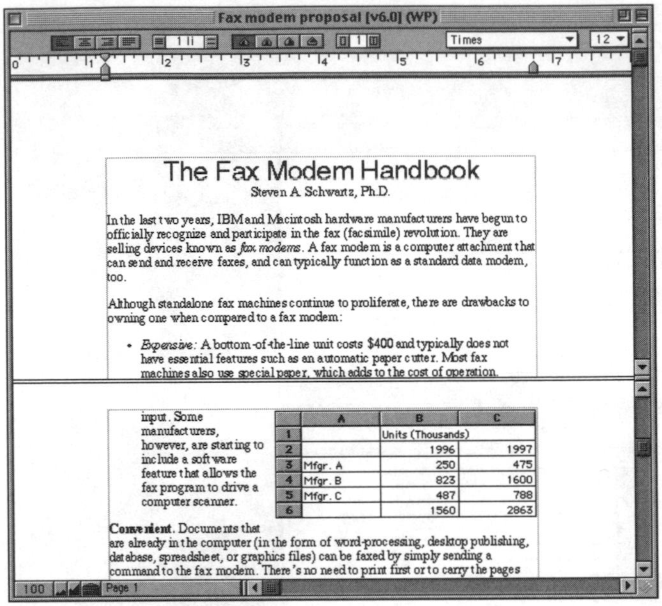

Figure 1-19: A split screen

Creating a new view of a document

If you want to open two copies of the same document, choose Window ➪ New View. Any changes you make in one copy are instantly reflected in the other copy. To distinguish between the copies, AppleWorks appends a colon and a number at the end of each document's name in the Title Bar. If the original document is called Memo (WP), for example, you end up with two documents onscreen: Memo:1 (WP) and Memo:2 (WP).

> **Note**   You also can open a text, spreadsheet, or paint frame as a window unto itself by selecting the frame and choosing Window ➪ Open Frame.

What's the point of having multiple copies of the same document onscreen? Creating multiple views of a document has the following major advantages, among many minor ones:

✦ It enables you to see a zoomed-out view (the entire document) and a 100 percent view (the normal view) at the same time. Editing changes are reflected in both views so you can see their effects, such as where page breaks will occur.

✦ If you have a spreadsheet frame in a word processing, draw, presentation, or database document, the only way to increase the number of rows and columns in the frame is by creating a new view of the frame (by choosing Window ➪ Open Frame).

✦ In the database environment, you can use two views to look at the document in both Browse and Layout modes at the same time. As you make changes to the layout, you can instantly see how they will affect the formatting of the data.

Printing

The final step for most documents is creating a printout — a printed copy of the spreadsheet, memo, graphic image, database report, or presentation slides and notes. Begin by opening or creating an AppleWorks document. Choose File ➪ Print. The Print dialog box appears. Select the print options you want to use for this printout. Click the Print button to send the print job to the printer.

Note Some options in the Print dialog box are specific to a particular AppleWorks environment. When working on a spreadsheet, for example, you can print or omit the row headings, column headings, and the cell grid.

The Print dialog box you see depends on the printer you select in the Chooser or on the Finder DeskTop, as well as the version of system software that is installed on your Mac. Figure 1-20 shows the Print dialog box for Apple LaserWriters under MacOS 9.

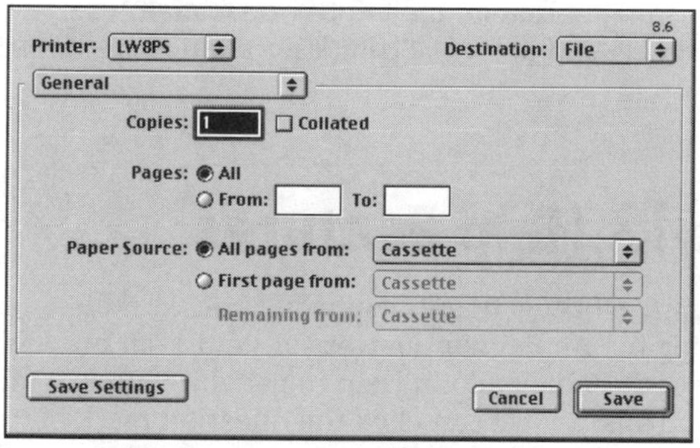

Figure 1-20: The Print dialog box for the LaserWriter 8 driver

Note Be sure you have selected a printer in the Chooser desk accessory or a desktop printer in the Finder, particularly if you have more than one printing device. The printer that is currently selected receives the print job. Whenever you change the printer selection, you should also use the Page Setup command to make sure the options are correct for the newly selected printer.

To select a printer, open the Chooser desk accessory (see Figure 1-21) by selecting it from the Apple menu. Click the appropriate printer driver icon from the left side of the window, and select the printer and other options from the right side of the window. (The printer must be turned on for its name to appear in the right side of the window.)

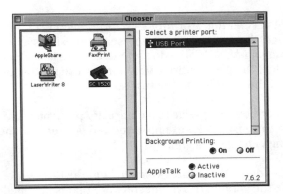

Figure 1-21: Use the Chooser desk accessory to select the printer and set other options.

 Note   You can specify a default printer by selecting a printer icon on the desktop and choosing Printing ➪ Set Default Printer (⌘+L). You also can print by simply dragging document icons onto the printer icon for the printer you want to use. (Note, however, that most inkjet printers and non-PostScript laser printers are not supported as Desktop Printers.)

Using the AppleWorks Help Features

AppleWorks 6 provides several ways for you to get help while you work. In addition to viewing AppleWorks Help using the Apple Help Viewer (or your Web browser, if you're running MacOS 8.1), you can enable Balloon Help to get assistance in identifying AppleWorks's tools and controls, or you can click the question mark button in any dialog box. You also can see ToolTips by hovering your mouse pointer over the Button Bar buttons or the Tools window items. ToolTips for the Button Bar can be disabled; however, they are always present in the Tools window.

Using AppleWorks Help

In early versions of ClarisWorks, all important program information was located in the manual. Beginning with ClarisWorks 3, major portions of the manual were moved into the online help system. You'll now find that almost all of the program information is available only in AppleWorks Help, and the manual is more of a marketing blurb and installation guide.

Note Apple Help Viewer is a separate program from AppleWorks. Although you can request help from within AppleWorks (which launches the Apple Help Viewer program), Apple Help Viewer also can be launched directly from the desktop — even if AppleWorks isn't running.

When you're running AppleWorks, you can invoke the Apple Help Viewer by doing any of the following:

✦ Choosing Help ⇨ AppleWorks Help (see Figure 1-22)

✦ Pressing ⌘+? or the Help key (if your keyboard has that key)

Figure 1-22: The Help menu

Help summoned from dialog boxes in AppleWorks 6 is context-sensitive. If you click the question mark (?) button in any dialog box, AppleWorks Help opens to a screen that is relevant to that dialog box.

When you open AppleWorks Help from the Help menu, on the other hand, you are presented with the opening screen (Table of Contents) of the AppleWorks Help system (see Figure 1-23).

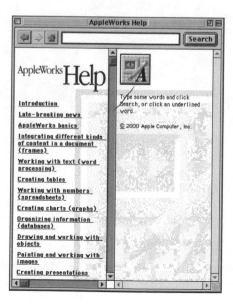

Figure 1-23: The opening Help screen

After AppleWorks Help opens, you can do any of the following:

✦ Display the Help Index by clicking the Index hyperlink.

✦ Display the most recent Help screen viewed by clicking the Go Back button (assuming you have been viewing different Help screens).

✦ Go to a Help screen that is related to the current topic by clicking a hyperlink on that screen.

✦ Search for help on a particular topic by typing an entry in the text box at the top and clicking the Search button.

✦ Go directly to any topic of interest by clicking text that contains a solid underline, or by clicking a topic in the Index.

✦ Print the current Help topic or all Help topics by choosing File ⇨ Print or File ⇨ Print One Copy.

One of the fastest ways to find help on a particular subject is to use the Index. The Index (shown in Figure 1-24) is an alphabetical list of all Help topics. Click the first letter of the topic you're interested in, scroll to an item of interest, and then click any of the links.

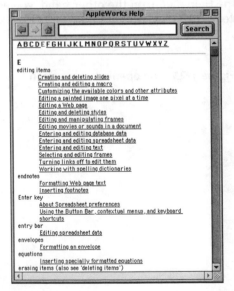

Figure 1-24: The Help Index

Help can remain onscreen while you continue to work on AppleWorks documents. When you are through with AppleWorks Help, you can dismiss it by choosing File ⇨ Quit.

Using Balloon Help

By choosing Help ➪ Show Balloons , you can get helpful descriptive information about AppleWorks components. Whenever the mouse pointer passes over an object that has a Balloon Help message attached to it, a cartoon-style balloon pops up, providing some general information about that object. Resizing controls, icons in the Tools window, menu items, dialog box buttons, and parts of the document window are some of the items within AppleWorks that have Help balloons. Figure 1-25 shows an example of a Help balloon.

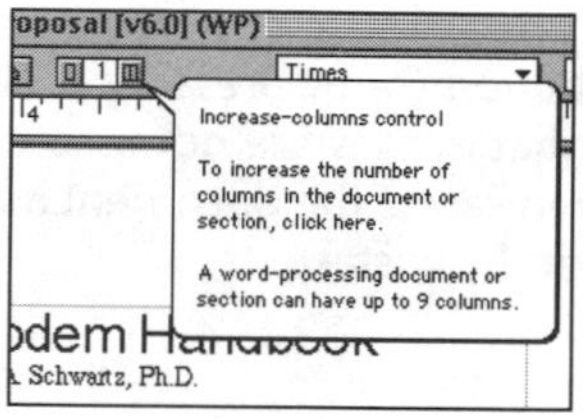

Figure 1-25: A Help balloon that explains a control in the ruler

To turn on Balloon Help, choose Help ➪ Show Balloons. Now, whenever you point to a Balloon Help object, a balloon will appear. Because most people find the balloons distracting when they are working, you might want to disable Balloon Help after you find out what you need to know.

To turn off Balloon Help, choose Help ➪ Hide Balloons.

Help-style balloons — called ToolTips — also are available for the buttons in the Button Bar and in the Tools window. Just let the mouse pointer rest on one of the buttons for a few seconds and a balloon will pop up. (See Chapter 12 for more information on Button Bars.)

Quitting the Program

After you finish using AppleWorks, choose File ➪ Quit (or press ⌘+Q). If you have new documents open that have never been saved, or documents with changes that haven't been saved, AppleWorks gives you an opportunity to save the files before quitting (see Figure 1-26). If a file has never been saved (that is, it's a new file you created in the current session) and you click the Save button in the Save Changes dialog box, AppleWorks presents the standard Save As dialog box (as described previously in this chapter in "Saving Documents"). If, on the other hand, the file has been saved before, clicking the Save button simply saves the new version of the file over the older version.

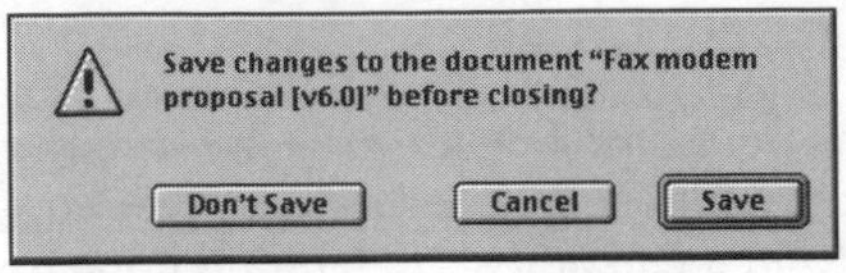

Figure 1-26: The Save Changes
dialog box

A Save Changes dialog box appears for every unsaved open document. If you change your mind about quitting, click the Cancel button. The AppleWorks session immediately returns to your work. Clicking Don't Save tells AppleWorks to close the document without saving it.

Caution

If you close a document by clicking the Don't Save button (or by pressing ⌘+D), all changes since the most recent save are ignored; that is, they are not recorded on disk. If this is a new document and it has never been saved, the document itself is discarded. Be sure not to click the Don't Save button by mistake.

Quick Tips

The following tips offer some helpful hints to:

✦ Ensure that you have enough memory for your AppleWorks sessions

✦ Immediately show an Open dialog box in front of the Starting Points window when you launch AppleWorks

✦ Optimally shrink and expand windows

✦ Print from the desktop

✦ Compensate for not having a translator for a file you want to open or insert

Changing the memory allocation for AppleWorks

While running AppleWorks, you might occasionally receive a message that the system has insufficient memory to open a document or run a presentation, or that a paint document will be opened in a reduced size. You can increase the memory available to AppleWorks and your documents by using the following procedure.

STEPS: Changing AppleWorks's Memory Allocation

1. Quit AppleWorks by choosing File ➪ Quit (or pressing ⌘+Q). If any open documents are new or have been changed, you are given an opportunity to save them. You are then returned to the desktop.

2. Select the AppleWorks program icon by clicking it and then choose File ⇨ Get Info ⇨ Memory (or control-click the icon and choose Get Info ⇨ Memory from the contextual menu). You see an Info window similar to the one shown in Figure 1-27. If you're using MacOS 8.x rather than MacOS 9, you'll need to choose File ⇨ Get Info (or ⌘+I) and then choose Memory from the pop-up menu.

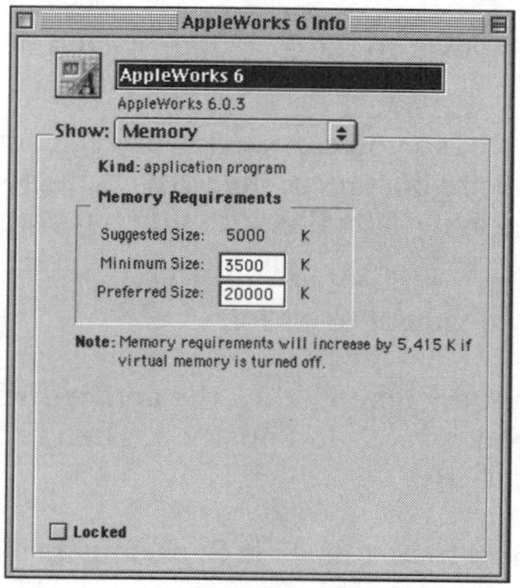

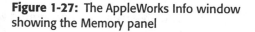

Figure 1-27: The AppleWorks Info window showing the Memory panel

3. Type a larger number into the Preferred Size box. (Increase the Preferred Size by 25 to 50 percent to start. Later, as you determine the amount of memory you require for a typical AppleWorks session, you can fine-tune the memory allocation.)

4. Click the close box in the upper-left corner of the Info window to save the changes. The next time you run AppleWorks, the additional memory will be available for your program and your documents.

Tip

Using a shareware control panel from Peirce Software called AppSizer, you can change the memory allocation for any application (such as AppleWorks) as you launch it. To learn more about AppSizer or to download a copy, use your Web browser to visit www.peircesw.com/AppSizer.html.

Showing an Open dialog box at start-up

If you want AppleWorks to display an Open dialog box when the program starts up, hold down the ⌘ key as you launch AppleWorks. After the program loads, it immediately presents the Open dialog box in front of the Starting Points window.

Note

If you've changed the General Preferences settings to make AppleWorks present the Open dialog box rather than the Starting Points window, holding down the ⌘ key as you launch the program makes nothing appear instead.

An alternative to tiled and stacked windows

If tiled or stacked windows don't appeal to you, you can take more control over your document window arrangement by shrinking and expanding individual windows.

STEPS: Shrinking and Expanding Document Windows

1. Using the size box, shrink each document window to the smallest possible size.

2. Manually arrange the document windows so the Title Bar of each one is exposed.

3. To make one of the documents active (so you can work with it), click once in its window. (When several windows are onscreen, the active window is the one with a series of horizontal lines in its Title Bar. The title bars for the other windows are blank.)

4. Click the zoom box to expand the document to its full size.

When you're ready to switch to a different document, click the active document's zoom box again; it shrinks back to its reduced size and position. Then repeat Steps 3 and 4 for the next document you want to use.

Alternatively, you can reduce each window to just its Title Bar using its window-shade box and then proceed from Step 3 previously.

Printing AppleWorks files from the desktop

If you aren't currently in AppleWorks and just want to print an existing document without making changes to it, you can do so by using a special procedure.

STEPS: Printing from the Desktop

1. Go to the desktop and select the file icon or icons that you want to print.

2. Choose File ➪ Print (or press ⌘+P).

   Instead of launching AppleWorks in the usual way, choosing Print from the desktop loads the selected document into AppleWorks and immediately presents the Print dialog box.

3. Set your print options, and then click the Print button.

   After the document has been printed, AppleWorks automatically quits and you are returned to the desktop.

You can use this printing procedure with most programs. The only drawback is that if you change your mind about printing the document or decide you need to make some changes before printing it, you need to restart the program and reload the documents.

More About Translators

Some earlier MacOS releases and ClarisWorks and AppleWorks 5 include an extensive set of MacLink Plus translators that, in conjunction with the File Exchange control panel (Macintosh Easy Open in MacOS 8.x), enable you to open a variety of foreign document types. In general, when you export a file to be used in AppleWorks, you should select one of the more specific translators that your copy of AppleWorks supports—that of a particular program such as Excel, Word, or other popular programs of the correct type. When AppleWorks (and MacLink Plus) translates such files, it attempts to retain the proper formatting, margins, styles, formulas, and so on. The next best solution is translating the file to a general format, such as ASCII text. Although much of the original formatting will disappear, at least you can work with the basic text of the document and save some retyping time. In the case of a word processing document, if you can't find a popular word processing format that's supported, see whether the program can create an *RTF* file (a Microsoft document format that has wide support in the computer industry). Unlike straight ASCII text, you'll find that the majority of the original formatting is retained. AppleWorks 6.0 did not include an RTF translator, but the 6.0.3 updater does.

Tip If your printer driver supports Apple's Desktop Printing software, you also can print from the desktop by dragging the files you want to print onto the appropriate Desktop Printer icon.

File conversion tips

Although AppleWorks can understand a few foreign file formats, many formats exist that AppleWorks can't read. What do you do if AppleWorks doesn't have a translator for the foreign file you want to open or insert? One solution is to use the original program to save or export the file into a format that AppleWorks does support.

Suppose, for example, that you have a word processing document that was created in a version of Microsoft Word. All you have to do is open the file in Word and save a new copy of the file in a format that AppleWorks supports, such as RTF (this requires that you have applied the AppleWorks 6.0.3 or later updater). Alternatively, if you don't have that version of Microsoft Word, see whether you have another program that understands Word files. Then load the file into that particular program and save or export it to a format that AppleWorks supports.

Summary

✦ You can launch AppleWorks in several ways. You can have the program open to a particular document on-screen (or several documents), present the Starting Points window, or present the Open dialog box—depending on your needs for the session.

✦ To make finding a particular document easier, the AppleWorks Open dialog box contains a Document Type pop-up menu that can restrict document choices to an environment of your choosing.

✦ Using QuickTime and MacLink Plus, AppleWorks can open or insert many types of non-AppleWorks files.

✦ You can use the Save command to save new versions of documents that are already stored on disk. You can use the Save As command to save new files and multiple generations or backup copies of existing files.

✦ To keep important documents from being easily viewed by others, you can assign passwords to them.

✦ When you're through with a particular document, you can close its window by clicking its close box or by choosing File ➪ Close. You can simultaneously close all document windows by holding down the Option key while clicking any close box or choosing the Close command.

✦ You can click icons in the Tools window's Frames panel to add different environment frames to a document, or the tool frame to select drawing, paint, and table tools. You can hide the Tools window to show more of your document.

✦ You can specify colors, patterns, wallpapers, gradients, and line styles for objects using the Accents windoid.

✦ The Button Bar enables you to quickly execute common commands. Its contents change to match the current environment.

✦ You can integrate two or more environments in a single document by using frames.

✦ You can drag selected text from one AppleWorks document to another, between drag-and-drop enabled programs, and to or from the Macintosh desktop.

✦ You can change the display for any document by hiding or showing tools, resizing the document window, and splitting the screen. If you're working with multiple documents, you can optimize their arrangement with the Tile Windows or Stack Windows commands from the Window menu.

✦ You can print documents from within AppleWorks or from the desktop.

✦ AppleWorks offers several forms of program help: the AppleWorks Help system (Apple Help Viewer), ToolTips, and Balloon Help.

✦   ✦   ✦

New Features in AppleWorks 6

CHAPTER
2

◆ ◆ ◆ ◆

In This Chapter

A history of the changes introduced in ClarisWorks 2.1, 3.0, 4.0, and 5.0

A summary of the new features introduced in AppleWorks 6.0

◆ ◆ ◆ ◆

If you have used an earlier version of AppleWorks or ClarisWorks and have just upgraded to AppleWorks 6.0, this chapter will acquaint you with the program's new features and enhancements. The description of each new feature is followed by a reference to the chapter in which it is fully discussed. Thus, this chapter leads you directly to the feature you want to learn about next.

> **Note** If you're still using any version of ClarisWorks prior to 6.0, you can contact Apple Computer at `www.apple.com/appleworks` for upgrade information.

ClarisWorks/AppleWorks Update History

AppleWorks 6 is the first version since ClarisWorks 2.0 to introduce a new environment, and the first version to drop an environment. You'll see New Feature icons in the margins of this book, making it easy to identify new features in AppleWorks 6.0. If you are upgrading from a version earlier than 5.0, however, you may not recognize other features that—although not new in 6—were new in subsequent versions of ClarisWorks or AppleWorks (and are new to you). To bring you up to date, the following sections briefly discuss the changes that were introduced in ClarisWorks 2.1, 3.0, 4.0, and 5.0. The chapter concludes with a list of the new features in AppleWorks 6 and provides references to the chapters in which the features are discussed. If you are upgrading from ClarisWorks 5 or AppleWorks 5.0, you can skip directly to this final section. With AppleWorks 6 at the vanguard of new OS X-ready applications, Apple has released updaters to improve performance, stability, and functionality as the OS X code base matures. At the time of this writing, AppleWorks 6.0.4 is the latest version.

Note   If this is your first version of AppleWorks, you can skip this entire chapter, because everything is new to you!

New in ClarisWorks 2.1

In February 1994, Claris released ClarisWorks 2.1, which included not only a handful of changes that made AppleWorks easier to use, but also included two important new features:

✦ **Hyphenation.** A custom hyphenation dictionary enabled you to set automatic hyphenation for any word processing document, database, or text frame. You also could enter discretionary hyphens (which appeared only when a word was split across two lines), keep certain words from being hyphenated, and you could edit the hyphenation dictionary. (Hyphenation is covered in Chapter 3.)

✦ **PowerTalk electronic mail support.** This feature enabled you to add a mailer (an address header) to a ClarisWorks document, making the document a letter you could send to other PowerTalk users. Documents sent via PowerTalk could include enclosures, such as other ClarisWorks documents. Support for PowerTalk messaging has been eliminated as of ClarisWorks and AppleWorks 5.0.

New in ClarisWorks 3.0

Although the main purpose of ClarisWorks 3.0 was to bring the Windows version of the program up to par with the Macintosh version, a few significant features and enhancements were added to the Mac version:

✦ **Introduction to ClarisWorks.** New users of ClarisWorks appreciated this guided tour of the program. This feature is no longer available in Apple-Works 6.0.

✦ **Welcome screen.** Rather than assume you always wanted to create a new document, a new Welcome screen enabled you to create a new document, load an existing document, invoke a ClarisWorks Assistant, or view an onscreen tour of ClarisWorks. The Welcome screen was removed in ClarisWorks 4.0.

✦ **Assistants.** Assistants — built-in "experts" — made it simple to perform tasks such as formatting footnotes, creating mailing labels and envelopes, and designing newsletters and presentations. Assistants are discussed in Chapters 1, 3, and 10.

✦ **Revised Help system.** The Help system was changed dramatically in ClarisWorks 3.0. The Help system and related features are discussed in Chapter 1.

✦ **Document Summary.** You could save identifying information with any file to show a more descriptive title, the name of the person who created the file, a version number, keywords, a category, a description, and so forth. This dialog box has been renamed the Properties dialog box in AppleWorks 6 and is discussed in Chapter 1.

✦ **Word count.** This feature provided a count of the number of characters, words, lines, paragraphs, and pages in the current document. Word counts in ClarisWorks 3.0, however, were always based on the entire contents of the document. In ClarisWorks 4.0 and higher, this feature also could perform a count on selected text. Word count is discussed in more detail in Chapter 3.

✦ **Improved Save As and Open dialog boxes.** The new Save As dialog box made it extremely simple to save any document as a stationery template. With Apple's QuickTime extension, the Open dialog box could show you a thumbnail preview of any graphic image or QuickTime movie before you opened the file. While more file types — including AppleWorks documents — can now be previewed in AppleWorks 6, the Create Preview button is no longer available. These dialog boxes are discussed in Chapter 1.

✦ **Automatic macros.** Certain macros could automatically play whenever you launched ClarisWorks, created a new document in a particular environment, or opened a document in a particular environment. Chapter 13 discusses automatic macros.

✦ **Clip art.** To help you create more interesting and attractive documents, ClarisWorks 3.0 included 75 clip art images. In ClarisWorks 4.0, as well as in ClarisWorks and AppleWorks 5, clip art images were organized in libraries. In AppleWorks 6, they are organized as clippings collections. Clippings are discussed in Chapter 13.

✦ **MacWrite Pro file filter.** ClarisWorks 3.0 added a filter that could translate files created with MacWrite Pro. In AppleWorks 6, most filters have been eliminated, and you will need to purchase a separate product such as MacLink Plus to provide this functionality. Translation filters are discussed in Chapter 1.

New in ClarisWorks 4.0

As in most previous ClarisWorks updates, version 4.0 introduced a few new, big features, plus a host of small tweaks, enhancements, and changes.

General enhancements

✦ **Stylesheet palette.** ClarisWorks 4.0 introduced a Stylesheet palette you could use to quickly format text, paragraphs, outlines, spreadsheet tables, and graphics. In addition to using the predefined styles, you also could create your own reusable styles. This has been redesigned in AppleWorks 6 as the Styles window and is discussed in Chapter 15.

✦ **Drag-and-drop support.** Many items that were previously moved using cut-and-paste could now be moved within a document or copied between documents by simply dragging. In version 4.0.3, ClarisWorks became capable of exchanging text and graphics with other drag-and-drop–enabled applications, such as the Scrapbook.

✦ **Libraries.** ClarisWorks 4.0 included 20 ReadyArt libraries of clip art, each organized around a theme, such as education, flags, and foods. Any of the supplied images could be dragged and dropped into your documents. You also could create new libraries in which to store your own graphics, important text, spreadsheet formulas, and QuickTime movies. These have been replaced in AppleWorks 6 by Clippings, which are discussed in Chapter 13.

✦ **New Assistants.** ClarisWorks Assistants made it simple to accomplish common personal and business tasks by guiding you through the process through a series of dialog boxes. ClarisWorks 4.0 added new Assistants for home finance, mailing labels, and certificates. Assistants are introduced in Chapter 1. You'll find additional information about the Mailing Label Assistant in Chapter 5, and Assistants for word processing-related task are described in Chapter 3.

✦ **HTML translator and stationery document.** Because people have continually expressed interest in the Internet and the World Wide Web, ClarisWorks 4.0 could be used to create and translate HTML (HyperText Markup Language) documents to present information and graphics on the Web. A stationery document with predefined HTML tag styles also was provided. Details on viewing, editing, and creating HTML documents is presented in Chapter 19.

✦ **Sample AppleScripts.** If you had Apple Computer's AppleScript software installed on your Mac, you could use the sample AppleScripts to print batches of documents, translate groups of non-ClarisWorks documents to ClarisWorks format, run remote slide shows, and even use FileMaker Pro data in a mail merge. In AppleWorks 6, a new set of sample AppleScripts has been provided, courtesy of T & B Enhancements (www.tandb.au).

Spreadsheet enhancements

✦ **Cell shading.** In previous versions of ClarisWorks, spreadsheet embellishments were largely limited to applying borders, choosing fonts, and adding a background color. ClarisWorks 4.0 enabled you to apply colors and patterns to individual worksheet cells. Cell shading is discussed in more detail in Chapter 4.

✦ **Fill Special command.** Spreadsheet users are familiar with the Fill Down and Fill Right commands, which enabled them to create mathematical sequences or to number a series of rows. Fill Special was a more powerful version of these two commands, making it easy to create a numerical sequence without having to determine the formula or to label a series of cells with dates, times, month names, days, and so on. The Fill Special command is discussed in Chapter 4.

Database enhancements

✦ **New field types.** ClarisWorks 4.0 introduced seven new field types: name, pop-up menu, radio buttons, checkbox, serial number, value list, and record info. Chapter 5 discusses these field types and the other changes to the database environment.

✦ **List mode.** In previous versions of ClarisWorks, all data entry, editing, and record viewing was done in Browse mode. By selecting List mode, any database could then be viewed and worked with in a spreadsheet-like grid.

✦ **Named searches and sorts.** ClarisWorks 4.0 enabled you to save Sort and Find instructions for each database so that they could easily be reexecuted whenever you liked.

✦ **Report generator.** Report creation instructions — including the name of the layout to be used, the Sort and Find instructions, and whether the report should automatically be printed — also could be saved.

✦ **Mailing Label Assistant.** ClarisWorks 4.0 provided a new Assistant for creating mailing labels.

Word processing enhancements

✦ **Sections.** Complex documents (such as books and reports) could be divided into logical sections. Each section could have its own title page, as well as different headers and footers. Left- and right-facing pages were also supported. Chapter 3 discusses word processing features.

✦ **Outlining.** In earlier versions of ClarisWorks, a word processing document could be displayed in normal or outline view. In ClarisWorks 4.0, outlining was fully integrated into the word processing environment, enabling you to create an outline inside a regular word processing document.

✦ **Endnotes.** In previous versions of ClarisWorks, only footnotes could be produced. With the added support for endnotes, users could move all in-text citations to the end of the current document.

✦ **Selective word count.** In addition to being capable of gathering word count statistics for an entire document, ClarisWorks 4.0 was the first version to also create a word count report based on the current text selection.

✦ **Paragraph Styles menu.** Paragraph and outline formats could be chosen and applied from this pop-up menu in the ruler bar. In ClarisWorks and AppleWorks 5.0, this pop-up menu was moved to the Button Bar. In AppleWorks 6, it is an optional pop-up menu button for the Button Bar.

✦ **New font styles.** ClarisWorks 4.0 added three new font styles: superior, inferior, and double underline.

✦ **Onscreen mail merge preview.** When performing a mail merge, users could preview how their documents would look and print using actual merge data.

Drawing enhancements

✦ **Free rotation.** In previous versions of the program, Draw objects could only be rotated in 90-degree increments. In ClarisWorks 4.0, objects could be rotated to any angle by using either the Free Rotation or Object Info command (called the Object Size command in ClarisWorks/AppleWorks 5.0 and AppleWorks 6.0). Chapter 6 provides more information on using these commands.

New in ClarisWorks and AppleWorks 5.0

No new environments appeared in ClarisWorks 5.0, but a terribly confusing marketing/renaming scheme resulted in three virtually identical versions of the product. ClarisWorks 5 — the core program — was available only to the educational market, as a product upgrade, or as bundled software on iMacs and iBooks. ClarisWorks Office — the core program, plus Internet- and business-related add-on software — was the sole retail product. When Apple updated the base product to version 5.0.3, it was renamed AppleWorks (or AppleWorks 5). The only important thing you should remember from this lengthy discussion is that all of the following products had the *identical* base program: ClarisWorks 5, ClarisWorks Office, AppleWorks, and AppleWorks 5.

The most significant features added to the base product were: the customizable Button Bars (replacing the former Shortcuts palette); bookmark, document, and URL links, plus the new Links palette; and, improved support for creating Web pages in AppleWorks.

ClarisWorks Office enhancements

✦ **Add-ons.** What distinguished ClarisWorks Office from ClarisWorks 5.0 was a series of add-on programs and templates that were available only as a part of ClarisWorks Office. Included were Netscape Navigator (a popular program for browsing the World Wide Web, and which also has been included with System software releases), Claris Home Page Lite (a Web-page design program, subsequently renamed as FileMaker Home Page Lite), and a series of business templates. These add-ons are not included in AppleWorks 6.

General enhancements

✦ **Button Bars.** In previous versions of the program, you could click buttons in the floating Shortcuts palette to perform common — and occasionally esoteric — tasks in any environment. Customizable button bars that were displayed above the current document took the place of the Shortcuts palette. Button Bars are covered in Chapter 12.

✦ **Bookmark, document, and URL links.** Text, objects, and frames could be designated as clickable links in AppleWorks 5.0 documents. Depending on the type of link, clicking could make the document automatically scroll to a bookmark in the same document, open a different document (including documents created by programs other than AppleWorks), or launch your Web browser and display a particular page on the World Wide Web. Links and the Link palette are discussed in Chapters 18 and 19.

✦ **Passwords.** To improve security, passwords could be assigned to documents, as explained in Chapter 1.

✦ **Default font.** You could now specify a default font to be used for all text, as explained in Chapter 11.

✦ **Compound styles.** By enabling compound styles, you could apply multiple styles from the current stylesheet to selected text. (Refer to Chapter 15.)

✦ **Business Card Assistant.** This new Assistant enabled you to quickly create business cards in several different styles.

✦ **Context-sensitive help for dialog boxes.** Every major dialog box sported a ? (Help) button that, when clicked, summoned help relevant to the dialog box.

✦ **Fonts.** Seven free TrueType fonts were included with AppleWorks 5.0. Many more are included with AppleWorks 6.

✦ **File translators.** To improve AppleWorks's file translation capabilities, a special version of the DataViz file translators, the control panel, and the extensions were provided. These translators do not ship with AppleWorks 6, but will continue to work with AppleWorks 6 if you are upgrading from an earlier release of AppleWorks or ClarisWorks.

Word processing enhancements

✦ **Ruler guidelines.** When setting margins and tabs in a word processing document, a temporary vertical line extended down the page from the margin or tab stop in the ruler.

✦ **Equation Editor.** Statisticians and others who worked with numbers were pleased to learn about the new Equation Editor. By selecting options from pop-up menus, you could create extremely complex equations and place them in your documents as resizable graphics.

✦ **Paragraph Sorter.** Using the Paragraph Sorter Assistant, you could arrange any selected group of paragraphs alphabetically or randomly. This Assistant is not part of AppleWorks 6.

✦ **Descent setting for in-line objects.** In previous versions of ClarisWorks, in-line graphics could be resized, but not moved up or down, to improve their appearance within the surrounding text. Using the Descent command, you could raise or lower the placement of any in-line graphic. This feature is discussed in Chapter 3.

Database enhancements

✦ **Multimedia fields.** The new multimedia field type was used to store QuickTime movies, graphics, and sounds in AppleWorks databases, as discussed in Chapter 5. The movies and sounds could be played by clicking the field in which they are stored.

Spreadsheet enhancements

✦ **Named ranges.** To make it simpler to identify key ranges in worksheets, users could now name ranges and refer to them in formulas by name (Quarterly Sales, for example), rather than by address (C3..C6, for example). Named ranges are discussed in Chapter 4.

Paint enhancements

✦ **New graphic file formats.** Graphic files could be opened or saved in BMP, GIF, and JPEG formats, improving compatibility with Microsoft Windows and the World Wide Web. While AppleWorks 6 will still open GIF files, it will not create them due to licensing restrictions on the compression technology. PNG graphics (another WWW standard) can be created with AppleWorks 6, as well as any graphic format that QuickTime supports.

Internet enhancements

✦ **URL links.** Hyperlinks to specific Web pages could be embedded in most AppleWorks documents. When the hyperlink was clicked, the user's Web browser was launched and the Web page was loaded from the Internet. URL links are covered in Chapters 18 and 19.

✦ **Improved HTML translator.** Any standard word processing document could be translated into HTML format — the language of pages on the World Wide Web. To make it even easier to design Web pages, a dozen new stationery templates for personal, business, and student Web pages were provided. During the process of translating the documents to HTML, embedded graphics were automatically converted to GIF or JPEG format. Support also was added for tables and page backgrounds. Chapter 19 discusses creating Web pages with AppleWorks.

✦ **Internet button bar.** AppleWorks 5.0 included a special Internet Button Bar that enabled you to configure your Macintosh for the Internet, launch a Web browser or e-mail program, add hyperlinks to a document, convert the current document into a Web page, or summon assistance from the Claris Web site.

New in AppleWorks 6.0

AppleWorks 6 is the first major upgrade to the product with a new environment: Presentations. In addition, the somewhat outdated Communications environment has been removed. Finally, AppleWorks 6 sports a totally new user interface to fit into the coming OS X environment.

Caution AppleWorks 6 is "carbonized." This means that it is ready to run on MacOS X and requires the CarbonLib system extension when used with earlier versions of the MacOS. Another kind of MacOS X-ready application exists, called "Cocoa," that cannot be made to run on earlier MacOS releases. A number of third-party add-ons, as described in the "Late Breaking News" document included with AppleWorks 6, are not Carbon-compatible and can cause problems when running AppleWorks. Apple included revisions of the CarbonLib system extension in its AppleWorks 6.0.3 and later updates to improve performance and increase stability, as well as to offer some new functionality (an RTF translator, for example). Further updates are expected, and you should check the Apple Web site to see what is current.

AppleWorks 6 is also the first version to directly use the Internet to distribute additional content and support. In addition, you can construct some fairly sophisticated Web sites with the Internet tools.

Inter-application document format conversion has largely been left to third-party tool providers such as DataViz, while reliance on and inclusion of QuickTime 4 has increased the number of supported graphic and multimedia formats.

AppleWorks 6 has significantly enhanced AppleScriptability, and includes a selection of third-party AppleScripts from T&B (www.tandb.au) in its new Scripts menu.

In addition, AppleWorks 6 provides the following changes.

Updated user interface

The new AppleWorks 6 interface relies heavily on tabbed floating windows, as described in Chapter 1. These windows include:

✦ **The Starting Points window** replaces the New Document window for basic document creation, as well as for accessing AppleWorks Assistants, template files (formerly called stationery), recently opened files, and Web content. The Starting Points window is discussed in Chapter 1.

✦ **The Clippings window** replaces the Libraries palette as the interface to a centralized clip art repository. The search feature in Clippings enables you to find the right art—whether it is located on one of your disks or on the Internet. You can download additional clip art from the AppleWorks Web site without requiring a separate browser. The Clippings window is discussed in Chapter 13.

✦ **A new Tools window** has been added consisting of two panels. These panels contain the various frame and work tools that were formerly placed on the Tool panel, as well as tools for the new Tables (covered later). The Frames panel contains framing tools for the Drawing, Word Processing, Spreadsheet, Painting environments, and Table frames. The Tools panel contains tools for creating and editing drawing and painting objects — as well as tables — to all environments. The Tools windoid is discussed in detail in Chapter 1.

✦ **The Accents window** collects the various pop-up and tear-off palettes that were formerly part of the (now defunct) Tool panel. The Accents window enables you to access colors, patterns, wallpapers, gradients, and line width adjustment panels with the click of a tab. Chapter 6 discusses the Accents window and how it is used to add enhancements to your graphic projects.

✦ **The Button Bar** has been resized and made easier to use. Most AppleWorks power users feel that although the new Button Bar is easier to use and the new buttons are easier to recognize, some power and functionality has been lost. The contents of the Button Bar have been streamlined. By default, it includes the most commonly used buttons for each of the six AppleWorks environments. You add or delete buttons from a new Button Bar preferences dialog box. Button Bars are described in Chapters 1 and 12.

✦ **Autosave** (a preference setting) specifies how often and when you would like AppleWorks to automatically create a backup copy of your document. File security is also enhanced. If your Mac crashes, AppleWorks will automatically launch at startup with the autosaved copy, enabling you to continue working on the last document you were using. Both features are described in Chapter 1.

✦ **Mail merge enhancements** enable you to merge data from databases into a single file, multiple files, or directly to the printer. Mail merge is discussed in Chapter 8.

Introducing a new environment: Presentations

AppleWorks 6 left the older slideshow capabilities of the Drawing environment intact, but duplicated much of the functionality and added significant enhancements to a new environment called Presentations. Presentations are covered in detail in Chapter 7. Some of the most important Presentation features and capabilities are as follows:

✦ AppleWorks provides a collection of prebuilt presentation templates to assist you in beginning a project. You also can build a presentation from scratch.

✦ Multiple master slides let you create themed Presentation groupings without many of the workarounds required by a single Master Page (although you have the equivalent of a Master Page, named Background, as well).

✦ A thumbnail view can be used to manage and order your slides. You can move slides around, rename them, and mark them as hidden or nonprinting using the viewer. You also can hide slides to personalize presentations for different audiences.

✦ A Notes View feature enables you to write speaker's notes directly onto sheets containing a copy of the slides.

✦ You can group pages together to ensure that when you reorganize slides, that individual pages do not get out of order.

✦ Presentations include robust playback features. You can add transitions between slides, use auto-advance and looping for continuous play, and add music, movies (such as QuickTime movies), and voice annotation.

Spreadsheet enhancements

✦ Formulas can now reference cells in other AppleWorks spreadsheets, documents, and frames by typing a name with an exclamation point into the Calculation text box. Spreadsheet references are described in Chapter 4.

✦ The Paste Function dialog box lets you choose from over 100 built-in functions to assist in building calculation formulas in spreadsheets and databases. Both the function name and a short description are displayed in the Insert Function dialog box. Functions are described in Chapters 4 and 5.

✦ Keyboard navigation in spreadsheets has been enhanced

✦ AppleWorks now adds a missing closing parenthesis in spreadsheet formulas if it has been inadvertently omitted, correcting a common user error.

Table enhancements

✦ You can now create tables in any environment without resorting to the use of spreadsheet frames. As with anything else in the Paint environment, however, it reverts to a bitmap as soon as you click out of it. Tables are discussed in terms of reports and charts in Chapter 9, and are specifically discussed in Word Processing documents in Chapter 3.

✦ You can draw a table directly into a document using the new table frame tool, and then specify how many rows and columns to place in your custom-built table. You also can convert from tab-delimited text to table and back again.

✦ You can add, delete, and resize table cells individually, as well as in ranges, rows, and columns. You can use the Cell tool or Table menu commands to merge, resize, split, add, format, or delete cells.

✦ Each cell is a word processing frame and accepts anything (other than another table frame) that any other text frame will hold, such as outlines, text, graphics, and multimedia.

✦ You can embed all types of frames within tables (except another table frame), as well as import movies, sounds, and graphics into table cells. You also can link a table's graphic image to a Web site.

✦ You can create the effect of complex nested tables in AppleWorks and convert them to HTML without any data loss. Chapter 19 discusses how to use AppleWorks to build Web pages.

Internet enhancements

✦ AppleWorks 6 provides extensive Internet integration. The new Web panel in the Starting Points window enables you to download templates from the Web to your desktop or to access AppleWorks documents (such as the AppleWorks Newsletter) stored on Web sites. You also can download clip art directly from the AppleWorks site using the new Clippings window, without having to use a browser. In addition to being able to link to pages on the Web from any document in AppleWorks using a browser, you can now share AppleWorks documents transparently over the Web. The Internet features of AppleWorks are described in Chapter 19.

✦   ✦   ✦

Using the AppleWorks Environments

◆ ◆ ◆ ◆

The Word Processing Environment

Everyone writes. Your parents make you write "Thank you" notes when you're a kid. Teachers assign you essays and reports when you're in school. You write love letters and diary entries as a teenager or young adult. At work, you write memos and reports. Whether you're working on a letter, memo, fax, report, or the Great American Novel, a word processor is the ideal writing tool.

About Word Processors

A word processing program makes it easy for you to edit, reorganize, and polish your writing. Spelling checkers, thesauruses, and grammar checkers can help you choose the best (and correct) words. Because you create documents onscreen, you can avoid paper waste by not printing until the document is exactly as you want it. Instead of making copies of documents for your hard copy files, you can simply save them on disk. If you ever need to refer to the original document again or want another printed copy, you just open the document in the word processor and, if desired, print it. Finally, you can store frequently used paragraphs on disk and reuse them whenever you like. You can copy and paste them into the document, move them from one document to another using drag-and-drop, or save them as reusable templates.

As you read this chapter, keep in mind that almost everything in it applies to word processing frames, as well as to documents. In addition, some of the features you traditionally associate with word processing, such as the spelling checker and text ruler, also are available in other AppleWorks environments. This chapter includes a discussion of these features (because this is where you'd normally expect to read about them), and other chapters refer you back to this chapter as necessary.

Word Processing Essentials

The first step in using the word processor is to create a new word processing document. In AppleWorks, you do this by choosing File ➪ New ➪ Word Processing (or by pressing ⌘+N). Alternatively, you could click either the Word Processing thumbnail on the Starting Points Basic panel or the Word Processing button on your Button Bar. A blank document opens (see Figure 3-1) with the cursor positioned at the top of the page, ready for you to start typing text.

Figure 3-1: A new word processing document

Text that you type, paste, or add with the Insert command always appears at the text insertion point. The insertion point is marked by a tiny vertical line. You can change the insertion point by moving the mouse and then clicking in a new location within the existing text. To help you accurately position the text insertion point, AppleWorks displays an I-beam cursor (shown in Figure 3-1) as you move the mouse pointer over the page.

Note

In AppleWorks 6, you also can add text to a word processing document or frame by simply dragging it from another open AppleWorks document or from any drag-and-drop-enabled application, such as SimpleText. This same technique also can be used to move text within a document, as well as to move objects between documents.

As you type, AppleWorks automatically handles line endings by wrapping extra text to the next line. When you approach the end of a line, the word processor checks whether the word you are typing, plus the other words in the line, exceed the printable page width. If so, the last word is automatically moved or wrapped to the next line. Unlike with a typewriter, you don't have to press the Return key to start a new line in a word processing document. You just keep typing. In fact, the only times you should press the Return key are to end a paragraph or to insert an extra blank line between paragraphs, although, as we'll discuss later in this chapter, you have a better way to accomplish the latter.

In addition to reformatting lines for you, the word processor automatically repaginates for you. As you insert, delete, or move text in the document, the program automatically adjusts the composition of the pages. Suppose, for example, you add a couple of paragraphs to the middle of a report. If you are using a typewriter, you have to retype most or all the pages that follow that insertion. In the AppleWorks word processor, however, any text following the two new paragraphs automatically shifts down, and the program forms new pages as required. Large deletions work the same way. When you delete, the word processor automatically closes up the space and repaginates the document.

As with all current word processing programs, the AppleWorks word processor is paragraph-oriented. Tabs, indents, and text alignment options that you apply always affect an entire paragraph, not just the line where the text insertion point happens to be. When you press the Return key, a new paragraph is started that — by default — contains the same settings as the previous paragraph. Because each paragraph is treated as a separate entity, you can change settings on a paragraph-by-paragraph basis.

You also can apply text formatting options such as fonts, sizes, and character styles to entire paragraphs or to selected text within a paragraph. You simply select some text and then choose the appropriate text formatting commands from the Font, Size, and Style menus.

Navigation

AppleWorks provides several ways to navigate through a document without changing the insertion point. If you're just reading a document onscreen or checking what was written on page 7, for example, you can use the techniques in Table 3-1 to move through the document. Again, when you are using these techniques, the text insertion point does not change.

Table 3-1 Navigational Techniques	
Navigation	Key or Action
Move up or down one line of text	Click the up- or down-arrow symbol on the scroll bar.
Move up or down one screenful of text	Press the Page Up or Page Down key, or click in the gray area of the vertical scroll bar.
Move up or down to an approximate location	Drag the box in the vertical scroll bar to a new position.
Move to the beginning or end of the document	Press the Home or End key, or drag the box in the scroll bar to the top or bottom.
Go to a specific page	Double-click in the page number area at the lower edge of the document, and then type a page number in the dialog box that appears.

Basic Text Editing

Few of us are blessed with the ability to write precisely what we want the very first time. In fact, depending on the type and complexity of the document, we might actually spend more time editing than doing the initial writing. This section describes some essential techniques for text editing in the word processing environment.

Selecting text

To manipulate text — to cut it, change the font or style, and so on — you first have to select it.

To select text, position the cursor where you want the selection to start and then either Shift+click where you want it to end, or simply drag to complete the selection. In addition to this basic text-selection technique, you also can use these shortcuts:

✦ To select a single word, double-click anywhere within the word

✦ To select the current line, triple-click anywhere within the line

✦ To select the current paragraph, quadruple-click anywhere within the paragraph

✦ To select the entire document, choose Edit ⇨ Select All (or press ⌘+A)

Inserting text in a word processing document or frame

Whether you type text, paste it, insert it with the Insert command, or drag it in from another document, it is always entered at the text insertion point (described previously). You can enter new text into a word processing document or a text frame.

Position the cursor over the spot where you want to insert the text and press the mouse button once, or use the arrow keys to move the cursor as described in Table 3-2. Type the text, paste it, or enter it with the Insert command from the File menu.

Table 3-2
Insertion Point Navigational Shortcuts

Cursor Movement	Keystroke
One character left or right	Left-arrow or right-arrow key
One line up or down	Up-arrow or down-arrow key
To the start or end of a line	⌘+left-arrow or ⌘+right-arrow key
One word to the left or right	Option+left-arrow or Option+right-arrow key
To the beginning or end of a paragraph	Option+up-arrow or Option+down-arrow key
To the beginning or end of the document	⌘+up-arrow or ⌘+down-arrow key
Continuous scrolling	Press and hold the up-arrow or down-arrow key

> **Tip**   Keyboard shortcuts also exist to create or extend a selection from the cursor's location. Holding down the Shift key while using any of the arrow key combinations extends the selection from the cursor's location to the point where the unshifted keystroke would move the cursor.

When you position the cursor, you need to place it immediately before, after, or within the current text of the document. In a new, blank document, for example, no matter where you click, the insertion point is set at the start of the first page. Similarly, even if you click several inches below the last paragraph in a partially written document, the insertion point is placed immediately following the last character of the document. If you want to start typing well below the current end of the document, you can press the Return key several times to add the necessary white space so you can position the insertion point where you want it.

> **Note**   When you use drag-and-drop to copy or move text, a small vertical insertion bar appears immediately above the cursor, indicating the exact position to which the dragged text will be inserted.

Deleting text from a word processing document or frame

Part of the writing process for anyone is deleting text — either character by character or for entire blocks of text.

To delete a character, position the cursor to the right of the character and press the Delete or Backspace keys. Each key press deletes one character to the left of the cursor. If your keyboard has a Del key, you can position the cursor to the left of the character you want to delete and press the Del key. Each press of the Del key deletes one character to the right of the cursor.

To delete a block of text, select the text, and then press the Delete, Backspace, Clear, or Del key (or choose Edit ➪ Clear). Each of these operations deletes the text selection without copying it to the clipboard. You also can choose Edit ➪ Cut (or press ⌘+X). This method simultaneously deletes the text selection and copies it to the clipboard. Use this approach when you want to paste the text elsewhere — either in the current document or another document.

Copying and reusing text

The Copy command comes in handy when you have text strings or phrases you want to use in several places in a document or copy to a different document. To copy text, select the text to be copied, and then choose Edit ➪ Copy (or press ⌘+C). A copy of the selected text is transferred to the clipboard, and the text is immediately available for pasting. Until you copy or cut (⌘+X) something else to the clipboard, you can paste the copied text repeatedly (⌘+V) in the current document, as well as in other documents.

Using the Macintosh Clipboard

Throughout this book, and in many other Macintosh books, magazines, and manuals, you see frequent references to the *clipboard*. What is the clipboard, and how does it work?

The clipboard is a file in your System folder that contains a copy of the *scrap*, a temporary storage area in Macintosh *RAM* (memory). The last object or text selection you copied with the Copy command (⌘+C) or removed with the Cut command (⌘+X) is stored in the clipboard. Each time you copy or cut a new object or text selection, the new object or text replaces the current contents of the clipboard.

The beauty of the clipboard is that its current contents are available for pasting using the Paste command (⌘+V). Not only can you paste the object or text into the current document, you also can paste it into other documents — even into documents in other programs. You can, for example, copy a name and address from a word processing document and paste it into an address book desk accessory (or vice versa).

The only actions that clear the contents of the clipboard are cutting or copying a new object or text selection or restarting the Mac. Otherwise, you can quit one program and start another, confident that the clipboard's contents are still intact. (Note, however, that a few Mac programs create their own clipboard that is separate from the Mac's clipboard. Information that is copied to or cut from a program-specific clipboard might not be available for pasting in other programs. See your program's documentation or help files for more information.)

Note

You also can use drag-and-drop to move text within the current document. This works like a cut-and-paste operation, but does not affect the contents of the clipboard. When text is dragged from one document to another, the effect is like a copy-and-paste operation. Again, the clipboard is unaffected.

Moving text in a word processing document or frame

In AppleWorks, moving text is usually a two-step process: cut and then paste. You cut selected text from the document and then paste it in another position in the document. To move text by cutting and pasting, select the text to be moved, and then choose Edit ➪ Cut (or press ⌘+X). The text is deleted and then moved to the clipboard. Move the text insertion point to the spot where you want to move the text. Choose Edit ➪ Paste (or press ⌘+V). The previously cut text is pasted at the text insertion point.

Tip

AppleWorks also provides a shortcut for directly moving a text selection to a new location without using the normal cut-and-paste or drag-and-drop routine. To use this method, select the text to be moved and hold down the ⌘ and Option keys while you use the mouse button to click the destination location in the document. The text is transferred from its original location to the destination.

Undoing your actions

While typing or editing a document, you'll probably make errors. You might find you've typed a phrase in the wrong spot — perhaps in the middle of a word — or you've chosen the wrong formatting command. You often can correct the damage by using the Undo command.

AppleWorks keeps track of the last thing you did to change the current document, such as cutting or inserting text, or by applying formatting to a selection. If Apple-Works can undo the last action, choosing Edit ⇨ Undo (or pressing ⌘+Z) puts the document back to the condition it was in immediately before you performed the action. The wording of the Undo command changes to reflect the last action. If, for example, the last change you made was a cut, the command reads Undo Cut.

After choosing Undo, you can still change your mind. The Undo menu command now reads Redo command (in this case, Redo Cut). Choose the Redo command, and the Undo is undone.

Caution   Undo tracks only the last change you made to the document. If you delete some text and then type new text, you cannot undo the deletion. For the Undo command to work, you have to catch the error immediately — before you make any other change to the document. Also, you cannot undo some actions. Saving a new version of a file over the existing file is one example. In those instances, the Undo command is grayed out and reads Can't Undo. Think carefully before you make major changes (and be sure to keep current backups).

If you've been experimenting with a document and want to undo all the changes you've made, choose File ⇨ Revert. Revert replaces the document onscreen with a copy of the most recently saved version of the file. It's as though you closed the current document without saving it and then reloaded the original document from disk. Be careful when you use the Revert command — you cannot undo it by using the Undo command. Also note that you can use the Revert command with any type of AppleWorks document, not just word processing files.

Formatting: Word Processing with Style

Formatting is what distinguishes an ordinary document from one with style. Sure, you can just pick a standard font (such as Times or Helvetica) and type the entire document, pausing only to press the Return key now and then to begin a new paragraph. But the word processor enables you to do much more. You can choose different fonts for headers and body text, apply italic to selected phrases to add emphasis, set left and right indents differently for different paragraphs, create hanging indents to format bullet lists, and use tabs to align items in a list or in columns of numbers. You will learn to master these — and other — formatting commands in this section.

The word processing environment has four classes of formatting:

✦ **Text formatting** is concerned with applying fonts, sizes, and styles to characters, words, phrases, sentences, and paragraphs.

✦ **Paragraph formatting** enables you to set tabs, indents, line spacing, and between-paragraph spacing for paragraphs.

✦ **Section formatting** enables you to divide a document into logical chunks (such as chapters), and specify whether a section begins with a title page, whether left- and right-hand headers and footers are different from each other, and whether page numbering should pick up where the last chapter ended or restart at a particular number. You also can set a different number of columns for text in different sections.

Note

You have your choice as to whether a section break starts on a new line (useful when you want a different number of columns for part of the page) or a new page (which is customary for a new chapter). In AppleWorks 5, the default section break started on a new page, but that default has changed to a New Line break in AppleWorks 6.

✦ **Document formatting** governs the look of the entire document. It includes setting margins, controlling the onscreen appearance of margins and page guides, setting a starting page number for the document, and specifying whether the document will have footnotes or endnotes.

Note

AppleWorks has two related features to help you consistently apply text and paragraph styles. They are the Styles windoid and the optional Styles pop-up button. Both are discussed briefly in this chapter. (For additional information about styles, see Chapter 15.)

Formatting words

Formatting words, as discussed here, refers to applying different fonts, sizes, and styles. Although you can apply these formats to individual characters within a document, you'll usually format words and phrases.

Changing fonts and styles

Most people format correspondence and reports using a single font in a single size. When you want to make some text stand out (for example, by applying italic to emphasize a phrase or by changing the font to differentiate a header from body text), AppleWorks enables you to apply different fonts, sizes, and styles.

To type text into a document using a specific font, size, or style, position the text insertion point and choose from the Text ⇨ Font, Text ⇨ Size, or Text ⇨ Style submenu before typing. To change existing text, select it and then choose a new font, size, or style from the corresponding submenu.

Although each character can have only one font and size combination (Helvetica 12 point, for example), you can assign multiple styles to any text. To apply additional styles, select some text and then choose the Style commands you want to apply to the text.

Styles you can combine include the following:

- ✦ **Bold** (⌘+B)
- ✦ *Italic* (⌘+I)
- ✦ Underline (⌘+U) or Double Underline
- ✦ Strikethrough
- ✦ Outline
- ✦ Shadow

In addition, you can do the following:

- ✦ Apply a color to selected text by choosing a color from the optional Text Color pop-up menu in the Button Bar or from the Text ➪ Color submenu. You also can click the Text box in your Accents windoid and select the desired color from the Color panel.
- ✦ Move letters in a text string closer together (Condense) or farther apart (Extend).
- ✦ Format characters so they appear higher (Superscript, ⌘+Shift+- [hyphen]), lower (Subscript, ⌘+Shift+- [hyphen]), higher in a reduced size (Superior), or lower in a reduced size (Inferior) than the surrounding text.

The following sets of styles are mutually exclusive: Condense and Extend; Underline and Double Underline; and Superscript, Subscript, Superior, and Inferior.

If the Button Bar is visible (choose Window ➪ Show Button Bar or press ⌘+Shift+X) and you have added the optional pop-up buttons, you can quickly set the font, size, style, and color of text by choosing options from the pop-up menus, as shown in Figure 3-2. See Chapter 12 to learn how to customize the Button Bar.

Note   The AppleWorks 6.0.3 (and 6.0.4) updater modified the text ruler to include font and size pop-up menus to the right of the column controls.

Removing styles

Each command in the Text ➪ Style submenu works as a toggle. To remove a single style from a text string, select the text and choose the style command you want to remove—italic, for example. This method of removing styles is particularly useful when a text string has several styles and you want to remove one or some of them, while leaving the other styles intact. You can instantly remove all styles (except color) from text by selecting the text and then choosing Text ➪ Style ➪ Plain Text (⌘+T).

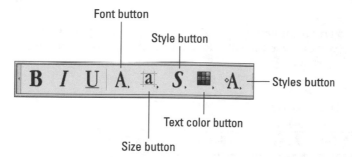

Figure 3-2: The Button Bar provides pop-up menus for common text-formatting options.

Formatting paragraphs

The AppleWorks word processor treats every paragraph as a distinct entity. If you like, you can give every paragraph different settings for tabs, indents, alignment, and the spacing between lines and between paragraphs. You can set these paragraph formatting options with the ruler or choose the Format ➪ Paragraph and Format ➪ Tabs commands.

Note

When you type new paragraphs, each time you press the Return key to end one paragraph and begin another, AppleWorks automatically applies the format of the previous paragraph to the new paragraph. These formatting options remain in effect for additional paragraphs until you specifically change them.

Choosing and Using Fonts

Regardless of the type of document you're working on, you'll do well to restrict your use of fonts to a small number — perhaps two. (Too many fonts can make a document look like a ransom note.) Within a selected font (Helvetica or Times, for example), you can freely apply other styles, such as italic, bold, and so on.

Body fonts can be divided into two general types that are referred to as *serif* and *sans serif*. A serif font, such as Times, has angular points and lines (called *serifs*) at the base and top of each character. Serif fonts are designed to be easy on the eyes and are regularly used to format body text. Sans serif fonts, such as Helvetica, are essentially smooth (they have no serifs) and are often used as headings (*sans* means *no* or *without*). Other special-purpose fonts also exist (script, picture, dingbat, and so forth), but they are primarily ornamental in nature and usage.

If you're new at selecting and using fonts (as most of us are), try these suggestions as a starting point:

✦ For body text, choose a serif font (such as Times, Palatino, or Adobe Garamond)

✦ For heads, use a sans serif font (such as Helvetica Bold, Arial Black, or Franklin Gothic)

Using the ruler

The text ruler serves a greater function than simply showing the page width. By clicking and dragging, you can use the ruler to set most paragraph formatting options, as shown in Figure 3-3.

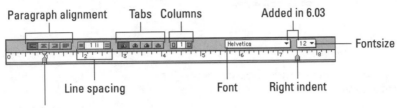

Figure 3-3: The ruler and its components

The options you can set with the ruler include:

✦ Paragraph alignment (left, center, right, or justified)

✦ Line spacing

✦ Indents (left, right, and first)

✦ Tab stops (left, center, right, or decimal)

✦ Number of columns (described in "Columns," later in this chapter)

✦ Font and font-size, if you have updated to AppleWorks 6.0.3

Custom Text Styles

As you work with the word processor, you might find that you frequently use some special text styles (12-point Helvetica Bold, for example). Text styles in the stylesheet are called *basic styles*. You can add custom text styles, edit existing styles, delete styles, and import or export styles (enabling you to share styles among documents and users) to the stylesheet. In addition to text styles, the stylesheet also can contain paragraph and outline styles that you can use in word processing documents.

To apply a text style to selected text, display the Styles windoid (choose Format⇨Show Styles ⌘+Shift+W) and click the name of the style in the Styles windoid. Paragraph styles can be selected from the Styles windoid or from the optional Styles pop-up button in the Button Bar. (See Chapter 15 for information about using stylesheets in the word processor, as well as in other environments.)

You can apply multiple text styles to the same text by clicking the Allow Compound Styles checkbox in the Styles windoid. When the Allow Compound Styles checkbox is not checked, each stylesheet text style you set for a particular text block automatically replaces the previously set style.

When you want to make minor changes to paragraph formatting, this visually guided approach is easy to use. Just change the ruler settings until the paragraph looks right. If the ruler isn't visible, choose Format ➪ Rulers ➪ Show Rulers (or press ⌘+Shift+U). To hide the ruler, choose Format ➪ Rulers ➪ Hide Rulers (or press ⌘+Shift+U).

Although most people prefer a ruler that measures in inches, you can change the measurement units, as well as specify the number of ruler divisions — up to 512. Regardless of how many divisions you set, the ruler will not display more tick marks than 8 per inch or 4 per centimeter, but the resolution is there for placement of tabs and other objects. Examples of the different measurement units are shown in Figure 3-4.

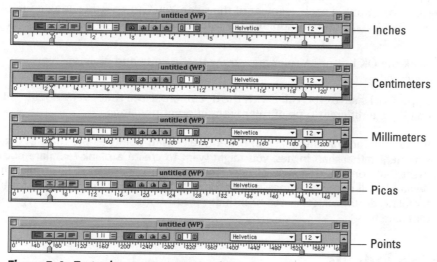

Figure 3-4: Text ruler measurement units

STEPS: Setting Ruler Measurement Units and Divisions

1. Open an existing word processing document or create a new document.

2. Choose Format ➪ Rulers ➪ Ruler Settings. The Rulers dialog box appears (see Figure 3-5).

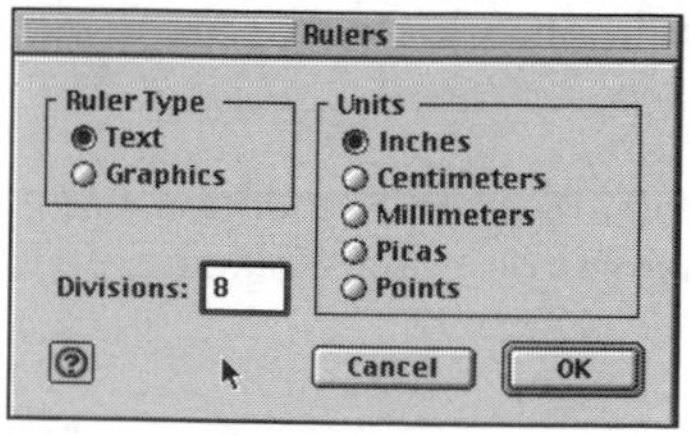

Figure 3-5: The Rulers dialog box

3. Select either the text ruler or the graphics ruler by clicking the appropriate radio button in the Ruler Type box.

   The text ruler is a standard horizontal ruler that appears at the top of the page. Selecting the graphics ruler creates a pair of rulers: a horizontal ruler across the top of the page, and a vertical ruler down the left side of the page. Graphics rulers, however, are only aids for positioning; they do not contain the same controls as text rulers. Thus, graphics rulers are not recommended for use with word processing documents — unless you are trying to position a frame or draw object precisely within a page (or something similar).

4. Select a unit of measurement by clicking the appropriate radio button in the Units box.

5. Type a number in the Divisions text box to indicate the number of minor divisions you want in each segment of the ruler. You can specify a maximum of 512 divisions, although AppleWorks will display only up to division marks on the ruler.

6. Click the OK button. A ruler appears with the units and divisions you specified.

   AppleWorks saves the ruler with the document. Note that every document can have a different type of ruler with different divisions.

Note   If you find, for example, that you prefer a ruler with points as the units of measurement rather than inches, you might want to create a blank template document that contains that style of ruler. You also can make that style of ruler the default for all new word processing documents by including the ruler in a default template document. (Chapter 10 includes instructions for creating both types of template files.)

Setting indents

Indents are paragraph-specific settings that indicate how far in from the left or right margins the text should be positioned. In AppleWorks, as in other word processors, you can set a first line indent so that the first line is treated differently from other lines in the paragraph. First line indents can be used to create hanging indents, as well as the more common indentation you were taught in school. Indents are useful for formatting bullet lists, numbered lists, and quotations, as shown in Figure 3-6.

To set indents with the ruler, select the paragraph or paragraphs for which you want to set the indents and drag the left, right, or first indent symbols to the appropriate locations on the ruler. As the indent symbols are placed, the selected paragraphs automatically reformat to match the new settings.

Note   As you drag the indent markers, AppleWorks 6 extends a dotted line down the page showing precisely where the new margins or indents will appear.

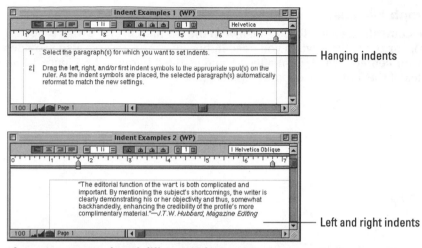

Figure 3-6: Examples of different indents

Hanging indents

Hanging indents are frequently used in documents, particularly for formatting numbered lists and bullet lists. (In a hanging indent, the first line begins farther to the left than the remaining lines.) To create a hanging indent, drag the left indent marker (upward-pointing pentagon on the left side of the ruler) to the right. Its location marks the spot where the text will begin. Drag the first line marker (the downward-pointing pentagon at the top of the ruler) to the desired position. Its location marks the spot where the numbers or bullets will appear. (If you want the numbers or bullets to be flush with the left margin, you don't need to change the position of the first line marker.) Refer to the ruler in the top half of Figure 3-6 for an example of a hanging indent.

Note The left indent marker can be moved with, or independently from, the first line marker. To move the left indent marker alone, click and drag the pentagonal portion of the marker. To move the left indent and first line markers together, click and drag the small rectangle beneath the left indent marker.

To form the hanging indent, start by typing the number or bullet symbol. Then press the Tab key and type the text of the step or point. If the text is longer than one line, the additional text automatically wraps to the position of the left indent marker.

Tip ClarisWorks 4 and 5, as well as AppleWorks 6, contain predefined styles you can use to instantly format paragraphs to show bullets or sequential numbers. Select the paragraphs, and then choose Bullet or Number from the optional Styles button in the Button Bar or from the Styles windoid. Note, however, that you're stuck with the style of bullets or numbers AppleWorks provides. You cannot change the bullet character (using a Zapf Dingbats character, for example), nor can you change the font or style of the numbers. You can, however, create a custom style based on the predefined styles and select it from the Styles windoid.

Paragraph alignment

Most documents are left-aligned (flush with the left margin and with a ragged right margin). For those times when you need it, however, AppleWorks also provides options for center-aligned, right-aligned, and justified paragraphs. Figure 3-7 shows examples of the four types of paragraph alignment.

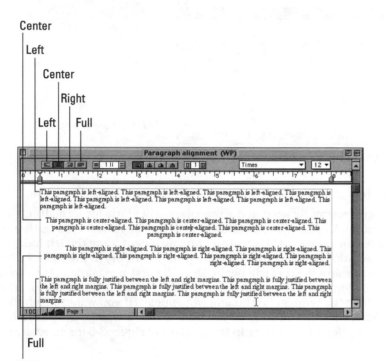

Figure 3-7: The four paragraph alignment icons on the ruler, with examples of aligned paragraphs

Center-aligning a document title centers the title text on the page; you don't need to use tabs or spaces to align the title. You also can use the right-align setting to position the current date in a letter, as an example.

Justified paragraphs are flush with both the left and right margins. AppleWorks automatically adds extra space between words to make each line edge (other than the last line of a paragraph) flush with each margin. Magazine articles often have justified paragraphs.

To set paragraph alignment, select the paragraph or paragraphs for which you want to set an alignment and click one of the four paragraph alignment icons in the ruler bar. The chosen alignment is then applied to the selected paragraphs.

Note

To be precise, alignment affects the selected paragraph within the current column. If you are working in a multicolumn page, a centered title will be centered within the column rather than across the entire page. If you want a centered title to span the full multicolumn page, you will need to create a section break (see "Formatting Sections," later in this chapter).

Line spacing

Most documents are printed single-spaced (with no blank lines between each line of text). Occasionally, however, you might need to alter the between-line spacing. High school and college homework, for example, is often double-spaced, with a single blank line between every pair of text lines. Manuscripts that are submitted to newspaper, magazine, and book publishers often must be double- or even triple-spaced, as well, to make it easier for an editor to edit and write comments on the printed copy.

To set line spacing, select the paragraphs for which you want to set between-line spacing. In the ruler bar, click the line spacing icon on the left to decrease the between-line spacing, or click the line spacing icon on the right to increase the spacing. Assuming you have not changed the measurement units from Lines (the default setting), line spacing always increases or decreases in half-line increments. The minimum line spacing is 1 line; the maximum is 10 lines. Figure 3-8 shows examples of several of the most common settings for line spacing. Line spacing also can be set using the Paragraph command, and is discussed later in this chapter.

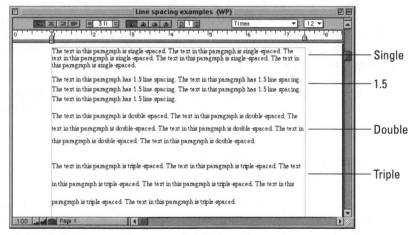

Figure 3-8: Line spacing examples

Note As with other ruler settings, line spacing can be different for every paragraph in an AppleWorks word processing document. If you want to set line spacing for the entire document, choose Edit ➪ Select All (or press ⌘+A) and then select a line spacing option.

Tab stops

If you're familiar with a typewriter (we haven't touched one in more than 20 years), you already know about tabs. Tabs are used to align text in columns, create tables, and to precisely position important text strings (enabling you to right-align a page number in a footer, for example). AppleWorks offers four tab-stop options: left, center, right, and align-on (sometimes called decimal because its most common use is to align a column of numbers on a decimal point). Figure 3-9 shows examples of the four types of tab stops.

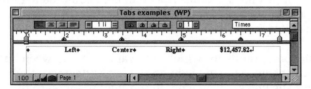

Figure 3-9: Left, center, right, and align-on tab stops

Tabs can be set in two ways: by dragging them onto the ruler or by typing their exact locations using the Tab command. After you set a tab, you can reposition it by simply dragging it to a new location on the ruler. You can remove a tab by dragging it off the ruler.

To set tab stops with the ruler, begin by selecting the paragraph or paragraphs for which you want to set tab stops. Click a tab icon and drag it into position on the ruler. As you manually position the tab stop, AppleWorks 6 extends a line down the page to show where the tab will appear.

Tip You can quickly create a new tab stop by clicking the desired tab type (left, center, right, or align-on) and then clicking the spot on the ruler where you want the tab stop to be set.

STEPS: Setting Tab Stops with the Tabs Command

1. Select the paragraph or paragraphs for which you want to set tab stops.

2. Choose Format ➪ Tabs command. The Tab dialog box appears. (If the Tab dialog box covers any of the paragraphs that will be affected by the command, you can drag the dialog box to a different position.)

   You can quickly summon the Tab dialog box by double-clicking any of the four tab icons on the ruler bar.

3. Choose the settings for the first tab stop you want to set. Click the radio button for the alignment desired, type a number in the Position text box, and (optionally) click a radio button to select a fill pattern (also called a *leader*).

   A leader is a character, such as a period, that fills the blank space leading up to the tab. Leader characters are particularly useful for formatting entries in a table of contents or for separating invoice items from prices (as in `Jello......$0.49`).

4. Click Apply to insert the new tab.

5. Repeat Steps 3 and 4 for additional tabs you want to set at this time.

6. Click the OK button to accept the new tab settings, or click the Cancel button to revert to the original tab settings.

The Tab dialog box does not provide a method for removing tab stops. Regardless of how you set tabs, you have to remove them manually by dragging them off the ruler.

Note The decimal tab (the Align On option) is followed by a text box. Although you normally set such a tab to align on a decimal point (.), you can specify any character you like. You might, for example, want a column of numbers to align on the percent sign (%).

When you are creating a document, such as a résumé, that uses many different indentations, use tabs instead of spaces between items. Although spaces might look as good as tabs on the screen, the printout will look quite different. Tabs are also much easier to adjust than spaces.

Using the Copy Ruler and Apply Ruler commands

After you set formatting options for a paragraph, you might want to reuse these settings in other paragraphs in the document. For example, when writing a report, you might create a paragraph format for long quotations. Manually recreating this format each time you have a new quote is time-consuming and prone to error. To simplify the transfer of paragraph formats, AppleWorks provides the Copy Ruler and Apply Ruler commands.

Note The stylesheet is also particularly useful for storing and applying paragraph styles. (See Chapter 15 for information about stylesheets.)

STEPS: Applying Ruler Settings to a New Paragraph

1. Move the cursor into the paragraph whose ruler settings you want to copy.

2. Choose Format ➪ Rulers ➪ Copy Ruler (or press ⌘+Shift+C).

3. Move the cursor into the target paragraph.

Alternatively, you can use normal text-selection techniques to select several contiguous paragraphs to which you want to apply the ruler settings.

4. Choose Format ➪ Rulers ➪ Apply Ruler (or press ⌘+Shift+V). The ruler settings from the copied ruler are applied to the selected paragraphs.

Note that the Apply Ruler command remains active even after you paste the settings. You can continue to paste these settings into additional paragraphs until you quit AppleWorks or you issue a new Copy Ruler command.

Tip   You also can use the Copy Ruler and Apply Ruler commands to transfer ruler settings between documents. If you frequently use certain ruler settings, you can create a document that contains them all and then copy them to new documents as necessary.

Using the Paragraph command

Although the ruler is handy, you also can use the Paragraph command from the Format menu to set paragraph indents, line spacing, and alignment. The advantages of using the Paragraph command over using the ruler include the following:

✦ The Paragraph command gives you improved precision in establishing settings.

✦ You can set several options in a single dialog box (as opposed to setting them one by one with the ruler).

✦ You can use any measurement system you like — not just the one shown on the current ruler — for line and paragraph spacing.

✦ You can select outlining label formats for paragraphs — such as diamonds, checkboxes, and Roman numerals — and choose a paragraph alignment.

✦ The only way you can set spacing above and below a paragraph is with the Paragraph command.

Tip   You can summon the Paragraph dialog box by double-clicking the line spacing indicator or the alignment icons on the ruler bar.

STEPS: Choosing Paragraph Settings with the Paragraph Command

1. Select the paragraph or paragraphs for which you want to alter paragraph format settings and choose Format ➪ Paragraph. The Paragraph dialog box appears, as shown in Figure 3-10.

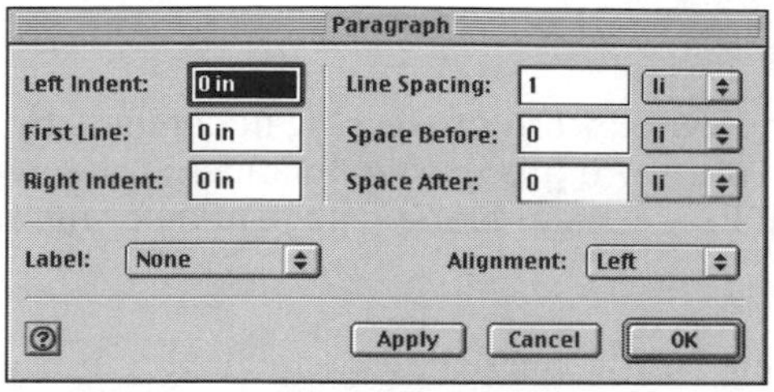

Figure 3-10: The Paragraph dialog box

2. Type numbers in the text boxes and choose options from the pop-up menus for the settings you want to change. Here are some pointers:

   • The only measurement settings in the Paragraph dialog box that do not appear on the ruler are Space Before and Space After. Fill in their boxes in the Paragraph dialog box to set the amount of blank space you want to appear before or after the selected paragraphs.

   • You can change the measurement system for Line Spacing, Space Before, or Space After by selecting an option from their respective pop-up menus. You can mix and match measurement systems, if you wish. (Be sure to change the measurement system before entering your numeric change, because AppleWorks will convert the existing setting to the new units. For example, if you had Space Before set to 2 lines and you changed the units to points, AppleWorks will change the 2 to a 24, if each line was 12 points high.)

   • You can choose a paragraph alignment from the Alignment pop-up menu.

   • If the selected paragraphs are outline topics or subtopics, you can choose a new label format from the Label pop-up menu. You also can make them into outline topics or subtopics by choosing a label format from the Label pop-up menu.

3. Click Apply to apply the new settings to the selected paragraphs. (Apply is a tentative option. You can remove changes made with Apply by clicking the Cancel button; the formatting instantly reverts to the original settings.)

4. Click the OK button to accept the paragraph formatting changes, or click the Cancel button to revert to the original settings.

Note

If you routinely want each paragraph to automatically be separated from the next paragraph by one blank line, set Space After to 1 li. With that setting, you don't have to press the Return key between paragraphs. This also makes your text easier to edit later, when your teacher, editor, or boss says that they don't want one blank line after each paragraph.

Formatting sections

You can create more complex and varied word processing documents by dividing them into sections. Each section of a word processing document can have a different title page, as well as different headers and footers, page numbering, and numbers of columns.

If you are writing a book, for example, you can define each chapter as a separate section and set the following options:

✦ Each chapter begins on a right-hand page and is treated as a title page (with no headers or footers).

✦ Page numbering is chapter-relative; that is, it restarts at 1, but is preceded by the chapter number and a dash, as in 5-1.

✦ The left and right headers and footers are different from each other (the book title is in the header of all left pages and the chapter title is in the header of all right pages, for instance).

You must individually specify the section options for each section in the document. To create a new section, move the insertion point to where you want the section to begin and choose Format ➪ Insert Section Break from the Format menu (or press Option+Return).

To set options for a section, place the insertion point anywhere within the section and then choose Section from the Format menu. The Section dialog box appears as shown in Figure 3-11.

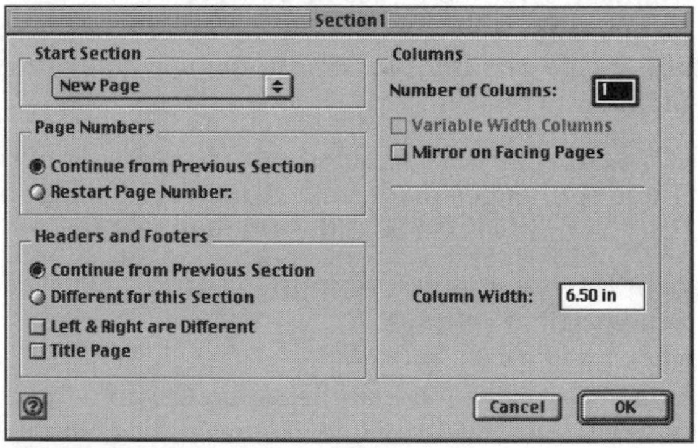

Figure 3-11: The Section dialog box

The meaning of each option in this dialog box is explained in the following sections. To remove a section break, position the text insertion point at the start of the section that follows the break and press Delete.

Note Many — perhaps most — documents have only one section. Nevertheless, you can still use the Section dialog box to specify page numbers, headers and footers, and column settings (in this example, for the entire document).

Start section

Depending on your selection from the Start Section pop-up menu in the Section dialog box, the current section can begin on a New Line, New Page, New Left Page, or New Right Page. (Book chapters often begin on a right-hand page, for example.) The default for each document is New Line, but after that, it is whatever setting you last chose for the current document.

Page numbers

To make page numbering pick up where the previous section left off, click the Continue From Previous Section radio button. If the last section ended on Page 17, for example, this section would start with Page 18.

If you want the page numbering in this section to start with some other number, click the Restart Page Number radio button and type a page number in the text box that appears to the right of this option, when selected.

Note If the current section started on a New Line, the Restart Page Number radio button will be disabled (grayed out).

Headers and footers

Click the Continue from Previous Section radio button if you want to use the same headers and footers that were used in the previous section; click the Different for this Section radio button if you want to specify new headers or footers. After making this choice, you can safely edit the headers and footers in the new section without changing the previous section's headers and footers.

Note When your section starts on a new line, you might wonder which headers and footers will be displayed when you choose the "Different for this Section" option. Well, headers match the settings for the first section to appear on the page. Footers work differently; the footer in effect for the last section to appear on a page is the footer that will be displayed.

If you want to have different headers and footers for left- and right-hand pages, click the Left & Right are Different checkbox. This is a common practice in books and in lengthy reports.

When you click the Title Page checkbox, AppleWorks treats the first page of the section as a title page. It eliminates the headers and footers for that page only. Normally, you do not want to display page numbers and date stamps (common items for a header or footer) on the first page of a chapter, for example. If the document doesn't have headers or footers, this setting is irrelevant.

Columns

AppleWorks enables word processing documents and document sections to have multiple columns. Newsletters, magazines, and church bulletins are often formatted with two or more columns, for example.

You can use the ruler bar to specify the number of columns for a section by clicking the Decrease Columns and Increase Columns controls (see Figure 3-12).

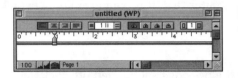

Figure 3-12: Setting the number of columns by using the ruler

You also can manually adjust column widths and the space between columns. To manually adjust the widths of two adjacent columns, move the mouse pointer into the space between a pair of columns and press the Option key. The mouse pointer changes to a pair of arrows surrounding a hollow box. Press the mouse button and move the pointer to the left or to the right. As you move the pointer, the widths of the two columns change. Release the mouse button to set the new column widths. Using this procedure, the space between the columns does not change. You are merely changing the combined widths of the two columns in a new way.

To manually change the space between two adjacent columns, move the mouse pointer so that it touches the inside or outside edge of a column and press Option. The mouse pointer then changes to a pair of arrows surrounding two vertical lines. Press the mouse button and move the pointer to the left or to the right. As you move the mouse pointer, the width of the column that the pointer is touching and the space between the columns change. Release the mouse button to set the new column width and between-column spacing.

You also can use the Section command to set columns, as described in the following steps.

STEPS: Setting Multiple Columns with the Section Command

1. Position the text insertion point within the section you want to format. (If the document contains only one section, position the text insertion point anywhere in the document.)

2. Choose Section from the Format menu. The Section dialog box appears, as shown earlier in Figure 3-11.

3. Type a number in the Number of Columns text box.

4. If you want all of the columns to be the same width, leave the Variable Width Columns checkbox unchecked. The default Column Width and Space Between for that number of columns are shown at the bottom of the dialog box. As long as you don't exceed the page width, you can alter either or both of these numbers.

or

If you want the columns to be different widths, click the Variable Width Columns checkbox. By default, all columns are set to the same width. To change the widths, select a column number (the columns are numbered from left to right) from the Settings for Column pop-up menu, and then enter values for Space Before, Column Width, and Space After. Repeat this procedure for the remaining columns.

When you set two or more columns, the Columns portion of the Section dialog box changes depending on your choice of variable-width or equal-sized columns (as shown in Figure 3-13).

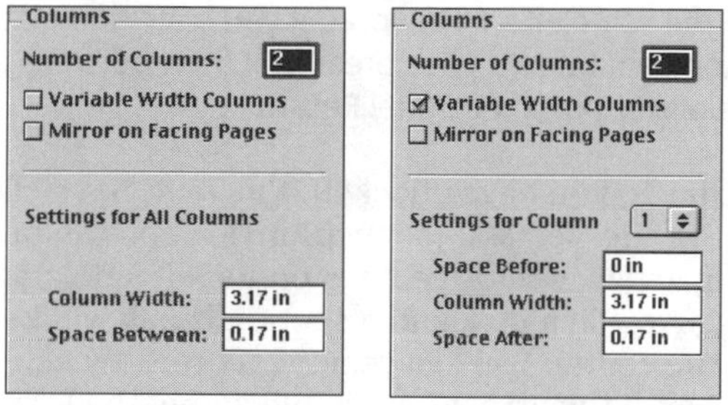

Figure 3-13: With equal-sized columns selected, Column Width and Space Between are set for all columns (left). With variable-width columns, Space Before, Column Width, and Space After can be set individually for each column (right).

5. *Optional:* If the section has multiple, variable-width columns and is intended to be printed like a book, click the Mirror On Facing Pages checkbox.

For example, if the left-hand pages have a two-inch column near the outside margin and a four-inch column beside the inner margin (also called the *gutter*), right-hand pages would be mirrored; that is, the four-inch column would still be beside the gutter and the two-inch column would be near the outer margin. If the Mirror On Facing Pages checkbox was unchecked, the four-inch column would always be on the right.

6. Click the OK button to use the new column settings, or click the Cancel button to revert to the column settings that were in effect before you chose the Columns command. If you click the OK button, AppleWorks automatically reformats the text to flow into the columns you created.

Note

If you specify an individual column width that is wider than the allowable maximum, the program displays an error message, and you will have to specify a new width value. Similarly, if the combined width of all columns and the space between columns exceeds the page width, you are asked to specify new values.

Page and column breaks

One feature that AppleWorks lacks is the capability to handle widows and orphans in text. A widow is a lone line of text that ends a page or column (the first or only line of a paragraph or a heading). An orphan is a lone line of text that starts a page or column (usually the final line of a paragraph). Widows and orphans make a document look unprofessional. To eliminate widows, you can manually insert breaks as needed as the final editing step before you print the document. To eliminate orphans, you would adjust either the font-size, line spacing, or paragraph spacing of the preceding material to reduce the space consumed.

To insert a page or column break, position the text insertion point at the beginning of the line you want as the first line in the new page or column and choose Format ➪ Insert Page Break (or press the Shift+Return keys) or Format ➪ Insert Column Break (or press the Return key). The break appears, and the line of text is then moved to the next page or column.

Note   AppleWorks 6 also includes a handy way to insert column breaks. Simply press the Return key. If the text insertion point is in a single-column section, a column break and a page break will have the same effect. However, if you later change the number of columns in the section, what was a page break will then become a column break. To guarantee a page break, press the Shift+Return keys.

If Show Invisibles is enabled (that is, you have checked it in Text, have clicked its button on the Button Bar, or have pressed ⌘+; [semicolon]), a column break is indicated by a tiny upward-pointing arrow with three lines on its left side, page breaks will have a downward-pointing arrow in a box, and a section break will be a box with a horizontal line through the center. You can remove a break by selecting the arrow and pressing the Delete key. If the arrow is invisible, move the text insertion point to the start of the first text line that begins after the break, and then press the Delete key.

Formatting documents

Document formatting controls the overall appearance of each page — both onscreen and when printed. Document options include:

✦ Margins (top, bottom, left, and right)

✦ Margin and page guides (shown or invisible)

✦ Onscreen page display (single pages or facing pages side by side)

✦ Starting page number

✦ Footnotes and endnotes

You set document formatting options by choosing Document from the Format menu. The Document dialog box appears, as shown in Figure 3-14. Set options and click the OK button to put your choices into effect, or click the Cancel button if you change your mind.

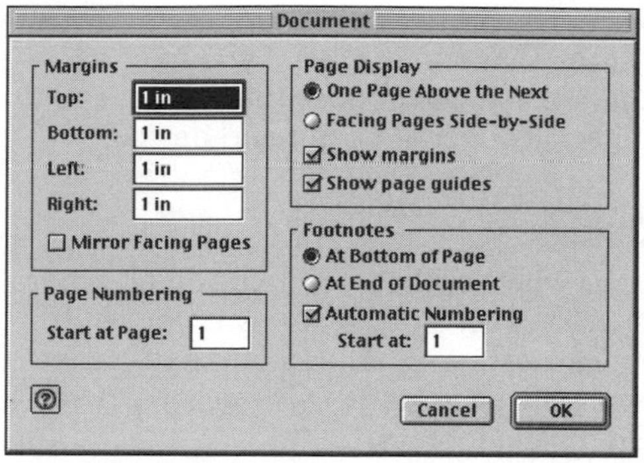

Figure 3-14: The Document dialog box

Note that several of the options (Margins, Footnotes, and Page Numbering) affect the way the document looks and prints. The remaining setting (Page Display) affects only the document's appearance onscreen.

Tip

All settings in the Document dialog box affect only the active document. When you create a new document, you have to reset the Document options. Although you can't save these options as preferences, you can avoid the boring, repetitious task of resetting the options. Create a new blank document, set the document preferences, and then save the file as a default template document, as described in Chapter 10. New word processing files then automatically use your preferred Document settings. (You can use this same technique for any AppleWorks environment you want to standardize.)

Margins

To change a margin setting in the Document dialog box, simply type a number in the appropriate margin text box.

You'll note that the units of measurement for each margin setting match those of the ruler. If you want to specify an amount in a different measurement unit, you can type in the abbreviation for that measurement unit and AppleWorks will do the unit conversion. If you want to change the units displayed, choose Format ➪ Rulers ➪ Ruler Settings and set the units you want displayed.

Note

If you intend to have your document printed double-sided (as you would with a bound book, for example), click the Mirror Facing Pages checkbox. The wording for the Left and Right margin settings then changes to Inside and Outside.

Number of pages displayed

By default, AppleWorks is set to display every document one page at a time (One Page Above the Next). If you would rather see pages side by side, click the Facing Pages Side-by-Side radio button in the Document dialog box.

The Facing Pages Side-by-Side option is particularly useful if you have a monitor that can display two complete pages at the same time. Even if you have a low-resolution monitor (800×600, for example), you can choose this option and then zoom the document to 50 percent to check its overall layout and design.

Show Margins and Show Page Guides

The setting for Show Margins determines whether the body text will be separated from the edges of the page by white space (when Show Margins is checked). Checking the Show Page Guides option causes the work area of the document to be outlined by a faint gray border. Having the page guides visible is particularly useful when you are working with headers and footers.

Start at Page

This option works in conjunction with the automatic page numbering feature (Insert Page # from the Edit menu). You can specify a starting page number by specifying a number in the text box. Although you usually want page numbering to begin with 1 (the default), this feature can be useful. For example, if you are writing a book with each chapter in its own document and you know Chapter 1 ended on Page 26, you can specify a starting page number of 27 for Chapter 2.

Footnotes and endnotes

Important in-text notes can be displayed at the bottom of each page as footnotes, or they can be grouped together at the end of the document as endnotes. If you want footnotes, click the At Bottom of Page radio button; for endnotes, click the At End of Document radio button. (Of course, if you don't intend to insert footnotes in the document, this setting is irrelevant.)

When you check the Automatic Numbering checkbox, AppleWorks automatically numbers footnotes and endnotes, beginning with the number specified in the Start At text box. Leave this option unchecked if you want to manually number footnotes or endnotes, or if you want to use characters other than numbers, such as asterisks (*).

Advanced Editing Tools and Techniques

The features and editing techniques discussed in this section are nonessentials. Although you can do without them initially, you'll eventually find many of the following tools and techniques helpful in creating clean, attractive, and readable documents:

- ✦ Finding and replacing text
- ✦ Inserting headers and footers
- ✦ Inserting footnotes and endnotes

✦ Inserting automatic date, time, and page numbers

✦ Using the spelling checker and thesaurus

✦ Performing a word count

✦ Using the hyphenation feature

✦ Creating outlines

Finding and replacing text

As with other word processing programs, the AppleWorks word processing environment includes a set of Find/Change commands. Use Find to quickly locate a particular section of a document (where you talked about Social Security, for example). Use the Change option to replace one text string with another. The Find/Change dialog box enables you to do the following:

✦ Find the next occurrence of a particular string of text.

✦ Find subsequent occurrences of the same text string.

✦ Replace a found text string with another text string (or simultaneously replace all instances of one text string with another text string).

✦ Find a text string that matches the currently selected text in the document.

STEPS: Finding a Text String

1. Choose Edit ➪ Find/Change (or press ⌘+F). The Find/Change dialog box shown in Figure 3-15 appears.

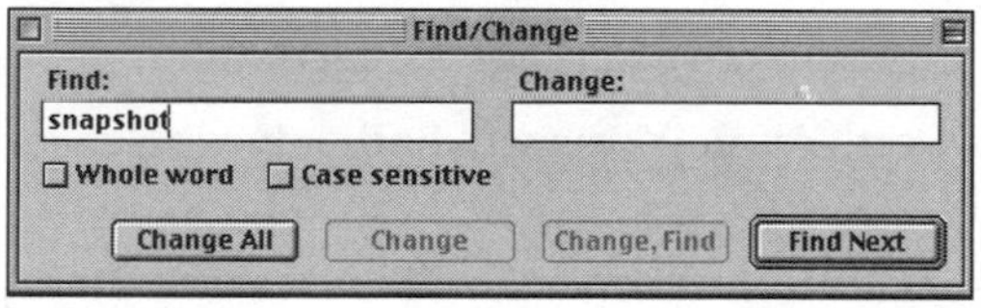

Figure 3-15: The Find/Change dialog box

2. In the Find text box, type the text string for which you want to search (leave the Change text box empty). You also can set these options:

   • **Whole word.** If you want to search only for complete words, click the Whole word checkbox. With the Whole word option checked, searching for "and" will find only "and" — not "sand" or "bandage."

   • **Case sensitive.** Click the Case sensitive checkbox if you want the case of each character in the Find string to be considered during the search. If you check this box, a search for "Young" would not match "young" or "YOUNG." If you're unsure of the capitalization, don't check the Case sensitive checkbox.

3. Click the Find Next button (or press the Return or Enter keys). The search commences downward from the current cursor position. Eventually, the search wraps around so the whole document is searched — including text that is above the initial cursor position.

   If the document contains a match, AppleWorks highlights the first instance of the text string. If no match is found, a message to that effect appears.

4. If the found text is not the instance for which you are searching, click the Find Next button again. Each click restarts the search from the point of the last found text.

5. When you are finished, close the Find/Change dialog box.

You can repeat a search by choosing Edit ⇨ Find/Change ⇨ Find Again (⌘+E).

You probably noticed the Find/Change dialog box also contains a Change box. Text you type into this text box can replace instances of found text — either one match at a time (with your approval) or globally (automatically replacing all instances without one-by-one approval).

Note   Sometimes the Find/Change dialog box obscures the found text. If necessary, you can move the dialog box to a different location by clicking its title bar and dragging the dialog box to a new position.

STEPS: Finding and Changing Text

1. Choose Edit ⇨ Find/Change ⇨ Find/Change (or press ⌘+F). The Find/Change dialog box (shown earlier in Figure 3-15) appears.

2. In the Find box, enter the text string to be located, and in the Change text box, type a replacement text string.

3. Set the Whole word and Case sensitive settings as desired:

   • If you check Whole word, AppleWorks will find only whole words that match the Find string.

   • If you check Case sensitive, the program will locate only strings that have capitalization identical to the Find string's capitalization.

4. To change all instances of the Find string to the Change string without prompting from the program, click the Change All button. A dialog box appears stating: "The Change All feature is not undoable." Click the OK button to continue, or click the Cancel button.

   or

   To examine each Find result before you change the text, click the Find Next button. As text is found, click one of the following:

   • Click the Change button to change only the current instance. Normally, you choose this option when you are ready to end the search (after you have found the single or final instance of text you want to change).

If you decide you want to continue the search after you click the Change button, click the Find Next button, or press the Return or Enter keys.

- Click the Change, Find button to change the current instance and then find the next one.

- Click the Find Next button, or press the Return or Enter keys, if the current instance is not one you want to change.

5. When you are finished, close the Find/Change dialog box.

On subsequent finds in this session, the Find/Change dialog box will contain the last set of Find/Change text strings and settings you used.

Finding special characters

Occasionally, you might want to locate — and optionally replace — some special AppleWorks characters, such as tabs, paragraph returns (end-of-paragraph markers), or automatic dates. To search for these characters or use them as replacements, type the symbols shown in Table 3-3 in the Find or Change text boxes of the Find/Change dialog box.

Table 3-3
Find/Change Symbols for Special Characters

Search Character	Characters to Type
Space	Spacebar
Nonbreaking space	Option+Spacebar
Tab	\t
Discretionary hyphen	\- or ⌘+- (hyphen)
Paragraph return	\p or ⌘+Return
Line break (soft return)	\n or Shift+⌘+Return
Column break	\c or ⌘+Return
Page break	\b or Shift+⌘+Return
Section break	\§ (Option+6)
Automatic date	\d
Automatic time	\h
Automatic page number	\#
Backslash	\\

Note Because the backslash character (\) is used to define many of the special characters in the table, you have to type a pair of backslashes (\\) to find a backslash
that appears in the text.

Because the need to search for such characters or use them as replacements might
not be readily apparent, consider the following examples:

✦ **Removing double spaces.** Modern typesetting conventions frown on double
  spaces between sentences. (we know you were taught to use double spaces
  when you learned to type, but double spaces are not necessary when using
  a computer, a word processing program, and a decent printer.) Use the
  Find/Change command to substitute a single space for every instance of a
  double space. In addition to eliminating double spaces between sentences,
  you'll also get rid of extra spaces between words.

✦ **Substituting spaces for tabs in communications text.** Some information services and bulletin boards aren't prepared to handle tabs in text files. Search
  for the tab character (\t) and replace each instance with a fixed number of
  spaces (1, 2, 5, or 8, for example). Be aware that your text will no longer line
  up on your tab stops unless all text blocks are the same length.

✦ **Eliminating extra space at the end of paragraphs.** Some publishers are stick-
  lers about this. Search for Space Return (\p) and replace with Return (\p).

✦ **Replacing an automatically inserted date and time with a fixed date or
  time.** Automatic dates or times (which you insert by choosing Edit ⇨ Insert
  Date ⇨ Auto-updating or Edit ⇨ Insert Time ⇨ Auto-updating) change every
  time you open the document. This is useful if you want to show a new date or
  time each time you print the document. If you want to show when a document
  was written, on the other hand, you can replace the automatic date and time
  with a fixed date and time.

New Feature In AppleWorks 5 and previous versions of ClarisWorks, Insert Date and Insert Time
placed auto-updating objects in your document and you had to convert them to
normal text. In AppleWorks 6, you get to choose from two alternatives in the Edit ⇨
Insert Date and Edit ⇨ Insert Time submenus: Auto-updating and Fixed.

If you can't remember what to type when you want to execute a search for a particular character, or if you don't have Table 3-3 handy, you can copy the special characters in your document and then paste them into the Find/Change dialog box. For
many of these characters, it is easier if you have Show Invisibles enabled. Show
Invisibles displays (in light gray) special characters showing formatting controls
such as (but not limited to) spaces, tabs, and paragraph/section/column breaks.

STEPS: Copying and Pasting Special Characters

1. Find an example of the character in your document.

To find characters that are normally hidden, click the Show/Hide Invisibles button (Figure 3-16) in the Button Bar, choose Edit ➪ Preferences ➪ General, and then check the Show Invisibles checkbox in the Text options dialog box, or press ⌘+; (semicolon).

 Figure 3-16: The Show/Hide Invisibles button

2. Select the character and choose Edit ➪ Copy (or press ⌘+C).

3. Choose Edit ➪ Find/Change ➪ Find/Change (or press ⌘+F). The Find/Change dialog box appears.

4. Press ⌘+V to paste the character into the Find or the Change text box, as appropriate. When pasting into a Find/Change text box, AppleWorks automatically substitutes the correct symbols for the special character.

Creating headers and footers

Headers and footers can contain any text or graphics you want to separate from the body of the document. Because they are printed on the top or bottom of every page, headers and footers are very useful for displaying document identification text such as the date, your name, a document file name, or the report title. You also can place logos and other graphics in headers and footers to save yourself the trouble of repeatedly pasting images into every page of the document. Figure 3-17 shows a header and a footer for a typical letterhead.

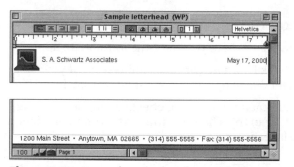

Figure 3-17: Examples of a header and footer

Page numbers are routinely placed in a header or footer. (For page numbers that automatically change to reflect pagination changes in the text, see "Inserting automatic date, time, and page numbers," later in this chapter.)

To create a header or footer, choose Format ➪ Insert Header or Format ➪ Insert Footer. A header or footer appears in the document, and the text insertion point moves into the header or footer area. You can then type the header or footer text.

As with other text, you can format header and footer text with different fonts, styles, sizes, and paragraph/ruler bar settings.

Caution

Unless you check the Show Page Guides checkbox in the Document dialog box (by choosing the Document command from the Format menu), you might have a difficult time distinguishing the header and footer text from the body text. After you check the Show Page Guides checkbox, faint gray outlines surround the header and footer.

If you later decide you do not need a header or a footer, you can delete them by choosing Remove Header or Remove Footer from the Format menu. Doing so instantly deletes all text in the header or footer.

Note

Remember that if a document is divided into sections, you can set different headers and footers for each section, if you like. Refer to "Formatting sections," earlier in this chapter.

Adding footnotes and endnotes

If you're working on a school report or a professional paper, you'll appreciate the AppleWorks features for managing footnotes and endnotes. You can choose whether to have AppleWorks automatically number them for you or just insert marking characters, whichever your teacher, editor, or boss prefers.

STEPS: Inserting a Footnote

1. Position the text insertion point where you want the footnote to appear.

2. Choose Format ➪ Insert Blank Footnote (or press Shift+⌘+F). If you chose Endnotes in your Document dialog box, the menu item will say Insert Endnote.

3. If you have enabled the Automatic Numbering checkbox in the Document dialog box (described earlier in this chapter), the next footnote number in sequence appears at the insertion point.

or

If you have not enabled the Auto Number Footnotes checkbox, the Footnote dialog box appears, as shown in Figure 3-18. Type the character you want to use to mark the footnote in the Mark With text box and click the OK button. The character appears at the insertion point.

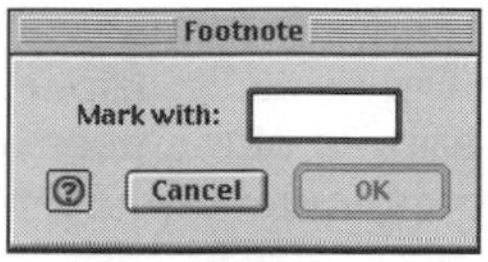

Figure 3-18: Use the Footnote dialog box to specify a special footnote character.

After the program inserts the footnote mark, the cursor automatically moves into the footnote area at the bottom of the current page or at the end of the document (depending on whether footnotes or endnotes were chosen in the Document dialog box).

4. Type the footnote or endnote, and then press the Return or Enter keys to return to the body text at the footnote location or click in the body text area to continue working elsewhere in the document. Figure 3-19 shows an example of a footnote.

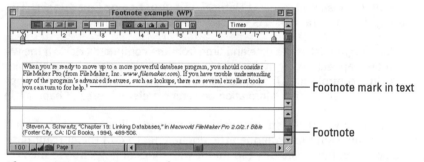

Footnote mark in text

Footnote

Figure 3-19: Footnote example

If you decide to create your own footnote symbols instead of using a simple numbered sequence, you might want to consider any the symbols shown in the following table. Some of these symbols might appear as an empty square in the Mark With dialog box, depending on whether they are present in your System font (usually Chicago or Charcoal).

Character	Keystroke
*	Shift+8
†	Option+T
‡	Shift+Option+7

To remove a footnote or endnote, select the footnote/endnote number or symbol where it appears in the body text, and then press the Delete or Backspace keys. The program automatically removes the reference at the bottom of the page or the end of the document and renumbers the remaining footnotes/endnotes as required.

Remember that the difference between footnotes and endnotes is simply where they are displayed in the document. Footnotes appear at the lower edge of the page in which the footnote is marked; endnotes appear in a single list at the end of the document. For more information about creating footnotes, see "Using the Word Processing Assistants," later in this chapter.

Inserting automatic date, time, and page numbers

Whether for record-keeping purposes or for use in headers and footers, you might want to date- or time-stamp certain documents to show when you printed or last updated them. To insert the current date or time in a document, position the insertion point. Choose Edit ➪ Insert Date ➪ Auto-updating or Edit ➪ Insert Time ➪ Auto-updating. The program inserts the current date or time for you.

Note   The program takes the date and time from the computer's clock. If the wrong date or time appears, you can correct it by specifying the proper information in the Date & Time control panel. The format for dates is taken from the setting in AppleWorks's Text preferences. (For information on setting preferences, see Chapter 10.)

Dates or times you insert in this manner automatically change to reflect the new date and time each time you open the document. To add the current date or time to the document permanently (so that it will not change), choose the Fixed option rather than the Auto-updating option from the submenu.

You use a similar command, Insert Page #, to add page numbers to documents. If you add them inside a header or footer, page numbering automatically carries through to every page in the document as described in the following Steps.

STEPS: Adding Page Numbers to a Document

1. Specify a starting page number in the Document or Section dialog box. (Access these dialog boxes by choosing Format ➪ Document or Format ➪ Section, as described earlier in this chapter.)

2. If the document already contains a header or footer, skip to Step 3.

or

If the document doesn't already contain a header or footer, choose Format ➪ Insert Header or Format ➪ Insert Footer.

3. Position the text insertion point in the header or footer.

4. Choose Edit ⇨ Insert Page #.

The Insert Page Number dialog box appears, as shown in Figure 3-20.

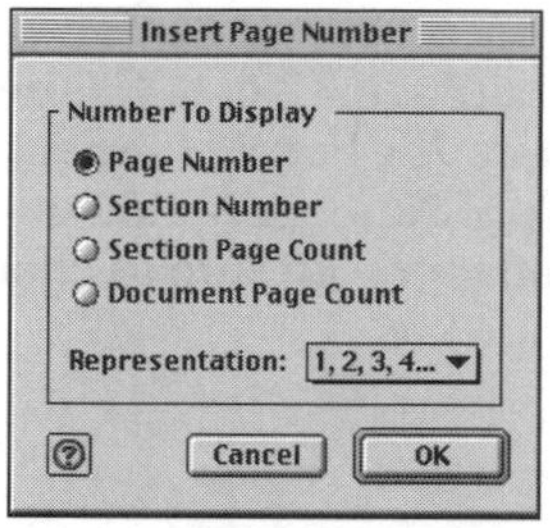

Insert Page Number

┌─ Number To Display ─┐
● Page Number
○ Section Number
○ Section Page Count
○ Document Page Count

Representation: [1, 2, 3, 4... ▼]

[⑦] [Cancel] [OK]

Figure 3-20: The Insert Page Number dialog box

5. Select the desired options from the Insert Page Number dialog box, as follows:

- To insert a page number, click the Page Number radio button.

- To insert the current section number, click the Section Number radio button.

- To insert the total number of pages in the current section, click the Section Page Count radio button.

- To insert the total number of pages in the document, click the Document Page Count radio button.

6. Choose a format for the number from the Representation pop-up menu.

7. Click the OK button to complete the command, or click the Cancel button if you change your mind. AppleWorks inserts the current page number and renumbers all subsequent pages in the document or section, beginning with the number specified in the Document or Section dialog box if you placed the page number in a header or footer.

Page numbers inserted in this manner automatically change as the document changes (that is, as you add, delete, or move pages).

Remember that you can add formatting to header and footer text, just as you can to body text. For example, you can right- or center-justify page numbers by clicking the appropriate alignment icon beneath the ruler or by using tabs. (If the ruler isn't visible, choose Format ⇨ Rulers ⇨ Show Rulers.) You also can apply different fonts or styles. After you apply formatting to an element of a header or footer, the program automatically repeats the formatting on every page for you.

Note   Depending on the type of document you're working on, plain numbers might look odd. You might prefer to precede each number with the word Page, for example. To do this, simply type Page, followed by a space, just before where you have inserted — or are about to insert — the automatic page number. Alternatively, you might want to insert a hyphen or tilde character on either side of the number (as in - 3 - or ~ 3 ~).

To create chapter- or section-relative page numbers (Page 4-2 or A-1, for example), choose Section Number in the Insert Page Number dialog box. In the Section dialog box (choose Format ⇨ Section), click the Restart Page Number radio button, and then type **1** in the text box (for the starting page number). Be sure to choose the same settings for each section in the document.

Using the spelling checker

The inclusion of a built-in spelling checker was one of the first great advancements in word processing. A spelling checker examines every word in a document and compares it to words found in its massive dictionary. The program then flags unknown words and gives you an opportunity to replace them, either by typing the replacement word or by selecting a word from a list of the most likely replacements. Now, with only a modicum of effort, every man, woman, and child can produce letters, memos, and reports consisting of correctly spelled words. Making sure that the right word is used, however, is still up to you. For example, your and you're are both correctly spelled, but are you talking about something you possess or something you are going to do?

Checking spelling

AppleWorks provides two spell-checking options: Check the entire document, or check only the currently selected text. The spelling checker is available for all AppleWorks documents that contain text. You initiate spell-checking by choosing one of the following options from the Edit ⇨ Writing Tools submenu:

✦ **Check Document Spelling (⌘+=).** Select this option if you want to spell-check the entire document. Note that when you choose this command, the position of the cursor doesn't matter. Spell-checking automatically starts at the beginning of the document.

✦ **Check Selection Spelling (Shift+⌘+Y).** Select this option if you want to spell-check only the currently selected text. Check Selection Spelling is particularly useful for checking a single word or just a paragraph or two you've recently edited.

Regardless of which command you use to start the spelling checker, AppleWorks displays the spelling checker's progress in the Spelling dialog box (see Figure 3-21).

Figure 3-21: The Spelling dialog box

As the spelling checker examines the document or selection, it stops at each word it doesn't find in its dictionary, or in any user dictionaries you have created. For each word, you can do the following:

✦ Correct the spelling by typing the proper word in the Word text box and clicking the Replace button. (After making a manual correction in this fashion, you can click the Check button to make sure the replacement word is spelled correctly.)

✦ Select a replacement by double-clicking any of the words in the list box, by typing its Command-key equivalent (C-1, C-2, and so on), or by highlighting the replacement and clicking the Replace button.

✦ Accept the spelling as correct by clicking the Skip button.

✦ Accept the spelling as correct and add it to the current User Dictionary by clicking Learn.

✦ End the spell-check by clicking the Cancel button.

Caution If you haven't yet selected or created a User Dictionary, the Learn button will be disabled. See the "Working with dictionaries" section later in this chapter for more information on specifying a User Dictionary.

You can click the tiny flag icon in the lower-right corner of the dialog box to toggle between showing the potentially misspelled word in context and showing only the word itself.

As the spell-check continues, AppleWorks reports the number of words checked, as well as the number of questionable words found. After you deal with each questionable word, the spell-checker proceeds through the document or selection until it finds the next questionable word, or until the spell-check is completed. When all words have been checked, the upper button in the dialog box changes to Done. Click the Done button to close the spelling checker.

Note As good as spell-checking is, it is not a substitute for proofreading. The AppleWorks spelling checker does not flag duplicate words (and and), grammatical errors, or errors in punctuation, nor will it find words that are spelled correctly but that happen to be the wrong words ("she one the game to many times," for example).

Working with dictionaries

At any given moment, you can have two dictionaries available for use with the spelling checker: a main dictionary and a user dictionary (one you've created). When you spell-check a document or selection, AppleWorks automatically uses the words in both dictionaries.

AppleWorks comes with a 100,000-word dictionary it normally uses as the main dictionary, although replacement dictionaries (most notably for foreign languages) are also available from Apple. In addition, both Spanish and U.K. English dictionaries are in the AppleWorks Extras folder on your AppleWorks 6 CD-ROM.

The User Dictionary contains a list of words you want AppleWorks to accept as correct, even though they are not in the main dictionary. Each time you click the Learn button in the Spelling dialog box, the spell-checker adds the current word it is questioning to the active User Dictionary. You also can add words manually by choosing Edit ➪ Writing Tools ➪ Edit User Dictionary. Examples of words you might want to add to a user dictionary include proper nouns (such as product names and company names), technical terms, frequently used acronyms, and current slang.

Creating and opening dictionaries

The following instructions tell you how to open a different main or user dictionary or thesaurus; create a new User Dictionary; and how to use no dictionaries at all. Remember that at most one dictionary of each type may be in use at a given time.

STEPS: Choosing a Dictionary

1. Choose Edit ➪ Writing Tools ➪ Select Dictionaries. The Select Dictionaries dialog box appears, as shown in Figure 3-22.

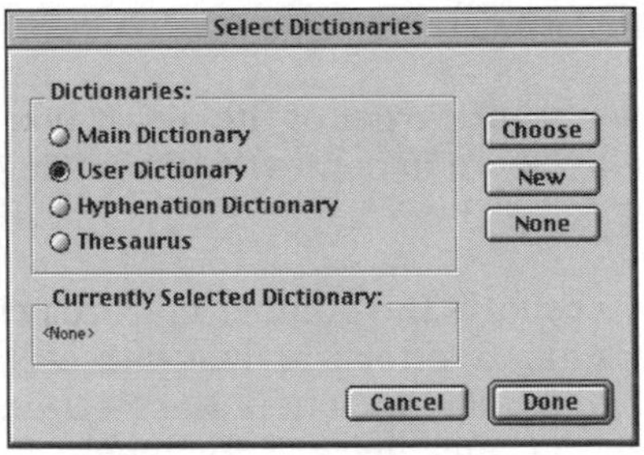

Figure 3-22: The Select Dictionaries dialog box

2. Choose one of the dictionary types using the radio buttons in the dialog box (Main Dictionary, User Dictionary, Hyphenation Dictionary, or Thesaurus) to indicate the type of dictionary you want to select or create. The name of the currently installed dictionary of the selected type appears in the lower portion of the dialog box.

3. Click the Choose button to pick an alternate dictionary file of the selected type. AppleWorks automatically navigates to the AppleWorks Essentials:Dictionaries folder within the AppleWorks folder, where all dictionaries are stored. A standard Open dialog box will appear.

4. Select the new dictionary file and click the Select button, or click the Cancel button to leave things as they are.

5. Click the Done button to close the Select Dictionaries dialog box. The program now uses the new dictionary.

Note

If you decide not to choose a new dictionary (because you intend to keep using the current one, for example), just click the Done or Cancel buttons without choosing a dictionary. If you don't want to use a User Dictionary, click the User Dictionary radio button, click the None button, and then click the Done button to close the dialog box.

To create a new user dictionary, choose Edit ➪ Writing Tools ➪ Select Dictionaries. The Select Dictionaries dialog box appears, as shown earlier in Figure 3-22. Click the User Dictionary radio button. The name of the currently installed User Dictionary appears at the bottom of the dialog box. Click the New button. A Save dialog box appears. Type a file name for the new User Dictionary. Then, click the Save button to create the new dictionary file, or click the Cancel button if you change your mind. After you create a new user dictionary in this fashion, AppleWorks automatically puts it into use.

Dictionary editing

As mentioned earlier, you can add words to the active User Dictionary during a spell-check by clicking the Learn button. Periodically, however, you might want to examine the contents of the User Dictionary to see whether it contains incorrect entries or words you no longer need. You also can add words while editing the dictionary.

Using Multiple User Dictionaries

If you like, you can create several user dictionaries, each for a particular type of writing. If you write about computers, for example, you might want to create a separate User Dictionary for computer terminology. If you write many interoffice memos, you might want a second User Dictionary that includes the spelling of each employee's name.

When you create multiple user dictionaries, keep in mind that only one can be active during a spell-check. If the writing in any document covers several dictionary content areas, you will have to check the document in multiple passes — one for each different User Dictionary you need. If this situation occurs frequently, you might be better off creating a single, composite User Dictionary.

STEPS: Editing a User Dictionary

1. If the appropriate User Dictionary is not already selected, choose Edit ⇨ Writing Tools ⇨ Select Dictionaries. Select the User Dictionary you want to edit, and then click the Choose button.

2. Choose Edit ⇨ Writing Tools ⇨ Edit User Dictionary. The User Dictionary dialog box appears (see Figure 3-23). The name of the current User Dictionary is shown in the upper portion of the dialog box.

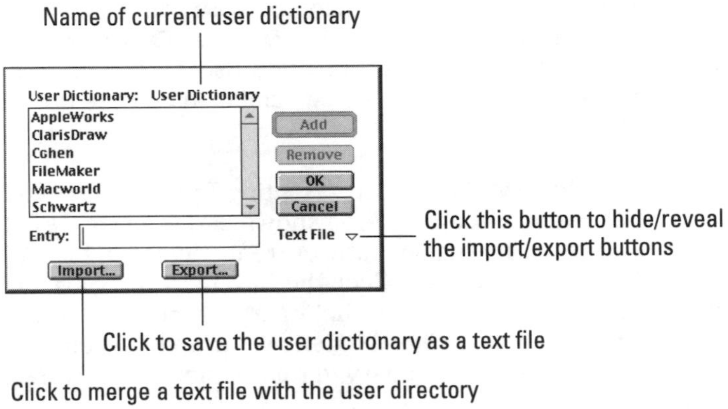

Name of current user dictionary

Click this button to hide/reveal the import/export buttons

Click to save the user dictionary as a text file

Click to merge a text file with the user directory

Figure 3-23: The User Dictionary dialog box

3. Add or remove words from the dictionary. To add a new word, type the word in the Entry text box and click the Add button. To remove a word, select the word in the list, and then click the Remove button.

4. After you finish editing the dictionary, click the OK button to save the changes and return to the document, or click the Cancel button to ignore the changes you made.

Importing and exporting user dictionaries

The User Dictionary dialog box has two more commands — Import and Export — that make it easy to add entire word lists to a User Dictionary or export the current dictionary to a text file. If you've already created a User Dictionary in another word processing program, for example, you can import the words into an AppleWorks dictionary without waiting for them to be individually flagged as questionable during a spell-check.

STEPS: Importing Words into a User Dictionary or Exporting a Word List

1. If the appropriate User Dictionary is not already selected, choose Edit ⇨ Writing Tools ⇨ Select Dictionaries. Select the User Dictionary, and then click the Choose button.

2. Choose Edit ➪ Writing Tools ➪ Edit User Dictionary. The User Dictionary dialog box appears. The name of the current User Dictionary is displayed in the upper portion of the dialog box.

3. To reveal the Import and Export buttons in the User Dictionary dialog box, click the small triangle beside Text File. The dialog box expands, as shown earlier in Figure 3-23.

4. To import a word list, click the Import button. Then choose a text file in the file dialog box and click the Open button. AppleWorks compares every word in the document with the words in the current user and main dictionaries and then adds every new word to the User Dictionary.

   or

   To export a User Dictionary to a text file, click the Export button. Navigate to the disk and folder where you want the exported text saved, type a name for the new file, and then click the Save button. AppleWorks exports the entire contents of the User Dictionary as a text file.

Tip You can use the Import command to import text other than word lists and dictionaries from other programs. Suppose, for example, that you have written a technical paper for work or school. Using the Import command to open the document (after you have saved it as Text rather than AppleWorks or some other word processor format), you can automatically add all the new technical words to your User Dictionary. Other words that are already in the main or current User Dictionary are ignored.

Using the thesaurus

When you're stuck for a word, or you find yourself using the same pet phrase over and over again, you can turn to the thesaurus for assistance. Because it contains more than 220,000 synonyms (words with the same or similar meanings), chances are excellent that you can find a new word or phrase that will add a little variety and style to your writing.

STEPS: Finding a Synonym

1. Invoke the thesaurus by choosing Edit ➪ Writing Tools ➪ Thesaurus (or by pressing Shift+⌘+Z).

   If you invoke the thesaurus while a word in the document is selected, the program displays definitions and synonyms for that word in the Thesaurus dialog box (see Figure 3-24).

   If no word is selected, the dialog box will be blank. In the Word box, type the word for which you want to display synonyms, and then click the Lookup button.

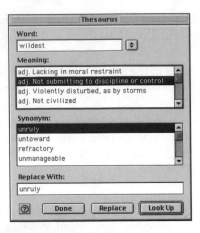

Figure 3-24: The Thesaurus dialog box

New Feature

In AppleWorks 6, the Thesaurus window also lists various definitions for the words it knows in the Meaning list. When you select one of these definitions, the Synonym list changes appropriately.

2. Scroll through the list of synonyms. If you find a word you want to use, select it and click the Replace button (or double-click the word). The dialog box closes, and the word is inserted at the current cursor position in the document. (If a word was highlighted in the document, that word is replaced by the synonym you selected.)

To exit from the thesaurus without replacing a word, click the Cancel button.

or

If you don't see a synonym you like, but you do see a word with a similar meaning, select it with the cursor. To see synonyms for that word, click the Lookup button. When you find a word you like, click the Replace button.

If you want to reexamine other words you've looked at during this thesaurus session, choose them from the pop-up button beside the Word text box. To recheck one of these words, select it and then click the Lookup button.

Performing a word count

By selecting Edit ➪ Writing Tools ➪ Word Count, you can get statistical information about the text in a document, including the number of characters, words, lines, paragraphs, pages, and sections. The Word Count feature is an enormous help to those who must write within a specific length limit (400 words or less, for example), as well as to writers who are paid by the word.

Note Be aware that Headers, Footers, and footnotes/endnotes count toward the statistics displayed, and that endnotes not only count as a section, but also count toward the characters, paragraphs, and lines. However, footnotes don't count as a section.

When the Word Count dialog box appears, its statistics are based on the entire contents of the current document. To obtain statistics on a portion of a document, select the text of interest, choose the Word Count command, and click the Count Selection checkbox in the Word Count dialog box. The statistics change to reflect only the current selection.

Using hyphenation

Sometimes the traditional "ragged right" formatting used in documents is just too ragged. Hyphenation can work wonders to improve the appearance of documents.

To enable auto-hyphenation for a document, choose Edit ➪ Writing Tools ➪ Auto-Hyphenate or, on the Button Bar, click the Auto Hyphenate button shown in Figure 3-25.

 Figure 3-25: The Auto-Hyphenate button

When auto-hyphenation is enabled, a checkmark appears in front of the command. Selecting the command again disables auto-hyphenation and removes the checkmark.

Note The Auto-Hyphenate button is not a standard part of the AppleWorks 6 default Button Bar. You must add the Auto-Hyphenate button manually, as explained in "Adding Buttons," located in Chapter 12.

After you enable auto-hyphenation, AppleWorks automatically examines line ends, consults its hyphenation dictionary, and then determines whether (and how) a word should be hyphenated.

Tip Auto-hyphenation is document-specific; that is, turning on auto-hyphenation affects only the current document. If you want to make auto-hyphenation the default for all new word processing documents, you can do so by creating a default template document, as explained in the "Using Template Documents to Set New Environment Defaults" section in Chapter 11.

Hyphenating a word your way

Auto-hyphenation is an all-or-nothing affair—that is, it affects the entire document, section, or text frame. If you decide you don't want a particular word hyphenated, or if AppleWorks fails to hyphenate a word because the word isn't in the hyphenation dictionary, you can edit the hyphenation dictionary.

Note   Only words of five or more letters can be added to the hyphenation dictionary.

STEPS: Editing a Hyphenation Dictionary

1. Choose Edit Hyphenation Dictionary from the Writing Tools submenu of the Edit menu. The Hyphenation File dialog box appears.

2. Edit the hyphenation dictionary as desired:

   • To specify a word's hyphenation, type the word in the Entry text box, inserting the appropriate hyphens. Then click the Add button.

   • To prevent AppleWorks from hyphenating a particular word, type the word in the Entry text box without hyphens. Then click the Add button.

   • To change the hyphenation for a word previously added to the hyphenation file, select the word and make the appropriate changes in the Entry text box. Then click the Replace button.

   • To remove a word previously added to the hyphenation file, select it and then click the Remove button. You cannot remove or change the hyphenation of words in the supplied dictionary.

3. Click the Done button to accept the changes to the hyphenation file and return to your document; otherwise, click the Cancel button.

Even when auto-hyphenation is enabled, you can adjust a word's hyphenation by manually inserting regular and discretionary hyphens:

✦ To insert a regular hyphen, set the text insertion point where you want the hyphen to appear, and then press the hyphen (-) key.

Note   A regular hyphen inserted in this manner will always show up at that spot in the word—regardless of where the word appears in the line. As a result, if the text is later edited or reformatted, regular hyphens can show up in the middle of a line. (If you ever see a word like "Mac-intosh" in the middle of a line, someone probably inserted a regular hyphen, edited the surrounding text, and then forgot to proofread the text.) You should insert a regular hyphen only if a word is always hyphenated, as in "double-click."

✦ To insert a discretionary hyphen, set the text insertion point where you want the hyphen to appear and then press ⌘+- (hyphen). Unlike regular hyphens, discretionary hyphens appear only when a word must be split between two lines; otherwise, they're invisible.

Installing a different hyphenation dictionary

In the United States, AppleWorks 6 is shipped with an English hyphenation dictionary. If you work in other languages, you can purchase other language-specific hyphenation dictionaries from Apple. The Spanish hyphenation dictionary is included on your AppleWorks 6 CD-ROM. To install a hyphenation dictionary, choose Edit ⇨ Writing Tools ⇨ Select Dictionaries. The Select Dictionaries dialog box appears, as shown previously in Figure 3-22. By default, the dialog box opens to the Dictionaries folder, where the various AppleWorks dictionaries are stored. Click the Hyphenation Dictionary radio button and click the Choose button. Select the hyphenation dictionary you want to use from the standard Open dialog box that appears, click the Select button, and then click the Done button. AppleWorks installs the new hyphenation dictionary, which will be used for all documents until you choose a different dictionary.

Note Although most users associate hyphenation with word processing, don't forget you can use it with database fields and text frames that are inserted into other types of documents, such as spreadsheets and presentations.

Working with outlines

Think back to your high school or college days. Remember making outlines — those numbered lists you used to help arrange your thoughts for a paper or speech into a coherent, meaningful order? Well, many of us still use outlines, and AppleWorks 6 makes outlining simple.

The main headings in an outline are called *topics*. Subordinate headings are called *subtopics*. Each subtopic is a point or idea that is related to the topic that precedes it, as shown in Figure 3-26. An AppleWorks outline can have up to 16 levels of subtopics.

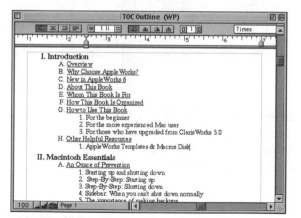

Figure 3-26: Outline topics and subtopics

Note   In versions of ClarisWorks prior to 4.0, the Outline View command worked as a toggle. Each time you chose the command, it toggled between an outline and normal view for the current document. In ClarisWorks 4 and 5, as well as AppleWorks, outlining is fully integrated into the word processing environment. An outline can now be a complete word processing document, or it can simply be incorporated as part of a word processing document or frame.

What defines a paragraph as being part of an outline — rather than normal word processing text — is that an outline format has been applied to it. When working in a word processing document or frame, you can choose from any of three predefined outline formats in the optional Styles pop-up button (in the Button Bar) or the Styles windoid (choose Format ➪ Show Styles or press Shift+⌘+W), as shown in Figure 3-27. The predefined outline formats are Diamond, Harvard, and Legal. Each format includes style definitions for between 5 and 12 outline levels.

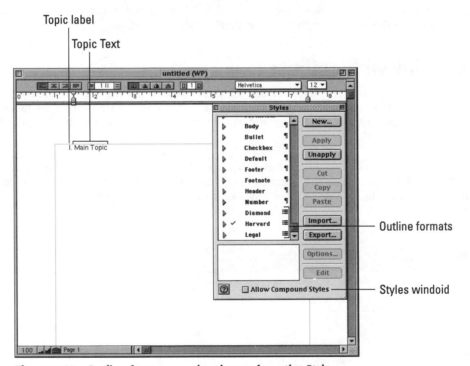

Figure 3-27: Outline formats can be chosen from the Styles windoid, the Outline ➪ Label Style submenu (not shown) or the Styles pop-up button (see Figure 3-2) in the Button Bar.

After choosing an outline format, you can immediately type your first topic. As you begin typing, a level-1 label automatically appears to the left. To create a new topic at the same level, press the Return key. To create a new topic to the left or the right of the current topic, choose Outline ⇨ New Topic Left or Outline ⇨ New Topic Right (or press ⌘+L or ⌘+R).

Caution

Each outline should have only one outline format — Diamond, Harvard, or Legal. If you select a topic in the middle of the outline and apply a different outline format to it, AppleWorks can get confused. It might treat the selected topic as a new outline (resulting in two topics labeled 1 and I, for example), or it might change the formatting and labels to something outlandish. Unless you really want nested outlines with different formats, immediately choose Undo from the Edit menu, or reapply the original outline style to the affected topics.

Outline formats and topic labels

Every outline has a general format, which you choose from the Styles windoid or the Styles pop-up button. Although you are free to customize individual topics or subtopics (by changing their font or style, for example), an outline format specifies a default style for every new topic and subtopic you create. Thus, you don't need to format individual topics and subtopics; their formatting is handled for you in the outline format definition.

On the other hand, if you want to get fancy, you can create a custom outline format or edit the formatting of the levels of an existing outline format (as explained in "Custom outline formats," later in this chapter).

Tip

To change from one outline format to another, select the entire outline and choose a new outline format — Diamond, Harvard, or Legal — from the Styles windoid or the Styles pop-up button.

As you work with outlines, you'll note that each predefined outline format has its own method of assigning topic labels (the symbol, letter, or number that precedes each topic and subtopic in the outline), as well as the particular font and style for each level. AppleWorks has 12 different topic label formats, as shown earlier in Figure 3-28. Although an outline format automatically assigns a topic label to every topic and subtopic, you can change any topic label.

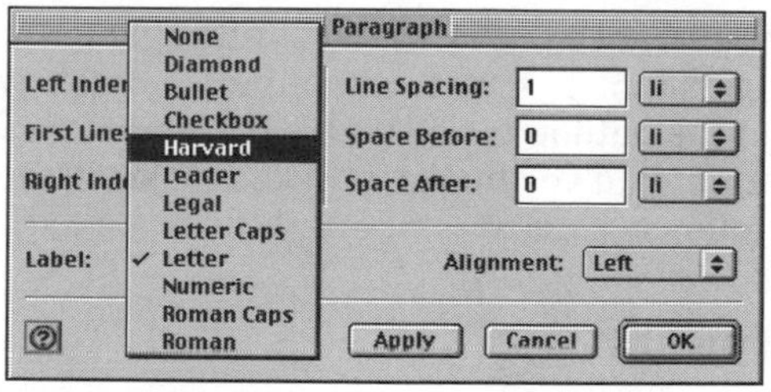

Figure 3-28: You can choose different topic labels in the Paragraph dialog box.

STEPS: Changing a Topic Label

1. Select one or more contiguous topics or subtopics in the outline by clicking and dragging through them.

2. Choose Format ⇨ Paragraph. The Paragraph dialog box appears.

3. Choose a label style from the Label pop-up menu, as shown in Figure 3-28. The label style is applied to the selected topics and subtopics.

4. Click the OK button to accept the new topic label style. (If you wish, you can first click the Apply button to see how the new label looks.)

When changing topic labels, it's usually best to restrict changes to one level at a time. Remember that the Paragraph command also sets line indents for all selected paragraphs. If you select topics that span two or more levels and then choose a new topic label (as described previously), the indenting of all selected topics is changed to match the new setting.

Note

As you work with outlines, you'll quickly discover that you cannot directly edit the topic labels (the numbers, letters, diamonds, and Roman numerals that precede each topic). These labels are governed by the level of each topic and are automatically handled for you by AppleWorks. In fact, the formatting of each topic label is directly connected to the first character in the topic name. If you change the font, size, color, or style of the first character, the topic label instantly changes to match. Thus, formatting only the first word of a topic as italic, for example, will also change the topic label to italic. Then again, if you change the format of an entire topic—as you would normally do when reformatting a level, for example—you probably want the label to change.

Custom outline formats

For a quick-and-dirty outline, stick with the level definitions that AppleWorks provides for the outline format you've selected. For presentations or formal papers, on the other hand, you might well want to design your own format for the outline so that you can select the topic labels, indents, fonts, styles, and sizes for each level.

Although you can manually alter the appearance of any topic or subtopic in the outline (by selecting the text and changing its font or size, for example), a better way to make the appearance of the levels in the outline consistent is to create a custom format. Regardless of which outline format you've chosen, you can make changes to the level formats, as described in the following steps.

STEPS: Creating a Custom Format

1. If the Styles windoid isn't visible, choose Format ⇨ Show Styles (or press Shift+⌘+W).

2. In the left side of the windoid, click the name of the particular outline format you want to change and then click its disclosure triangle. The outline format is selected and expands to show all outline levels.

3. In the Styles windoid, click the Edit button. The palette expands to show a Properties list. The pointer changes to the style-editing pointer—a shadowed S.

4. Scroll down and select the level you want to change. The level's current properties are listed, as shown in Figure 3-29.

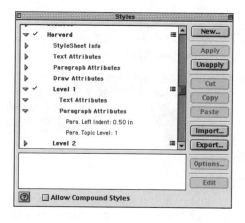

Figure 3-29: The expanded Styles windoid shows the properties of the selected level.

5. Choose Format ⇨ Paragraph. In the Paragraph dialog box that appears, you can change the line indents, line spacing, alignment, and label style of the new level format. (Note that several of these settings also can be selected by simply clicking icons in the ruler bar.)

6. Change any Text settings you want to alter for the level by choosing options from the Text ⇨ Font, Text ⇨ Size, Text ⇨ Style, and Text ⇨ Color submenus.

7. When you finish making changes for one level, repeat Steps 4 through 6 for each additional level you want to change. Click Done when you've made all necessary changes.

When you click the Done button, existing topics and subtopics for any changed levels are instantly updated to match the new styles. Any new topics and subtopics you create for levels you've just modified will have the attributes you have just specified.

Note   Using different text colors is an excellent way to differentiate levels. In a presentation, for example, lecture items could all be one color, and points you want to demonstrate could be formatted in another color.

For more information about creating and modifying styles (you might want to define new outline styles rather than edit the existing ones, for example), see Chapter 15.

Tips for Expanding and Collapsing

When the subtopics of a main topic have been collapsed, the topic label is usually under-lined. In a Diamond outline, however, collapsed subtopics are indicated by a gray diamond. Double-click it to reveal the subtopics hidden beneath it.

Although checkboxes are excellent for to-do lists, they pose a special problem when you expand or collapse levels. In a normal outline that uses diamond symbols, bullets, or num-bers as topic labels, you can expand or collapse levels by double-clicking the label. (Double-clicking is much easier to remember than the keyboard shortcut — Ctrl-Spacebar — and handier than pulling down the Outline menu.) Unfortunately, double-clicking in a checkbox merely toggles the checkmark on and off. The trick to collapsing a checkbox level is to double-click to the left of the checkbox, rather than directly in the checkbox.

To collapse or expand a single topic and all associated subtopics, select the topic you want to collapse or expand. Double-click the topic label, choose Outline ➪ Collapse or Outline ➪ Expand, or press Ctrl-Spacebar. If a topic cannot be collapsed or expanded, nothing hap-pens. (For example, you cannot collapse the lowest level topic because it has no subtopics.)

Creating new topics and subtopics

Now that you know about the components of an outline and how to assign formats and labels to topics, you need to step back and examine the mechanics of typing outline topics and subtopics.

After you type a new topic, you can do the following:

✦ Create a new topic at the same level by pressing ⌘+Return, or by choosing Outline ➪ New Topic. (These methods apply the default format for the level.)

✦ Create a new topic at the same level with the same formatting as the previous topic by pressing Return.

✦ Create a new topic below and to the right of the current topic (a subtopic) by pressing ⌘+R or choosing Outline ➪ New Topic Right.

✦ Create a new topic below and to the left of the current topic (at a higher level) by pressing ⌘+L or choosing Outline ➪ New Topic Left.

Collapsing and expanding an outline

AppleWorks enables you to expand and collapse the entire outline or just selected topics and subtopics. You might want to collapse the outline to show only one or two levels of topics so that you can focus on the main points without the clutter of additional subtopics. Similarly, you might want to collapse only the levels below a particular topic or subtopic. When we're working with a book outline, we often use this approach to show that a chapter has been completed.

STEPS: Collapsing or Expanding the Outline

1. Select the topics and subtopics you want to collapse or expand.

   To choose multiple topics, click in the first topic to set the text insertion point, and then drag to choose the additional topics. Select all outline topics if you want to collapse or expand the entire outline.

2. Choose Collapse or Expand from the Outline menu. The selected portion of the outline collapses to show only the highest level or expands to show all subordinate levels, respectively.

   or

   Choose Outline ⇨ Expand All or Outline ⇨ Collapse All. As in previous versions of both ClarisWorks and AppleWorks, you can press the Option key as you open the Outline menu, and Expand and Collapse change to Expand All and Collapse All, giving you two of each choice. For each topic selected, AppleWorks reveals (Expand All) or conceals (Collapse All) all the subtopics.

   or

   Choose Outline ⇨ Expand To. The Expand To dialog box appears.

   In the Expand To text box, type the number of outline levels you want to display, and then click the OK button. The selected portion of the outline changes to show only that number of levels. Type 1, for example, to display only the main topics for the selected portion of the outline. Type a larger number (the maximum is 16) to display all levels.

Rearranging topics and subtopics

One of the nice things about working with outlines in AppleWorks is the ease with which you can rearrange topics and subtopics. AppleWorks provides a variety of features for rearranging topics, including dragging them to different levels and using keyboard or menu commands.

Moving topics

By using the mouse, you can easily move a topic and its subtopics to a new position in the outline.

STEPS: Moving a Topic by Using the Mouse

1. Click the topic label to choose the topic and its associated subtopics. (If the topic has a checkbox label, click to the left of the checkbox.)

2. Click to the left of the selected topic and press the mouse button. As you drag up or down, the cursor changes to a double-headed arrow, with a tiny horizontal line that separates the arrowheads. A thick horizontal line (called the *insertion marker*) appears, showing the position to which the selected topic will move.

3. When the insertion marker is in the location to which you want to move the topic, release the mouse button. The topic and associated subtopics move to the new position, and the outline is relabeled as necessary.

You also can use the Outline ➪ Move Above (Ctrl+up arrow) or Outline ➪ Move Below (Ctrl+down arrow) commands from the Outline menu to move a selected topic above or below adjacent topics while retaining the same level in the outline hierarchy.

If you want to move a topic up or down without also moving its subtopics, press the Option key when you choose Outline ➪ Move Above or Outline ➪ Move Below (or press Option+Ctrl+up arrow or Option+Ctrl+down arrow). This will assign the subtopics to the topic formerly above the moved topic.

Concentrate on the Important Outline Commands

Because so many different commands exist for raising, lowering, moving, and creating new topics, it is unlikely you will remember them all unless you use the commands on a daily basis. Instead, you are better off doing the following:

✦ For reorganizing topics and subtopics, try the visual approach. Select the topics and subtopics and drag them to where they should go, or press ⌘+Option+click where you want them moved (to the left of the topic label before which you want them to appear).

✦ Expand and collapse topics by double-clicking their labels (to the left of checkbox labels).

✦ Concentrate on memorizing only the most important keyboard shortcuts, and choose the others from the Outline menu. The commands listed in the following table are the ones you are most likely to use.

Procedure	Keystroke
New topic at the same level	⌘+Return
New topic at the same level with the same formatting	Return
New topic to the left	⌘+L
New topic to the right	⌘+R
Shift topic to the left	Shift+⌘+L
Shift topic to the right	Shift+⌘+R

Raising or lowering topic levels

Although you can use the mouse to move a topic anywhere in the outline, you cannot change a topic's level by moving it with the mouse. If a topic was at Level 3 before the move, it will still be at Level 3 after the move. To change a topic's level, you need to use the Move Left or Move Right command (or the keyboard equivalents).

Select the topic whose level you want to change by clicking anywhere within its text. Choose Outline ⇨ Move Left ⇨ With Subtopics (Shift+⌘+L or Ctrl+left arrow) or Outline ⇨ Move Right ⇨ With Subtopics (Shift+⌘+R or Ctrl+right arrow). The selected topic and all associated subtopics are promoted or demoted one level in the outline hierarchy. If you want to promote or demote a topic without affecting its subtopics, choose Outline ⇨ Move Left ⇨ Without Subtopics (Option+Ctrl+left arrow) or Outline ⇨ Move Right ⇨ Without Subtopics (Option+Ctrl+right arrow).

Note
You also can promote a topic and its associated subtopics by selecting it and then choosing Raise Topic from the Outline menu.

Deleting topics

As you work, you might decide to delete some topics or levels in the outline. The procedure you use to do this depends on whether you want to delete a topic and its subtopics or just delete a single level in the outline without eliminating its subtopics.

To delete a single level, triple-click in the text of the level you want to delete. The entire line of text is selected. If the topic contains more than one line, quadruple-click to select it. You also can drag to select all the text in the level. Then press the Delete, Clear, Del, or Backspace keys to delete the line. If the topic was one of several topics at the same level, the other topics beneath it move up and are renumbered as necessary.

Outline Ideas

Although the outlines you created in high school or college were usually designed to organize points for a paper or speech, there's no reason you can't write the entire paper or speech with outline formatting. Why use an outline just for notes? After all, a topic doesn't have to be a point. It can just as easily be an entire paragraph.

Outline formats are also excellent for creating presentations. You can use the diamond or bullet format to design standard text charts, or you can create a custom format, if you prefer. When you finish the charts, you can use a laser or inkjet printer to print transparencies or handouts. (See Chapter 7 for more on Presentations.)

Although a word processing document is normally used for outlines, you can also create an outline in a text frame or in a table cell (covered later). Insert a text frame onto a Presentation slide, and you can quickly create a bullet list or text chart.

To delete a topic and associated subtopics, click the topic label. (If the topic has a checkbox label, click to the left of the checkbox.) The topic and all associated subtopics are selected. Press Delete, Clear, Del, or Backspace. The topic and its subtopics are eliminated. Labels for topics below the deleted topic are automatically renumbered, as necessary.

Adding Graphics to Word Processing Documents

The selective use of graphics can go a long way toward enhancing a report or memo. For example, you can add a company logo to letterhead or presentation pages and embed spreadsheet charts in reports. AppleWorks enables you to add graphics to a word processing document or frame in two ways: as free-floating objects or as in-line graphics (part of the text).

Because floating objects are not part of the text, you can move them wherever you like. And because they are objects, you can add a new background color, pattern, wallpaper, gradient, or bounding lines to them. Finally, you also can specify a text wrap for each object (none, regular, or irregular). Figure 3-30 shows examples of both types of graphics.

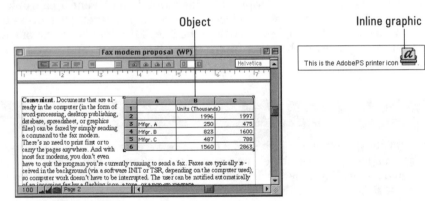

Figure 3-30: An in-line graphic (right) and an object for which regular text wrap has been set (left)

In-line graphics

An in-line graphic in a word processing document is treated exactly the same as a text character. For all practical purposes, you can think of it as just another character. As a result, if the graphic is in a paragraph by itself, you can use paragraph formatting commands to align the graphic to a tab stop or to center it, for example.

Tip In most cases, the best place for an in-line graphic is in a paragraph by itself — without any surrounding text. An in-line graphic that is in the same line with text can sometimes cause serious problems with spacing between lines because line height is defined by the largest font or image in the line.

STEPS: Adding an In-Line Graphic

1. Set the text insertion point where you want to insert the graphic.

2. To insert a graphic from a file, choose File ⇨ Insert and choose a graphic file to insert. The entire contents of the file appear at the text insertion point.

   or

   To insert a graphic from the clipboard, select and copy the graphic (⌘+C) from an AppleWorks paint or draw document, from within another graphics program, or from the Scrapbook. In the AppleWorks document, choose Edit ⇨ Paste (or press ⌘+V). The graphic appears at the text insertion point.

   If the program or desk accessory supports drag-and-drop, you can drag the graphic into the AppleWorks document (without using cut-and-paste) and drop it in place.

   To insert a graphic from your AppleWorks Clippings, choose File ⇨ Show Clippings (⌘+2) if the Clippings windoid isn't showing, and use either the Search panel to find the clipping you desire or click the tab that holds the clipping you want. Select the clipping's thumbnail and drag it to the document window, until the insertion cursor is where you want it. Then release the mouse button

3. *Optional:* Resize the graphic as needed by dragging its handle to a new position. You can maintain the original proportions by pressing Shift as you drag. To resize the graphic by a specific percentage, choose Format ⇨ Scale by Percent.

After placing and optionally resizing an in-line graphic, you can use the Descent command to vertically align the graphic with the surrounding text. Select the in-line graphic and choose Format ⇨ Descent (or just double-click the graphic). The Descent dialog box appears. Type a negative number (in points) to raise the graphic in relation to the text baseline; type a positive number to lower the graphic.

Graphic objects

You can paste graphic objects into a document, insert them with the Insert command, create them from scratch with the drawing tools, or embed them in a paint frame.

STEPS: Pasting a Picture from the Clipboard as a Free-Floating Graphic

1. In the AppleWorks graphics environment, another graphics program, or in the Scrapbook desk accessory, select the picture.

2. Choose Edit ➪ Copy from (or press ⌘+C). A copy of the image is temporarily stored in the clipboard.

3. Select the pointer tool from the AppleWorks Tools window's Tool panel. (If the Tools window isn't visible, click the Show/Hide Tools control in the lower-left corner of the document window, and then click the Toolbox tab.)

   Selecting the pointer tool takes you out of word processing mode and instructs AppleWorks to treat the graphic to be pasted as a free-floating object rather than as an in-line graphic.

4. Choose Edit ➪ Paste (or press ⌘+V). The picture is pasted as an object that you can resize or move.

   After the picture has been pasted, it should be surrounded by handles. If the handles are not visible, the picture has probably been pasted as an in-line graphic (part of the text), rather than as an object. Press the Delete, Clear, or Del keys to remove the picture, and then go back to Step 3.

STEPS: Inserting a Picture from a File as a Free-Floating Graphic

1. Select the pointer tool from the AppleWorks Tools window's tool panel as in Step 1 previously.

   Selecting the pointer tool takes you out of word processing mode and instructs AppleWorks to treat the graphic to be pasted as a free-floating object rather than as an in-line graphic.

2. Choose File ➪ Insert. A standard Open dialog box appears.

3. Navigate to the proper drive and folder and choose the graphics file you want to insert in the document.

4. Click Insert. The program inserts the file into the document as an object that you can resize or move about.

   After the picture has been inserted, it should be surrounded by handles. If the handles are not visible, the picture has probably been inserted as an in-line graphic (part of the text), rather than as an object. Press the Delete, Clear or Del key once to remove the picture, and then go back to Step 1.

Inserting Free-Floating Graphics

In AppleWorks 6, you'll also find it remarkably easy to insert free-floating graphics using drag-and-drop. Begin by selecting the pointer tool in your AppleWorks word processing document or frame. Then open any drag-and-drop-enabled application or desk accessory (such as the Scrapbook) and drag the graphic onto the word processing document or frame. If you don't select the pointer tool, the graphic will be inserted as an in-line object.

AppleWorks also includes hundreds of clip-art images you can place in your documents, both on your disk and accessible via the Web. To insert any of these images into a word processing document, decide whether you want an in-line graphic or a floating graphic by setting the text insertion point or by choosing the pointer tool, choose File ➪ Show Clippings (⌘+2), choose a graphic from one of the Clippings panels or search for it on the Web, and then drag its thumbnail representation into your document. (For more information about using AppleWorks Clippings, see Chapter 6.)

Chapter 6 also discusses the details of creating a picture from scratch. In general, you select drawing tools from the Tool panel of the Tools windoid and drag to create different shapes.

Wrapping text around graphic objects

If you are going to surround the graphic object with text, you can specify how (or whether) the text should wrap around the object (see Figure 3-31).

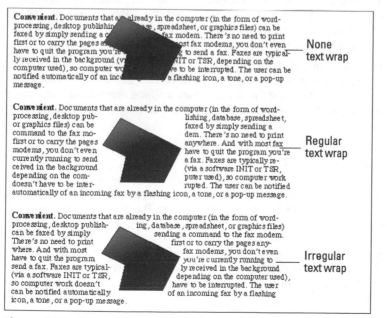

Figure 3-31: Text wraps

You can choose from the following text wrap options:

✦ **None.** The object obscures any text it is covering. If you move the object to the back, the text appears over the object.

✦ **Regular.** An invisible rectangle is drawn around the object, and text wraps to the edges of the rectangle.

✦ **Irregular.** Text wraps as closely as you specify to the original edges of the object.

In the Gutter text box, type a number (in points) for the amount of space you want between the object and the surrounding text.

You also can specify a text wrap for other objects, such as spreadsheet frames.

Text wrap can be set for floating objects, but not for in-line graphics. To set text wrap for a floating object or frame, begin by selecting the object with the pointer tool. Choose Options ➪ Text Wrap. In the Text Wrap dialog box that appears, click the icon for None, Regular, or Irregular, depending on the type of wrap you want. Then, specify the gutter (if you chose Irregular) and click the OK button. The text wraps around the object or frame in the manner you specified.

Tip

When you try to do an irregular text wrap around an imported PICT image, the object often appears to be embedded in a large rectangle—regardless of the actual shape of the image. To get the wrap you want, ungroup the object in AppleWorks and then group it again (the Ungroup and Group commands are in the Arrange menu). The text should wrap correctly. (Note, however, that if the object really is surrounded by a rectangular box—most scans, for example—this procedure might change nothing.)

This tip will work only if the graphic is a draw object made up of QuickDraw shapes. If the image is a bitmap, the handles will define the image area. A workaround to this is to insert the bitmap, draw a shape around the text wrap area (using the polygon tool), assign the appropriate text wrap, and then make the polygon transparent.

Layering pictures and text

Of course, text does not have to be wrapped around graphic objects. You can place a picture behind or in front of text by selecting the picture and choosing the Move Forward, Move to Front, Move Backward, or Move to Back command from the Arrange menu.

With Text Wrap set to None, a graphic can float on top of the document, hiding the text beneath it. And by using the Move to Back command, text can print over a graphic. This technique is useful for creating a watermark or rubber stamp effect, as shown in Figure 3-32.

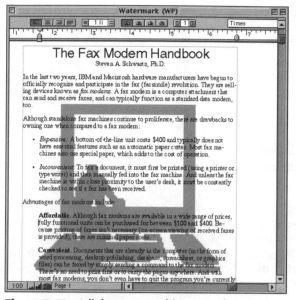

Figure 3-32: A light gray graphic can make an interesting watermark for a document.

Note

Objects that have been moved to the back of a word processing document usually work best if they are light in color. Dark objects, or objects with dark areas, can make reading the overlaying text difficult or impossible.

Caution

If you are working in a word processing frame rather than a word processing document, you will need to select the word processing frame and choose Options ⇨ Frame Links (Shift+⌘+L) to force the text-wrap settings to take effect. (Frame Links will be covered in more depth in Chapter 6.)

Adding Equations to a Word Processing Document

Using the Equation Editor, you can create mathematical and scientific equations and insert them into word processing documents or frames. Figure 3-33 shows two complex equations that were created with the Equation Editor.

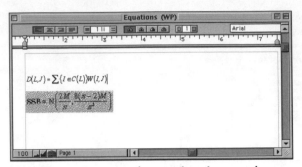

Figure 3-33: Two sample equations in a word processing document

Equations are treated as objects — not as text. As such, they can be added as in-line graphics or as floating graphics (discussed previously in "Adding Graphics to Word Processing Documents," earlier in this chapter). Similarly, because they are graphic objects, all changes you want to make to the equation must be done in the Equation Editor, and not in the AppleWorks document in which the equation is placed.

STEPS: Creating an Equation

1. To create an equation as an in-line graphic, set the text insertion point in the text where you want the equation to appear.

   or

   To create an equation as a floating object, select the pointer tool.

2. Choose Edit ➪ Insert Equation. The Equation Editor launches, as shown in Figure 3-34.

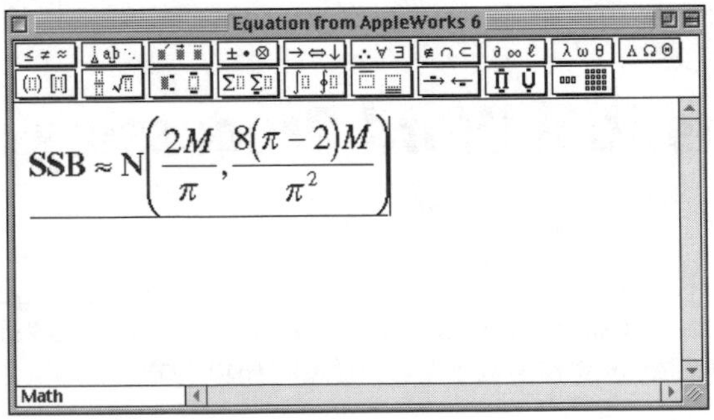

$$SSB \approx N\left(\frac{2M}{\pi}, \frac{8(\pi - 2)M}{\pi^2}\right)$$

Figure 3-34: The Equation Editor

3. Design the equation by typing and choosing options from the symbol pop-up menus.

4. To complete the equation, click the equation window's close box. The AppleWorks document is displayed, and the equation is inserted as an in-line or floating graphic, as appropriate.

As with other objects, you can change the size of an equation by clicking and dragging a handle. If you want to embellish an equation by adding a bounding box or a background color, pattern, wallpaper, or gradient, place it as a floating object rather than as an in-line graphic. You can then select the object in the document and set options for it by choosing from the Pen and Fill settings in the Accents windoid.

If you later need to modify an equation, double-click it. The Equation Editor opens and displays the selected equation. Make any necessary changes, and then close the Equation Editor window to return to the AppleWorks document.

Note

You can alter the vertical placement of an in-line equation relative to the surrounding text by choosing the Descent command from the Format menu.

You can change an existing in-line graphic equation to a floating one or vice versa by cutting it, selecting the pointer tool or by setting the text insertion point (as appropriate), and then pasting.

Using Tables

Prior to AppleWorks 6, unless you were using a Japanese version of ClarisWorks 4.1 or later, you had to use spreadsheet frames or laboriously drawn graphic boxes to place tables into word processing and other documents. An enhanced version of these Japanese (Keisen) tables are new in AppleWorks 6.

Unlike spreadsheets, where every cell in a row is the same height and every cell in a column is the same width, tables enable you to create relatively free-form grids, where each cell is a word processing frame that can contain outlines, graphics, multimedia, styled text, and so forth. When your text outgrows the cell, the cell expands to accommodate your text.

You can add a table as an inline object at the cursor position by choosing Table ➪ Insert Table or as a free-floating object by clicking on the Table tool on the Frames panel of the Tools window and either dragging it onto your document or clicking and dragging where you want it to appear in your document.

Previously, you would create a table by creating tab stops and typing away. These rather plain tables are functional, but they do not stand out. If you want to embellish a table of this type, select the entire table and choose Table ➪ Convert to Table. You also can select an AppleWorks table and choose Table ➪ Convert to Text.

Caution   Be aware that your table cell widths and your tab stops will not correspond. These commands simply provide quick movement from one format to another.

In addition to all the text formatting options we cover here for word processing, you have some extra capabilities in a table cell. For example, you can set the vertical alignment of the text to hug the lower or upper portion of the cell or, if you like, to be vertically centered in the cell.

Tables are also a very important aspect of formatting a word processing document that will become a Web page. Because HTML (the language interpreted by Web browsers) does not understand tabs or columns, which you use to align your text and images, Web designers make heavy use of HTML tables to provide these effects. AppleWorks tables translate directly into HTML tables when you use the Save As HTML option from the File menu.

Note   Unfortunately, the HTML translator does not translate HTML tables into AppleWorks tables, so be sure to save a copy in AppleWorks format if you think you might want to modify your Web page at a later time.

Tables will be covered in much greater detail in Chapter 14, and Table Styles will be covered in Chapter 15.

Adding Document Links

Using the Links windoid (Format ⇨ Show Links Window or Shift+⌘+M), you can create three types of linked text, plus images, objects, and frames in AppleWorks 6 documents: anchors (bookmarks in AppleWorks 5), document links, and URL links.

Anchors are placemarkers — text strings, objects, paint images, spreadsheet cells, or frames — to which you can quickly jump to by double-clicking their names in the Links windoid or by clicking an associated document link in an AppleWorks document. Document links are text strings, objects, paint images, spreadsheet cells, or frames in another AppleWorks document that, when clicked, transport you to an anchor in the same document (or that instruct AppleWorks to open a different document). URL links are text strings, objects, paint images, spreadsheet cells, or frames in an AppleWorks document that, when clicked, connect you to a particular page on the World Wide Web.

By adding document links to a Table of Contents page, for example, you can click chapter headings and jump to that location in a document. Company memos can contain URL links to related information on the World Wide Web, as well.

To create a link, choose Format ⇨ Show Links Window (Shift+⌘+M). In the Apple-Works document, select the text string, object, paint image, spreadsheet cell, or frame that will serve as the link. In the Links windoid, choose a link type from the tabs at the bottom of the windoid. To create the link, choose the New command on the selected panel, name the link, and set additional options, as necessary.

To learn more about creating, editing, and using links, see Chapter 18.

Using the Word Processing Assistants

When you're working in a word processing document or frame, you can add a word processing AppleWorks Assistant to your Button Bar to get assistance with one common task: inserting and formatting citation footnotes.

Using the Insert Citation Assistant

Whether you are writing a college term paper, a professional article, or any other work in which you include footnotes, the Insert Citation Assistant is an enormous help in ensuring that each footnote contains the necessary information. Unlike footnotes you create manually with the Format ➪ Insert Blank Footnote (Shift+⌘+F), the Insert Citation Assistant steps you through the process of composing the footnote, and then formats it according to the footnote style you've chosen.

STEPS: Adding a Footnote with the Insert Citation Assistant

1. In a word processing document, position the cursor where you want to insert the footnote.

2. Click the optional Insert Citation button in your Button Bar (see Chapter 12 for information on adding a button to the Button Bar). The Insert Footnote Assistant dialog box appears. Click the Next button to present the Insert Footnote dialog box shown in Figure 3-35.

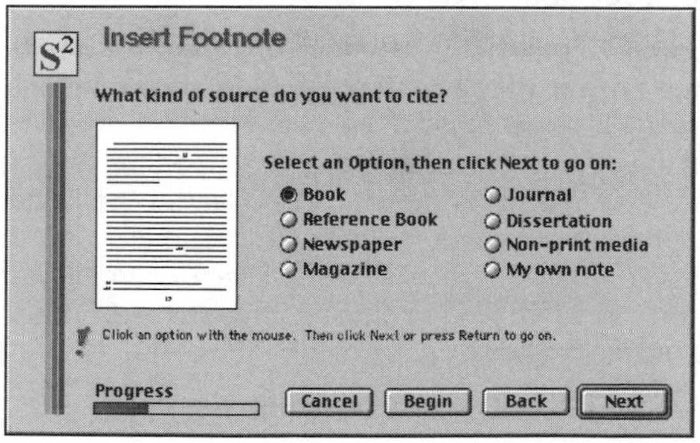

Figure 3-35: The Insert Citation Assistant dialog box

Note The button is called Insert Citation, but the Assistant is named Insert Footnote. To avoid confusion with the Insert Footnote button or the Format ⇨ Insert Blank Footnote command, we'll refer to it as the Insert Citation Assistant (because that is the button that calls it to action).

3. Click the radio button for the type of source you want to cite, and then click the Next button.

4. A second Insert Footnote dialog box appears (such as the one shown in Figure 3-36), where you type in the appropriate information for your source. The information requested varies with different types of sources. Any field you leave blank is marked with a placeholder in the footnote, which you can later complete.

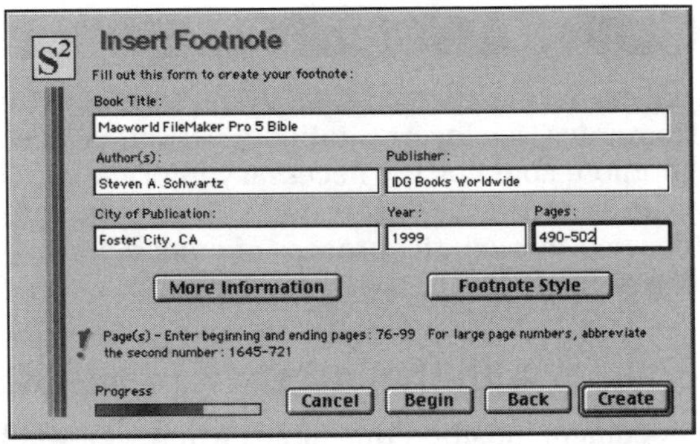

S^2 **Insert Footnote**

Fill out this form to create your footnote :

Book Title :

Macworld FileMaker Pro 5 Bible

Author(s) :   Publisher :

Steven A. Schwartz   IDG Books Worldwide

City of Publication :   Year :   Pages :

Foster City, CA   1999   490-502

[More Information]   [Footnote Style]

Page(s) - Enter beginning and ending pages : 76-99 For large page numbers, abbreviate the second number : 1645-721

Progress   [Cancel] [Begin] [Back] [Create]

Figure 3-36: Fill in the blanks with your source information.

5. *Optional:* Some source forms include a Footnote Style button you click to select one of two footnote styles: Modern Language Association or *Chicago Manual of Style*. Click the OK button to continue. If you do not select a style, the Modern Language Association style is used.

6. Click Done. The new footnote number is inserted at the cursor position, and the footnote is added to the bottom of the current page, as shown in Figure 3-37.

Note If you want endnotes in the document (notes that are grouped together at the end of the document) rather than footnotes (notes that appear at the bottom of the pages on which they are referenced), choose Format ⇨ Document, click the At End of Document radio button (in the Footnotes section of the Document dialog box), and click the OK button. All footnotes—including those created by the Insert Citation Assistant—are moved to the last page of the document.

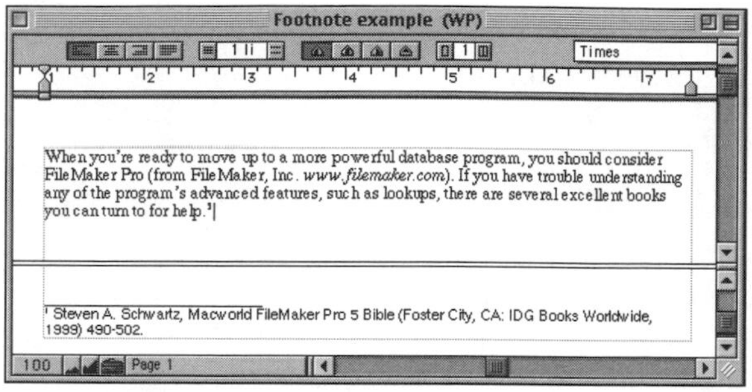

Figure 3-37: A footnote automatically appears at the bottom of the current document page.

Although the Insert Citation Assistant is also available when you invoke this dialog box from a word processing frame, you can use this Assistant only in a word processing document. (An error message appears if you select the Assistant from within a word processing frame.)

Down to Business: An Improved Fax Form Template

Although AppleWorks includes a fax form template, you might want to design one of your own.

We prefer to combine the cover page information with the body of the fax. As you can see in the finished fax form shown in Figure 3-38, the essential To:/From: information takes up less than a third of the page, leaving plenty of room for the fax message. If you use this form rather than a cover page, you can probably reduce most transmissions to a single page.

This exercise illustrates the following AppleWorks features:

- ✦ Placing and drawing graphics in a word processing document
- ✦ Locking graphic elements (so they cannot be moved or inadvertently altered)
- ✦ Using multiple fonts, styles, and sizes
- ✦ Paragraph formatting
- ✦ Creating a footer
- ✦ Automatic page numbering
- ✦ Using a table

✦ Changing table column widths

✦ Using page numbering and page counts

✦ Automatic date stamping

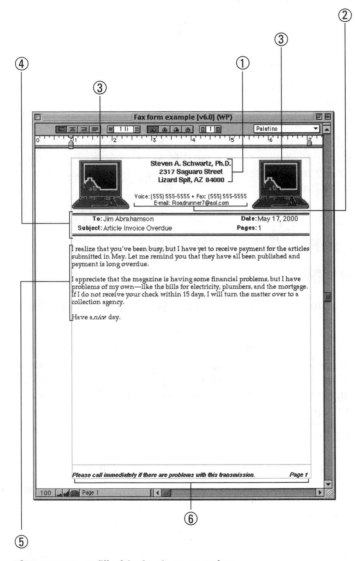

Figure 3-38: A filled-in fax form template

Designing the template

To create the template, begin by creating a new word processing document (choose File ⇨ New or press ⌘+N). Then choose Format ⇨ Document. In the Document dialog box that appears, set the Left and Right Margins to 1 in. This setting ensures you will not lose text from the sides of the document when you send it as a fax.

The key elements of the fax form are numbered in Figure 3-38, shown earlier. The discussion that follows refers to each element by number.

1. Name/Company Name/Return Address

Center your name, company name, and return address on the page. (Click the center-alignment icon in the ruler bar to center text between the margins.) Use 12-point Helvetica Bold for the font.

2. Fax and Voice Phone Numbers

Center these lines just as you centered the address information. The phone numbers and the electronic mail account information (America Online) are in 10-point Helvetica.

You can replace this e-mail address with your own electronic mail address (if you have one) or with other pertinent information, or you can simply delete it. Choose Format ⇨ Paragraph and set Space After to 2 li. Press the Return key once so that you'll be positioned for the next object — the table.

3. Logo or Graphic

We like to use graphics or logos in our faxes. The logos shown earlier in Figure 3-38 are pasted into the document as objects rather than as in-line graphics.

STEPS: Adding a Graphic to a Template

1. In the Scrapbook, AppleWorks Clippings, or a graphics program (the AppleWorks draw environment, for example), select the image you want to copy.

2. Choose Edit ⇨ Copy (or press ⌘+C).

3. Return to the fax form in AppleWorks and select the pointer tool from the Tool panel.

4. Choose Edit ⇨ Paste (or press ⌘+V). The graphic appears onscreen, surrounded by handles to show that it is selected. (If the handles are not visible, the graphic has been pasted as in-line text rather than as an object. Press Delete to remove the image and return to Step 3.)

If the graphic is in a drag-and-drop-enabled application or desk accessory (such as the Scrapbook or in the Clippings), you can drag it onto the fax form rather than using the copy-and-paste procedure just described.

5. With the image still selected, drag it to the upper-left corner of the fax form. If the image is too large or too small, click its lower-right handle and, while pressing the Shift key, drag to resize the image. (Using Shift while resizing a graphic tells AppleWorks to maintain the same proportions.)

6. *Optional:* To make an exact copy of the graphic for use in the upper-right corner of the fax form, select the graphic and choose Edit ➪ Copy (or press ⌘+C).

Choose Edit ➪ Paste (or press ⌘+V). A copy of the graphic is pasted directly on top of the original graphic.

Select the new graphic and, while pressing Shift, drag it horizontally to the right edge of the fax form. (Pressing Shift while dragging an image ensures that all movements are exactly horizontal or vertical and keeps the two graphics perfectly aligned.)

Tip   You can also achieve the results of Step 6 by selecting the graphic, pressing the Option key, starting to drag, and then also pressing the Shift key while continuing to drag to the right edge. In this way, you duplicate the object, start the drag, constrain it, and it retains the clipboard contents if you have something on it you still want.

4. The Table (Addressee Information)

The addressee information is a table. Figure 3-39 shows what the table looks like as you work with it.

| To: | Jim Abrahamson | Date: | May 17, 2000 |
| Subject: | Article Invoice Overdue | Pages: | 1 |

Figure 3-39: The table

STEPS: Creating the Addressee Table

1. Choose Table ➪ Insert Table.

2. Tell AppleWorks that you want two rows and four columns.

3. Place the From:, To:, Date:, and Pages: strings in the cells.

4. Select the first and third columns by clicking and dragging in each of the cells while holding down the ⌘ key. Format the four cells with 12-point Helvetica Bold and right-align them. To set the font (Helvetica), style (Bold), and point size (12), choose the appropriate options from the Text ➪ Font, Text ➪ Style, and Text ➪ Size submenus. To set the alignment, choose Right from the Alignment submenu in the Format menu. You should also choose the bottom alignment choice from the Table ➪ Vertical Alignment submenu.

5. Use a 12-point font (Helvetica, for example) and left alignment (the default setting) for the cells in the second column, and your choice of left or right alignment for the cells in the fourth column (left used here). Set the font and point size for these cells by using the procedure described in Step 2.

6. Click in the top cell in the fourth column and choose Edit ⇨ Insert Date ⇨ Auto-updating.

7. *Optional:* If you wish a different date format, choose Edit ⇨ Preferences ⇨ General, choose Text from the pop-up menu to display the Text preferences and then choose the date format you prefer from the Date Format pop-up menu. Click the OK button.

8. Click in the bottom-right cell and choose Edit ⇨ Insert Page #. Click the Document Page Count radio button and click the OK button.

9. When you first created the table, the column widths were all uniform. To change them to their final sizes, select the first column's right edge (the cursor turns into parallel lines with outward-pointing arrows), and drag left to the desired width. Repeat the process, dragging to the right, with the second column's right edge. Set the widths however you would like to modify them.

10. Now, you're ready to select the top and bottom table borders and choose the appropriate styles from the Tables ⇨ Line Styles submenu. Select the other cell borders and set their thickness to None in the Accents window.

12. Position the text cursor after the table, press the Return key, and then set your alignment to left-justified to prepare for your body text.

5. The Body Text

Enter a dummy line of body text (such as Message goes here) so that you can set the paragraph format and choose a font for the fax text. Choose a font for the body text from the Text ⇨ Font submenu or the Font pop-up menu in your ruler and use it to format the dummy text line. Make sure the font you choose is very legible so that your recipient's copy will be clear. Times is a good choice in 10 point or larger text.

Every paragraph of the body text uses the same font and paragraph format settings. To set the paragraph format, choose Format ⇨ Paragraph. The Paragraph dialog box appears. Set Line Spacing and Space After to 1 li; all other settings can be left at their defaults.

6. The Footer

The footer repeats on every page of the fax, displaying a standard message and the page number for each page. To create the footer, choose Format ⇨ Insert Footer. A blank area at the bottom of the page is now reserved for the footer. Press the Return key once to add a blank line at the top of the footer (to separate it from the body text). Set the font, style, and size as Helvetica, Bold and Italic, and 10 point, respectively. Type the following message: "Please call immediately if there are problems with this transmission." Then, press the Tab key once and type Page, followed by a space. Drag a right tab—the third tab icon—to the 7-inch mark on the ruler. Doing so causes the page number information to align with the right margin. To complete the footer, insert the automatic page number. With the text insertion point at the end of the footer text, choose Edit ➪ Insert Page #, click the Page Number radio button in the Insert Page Number dialog box, and then click the OK button.

Because you want to have ready access to the template and ensure you do not change it by mistake, save it as a template rather than as a document.

STEPS: Saving the Template as an AppleWorks Template Document

1. Choose Save As from the File menu. The standard Save file dialog box appears.

2. Click the Template radio button. By default, AppleWorks automatically selects the AppleWorks Templates folder. Saving the template in the AppleWorks Templates folder will enable you to choose the template easily from the Starting Points window's Templates panel when creating new files.

3. Type a name for the document, such as **Fax Form Template**.

4. Click the Save button.

To open this—or any other—template in AppleWorks 6, File ➪ Show Starting Points (or press ⌘+1), click the Templates tab if Starting Points isn't already showing that panel, and then click the correct thumbnail to start a new document based on that template.

Using the template

Now that you have created the fax form template, you need to know how to use it.

STEPS: Creating a Fax

1. Choose File ➪ Show Starting Points and click the Templates tab if that panel is not already showing.

2. Click the Fax Form Template's thumbnail and an untitled copy of the fax form template appears.

3. Fill in the address information. Begin by double-clicking to the right of the To: field. Type the name of the fax recipient and press ⌘+down arrow. The cursor moves to the cell below, where you can now type the subject of the fax.

4. Select the line of text that reads "Message goes here" and type the body of the fax. You'll notice each time you press the Return key to start a new paragraph, the program automatically inserts a blank line for you.

5. When you've completed the body text, notice that the cell to the right of the Pages: field contains the total number of pages for the fax.

6. If you are going to transmit the fax on a standard fax machine, turn on the printer and choose File ➪ Print. The Print dialog box appears. Change settings as necessary (you can usually accept the default settings) and click the OK button to print the fax.

   or

7. If you are going to transmit the fax using your fax modem, select the Chooser desk accessory from the Apple menu. The Chooser dialog box appears. (The specific procedure for sending a document with your fax modem might differ, depending on the fax software installed on your Mac. See your Fax software's manual for exact instructions.)

8. Select the fax modem driver from the left side of the Chooser dialog box and click the close box to select that driver as the current driver.

9. In AppleWorks, choose Page Setup from the File menu and change settings as needed. Click the OK button to return to the document.

10. Choose Print from the File menu, change settings as necessary, specify a recipient for the fax, and then click the OK button. The document is now translated into fax format and transmitted to the recipient.

Quick Tips

The following quick tips describe how to create glossary terms and suggest ways to improve the quality of your documents by using special papers.

A do-it-yourself glossary

You might have noticed that the AppleWorks word processor lacks a glossary feature. (A glossary enables you to easily insert frequently used terms and phrases into documents by selecting them from lists or by pressing hot keys.) However, with minimal effort, you can create glossary terms. Two approaches work fairly well: using the Find/Change command and using macros.

To use the Find/Change method, you define one or more abbreviations to represent a longer word or phrase, use them in the text, and then issue the Find/Change command to replace each abbreviation with the expanded phrase.

Decide on a term or phrase for which you want to define an abbreviation. The phrase can contain up to 255 characters, including spaces. Pick an abbreviation for the phrase. Ideally, the abbreviation should not be a real word or a portion of a word. For example, you can use three asterisks (***) or a nonsense syllable (such as cpt).

When typing the document, use the abbreviation, rather than the full word or phrase it represents. After you finish typing the document, replace all abbreviations with the full word or phrase. Do so by choosing Edit ➪ Find/Change ➪ Find/Change (or by pressing ⌘-F), entering the abbreviation in the Find text box, typing the expanded word or phrase into the Change text box, and then clicking the Change All button.

Alternatively, you can create a macro, as described in the following steps:

STEPS: Creating a Glossary Term Macro

1. Open a new or existing word processing document.

2. Choose File ➪ Macros ➪ Record Macro (or press Shift+⌘+J). The Record Macro dialog box appears, as shown in Figure 3-40.

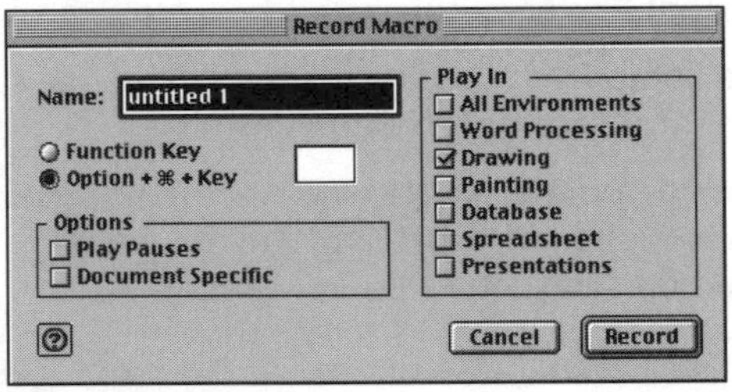

Figure 3-40: The Record Macro dialog box

3. Type a name for the macro and specify an Option+⌘ key or function key with which to execute the macro.

> **Note**
>
> If you hold the Shift key down when choosing a character to invoke your macro in combination with the ⌘ and Option keys, you will have to press it each time you need to use the macro. In other words, ⌘+Option+C is not the same as ⌘+Option+c.

4. Choose from the following options:

   • If you don't intend to use the glossary term anywhere other than in the present document, click Document Specific. If you want the macro to be available in other documents, leave that checkbox blank.

   • If you want to use the glossary term in other environments (in addition to the word processing environment), click their Play In checkboxes.

5. Click Record. You are returned to the document, and the macro recorder starts.

6. Type the term or phrase you want to record. In most cases, you will probably want to end the macro term or phrase with a space (that is, you will type "AppleWorks " rather than "AppleWorks"). If you include a space at the end of the macro term or phrase, you don't have to press the spacebar before you type the next word after you execute the macro.

7. Choose Macros ⇨ Stop Recording (or press Shift+⌘+J).

Whenever you want to insert the new glossary term, simply press the Option+⌘ key or function key you assigned to the macro.

Note If you wish, you also can create a custom button for the macro and add it to one or more Button Bars. (See Chapter 12 for information on creating and using buttons.)

Paper, paper . . . who's got the paper?

Letterhead and fan-fold computer paper do not meet every word processing need. Whether you just want to make a document look its best or you have something different in mind (such as a brochure, an imprinted postcard, or an award certificate), a special paper might be exactly what you need.

Unless you happen to have a heavy-duty stationery shop nearby, one of the best sources of specialty papers is Paper Direct (800-272-7377 or www.paperdirect.com). Call and ask for a copy of the current catalog. If you own a laser printer or a high-quality inkjet printer, you'll be amazed at the printing capabilities you have but don't know about.

Summary

✦ Word processing text can contain any combination of fonts, sizes, and styles. You can apply multiple styles to the same text string. If you use certain text styles often, you can add their definitions to the stylesheet.

✦ Paragraph formatting controls the look of a particular paragraph. It includes settings for tabs, indents, line spacing, and text alignment. You can set most paragraph options directly on the ruler, or you can choose the Paragraph command from the Format menu.

✦ AppleWorks offers four kinds of tab stops: left, centered, right, and align-on. Align-on tab stops are frequently used to align a column of numbers on the decimal point. You also can specify a fill or leader character for tab stops.

✦ The four alignment options enable you to create left-, right-, center-, or full-justified paragraphs.

✦ Section commands are used to break a document into logical sections, such as book chapters. They are also used when you want to have a different number of columns in multiple parts of the same page. Each section can have a different number of columns, a separate title page, and different headers and footers from other sections.

✦ Document commands enable you to see multiple pages of text onscreen at the same time, set margins, and choose footnotes or endnotes for the document.

✦ If you want to lay out a newsletter or a magazine article, you can easily change to a multicolumn layout. You can use the various Insert Break commands to manually adjust page, section, and column breaks and to avoid widowed and orphaned lines.

✦ The Find/Change commands enable you to search for words or character combinations and, optionally, to replace them with other words or characters.

✦ Headers and footers are document parts that appear on every page of a section or a document. They are useful for displaying page numbers, a company logo, and so on.

✦ AppleWorks can automatically number and manage footnotes, or you can mark them with special characters you have selected.

✦ You can insert automatic dates, times, or page numbers into any document. Such dates and times automatically update each time you open the document. Page numbers automatically adjust as the pagination for the document changes. You also can insert the current date or time as a fixed string.

✦ The spelling checker enables you to check the entire document or just text that is currently selected. You can create user dictionaries that contain the spellings of words that are not in the main dictionary. The thesaurus helps you find synonyms when you're stuck for a word or phrase.

✦ Use the Word Count command to view summary statistics on an entire document or just for the selected text.

✦ AppleWorks has an auto-hyphenation feature that can dramatically improve the appearance of documents.

✦ Outlines can be incorporated within a normal AppleWorks word processing document. You have three general outline formats to choose from, as well as 12 styles of topic labels.

✦ You can add pictures to word processing documents as in-line graphics or as objects. AppleWorks treats the former as characters. The latter are free-floating, and you can position them next to, behind, or in front of text. You can wrap text around free-floating graphics and adjust the vertical alignment of in-line graphics.

✦ AppleWorks 6's new Tables make it easy to place attractive tables in your documents. These are especially useful when you are creating Web pages.

✦ AppleWorks 6's Equation Editor makes it possible to create equations for inclusion in scientific, business, and school reports.

✦ You can add a Word Processing Assistant to your Button Bar. This Assistant makes it easy to insert properly formatted citation footnotes or endnotes.

✦　✦　✦

The Spreadsheet Environment

A spreadsheet program is like an electronic version of a bookkeeper's ledger page. A spreadsheet document (spreadsheet) is a grid composed of numbered rows and lettered columns. You type data into spreadsheet cells — the intersections of the rows and columns. The default size for an AppleWorks spreadsheet is 500 rows by 40 columns. Figure 4-1 shows the components of a spreadsheet.

The Function button and the Named Range pop-up menu were new additions to the entry bar in ClarisWorks and AppleWorks 5. You click the Function button to incorporate a spreadsheet function into the current cell's formula. You use the Named Range pop-up menu to create or modify names of cell *ranges* — rectangular blocks of one or more cells.

The real power of the spreadsheet lies in its calculation capabilities. You can mathematically combine the contents of numeric cells by creating formulas that add, subtract, divide, or multiply cells by each other or by constants. The AppleWorks spreadsheet environment also offers a large number of mathematical, statistical, time, text, financial, and logical functions that enable you to perform complex calculations, such as determining the average of a group of numbers or computing a modified internal rate of return.

The spreadsheet is the ideal environment for data that requires calculations. As such, it is frequently used for accounting, bookkeeping, and record-keeping. You can use the charting capabilities to pictorially summarize any portion of your data. And although the AppleWorks spreadsheet does not contain the database commands some other spreadsheet programs offer, you can still keep simple lists in a spreadsheet and sort them as needed. You also can use spreadsheet frames as tables in other AppleWorks environments if you want to have calculated values in cells or to create charts based on the table's contents.

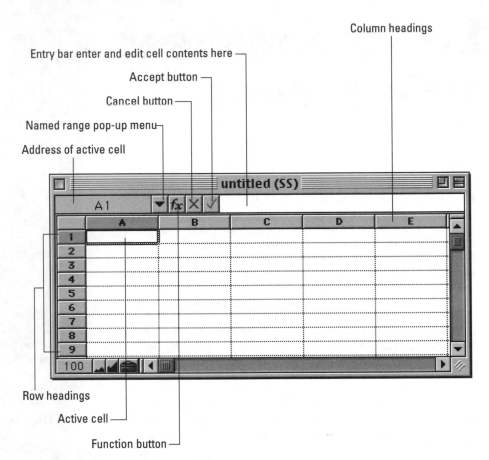

Figure 4-1: The parts of a spreadsheet

Understanding Spreadsheet Basics

Spreadsheet cells are identified by the letter and number combination of the intersection of the cell's column and row. For example, the cell in the upper-left corner of every spreadsheet is A1 (column A, row 1). The current cell has a thick border and is called the active cell. To make a different cell active, you can click the cell with the mouse, move to it by using the cursor keys, or choose the Go to Cell command (⌘+G) from the Options menu.

The letter and number combination for a cell is called its *cell address*. A cell address uniquely identifies every cell in the spreadsheet. You can use cell addresses in formulas. For example, to add the contents of cells A1 and B1 and display the result in cell C1, you enter this formula in C1: **=A1+B1**.

> **Note** The equal (=) sign tells AppleWorks that you are typing a formula.

You can use a combination of cell addresses and constants in formulas, as shown in the following formulas: =B3*15 and =(A17/5)+2.37.

> **New Feature** AppleWorks 6 even lets you use cell addresses from other spreadsheets in your formulas. See "Referencing other spreadsheets," later in this chapter.

You also can work with a rectangular group of cells known as a range (see Figure 4-2). You can include ranges in some types of formulas, such as =SUM(A1..A4), where A1..A4 is a range that represents the four cells from A1 to A4 (that is, A1, A2, A3, and A4). This formula adds the contents of the four cells. When you want to quickly apply a format (a font, style, size, or numeric format, for example) to a large number of cells by using a single command, you can select a range prior to issuing a formatting command.

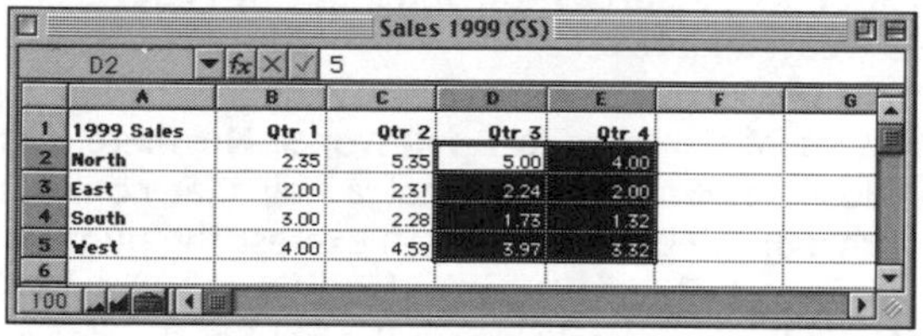

Figure 4-2: A range is a rectangular selection of contiguous cells.

To specify a range in a formula, you specify the upper-left and lower-right cells in the range (called anchors or anchor cells, as shown in Figure 4-2) with a pair of periods, as in =SUM(A1..A5).

To make it simpler for you to work with ranges, AppleWorks 6 enables you to assign names to ranges (such as Qtr 1, Monthly Sales, or Test Scores). Using named ranges often makes it easier to understand the assumptions that underlie a spreadsheet and communicate what the spreadsheet is about. (For information about using named ranges, see "Working with named ranges," later in this chapter.)

Selecting cells

Many actions in a spreadsheet program require that you first select one or more cells and then choose the action you want to perform on those cells. After you choose cells, you can apply formats to them, fill them to the right or down, clear them, create a chart based on the selected values, sort them, and so on.

You use the following methods to select cells:

✦ To select a single cell, click it. The cell is surrounded by a thick border and becomes the active cell.

✦ To select a cell range, click to select the first cell, and then drag the cursor or Shift-click to choose the remaining cells.

✦ To select an entire row or column, click the heading for that row or column, or drag through the row or column.

✦ To select the entire spreadsheet, click the blank box above the heading for row 1 or choose Select All (⌘+A) from the Edit menu.

✦ To select the active area of the spreadsheet (the cell range that contains entries), press the Option key while clicking the blank box above the heading for row 1.

Cell contents

Every cell can contain a text string, a number, or a formula. Numbers can be positive or negative, and you can type them directly (as in 43 and –123.654). You also can type directly any entry that begins with a letter (as in Sam Jones and Social Security #123-45-6789). As soon as you press the spacebar or type another text character, that cell is treated as text.

Note   Dates and times are special cases of numbers to AppleWorks. Nowhere is this more obvious than in a spreadsheet. When you format a cell that contains a number, you'll be presented with a dialog box that lets you express the number as a date or time, as well (and vice versa). The digits to the left of the decimal point are days since January 1, 1904 and the fractional part (to the right of the decimal) is the fraction of a 24-hour period. Thus 16880.75, when displayed as a date, would be March 20, 1950. When shown as a time, it would be displayed as 6:00 p.m. (1800 in military parlance, or three-fourths of a day).

To create a formula, you must precede it with an equal (=) sign (as in =A5+B4). If you want to treat a number as text, type it as if it were a formula; that is, precede the number with an equal sign and enclose it in quotation marks (as in ="1997").

Caution   AppleWorks treats cell data and the formatting that has been applied to the data as separate entities. If you delete the contents of a cell, the formatting remains. Understanding this concept is particularly important when you want to print a spreadsheet. The print range defaults to printing all cells that have data in them (actually, all cells from A1 to the lower rightmost cell containing data) — which is interpreted by AppleWorks to mean all cells that have data or formatting. For example, if you use the Select All command to apply a different font or size to all cells when you create the spreadsheet, every cell in the spreadsheet will be printed — resulting in pages and pages of blank printout. As you'll see later in this chapter, you can override this setting by defining your own print range.

Typing and editing data

To type data into a cell, begin by selecting the cell. The cell is surrounded by a thick border, which shows that it is the active cell. Type the text, number, or formula you want to type into the cell. Whatever you type appears in the entry bar at the top of the document window. To accept the entry, press the Return, Enter, Tab keys, press an arrow key, or click the Accept button (the checkmark button) in the entry bar. To cancel the entry, click the Cancel button (the X) in the entry bar or press the Esc key.

Note

In AppleWorks 6, the way the arrow and Option-arrow keys work is determined by the setting chosen in Spreadsheet Preferences. One set of these key commands moves the cursor in the entry bar (when typing or editing cell data); the other set of key commands moves the cursor from the current cell to an adjacent cell. (See Chapter 11 for more information on spreadsheet references.)

If you press a key other than the Enter or Esc keys to complete a cell entry, the cursor moves to an adjacent cell and makes that cell the active cell. The direction in which the cursor moves depends on the key you press, as described in Table 4-1.

Table 4-1 Spreadsheet Cursor Movement	
Key/Button	*Cursor Movement*
Esc, Cancel button	Stays in the current cell and cancels the entry
Enter, Accept button	Stays in the current cell and accepts the entry
Return, down arrow (or Option+down arrow)	Moves one cell down
Right arrow (or Option+right arrow), Tab	Moves one cell to the right
Left arrow (or Option+left arrow), Shift+Tab	Moves one cell to the left
Up arrow (or Option+up arrow), Shift+Return	Moves one cell up

You also can edit or clear the cell contents. To edit the contents of a cell, click the cell you want to edit. The contents of the active cell appear in the entry bar. In the entry bar, click to position the text insertion point. Use normal editing procedures to add or delete characters and to insert new cell references. (You are always in insertion mode when you are editing or typing text.) To move the cursor within an entry, press the left- or right-arrow key (or the Option+left-arrow or Option+right-arrow keys — depending on the setting you've chosen in Preferences, General; see Chapter 11 for details). To complete the entry, press the Return, Enter, Tab keys, press an arrow key (or Option+arrow key); or click the Accept button.

STEPS: Clearing the Contents of a Cell or Range of Cells

1. Select the cell or cell range you want to clear.

2. Choose Edit ⇨ Clear, or press the Clear key if your keyboard has that key. The cell contents, as well as any formats that were applied to the selected cells, are cleared.

   or

   Choose Edit ⇨ Cut (or press ⌘+X). The program copies the cell contents to the clipboard and then clears the cells, as well as any formats that were applied to the selected cells.

   or

   Press the Delete key. AppleWorks clears the cell contents, but leaves the formats applied to the selected cells intact.

Spreadsheet navigation

The AppleWorks spreadsheet environment offers a number of ways for you to move about the spreadsheet:

✦ Use the horizontal or vertical scroll bars.

✦ Press the Page Up or Page Down keys to move up or down one screen.

✦ Press the Home or End keys to move to the top or bottom of the spreadsheet.

✦ Press the Enter key to make the spreadsheet scroll to display the active cell.

None of these commands changes the active cell. They are pure navigational commands. If you want to change your view of the spreadsheet and also change the active cell, do one of the following:

✦ Choose Options ⇨ Go to Cell (⌘+G) to go to a specific cell and make it active.

✦ Press an arrow key, or press the Tab, Return, Shift+Tab, or Shift+Return keys, to move one cell in the appropriate direction, as described previously.

Specifying Cell Names and Ranges by Pointing

To prevent inaccuracies when you type or edit formulas, you can use the mouse pointer to point to cell addresses and ranges instead of typing them. Suppose, for example, that you want to add the contents of cells A2 and A3. After selecting the destination cell (A4, for example), you would normally type the following formula: = A2 + A3. Or, you can accomplish the same task using the pointing method, as described in the following steps.

Steps: Using the pointing method to add two cells

1. Select cell A4 and press the equal (=) key.

2. Using the mouse pointer, click cell A2, press the plus (+) key, and then click cell A3. (Clicking a cell has exactly the same effect as typing its cell address.)

In fact, you can even skip typing the plus key, if you want. If no symbol separates the two selected cell addresses or ranges, AppleWorks assumes you want to add them, and it then inserts the plus for you.

Pointing is particularly useful for selecting a range. To compute the sum of a particular range (A1 through A6, for example), you can type this formula: **=SUM(A1..A6)**. Or, you can accomplish the same thing using the pointing method, as described in the following steps.

Steps: Using the pointing method to add a range of cells

1. Select the destination cell and press the equal (=) key.

2. Choose Paste Function from the Edit menu, choose SUM, and then click the OK button. The SUM function appears in the entry bar.

3. Highlight the arguments in the SUM function and then use the mouse pointer to highlight the desired range (A1 through A6, for example).

4. Click the Accept button (you also can press the Return, Enter, or Tab keys, or press an arrow key) to complete the entry.

Formulas

Formulas are the spreadsheet's raison d'être. A formula can be as simple as adding the contents of two cells (for example, =A1+A2) or complex due to several nested spreadsheet functions. As mentioned earlier in this chapter, you need to begin every formula with an equal (=) sign.

Table 4-2 lists the numeric operators you can use in formulas.

Table 4-2
Numeric Operators in Formulas

Symbol	Meaning	Examples
+	Addition	= A5+3
-	Subtraction or negative number	= B7-6; -15
*	Multiplication	= A2*A3
/	Division	= A7/3
^	Exponentiation (raise to the power of)	= A1^2

The ampersand (&) character is the only text operator. You use it to concatenate (combine) pairs of text strings. For example, if A1 contains the word Steve and B1 contains Schwartz, you can place a formula in C1 that creates a full name, as in **=A1 & " " & B1** (that is, Steve, a space, and Schwartz). Note that you need to surround text constants in formulas — such as the space in the preceding example — with double quotation marks.

Precedence in formulas

When a formula contains multiple operators, the precedence of the operators determines the order in which the program performs calculations. Higher precedence operations are performed before lower precedence operations. If all operators have the same precedence level, the program evaluates the formula from left to right.

Note You can use parentheses to change the precedence level. When you use parentheses, AppleWorks first performs calculations on the innermost set of parentheses.

The precedence levels for different operators are listed in Table 4-3.

Table 4-3
Precedence of Operators

Operator	Precedence Level
% (divide by 100)	7
^ (exponentiation)	6
+, – (sign)	5
*, / (multiplication, division)	4

Operator	Precedence Level
+, – (addition, subtraction)	3
& (text concatenation)	2
=, >, >=, <, <=, <> (logical comparison)	1

The examples in Table 4-4 illustrate how AppleWorks evaluates different formulas:

Table 4-4
Formula Evaluation Examples

Formula	Result
=7+2–5	The result is 4. Because addition and subtraction have the same precedence, the program evaluates the formula from left to right.
=5+4*3	The result is 17. Because multiplication has a higher precedence than addition, the program evaluates 4*3 first and then adds 5 to produce the result.
=(5+4)*3	The result is 27. The parentheses change the calculation order, forcing the program to evaluate 5+4 first and then multiply that result by 3.
=3+(2*(4+5))–5	The result is 16. The program evaluates the contents of the innermost parentheses first, giving a result of 9. Then it evaluates the next set of parentheses, producing 18. Finally, because the formula contains no more parentheses and the remaining operators are the same precedence level, it evaluates the rest of the formula from left to right, giving a result of 16.

Using functions in formulas

AppleWorks provides more than 100 built-in functions you can use in formulas. Function categories include business and financial, numeric, statistical, text, trigonometric, logical, date/time, and information. For additional information on using the AppleWorks database and spreadsheet functions, refer to Appendix B or AppleWorks Help.

STEPS: Entering a Formula That Contains a Function

1. Select the cell in which you want to enter the formula.

2. Type an equal (=) sign.

3. Choose Edit ⇨ Insert Function or click the Function button in the entry bar. The Insert Function dialog box appears, as shown in Figure 4-3.

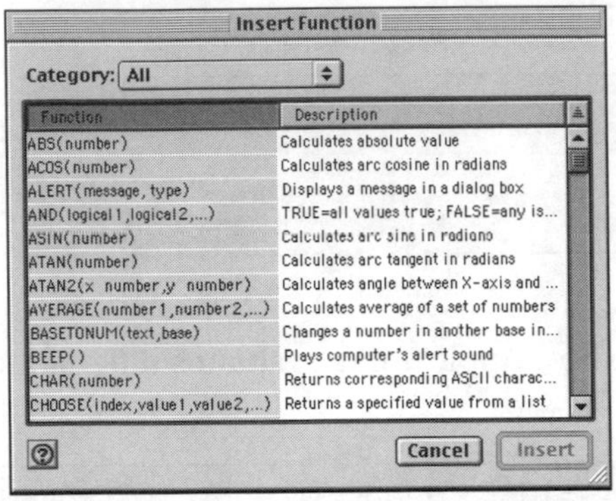

Figure 4-3: The Insert Function dialog box

You can quickly move to the vicinity of any function in the list by pressing the letter key for the first letter in the function name.

4. *Optional:* To restrict the displayed functions to a particular type (Text or Numeric, for example), choose a function category from the Category pop-up menu.

5. Choose a function from the scrolling list. (To choose a function, click the OK button or double-click the function name.) The function and its arguments appear at the text insertion point in the entry bar, as shown in Figure 4-4. The first argument is automatically selected for you.

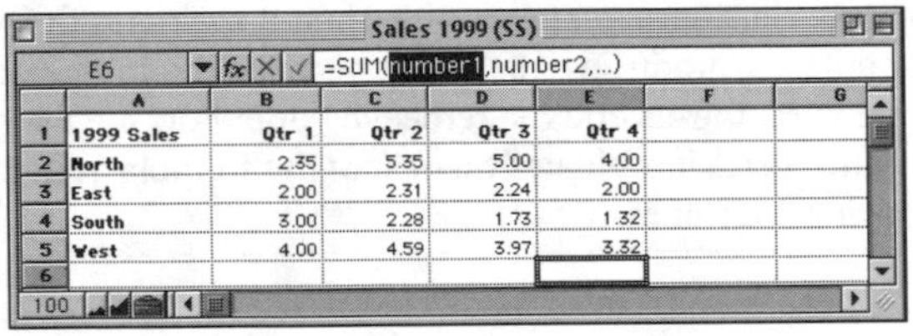

Figure 4-4: Inserted functions include the arguments to the function.

6. Replace the arguments in the function with real numbers and/or cell references.

7. To add more functions to the formula, click in the entry bar to set the text insertion point, and then repeat Steps 3 through 6.

8. Click the Accept button (you also can press the Return, Enter, or Tab keys, or press an arrow key) to complete the entry.

You can manually type functions into formulas. Simply type the function and its arguments at the appropriate position in the formula.

Tip

You can nest functions (have one function act upon another one). An example is =DAYOFYEAR(NOW( )). The NOW( ) function returns a number from the system clock that represents this moment in time. The DAYOFYEAR function converts the number to the day of the current year. For example, if today was July 26, 1997, the result would be 207. Note that the inner function—NOW( )—is surrounded by parentheses to set it apart from the outer function, DAYOFYEAR.

Working with named ranges

In ClarisWorks 4 and earlier, if you wanted to refer to a range of cells in a formula, you had to type the formula like this: =SUM(B3..B6). The cell address or range had to be typed in this less-than-obvious manner. ClarisWorks and AppleWorks 5 caught up with other spreadsheet programs by supporting named ranges (also referred to as range names), enabling you to assign a common name to any important cell or range and then use that name in formulas to refer to that cell or range. In the previous example, if B3..B6 represented company sales for the first quarter, you might name it Qtr 1 and then change the formula to read: =SUM(Qtr 1). Using named ranges rather than cell references makes it simpler to understand the cell or range to which the formula refers.

Note

Range names have some restrictions. Each range name must be unique; the first character must be a letter; it cannot contain operators or punctuation marks; and it cannot resemble a cell reference. It can, on the other hand, contain multiple words, such as Sales 97.

You assign names to ranges by choosing options from the entry bar's Named Range pop-up menu (see Figure 4-5). Menu commands enable you to name ranges either manually or automatically; edit or replace range names; replace cell references in formulas with range names and vice versa; and refer to existing range names.

Click to pop up the Named Range menu

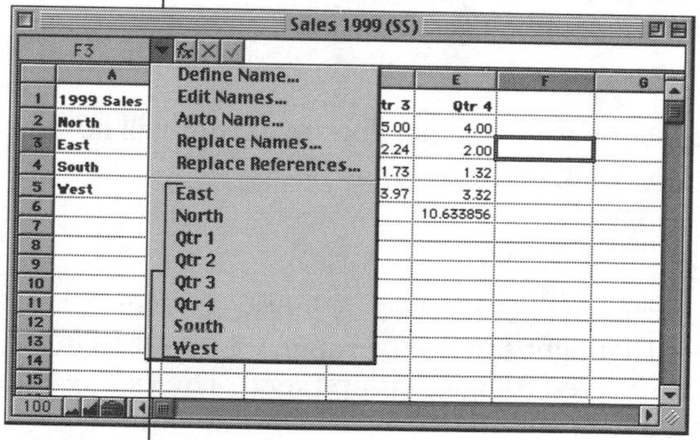

Currently defined range names

Figure 4-5: Use the Named Range pop-up menu to create or modify range names.

Auto-naming ranges

If a range already has a row or column label, AppleWorks can automatically use that label as the range name. To automatically name one or more ranges, select them in the spreadsheet—including the row or column labels with which you will name the ranges. Click the Named Range pop-up menu in the entry bar, and then choose Auto Name. The Auto Define Names dialog box appears (see Figure 4-6). Examine the list to be sure the names and cell ranges are correct. Remove the checkmarks from ranges or names that are incorrect, and then click the Define button. All names that you accept are inserted alphabetically into the list of range names that appears at the lower edge of the Named Range pop-up menu. (Note that when you auto-name a range, AppleWorks does not include the label within the actual range.)

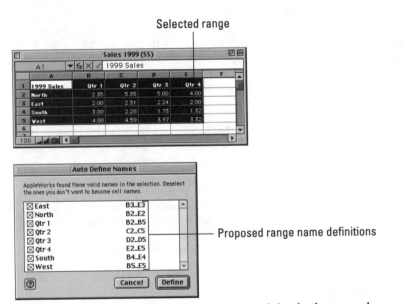

Figure 4-6: Selecting a spreadsheet area containing both row and column labels lets you quickly name a series of ranges.

Note   Any labels that violate the previously discussed naming restrictions will not be listed in the Auto Define Names dialog box.

Manually naming ranges

In those instances where a cell or range is not headed by a row or column label, you can manually define range names. Highlight the cell or range you want to name, and then choose Define Name from the Named Range pop-up menu. The Define Named Range dialog box appears. Type a name, and then click the Define button.

Tip

To see the range to which a particular range name refers, select it in the Named Range menu. AppleWorks automatically highlights the matching range.

Using range names in formulas

After defining range names, you can use them in formulas in either of these ways:

✦ Type them by hand. (Case is ignored. For example, Sales and sales are considered the same range name.)

✦ Choose them from the Named Range pop-up menu. (Type the formula in the entry bar up to the point where the range name is needed, and then select it from the Named Range pop-up menu.)

Note

You also can create range names on the fly. Type a formula using an undefined range name, such as =AVERAGE(Sales), where Sales has yet to be defined as a range name. When you complete the formula, AppleWorks responds with a #NAME! Error in the cell. Now, define the referenced range name (as explained in "Auto-naming ranges" or in "Manually naming ranges," earlier in this chapter). The formula will now calculate correctly using the newly defined range name.

Editing range names

You can delete unneeded range names, change range names, or modify the range referred to by any range name by following these steps.

STEPS: Modifying Existing Range Names

1. Choose Edit Names from the Named Range pop-up menu. The Edit Names dialog box appears (see Figure 4-7).

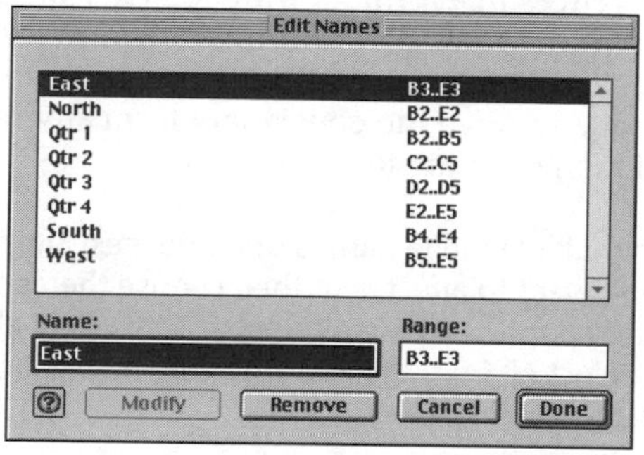

Edit Names	
East	B3..E3
North	B2..E2
Qtr 1	B2..B5
Qtr 2	C2..C5
Qtr 3	D2..D5
Qtr 4	E2..E5
South	B4..E4
West	B5..E5

Name: East   Range: B3..E3

Modify   Remove   Cancel   Done

Figure 4-7: The Edit Names dialog box

2. From the list of all the defined range names for the current spreadsheet, select the range name you want to modify.

3. If you want to delete (or undefine) the range name, click the Remove button. Note that range names currently in use in one or more formulas cannot be removed.

4. To change the name of the range, type the new name in the Name text box and click the Modify button.

5. To alter the range to which the range name applies, type the new range — properly formatted — in the Range text box and click the Modify button.

6. Repeat Steps 2 through 5 for any additional range names you want to edit.

7. To accept all changes, click the Done button. To ignore all changes, click the Cancel button.

Note   If you insert cells in the middle of a named range, the range automatically adjusts to include the new cells, and the definitions of all other affected named ranges will be updated. If you insert cells immediately above, below, to the left, or to the right of an existing named range, however, those cells are not appended to the named range. You must edit the named range if you want to include the new cells.

Replacing names and references in formulas

Although the purpose of using range names is to avoid displaying or having to type range references in formulas, AppleWorks enables you to replace range names with range references, and vice versa.

To replace the use of a range name in a formula with the normal range reference (changing =AVERAGE(Grades) to =AVERAGE(B2..B12), for example), select the cell containing the formula, and then choose Replace Names from the Named Range pop-up menu. To replace range references in a formula with defined range names, select the cell containing the formula, and then choose Replace References from the Named Range pop-up menu. In either case, a dialog box appears that shows the appropriate range names. If necessary, remove the checkmark from any range name that you do not want to affect, and then click the Replace button.

Tip   You can simultaneously replace multiple range names or references. Simply select all cells that contain formulas you want to affect, and then choose the appropriate command from the Named Range pop-up menu. Alternatively, to affect all formulas in the spreadsheet, choose Select All from the Edit menu prior to choosing the Replace Names or Replace References command.

Absolute and Relative Cell References

When a formula in a cell refers to another cell or range of cells, it is called a *cell reference*. For example, you might have a formula in cell B1 that multiplies the contents of cell A1 by 0.15, as in =A1*0.15. If you copy cell B1 and then paste it into cell B2, the formula updates to read =A2*0.15. The cell the formula refers to is no longer the original cell. The reason for the change is the initial cell reference is a *relative reference*; that is, the reference is relative to the position of the active cell. AppleWorks interprets the formula in B1 to mean: "Take the contents of the cell to my immediate left and multiply it by 0.15." No matter which cell you copy this formula to, AppleWorks interprets it in the same manner.

Normally, a relative cell reference is what you want. When you copy a cell that contains a formula or you apply the Fill Down or Fill Right commands to a group of cells beginning with a cell containing a formula, you want the new cells to contain the same formula — but with the appropriate cell references. Occasionally, however, you might want the row or column reference to remain unchanged — pointing to the original row and/or column of the cell. Any reference that does not change when you copy the cell elsewhere is called an *absolute reference*.

Suppose cell A1 contains an estimate of inflation (.15, for example), and the range from A2 to A7 contains various expense figures, as shown in the following figure. In cells B2 through B7, you want to calculate new expense figures after taking inflation into account. If you were using relative cell references, the formula in B2 would read =A2+(A1*A2). However, to keep the reference to cell A1 from changing when you copy or fill the formula in B2 to the remaining cells (B3 through B7), you need to make it into an absolute reference, as in =A2+(A1*A2). The $ in front of the *A* makes the column reference absolute. The $ in front of the *1* makes the row reference absolute. When you copy the new formula to cells B3 through B7, every instance refers directly to cell A1. The references to A2, on the other hand, are still relative and are updated to point to the correct relative cell.

When you type a formula, you can automatically make a reference absolute by holding down the Option and ⌘ keys as you click the cell.

You also can create *mixed references*, in which the row reference is absolute and the column reference is relative (or vice versa), as in =B$1+7.

Circular references, on the other hand, are errors, and you should avoid them. They occur when two or more cells depend on the contents of each other, either directly or indirectly. The following formulas contain circular references: A1=B3+7 and B3=A1/5. Because cells A1 and B3 are mutually dependent, the program cannot calculate the results. Cells that contain circular references are indicated by bullets that surround the cell contents, as in •8.75• or •#REF!•.

Filling Cells

AppleWorks provides two commands for quickly copying a formula into a series of cells: Fill Down and Fill Right. (You also can use Fill Down and Fill Right to copy a single number or text string into a series of cells.) To fill cells down or to the right, select the source cell whose formula you want to copy. Drag the cursor or press the Shift key to select the additional cells to the right or below that will serve as the destination for the copied formula. Choose Calculate ⇨ Fill Right (⌘+R) or Calculate ⇨ Fill Down (⌘+D), as appropriate. The program copies the formula into every selected cell to the right or below the source cell.

In other spreadsheet programs, you can use Fill Right or Fill Down to number a series of cells conveniently, increasing each one by an increment of your choice. In AppleWorks 6, you can achieve the same effect by using the Fill Special command. Fill Special can fill cells with a repeating pattern, as well as with a series of dates or times.

Tip   Rather than start with a blank range, you might prefer to type the initial value or pair of values in the range before choosing the Fill Special command. If the first cell contains a date, for example, AppleWorks will try to select the proper sequence for you.

The Fill Special command also can be used to duplicate a pattern. Suppose, for example, that you have two column headers labeled Yes and No. If you need to repeat this same set of headers several times, just select the range to which the pattern is to be applied, choose the Fill Special command, click the Pattern radio button, and then indicate the number of cells in the pattern (two, in this instance).

STEPS: Filling Cells with a Special Sequence

1. Drag the mouse pointer to select the cells you want to fill. The selected range must be contained within a single row or column; otherwise, you cannot choose the Fill Special command.

2. Choose Calculate ⇨ Fill Special. The Fill Special dialog box appears (see Figure 4-8).

3. On the left side of the dialog box, click a radio button to indicate the type of data the series will contain: numbers, times, dates, and so on.

4. Depending on the data type selected, either type a starting number or select a start pattern (Quarter 1, Sunday, and so on).

5. Type or select an increment. (Note that some sequences present additional increment options. Dates, for example, can be incremented by days, weeks, months, or years.)

6. Select additional options, if any are shown.

7. Click the OK button.

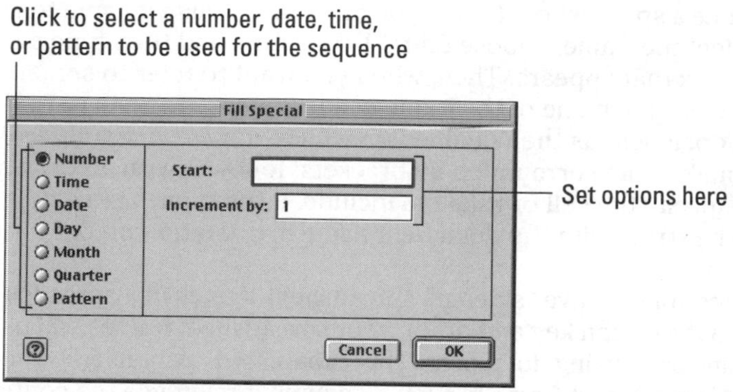
Click to select a number, date, time, or pattern to be used for the sequence
Fill Special
Number
Time
Date
Day
Month
Quarter
Pattern
Start:
Increment by: 1
Set options here
Cancel
OK

Figure 4-8: The Fill Special dialog box

New Feature

New in AppleWorks 6 is the ability to create *intersheet references,* (replacing the Publish and Subscribe commands available in previous versions of AppleWorks and ClarisWorks). What this means is that if you have two or more spreadsheets or spreadsheet frames (either in the same or other documents), you can have formulas from one spreadsheet work with cells and ranges from another spreadsheet.

Referencing other spreadsheets

When you want to reference the cell or range in another spreadsheet, type the document name, followed by an exclamation point, and then type the cell address or range name. For example, if you have a spreadsheet named "Inventory" containing your stock on hand, you could have a spreadsheet that automatically calculated orders when stock fell below a certain level by including the formula in the cell for the number of widgets to order:

```
=IF ("Inventory"!widgets<"Inventory"!minwidgets,
"Inventory"!minwidgets - "Inventory"!widgets, 0)
```

When AppleWorks calculates the value of this formula, it will provide a standard Open dialog box to the referenced document.

Caution

If the document or frame name contains special characters (punctuation, spaces, and so on) or it might be misinterpreted as a function name, cell address, or a named range in the current spreadsheet, the name must be enclosed in double quotation marks. You should get in the habit of always adding double quotation marks – both for consistency and to prevent unexpected errors from appearing as you name new ranges.

If you want to reference a spreadsheet frame, you must first assign a name to that frame. To do this, select the frame, choose Edit ➪ Frame Info, and then type a name in the Display dialog box that appears. Then, when you want to refer to something in that frame, you enclose the name of the frame inside square brackets ([ ]). If the frame is in the same document as the document in which you are currently working, just type the frame's name surrounded by brackets, follow it with an exclamation point, and then specify the cell or range to include. If the frame is in a different document, precede the string with the document name in quotation marks.

While it is certainly possible to have "sidebar" spreadsheet frames in a spreadsheet document (hold down the option key and drag), your spreadsheet frames will usually be in a word processing or drawing document. This capability is very useful when you wish to have one spreadsheet frame in such a document reference the contents of another spreadsheet frame.

Note With the elimination of support for Publish and Subscribe in AppleWorks 6, intersheet references give you a way to include such "live" information.

Rearranging Spreadsheets

Creating a useful spreadsheet is an evolving process. The basic structure can change frequently. New rows and columns are inserted, ranges are moved, and columns are sorted as you determine the best way to display the data. AppleWorks provides all the commands necessary to ensure that rearranging the spreadsheet is as easy and trouble-free as possible.

Inserting and deleting cells, columns, and rows

Clearing the contents of a cell or a range of cells has no other effect on the spreadsheet (unless formulas in other cells refer to the cleared cells). Sometimes, however, you might want to add one or more new cells, a new row, or a new column to a spreadsheet; or you might want to delete cells, rows, or columns.

When you add cells, you need to shift other cells lower or to the right to make room for the new cells. (The shift is automatic if you insert entire rows or columns.) When you delete cells, you need to close up the hole that is left by the departing cells. (The shift is automatic if you delete entire rows or columns.)

Using the Insert Cells or Delete Cells command (described in the following steps) is much faster than the alternative: cutting, pasting, and otherwise manually rearranging the spreadsheet. You might find, for example, that you haven't left sufficient space at the top of a spreadsheet for a general label (for example, Budget Spreadsheet for Fall 1997) or other identifying information. You can use the Insert Cells command to insert a row or two easily.

STEPS: Inserting New Cells

1. Select the cell or range where you want to add the new cells.

2. Choose Format ➾ Insert Cells (or press Shift+⌘+I). The Insert Cells dialog box appears, as shown in Figure 4-9.

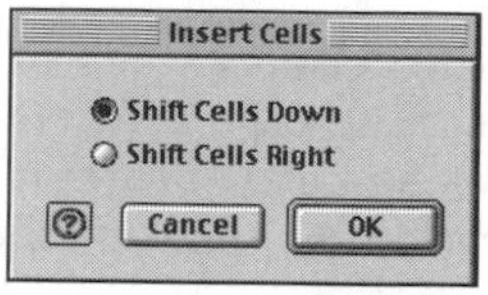

Figure 4-9: The Insert Cells dialog box

3. Choose Shift Cells Down if you want the selected cells and all cells directly below the selection to move down.

   or

   Choose Shift Cells Right if you want the selected cells and all cells directly to the right of the selection to move to the right.

4. Click the OK button. The program inserts the new cell or cells and rearranges the spreadsheet as requested.

To insert new columns or rows, select the headings for the columns or rows where you want to insert the new columns or rows. Choose Format ➾ Insert Cells (or press Shift+⌘+I). New blank columns or rows are inserted in place of the selected columns or rows, and the originally selected columns or rows automatically shift to the right or down to make room.

Caution

Be aware that if you insert or delete whole rows or columns, your spreadsheet's size will change, but if you insert smaller ranges and data exists that would be moved out of the sheet's bounds, AppleWorks beeps at you and refuses to insert the cells.

STEPS: Deleting Cells

1. Select the cell or range you want to delete.

2. Choose Delete Cells from the Calculate menu (or press Shift+⌘+K). The Delete Cells dialog box appears.

3. Choose Shift Cells Up if you want the cells below the selection to move up to fill the hole left by the deletion.

   or

   Choose Shift Cells Left if you want the cells to the right of the selection to move left to fill the hole left by the deletion.

4. Click the OK button. The program deletes the cell or cells and rearranges the spreadsheet as requested.

To delete entire columns or rows, select one or more columns or rows to be deleted by clicking the column or row headings. Choose Delete Cells from the Calculate menu (or press Shift+⌘+K). The program removes the selected columns or rows, and the columns to the right or rows below automatically move to close the gap.

Copying and pasting cells

One way to duplicate or move cells is to copy or cut the cells and then paste them into a new location. To copy and paste, you select the cells of interest, choose Edit ➪ Copy, select a destination, and then choose Edit ➪ Paste. When you copy a formula, the program reflects the new location by updating the cell references that the formula contains.

Note You cannot paste the copied contents of a single cell into more than one cell at a time. During a paste operation, the program automatically replicates the shape of the copied cell grouping. Thus, if you copy a single cell and select multiple cells for the paste, the data or formula is copied only to the first cell in the destination range. If you select a vertical string of three cells when copying (A1 through A3, for example), regardless of the area selected for pasting, AppleWorks fills the first cell of the destination range and the two cells immediately below it.

You also can paste formula results (or values), leaving the formulas behind. To paste values, select the cell or cells you want to copy, and then choose Edit ➪ Copy (or press ⌘+C). Select a destination, and then choose Edit ➪ Paste Special. The Paste Special dialog box appears. Click the Paste Values Only radio button and click the OK button.

Note When pasting values only, the cell formatting from the copied cell is ignored. The pasted information is displayed in the spreadsheet's default font.

You also can move cells from one spreadsheet location to another by choosing Calculate ➪ Move or by using drag-and-drop, which we discuss in the next section, "Moving cells."

Moving cells

When you use the cut-and-paste method to move cells from one spreadsheet location to another, the program updates the relative cell references contained within the moved cells so that they refer to the new locations. If you want the cell references to remain unchanged, use the Move command instead.

Suppose, for example, cell A1 contains 10 and cell B1 contains the formula =A1+5 (which evaluates as 15). If you use the Move command to move cell B1 to D10, the formula remains unchanged (=A1+5). On the other hand, if you simply cut cell B1 and paste it into D10, the formula reads =C10+5 and evaluates incorrectly — assuming you still wanted the cell to reflect the contents of cell A1 plus 5.

In this same example, if you want to move both cells A1 and B1, you can use either the Cut and Paste or Move commands. The result is the same. If a move contains all cells that are referred to by other cells in the move, the program updates the references, just as it does when you cut and paste.

Caution When executing a move or a paste operation, be sure that room exists at the destination for the moved or pasted cells. Existing data in the destination cells will be overwritten by the moved or pasted data. If you make this mistake, immediately choose Undo Move from the Edit menu.

To move the contents of one or more cells, begin by selecting the cell or range you want to move, and then choose Calculate ➪ Move. The Move dialog box appears, as shown in Figure 4-10. Type a destination cell address (the cell in the upper-left corner of the destination range) for the move, and click the OK button to move the cell or range to the new location.

Figure 4-10: The Move dialog box

Tip You can quickly accomplish a move by pointing or by using drag-and-drop. For either method, begin by selecting the cell or range you want to move. To move the cells by pointing, hold down the ⌘ and Option keys while clicking the destination cell. To move the cells using drag-and-drop, simply drag the cells to the desired destination. If you hold down the Option key, you will move a copy, leaving the original intact. (When the spreadsheet cursor changes from the plus (+) symbol to an arrow above a tiny box, it is in drag-and-drop mode.)

Sorting

AppleWorks has flexible sorting options that enable you to perform one- to three-level ascending or descending sorts on columns (vertical) or rows (horizontal). At the simplest level, a sort can affect a single string of cells in a row or column. To perform this type of sort, you select the cells, issue the Sort command, select an order key (a cell within the string), choose ascending or descending order, and then specify whether the sort is horizontal or vertical.

More common, however, is sorting a range of cells that consists of several columns and rows, based on the values in one or more of the columns or rows.

STEPS: Performing a Sort

1. Select the area of the spreadsheet you want to sort.

2. Choose Calculate ➪ Sort (or press ⌘+J). The Sort dialog box appears, as shown in Figure 4-11.

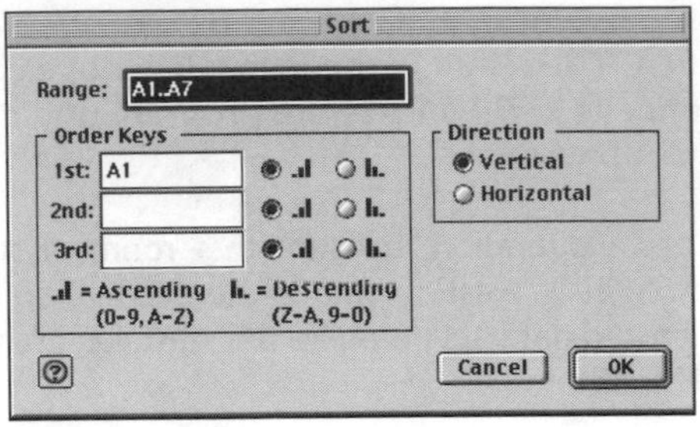

Figure 4-11: The Sort dialog box

3. If the range selected in Step 1 is incorrect, type the range in the Range box. Separate the two anchor cells with a pair of periods, as in A1..D7.

4. Click the Vertical radio button to sort columns or the Horizontal radio button to sort rows.

5. In the 1st Order Keys text box, type a cell address from the first column to perform a vertical sort, or type a cell address from the first row to perform a horizontal sort.

6. If you want to perform additional sorts, type a cell address for a second and third column or row on which you want to base the sort.

7. For each order key, click a radio button to indicate whether you want to sort in *ascending order* (from A to Z and lowest to highest number) or *descending order* (from Z to A and highest to lowest number).

8. Click the OK button. The program performs the requested sort or sorts.

When sorting on a single order key, the program sorts the selected range on the basis of the contents of the key's column (vertical sort) or row (horizontal sort).

When performing a multikey sort, the program sorts the selected range on the basis of the contents of the first key's column (vertical sort) or row (horizontal sort). It then performs a subordinate sort on the basis of the second key, where all ties (duplicate values) in the first key sort are reordered according to the second key. If you selected a third key, records that are still tied after the program sorts on the second key are reordered according to the third key.

As an example, Figure 4-12 shows a simple address database with fields in columns A through F (First Name, Last Name, Street, City, State, Zip Code). Each row is a record.

To sort the data records by Zip code, you would select the data range A2..F7 and choose Sort from the Calculate menu. (You would not include the labels in Row 1 as part of the sort, because you don't want the labels to change positions.) Type a key (cell address) from the Zip Code field (F2, for example), click the Ascending radio button, and then click the OK button.

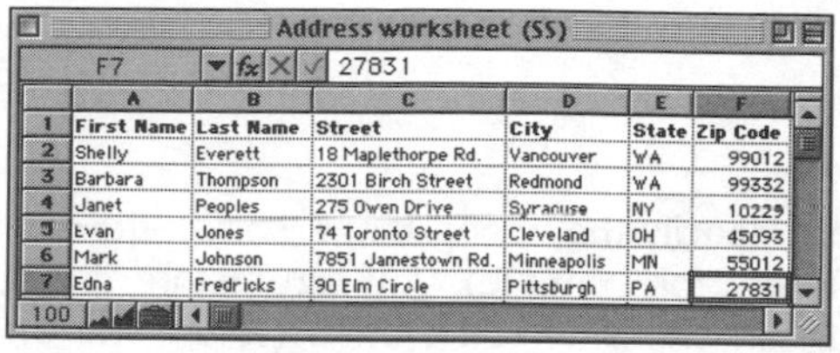

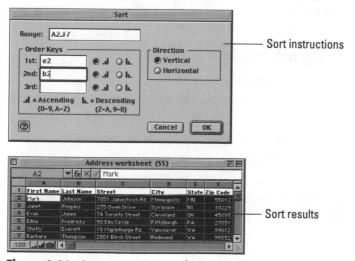

Figure 4-12: The original address spreadsheet

The result of the sort is shown in Figure 4-13. Because you are simultaneously sorting columns A through F, each entire record changes position — not just the Zip code. If you set the range as F2..F7, on the other hand, the program reorders only the Zip codes — not the accompanying data in columns A through E.

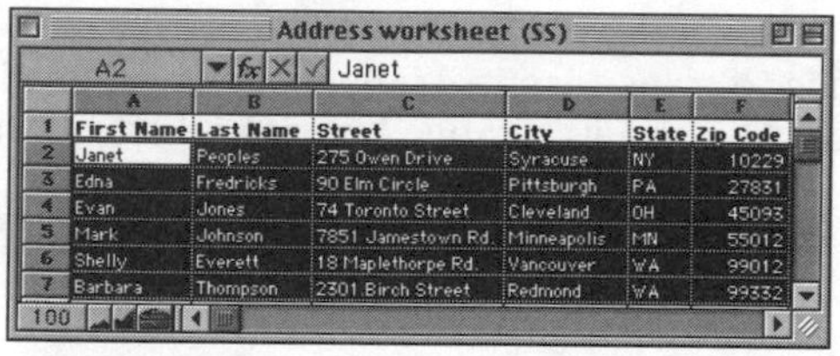

Figure 4-13: The spreadsheet reordered by Zip code

Figure 4-14 shows the settings for and the results of a two-way sort of the same spreadsheet. The first sort is on State (Column E), and the second sort is on Last Name (Column B). When the program executes the sort instructions, it sorts the entire spreadsheet (A2..F7) alphabetically based on State. It then re-sorts any duplicate entries (WA, in this case) alphabetically according to the person's last name.

Sort instructions

Sort results

Figure 4-14: A two-way sort on the same data

Note   When performing a multilevel sort, list the sort keys in order of decreasing importance.

Tip   If you make a mistake during a sort (specify the wrong range, sort in the wrong order, or sort rows instead of columns, for example), you can restore the data to its original condition by immediately choosing Edit ➪ Undo (⌘+Z). The Undo command should read Undo Sort.

If you've gone a few steps too far, you can choose the Revert command from the File menu to revert to the most recently saved version of the document. This is another reason to save often.

Transposing a range

Another way to rearrange information is to transpose it. Transposing a range swaps columns for rows and vice versa. Figure 4-15 shows a range before and after it has been transposed.

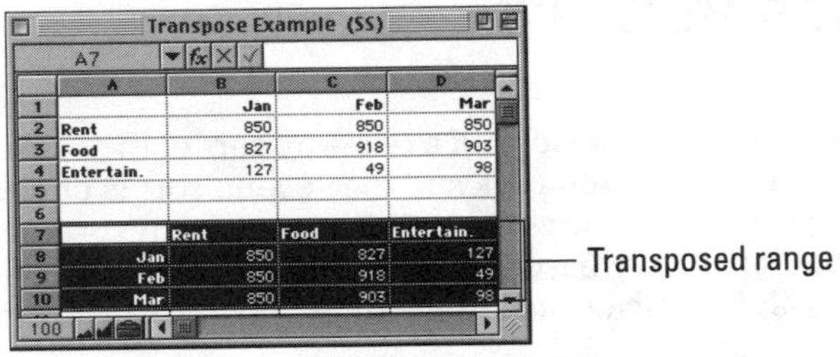

	A	B	C	D
1		Jan	Feb	Mar
2	Rent	850	850	850
3	Food	827	918	903
4	Entertain.	127	49	98
5				
6				
7		Rent	Food	Entertain.
8	Jan	850	827	127
9	Feb	850	918	49
10	Mar	850	903	98

— Transposed range

Figure 4-15: Range A7..D10 contains transposed information from the range A1..D4.

STEPS: Transposing Information

1. Select the area you want to transpose.

2. Choose Edit ➪ Copy (⌘+C) or Edit ➪ Cut (⌘+X) to place a copy of the range on the clipboard.

3. Select a destination cell for the range.

4. Choose Edit ➪ Paste Special. The Paste Special dialog box appears, as shown in Figure 4-16.

5. Click the Transpose Rows and Columns checkbox and then click the OK button. The range is transposed and pasted into place, starting at the chosen destination cell.

Figure 4-16: The Paste Special dialog box

Caution

When you select a destination for the transposed range, be sure to leave enough room in the cells to the right and below. The transposed range overwrites data in the cells it covers. If you overwrite important data, immediately choose Edit ⇨ Undo (⌘+Z), and then select a different destination.

Tip

In some instances, the reason you want to transpose a range is because — after looking at the original data — it simply makes more sense to display it transposed. If — within the range — the number of rows is the same as the number of columns (a five-cell by five-cell range, for example), you can safely paste the transposed data over the original range without fear of overwriting other cells in the spreadsheet.

Changing the size of the spreadsheet

When you create a new AppleWorks spreadsheet, it contains 40 columns and 500 rows. (A new spreadsheet frame in another AppleWorks document contains 20 columns and 50 rows — this is an increase from the 10×50 default in previous versions of AppleWorks and ClarisWorks.) Although these dimensions are adequate for most spreadsheets, you might occasionally find you've run out of room. AppleWorks enables you to increase or decrease the number of spreadsheet rows and/or columns as your needs change.

To change the size of a spreadsheet, select Format ⇨ Document. The Document dialog box appears, as shown in Figure 4-17. Specify the number of columns and rows you want the resized spreadsheet to contain by typing numbers in the Size section of the dialog box. Click the OK button to close the dialog box. The spreadsheet is resized according to your specifications. (Keep in mind that you can use this command to either reduce or increase the size of a spreadsheet.)

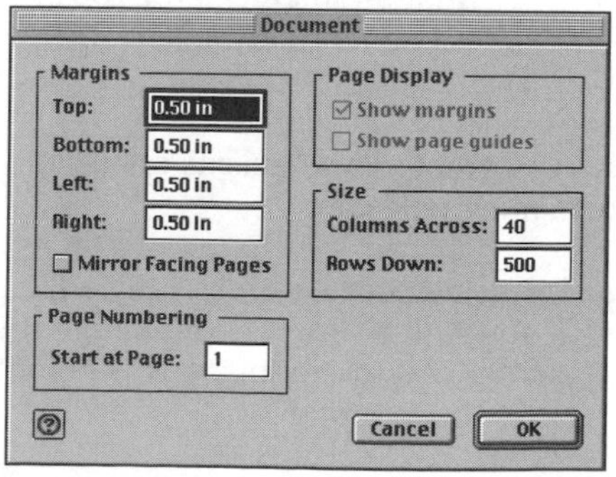

Figure 4-17: The Document dialog box

To reach the Document dialog box from a spreadsheet frame, on the other hand, you first must open the frame to full size by choosing Window ➪ Open Frame, and then choose Format ➪ Document.

Formatting Cells

As recently as a few years ago, spreadsheets were fairly drab. They were usually restricted to a single font in a single point size. Modern spreadsheet programs, such as the AppleWorks spreadsheet environment, encourage you to be creative when you format spreadsheets. For example, you can:

✦ Use multiple fonts, sizes, and styles (although you are limited to one combination per cell)

✦ Add color to text

✦ Surround cells with border lines

✦ Hide the cell gridlines or row and column headings

✦ Change the width and height of individual columns and rows

✦ Format cell backgrounds with colors and patterns

Setting cell formats

AppleWorks provides a host of methods for dressing up the contents of any cell:

✦ Assigning a font, size, and style

✦ Applying a color

✦ Setting an alignment (general, left, right, or center)

✦ Making text wrap in the cell if it is too wide to fit

✦ Assigning a number format for displaying numbers, dates, or times

To assign text formatting attributes to cells, select a cell or range of cells. Then, choose options from any of the following of the Format submenus: Font, Size, Style, Text Color, or Alignment. The program applies the new settings to the entire contents of the selected cells.

Note   The General Alignment option (the default) automatically left-aligns cells that contain text and right-aligns cells that contain numeric data.

If you set a large point size for a cell, AppleWorks does not automatically adjust the row height to accommodate the largest font in the row. If you do not change the row height, some of the text might be clipped. (Instructions for changing row heights are provided in "Making cell contents fit," later in this chapter.)

STEPS: Adding or Removing Cell Borders

1. Select a cell or range of cells.

2. Choose Format ⇨ Borders. The Borders dialog box appears, as shown in Figure 4-18.

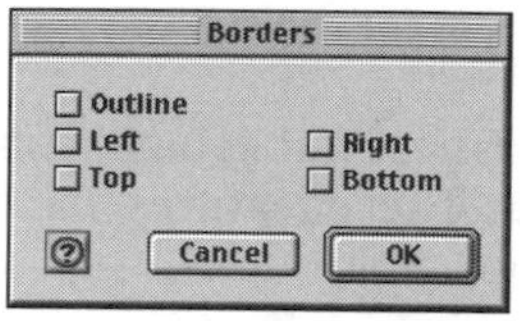

Figure 4-18: The Borders dialog box

3. Place checkmarks in the checkboxes to indicate the sides on which the program should apply border lines. (Each checkbox works as a toggle.)

   A dash in a checkbox means that some—but not all—of the selected cells have that particular border option set.

   Removing a checkmark clears the border on that side of the selected cell or cells.

4. Click the OK button. The program applies the selected border options individually to every selected cell.

Note

The exception to this rule is the Outline option. If you checked this box in Step 3, an outline border appears around the group of cells you selected, not around every individual cell.

To set a numeric format for one or more cells, select the cell or range of cells and choose Format ⇨ Number (or press Shift+⌘+N). The Format Number, Date, and Time dialog box appears, as shown in Figure 4-19. Set options and click the OK button to apply the options to the selected cell or cells.

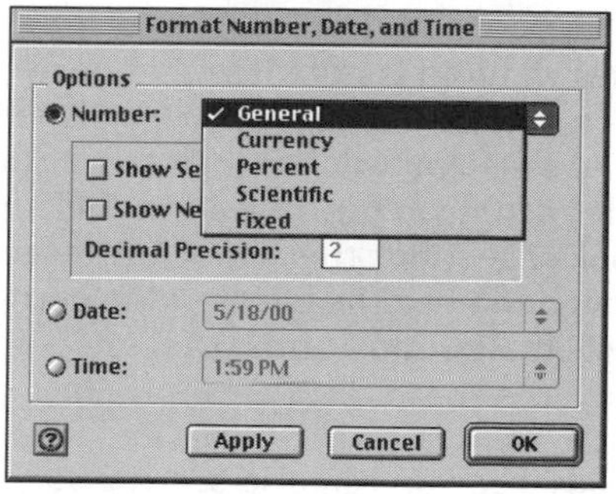

Figure 4-19: Use this dialog box to assign a number, date, or time format to any cell or range of cells.

Tip   You can directly summon the Format Number, Date, and Time dialog box for an individual cell by double-clicking that cell.

Tip   If you just want to test a numeric format, click the Apply button in the Format Number, Date, and Time dialog box. The selected format is applied to the chosen cells. To accept the new formatting, click the OK button. Otherwise, click the Cancel button to revert to the original number format for the cell or range.

AppleWorks provides the tools necessary for spreadsheet publishing, enabling you to apply colors and/or patterns to selected cells. These features can be used whether the spreadsheet is a document or in a frame.

To assign a cell color or pattern, if the Accents windoid is not visible, choose Window ➪ Show Accents (or press Shift+⌘+K). Select the cell or range of cells you want to format. Choose a fill color or fill pattern from the color and pattern panels. The color or pattern is then applied to the selected cells. Figure 4-20 shows a simple example of a colored, patterned spreadsheet range.

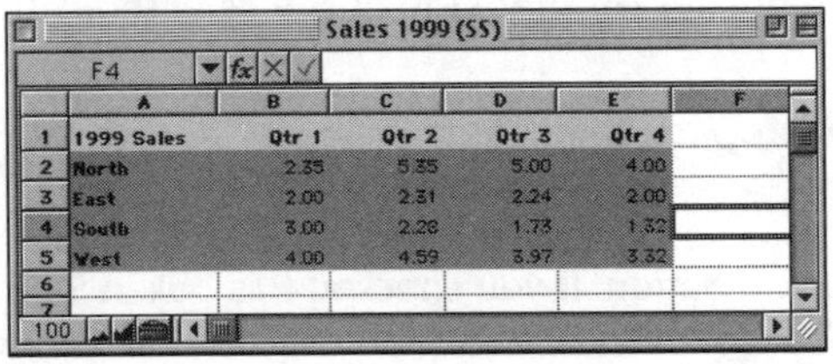

Figure 4-20: A section of this spreadsheet has been embellished with solid and patterned colors.

If you'd like to dress up your spreadsheets but aren't very design oriented, you can use one of the AppleWorks predefined SS table styles in the Styles windoid.

Note   In previous versions, these were called Table styles. That name has been assigned to the new AppleWorks Tables and an "SS-" has been prepended to let you know that these table styles are for spreadsheets.

To format cells with the stylesheet, if the Styles windoid is not visible, choose Format ➪ Show Styles (or press Shift+⌘+W). The Styles windoid appears, listing the available SS-table styles. Select the range of cells you want to format. (SS-Table styles are meant to be applied to a range.) Click a style in the Styles windoid and view the preview box to see what the style looks like. Click the Apply button and the style is applied to the selected range. If you don't like the effect of the current SS-table style, either choose Edit ➪ Undo (it will read Undo Format), or select the same range again and choose another table style.

Tip   If the Button Bar is visible above the spreadsheet, you can also select a spreadsheet style from the (optional) Styles pop-up menu button on the Button Bar.

After applying an SS-table style, some tweaking is often required, particularly with number formats, which are often defined as part of the style. For example, you might have to change a column of quantities from Currency format (as applied by the table style) to the more appropriate General format.

Tip The Styles windoid initially shows seven table styles, in addition to the default. Unlike ClarisWorks and AppleWorks 5, which included more than two dozen table styles you could import, AppleWorks 6 doesn't include any. However, if you have upgraded from a previous version of AppleWorks or ClarisWorks, you can import those styles. To use the others, click Import in the Styles windoid, select the file named More Table Styles (located in the AppleWorks 5:AppleWorks Styles or ClarisWorks 5:ClarisWorks Styles folder), and choose the additional styles you want to import. (To learn more about styles and using the Styles windoid, see Chapter 15.)

Reusing cell formats

When you are formatting cells, AppleWorks also provides a pair of commands that enable you to copy an existing cell format and apply it to other cells without creating styles and applying styles.

STEPS: Copying and Pasting Cell Formats

1. Select a cell that contains the format options you want to duplicate.

2. Choose Edit ⇨ Copy Format (or press Shift+⌘+C). All formatting in the cell is copied — including font, size, style, alignment, color, number format, borders, and cell color and pattern.

3. Select the cell or range to which you want to apply the format options.

4. Choose Edit ⇨ Paste Format (or press Shift+⌘+V). The program applies the formats to the target cell(s).

Making cell contents fit

When you type an entry into a cell, it sometimes doesn't fit. If the cell contains text, it might overflow into blank cells to the right, left, or both the right and the left — depending on the alignment option you choose for the too-small cell. If the cell next to the current cell is not empty, only as much of the text string as will fit in the current cell is displayed.

Note If a number doesn't fit in its cell, the program converts it to scientific notation or displays it as a string of # symbols, depending on what numeric format you've chosen.

You can fit text horizontally within a cell by applying the Wrap option from the Alignment submenu of the Format menu. Wrap works similarly to the word wrap feature in a word processing program. You might have to change the row height to see all the wrapped text, however. Further, if a word on a line by itself is too long to fit in the cell, it will be broken into smaller character sequences that do fit.

In many cases, you might simply prefer to change the width of the column that contains the cell. AppleWorks enables you to widen or narrow columns selectively. You also can change the height of rows.

STEPS: Using the Row Height and Column Width Commands

1. Select a cell or group of cells from the rows or columns whose height or width you want to change.

2. Choose Format ➪ Row Height or Format ➪ Column Width. The Row Height or Column Width dialog box appears, as shown in Figure 4-21.

Click to reset to the default height or width

Figure 4-21: The Row Height and Column Width dialog boxes

3. Type the number of points for the desired height or width. (One inch equals 72 points.) As an alternative, if you click the Use Default checkbox, AppleWorks uses the default height (14 points) or width (72 points).

4. Click the OK button. The program applies the new height or width to the selected rows or columns.

   If you prefer, you can use other units of measurement when setting a new row height or column width. To indicate the unit of measurement, type one of these abbreviations after the numeric entry: inches (in), centimeters (cm), millimeters (mm), picas (pc), or points (pt).

You also can manually set row heights and column widths. Move the mouse pointer into the heading area at the top or left side of the spreadsheet. Whenever the mouse pointer is over the dividing line between a pair of rows or a pair of columns, it changes into a special cursor, as shown in Figure 4-22. Click and drag to change the width or height of a column or row.

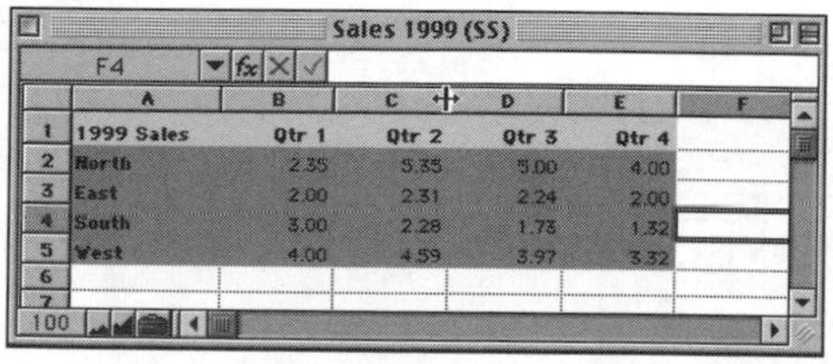

Figure 4-22: The mouse pointer changes when you manually change a column width or row height.

> **Tip**
>
> In many cases, what you really want to do is set a column width so that it is just wide enough to accommodate the widest cell in the column or set a row so it can display the highest cell in the row. To accomplish this, double-click the right edge of the column or the lower edge of the row. Alternatively, you can select the column or row and click the Autosize Row or Autosize Column buttons from the Button Bar.

Making Charts

Question of the Day: If a picture is worth a thousand words, how much data is a chart worth?

Charts and graphs provide a pictorial representation of data, making it easy to see significant trends. AppleWorks has the capability to produce the following charts: bar, area, line, scatter, pie, pictogram, stacked bar, stacked area, X-Y line, X-Y scatter, hi-low, stacked pictogram, and combination.

> **Note**
>
> As long as a chart is attached to a spreadsheet, changes you make to the data are instantly reflected in the chart. If you copy a chart to another AppleWorks document, however, the chart loses its link with the data. If the data changes, the chart remains the same.

STEPS: Creating a Chart

1. Select the data range you want to express as a chart.

   If you also select the labels above and to the left of the data, they will appear in the chart and be used in the legend. Any text in the upper-left corner of the range becomes the chart title.

2. Choose Options ⇨ Make Chart (or press ⌘+M). The Chart Options dialog box appears, as shown in Figure 4-23.

3. Select a chart type from the Gallery section of the dialog box.

4. *Optional:* Choose chart enhancements at the bottom of the dialog box by clicking the checkboxes. The enhancements that are listed vary according to the type of chart selected.

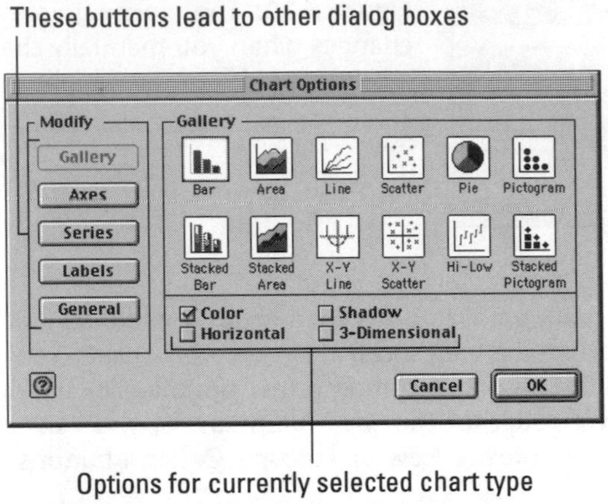

These buttons lead to other dialog boxes

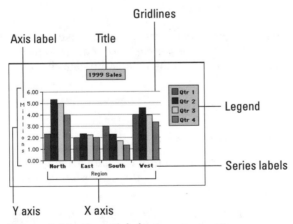

Options for currently selected chart type

Figure 4-23: The Chart Options dialog box

5. *Optional:* Set other chart options by clicking the Axes, Series, Labels, or General buttons (these options are discussed in the next section). A different dialog box appears for each button.

6. Click the OK button. A chart appears with the characteristics you chose.

Figure 4-24 shows the parts of a chart.

Figure 4-24: Essential chart components

Chart options

If a chart doesn't look exactly the way you want it to look, AppleWorks provides plenty of options for changing it without starting over. The following sections discuss chart options according to the Chart Options dialog box that is displayed.

Gallery options

AppleWorks presents Gallery options (refer to Figure 4-23, shown earlier) whenever you choose the Options ➪ Make Chart command (to create a new chart) or choose Edit ➪ Chart Options (to edit an existing chart). The Gallery options enable you to accomplish the following:

✦ Select an initial chart type.

✦ Change an existing chart to another chart type.

✦ Set basic display options for the chart such as:

• Color versus black and white

• Horizontal versus vertical

• Two-dimensional versus three-dimensional

• Whether shadows appear behind each plotted data series

The display options presented in the Chart dialog box vary according to the chart type chosen.

Axes options

Axes options (see Figure 4-25) enable you to do the following:

✦ Add labels to the *X* (horizontal) and *Y* (vertical) axes

✦ Specify whether grid lines are displayed

✦ Set minimum, maximum, and/or step values for axis divisions

✦ Use a log scale

✦ Specify whether tick marks are shown and, if so, how they appear

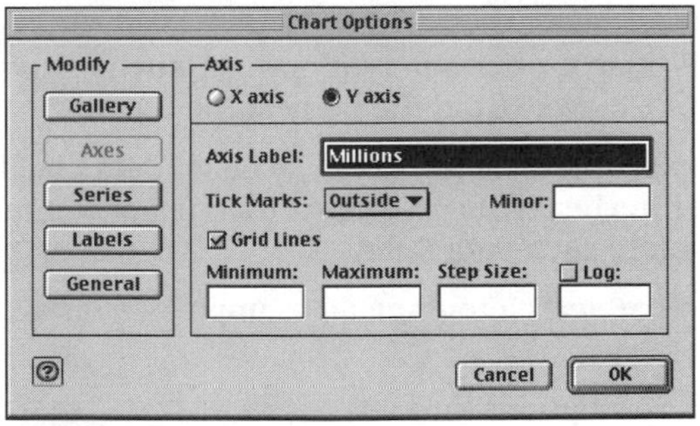

Figure 4-25: Axes options

You have to change the elements of each axis individually. Select an axis by clicking the *X* axis or *Y* axis radio button at the top of the Chart Options (Axes) dialog box. All other settings you choose affect that axis only.

> **Note** The *X* axis is the horizontal axis, running along the lower portion of the chart; the *Y* axis is the vertical axis, running along the left side of the axis. (Pie charts do not have axes.)

To change the color, pattern, or line width for an axis and its gridlines, select the axis on the chart, and then modify it using the Accents windoid. To alter the font attributes for the axis text, select the axis on the chart, and then choose the appropriate attributes from the Format menu's submenus.

Series options

You use the Series options to specify settings for one or all of the data series included in the current chart. You can label data points with their values and change the type of display for individual data series. The latter option enables you to create combination charts. For example, you can show the first data series with bars and the second data series as a line.

STEPS: Specifying a Series Option

1. In the Edit Series pop-up menu, choose All or the specific series you want to change.

2. *Optional:* Choose a graph type for the series from the Display pop-up menu.

   Some graph types also enable you to choose a symbol to use for data points, as shown in Figure 4-26. To select a symbol for the data points for a particular series, choose a series from the Edit pop-up menu, and then click a new symbol. To change a symbol's color, click the box to the right of the Symbol checkbox and select a color from the pop-up palette. To change the size of a symbol, type a new number (in points) in the Size text box. (One inch equals 72 points.)

   Other graph types, such as pie charts, offer different options, such as the capability to *explode* a slice (pull it away from the body of the pie).

3. *Optional:* To label data points with their values, click the Label Data checkbox. Click any of the nine radio buttons below the checkbox to indicate where the data label will appear in relation to each data point.

   For some graph types, such as bar and pictogram, an example of a data label is shown in a Sample box.

4. Click the OK button to put the new options into effect.

Click to change the symbols color

Choose a series to edit

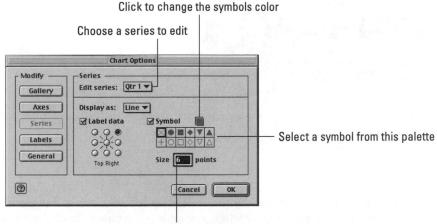

Select a symbol from this palette

Specify a size for the symbol

Figure 4-26: Use the Chart Options dialog box to choose the shape, size, and color of the symbol for data points.

Note

To change the color or pattern of any series, select its box in the chart legend, and then select another color, pattern, wallpaper, or gradient from the Accents windoid. (Wallpapered—textured—graph objects are a feature found only in AppleWorks 5 and 6.)

Labels options

Use the Labels options to specify settings for the chart title and legend.

If a title was in the upper-left corner of the selected chart range, it appears in the Title box. You can change it in the spreadsheet or in the Chart Options (Labels) dialog box. If the chart has no title, you can create one in the dialog box. To display the title horizontally, check the Horizontal checkbox. To display the title vertically, clear the checkmark. To add a drop shadow behind the chart title, check the Shadow checkbox. To specify a different location for the chart title, click one of the eight title placement radio buttons to the right of the Title box. To remove the title, delete it from the cell. Figure 4-27 displays label options for chart title and legend.

Text characteristics (such as the font and size), the background color, and the pattern for the title come directly from the formatting you apply (or change) in the title's cell in the spreadsheet. You also can change the title's attributes by selecting it in the chart and then choosing options from the Format menu. You can alter the title's bounding box or background by selecting the title in the chart and then choosing a background (fill) color, pattern, wallpaper, gradient, line width, or pen color from the Accents windoid.

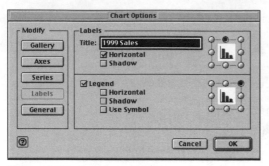

Figure 4-27: Labels options

Labels in the legend are determined by the series labels to the left and upper part of the spreadsheet range you specify when you create the chart. To change any of the labels, change the contents of the appropriate cells.

You can alter the legend's background and bounding box by selecting the legend in the chart and then choosing a background color, pattern, wallpaper, gradient, line width, or pen color from the Accents windoid. If you don't like the way series names are displayed in the legend, you can select the legend in the chart and then choose new text attributes from the Format menu.

STEPS: Modifying the Legend

1. To change from the labels of one series to the labels of another series, click the General button in the Chart Options dialog box. Click the radio button for Series in Rows or Series in Columns to change the series used for the legend. (This action also changes the chart layout.)

2. To change the position of the legend relative to the chart, click one of the eight position radio buttons in the Chart Options (Labels) dialog box.

3. Use the Horizontal checkbox in the Chart Options (Labels) dialog box to designate whether the legend elements are to be displayed in a vertical or horizontal list.

4. To place a shadow behind the legend box, click the Shadow checkbox.

5. Some chart types, such as line graphs, use symbols to represent data points. If you want the symbols to be displayed in the legend, click the Use Symbols checkbox.

6. To hide the legend, remove the checkmark from the Legend checkbox.

General options

Use the General options (see Figure 4-28) to do the following:

✦ Change the data range for the chart

✦ Use numbers as axis labels

✦ Indicate whether the data series in the selected range is in rows or in columns

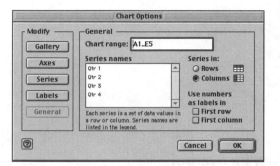

Figure 4-28: General options

To specify a new chart range, type it into the Chart Range text box. Remember to separate the anchor points in the range with a pair of periods, as in A1..D7.

In most cases, you will use text from the spreadsheet as axis labels. If the first row or first column of the selected chart range contains numbers you want to use as labels, click the (Use numbers as labels in) First Row or First Column checkbox, as appropriate.

To indicate whether the data series in the selected range is arranged in rows or in columns, click the Series in Rows or Columns radio button, as appropriate. The labels that appear in the Series Names list box represent the data that will be plotted.

Pictograms

Pictograms use pictures — rather than bars, lines, and so on — to represent data. Pictogram images can be a single image or a series of repeating images, one above the other. To use pictogram images in a chart, you must do one of the following:

✦ Select Pictogram or Stacked Pictogram as the chart type

✦ Set one or more of the series to display as pictograms in the Chart Options (Series) dialog box

The default pictogram symbol is a large arrow, but you can provide your own symbols, as described in the next section and as shown in Figure 4-29.

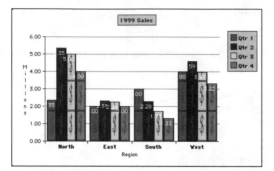

Figure 4-29: A pictogram with a repeating custom symbol (a dollar sign)

STEPS: Changing a Pictogram Symbol

1. In the Scrapbook, a graphics program, or an AppleWorks draw document, select the image you want to use as a pictogram. (Apple recommends using a draw image or a clipping rather than a paint picture, as they generally consume less memory.)

2. Choose Edit ➪ Copy to place a copy of the image on the clipboard.

3. In the Chart Options (Series) dialog box, choose All or a specific data series from the Edit Series pop-up menu. (You can use the same image for all series or a different image for each series.) The current pictogram image appears in the Sample box.

4. Click the Sample box. A dark border surrounds the box.

5. Choose Edit ➪ Paste (or press ⌘+V). The image on the clipboard replaces the one in the Sample box and is used for the selected series or all series, depending on the choice you made in the Edit Series pop-up menu.

6. Click the Repeating checkbox to have a constantly sized symbol repeat in each bar. If you want repeating symbols to overlap each other, type a number in the % Overlap text box. Leave the Repeating checkbox cleared if you want the symbol to be sized to match the height of the bar.

7. If you want to use the same image for other data series, repeat Steps 3 through 6 as required.

Tip   To display only a pictogram symbol without the usual bounding box, click the box in the legend associated with that data series and then set the line width to None in the Tool panel.

Chart-Editing Shortcuts

So you can avoid wading through dialog boxes and buttons, AppleWorks provides several shortcuts that take you directly to the appropriate Chart Options dialog box:

✦ Double-click an open area of a chart to make the Chart Options (Gallery) dialog box appear. This action is equivalent to choosing Edit ➪ Chart Options. The Chart Options (Gallery) dialog box enables you to change the chart type or to set basic display options.

✦ Double-click the X or Y axis of a chart to make the Chart Options (Axis) dialog box appear.

✦ Double-click a chart symbol in the legend to make the Chart Options (Series) dialog box appear.

✦ Double-click the chart title (if the chart has a title) or the legend to make the Chart Options (Labels) dialog box appear.

Other chart changes and embellishments

In addition to using the options in the Chart Options dialog boxes, you can use other methods to modify and embellish charts. After you create a chart, it acts like any other AppleWorks object. When you first click a chart, handles appear at its corners. You can drag it to a new location or resize it by dragging a handle.

You can embellish the chart by adding text (as callouts, for example) and graphics. You can draw attention to an important element in the chart, such as an outstanding quarterly sales figure, by using the drawing tools to add an arrow pointing to the bar or data point. Finish off the effect by selecting the text tool to create a comment (for example, "Best quarter since the company's inception!"), and then surround the comment with a colored box or oval.

You also can add a background color, pattern, texture, or gradient to the chart; color the legend box; and change the line width or color of the box that encloses the chart by choosing options from the panels in the Accents windoid. Because a chart is just another object, to achieve an uncluttered look, you can use the chart to hide the data used to create it. When you copy a chart into a word processing document, you can specify a text wrap for a more professional appearance.

Tip   Remember that when a chart is simply pasted into a document, it loses its link with the spreadsheet in which it was created. You might prefer to add the spreadsheet to the document as a frame and display only the chart portion.

Printing

AppleWorks has several features that apply only to printing spreadsheets. These features can be used to do the following:

✦ Add manual page breaks

✦ Specify a print range

✦ Decide whether to print or omit the cell grid, as well as the column and row headings

Adding page breaks

Although AppleWorks automatically determines where page breaks occur based on full pages, you might want to force a page break at a strategic spot in the spreadsheet — usually to keep important information from being split across pages.

To insert a page break, select the cell you want to print as the last (lower-right) item on a page and choose Options ➪ Add Page Break. Any cells to the right or below the selected cell will print on succeeding pages.

You can remove a manual page break by selecting the same cell and choosing Remove Page Break from the Options menu. To remove all manual page breaks simultaneously, choose Remove All Breaks from the Options menu.

Tip   If you want to see how the spreadsheet will print (and where the page breaks will occur), choose Page View (Shift+⌘+P) from the Window menu.

Specifying a print range

When the time comes to print the spreadsheet, AppleWorks intelligently defaults to printing the entire active portion of the spreadsheet; that is, it prints all areas of the spreadsheet (beginning with cell A1) to the lower rightmost cell that contains data. You also can specify a different print range. Choose Options ➪ Set Print Range. A Print Range dialog box appears. Click the Print Cell Range radio button and type the specific range you want to print. If you have a range selected where you chose Options ➪ Set Print Range, that range will be automatically filled in for you. (Remember that a range consists of the upper-left cell coordinate and the lower-right cell coordinate, separated by a pair of periods.) Click the OK button to set the new range.

Tip   If you preselect a range by dragging and then go directly to the Print command, you do not have to use the Print Range command. The program automatically prints the highlighted range.

Working with a modified Print dialog box

When you choose File ➪ Print (or press ⌘+P), you'll notice that the Print dialog box has been modified slightly, as shown in Figure 4-30. In the lower portion of the dialog box (or in a different panel for application-specific settings, such as with the LaserWriter 8 printer driver), you will find a series of checkboxes that appear only when you are printing a spreadsheet. Depending on the boxes that are checked, you can print or omit column headings, row headings, and the cell grid. Initially, these settings match the options you have chosen in the Display dialog box (which is discussed in "Changing display options," later in this chapter).

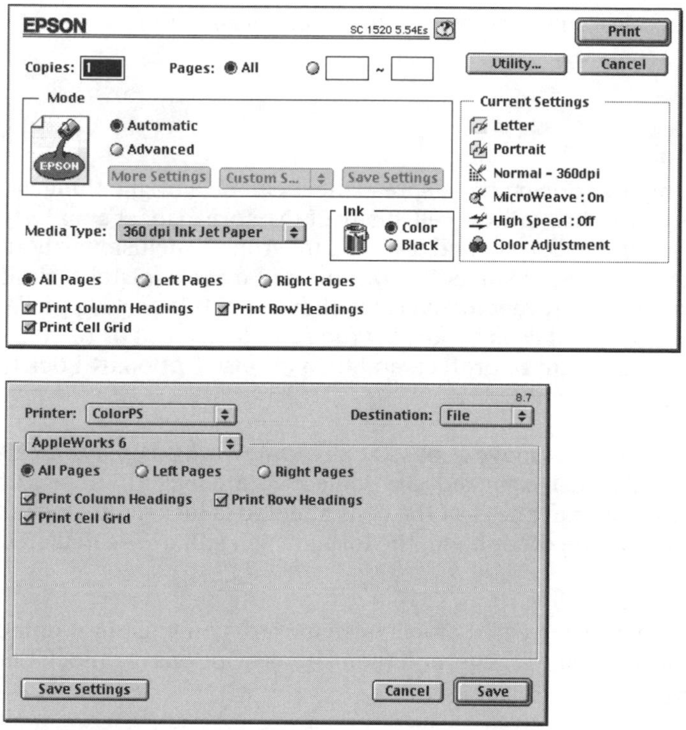

Figure 4-30: When you print a spreadsheet, a modified Print dialog box appears.

Other Procedures and Options

This section explains the remaining commands, procedures, and options available to you in the spreadsheet environment (in short, other stuff). Although you don't have to use any of these features (some you might never use), knowing they're available is nice.

Automatic and manual recalculation

Normally, AppleWorks recalculates the spreadsheet whenever necessary. If a cell contains a formula that refers to another cell (B17, for example) and you change the contents of that cell (B17), the program automatically recalculates the formula. In very large spreadsheets or on slower Macs, recalculation can be time-consuming. If you like, you can disable automatic recalculation by choosing Auto Calc from the Calculate menu and clearing its checkmark.

When Auto Calc is disabled, AppleWorks recalculates the spreadsheet only when you choose Calculator ➪ Calculate Now (or press Shift+⌘+=).

Note   If you select Auto Calc, you will never need to use Calculate Now.

Locking cells

As with any other computer document, a spreadsheet can be a fragile thing. If you type an incorrect entry in a critical cell, many of the spreadsheet's underlying assumptions might become incorrect and lead you to wrong conclusions about the data or its summary figures. If you edit a formula and make a mistake, similar consequences can result. To prevent inadvertent changes of this sort, AppleWorks enables you to protect selected cells by locking them. To lock a cell or range, select the cell or range you want to protect, and then choose Options ➪ Lock Cells (or press ⌘+H).

If you attempt to edit, delete, or move a locked cell, AppleWorks displays an alert box with the message "This cell is locked" or "Some cells are locked," depending on whether one — or more than one — of the cells affected is locked. If a locked cell contains a formula, on the other hand, the formula will still be recalculated as necessary.

If you need to type data into any cell that has been locked, you must first unlock that cell. Select the locked cell or range, and then choose Options ➪ Unlock Cells (or press Shift+⌘+H).

Locking titles

Depending on the nature of the spreadsheet, locking row or column titles in place can sometimes be useful. To lock titles, do one of the following:

✦ To lock a set of row and column titles in place, select the cell that intersects the row and column titles and choose Options ➪ Lock Title Position.

✦ To lock a set of column titles in place, select the entire bottom row of the titles (by clicking the row number heading) and choose Options ⇨ Lock Title Position.

✦ To lock a set of row titles in place, select the entire rightmost column of the titles (by clicking the column number heading) and choose Options ⇨ Lock Title Position.

As you scroll the spreadsheet, the titles remain in view. Figure 4-31 shows a spreadsheet with Column A and Rows 1 and 2 locked in place.

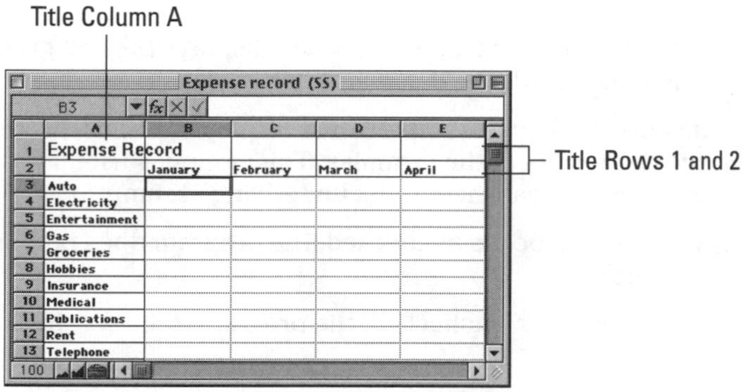

Title Column A

Title Rows 1 and 2

Figure 4-31: Solid lines surround the cells in the locked rows (1 and 2) and column (A).

To unlock the titles (to choose a different set of locking titles, to edit a cell in the title region, or to remove the locking titles), choose Lock Title Position again.

Setting a default font

Normally, the default font for spreadsheets is 9-point Geneva. Unless you manually select another font for a cell, the program uses the default font for all formatting. To set a different default font for the current spreadsheet, choose Options ⇨ Default Font. The Default Font dialog box appears. Select a new font from the list box (all fonts installed in the system are displayed in the list) and type a point size in the Size text box. Click the OK button. All cells that have not had a different font or size manually applied to them change to the new default font and size. Cells you have manually set to a specific font or size retain that font or size.

Tip

If you don't like having Geneva 9 as your default font in every new spreadsheet, create a new spreadsheet and choose Options ⇨ Default Font and set your preferred choices. Now, save that spreadsheet as your default options template — "AppleWorks SS Options."

Changing display options

The Options ⇨ Display command enables you to exert some control over the way AppleWorks displays the current spreadsheet. For example, you might want to alter the display before printing a spreadsheet or using it as part of a presentation or report.

In the Display dialog box (see Figure 4-32), checking or clearing a particular checkbox has the following effects:

✦ **Cell Grid.** When this box is unchecked, AppleWorks displays the spreadsheet without a cell grid.

✦ **Solid Lines.** When this box is checked, the program displays the cell grid as solid lines. When it is unchecked (the default), a dotted cell grid is displayed.

✦ **Formulas.** When this box is checked, AppleWorks displays formulas in cells, instead of displaying the results of the formulas. This option is useful for checking the accuracy of a spreadsheet or its underlying assumptions.

✦ **Column Headings.** When this box is unchecked, the program does not display column headings (letters).

✦ **Row Headings.** When this box is unchecked, the program does not display row headings (numbers).

✦ **Mark Circular Refs.** When this box is checked, data in a cell that contains a circular reference is surrounded by bullet characters (•).

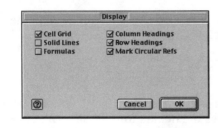

Figure 4-32: Set options for viewing and printing the current spreadsheet.

Tip

When the row or column headers are hidden, you might think that you can't select a whole row or column. This is usually the case, but if you have enabled Lock Title Position, clicking in the title area will select the entire row or column to which that title cell refers.

Down to Business: Creating a Check Register Spreadsheet

As an illustration of some of the AppleWorks spreadsheet capabilities, you can create a spreadsheet that fulfills the reason many new users say they bought their computers: to balance their checkbooks. (Of course, when you think about it, paying over $1,000 for slightly more power than a hand calculator doesn't make a great deal of sense, does it?)

This spreadsheet is useful if you don't like to manually balance your checking account, or if you want a clean, printed copy of your check register. But because the spreadsheet duplicates your written check register, you have to post your checks and deposits twice—once in the check register and once in the spreadsheet.

In addition to duplicating a standard check register, the spreadsheet tosses in a few extra features:

✦ Separate Payee and Description columns, so you can record to whom each check was made payable, as well as what it was for

✦ Automatic calculation of your balance

✦ Automatic calculation of the total of uncleared checks, withdrawals, and deposits (the uncleared total)

Creating the spreadsheet

Figure 4-33 shows the check register spreadsheet with a half dozen sample entries.

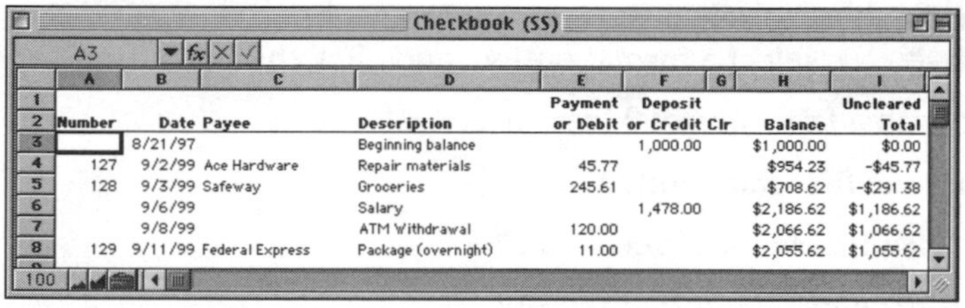

Figure 4-33: The check register spreadsheet

Use the following steps to create a working copy of the spreadsheet.

STEPS: Laying Out the Spreadsheet

1. Create the column labels in Rows 1 and 2. All label text is 9-point Geneva bold, and all other text is 9-point Geneva.

2. Set the alignment for each column. To do this, click a column heading to select the entire column, and then choose an option from the Format ⇨ Alignment submenu. If the default Button Bar is displayed, you might find it faster to click alignment settings in the Button Bar.

   Set Columns A, B, E, F, H, and I as right-aligned (⌘+]).

   Set Columns C and D as left-aligned (⌘+[).

   Set Column G as center-aligned (⌘+\).

3. Use Format ⇨ Column Width to set the column widths as follows (all settings are in points):

   - A (44)
   - B (52)
   - C (104)
   - D (124)
   - E and F (56)
   - G (22)
   - H and I (64)

4. Add a bottom border to cells A2 through I2 by using Format ⇨ Borders.

5. Set the number formats for data in the spreadsheet as follows. To do this, click a column heading to select the entire column, choose Format ⇨ Number (or press Shift+⌘+N), select a format option, and click the OK button.

   - A (Fixed with a Precision of 0 [zero])
   - B (choose the first Date option)
   - E and F (Fixed, Commas, Precision 2)
   - H and I (Currency, Commas, Precision 2)

6. The record in Row 3 is reserved for the beginning balance. For now, type the following:

   - Today's date in B3
   - Beginning balance in D3
   - 1000 in F3
   - =F3 in H3
   - 0 in I3

You can change this information later to match your real beginning balance.

7. Type this formula into cell H4 to calculate the running balance (Balance):

```
=IF(B4<>"",H3-E4+F4,"")
```

After entering the formula, copy it to the remaining cells in Column H by selecting cells H4 through H500 and choosing Calculate ➪ Fill Down (⌘+D).

8. Type this formula into cell I4 to calculate the running total of uncleared checks, withdrawals, and deposits (Uncleared Total):

```
=IF(B4="","",IF(G4<>"x",I3-E4+F4,I3))
```

After typing the formula, copy it to the remaining cells in Column I by selecting cells I4 through I500 and choosing Calculate ➪ Fill Down (⌘+D).

9. To keep the labels in Rows 1 and 2 from scrolling off the screen as additional transactions are entered, change them into titles. Select Row 2 by clicking the row heading (the number 2) and choose Options ➪ Lock Title Position.

After you lock the rows, you cannot edit any of the cells in Rows 1 or 2. Later, if you need to make changes in either row, choose Lock Title Position again to remove the checkmark.

10. *Optional:* Select Columns H and I by clicking their headings, and then choose Options ➪ Lock Cells (or press ⌘+H) to keep the entries in these columns from being accidentally altered. (The entries in Columns H and I are all calculated automatically, based on your transactions.)

Understanding the formulas

The formulas are fairly complex, so they require further examination. The formula in H4 is as follows:

```
=IF(B4<>"",H3-E4+F4,"")
```

First, the formula checks cell B4 — the date for the current record — to see whether it is empty. If B4 is nonempty (for example, it contains something such as a date), the first action is performed. That is, the formula takes the previous balance (H3), subtracts any payment entered for this record (E4), and adds any deposit entered for this record (F4). If, on the other hand, the date field is blank for the record, the second action is taken: the Balance entry is left blank. (You test for the existence of a date because every legitimate record should contain one. If no date is found, you assume the record does not yet exist.)

This formula could have been written as =H3-E4+F4. When filled down to the remaining records, however, transactions that didn't yet exist would all display the current balance. Using this more complex approach to test whether a transaction exists produces a more attractive spreadsheet.

The formula in I4 is even more complex. It contains an IF function nested within another IF function:

```
=IF(B4="","",IF(G4<>"x",I3-E4+F4,I3))
```

The formula performs two actions. First, if the Date field is blank—(B4=""—it assumes the record does not yet exist and leaves the Uncleared Total entry blank, just as the previous formula left the Balance entry blank. Because the first test has been met, the remainder of the formula is not evaluated.

On the other hand, if the Date field (B4) is not blank, the formula checks the Clr entry (G4) for the current record to see whether it contains an x. (You use an *x* to indicate—according to the bank statement—that a check, withdrawal, or deposit has cleared.) If an *x* is not found, the formula takes the previous Uncleared Total (I3), subtracts the current Payment (E4) from it, and adds the current Deposit (F4) to it. Thus, if an entry has not cleared, its payment or deposit is reflected in the Uncleared Total. If an *x* is found, on the other hand, the previous Uncleared Total in I3 is simply copied to the cell.

Using the spreadsheet

The best time to begin using this spreadsheet is when you open a new account or immediately after you've received a bank statement and have balanced your checkbook.

Begin by editing the first record (Row 3). Replace the temporary date (B3) and starting balance (F3) with today's date and your balance. Placing the balance in F3 automatically copies it to the Balance column (H3). Because the beginning balance won't be part of a later reconciliation, type a lowercase *x* in the Clr column (G3) for the entry.

Now go back through your check register and, beginning in Row 4, type an entry for every outstanding check, withdrawal, and deposit. (If you don't want gaps in the register, you can go back to the oldest outstanding check, withdrawal, or deposit, and type every transaction up to the current date. If you do so, be sure to add an *x* in the Clr field for every item that has cleared.)

When a bank statement arrives, the Checkbook spreadsheet can help with the reconciliation process. Going down column G (the Clr column), add an *x* for every item that has cleared. When you are through, the last figure in the Uncleared Total column will represent the total of the outstanding deposits minus the outstanding checks.

Quick Tip: Speeding Data Entry by Preselecting a Range

Although you can tab and click to move from cell to cell when you type data, you can use a faster method to add data into a specific section of a spreadsheet. Start by preselecting the range into which you will be typing data. The range might look like the one in Figure 4-34, for example.

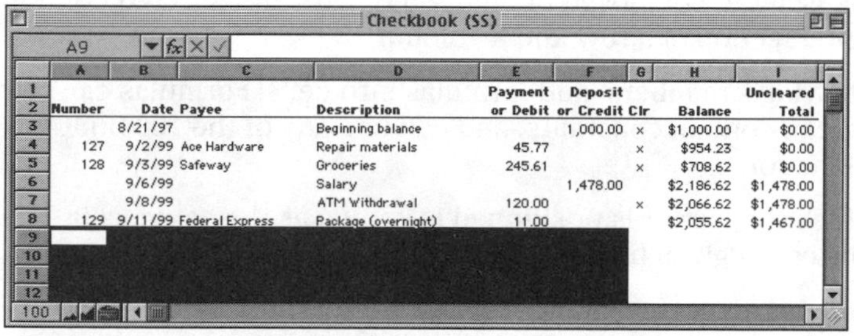

Figure 4-34: A preselected range

In a preselected range, the active cell is white, while all other cells are dark. After typing information in the first cell, press the Tab key. The cell to the right becomes active. If you continue to press Tab after each cell entry, the active cell shifts across each row, one cell at a time. When a row is completed, the cursor drops down to the first cell in the next row. (If you press the Return key rather than the Tab key after each cell entry, the cursor moves down one cell at a time through each selected column.)

Moving On Up

Although the AppleWorks spreadsheet environment is sufficient for many users, as your needs become more complex, you might want to check out a more full-featured spreadsheet program. Features such as a programming (sometimes called "macro") language, the capability to define your own functions, additional chart types and functions, and linked and three-dimensional spreadsheets are all commonplace in commercial spreadsheets. Currently, the leading Mac spreadsheet program is Microsoft Excel (Microsoft Corporation, www.microsoft.com). You might also want to consider Spreadsheet 2000 (Casady & Greene, www.casadyg.com), a distinctly different type of spreadsheet program. If you're looking for additional charting capabilities, check out DeltaGraph (DeltaPoint).

Caution

The lack of export capabilities in AppleWorks 6 makes moving to other spreadsheets less than easy. You can no longer save an AppleWorks spreadsheet in Excel 3, Excel 4, or SYLK format, which most other spreadsheet programs can correctly interpret. Unless you use a product such as MacLink Plus, you will probably have to save your spreadsheet as ASCII text, losing formatting, formulas, and charts.

Summary

✦ A spreadsheet is a grid composed of numbered rows and lettered columns. A cell is the intersection of a row and a column.

✦ You type text strings, numbers, and formulas into cells. Formulas can refer to other cells, can contain constants, and can use any of the 100 built-in AppleWorks functions.

✦ The cell in which the cursor is positioned is known as the active cell. The location of any cell is given by its cell address.

✦ A group of cells is known as a range. A range is identified by its anchor points — the upper-left and lower-right cells in the range.

✦ Formulas are normally evaluated from left to right. The precedence levels of the operations performed within the formula can change the calculation order, however, as can the use of parentheses to enclose operations.

✦ You can type functions directly into formulas, or you can paste them there (along with dummy arguments) by using the Paste Function command.

✦ To save typing time, or to make it simpler to understand the assumptions that underlie your spreadsheet, you can use range names in formulas rather than normal cell references.

✦ You can copy and paste formulas to other cells. You also can paste just the values contained in cells, ignoring the formulas. The Fill Down and Fill Right commands expedite copying a formula to a large range.

✦ The Fill Special command makes it easy to create sequences of numbers and dates. This feature is particularly useful for generating a set of ordered row or column headings.

✦ You can reference cells and ranges in other spreadsheets and spreadsheet frames using AppleWorks 6's new intersheet references.

✦ AppleWorks provides many commands that make reorganizing a spreadsheet simple. It has commands that insert and delete cells, columns, and rows; move ranges of cells to new locations; sort data; and transpose a range (swapping the positions of rows and columns).

✦ To make spreadsheets more attractive, you can selectively apply font, size, style, color, and alignment options to the text in cells. You also can apply colors and patterns to cells (cell shading).

✦ To make the contents of the cell fit inside the cell borders, you can widen column widths, change row heights, or apply a Wrap format.

✦ You can control the way the program displays numbers, dates, and times by choosing options in the Format Number, Date, and Time dialog box.

✦ The Copy Format and Paste Format commands enable you to easily apply existing cell formats to other cells.

✦ AppleWorks provides a dozen different styles of charts you can use to embellish a spreadsheet. Because every chart is also an object, you can copy and paste charts into other documents.

✦ When printing a spreadsheet, AppleWorks defaults to selecting the entire active area of the spreadsheet. However, you can specify a particular print range, add manual page breaks, and disable the printing of some spreadsheet elements, such as the cell grid and row or column headings.

✦ You can lock important cells to prevent them from being inadvertently changed. You can lock important information (titles, for example) at the upper and left sides of the spreadsheet so that it doesn't disappear when you scroll the spreadsheet.

✦　　✦　　✦

The Database Environment

A database is an organized set of information, usually on one particular topic. One common example of a database is a card file that contains the names, addresses, and phone numbers of business associates, customers, or friends. Other everyday examples of databases you can find around the office or home include employee records, inventory records, recipes, and videotapes.

Every database is composed of records. In the preceding examples, each record contains all the pertinent information about one friend, one employee, one inventory part, one recipe, one videotape, and so on.

Each record is composed of fields. A field contains one piece of information about the employee (a social security number or date of hire, for example), videotape (the name of the star or the show's length), recipe (ingredients and cooking time), or friend (birthday or telephone number). In an address database, you might have separate fields for each person's first name, last name, street address, city, state, and Zip code.

Unlike a word processing document (which is relatively free-form), a computer database has an order that comes from its use of fields. Every field holds one particular type of information (an employee identification number, for example). As you skim through the records of the database, you see that the same type of information is in that field in each record. Figure 5-1 shows the relationship between a database, records, and fields.

Although you can keep database information in a word processing document, you lose the data manipulation advantages that a database provides, such as the capability to select subsets of records (for example, only employees who make between $20,000 and $30,000 per year), sort records by one or more fields (for example, by last name, years of employment, or cost of ingredients), create fields that perform calculations and computations (for example, totaling all items ordered or combining two text fields), and generate custom reports.

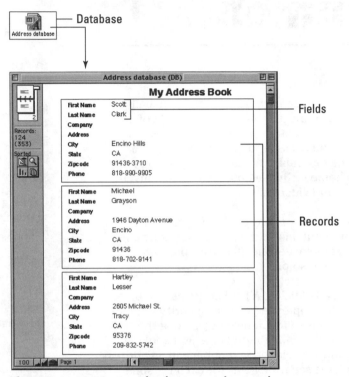

Figure 5-1: A computer database contains a series of records; each record is composed of a set of fields.

Another great thing about a computerized database, as compared to a paper version, is the ease with which you can modify and reorganize its contents. Early database programs required you to define every field before you started to add records. If you later decided to add a field, delete a field, or change a particular field's type (from text to numeric, for example), you had to execute a complex procedure to reorganize the database. Current database programs, such as the AppleWorks database environment, make reorganizing a database remarkably easy. If you need a new field, for example, you simply define it and add it to the appropriate layouts.

Working with the AppleWorks Database

You use an AppleWorks database in four modes: Layout, Browse, Find, and List. In Layout mode, you arrange fields and other database objects on a screen page so that the program will display and print them the way you want. You use Browse or List mode to view, edit, add, delete, and sort records. You do all data entry in Browse or List mode. Find mode enables you to search for records that meet one or more criteria (Last Name = Smith, for example).

Using the AppleWorks database, you can do the following:

- ✦ Quickly identify records that match simple criteria (for example, Name = Sam Jones) or very complex criteria (for example, Salary <= $40,000 and Age > 45).

- ✦ Sort the records by the contents of one or more fields (for example, by Last Name within City).

- ✦ Create multiple layouts for any database (for example, create data entry, phone directory, and label layouts for the same database).

- ✦ Set data validation criteria for some fields (such as unique data or data within a particular range).

- ✦ Specify a data type for each field (such as text, number, date, time, multimedia, calculation, or summary).

- ✦ Automatically enter certain data (today's date or an invoice number).

- ✦ Perform calculations (totals or averages for each record, a subset of records, or the entire database).

Defining Fields

Every database is composed of fields into which you enter information. In fact, you cannot begin to enter data until you have defined at least one field by specifying its name and the type of data it will contain.

To create new fields, delete fields, or modify the definitions or options for existing fields, choose Layout ➪ Define Fields (or press Shift+⌘+D). The Define Database Fields dialog box appears, as shown in Figure 5-2. Click the Done button when you have finished.

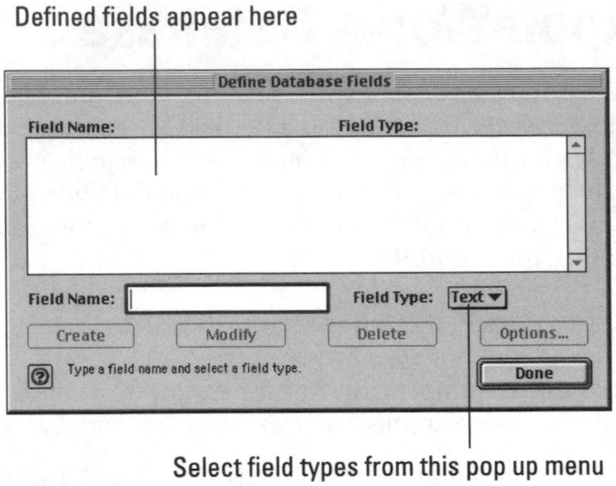

Defined fields appear here

Figure 5-2: You use the Define Database Fields dialog box to specify a name, field type, and options for every field in the database. You also can use it to modify a field definition or delete a field.

Select field types from this pop up menu

Although the database environment is packed with fancy features, sometimes simple is best. You can define the necessary fields, accept the default layout, and start entering data. The following example shows the steps for designing a basic address book database. As you progress through this chapter, you will learn how to customize layouts and work with special data types and options.

STEPS: Creating a Simple Database

1. Choose File ➪ New ➪ Database, click the New Database button on the Button Bar, or click the Database thumbnail on the Starting Points window's Basic panel.

2. A new database is created, and the Define Database Fields dialog box appears, as shown earlier in Figure 5-2.

3. Define the fields you want to use in the database. For the address book database, you'll define the following fields (in order): First Name, Last Name, Address, City, State, Zip, and Birthdate. Birthdate is a date field; all others are text fields.

> **Note** You might wonder why Zip is a text field. The first reason is that some Zip codes start with a zero. If you define the field as a numeric field, the leading zero won't display. Second, you might have some addresses in countries other than the United States (such as Canada) where the postal codes often include letters.

For each field, type its name in the Field Name text box, choose the appropriate field type from the pop-up menu, and then click the Create button. The field is added to the list box.

The name of the field just defined is still in the Field Name text box. When you begin typing a name for the next field, the Field Name text box automatically clears.

Tip

When you design any database, you should always try to plan ahead. By separating first and last name fields, for example, you'll have an easier time doing searches and sorts in the future. Try not to combine important bits of information into a single field.

4. After you have defined all fields, click the Done button. A database with the default layout (field sizes, placements, fonts, and so on) appears, as shown in Figure 5-3, ready for you to add the first record.

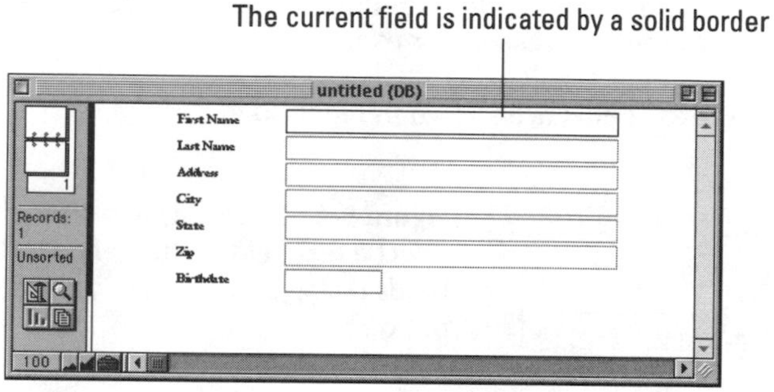

The current field is indicated by a solid border

Figure 5-3: After you define the database fields, AppleWorks displays the first blank record.

After completing an entry for a field, you can move to the next field by pressing the Tab key. To create additional records, choose New Record from the Edit menu (or press ⌘+R).

Field types

AppleWorks 6 offers 14 types of fields, each for a different category of data or a specific presentation format: text, number, date, time, name, pop-up menu, radio buttons, checkbox, serial number, value list, multimedia, record info, calculation, and summary. By assigning the correct data type to each field, you can let AppleWorks do some simple validation (for example, making sure only dates are typed into date fields and only numbers are typed into number fields).

Note

Users of earlier versions of AppleWorks should read this chapter carefully. ClarisWorks 3.0 and earlier provided only six field types. In ClarisWorks 4.0 and 5.0, however, things that were previously considered formatting options — pop-up menus, checkboxes, and radio buttons — have been defined as separate field types. By selecting any of these field types, you can create more attractive databases, while making it easy for you to complete the field — without having to type the complete entry! In addition, ClarisWorks and AppleWorks 5 introduced a multimedia field type, which enables you to store QuickTime movies, pictures, and sounds in your database.

Although you could define every field as a text field, you won't be using AppleWorks to its fullest potential if you don't take advantage of the other field types. The following sections describe how each field type works.

Text fields

Although it's called a text field, you can type any character into this field. Letters, numbers, punctuation marks, spaces, and so on are all legal characters. Data you type into a text field will word wrap, just as it does in a word processing document. You can even press the Return key to begin a new line. This flexibility makes text fields ideal for notes, as well as for any type of information that contains a mixture of letters and numbers (street addresses, for example).

Options you can set for text fields are shown in Figure 5-4.

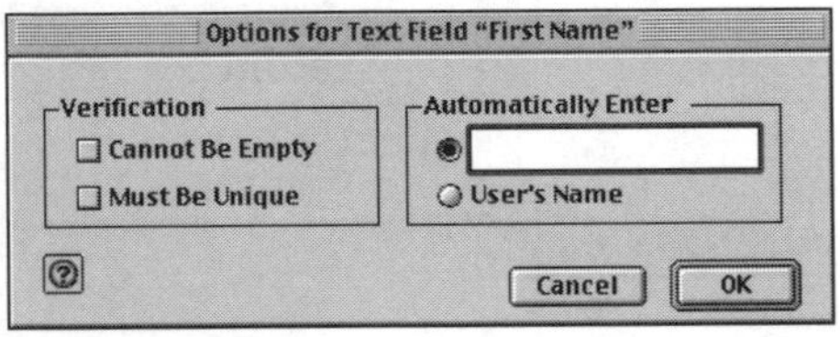

Figure 5-4: To display this dialog box, select a text field in the Define Database Fields dialog box and click the Options button.

The left side of the dialog box contains two text verification options:

✦ **Cannot Be Empty.** Click this checkbox if the field must be filled in for every record. If you attempt to switch to another record, create a new record, change to another mode, or close the database without filling in the field, AppleWorks presents a warning.

✦ **Must Be Unique.** Click this checkbox if you don't want to accept duplicate values for a field. (This is a useful option for part numbers in a company catalog or an inventory database, for example.) If you attempt to type a text string that already exists in the same field in another record, AppleWorks presents a warning.

Either warning can be overridden by clicking the Yes button in the warning message box.

If you have a text string you frequently use, type that string in the Automatically Fill In text box. All new records will automatically have that value inserted into the field. Alternatively, you can click the User's Name radio button and AppleWorks will initialize the field with the name, from the File Sharing control panel, of the Mac's owner when the record is created. You can edit this in the record if the default value is not appropriate for the current record.

As with other fields in an AppleWorks database, you can apply selective formatting to any portion of the text field's contents. For example, if you create a Comments field that you define as a text field, you can selectively change the font for some words or add a style such as italic to others.

The size of the bounding box for a text field does not restrict the amount of text you can type into the field. As you type, the bounding box expands vertically as needed to accommodate additional text. When you exit the field (by pressing the Tab key or by clicking in a different field), the bounding box returns to its normal size, obscuring any overflow text. The field expands again whenever you move the text insertion point into the field.

Note

If a text field contains overflow text, you should expand the size of the field on the layout before printing the database. Otherwise, the text in the printout will be truncated.

An AppleWorks 6 text field can hold a maximum of about 1,020 characters — more than twice as much text as allowed in ClarisWorks 4.0 and earlier text fields. If you exceed this limit, a message to that effect appears. You will have to manually edit the contents of the field by removing some of the text or style formatting before AppleWorks will accept the entry.

Number fields

Number fields are for numeric data only, such as prices, quantities, and so on. Legitimate numeric characters can include the digits 0 through 9, a decimal point, parentheses or a minus sign (for negative numbers), the plus (+) sign, a percent (%) sign, and an e (for scientific notation). AppleWorks automatically flags other characters and requests that you retype the number. It ignores commas or dollar signs during data entry. In addition, number fields cannot contain Returns — in every number field, the entire number must be typed as a single, continuous string. The maximum length for a number field is 255 characters.

If you type a number that exceeds the width of the field, the program converts the number to scientific notation (1.234571+e19, for example). As with overly long text entries, you have to move the text insertion point into the number field to see a number that exceeds the field's width.

As with the other field types, several verification and default options can be set for number fields. The Options dialog box for number fields is shown in Figure 5-5.

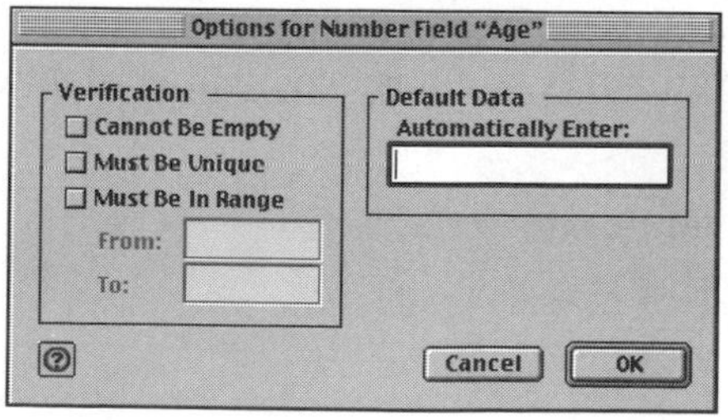

Figure 5-5: To display this dialog box, select a number field in the Define Database Fields dialog box and click the Options button.

The left side of the dialog box contains three verification options.

✦ **Cannot Be Empty.** Click this checkbox if the field must be filled in for every record. If you attempt to change to another record, create a new record, change to another mode, or close the database without filling in the field, AppleWorks presents a warning message box.

✦ **Must Be Unique.** Click this checkbox if you don't want to accept duplicate values for a field. If you attempt to type a number that already exists in another record for this field, AppleWorks presents a warning message box.

✦ **Must Be In Range.** Click this checkbox and type a pair of numbers into the From and To text boxes if you want to specify a range of allowable numeric entries. If you later type a number in this field that is outside the specified range, a warning message box appears.

Note All three warning messages can be overridden by clicking the Yes button in the warning message box.

You can assign a display format (such as Currency) or a particular number of decimal places to any field. (See "Field formatting," later in this chapter, for more information.)

If a particular number is typed more frequently than others in a number field (for example, you might have a default order quantity of 1), you can instruct AppleWorks to automatically insert that number for you each time you create a new record. Type the number in the Automatically Enter text box in the right side of the Options dialog box. As with the data in other number fields, auto-entered data can be edited as necessary.

Tip You should define some fields as text fields, even though they are composed entirely of numbers. Zip codes are a perfect example. Because number fields cannot display leading zeros, a Zip code of 01535 would display as 1535 in a number field. Similarly, numbers that contain parentheses or dashes are not allowed. Thus, Social Security numbers and phone numbers are best defined as text fields, too. In general, if numeric data will not be used in calculations, define it as a text field rather than as a number field.

Date fields

You use date fields, of course, to record calendar dates, such as 7/19/97. Examples include birthdates, the date a product was ordered, the date an employee was hired, or the date a school paper is due. You can type dates in a number of different ways. All of the following are acceptable:

✦ 7/19/00

✦ 7-19-00

✦ July 19, 2000

✦ Jul 19, 00

✦ 7/19

✦ Jul 19

As you can see, the methods for adding information to a date field are extremely flexible. As long as you type enough information to identify each portion of the date (the first three letters of the month's name, for example), AppleWorks will do its best to interpret what you type. If you omit the year, as in the last two examples, AppleWorks assumes you are referring to the current year and inserts it for you.

Note   If you type only one or two digits for the date, AppleWorks will assume that 00-90 should be 2000-2090, but that 91-99 should be 1991-1999.

Options available for date fields are shown in Figure 5-6. If you choose Must Be In Range as one of the verification options, you must type valid dates in the From and To boxes. (See "Number fields," earlier in this chapter, for more information on verification options and overriding verification warning message boxes.)

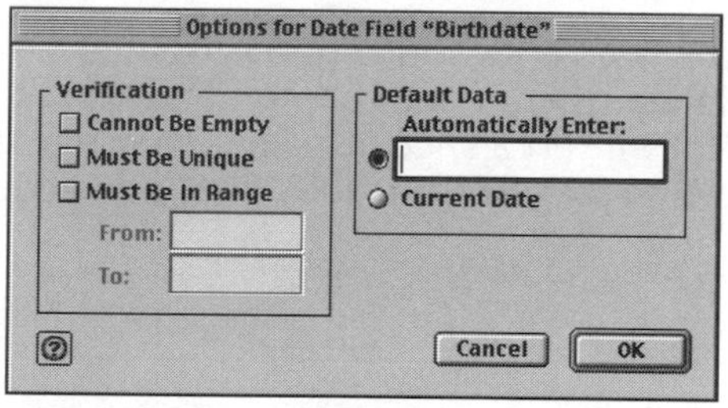

![Options for Date Field "Birthdate" dialog box with Verification section containing Cannot Be Empty, Must Be Unique, Must Be In Range checkboxes, From and To fields, and Default Data section with Automatically Enter text box and Current Date radio button, plus Cancel and OK buttons]

Figure 5-6: Date field options

In the right side of the Options dialog box, you can type a default date, if you like. If there's a particular date that should normally be entered, type it in the Automatically Enter text box. If you want to enter the current date when each record is created, click the Current Date radio button. As with other default values, you can edit or replace them in the records as necessary.

You can display dates within their fields in several ways. For a discussion of formatting options, see "Field formatting" later in this chapter.

Time fields

Time fields enable you to record times in hours, minutes, and seconds. The options for time fields are identical to those for date fields, as described earlier in "Date fields." The various time formats (discussed in "Field formatting," later in this chapter) enable you to record times with AM and PM suffixes, as well as in 12- or 24-hour formats.

Name fields

People's names are frequently recorded as two or more fields (First Name and Last Name, for example) because sorting a complete name is difficult. Generally, you sort by the person's last name, but you don't want to type a full name such as "Smith Bill," for example, to sort correctly. By using AppleWorks' name fields, however, you can gracefully handle complete names as a single field.

By default, entries in name fields are sorted by the last word in the field rather than the first. To force a particular name to be sorted by the first word, insert an @ symbol as the first character (@John Simms, for example). To force a particular name to be sorted by the next-to-last word (ignoring the final word), separate the next-to-last and the last word with an Option+space rather than a regular space. This enables a name prefix (such as Jr.) to be ignored during the sort, or a multiword surname (such as von Steubing) to be correctly sorted.

Name options are shown in Figure 5-7. The two verification options (Cannot Be Empty and Must Be Unique) were explained earlier in this chapter. The default options enable AppleWorks to automatically insert a specific name (your top salesperson, for instance) or your name (User's Name), as set in the File Sharing control panel.

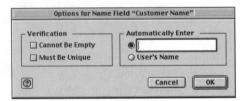

Figure 5-7: Name field options

> **Tip**
>
> If an incorrect user name appears in the name field, check the name that appears in the File Sharing control panel. Change it to reflect the name that should be used — your name, in most cases.

Pop-up menu fields

Setting a field type as a pop-up menu adds a menu to the field, as shown in Figure 5-8.

STEPS: Creating a Pop-Up Menu Field

1. Choose Layout ⇨ Define Fields (or press Shift+⌘+D). The Define Database Fields dialog box appears (see Figure 5-2, shown earlier in this chapter).

2. Type a name for the field in the Field Name text box, choose Pop-up Menu from the Field Type pop-up menu, and then click the Create button. The Options dialog box appears, as shown in Figure 5-9.

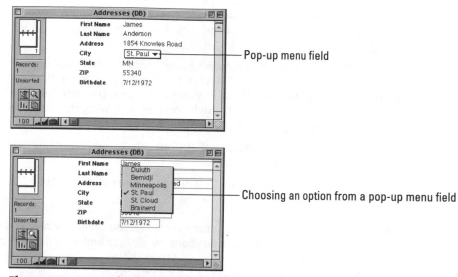

—Pop-up menu field

—Choosing an option from a pop-up menu field

Figure 5-8: A record with a pop-up menu field for City

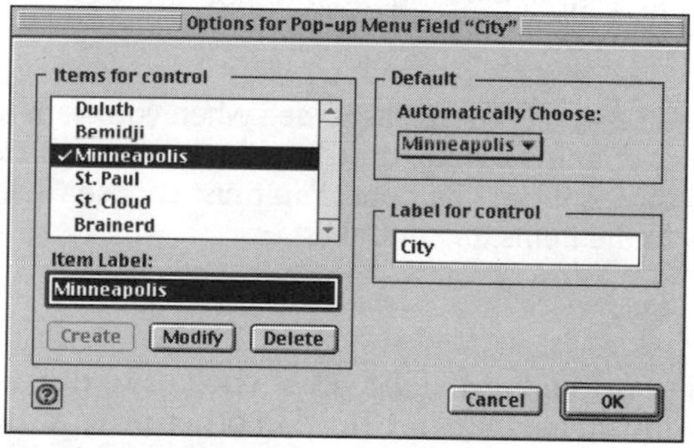

Figure 5-9: The Options dialog box for a pop-up menu field

3. To create a choice for the pop-up menu, type a name or value into the Item Label text box.

4. Click the Create button to add the choice to the Items for control list.

5. Repeat Steps 3 and 4 for all additional menu choices you want to create.

6. From the right side of the Options dialog box, choose a default item from the Automatically Choose pop-up menu. That item will be automatically selected when a new record is created.

7. *Optional:* Create a new label that will be attached to the pop-up menu field. By default, the field's name is used. You are free to change the label to something else.

As previously illustrated in Figure 5-8, the normal field label is removed when you display a pop-up menu field, and it is replaced by a label directly tied to the pop-up menu field. Optionally, you can remove the automatic field label, as well as the pop-up menu's triangle icon, by following the instructions in "Field formatting," later in this chapter.

8. To accept the field's definition and options, click the OK button. To cancel the changes, click the Cancel button.

9. Continue defining fields and editing definitions, or click the Done button to return to the database.

Note

Although entries in the Items for control list reflect the order in which you created the values, you can change their positions by clicking and dragging items in the list. Items also can be replaced or deleted by selecting the item and then clicking the appropriate button (the Modify or Delete button).

When you create a new record, the default entry is automatically chosen for any pop-up menu field in the layout. Tabbing into a pop-up menu field does nothing; to change the default entry to a different value, you must deliberately click the pop-up menu and drag to select another value.

Note

Setting a field type to pop-up menu is an excellent idea when you want to restrict the choices to a specific set of entries. Note, however, that if you or anyone else wants to type an unlisted choice, it can't be done. You must choose Define Fields again and add that choice to the Items for control list.

Radio buttons fields

Radio buttons fields are used to present a specific set of choices to the user, each with its own radio button (as shown in Figure 5-10). As in other programs, the choices are mutually exclusive — only one radio button can be selected. For help creating a radio buttons field, see "Pop-up menu fields," earlier in this chapter. The options and procedures are identical.

Figure 5-10: A radio buttons field

You can change the size or shape of the radio buttons field by switching to Layout mode and dragging one of the field's handles. You also can alter the appearance of the field by choosing options from the Radio Buttons Style dialog box (described in "Field formatting," later in this chapter).

AppleWorks provides several interesting keyboard shortcuts for choosing options in a radio buttons field (in addition to simply clicking the button of your choice). You can tab into the field and then:

✦ Press the spacebar repeatedly to cycle through the choices.

✦ Press any of the arrow keys (up, down, right, or left) to cycle through the choices.

✦ Press the Tab key again to leave the field, press the Enter or Return key, or choose Edit ➪ New Record (⌘+R) to complete the record.

Checkbox fields

Use a checkbox field to present a single label preceded by a checkbox, as shown in Figure 5-11. Checkbox fields are most appropriate for yes/no, true/false, and on/off types of data. Because they are simple to respond to, checkbox fields can be extremely useful as parts of data collection forms, such as surveys and business forms.

☒ Product shipped?   **Figure 5-11:** A checkbox field

The checkbox can be either checked or unchecked, and you can specify either as the default state for the field. The checkmark can be toggled between checked and unchecked by clicking it with the mouse, pressing the spacebar, or pressing any of the arrow keys.

Click the Options button in the Define Database Fields dialog box to set a different label for the field and to indicate whether the checkbox in new records should initially be checked or unchecked. To set formatting options for the field—including whether a ✓ will be used as the checkmark (an × will be used if the box is unchecked)—change to Layout mode, and then choose Edit ➪ Field Info to display the Checkbox Style dialog box.

Serial number fields

Serial number fields are used to assign numbers to records. Each record—including every record already in the database—is automatically given a number that reflects the order in which it was created. Although serial numbers can be edited, deleting records or sorting them does not affect the contents of a serial number field in other records. Serial number fields are often used to number invoices, purchase orders, statements, and checks.

Note   For data entry and editing purposes, an entry in a serial number field is treated like any other number. Only numeric entries are permitted. This means a serial number field cannot be used for part numbers such as 14B73, for example.

After defining a field as a serial number field, you can set options for the field by clicking the Options button in the Define Database Fields dialog box. The Options dialog box appears, as shown in Figure 5-12.

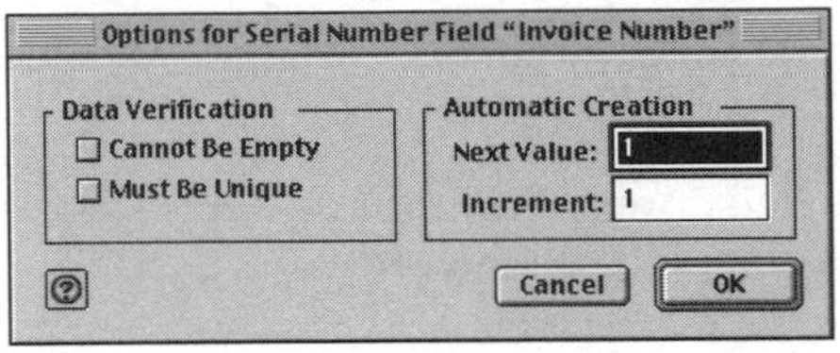

Figure 5-12: The Options dialog box for a serial number field

Checking the Cannot Be Empty checkbox enables AppleWorks to present a warning if you attempt to leave or close the current record and no serial number is present. If you don't check the Cannot Be Empty checkbox, you can delete serial numbers. Click the Must Be Unique checkbox if you want to disallow duplicate numbers. As with the options for other field types, you can override either of these restrictions on a record-by-record basis.

In the right side of the dialog box, type numbers for the next value (the serial number to be assigned to the first record in the database) and the increment value (how much you want each new serial number to increase over the previous number). When a serial number field is created, AppleWorks offers 1 as the default next value and 1 as the increment value.

Tip   If frequent breaks occur in a serial number field (purchase order numbers that are skipped or checks that are voided, for example), you can go to the Options dialog box for the serial number field and reset the value in the Next Value text box to jump to the next purchase order or check number. Doing this has no effect on the numbers for existing records.

Value list fields

Defining a field as a value list field causes it to present a drop-down list of values from which the user can select. Unlike pop-up menu fields, the list is automatically presented each time you tab into the field. You can manually insert unlisted values, and you can set several data validation options. Figure 5-13 shows a record that contains a value list field.

A default value appears here,
if one has been specified

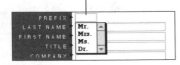

Figure 5-13: When a user tabs into the Prefix field of the Address List database, this value list automatically drops down.

The basic steps and options for creating a value list field are identical to those for pop-up menu fields (described earlier in this chapter). In addition to creating the list of values and optionally selecting a default value, you also can set any of the following data verification options:

✦ **Cannot Be Empty.** When this option is selected, AppleWorks presents a warning if you leave the field empty and then attempt to move to another record, accept the record (by pressing the Enter or Return key), or create a new record. (This warning can be overridden.)

✦ **Must Be Unique.** AppleWorks presents a warning if your choice or manual value for this field is already contained in another record. (This warning can be overridden.)

✦ **Alerts for Unlisted Values.** If you manually insert a value that is not contained in the value list, the warning in Figure 5-14 appears. The buttons enable you to continue editing the field's data (Continue), accept the entry as valid for this record only (Accept), or accept the entry and add it to the field's value list (Add to List). The Add to List option appends the current value to the bottom of the value list and makes the value an acceptable choice for all new and existing records.

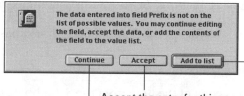

Accept the entry for this and every other record in the database

Accept the entry for this record only

Continue editing the contents of the field (that is try again)

Figure 5-14: This message appears when you manually insert a value into a field for which the Alerts for Unlisted Values option has been selected.

When entering or editing data in a value list field, you can choose a value in several ways:

✦ Double-click the value with the mouse pointer

✦ Scroll to the value with the up- and down-arrow keys

✦ Type the first character or two of the value's text

To complete the selection, you can double-click the value, or you can press the Return or Enter keys.

When all of the following circumstances are true, AppleWorks 6 ignores the default value set for a value list field:

✦ You are working in AppleWorks 6 with a converted database (one that was created in an earlier version of the program)

✦ The original database contained a text field that had a value list attached to it

✦ You have specified a different default value for the field in the Options dialog box

Multimedia fields

AppleWorks 6's multimedia fields enable you to store QuickTime movies, sounds, and pictures in any database.

Multimedia fields have no options that can be set in the Define Database Fields dialog box. You can change the size of a multimedia field for all records by changing to Layout mode, selecting the field, and then dragging one of its handles. If you want to maintain the original proportions of the field, press the Shift key as you drag. Field formatting options (such as scaling, cropping, and alignment) can be set for a multimedia field by changing to Layout mode, double-clicking or selecting the field, and then choosing Edit ⇨ Field Info.

You have several ways to add movies, pictures, or sounds to a multimedia field:

✦ Copy the item from another program or the Scrapbook and then paste it into the field.

✦ Add items from any of the Clippings tabs.

✦ Use drag-and-drop to move a copy of the item from the Scrapbook, another AppleWorks document, or a drag-and-drop-enabled program into the field.

✦ Select the field, choose File ⇨ Insert, and then select the movie, picture, or sound file you want to insert into the field.

Tip   Sound files must be in QuickTime format to be inserted, copied, or dragged into a multimedia field. To convert a sound file to this format, choose the Insert command from the File menu, select the sound you want to convert, and then click the Convert button.

To play a sound or movie that is stored in a multimedia field, double-click the field.

Caution   To save space, QuickTime movies and sounds are not stored in the database. Instead, AppleWorks merely records a reference to where they are located (your hard drive, for example). Pictures, on the other hand, are stored in the database. For this reason, when you give a copy of your database to someone else, you need to be sure to copy actual multimedia files, as well.

Record Info fields

As shown in the Options dialog box in Figure 5-15, Record Info fields enable you to automatically stamp each record with any of the following information:

✦ The date or time the record was created

✦ The date or time the record was last modified

✦ The name of the individual who created or last modified the record

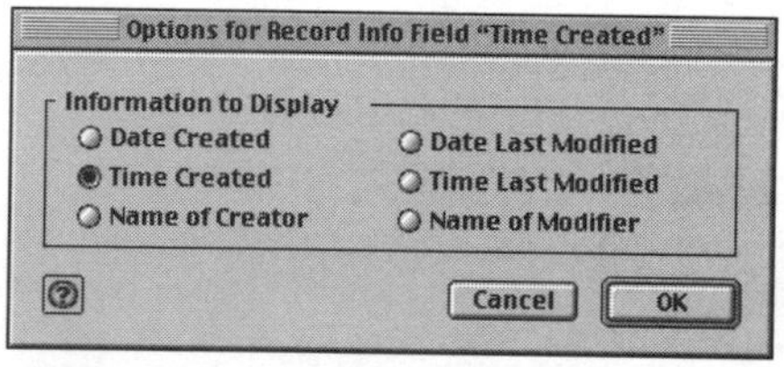

Figure 5-15: Options for a Record Info field

Data in a Record Info field is automatically inserted by AppleWorks when a record is first created (the Creation and Creator options) or edited (the Modified and Modifier options). Data in a Record Info field cannot be altered or deleted.

Calculation fields

The availability of calculation fields sets an AppleWorks database apart from a paper-based database or one created in a word processor. A calculation field is based on a formula you specify. You can use calculation fields to perform simple math, such as the computation of state sales tax (for example, `'Price'*.0825`), a product mark-up (for example, `'Cost'*1.5`), or the sum of several fields (for example, `'Qty1'+'Qty2'+'Qty3'`). Calculation fields also can incorporate any of the AppleWorks database functions described in Appendix B.

When a database contains a calculation field, a separate result is computed for each record in the database. For example, in a sales database, a calculation field named Total could sum the quarterly sales data for each salesperson, as in: `'Qtr1' + 'Qtr2' + 'Qtr3' + 'Qtr4'`.

STEPS: Defining a Calculation Field

1. Choose Layout ⇨ Define Fields (or press Shift+⌘+D). The Define Database Fields dialog box appears, as shown earlier in Figure 5-2.

2. Type a name for the calculation field in the Field Name text box and choose Calculation from the Field Type pop-up menu.

3. Click the Create button. The Enter Formula for Field dialog box appears, as shown in Figure 5-16.

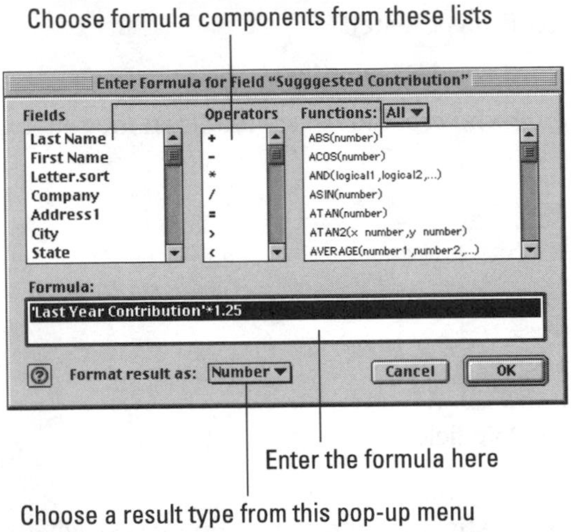

Choose formula components from these lists

Enter the formula here

Choose a result type from this pop-up menu

Figure 5-16: The Enter Formula for Field dialog box

4. Type the formula into the Formula text box. You can create formulas using any of the following methods:

   • Type directly into the text box.

   • Select fields, operators, and functions from the three scrolling list boxes. (Click an option to insert it into the formula at the text insertion point.)

   • Combine the first two approaches (type some parts of the formula and select others).

5. Choose a result type from the Format Result As pop-up menu. The choices are Text, Number, Date, and Time.

6. Click the OK button to accept the formula. AppleWorks notifies you if an error exists in the formula. Otherwise, you are returned to the Define Database Fields dialog box where you can define, modify, delete, or set options for additional fields.

> **Note**
>
> You cannot insert data into a calculation field. The program automatically fills it in based on the results of the formula for the field. Consequently, during data entry or editing, you cannot move into a calculation field by tabbing or by selecting it with the mouse. To show which fields in a database are user-modifiable and which fields are calculation fields, AppleWorks surrounds normal fields with a light gray bounding box while you're in Browse or List mode (for data entry and editing). Calculation fields have no bounding box.

Summary fields

Summary fields play an important role in AppleWorks databases. They can change a database from a static collection of data to something that really works for you — providing information that cannot be gleaned from a simple scan of the records.

A calculation field makes a computation within each record (adding the total of three invoice fields, for example). Summary fields, on the other hand, make calculations across a group of records — either a subset of records (for a sub-summary), or all visible records in the database (for a grand summary).

Every summary field is based on a formula. The built-in database functions in AppleWorks make it easy to calculate totals, averages, and counts to summarize groups of records or the entire database. Where a summary field is placed in the layout determines whether it summarizes each group of records (the field is in a sub-summary part) or the whole database (the field is in a leading or trailing grand summary part).

When you place a summary field in a sub-summary layout part, you have to specify a sort field for the summary field. The sort field serves to group the records. Suppose, for example, that you run a state-wide business and want to track total sales in different cities. You can create a summary field called Sales Total, define its formula as SUM('Sales'), and set the City field as the sort-by field for the summary field. Then, after you sort the database by city, the records for each city form a separate group (all customers from Chicago are listed together, for example).

At the end of every city group, the total sales for only that particular city are shown — above or below all the individual records for that city (the location of the summary figure depends on where you place it in the layout). You also can nest summary fields. For example, you might use two summary fields to look at total sales within each city or within each state.

When you place a summary field in a grand summary layout part, the summary field summarizes all the records in the database (or the found set of records, if you're viewing only a subset of the database). Two types of grand summaries exist: leading and trailing. A leading grand summary appears above the data it summarizes. A trailing grand summary appears below the data.

The Credit Card Charges database (described later in this chapter) provides additional examples of summary fields — in both sub-summary and grand summary layout parts.

Note

As with calculation fields, you cannot type information into a summary field. Instead, AppleWorks automatically calculates results for the field based on the criteria you set. To see the results for a summary field, you need to either be in Page View, in Browse or List mode and choose Window ➪ Slide Show, or you need to print the database. To ensure that summary fields in a sub-summary part contain the correct information, you need to sort the database by the sort field (the field specified in the Insert Part dialog box when the sub-summary part was created). To be safe, you should always sort the database just before printing a report.

Creating a summary field requires several steps: creating a new field to hold the summary information (similar to the way you create a calculation field), adding a summary part to the layout, placing the summary field in the summary part, and — if the field has been added to a sub-summary part — sorting the records.

STEPS: Creating a Summary Field

1. Choose Layout ⇨ Define Fields (or press Shift+⌘+D). The Define Database Fields dialog box appears.

2. Type a name for the summary field, choose Summary from the Field Type pop-up menu, and click the Create button. The Enter Formula for Field dialog box appears — the same dialog box that appears when you create a calculation field.

3. Type the formula for the summary field in the Formula text box. You can create formulas by typing them directly into the text box; by selecting fields, operators, and functions from the three scrolling list boxes (click an option to insert it into the formula at the text insertion point); or by combining the two approaches.

4. Choose a result type from the Format Result As pop-up menu. The choices are Text, Number, Date, and Time.

5. Click the OK button to accept the formula (AppleWorks notifies you if the formula contains an error), and then click the Done button to exit the dialog box.

6. From the lower portion of the Layout menu, choose the layout to which you want to add the summary field.

7. Choose Layout from the Layout menu (or press Shift+⌘+L).

   If an appropriate summary part already exists in the layout, you can skip to Step 11.

8. Choose Layout ⇨ Insert Part. The Insert Part dialog box shown in Figure 5-17 appears.

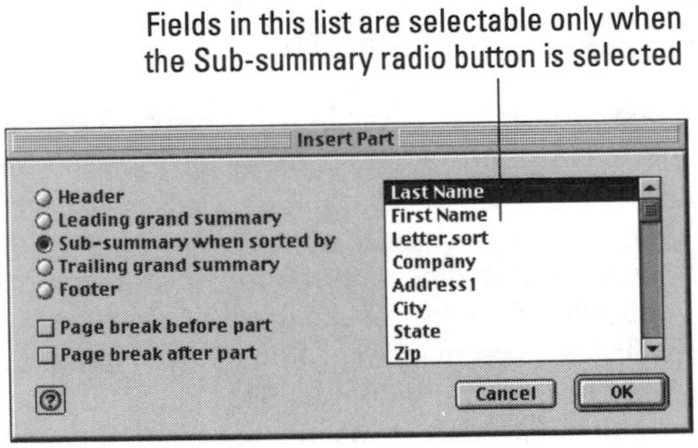

Fields in this list are selectable only when the Sub-summary radio button is selected

Figure 5-17: The Insert Part dialog box

9. Choose Leading grand summary, Sub-summary when sorted by, or Trailing grand summary. (Summary fields cannot be placed in header or footer parts.)

 You use the Leading and Trailing options to provide a summary for the entire database. In a sales database, for example, you can use either of these choices to total or average all sales for the database.

 If you choose the Sub-summary option, you have to choose a sort field from the list on the right side of the dialog box. When you sort the database by the contents of the selected field, the program groups the records by the sort field and calculates a subtotal of the found set for each group. If you want to examine sales on a state-by-state basis, for example, you can create a sales sub-summary sorted by state.

10. Click the OK button to leave the dialog box. (If you selected the sub-summary option, the program asks whether you want the sub-summary part to appear above or below each record group. Choose Above, Below, or Cancel.) The program adds the summary or sub-summary part to the appropriate location in the current layout.

11. Add the summary field to the layout by selecting Layout ⇨ Insert Field. The Insert Fields dialog box appears, as shown in Figure 5-18.

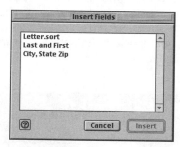

Figure 5-18: The Insert Fields dialog box

12. Select the summary field in the list box and click the OK button. (You also can double-click the summary field.) In either case, the field and its label appear in the current layout. Drag the summary field and its label into the summary or sub-summary part.

13. Switch to Browse mode by selecting Layout ⇨ Browse (or press Shift+⌘+B).

14. If the database is not in Page View, you won't see summary fields. If necessary, choose Window ⇨ Page View (or press Shift+⌘+P).

15. If the field is a sub-summary field (rather than a grand summary field), you need to sort the database by the field specified in the Insert Part dialog box. Choose Organize ⇨ Sort Records (or press ⌘+J). The Sort Records dialog box appears, as shown in Figure 5-19.

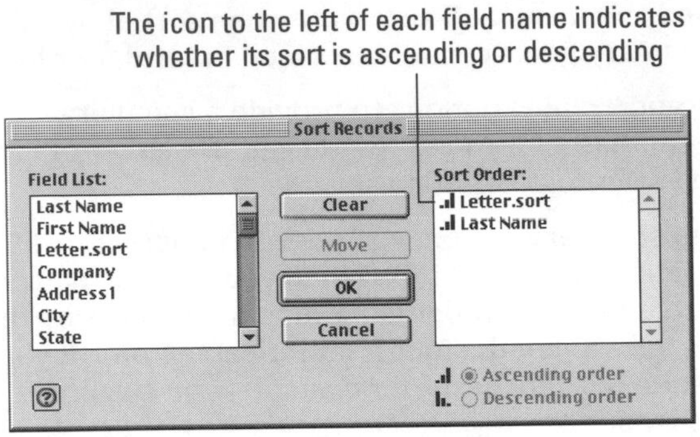

The icon to the left of each field name indicates
whether its sort is ascending or descending

Figure 5-19: The Sort Records dialog box

Click the Move and Clear buttons, as appropriate, to select the sort fields. You can sort each field in ascending or descending order, depending on which radio button you click. Click the OK button to perform the sort. The sub-summary information is displayed, grouped according to the contents of the sort-by field.

Tip

If you want to see all the summary data at one time or want to move it into another environment (such as the spreadsheet or word processor), change to Page View (Shift+⌘+P) and choose Edit ⇨ Copy Summaries. AppleWorks transfers the contents of summary fields to the clipboard, where the data is then available for pasting into other documents and applications.

The Fine Points of Calculation and Summary Formula Creation

You need to keep the following points in mind when creating formulas:

✦ Only calculation or summary fields can contain formulas. The program computes the results of a calculation field individually for each record in the database. Summary field formulas, on the other hand, summarize information across all or a subset of records. In a product catalog database, for example, you can use a summary field to calculate the total price of every product in the database.

✦ You need to surround field names with single quotation marks (for example, `'Sales'`) and text strings with double quotation marks (for example, `"Smithers"`).

✦ You can add extra space around operators (+ , – , and so on) you manually insert to improve readability when you are creating the formula, but AppleWorks removes extra spaces when it checks and saves the formula.

✦ When evaluating a formula, AppleWorks examines the elements from left to right. Different mathematical and logical operators (+, >, and so on) have different precedence, however. When you include more than one operator in a formula, the precedence of the operators determines the order in which AppleWorks performs the calculations.

You can add parentheses to a formula to improve readability or to change the precedence for performing a calculation. If, for example, A=2 and B=3 in a given record, the formula A+B*2 gives a result of 8. Because multiplication has a higher precedence than addition, AppleWorks evaluates the formula in this order: (B*2) equals 6, to which A is added, giving an answer of 8. By adding parentheses to the formula, as in (A+B)*2, you can change the precedence. Now the program adds A to B first (because elements that are enclosed in parentheses have a higher precedence than elements that are not enclosed in parentheses), giving a result of 5. Next, the program multiplies 5 by 2, giving an answer of 10.

Note: A common error is to have unbalanced parentheses in a formula. The number of left and right parentheses must always be equal.

Precedence levels in database formulas are as follows:

Operator	Meaning
%	Percentage (divide by 100)
^	Exponentiation (raise to a power, such as 'Length'^2)
+, -	Change sign (for example, -'Cost')
*,/	Multiplication, division
+, −	Addition, subtraction
&	Concatenate text strings ("Jim" & " " & "Uris" results in Jim Uris)
=,>,>=,<,<=,<>	Comparison operators (equal to, greater than, greater than or equal to, less than, less than or equal to, not equal to)

Selecting a function from the Function list inserts the function (as well as any appropriate arguments to the function) at the text insertion point. An example of a function is `AVERAGE(number1,number2,...)`, where number1, number2, and ... are the arguments to the function. The number1,number2, ... means you must replace the arguments with numbers or number fields, and you can have as many of them as you like.

Arguments are placeholders. You often replace them with field names. The fastest way to replace an argument with a field name is to double-click the argument to select it, and then click a field in the Fields list.

Continued

Continued

An ellipsis (. . .) in an argument list means the number of elements of the specified data type you use is up to you. In the Average example, a completed formula might read AVERAGE('Qtr1','Qtr2','Qtr3','Qtr4'), where each of the Qtr fields contains a sales figure or a numeric grade for the quarter.

Note: You also can replace any or all number arguments with real numbers by typing them directly into the formula, as in AVERAGE('Sales',25000).

Although most of the functions are available for use in both spreadsheet and database environments, database functions cannot refer to a range of fields. You must include every individual field name in a database formula, and separate the field names with commas. You can use this formula in a database:

    SUM('QTY1','QTY2','QTY3')

But you cannot use this formula:

    SUM('QTY1'..'QTY3')

A formula can consist entirely of a single function. You also can embed functions within a larger formula, as well as use one function to modify the result of another function. An example of the latter use is 'Due Date'-TRUNC(NOW()). This formula computes the number of days from the current date until the due date. The decimal portion of today's date and time (NOW()) is eliminated by the TRUNC function, and the result is subtracted from Due Date. (For additional information on using the AppleWorks database and spreadsheet functions, refer to Appendix B and AppleWorks Help.)

Modifying field definitions

After you define a field, you can change its type, name, or options. You also can change the formula for a calculation or summary field.

Tip
Changing a field definition from one data type to another sometimes has unfortunate effects, and you cannot use the Undo command to undo such changes. Saving the database before you alter a field definition is a smart idea. If the transformations don't work as you intended, you can simply close the database without saving the changes.

STEPS: Changing Field Types

1. Choose Layout ⇨ Define Fields (or press Shift+⌘+D). The Define Database Fields dialog box appears, as shown in Figure 5-20.

2. Select the field for which you want to set a new type. The field's name appears in the Field Name text box.

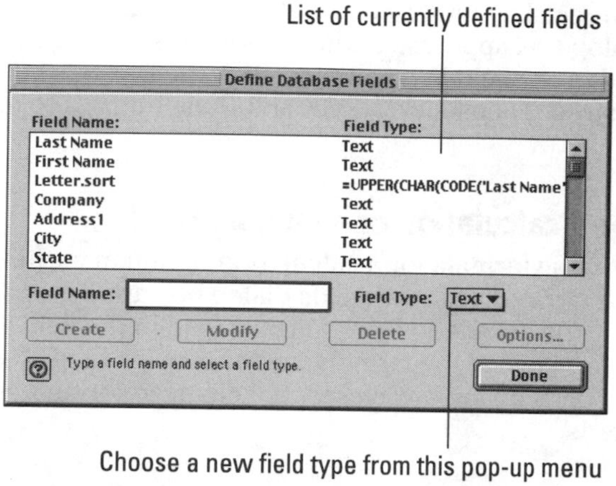

List of currently defined fields

Choose a new field type from this pop-up menu

Figure 5-20: The Define Database Fields dialog box

3. From the Field Type pop-up menu, choose the new type you want to assign to the field, and then click the Modify button.

   The following warning message box appears: "When modifying the field type, any data that cannot be converted will be lost."

4. Click the OK button to continue, or click the Cancel button to leave the original field type unchanged.

5. Click the Done button to return to the database.

Renaming fields

Once created, field names are not set in stone. To change a field name, choose Layout ➪ Define Fields, select the field name in the field list (in the Define Database Fields dialog box), type a new name, and then click the Modify button. If the field was referenced in any calculation or summary formulas, references to the old field name are automatically changed to reflect the new field name.

Tip   If you want to change a field name to make it more understandable when viewed in the layout, you can simply retype its field label in the layout. The field label has no effect on the actual field, so you can have a field called "tot sls" and label it Total Sales, for example.

Changing field options

As explained in "Field types," earlier in this chapter, most field types have options that can be set, such as setting a default value and choosing data validation measures. Field options can be altered at any time—not just when you first define the field.

To change field options, choose Layout ⇨ Define Fields (or press Shift+⌘+D). The Define Database Fields dialog box appears, as shown previously in Figure 5-20. Select the name of the field in the field list, and then click the Options button. Change the options, as desired. Then, click the OK and Done buttons to dismiss the dialog boxes.

Changing a formula for a calculation or summary field

You also can change an existing formula for a calculation or summary field. Choose Layout ⇨ Define Fields. The Define Database Fields dialog box appears, as shown earlier in Figure 5-20. Select the calculation or summary field in the field list, and then click the Modify button. Change the formula, and then click the OK and Done buttons. When the Define Fields dialog box closes, the changed formula is recalculated for all database records.

Deleting fields

Some fields outlive their usefulness, and you can easily delete them. However, deleting a field also deletes all information contained in that field from every record in the database.

STEPS: Deleting a Field

1. Choose Layout ⇨ Define Fields (or press Shift+⌘+D). The Define Database Fields dialog box appears, as shown earlier in Figure 5-20.

2. Highlight the field you want to delete.

3. Click the Delete button. A dialog box appears with the following question: "Permanently delete this field and ALL of its contents?"

4. Click the OK button to delete the field, or click the Cancel button if you change your mind.

5. Repeat Steps 2 through 4 for any additional fields you want to delete.

6. Click the Done button to exit the Define Database Fields dialog box.

> **Note**
>
> To remove a field from a layout, it is not necessary to use the preceding method. Instead, change to Layout mode, select the field, and then press the Delete key. Although the field is now gone from the layout, its data remains available for use in other layouts.

Adding new fields

You can add new fields to the database at any time. Choose Layout ⇨ Define Fields (or press Shift+⌘+D). The Define Database Fields dialog box appears, as shown earlier in Figure 5-20. Type the name of the new field in the Field Name text box, choose a type for the field from the Field Type pop-up menu, and then click the Create button. The new field is added to the list box.

You can continue to create new fields, or you can click the Done button to dismiss the Define Database Fields dialog box. When you are finished, AppleWorks adds the new fields and their labels to the database and to the currently selected layout. Edit the layout to accommodate or omit the new fields, as you prefer (as described in the next section, "Organizing Information with Layouts").

Organizing Information with Layouts

In many database programs, every database has a single screen on which you perform data entry, and you create reports in a separate part of the program. AppleWorks doesn't force you to make a distinction between data entry forms and reports. Instead, it uses the concept of layouts.

A layout is a particular arrangement of fields you've defined for a database. In each layout, you can use as many or as few of the defined fields as you like. There are no fields you must use. And you can have as many layouts for each database as you need. Using an address database as an example, you can create the layouts shown in Figure 5-21.

To create a new layout for a database, choose Layout ➪ New Layout, or choose the Layout pop-up menu in the Tool panel (see Figure 5-22). The New Layout dialog box appears, as shown in Figure 5-23.

Type a name for the new layout or accept the default name AppleWorks proposes (Layout #), click a radio button to choose one of the five layout formats, and then click the OK button. Depending on the type of layout chosen, AppleWorks creates it immediately or asks you to first choose fields and settings, as follows:

✦ If you choose a Labels layout, you can choose from any of the predefined label layouts in the pop-up menu, or you can create your own layout by selecting the Custom choice. (See "Working with mailing labels," later in this chapter, for a complete discussion of label options.)

✦ If you choose Standard, AppleWorks creates a default database layout that contains every field you defined for the database. The fields appear one above the other in a vertical list, ordered as shown in the Define Database Fields dialog box.

✦ If you choose Duplicate, AppleWorks creates an exact copy of the currently selected layout. This option is useful if you want to make a variation of the current layout — perhaps adding a few fields or rearranging the fields. You also can create a duplicate when you want to experiment with the layout. If the experiment doesn't work out, you can simply delete the layout.

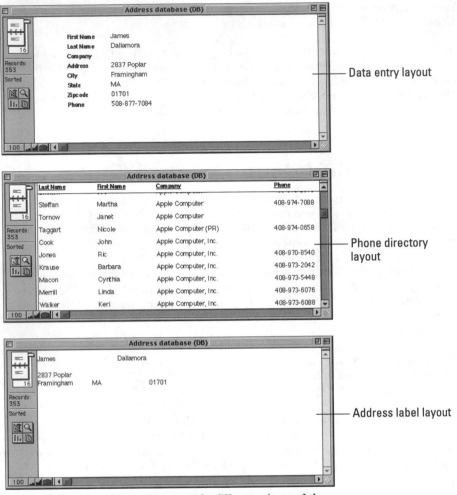

Data entry layout

Phone directory layout

Address label layout

Figure 5-21: Different layouts provide different views of the same data.

Layout pop-up

Search pop-up

Report pop-up

Sort pop-up

Figure 5-22: These four pop-up menus appear in the Tool panel in every mode except Layout mode. Use them to work with layouts, searches, sorting, and reports.

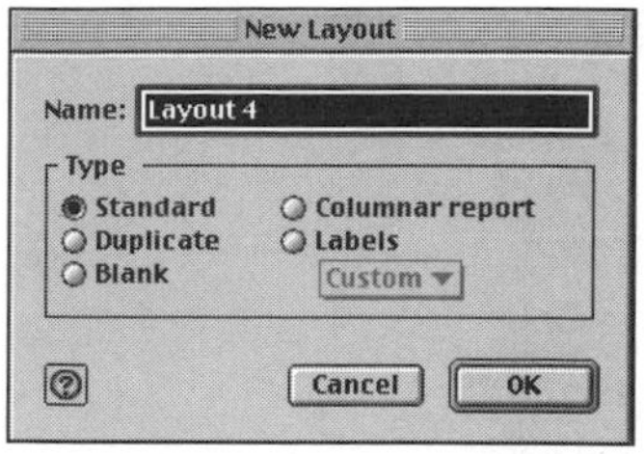

Figure 5-23: The New Layout dialog box

✦ If you choose Blank, AppleWorks creates a blank layout. You add all fields by choosing the Layout ➪ Insert Field command. (This option is useful when you want to design a layout from scratch.)

✦ If you choose Columnar Report or Labels (see the phone directory and label layouts in Figure 5-21, shown earlier, for examples), the Set Field Order dialog box appears, as shown in Figure 5-24.

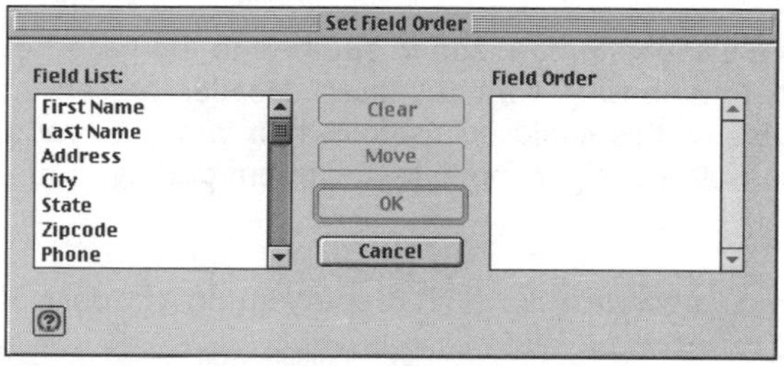

Figure 5-24: The Set Field Order dialog box

The purpose of the Set Field Order dialog box is to specify the fields you want to include in the new layout and to designate their order. Choose a field from the Field List (on the left side of the dialog box), and then click the Move button to add it to the Field Order list on the right. You can use as many or as few fields in the layout as you like.

Layout parts

As shown in Figure 5-25, every layout is composed of one or more labeled parts. The *body* is the main (and only mandatory) part of any layout, and it holds the bulk of the data fields — primarily those into which you enter data.

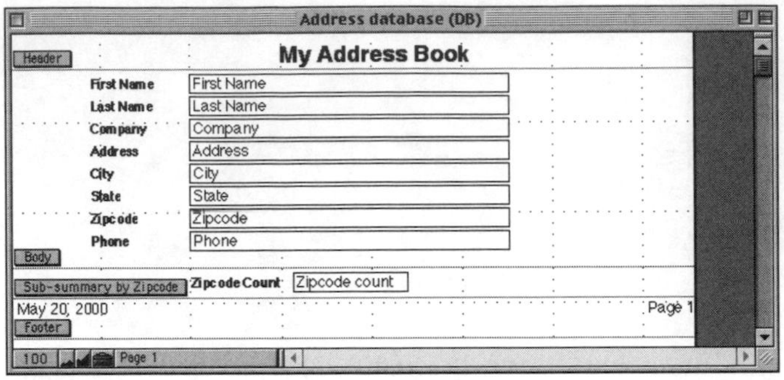

Figure 5-25: The parts of a database layout

All other parts of a layout are optional. The optional parts include:

✦ The *header* and *footer* (which hold information that repeats on every page of the layout)

Note The header and footer are separate from and in addition to the page header and footer you can create by choosing Format ➪ Insert Header or Format ➪ Insert Footer. While not necessary, this could be useful when you are producing the database report as a subset of a larger, multiple document package (for example, an annual report).

✦ Leading or trailing *grand summaries* (which display summary data at the beginning or end of a report)

✦ One or more *sub-summaries* (which display summary information for groups of records — all records from the same state, for example)

You can change the size of any part by simply clicking the dividing line for the part and dragging to make the part smaller or larger. As long as a part doesn't contain any fields or other objects, you can remove the part by dragging it up into the part immediately above it. (If the part does contain fields or other objects, you must delete the fields and objects or move them into other parts before you can remove the part.)

Note Although you can place any field in the body or in the header and footer, you can place only summary fields in a grand summary or sub-summary part.

Arranging fields in a layout

Initially, AppleWorks arranges fields in the layout according to the layout type you selected when you created the layout (Standard, Duplicate, Blank, Columnar Report, or Labels). Everything you place in a layout — fields, field labels, text, and graphics — is considered a draw object. As such, you can do anything with items in the layout that you can do with an object. Click any object and you see its handles. You can drag a handle to resize a field (making it larger or smaller); drag fields to different positions; change or delete field labels; align fields with each other or the grid (using the Align commands in the Arrange menu); change the font, size, or style of text in the field or the label; place graphics in the layout; and so on. (See Chapter 6 for additional information on working with objects.)

Adding graphics to a layout

Many layouts can be made more attractive by adding a graphic or two — a logo or some clip art, for example. To add a graphic to a layout, you can do any of the following:

✦ Choose File ➪ Insert and open a graphic file.

✦ Copy an image from the Scrapbook, an AppleWorks paint or draw document, or another graphics program, and then paste it into a layout.

✦ Drag the image from the Scrapbook, an AppleWorks paint or draw document, or another drag-and-drop-enabled graphics program into a layout.

✦ Select an image from AppleWorks Clippings.

✦ Use any of the standard AppleWorks draw tools to add lines, rectangles, and so on.

Field formatting

The default layouts create serviceable databases, but they aren't particularly attractive. The following instructions describe how to improve a layout by changing the text attributes for field contents and labels; by setting numeric, date, and time formats for fields; and by adding borders around fields.

To set text attributes for fields or labels, begin by choosing the layout in which you want to work from the lower portion of the Layout menu. Next, choose Layout ➪ Layout (or press Shift+⌘+L). Click or Shift+click to select the fields and field labels for which you want to set new text attributes. Choose options from the Font, Size, Style, Text Color, and Alignment submenus of the Format menu. The selected fields and labels change to match the new settings.

Tip
> By selecting a text, name, popup menu, radio buttons, checkbox, value list, or Record Info field, and then choosing Field Info from the Edit menu (or by double-clicking one of these field types), you can summon a special Text Style dialog box in which you can simultaneously set the font, size, and text color for the field (see Figure 5-26). Additional formatting options are also presented for some of these field types.

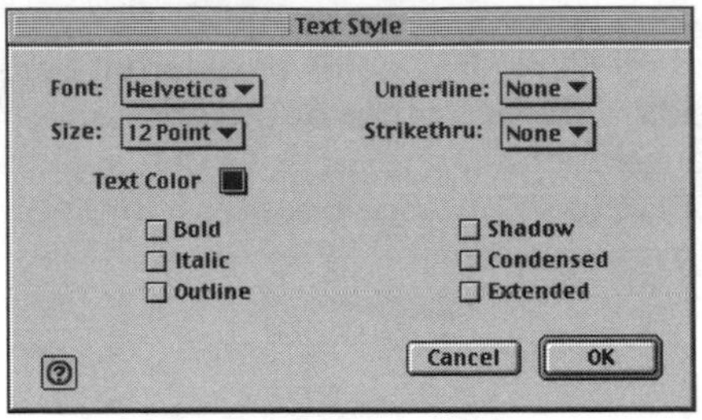

Figure 5-26: The Text Style dialog box

New Feature

In AppleWorks 6, you have some new options for underlining and strikethrough formatting. In previous versions, you had a simple strikethrough style and either single or double underlining. Now, you have a choice of multiple formats for both of these text styles in the Text Style dialog box.

Note

If a field will contain multiple lines of data (a Comments or Notes field, for example), you also can change the field's line spacing by choosing a setting from the Format ➪ Spacing submenu.

You can change the display format for number, date, time, and serial number fields, as well as for calculation and summary fields that produce a number, date, or time result. To set a number, date, or time format for a field, choose the layout in which you want to work from the lower portion of the Layout menu. Next, choose Layout ➪ Layout (or press Shift+⌘+L). Click to select a number, date, time, serial number, calculation, or summary field, and then choose Edit ➪ Field Info (or double-click the field). Depending on the field type, one of the three dialog boxes in Figure 5-27 appears. Choose options in the dialog box, and then click the OK button. AppleWorks formats the field according to your selections.

Date format options include slashes, abbreviations, and day names. Time format options include AM/PM, the display of seconds, and normal versus military (24-hour) time.

Note

The date formats that are offered will vary somewhat if you have chosen a separator other than a slash in your Date & Time control panel. AppleWorks takes its cue from your System settings.

The various number format options produce the following results:

✦ **General.** Displays numbers without commas, and displays the number of decimal places specified, or which are required by a calculation.

✦ **Currency.** Displays a dollar sign and two decimal places, as in $19.81. (You can change the display of commas, negative amounts, and number of decimal places with the Commas, Negatives, and Precision options.)

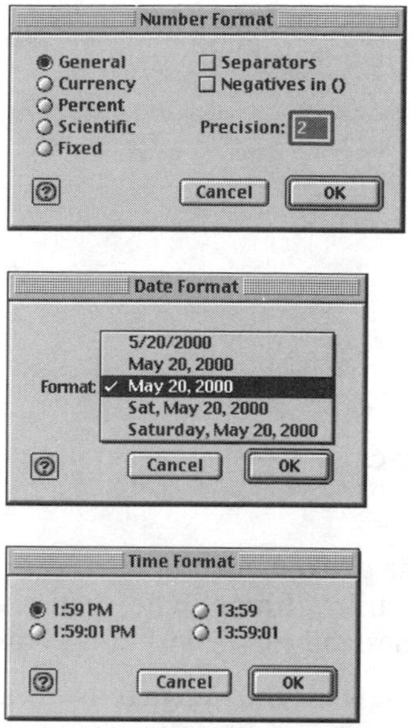

Figure 5-27: Use these dialog boxes to set the display format for number, date, and time fields.

✦ **Percent.** Adds a percent sign as a suffix, and then multiplies the field's contents by 100 (for example, 0.1235×100 is 12.35 percent). The Precision setting determines the number of decimal places.

✦ **Scientific.** Uses exponential notation, as in 1.245e+3 (for 1,245), which is useful for displaying very large or small numbers.

✦ **Fixed.** Rounds the results to the number of decimal places shown in the Precision box, as in 21.433 (for a precision setting of 3).

✦ **Commas.** Inserts commas every three digits, as in 18,221.

✦ **Negatives in ().** Surrounds numbers less than zero with parentheses, as in (24), instead of using a minus (–) sign.

✦ **Precision.** Sets the number of decimal places to be shown.

Because they are primarily used to store movies and graphics, the multimedia field options determine how images will be displayed onscreen. To set options for a multimedia field, change to Layout mode and either double-click the field or choose Edit ➪ Field Info. The Multimedia Field dialog box appears, as shown in Figure 5-28.

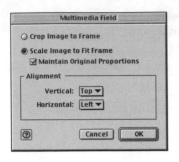

Figure 5-28: Set display options for a multimedia field in the Multimedia Field dialog box.

The following options—the first two are mutually exclusive—can be set in the Multimedia Field dialog box:

✦ Crop Image to Frame. When this radio button is clicked, images or movies will be trimmed as necessary to fit inside the current frame. When you play a cropped QuickTime movie, the movie is automatically scaled to fit the frame.

✦ Scale Image to Fit Frame. Click this option if you want the image to be as large as possible, given the size of the bounding frame. Images smaller than the frame will automatically be enlarged; larger images will be reduced in size to match the size of the frame. To maintain the horizontal and vertical proportions of the image, click the Maintain Original Proportions checkbox.

✦ Alignment. Choose options from the Vertical and Horizontal pop-up menus to specify how images should be aligned within the frame.

Note   You can change the size of any multimedia field by switching to Layout mode, selecting the field, and then dragging one of the four handles. To maintain the field's original proportions, press the Shift key as you drag. (Initially, all multimedia fields are one-inch square. A fairly typical QuickTime movie, however, is 2.22 by 1.67 inches (160 by 120 pixels) or some other proportionate fraction of 640 by 480 pixels. You might want to use 160 by 120 pixels as the starting dimensions for any field designed to hold movies.)

In Browse mode, AppleWorks database fields are surrounded by thin gray borders. If you like, however, you can change the appearance of any field border by following these steps.

STEPS: Creating Field Borders

1. From the lower portion of the Layout menu, choose the layout in which you want to work.

2. Choose Layout ➪ Layout (or press Shift+⌘+L).

3. Using the pointer tool, select the fields to which you want to add a border.

4. In the Accents windoid, set the pen pattern to opaque (the overlapping white and black square). You also can select a different pen color or line width. After you change to Browse mode (Shift+⌘+B), the fields appear with a border.

 Note You also can set the background for any field by switching to Layout mode, selecting the field, and then choosing options from the Fill Color, Pattern, Wallpaper, or Gradient panels of the Accents windoid.

Adding and deleting fields from a layout

As mentioned earlier, you can have as many or as few fields in each layout as you like. You can add fields to any layout that doesn't already display every defined field, and you can remove unnecessary fields.

STEPS: Adding a Field to a Layout

1. From the lower portion of the Layout Menu, choose the layout to which you want to add a field.

2. Choose Layout ⇨ Layout (or press Shift+⌘+L).

3. Choose Layout ⇨ Insert Field. The Insert Fields dialog box appears, as shown in Figure 5-29. Its list box contains only the defined fields that are not already in use in the current layout.

```
┌─────────────────────────────────┐
│         Insert Fields           │
│ ┌───────────────────────────┐▲  │
│ │ First Name                │   │
│ │ Last Name                 │   │
│ │ Address                   │   │
│ │ City                      │   │
│ │ State                     │   │
│ │ ZIP                       │   │
│ │ Birthdate                 │   │
│ │                           │▼  │
│ └───────────────────────────┘   │
│ ⦾        [ Cancel ] [ Insert ]  │
└─────────────────────────────────┘
```

Figure 5-29: The Insert Fields dialog box

4. Select a field, and then click the Insert button. AppleWorks inserts the field and its label into the layout.

5. If necessary, move and resize the field and its label.

To remove a field from a layout, begin by choosing the appropriate layout from the lower portion of the Layout menu. Change to Layout mode by choosing Layout ⇨ Layout (or pressing Shift+⌘+L). Use the pointer tool to select the fields you want to remove, and then press the Delete, Clear, or Del keys, or choose Edit ⇨ Clear or Edit ⇨ Cut (⌘+X). AppleWorks removes the selected fields from the layout.

Removing a field from a layout is not the same as deleting the field. Removing a field from a layout does nothing to the data in the field. The field can still appear in other layouts with its data intact. If you insert the field back into a layout, its data reappears. On the other hand, after you delete a field in the Define Database Fields dialog box (Shift+⌘+D), AppleWorks removes the field from all layouts and permanently deletes the field's data from the database (as soon as you click the Save button). Recreating that field will not bring back its data, only issuing a Revert command will restore the data (if you haven't yet saved your changes).

Deleting a layout

You can delete any layout you no longer want to use. Choose Layout ➪ Edit Layouts or choose Edit Layouts from the Layout pop-up menu in the Tool panel. The Edit Layouts dialog box appears, as shown in Figure 5-30. Choose the layout by name from the Current Layouts list, and then click the Delete button. A dialog box appears and asks "Permanently delete this layout?" Click the OK button to delete the layout, or click the Cancel button to leave it intact.

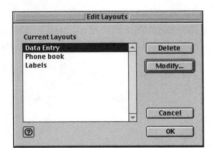

Figure 5-30: The Edit Layouts dialog box

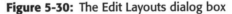

A layout can only be deleted if two or more layouts are currently defined. AppleWorks will not let you delete the only layout for a database. Thus, if you want to eliminate the original layout, you first have to create at least one additional layout.

Deleting a layout does not delete the fields you defined for the database or any of the data that appeared in the layout. It merely deletes one possible view or arrangement of the data. To delete a field, select the field in the Define Database Fields dialog box (Shift+⌘+D), and then click the Delete button. To delete data, remove it from the record or delete the record.

Layout modification options

You can assign a new name to a layout, specify the number of columns that appear in Page View, and close up the space between fields when printing (a particularly useful option for labels).

STEPS: Modifying a Layout

1. Choose Layout ⇨ Edit Layouts, or choose Edit Layouts from the Layout pop-up menu in the Tool panel. Select the name of the layout you want to change, and then click the Modify button. The Layout Info dialog box appears, as shown in Figure 5-31.

Layout Info

Name: [Labels]

Columns

Number of: [2]

● Across first
○ Down first

Slide

Select to remove space between objects when printing.

☑ Slide objects left
☑ Slide objects up

Cancel   OK

Figure 5-31: Use the Layout Info dialog box to choose optional settings for the current layout.

2. *Optional:* Enter a new name for the layout by typing it in the Name text box.

3. *Optional:* In the Columns section of the dialog box, set the number of columns to be displayed in reports and onscreen (in Page View only) by typing a number in the Number Of box. Then click a radio button (Across First or Down First) to indicate the order in which records will be displayed in the columns.

4. *Optional:* Use options in the Slide section of the dialog box to close up space between fields or lines when printing. This option is often useful for labels and addressing envelopes. The Slide Objects Left checkbox closes up space between objects on the same line. For example, the following address line

```
Bemidji   , MN 56601
```

would print as

```
Bemidji, MN 56601
```

The Slide Objects Up checkbox eliminates blank lines in records. For example, when you print an address label layout that contains fields arranged in five lines (1 – name; 2 – company name; 3 – first address line; 4 – second address line; and 5 – city, state, and Zip code), labels that contain only one address line or no company name print without blank lines in those positions.

Note   To make sure the objects slide left, the tops of the fields must be aligned.

5. Click the OK button to accept the layout options and return to the database.

Setting a tab order

You can use the Tab key to move from field to field when adding records. The Tab Order command enables you to set a new order for navigating between fields when you press the Tab key.

By default, AppleWorks sets the tab order for a database to match the order in which you created the fields. If you have altered the default layout by rearranging fields onscreen, the tab order might cause the cursor to jump willy-nilly all over the screen. You can change the tab order so that the cursor moves more efficiently.

STEPS: Setting a New Tab Order

1. From the lower portion of the Layout Menu, choose the layout for which you want to specify a new tab order.

2. Choose Layout ⇨ Layout (or press Shift+⌘+L).

3. Choose Layout ⇨ Tab Order. The Tab Order dialog box shown in Figure 5-32 appears. The current (or default) tab order is shown in the Tab Order list box on the right side of the dialog box.

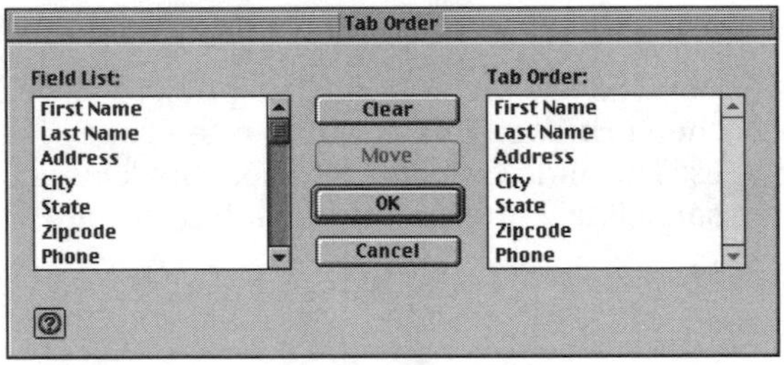

Figure 5-32: The Tab Order dialog box

4. To create a tab order from scratch, click the Clear button. AppleWorks clears the Tab Order list box.

5. To specify the new order, choose a field name from the Field List, and then click the Move button (or double-click the field name). The program adds the field to the lower portion of the Tab Order list. Continue selecting fields, in the order you prefer, until you have copied all the desired fields into the Tab Order list.

> **Tip**
>
> You also can Shift+click to choose several contiguous field names simultaneously, or ⌘+click to choose several noncontiguous field names.

The tab order for a database layout in List mode matches the order in which the columns are displayed. To set the tab order for a database in List mode, choose Layout ⇨ List (or press Shift+⌘+I), and then drag columns (by selecting their headings) to new positions in the layout.

Tip

If you don't want users to be able to tab into some fields, leave those fields out of the list. When a user is in Browse mode, a press of the Tab key skips right over the fields. Note, however, that users can still enter data in those fields by clicking in the field (unless, of course, the fields are calculation, summary, or Record Info fields). Note, too, that settings in the Tab Order dialog box have no effect on a database when it is in List mode.

Viewing, Adding, and Editing Data in Browse and List Modes

After you have designed a database and created your layouts, you will spend most of your time in Browse and List modes — adding, editing, and viewing the data.

Note

List mode displays the database in a spreadsheet-like grid, where each row is a record and each column is a field. Unlike a normal layout that is viewed in Browse mode — which only displays the fields you have placed in that layout — List mode presents every field that has been defined for the database. Regardless of the layout you were previously viewing, when you change to List mode, the arrangement of data is always the same.

Any database can be viewed in List mode by choosing Layout ⇨ List or by pressing Shift+⌘+I. You learn about List mode later in this chapter.

Browse mode

Whether you need to add and edit data, or you just want to flip through records, you can use Browse mode (choose Layout ⇨ Browse or press Shift+⌘+B). The advantage of using Browse mode — as opposed to List mode — is that you can display your data in any layout you've designed for a database, meaning that you can restrict the set of fields to only those you need at the moment. To select a layout in which to work, choose its name from the lower portion of the Layout menu.

Viewing records

When you are working on and viewing records in Browse mode, records can be displayed in any of three ways:

✦ Continuous scrolling list (choose Layout ⇨ Show Multiple)

✦ One record per screen (remove the checkmark from the Layout menu's Show Multiple command)

✦ Only as many records as can fit on the current page size as defined in the Page Setup dialog box (choose Window ⇨ Page View)

Note

Viewing records in Page View shows exactly how the records will appear when they are printed. Page View is similar to choosing the Print Preview command in many programs.

Adding and deleting records

To create a new record for the current database you must be in Browse or List mode. Choose Edit ➪ New Record (or press ⌘+R). The new record appears with the text insertion point in the first field.

To delete a record, select the record (in Browse or List mode) by clicking anywhere in the record other than inside a field. (To show that the record is selected, Apple-Works highlights the entire record.) Choose Delete Record, Cut, or Clear from the Edit menu, or press the Clear key. AppleWorks then removes the record from the database.

Entering and editing data

When a new record appears onscreen in Browse mode, the cursor automatically appears in the first field (or in the field which you set as first with the Tab Order command). Complete the field, and then press the Tab key to move to the next field. You also can move directly to any field by clicking it with the mouse. Note, however, that you cannot click in or tab to a field that does not allow user input — namely calculation, summary, and Record Info fields.

You edit data in exactly the same manner as in other text-oriented environments. After entering Browse mode (Shift+⌘+B) and tabbing or clicking into a field, you use normal editing techniques to add to, delete from, or otherwise alter the information in any field.

Tip

If a record is substantially similar to an existing record, you can save typing time by creating a duplicate of the existing record and then making the necessary editing changes to the duplicate. To create a duplicate record, select the record and then choose Edit ➪ Duplicate Record (or press ⌘+D).

Navigating among records

You can move among the database records in Browse mode in a number of ways. The following options are available:

✦ To move to the next or preceding record, click the lower or upper page of the book icon (see Figure 5-33). In normal view, this action moves to the next or previous record. In Page View, it merely scrolls the records in the appropriate direction.

✦ To move to the next or previous record while leaving the cursor in the same field, press ⌘+Return or Shift+⌘+Return, respectively.

Click to move to the next record

Click to move to the previous record

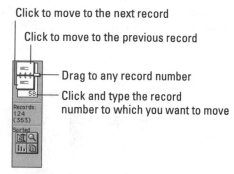

Drag to any record number

Click and type the record
number to which you want to move

Figure 5-33: The book icon

✦ To move to a specific record (by number), drag the tab on the right side of the book icon until you see the record number, or choose Organize ➪ Go to Record (or press ⌘+G). You also can click once to select the record number at the lower edge of the book icon, type a record number, and press the Return or Enter keys.

✦ To move up or down through the records, use the scroll bar at the right side of the database window, or press the Page Up or Page Down keys (if you are in Page View).

✦ To move to a specific page in the database, double-click the page number indicator at the lower portion of the database window (you must be in Page View). The Go to Page dialog box appears. Type a page number and click the OK button.

✦ To move to the beginning or end of the database, press the Home or End keys (if you are in Page View), or drag the tab on the right side of the book icon until you reach the beginning or the end.

Note

Below the current record number is a display area that tells how many records are in the database. If the found set (visible records) is smaller than All Available, the number of records in the found set is displayed and the total number of records is shown in parentheses.

List mode

Everything you can do in Browse mode also can be done in List mode, such as adding and editing data, adding and deleting records, and so on. Working in List mode is a lot like using a spreadsheet: each row represents a single record, and each column represents a single field. In normal view, fields are displayed in a continuous list that you can scroll to the right and left. In Page View (choose Page View from the Window menu), columns are separated by page breaks.

As the example in Figure 5-34 shows, all field types are normally displayed in List mode. You can still choose options from pop-up menu fields and value list fields, enable checkbox fields, and play movies in multimedia fields.

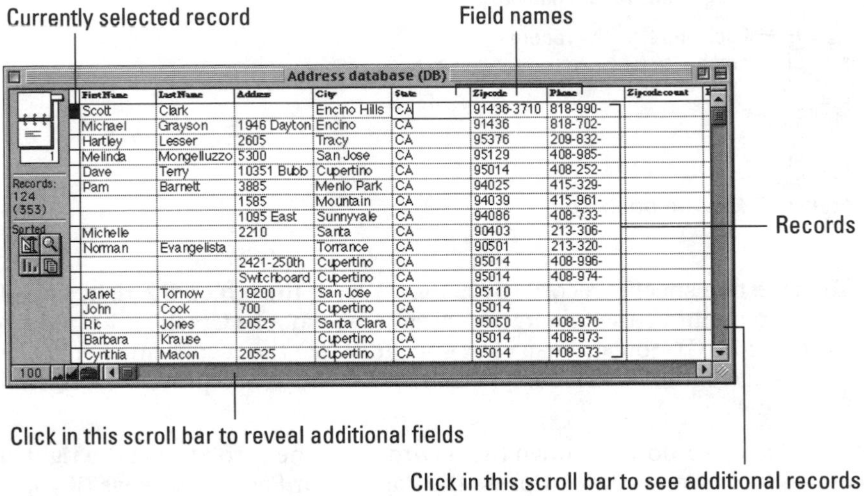

Currently selected record   Field names

Records

Click in this scroll bar to reveal additional fields

Click in this scroll bar to see additional records

Figure 5-34: A database displayed in List mode

Here are a few other things you can do in List mode:

✦ **Change column widths and record heights.** To change the width of a column, move the mouse pointer into the column label area until it is over the right edge of the column whose width you want to change. The mouse pointer changes to a tall double-arrow. Click and drag to change the column's width.

To change the height of any record, move the mouse pointer into the area to the left of the first field for the record. The pointer changes to a tall double-arrow. When the mouse pointer is over the bottom edge of the record, click and drag to change the height of the record.

✦ **Move columns.** To move a column to a new position, move the mouse pointer into the area just above the column. The pointer changes to a short double-arrow. Click and then drag the column to a new position. Release the mouse button to complete the move.

✦ **Change the format of an entire column.** Double-click the column name. Depending on the field type of the column, the Text Style, Number Format, Date Format, Time Format, or Multimedia Field dialog box appears. Set options and click the OK button. Alternatively, for any field type other than multimedia, you can select the column and then choose font, alignment, and spacing options from the Format menu's submenus.

You might occasionally find it necessary to select individual or multiple rows or columns. To select an individual row or column, click in the area to the left of the row, or click in the column label.

To select several records (to format, hide, or delete them all at the same time, for example), select one record, and then Shift+click to select the others. To select multiple, noncontiguous records, hold down the ⌘ key as you click in each record. To select multiple columns (fields), Shift+click as you select the columns. (You cannot select noncontiguous columns.)

Finding and Selecting Records

Flipping through a database one record at a time is the hard way to find specific information. AppleWorks has two different commands you can use to find and select records, based on criteria you supply. You use the Find command to restrict displayed records to a particular subset (the program temporarily hides all other records). For example, you might want to look only at records in which State equals Ohio. The Match Records command leaves all records visible and simply selects (highlights) those records that match the criteria.

> **Note**   AppleWorks enables you to save search criteria so you can easily execute the search again whenever you like. Saved searches also can be used to create reports in the database report generator. Instructions for saving and reusing search criteria are presented later in this chapter.

Using the Find command

To search for records, you type search criteria on a blank copy of a record that appears when you issue the Find command. To find an exact or partial match, you simply type the text or number you want to search for in the appropriate field. To find all address records for people whose last name contains the string "Sch," for example, you type **Sch** in the Last Name field. In this type of search, the program considers a record a match if it contains the string anywhere within the field, not just at the beginning of the field.

You also can use logical operators to specify search criteria, as described in Table 5-1.

> **Tip**   To search for a blank database field, type only an equal (=) sign in a field.

Table 5-1
Logical Search Operators

Operator	Meaning	Examples
=	Find records that exactly match the contents of this field.	(=435; =18 Apple Street)
<	Find records that are numerically or alphabetically less than this value.	(<100; <S)
>	Find records that are numerically or alphabetically greater than this value.	(>180; >Bob)
≤ (Option+<)	Find records that are numerically or alphabetically less than or equal to this value.	(≤2000; ≤D)
≥ (Option+>)	Find records that are numerically or alphabetically greater than or equal to this value.	(≥4/19/93; ≥3000)
<> or ≠ (Option+=)	Find records that are not equal to this value.	(<>10; ≠CA; ≠11:15)

STEPS: Finding Records

1. From the lower portion of the Layout Menu, choose the layout you want to use as a search template. (Be sure the fields you intend to use as criteria appear in the layout.)

2. Choose the Layout ➪ Find command (or press Shift+⌘+F). A screen with a blank record appears, as shown in Figure 5-35.

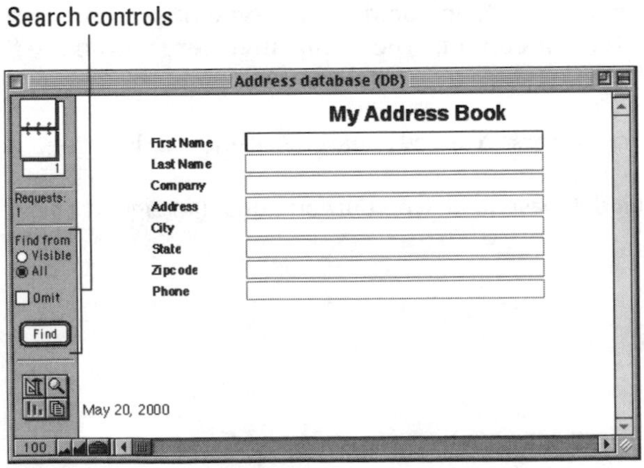

Search controls

Figure 5-35: You type search criteria into fields in a blank record.

3. Type the search criteria into the appropriate fields.

4. *Optional:* If you want to find all records that do *not* match the search criteria, click the Omit checkbox.

5. Click the All radio button to search the entire database, or click the Visible radio button to search only visible records; that is, those that are not currently hidden. AppleWorks conducts the search. It displays matching records and hides all others.

> **Note** After you're through examining the records that match the criteria, you can make the entire database visible again by choosing Organize ⇨ Show All Records (Shift+⌘+A).

When you specify multiple criteria in a single Find request, you are conducting an AND search. In an AND search, AppleWorks finds only records that satisfy all the criteria. For example, typing Santa Clara for the city and CA for the state identifies only the address records for people who come from Santa Clara, California. It does not find records for people from other California cities or from cities named Santa Clara in other states.

Sometimes, you might want to conduct an OR search — searches in which the program finds a record if the record matches any one of several criteria. To conduct this type of search, you have to issue multiple Find requests.

STEPS: Conducting an OR Search

1. From the lower portion of the Layout Menu, choose the layout you want to use as a search template. (Be sure the fields you intend to use as criteria appear in the layout.)

2. Choose Layout ⇨ Find (or press Shift+⌘+F). A screen with a blank record appears. (Note that even if you were previously in List mode, the Find screen is displayed as it would be in Browse mode for that layout.)

3. Type a set of search criteria in the record.

4. Before clicking the All or Visible radio buttons, choose Edit ⇨ New Request (or press ⌘+R). Another blank record appears.

5. Type the next set of search criteria in the new record.

6. Repeat Steps 4 and 5 for each additional set of criteria you want to specify.

7. Click the All radio button to search the entire database, or click the Visible radio button to search only the visible records; that is, those that are not currently hidden.

8. Click the Find button to execute the search. Records that satisfy any of the search requests are displayed and all others are hidden.

Tip You can issue a Find command from any layout as long as the fields on which you want to base the search are present. Some layouts, however, are easier to search from than others. A layout that is designed to print mailing labels, for example, makes the task more difficult because the fields are not labeled. Change to a better layout by selecting a layout from the lower portion of the Layout menu before initiating the search. After the program finds the records, you can change back to the original layout to view or print the records.

Creating a named search

Although some Find requests are issued only once (when you are searching for a particular record, for example), it's not uncommon to discover you are manually recreating many of the same Find requests over and over. Whether you are selecting important subsets of data to be used in a report or you simply want to look at all sales in a particular region of the country, you can save these Find requests — enabling you to instantly execute them whenever you want.

STEPS: Saving a Search Request

1. Choose New Search from the Search pop-up menu (the magnifying glass) in the Tool panel. The dialog box shown in Figure 5-36 appears.

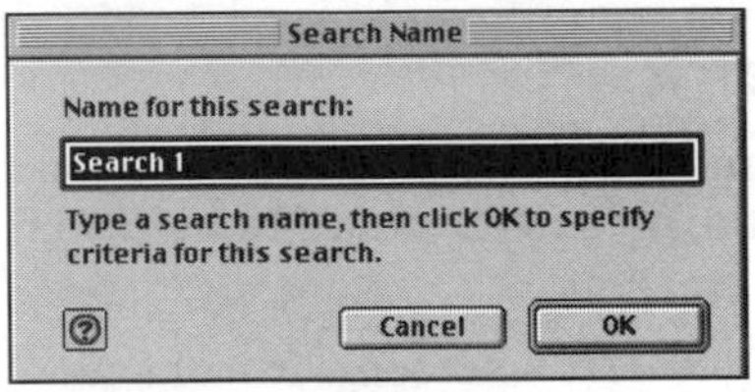

Search Name
Name for this search:
Search 1
Type a search name, then click OK to specify criteria for this search.

Figure 5-36: This dialog box appears when you create a new search.

2. Enter a descriptive name for the search, and then click the OK button to continue. A Find request form appears.

3. Type the search criteria.

4. If you need to use additional Find requests (creating an OR request, as previously), choose Edit ➪ New Request (⌘+R) and type the search criteria.

5. Click the Store button in the Tool panel, or press the Enter key. The search name is appended to the Search pop-up menu.

After one or more named searches has been created, you must follow special procedures for using and modifying those searches:

✦ To execute a named search, choose its name from the Search pop-up menu.

✦ To rename a named search, choose Edit Searches from the Search pop-up menu, choose the named search from the Edit Searches dialog box (shown in Figure 5-37), click the Modify button, type a new name for the search, and then click the OK button twice to dismiss the two dialog boxes.

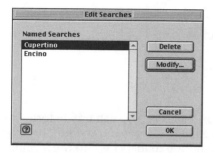

Figure 5-37: The Edit Searches dialog box

✦ To delete a named search, choose Edit Searches from the Search pop-up menu, choose the search you want to delete from the Edit Searches dialog box (shown in Figure 5-37), click the Delete button, and then click the OK button.

✦ To edit the Find criteria associated with a named search, change to Find mode (choose Layout ⇨ Find or press Shift+⌘+F), choose the named search from the Search pop-up menu, modify the search criteria, and then click the Store button (or press the Enter or Return key).

Tip   There's one general type of named search you might want to add to every database you make — you could call it the All search. Instead of trying to remember the command for Show All Records, just create a named search called All or All Records that finds all records in the database. In the Find request form, leave all the fields blank and click the Find from All radio button in the Tool panel.

Using the Match Records command

The Find command is intended for simple searches. If you want to perform a more complex search, you can use the Match Records feature. A Match Records search selects (highlights) all records that meet the criteria, but it leaves the other records onscreen. Because the records are selected (highlighted), using Match Records is an ideal way to identify and delete records you no longer need.

STEPS: Selecting Match Records

1. Choose Organize ⇨ Match Records (or press ⌘+M). The Enter Match Records Condition dialog box appears, as shown in Figure 5-38. It is identical to the dialog box you use to define a formula for a calculation field or a summary field.

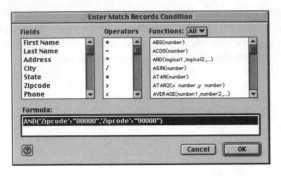

Figure 5-38: Use this dialog box to specify the search conditions formula.

2. Enter the match formula in the Formula box. You can create formulas by typing them into the box; by selecting fields, operators, and functions from the three scrolling list boxes (click an option to insert it into the formula at the text insertion point); or by combining the two approaches. Field names must be enclosed in single quotation marks (') and text strings in double quotation marks ("). The formula shown in Figure 5-38 instructs AppleWorks to select all records with Zip codes that are greater than 80000 and less than 90000.

3. Click the OK button. AppleWorks evaluates the formula. If it finds an error, it displays the message "Bad formula." Otherwise, it highlights the records that match the formula.

After using the Match Records command to select a set of records, you can use two additional commands from the Organize menu to help you focus your attention on the new record subset: Hide Selected (⌘+([left parenthesis]) and Hide Unselected (⌘+) [right parenthesis]). Hide Unselected has the same effect as the normal Find command. It hides all records that do not match the Match Records formula; that is, the ones that were not selected. Hide Selected has the same effect as a Find command with the Omit checkbox checked—it displays only those records that were not selected.

You also can use the Hide Selected and Hide Unselected commands after you manually select records. To select a single record, click anywhere in the record except in a field. To select multiple, contiguous records, hold down the Shift key as you select the records. To select noncontiguous records, hold down the ⌘ key as you select the records.

Perhaps the most important reason for using the Match Records command is you want to do something to all members of the selected (or unselected) group. You can view them in context in Browse or List mode (viewing the records of all employees who have not had raises in the last two years, for example).

You also can use Match Records to help purge the database of unwanted records. For instance, you might want to eliminate all invoice records that are more than three years old. After using Match Records to identify the correct records, choose Edit ⇨ Delete Record.

In previous versions of AppleWorks and ClarisWorks 4.0 (and earlier versions), deleting a record or group of records was difficult to reverse. As long as you had not saved the changes, the best you could do was to restore the database to its state from the last time it was saved by choosing File ⇨ Revert or by closing the database without saving the changes. In AppleWorks 5 and 6, however, after deleting one or more records, the Undo command now reads Undo Clear. You can choose this command to restore the deleted records.

Changing the display order of records

You can change the order in which records are displayed by sorting them by the contents of one or several fields. You can do an ascending (A to Z) or descending (Z to A) sort for each sort field. AppleWorks sorts the database once for each sort field, using the order in which you selected the sort fields. Sorting changes the order of records in the database for all layouts, not just for the one currently displayed.

STEPS: Sorting Records

1. Choose Organize ⇨ Sort Records (or press ⌘+J). The Sort Records dialog box appears, as shown in Figure 5-39. (If you have previously sorted the database, the program displays the most recent sort instructions.)

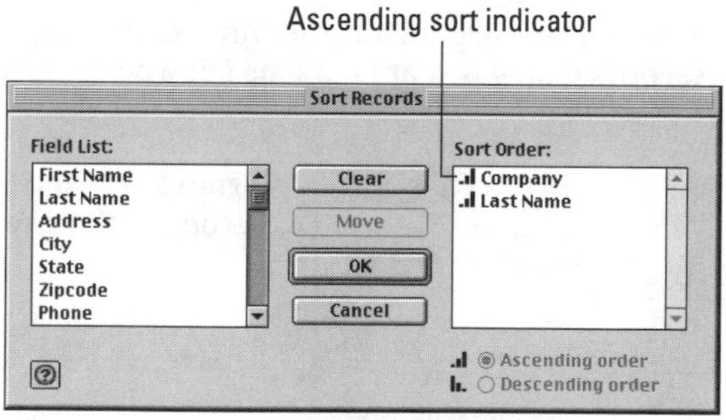

Figure 5-39: The Sort Records dialog box

2. Choose the first sort field from the list on the left. To add the field to the Sort Order list, click the Move button, or simply double-click the field name in the Field List. AppleWorks adds the field to the Sort Order list on the right.

If you make a mistake (choosing fields in the wrong order, for example), you can start over by clicking the Clear button, or you can remove individual fields by selecting them in the Sort Order list and then clicking the Move button.

3. To specify an ascending or descending sort for each chosen field, select it in the Sort Order list and then click the Ascending Order or Descending Order radio button.

    Alternatively, you can specify an ascending or descending order sort by clicking the appropriate radio button *before* moving the field into the Sort Order list.

4. Choose additional sort fields by repeating Steps 2 and 3, as required.

5. Click the OK button to execute the sort instructions. The program displays the records in the new order.

Note   If a layout has sub-summary fields, you have to sort the database by the designated sort field if you want the summary information to be displayed. For example, if you have created a sub-summary when sorted by last name, you must sort by last name. (See "Summary fields," earlier in this chapter, for more information.)

You also can manually reorganize records using drag-and-drop. Simply select the records you want to move and drag them to the desired position in the database. You can accomplish this maneuver in List mode or in Browse mode (when Show Multiple is checked in the Layout menu).

You can save sort criteria so you can easily execute the same sort whenever you like. Named (saved) sorts also can be used to create reports in the report generator (discussed in "Creating and using named reports," later in this chapter).

STEPS: Creating Named Sorts

1. Choose New Sort from the Sort pop-up menu (the three rising bars) in the Tool panel. The Sort Records dialog box appears, as shown in Figure 5-40.

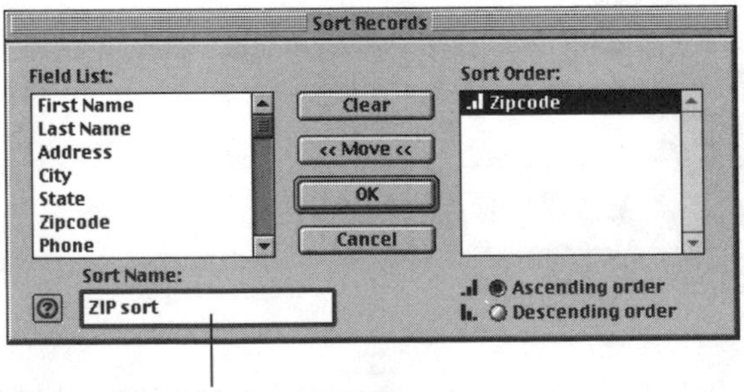

Figure 5-40: The Sort Records dialog box

The name of the sort appears and can be changed in this text-edit box

2. Type a descriptive name for the sort.

3. Select the sort fields and set ascending or descending order for each one.

4. Click the OK button. The sort name is appended to the Sort pop-up menu.

After one or more named sorts has been created, you must follow special procedures for using and modifying the sorts:

✦ To execute a named sort, choose its name from the Sort pop-up menu.

✦ To rename or edit a named sort, choose Edit Sorts from the Sort pop-up menu, choose the sort from the Edit Sorts dialog box, and then click the Modify button. The Sort Records dialog box appears (shown earlier in Figure 5-40). Type a new name for the sort and/or modify the sort instructions, and then click the OK button twice to dismiss the two dialog boxes.

✦ To delete a named sort, choose Edit Sorts from the Sort pop-up menu, select the name of the sort you want to eliminate from the Edit Sorts dialog box, click the Delete button, and then click the OK button.

Creating Reports

One of the main reasons for building a database is the ease with which you can create custom reports and mailing labels. Although you can print any layout, creating special layouts for reports often makes more sense, especially if you design layouts that show the particular fields and summary information you require, organized in a manner that makes sense for a report.

To make it easy to recreate a given report, you can select report elements — including sort instructions, record selection criteria, and the appropriate layout — and save them as a custom report. Details are provided later in this chapter.

Adding headers and footers

You can add a header and a footer to a database layout. A header or footer appears in every report page and can be used to show a title or page numbers, for example. To create a header or footer, switch to the appropriate layout, and then change to Layout mode. Choose Layout ➪ Insert Part. The Insert Part dialog box appears. Click the Header or Footer radio button, and then click the OK button. A header or footer area is inserted per your request at the top (header) or bottom (footer) of the current layout.

Tip   You can actually create two headers and two footers for your database, if you are so inclined. AppleWorks lets you create a Header or Footer while in Browse or List mode as part of the document description. These page elements appear above (header) and below (footer) the layout's header and footer.

You can add graphics or text in the header or footer area. Whatever you insert will appear in that position at the top or bottom of every page. To see how the header or footer will look when it is printed, change to Browse mode (Shift+⌘+B) and choose Window ⇨ Page View (Shift+⌘+P).

Note

Headers and footers frequently include a report date and page numbers. To add automatic page numbering (so page numbers increment by one for each new page) and date- or time-stamping, select the appropriate layout, change to Layout mode, select the text tool, click the position in the header or footer where you want to place the element, and then choose Insert Page #, Insert Date (either Fixed or Auto-updating), or Insert Time (either Fixed or Auto-updating) from the Edit menu. You should note, however, that every time you open the database, the date and time change to match the current date and time (if you choose Auto-updating). If you want to insert the current date or time and make sure it does not change, use the Fixed choice from the submenu.

Calculating summary and sub-summary information

By creating summary fields and adding them to a layout, you can calculate statistics that span the entire database or that summarize data based on record groupings (generating subtotals for each type of household expense, for example). Summary information can come at the beginning or end of a report or be displayed at the break between each group of records. You aren't restricted to just totals. You can use any formula you like, as well as take advantage of the dozens of database functions AppleWorks offers. For instructions on adding summary and sub-summary fields to a database, see "Summary fields," earlier in this chapter.

Creating and using named reports

Using the Report pop-up menu in the Tool panel, you can save reporting options and later use them to quickly produce complex reports. To create a named report, choose New Report from the Report pop-up menu (the icon displaying overlapping sheets of paper) in the Tool panel. The New Report dialog box appears, as shown in Figure 5-41.

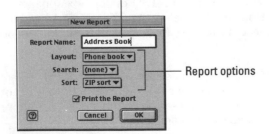

Enter a name to the report here

Report options

Figure 5-41: The New Report dialog box

As you can see in Figure 5-41, creating a report consists of the following tasks:

✦ Naming the report (in the Report Name text box)

✦ Choosing a layout for the report, search criteria, and sort instructions

✦ Deciding whether the report should automatically be printed

Layout choices are restricted to the names of existing layouts, List mode, and None. Search and sort criteria are limited to None or existing named searches and sorts that have been saved for the database. After making your choices, click the OK button. The name of the new report is added to the Report pop-up menu for the database.

To produce a named report, choose its name from the Report pop-up menu in the Tool panel. The database instantly changes to the selected layout and executes the designated search and sort instructions, if any. If you also clicked the Print the Report checkbox in the New Report dialog box, a standard Print dialog box appears. Turn your printer on (if necessary), change options in the Print dialog box (if necessary), and then click the Print button.

To modify any of the elements of the report, choose Edit Reports from the Report pop-up menu, select the name of the report in the Named Reports dialog box that appears, click the Modify button, make the changes, and then click the OK button twice to dismiss the dialog boxes.

To delete a report, choose Edit Reports from the Report pop-up menu, select the name of the report in the Named Reports dialog box that appears, click Delete, and then click the OK button.

Working with mailing labels

Although you can design your own layouts for printing labels, AppleWorks comes with more than 100 predefined layouts for popular Avery labels (actually 101 layouts). If you don't find a layout to match the size of labels you use, you can easily create a custom layout.

STEPS: Using a Predefined Label Layout

1. Choose Layout ➪ New Layout or New Layout from the Layout pop-up menu in the Tool panel. The New Layout dialog box appears.

2. Click the Labels radio button and then click its pop-up menu. A list of the supported label formats pops up. (If you aren't using an Avery label, measure your label and match it to the equivalent Avery label format, or create a custom label layout by following the instructions in "Steps: Creating a Custom Label Layout," later in this chapter.)

3. Choose a label format and click the OK button. The Set Field Order dialog box appears, as shown in Figure 5-42.

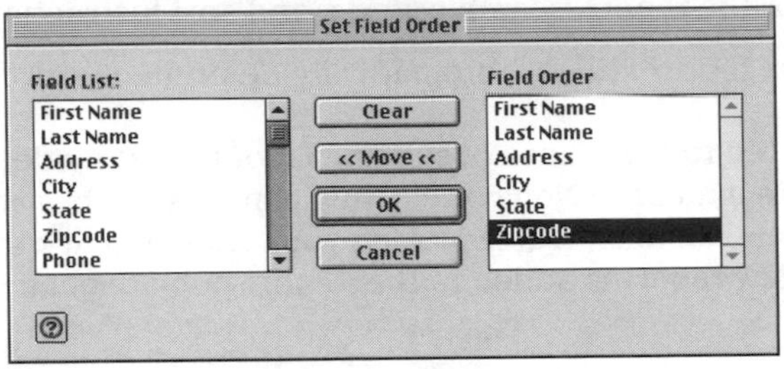

Figure 5-42: The Set Field Order dialog box

4. Select fields in the order in which you want them to appear on the labels, and then click the Move button to transfer each field to the Field Order list box.

5. Click the OK button. The label layout appears.

   In Step 1, if you chose New Layout from the Layout pop-up menu rather than choosing this command from the Layout menu, you will now be in Browse mode. Change to Layout mode by choosing Layout ➪ Layout.

6. Resize and move the fields to correspond with the way they should appear on the labels. Figure 5-43 shows a typical layout after editing.

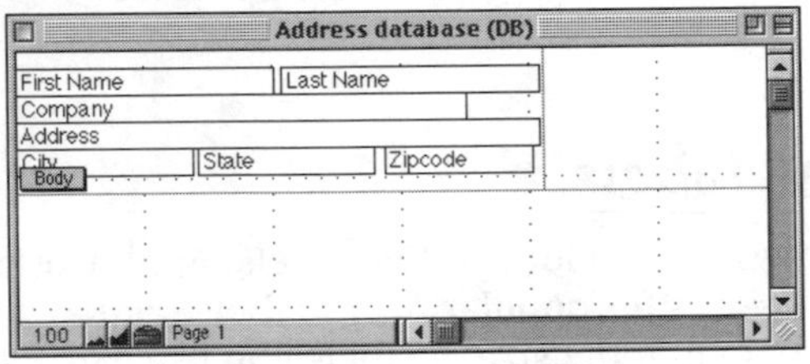

Figure 5-43: A sample label layout

7. If you want an idea of how the labels will look, choose Layout ➪ Browse (or press Shift+⌘+B). Make sure Page View (Shift+⌘+P) is also in effect. (Note that the space between fields, as well as blank lines, will be closed up when you print the labels, but not when you view them onscreen.)

   As an alternative, you can create a new view, tile windows, and have one view in Layout mode and one in Browse mode — giving instant feedback.

If you don't see a predefined label format that matches the labels you want to use, you can create a custom label layout.

Some Notes on Printing Labels

To print properly, many of the label layouts require that you set Larger Print Area (or US Letter rather than US Letter Small) in the Page Setup dialog box using the LaserWriter 8 printer driver.

AppleWorks has unusual requirements you need to adhere to when attempting to close up space during printing. These requirements apply not only to labels but also to any other type of database layout:

✦ Objects do not slide toward other objects that are smaller. Therefore, for a field to slide left, the field to the left must be exactly the same size or larger than the sliding field. Also, the top edges must be aligned if the fields are on the same line. The left edges must be aligned if fields are stacked one above the other (on different lines), and the upper field must be at least as wide as the one you want to have slide up.

✦ To check the dimensions of each field, choose Options ⇨ Object Size and then click each field. The Object Size windoid lists each field's distance from the margins, as well as its height and width. (See Chapter 6 for information on using the Object Size windoid to set the dimensions of an object.)

✦ Fields will not slide at all if their edges are touching on the layout.

Also, if you are using a laser or an inkjet printer, you should note that the printer cannot print on the entire page. Most laser printers require a minimum margin of between 0.2 and 0.25 inches all around the page. To ensure you can print as close to the edges as possible, choose Page Setup from the File menu, click the Options button, and then click the checkbox for Larger Print Area (Fewer Downloadable Fonts). Note that if you have the LaserWriter 8 installed (standard with OS 8 and later), you should choose US Letter rather than US Letter Small under Page Attributes.

Finally, because it's difficult to get text to align perfectly on labels, you're well advised to print a test page on standard paper and then place the test printout over a page of labels to see how they align. Continue to adjust the fields and make test printouts until the alignment is correct.

STEPS: Creating a Custom Label Layout

1. Choose Layout ⇨ New Layout or New Layout from the Layout pop-up menu in the Tool panel. The New Layout dialog box appears.

2. Click the Labels radio button and be sure the Custom option is selected.

3. Type a descriptive name for the label layout in the Name text box, and then click the OK button. The Label Layout dialog box appears, as shown in Figure 5-44.

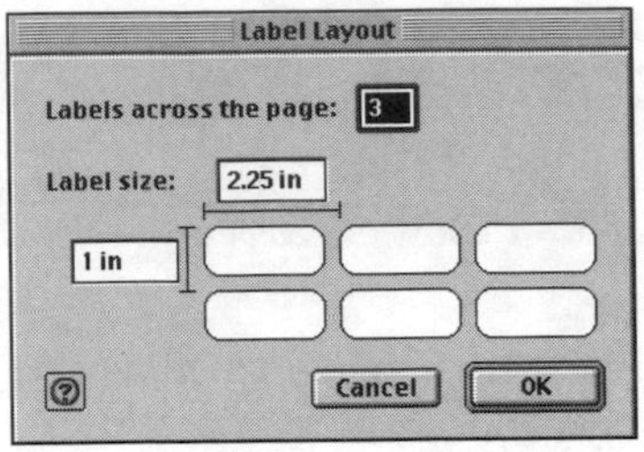

Figure 5-44: The Label Layout
dialog box

4. Specify the number of labels across (choose 3 for a page with three labels across it, for example) and the dimensions for a single label, and then click the OK button. The Set Field Order dialog box appears (refer to Figure 5-42, shown earlier in this chapter).

   You measure the width of a label from the left edge of the first label to the left edge of the next label. Similarly, you measure label height from the top of one label to the top of the label below it. That is, the gaps that follow each label to the right and below are considered part of the label's size.

5. Select the fields you want to appear on the labels, click the Move button to transfer them to the Field Order list, and then click the OK button. The new layout appears.

   In Step 1, if you chose New Layout from the Layout pop-up menu rather than choosing this command from the Layout menu, you will now be in Browse mode. Change to Layout mode by choosing Layout ➪ Layout.

6. Resize and move the fields to correspond with the way they should appear on the labels. The initial placement of the body dividing line is correct for the size of label specified. Do not move it, and be sure all fields stay within its boundaries.

7. If you want an idea of how the labels will look, choose Layout ➪ Browse (or press Shift+⌘+B). Make sure Page View (Shift+⌘+P) is also in effect. (Note that the space between fields, as well as blank lines, will be closed up when you print the labels, but not when you view them onscreen.)

Tip   If you want to eliminate some of the fuss of creating mailing labels, you can use the Create Labels Assistant. From any database, choose New Label Layout from either the Layout menu or the Layout pop-up menu. Follow the steps in the series of dialog boxes that are presented. When you are finished, the Assistant generates a new label layout that matches the specifications you provide.

Creating and Saving Custom Label Definitions

All permanent label layout definitions are stored in a text file named AppleWorks Labels that is located in the AppleWorks Essentials folder. By editing this file, you can add your own custom label definitions, as well as change the names of existing layouts ("Diskette Label — 3-up," rather than "Avery 5096, 5196, 5896," for example). After you make the changes to the file, you can choose your own label definitions from the Labels pop-up menu in the New Layout dialog box.

To create a new label definition:

1. Locate the AppleWorks Labels file. It is inside the AppleWorks Essentials folder, located inside your AppleWorks 6 folder.

2. Select the AppleWorks Labels icon and choose File ⇨ Duplicate (or press ⌘+D). The file is copied and named AppleWorks Labels Copy. (Making a duplicate protects the original file.)

3. To protect the original AppleWorks Labels file, change its name (to AppleWorks Labels.bak, for example). Keep it as a backup copy in case you have problems with the editing.

4. Load the duplicate copy of the AppleWorks Labels file into AppleWorks using the Open command. The file is loaded and converted from plain text to AppleWorks format. The following figure shows the contents of the AppleWorks Labels file.

Continued

Continued

As you can see in the figure, every label definition consists of eight lines: the label name enclosed in brackets, the number of columns, the horizontal pitch (label width), the vertical pitch (label height), the top margin, the bottom margin, the left margin, and the right margin. (Ignore any information that is preceded by two or more slashes [//]; it is a comment.)

5. Use one of the existing label definitions as a template for designing a new label. Select any eight-line segment, starting with a label name and ending with its right-margin data. Choose Edit ➪ Copy (or press ⌘+C).

6. Select the position in the label list where you want to insert the new label definition. You might want to keep your own definitions together—at the end of the list, for example.

7. Place the text insertion marker at the position where you want to insert the definition, and then choose Edit ➪ Paste (or press ⌘+V). Be sure you do not break up an existing definition when you paste the definition.

8. Edit the pasted text by entering your own label name within the brackets and replacing the other lines with the number of columns, width, height, top margin, bottom margin, left margin, and right margin for your label.

9. Save the file by choosing File ➪ Save As (or pressing Shift+⌘+S). Choose Text in the File Format pop-up menu, click the Document radio button, and enter **AppleWorks Labels** as the new file name.

10. Quit AppleWorks. The next time you launch AppleWorks, the new label layouts will be available.

Changing the name for any of the existing label layouts is even easier. Simply follow the preceding steps, but—instead of adding an entirely new layout—just change the text string between any pair of brackets to something more meaningful, such as [Audio Cassette 2-up] rather than [Avery 5198]. After you change the name for a label layout and save the file, the new name appears in the Labels pop-up menu.

Database printing

To generate a printed database report or other printout from a database, you can just select an appropriate layout and choose Print. However, you also can set other options to make reports and printouts more meaningful. (Every printout can consist of all visible—nonhidden—records, or only the currently selected record.)

STEPS: Printing from a Database

1. From the lower portion of the Layout menu, choose the layout you want to use to generate the printout.

2. Use the Find command (see "Finding and Selecting Records," earlier in this chapter) to select the records you want to include. If you want to use all of the records, choose Organize ➪ Show All Records (or press Shift+⌘+A).

3. If you want the records to display in a particular order, sort the records (as described in "Changing the display order of records," earlier in this chapter).

4. Choose File ➪ Print (or press ⌘+P). The Print dialog box appears, as shown in Figure 5-45.

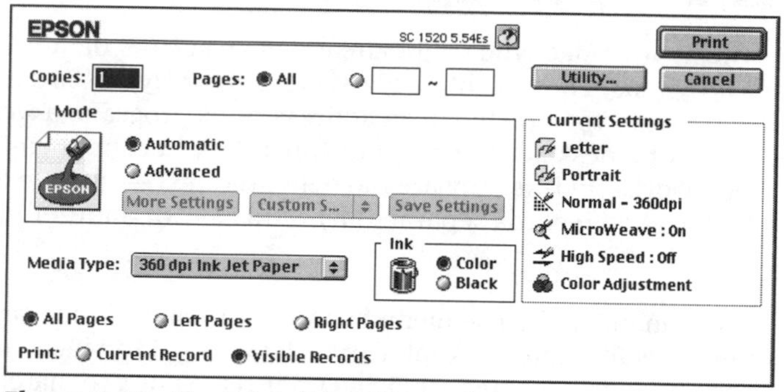

Figure 5-45: The Print dialog box, as it appears when you are printing an AppleWorks database

5. Click the Current Record or Visible Records radio button in the lower portion of the dialog box, depending on what you want to print.

6. Click the Print button to send the report to the printer. (Chapter 1 explains other print and page setup options.)

Saving Changes

If you've used FileMaker Pro or any of its earlier incarnations, you've undoubtedly noticed the many features it shares with the AppleWorks database environment. One of the major differences, however, is the way the two programs handle data and layout storage.

FileMaker Pro automatically saves any database changes, whether they are layout modifications or data additions, deletions, or alterations. In fact, FileMaker Pro doesn't even have a Save command. The plus side of this feature is that you never have to worry about whether your changes have been saved. The minus side is that the program saves all changes — both deliberate changes and unintentional or ill-advised changes. Unless you have a backup of your important FileMaker files, experimentation can be dangerous.

AppleWorks, on the other hand, does not have an automatic save feature (other than the autosave in case of a crash). You can experiment to your heart's content, secure in the knowledge that you can close the file at any time without saving changes. When you do want to save, on the other hand, choose the Save or Save As command from the File menu.

Importing and Exporting Data

Unless you just bought your Mac, you might already have several databases you designed in other programs. They might be FileMaker Pro or HyperCard databases, or they might be databases you created in an address book program, a word processor, a spreadsheet, or a desk accessory. Unfortunately, you cannot easily import databases into AppleWorks (unless they are tab-delimited text — plain text with fields separated by tabs and records separated by returns — or another Apple-Works file).

You use the Insert command in the File menu to add information from other databases or AppleWorks files into an AppleWorks database. If the file you're importing is a text file, you use the Import Field Order dialog box to match fields between the two databases — regardless of their order, or whether the databases have the same number of fields.

Caution AppleWorks 6 enables you to insert any AppleWorks file into an AppleWorks database and does so without bringing up the Import Field Order dialog box. It just inserts the data that it encounters one chunk at a time, as if it were tab-delimited. This can be convenient when you have a word processing document or a spreadsheet and the receiving database has enough fields to handle the data until the paragraph marker (return) or last cell in the spreadsheet row. Unfortunately, if you have a serious mismatch, AppleWorks could crash.

STEPS: Importing Information into an AppleWorks Database

1. In the source program, save or export the data file as a tab-delimited text file. Some programs, such as spreadsheets, might call this a Text file, an ASCII Text file, or a Text Only file. See the program's manual for instructions. (In a tab-delimited text file, each record is a separate paragraph. Every field in a record is separated from the next field by a tab character.)

2. Open or create an AppleWorks database to receive the imported data. Switch to Browse mode.

3. In AppleWorks, choose the Insert command from the File menu, choose the tab-delimited text file created in Step 1, and click the Insert button. The Import Field Order dialog box appears, as shown in Figure 5-46. The fields in the left side of the dialog box are from the file you're importing (the source file). The fields on the right are in the AppleWorks database (the destination file).

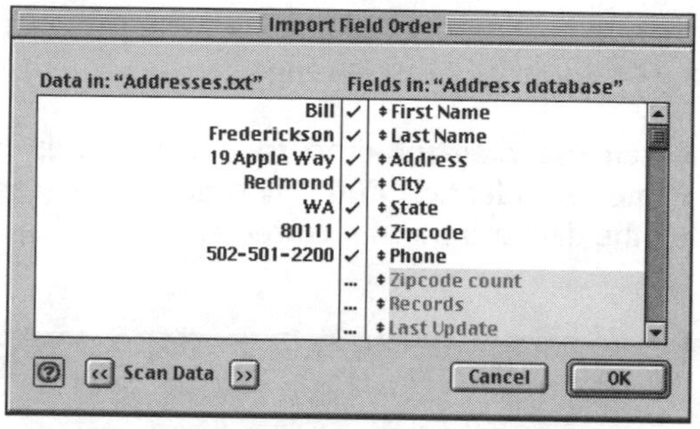

Figure 5-46: The Import Field Order dialog box

4. Drag to rearrange the fields in the right side of the dialog box so that they match the appropriate fields on the left side. Fields with a counterpart you want to import should have a checkmark in front of them. Fields with no counterpart are indicated by ellipses (. . .) and are not imported. You can click the checkmark or ellipses to toggle to the opposite state.

Note

Not every field needs to have a counterpart. You might well have more fields in one database than in the other. No restrictions govern how many or how few fields you can import. If you find, however, that the target AppleWorks database lacks a key field that the source file possesses, you might want to cancel the import, add the new field to the AppleWorks database, and then proceed with the import.

5. Using the Scan Data buttons, check several records of the source file to see whether the fields match correctly. If you're satisfied with the way they match, click the OK button to import the data. The new records are imported into the database.

As with importing data, when you export data from an AppleWorks database to use in another program, tab-delimited ASCII text is often the best format to use. Virtually every type of Macintosh program (including word processors) can correctly handle such a file. (A tab-delimited text file contains one record per line, and each field in the record is separated from the next field by a tab character.)

STEPS: Exporting an AppleWorks Database File

1. Open the AppleWorks database by choosing File ➪ Open (or press ⌘+O).

2. Choose File ➪ Save As (or press Shift+⌘+S).

3. Choose ASCII Text from the File Format pop-up menu, click the Document radio button, and then type a new file name for the export file. If the receiving program can read one of the following formats and you have an appropriate translator (not included with AppleWorks 6), you also can choose a DBF, DIF, or SYLK format for the exported data.

4. Click the Save button to save the file.

5. In the destination program, open or import the file. (See the program's manual for instructions on opening or importing foreign files.)

Tip   In AppleWorks 6, you also can use drag-and-drop to move records between databases. Wherever field names are identical in the two databases (Last Name and Last Name, for example), the data will transfer correctly.

Using a Spreadsheet to Clean Up Import Data

Although you can use the Import Field Order dialog box to match fields as well as possible when you import data into a database, the match between fields isn't always as clean as it could be. When you import address data, for example, two problems are common:

✦ The address, phone number, or name fields in the import file are split into two fields (address line 1 and address line 2, area code and phone number, and first name and last name), but they are in one field in the AppleWorks database — or vice versa.

✦ Zip codes shorter than five digits are missing the leading zero (1276 rather than 01276).

Instead of importing the data as is and cleaning it up in the database afterward, you can use the AppleWorks spreadsheet to make the necessary transformations to the data more efficiently. Using the spreadsheet changes the steps in the AppleWorks database import process.

To use a spreadsheet to import data:

1. Export the data from the database, spreadsheet, or address book program as a tab-delimited ASCII text file.

2. Open the ASCII text file as an AppleWorks spreadsheet; make the transformations to the data, creating new fields as necessary; and save the spreadsheet.

3. Open the AppleWorks database and use the Insert command to import the AppleWorks spreadsheet into the database.

The simplest way to make the transformations in the spreadsheet is to create additional columns to the right side of the spreadsheet. Each column will contain a formula that combines or converts one or more columns of the original data. After you create the appropriate formula, use the Fill Down command (⌘+D) to copy it into the remaining cells in the column. The following figures illustrate three typical conversions.

In the first figure, Column A contains first names, and Column B contains last names. The combination formula in the entry bar, =A2&" "&B2, takes the first name in cell A2 (Jim), adds a space to it (" "), and then adds the last name from cell B2 (Abrams) to the end of the text string. The combined fields appear in Column C as one name.

The second figure is an example of combining two address fields into a single address field. Unlike the names in the preceding example, some addresses contain only one part. The equation =IF(B2<>"",A2&", "&B2,A2) checks to see whether the address has a second part (B2<>""). If the second portion is not blank, the formula combines the two portions, separating them with a comma followed by a blank—for example, "18 Maple Terrace, Box 432." If the address does not have a second part, the formula simply copies the first address part (A2) into the cell.

In the example in the third figure, a leading zero is added to four-digit Zip codes. Because Zip codes are often treated as numbers, the leading zero might disappear, resulting in an improper four-digit code. The lengthy formula =IF(LEN(A2)=4,"0"&A2, NUMTOTEXT(A2)) checks to see whether the length of the Zip code is four digits—LEN(A2)=4. If so, a leading zero is prepended to the Zip code—"0"&A2, and the Zip code is converted to text. If the Zip code does not contain four digits, it is converted to text and passed through unaltered—NUMTOTEXT(A2). Converting Zip codes to text is necessary to display leading zeroes and to handle blank Zip codes. If the formula simply ended with A2, rather than with NUMTOTEXT(A2), a blank Zip code would translate as a 0 (zero).

Down to Business: Creating a Credit Card Charge Tracker

If all you want to do is keep track of how you're doing on your credit cards, you don't need a dedicated home finance program. You can use a simple AppleWorks database to record charges and payments, as well as to show how you're doing overall. Figure 5-47 shows what the charge card database you're about to create looks like.

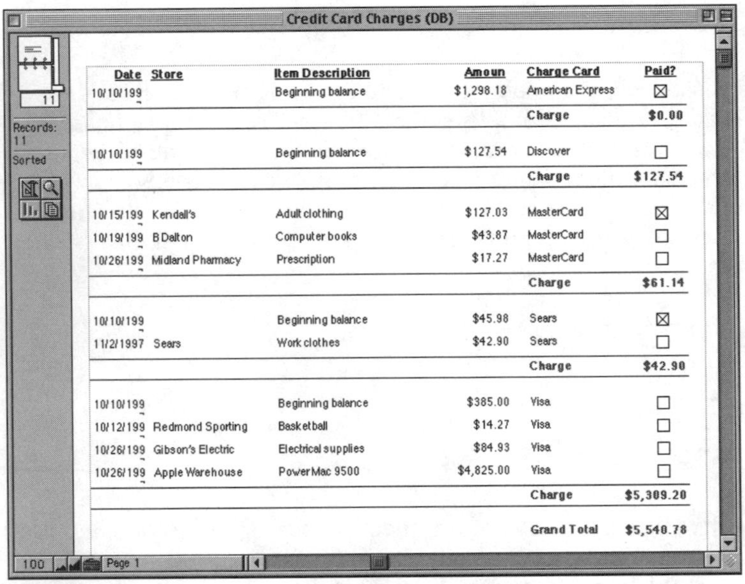

Figure 5-47: The Credit Card Charges database

This database enables you to record the following information for every charge: the date of the transaction, the store or business where the charge was made, a description of what was charged, the amount of the charge, and the particular credit card that was used.

Defining fields for the database

Before you can add data, you need to create a new database and specify the fields it will contain. We'll do this by creating a new database, and then defining the fields listed in Table 5-2.

Table 5-2
Fields for the Credit Card Charges Database

Field Name	Type	Formula/Description
Date	Date	
Store	Text	
Item Description	Text	
Amount	Number	
Charge Card	Value List	American Express, MasterCard, Discover, Visa, and so on
Paid?	Checkbox	
Outstanding Amount	Calculation	IF('Paid?'=1,0,'Amount')
Charge Total	Summary	SUM('Outstanding amount') **as a Sub-summary sorted by Charge Card**
Grand Total	Summary	SUM('Outstanding amount') **as a Trailing grand summary**

The first four fields (Date, Store, Item Description, and Amount) are self-explanatory. To save typing time and to ensure accurate, consistent spelling, Charge Card is declared as a value list field and contains a list of the names of all charge cards you intend to track. When you select the Charge Card field in the database (by clicking the field or tabbing into it), the Charge Card field displays a drop-down list of your credit cards.

When you define Charge Card as a value list field, the Options dialog box automatically opens. Create a value list that consists of the names of all the credit cards you intend to track. If you like, you also can specify a default charge card by typing its name in the Default Data section of the dialog box. Finally, click the Cannot Be Empty and Alerts for Unlisted Values checkboxes in the Data Verification section of the dialog box. This ensures that you will receive a warning if you neglect to choose a credit card for a record or if you type the name of an unlisted card. (If you later get a new credit card, you should edit this value list to include that card.) Click the OK button to dismiss the Options dialog box.

Paid? is a checkbox field. After defining the Paid? field, select it in the Field Name List, and click Options. In the Options dialog box, delete the text in the Label for Checkbox box, remove the checkmark from Initially Checked, and click the OK button.

Outstanding Amount is a calculation field used to determine whether each charge has already been reconciled (paid). If paid (that is, a check exists in the Paid? checkbox, which is interpreted as a 1), Outstanding Amount is set to 0 (zero). Otherwise, it is set to whatever number is currently in the Amount field for the record. Unlike the other database fields, Outstanding Amount is not displayed in the layout. It is, however, used to generate the Charge Total for each credit card, as well as the Grand Total (the total amount of all outstanding charges for all cards). Define Outstanding Amount as a calculation field, using the formula shown earlier in Table 5-2.

Charge Total is a summary field that calculates an individual charge total for each credit card when the database is sorted by Charge Card. To create the Charge Total field, type its name in the Define Database Fields dialog box, choose Summary as the field type, and then click the Create button. A new dialog box appears in which you can enter the formula shown earlier in Table 5-2. Indicate that you want the result to be formatted as a number.

Define Grand Total using the same technique just used for Charge Total. As Table 5-2 shows, Grand Total uses the same formula as Charge Total.

After creating all the fields and clicking Done, a default layout appears. You won't actually use this temporary layout in the database. The next section describes how to create the real layout.

Making the layout

This database requires only one layout. Not only will it serve for data entry, it will also display onscreen and printed reports.

STEPS: Designing the Layout

1. Choose Layout ⇨ New Layout or choose New Layout from the Layout pop-up menu in the Tool panel.

2. In the dialog box that appears, name the layout **Data Entry**, click the Columnar Report radio button, and then click the OK button.

3. In the Set Field Order dialog box that appears, select every field except Outstanding Amount and click the Move button. In order, the fields should be Date, Store, Item Description, Amount, Charge Card, and Paid?. Click the OK button to create the columnar layout.

4. Change to Layout mode and arrange these fields (in the body) and their respective labels (in the header) so they look like the layout in Figure 5-48.

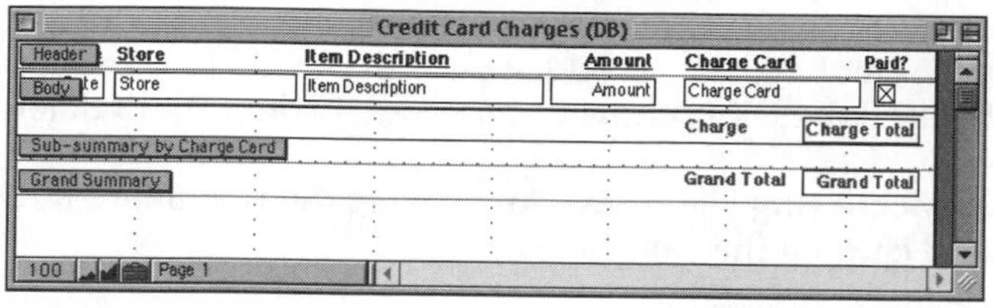

Figure 5-48: The final layout

5. To create the Charge Total sub-summary (shown earlier in Figure 5-48), choose Layout ⇨ Insert Part. Then choose Sub-summary when sorted by Charge Card, and then click the OK button. Click the Below button in the dialog box that follows. The sub-summary part is added to the layout.

6. To create the Grand Total summary, choose Layout ⇨ Insert Part. Then choose Trailing Grand Summary and click the OK button. The grand summary part is added to the bottom of the layout.

7. To insert the two summary fields into the layout, choose Insert Field from the Layout menu and then double-click Charge Total and Grand Total. After the fields are placed in the layout, drag them to the locations shown earlier in Figure 5-48.

You can add several finishing touches to embellish the database layout:

✦ Set the font and size of all fields to Helvetica 10 point. (Choose Select All from the Edit menu, choose Format Font ⇨ Helvetica, and choose Format ⇨ Size ⇨ 10.)

✦ Add boldface to the Charge Total and Grand Total fields by selecting the fields and choosing Format ⇨ Style ⇨ Bold, or by clicking the Bold button on the Button Bar.

✦ Set right justification as the text alignment for the Date, Amount, Charge Total, and Grand Total fields; set center justification for the Paid? field.

✦ Apply the Currency format to all monetary fields (Amount, Charge Total, Grand Total) by selecting the fields and then choosing Edit ⇨ Field Info.

✦ Change the height of all the fields in the body of the layout by selecting them, choosing Options ⇨ Object Size, and typing .18 in the Height box of the Object Size windoid. (The Height box is the second box in the right column of the windoid.)

✦ Above and below the Charge Total field, add solid lines that extend the full width of the page.

✦ Drag the Header and Body dividers up to reduce the space they take up in the layout.

Now that the real layout has been created, you can safely discard the original layout. Choose Layout ⇨ Edit Layouts, select Layout 1 in the Current Layouts list, and then click the Delete and the OK buttons when asked if you want to delete Layout 1.

Save the database by choosing File ⇨ Save As, clicking the Document radio button, entering a name, and clicking the Save button.

Using the database

Using the database is fairly simple. The basic procedures include starting up, entering new records, establishing a sort order in which to display the records, reconciling the individual charges with payments made to the credit card companies, and deleting records.

Starting up

The first time you use the database, you are likely to have outstanding balances on some of your credit cards. If so, create a Beginning balance record for each charge card, as shown earlier in Figure 5-47. As you pay off (or pay down) the balance, you will reduce it by your payment amounts (as described in "Reconciling the charge statement," later in this chapter).

Entering new charges

Whenever you have a new charge to post, choose Edit ⇨ New Record (or press ⌘+R). A new record appears, and you can add the charge details. Leave the Paid? field blank (unchecked).

> **Note**   When entering and editing data, you can work in Page view (Page View is checked in the Window menu) or in Normal view (Page View is unchecked in the Window menu). The choice is up to you.

Establishing a sort order

Although you can leave the records in the order in which you add them, this order complicates reconciliation and makes finding specific records difficult. Furthermore, the Charge Total summaries won't be available to you. You can solve all of these problems by specifying a sort order for the database.

Choose Organize ⇨ Sort Records (or press ⌘+J), set ascending sorts for the Charge Card and Date fields (in that order), and then click the OK button. AppleWorks sorts the database by charge card and, within each charge card, by date of purchase. If the Charge Totals are still not visible, make sure you have selected Page View from the Window menu.

Note   Each time you finish entering new records, be sure to sort the database again.

Reconciling the charge statement

When a charge statement arrives in the mail, you can reconcile it in one of two ways, depending on whether you pay off the entire balance or pay less than the balance due.

STEPS: Reconciling a Statement When You Pay Off the Entire Balance

1. Check each record against the statement to make sure it contains no mistakes.

2. Click in the Paid? checkbox for each record on the statement (marking them as paid). The Charge Total for that credit card should now show as 0 (zero).

STEPS: Reconciling a Statement When You Pay Off Less Than the Entire Balance

1. Check each record against the statement to make sure it contains no mistakes.

2. Subtract the amount you intend to pay on this statement from any of the outstanding charges for that credit card.

   For example, suppose you have $500 worth of Visa charges in your database ($300 of it as the beginning balance and two other charges of $100 each). If you are paying $75 today, you can edit any of the original Amount fields for that card by subtracting the $75 payment. Thus, you could reduce the $300 beginning balance to $225, for example.

   If you are paying $100, you can simply mark one of the $100 charges as paid (which would instantly remove that amount from the Charge Total for the credit card).

   Remember, the object is to show the correct outstanding amount for each card (the Charge Total). What the individual charges show is irrelevant — at least after you've verified that the credit card company has recorded them correctly.

Tip   You also can make new entries for your payments as negative dollar purchases, –$75 and –$100 in the preceding examples, if you want to keep a complete record of credits and debits.

Deleting records

After you've paid off some charges, you can, at your option, delete their records to prevent them from cluttering up the database. (However, you might want to make a printout of the database for your permanent records first.) The simplest way to remove all the paid records is to use the Match Records command.

STEPS: Selecting and Deleting the Paid Records

1. Choose Organize ⇨ Match Records (or press ⌘+M). The Match Records dialog box appears.

2. Type the following formula, and then click the OK button. The records that have been paid are selected.

    'Paid?'=1

3. Choose Clear from the Edit menu. The paid records are removed from the database.

> **Tip**   Instead of trying to remember this formula, you can create an AppleWorks macro to type it for you and delete the paid records. (See Chapter 13 for instructions.)

Quick Tips

The following quick tips suggest some simple ways to empty a database field for an entire database; perform date calculations; and use the spelling checker, thesaurus, and stylesheet in databases.

In addition, a final tip lists several programs to consider when you're ready for a more powerful database.

Emptying a database field for an entire database

Suppose you want to erase the contents of a single field within every record in a database. The database environment does not provide an easy way to perform this task, but you can do it if you enlist the spreadsheet to help.

STEPS: Emptying a Database Field

1. Create a new spreadsheet in AppleWorks.

2. Choose File ⇨ Insert, choose your database file from the standard file dialog box, and then click the Insert button.

    The database file is inserted into the spreadsheet with one database field in each column and one record in each row.

3. Select the column of data that corresponds to the database field you want to empty — "Phone" in this example. (Click the letter at the top of a column to select the column.)

4. Choose Edit ➪ Clear, or press the Clear, Delete, or Del keys. The cells are cleared.

5. Save the file as text by choosing File ➪ Save As, choosing ASCII Text in the File Format pop-up menu, and giving it a name. This step saves an ASCII text file with the modified version you just created in the spreadsheet.

6. Switch to the database screen. Choose Organize ➪ Show All Records (Shift+⌘+A), followed by Edit ➪ Select All (⌘+A). All records in the database are selected.

7. Choose Edit ➪ Clear, or press the Clear key to simultaneously remove all records.

8. Choose File ➪ Insert and choose the ASCII text version of the spreadsheet you saved in Step 5. Click the Insert button. The Import Field Order dialog box appears, as shown in Figure 5-49. This box shows you, one record at a time, how the imported data will be inserted into the database fields. The match should be perfect. (Of course, the field you just emptied — Phone, in this example — should be blank.)

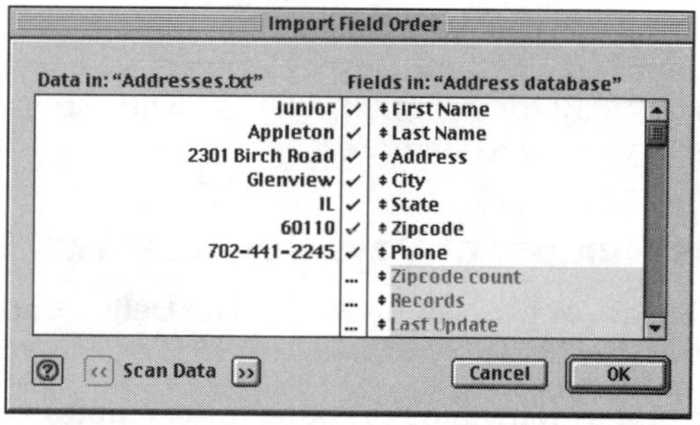

Figure 5-49: The Import Field Order dialog box

9. After using the Scan Data buttons to check several records, click the OK button. The procedure is now complete. Figure 5-50 shows the results of clearing the Phone field for all records.

> **Tip**
>
> If you are absolutely certain that your spreadsheet in Step 3 exactly matches what you want your database to hold (and it should), you can save the spreadsheet as a spreadsheet in Step 5 and shorten Step 8 to insert the spreadsheet. Voila! The data is back with the Phone field emptied.

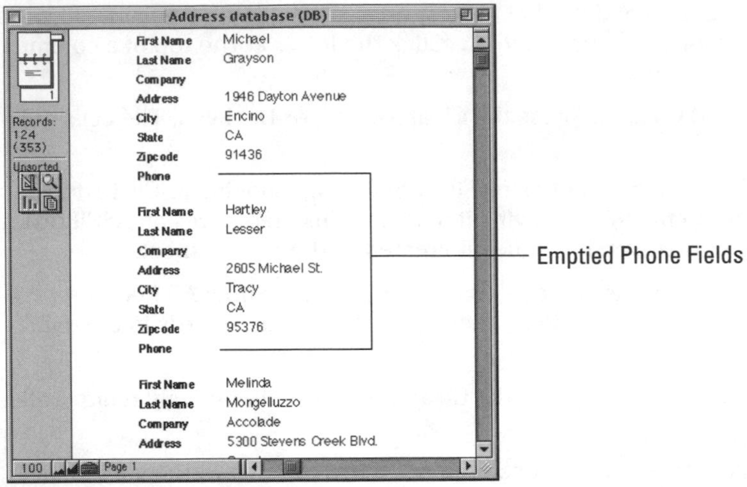

Figure 5-50: The revised database records

Date calculations

Because the AppleWorks database environment also enables you to create calculation fields, you might sometimes want to record two dates and then determine the number of days between them. You can calculate the number of days that completing a project required or the number of days until a special event will occur (days until your mother's birthday or payday, for example). The following steps show how to accomplish these tasks in your own databases.

STEPS: Calculating the Number of Days Between Two Dates

1. Choose Layout ⇨ Define Fields (or press Shift+⌘+D). The Define Database Fields dialog box appears.

2. Create a pair of date fields (Start Date and End Date, for example).

3. Create a calculation field to compute the difference between the dates (Total Days, for example). The formula for the field is `'End Date'-'Start Date'`. Set Number as the result type in the Format Result As pop-up menu.

STEPS: Calculating the Number of Days Until an Upcoming Event

1. Choose Define Fields from the Layout menu (or press Shift+⌘+D). The Define Database Fields dialog box appears.

2. Create a date field (such as Due Date) in which to record the target date.

3. Create a calculation field to compute the number of days between today and the target date. The formula for the field would be `'Due Date'-TRUNC(NOW())`. In the Format Result As pop-up menu, choose Number as the result type.

The `NOW( )` function takes the current date and time from the Mac's internal clock. When you truncate the date and time with the TRUNC function, the program discards the fractional portion of the day. Because you want to know only how many full days remain until the event, this formula produces a whole number as the result (7 days, rather than 7.1852 days, for example).

If the due date has already occurred, the result of this formula is a negative number. A result of –5 indicates the event occurred five days ago.

Formatting with style

Although the default stylesheet doesn't contain any useful styles that can be applied to fields, labels, or static text in a database, there's nothing stopping you from creating your own field styles.

STEPS: Creating Styles for Fields

1. Select a field and format it as desired. Formatting settings can include font, size, style, alignment, text color, pen color and line width (for a border), fill color, fill pattern, wallpaper, gradient, and so on.

2. If the Styles windoid isn't open, choose Format ⇨ Show Styles (or press Shift+⌘+W).

3. Click the New button at the top right of the Styles windoid. The New Style dialog box appears, as shown in Figure 5-51.

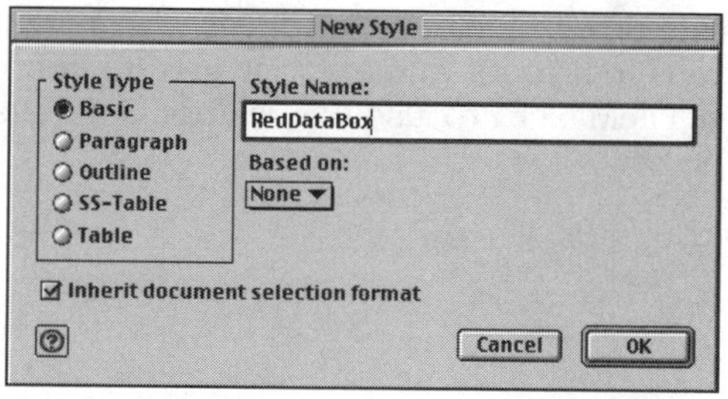

Figure 5-51: The New Style dialog box

4. Be sure the Basic radio button is selected and the "Inherit document selection format" checkbox is checked, and then type a name for the style.

5. Click the OK button to close the dialog box. The new style is added to the document's stylesheet.

To format other fields, labels, or static text using this new style definition, select the items in the layout and then click the style's name in the Styles windoid and click the Apply button. Note that the modified stylesheet is automatically saved when you save the database. (For more information on using styles, see Chapter 15.)

Don't forget the spelling checker and thesaurus!

The name of this section says it all. Although you normally think of the spelling checker and thesaurus in connection with word processing documents, you also can use them in other AppleWorks environments, such as the database. You might even want to create special user dictionaries for some databases. A dictionary that contains the spellings for company and customer names would be useful for a contacts or client database, for example, and would help to ensure the accuracy of the data you enter.

If your database includes large text fields, such as fields for notes or comments, you might want to turn on the auto-hyphenation feature. To do so, choose Edit ⇨ Writing Tools ⇨ Auto-Hyphenate.

Tip If you run a spell check in Browse mode, the spell-checker will check spellings in your fields. If you want to check the spelling of the labels and other text on your layout, you should run the spell-checker in Layout mode.

Moving On Up

If you're lusting for more database power, you'll find the transition to FileMaker Pro (from FileMaker, Inc. at www.filemaker.com) an easy one. The features in the AppleWorks database environment are a subset of the features in FileMaker Pro. FileMaker Pro enables you to create powerful database scripts with a simple-to-use scripting system, add script buttons to layouts, and exercise greater control over the way layouts display onscreen. FileMaker Pro also has relational database capabilities.

Summary

✦ A database is an organized set of information on one particular topic. Every database is composed of records, and each record is made up of fields.

✦ The AppleWorks database has four essential modes: Browse, Layout, Find, and List. Both Browse and List modes can be used to edit, add, and view data. List mode is layout-independent; instead of just showing the fields present in a single layout, List mode simultaneously shows all fields that have been defined for the database.

✦ AppleWorks offers 14 types of database fields: text, number, date, time, name, pop-up menu, radio buttons, checkbox, serial number, value list, multimedia, record info, calculation, and summary. You use different field types to allow only certain types of data to be entered into the fields and to present the data in special ways (as checkboxes, radio buttons, or pop-up lists or menus, for example). The multimedia fields in AppleWorks 6 enable you to store QuickTime movies, pictures, and sounds in your databases.

✦ Entries in calculation and summary fields are always the result of a formula you have specified. You cannot manually enter data into a calculation or summary field. AppleWorks also automatically fills in the data in Record Info fields. As with calculation and summary fields, you cannot enter or modify data into a record info field.

✦ The AppleWorks database environment includes several data validation and auto-entry options you can set for fields. These options can help ensure the accuracy of the data you enter and speed up the data entry process.

✦ For each database, you can create as many layouts (arrangements of data fields and other objects) as you need. Each layout can offer a different view of the data and use different subsets of fields.

✦ In addition to the body part of each layout (where most of the fields are placed), you can create header and footer parts (for information you want to appear on every page of the database), as well as summary and sub-summary parts (where you can calculate statistics or formulas for the entire database or selected record groupings).

✦ By sorting the database on the contents of one or more fields, you can change the order in which the records are displayed and the way in which they are grouped.

✦ You can search for records by using two commands: Find and Match Records. The Find command displays the subset of records that match the search criteria, while hiding all other records. Match Records merely selects the subset without hiding the other records.

✦ Entering multiple criteria in a single Find request results in an AND search (finding records that match this criterion and that criterion). You also can issue multiple Find requests to execute an OR search (finding records that match this criterion or that criterion).

✦ AppleWorks provides more than 100 layouts for Avery labels. You also can create custom label layouts.

✦ You can import and export data in a few formats. Importing enables you to merge records from other data files with an existing AppleWorks database. Exporting data is useful when you want to examine or use the database data in another program (a spreadsheet or desktop publishing program, for example).

✦ You can click the pop-up menus in the Tool panel to create and switch to layouts, as well as save and execute complex searches, sorts, and reports.

✦   ✦   ✦

The Draw and Paint Environments

AppleWorks has three graphics environments: draw, paint, and presentations. Draw and paint are basic environments and are the subject of this chapter. Presentations are a new feature in AppleWorks 6 and have their own chapter—Chapter 7.

Using the draw tools, you create objects—graphics you can move, resize, and place in layers over each other. Because the graphics are objects, they maintain a separate identity from everything else on the page. You can select any draw object separately from other images. However, editing affects the entire object. You cannot, for example, remove a few dots from an object or cut a section away. But changing the color, pattern, or line width for an object is simple.

In paint documents or frames, on the other hand, images are composed entirely of dots (or pixels), and you can edit them at the dot level. This capability makes the paint environment excellent for creating detailed images such as illustrations.

Here are the major differences between the two basic graphic environments:

✦ Draw tools are always available. The paint tools remain hidden until you select the painter's palette tool (to work in or create a paint frame) or open a paint document or frame.

✦ Draw objects are solid; you can edit them only as a whole. Paint images are composed of dots; you can edit them at the dot level.

✦ Selecting and manipulating draw objects is easy. Working with portions of paint images can be more difficult because they do not maintain a separate identity. (A paint image is just a mass of dots.)

✦ You can place draw objects in layers, with some objects obscuring portions of other objects. The objects retain their independence, enabling you to change their attributes and their position in the layers. In the paint environment, after you cover part of an image with another image, the obscured portion is gone forever (unless you immediately choose the Undo command).

✦ No such thing as a draw frame exists. You can place draw objects directly onto the pages of most AppleWorks documents. Paint images, however, must be in a paint document or in a paint frame. If you copy and paste a portion of a paint image into another document, AppleWorks automatically embeds it in a rectangular paint frame.

✦ You can align draw objects to each other or to the grid.

✦ You can rotate either type of image, flip them horizontally or vertically, and scale them to a different size.

✦ The paint environment enables you to apply a variety of special effects to selections. Some of the effects are invert, blend, tint, shear, distort, and perspective.

✦ You can alter the resolution and depth of paint documents.

Because the two environments share similar purposes and capabilities, this chapter discusses both of them.

The Draw Environment

The draw environment enables you to create graphics objects that you can easily move, resize, and combine. You can place these objects on any document page, copy them to other applications, and store them in the Scrapbook or in your Clippings folder.

The draw tools are available in every environment. Because everything on a draw page is treated as an object (including frames from other environments), the draw environment is excellent for laying out newsletters and ad copy.

Creating objects with the draw tools

AppleWorks provides draw tools for the following objects:

✦ **Lines.** A line has two endpoints. You can draw lines at any angle, or you can restrict them to multiples of the Shift constraint angle (as set in Preferences). You can apply only *pen attributes* (pen color, pen pattern, line width, and arrowheads) to a line.

✦ **Rectangles.** A rectangle is an object with four sides, and every corner angle is 90 degrees. In addition to normal rectangles (and squares), AppleWorks also supports rounded rectangles (rectangles with rounded corners). You can apply *fill attributes* (color, pattern, wallpaper, and gradient) to the interior and pen attributes to the border.

✦ **Ovals.** An oval is a closed object shaped as an ellipse or a circle. You can apply fill attributes to the interior and pen attributes to the border.

✦ **Arcs.** An arc is a curved line. Although arcs are typically drawn as open objects, you can assign fill attributes to the interior, which is the quarter-ellipse formed by the arc.

✦ **Polygons.** A polygon is any figure with a fixed number of sides. Polygons can be closed or open, contain uneven sides, or have sides of equal length (regular polygons).

To create any of these draw objects, you select the appropriate drawing tool from the Tools windoid's Tool panel (see Figure 6-1) and then click and drag in the current document. When you release the mouse button, the object is surrounded by tiny dark squares called handles (see Figure 6-2). By dragging the handles, you can change the object's size and proportions.

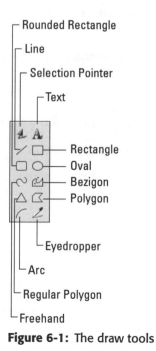

Rounded Rectangle

Line

Selection Pointer

Text

Rectangle

Oval

Bezigon

Polygon

Eyedropper

Arc

Regular Polygon

Freehand

Figure 6-1: The draw tools

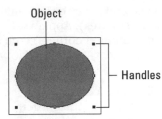

Object

Handles

Figure 6-2: A simple draw object

Note

Throughout this chapter, when we say "Tool panel," we are referring to the Tools windoid's Tool panel, and when we say "Frames panel," we are writing about the Tools windoid's Frames panel.

Tip

After you create an object, AppleWorks normally selects the pointer tool from the Tool panel. To keep the original drawing tool selected, double-click it—instead of single-click—when you select it. When you select a tool by double-clicking it, the tool's symbol in the Tool panel becomes blue (instead of simply becoming darkened), and you can draw multiple objects of the same type without reselecting the tool each time.

Pressing the Shift key as you create an object constrains the effects of the following drawing tools:

✦ Rectangle or rounded rectangle tool. A square or rounded square is drawn.

✦ Oval tool. A circle is drawn.

✦ Arc tool. A quarter circle is drawn.

✦ Line tool. A straight line is drawn. Only lines that are a multiple of the Shift constraint angle (as set in the Graphics section of the Preferences dialog box) can be drawn. (To find out how to change the Shift constraint, refer to Chapter 11.)

Creating or adjusting round corners on a rectangle

You can adjust the roundness of corners or add round corners to a standard rectangle.

Begin by selecting an existing rectangle or a rounded rectangle. Choose Edit ➪ Corner Info, or double-click the rectangle. The Corner Info dialog box appears, as shown in Figure 6-3. To create a rectangle with semicircles at the left and right ends (similar to what the pharmaceutical folks call a caplet), click the Round Ends radio button, and then click the OK button. If you prefer to specify a different curvature at just the corners, click the Radius radio button, specify a new radius (in the text box) for the circle, a 90-degree arc of which will form the curve, and then click the OK button.

Figure 6-3: The Corner Info dialog box

Reshaping an arc

The direction in which you drag when creating an arc determines the arc's curve.

Normal drawing results in a quarter ellipse. To increase or decrease an arc angle, you must modify it. You can reshape an arc in three different ways:

✦ Select a handle and drag. This changes the size (major and minor axes) of an arc.

✦ Use the Reshape command. This enables manual resizing of the arc angle.

✦ Use the Modify Arc command. This enables precise angle adjustment and permits framed edges.

To reshape an arc, select the arc with the pointer tool. Choose Arrange ⇨ Reshape (or press ⌘+R). A special reshape cursor appears. Click one of the arc's handles and drag to change the angle the arc subtends (the fraction of an ellipse that is drawn). The cursor is constrained to the arc's diameter. To complete the editing, select another tool or choose the Reshape command again.

Note The preceding behavior is best visualized if you fill the arc with a color, pattern, wallpaper, or gradient before experimenting.

To modify an arc, select the arc with the pointer tool. Choose Edit ⇨ Arc Info, or double-click the arc. The Arc Info dialog box appears, as shown in Figure 6-4. Choose Normal for a normal arc, or choose Frame Edges to create a pie wedge (closing the arc). Type numbers in the Start Angle and Arc Angle fields. Then, click the OK button to execute the instructions and close the dialog box.

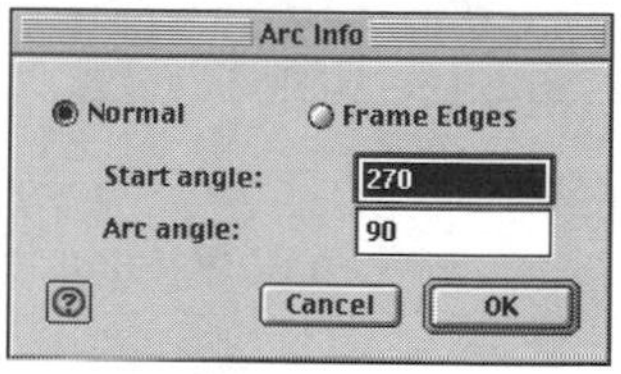

Figure 6-4: The Arc Info dialog box

Note Straight up is 0 degrees and the start angle is measured clockwise from that point. The arc angle is measured clockwise from the start angle.

Drawing and reshaping polygons

The tool you use to draw a polygon depends on whether the polygon will have sides of equal length.

To draw a polygon with uneven sides, select the polygon tool in the Tool panel. Click the document page once to select the starting point, and then move the mouse pointer to create the first line of the polygon. (If you press the Shift key as you move the mouse, the angle of the line will be restricted to an increment of the Shift constraint set in the Graphics preferences.) Click once to set the endpoint for the line. Move the mouse again and click to complete the next line. Repeat this step as many times as necessary to complete the polygon. To finish the polygon, click the starting point (to create a closed polygon), double-click, or press the Return key.

Tip To make polygons close automatically (the equivalent of clicking the starting point), choose the Graphics preferences option for Automatic Polygon Closing. (For information on setting preferences, see Chapter 11.)

To draw a polygon that has equal sides, use the regular polygon tool. A regular polygon has three or more sides, and all sides are equal in length. The default setting in a new document is for a three-sided polygon (an equilateral triangle).

To draw a regular polygon, select the regular polygon tool in the Tool panel. To set the number of sides for the polygon, choose Edit ➪ Polygon Sides. (The Polygon Sides command is available only when the Regular Polygon tool is selected.) In the dialog box that appears, specify the number of sides desired and click the OK button. Click the document page once to select the starting point, and then drag to create the polygon. You can rotate the polygon as you drag. When you release the mouse button, the polygon is completed.

Note Once you have set a number of sides, that default will be used in the current document until you change it again.

If you press the Shift key as you draw the regular polygon, its angle of placement on the page is restricted to the Shift constraint that is set for the mouse in the Graphics section of the Preferences dialog box. By default, the angle is set to 45-degree increments.

You can use the Reshape command to change the angles between polygon sides, add anchor points, or change a straight line into a curve.

STEPS: Reshaping a Polygon

1. Select the polygon with the pointer tool.

2. Choose Arrange ➪ Reshape (or press ⌘+R). The reshape pointer appears.

3. Drag a handle to reshape the polygon.

or

Click an anchor point and, while pressing the Option key, drag to create a curve.

or

Click between any pair of anchor points to add a new anchor point. The new anchor point can now be dragged or Option-dragged, as described previously.

4. To complete the editing, select another tool or choose the Reshape command again.

Drawing other shapes

You can use the freehand tool to create free-form objects. Unlike other objects, which are set to have a white fill, freehand objects have a transparent fill. They can, however, be made solid by assigning a fill color, pattern, wallpaper, or gradient to them.

By default, AppleWorks automatically smoothes freehand shapes (removes some of the irregularities in the lines and curves). To avoid smoothing, clear the Automatically Smooth Freehand checkbox in your Graphics preferences settings. (For information on setting preferences, see Chapter 11.)

The bezigon tool (some folks call it Beziér) enables you to draw complex shapes composed of curves and straight lines.

STEPS: Drawing with the Bezigon Tool

1. Select the bezigon tool in the Tool panel.

2. Click to select the starting point, and then move the mouse pointer to select the endpoint for the first line or curve.

3. Click to set the endpoint. To create an angular point, press the Option key as you click. To create a more dramatic curve, click and drag.

4. Repeat Steps 2 and 3 as required.

5. Double-click to close the shape.

To reshape any of the curves in a bezigon shape, choose Arrange ⇨ Reshape (or press ⌘+R) and click the object. Select any of the hollow handles that appear and drag to reshape. To add a new anchor point, click anywhere on a line. To delete an anchor point, select it and press the Delete or Backspace key. When you've finished reshaping the object, choose the Reshape command again or select another tool.

Note that two types of hollow handles exist: circles for curved points and squares for sharp points. Pressing the Option key while clicking a square handle enables you to change it to a curve. Click the handle and then drag right or left. Option-clicking a handle (one of the tiny dots that appear when creating or modifying a curve) resets the curve to a sharp point. (The bezigon editing procedures also can be applied to freehand shapes.)

Editing objects

Drawing an object is often only the first step. You can use the different commands, procedures, and windoids to change an object's size, shape, color, pattern, and so on.

Selecting and deselecting objects

In order to do anything with an object (change its size, position, or attributes, for example), you must first select it. To select an object, choose the pointer tool from the Tool panel and click the object. Handles appear around the object's border to show that it is selected. (Normally, eight handles appear, but you can change that to four by changing the Graphics preferences. See Chapter 11 for details.)

Note To select a transparent object, you have to click its border.

You also can select multiple objects. This capability is useful when you want to apply the same command or formatting to a number of objects. To select more than one object, do one of the following:

✦ Select the pointer tool and press the Shift key as you click objects

✦ Select the pointer tool and drag a selection rectangle around the objects

✦ Select the pointer tool and press ⌘ as you drag through the objects

✦ Choose Edit ⇨ Select All (or press ⌘+A) to select all objects in the current document

✦ Click an object type in the Tool panel and then choose Edit ⇨ Select All to select all objects of that type

Note The last technique works differently with bezigons, polygons, regular polygons, and freehand shapes. If you select one of these objects from the Tool panel and issue the Select All command, objects of all of these types are selected.

To deselect an object, click anywhere outside the object. To deselect individual objects when several have been selected, Shift-click them. Remember that for transparent objects you must Shift-click their border.

Changing the size of an object

You can change the size of a selected object in three ways:

✦ Dragging one of its handles

✦ Using the Scale By Percent command

✦ Using the Object Size command

When dragging one of an object's handles to change the size of the object, you can constrain the angle of movement by pressing the Shift key as you drag. You can change the Shift constraint in the Graphics preferences. By default, the angle is set to 45-degree increments.

STEPS: Changing an Object's Size Using the Scale By Percent Command

1. Select the object or objects whose size you want to change.

2. Choose Arrange ➪ Scale By Percent. The Scale By Percent dialog box appears (see Figure 6-5).

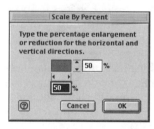

Figure 6-5: The Scale By Percent dialog box

3. Type new figures for the vertical or horizontal dimensions of the selected object. (To change the dimensions proportionately, type the same percentage for both dimensions.)

4. Click the OK button.

You can easily change an object's size or rotation with the Object Size command. Select the object whose size you want to change, and then choose Object Size from the Options menu. The Object Size windoid appears (see Figure 6-6). To change the horizontal or vertical dimensions (width or height) of the selected object, type new figures in the Width and/or Height text boxes. To change an object's orientation (rotation), type a new figure in the Rotation angle text box.

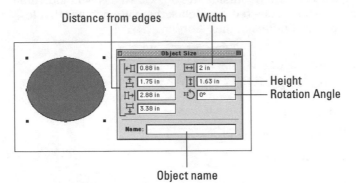

Figure 6-6: The numbers in the Object Size windoid refer to the currently selected object.

New Feature   In AppleWorks 6, you are now able to name objects in the drawing layer (including frames). Although there are currently no tools to search for named objects, the capability is useful as a place to store reference information such as a source material reference, a modification date, or some other reminder.

Smoothing and unsmoothing objects

You can smooth or unsmooth polygons, regular polygons, bezigons, and freehand shapes. Smoothing an object converts all angles into curves. Unsmoothing an object changes all curves into angles. To smooth an object, select it and choose Edit ➪ Smooth or press ⌘+(. To unsmooth an object, choose Edit ➪ Unsmooth or press ⌘+).

Caution   When you are working with a bezigon, smoothing and unsmoothing are not necessarily opposites. You might prefer to use the Edit ➪ Undo command to return to the original shape after you use the Smooth or Unsmooth command for a bezigon.

Setting object attributes: The Accents windoid

You can set the following object attributes to draw objects:

✦ Fill color

✦ Fill pattern

✦ Fill wallpaper (formerly called texture)

✦ Fill gradient

✦ Pen color

✦ Pen pattern

✦ Line width

✦ Arrowheads for lines

You can set these attributes before or after you create an object. To set attributes beforehand, select them from the Accents windoid's various panels (see Figure 6-7) and then draw the object. The object automatically uses the current attributes.

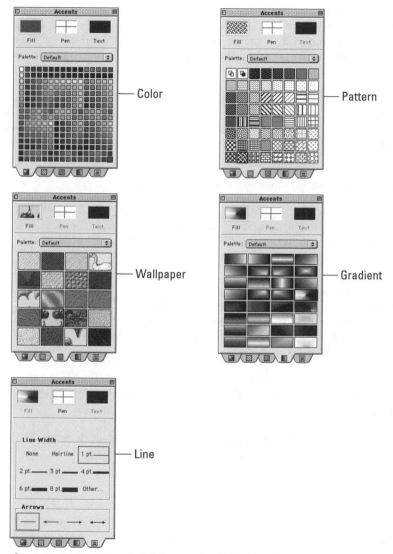

Figure 6-7: Accents windoid's panels: Color, Pattern, Wallpaper, Gradient, Line

To assign or change attributes for an existing object, select the pointer tool, select the object, and then select the new attributes from the various Accents windoid panels.

Tip   Although lines are normally solid, you can apply a pen pattern to a line to achieve interesting effects. For example, try different dot pen patterns to create dotted or stippled lines.

Transparent and opaque objects

Every object can be either transparent or opaque. An opaque object has a fill pattern and color, a wallpaper, or a gradient, and it obscures anything on the page that it covers. A transparent object, on the other hand, has no fill color, pattern, wallpaper, or gradient, and you can see anything on the page that it covers.

To make an object transparent, select the first fill pattern in the palette (the two linked blank squares). Any fill color, pattern, wallpaper, or gradient is temporarily removed. If you set the default fill pattern to transparent, the transparent icon is displayed in the Accent windoid's Fill text box as a reminder (see Figure 6-8).

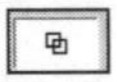

Figure 6-8: The default fill pattern is now transparent.

To make an object opaque (the default for all objects other than freehand shapes), select the second fill pattern in the palette (the linked blank and black squares). Any fill color that was previously applied to the object is restored.

Copying object attributes with the eyedropper tool

After setting attributes for an object, you can copy those attributes to other objects by using the eyedropper tool. To use the eyedropper tool, select the eyedropper tool from the Tool panel. Click the object whose attributes you want to copy. Select the eyedropper tool again and ⌘+click the objects to which you want to apply the attributes.

As with other draw tools, you can use the eyedropper repeatedly by double-clicking its icon in the Tool panel.

Tip   If a destination object has a transparent fill, you need to ⌘+click its border with the eyedropper to apply the attributes.

Arranging objects

The Arrange menu contains commands for moving, aligning, and reorienting objects. You also can move objects manually by dragging them, as well as make fine adjustments by using the arrow keys.

Moving objects

To manually reposition an object, select it with the pointer tool and drag the object to a new location. When you move a line, arc, rectangle, or oval, an outline of the object is visible as you drag. When you move other objects, only the bounding box is displayed as you drag.

To see the actual outline of a polygon, bezigon, or freehand shape as you drag it (rather than a rectangular bounding box), press ⌘ as you drag. To restrict movements to the current Shift constraint angle (set in the Graphics preferences), press the Shift key as you drag. (The Shift technique is particularly useful when you want to keep objects aligned with each other.)

You also can move a selected object by pressing any of the arrow keys. When Autogrid is disabled, the object moves one pixel in the direction of the arrow key. When Autogrid is enabled, the object moves one grid division (determined by the ruler type currently set). To enable or disable Autogrid, press ⌘+Y, or choose the appropriate command from the Options menu (Turn Autogrid On or Turn Autogrid Off).

One other way to move an object is to use the Object Size windoid (previously shown in Figure 6-6), which is displayed when you choose Options ⇨ Object Size. To change the position of a selected object, simply type new numbers in the Object Size windoid to set the object's distance from the left, top, right, or bottom edge of the page.

About the graphics grid

The dotted lines you see on a new draw document are called the graphics grid. The ruler type in effect and the number of divisions specified for that ruler govern the spacing of the dots. (By default, the unit of measurement is inches, and each inch has eight divisions.) When you use the Format ⇨ Rulers ⇨ Ruler Settings command to change the ruler or the number of divisions, you change the grid.

The grid can be shown or hidden. To hide the grid, choose Options ⇨ Hide Graphics Grid. To make it visible again, choose Options ⇨ Show Graphics Grid.

Only a portion of the grid is visible. You can think of the visible portion (grid points) as being grid border markers. As Figure 6-9 illustrates, many additional grid points are inside each rectangular grid section.

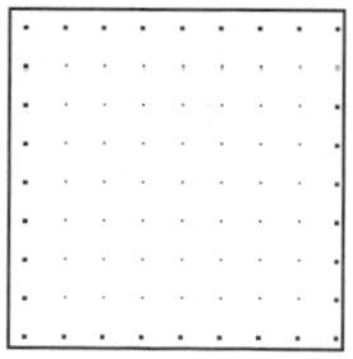

Figure 6-9: This single grid section is magnified 200 percent. The small dots inside the grid represent the grid points you cannot see.

Aligning objects

The Autogrid feature causes objects to align with the nearest point on the grid. When Autogrid is disabled, you can place objects without being constrained to a grid point. Choose Options ⇨ Turn Autogrid On or Options ⇨ Turn Autogrid Off (or press ⌘+Y) to change the state of the grid.

When Autogrid is disabled, you can still make objects align with the grid by using the Arrange ⇨ Align to Grid (Shift+⌘+L) command.

In many cases, having a set of objects align perfectly with one another is more important than having them align with the grid.

STEPS: Aligning Objects to Each Other

1. Select the objects you want to align to one another (drag or Shift-click to select multiple objects).

2. Choose Arrange ⇨ Align Objects (or press Shift+⌘+K). The Align Objects dialog box appears, as shown in Figure 6-10.

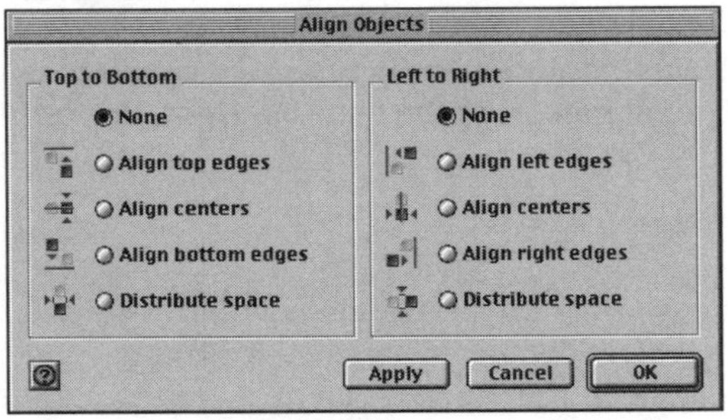

Figure 6-10: The Align Objects dialog box

3. Click the radio buttons for the desired alignment options.

4. Click the OK button to perform the alignment.

If the result is not what you intended, immediately choose Undo from the Edit menu and perform the steps again.

Object layers

You can place draw objects over one another, creating layers. Using the appropriate menu command, you can move an object to the top or bottom layer of a drawing or one step up or down in the layer hierarchy. Figure 6-11 shows two different stacking orders for the same set of objects.

To change an object's layer, start by selecting the object. To move one layer toward the front or the back, choose Arrange ➪ Move Forward (Shift+⌘++ [plus sign]) or Arrange ➪ Move Backward (Shift+⌘+– [minus sign]). To move the object directly to the top or bottom layer, choose Arrange ➪ Move to Front or Arrange ➪ Move to Back.

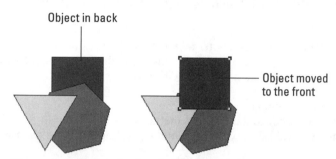

Figure 6-11: Bring the box in back to the front layer by choosing the Move to Front command.

Flipping and rotating objects

The Arrange menu has other commands you can use to change the orientation of selected objects:

✦ Flip Horizontally creates a mirror image of an object, reversing the left and right sides

✦ Flip Vertically creates a reflection of the object (as though it was sitting on the edge of a lake), reversing the top and bottom

Figure 6-12 shows the result of applying these commands to an object.

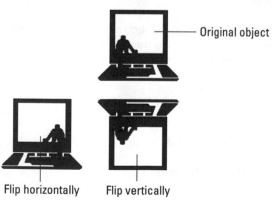

Figure 6-12: The original object and the object after the Flip Horizontally and Flip Vertically commands are applied to it

Draw objects also can be rotated — either manually or by typing a specific angle of rotation.

To rotate an object manually, click to select the object. Choose Arrange ➪ Free Rotate (or press Shift+⌘+R). The cursor changes to a ✕. Click one of the object's handles and drag to rotate the object. When the object is correctly rotated, release the mouse button.

To rotate an object to a specific angle, click to select the object. Choose Arrange ➪ Rotate. The Rotate dialog box appears. Specify the angle to which the object should be rotated (counterclockwise), and then click the OK button.

Note

It is important that you remember that rotation commands measure in a counter-clockwise direction from a horizontal axis and that arcs are measured in a clock-wise direction from a vertical axis or you will spend a great deal of time choosing Edit ➪ Undo.

You also can rotate an object to a specific angle using the Object Size windoid (shown earlier in Figure 6-6). Choose Options ➪ Object Size. In the Object Size windoid, type a rotation angle in the lower-right text box. Type a positive number to rotate the object counterclockwise, or a negative number to rotate it clockwise.

Duplicating objects

In addition to the normal copy-and-paste routine, you can use the Duplicate command to make a copy of an object and simultaneously paste it. To duplicate an object, select it and choose Edit ➪ Duplicate (or press ⌘+D). A copy of the object appears. If you immediately move the duplicate to its new position and then choose the Duplicate command again, the new duplicate will be offset the same distance and direction as the preceding one, provided that it will still fit within the document's borders. Duplicate is extremely useful for quickly creating a series of parallel, equidistant lines or other objects.

Tip

Here's a fun tip: The duplicate object will change direction if you place it where it otherwise might touch a page margin. With this in mind, if you use the Duplicate command repeatedly with the same object, you can create interesting graphic effects, such as the 3D tube shown in Figure 6-13.

Deleting objects

To delete an object, select it and use one of the following methods:

✦ Press the Delete, Backspace, Del, or Clear keys.

✦ Choose Edit ➪ Clear.

✦ Choose Edit ➪ Cut (or press ⌘+X).

The Cut command places a copy of the object on the clipboard. The other procedures delete the object without copying it to the clipboard.

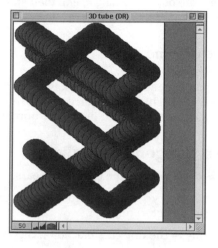

Figure 6-13: Dozens of repetitions of the Duplicate command can have surprising results.

 Note You also can use any of these procedures to delete several selected objects at the same time. If any of the objects are Locked (see the "Locking and unlocking objects" section that follows later in this chapter), you will receive an error message.

Combining objects

Sometimes, combining objects is useful. AppleWorks provides two methods of combining objects: grouping (which enables you to treat several objects as a single object) and reshaping (which links objects end to end).

Combining objects with the Group command

After you painstakingly create a complex series of interrelated objects, dealing with the objects as a whole is often easier and safer than dealing with the individual objects. After you select all the components of the image, you can create a single object with a single set of handles by choosing Arrange ➪ Group (or pressing ⌘+G). You can then, for example, move all the objects at the same time without fear of leaving a piece or two behind. You also can apply other Arrange commands to the new object group to flip or rotate it, or you can choose a new color, gradient, wallpaper, or pattern.

If you ever need to work with the component parts, simply select the grouped object and choose Arrange ➪ Ungroup (or press Shift+⌘+G). The components reappear, and you can work with them individually again.

Tip

You can create groups of objects where some of the constituent objects are themselves groups. This enables you to create a hierarchy of objects. Such a technique is useful when you are assembling complex diagrams, such as organizational charts where you might group the text with the box containing it, and then group the department before adding it to the division, and so on.

Combining objects with the Reshape command

The Group command enables you to treat several distinct objects as a united group. The Reshape command, on the other hand, enables you to link two or more freehand shapes, polygons, or bezigons end to end. This technique can be useful when you are designing repeating patterns, such as those used in picture borders.

STEPS: Linking Freehand Shapes, Polygons, or Bezigons

1. Choose Arrange ⇨ Reshape (or press ⌘+R). The reshape cursor appears.

2. Select the freehand shape, polygon, or bezigon you want to attach to another object. Hollow handles appear around the selected object.

3. Choose Edit ⇨ Copy (or press ⌘+C). A copy of the object is placed on the clipboard.

4. Select the second object (the one to which you want to attach the first object).

5. If you want to attach the object to the second object's starting point, select the starting point. Otherwise, the object will be attached to the endpoint.

6. Choose Edit ⇨ Paste (or press ⌘+V). A copy of the first object is connected to the second object.

7. If required, repeat Step 6 to attach additional copies end to end.

8. Choose Arrange ⇨ Reshape or select another drawing tool to complete the process.

Tip

If you press the Option key while choosing the Paste command in Step 6, the last point — rather than the first point — of the copied object will be attached to the second object.

Locking and unlocking objects

If the position or attributes of a particular object are critical to a document, you can lock the object in place and keep it from being altered by selecting the object and choosing Arrange ⇨ Lock (or pressing ⌘+H). If you later want to modify, delete, or move the object, choose Arrange ⇨ Unlock (or press Shift+⌘+H).

Creating custom colors, patterns, textures, and gradients

If you want to use special colors, patterns, wallpapers, or gradients (fills that blend from one color to another) that are not already in the palettes on the various Accents windoid panels, you can create new ones.

Custom colors, patterns, wallpapers, and gradients are automatically saved with the document in which they are created. You also can save the palette separately for use with other documents. To create a reusable color palette, choose a palette from the Color panel's Palette pop-up menu and make modifications as described here.

STEPS: Creating a Custom Color for the Current Document

1. Open the Accents windoid, if it is not already open (Window ⇨ Show Accents or ⌘+K) and click the Color tab (the leftmost tab).

2. Choose your starting palette from Palette pop-up menu.

3. Double-click the color you want to replace. A color chooser dialog box appears, as shown in Figure 6-14.

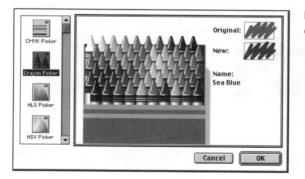

Figure 6-14: Select a new color from the color chooser.

4. To select a replacement color, you can do any of the following, or use a combination of these approaches (the options depend on the color chooser in use):

   • Click a different color on the wheel or other color chooser

   • Drag the scroll bar to change the lightness (brightness) of the colors

   • Specify new numbers for Hue Angle, Saturation, or Lightness

5. Click the OK button to save the change. The new color replaces the original color in both the Fill Color and Pen Color palettes. (To revert to the original color, click the Cancel button.)

6. Repeat Steps 3 through 5 for any additional colors you want to modify.

If you want this palette to be usable in other documents, choose Save as from the Palette pop-up menu, name the palette (AppleWorks will automatically navigate to the Palettes folder within the AppleWorks Essentials folder), and then click the Save button.

Note   All color palettes available for use appear in the Color panels Palette pop-up menu. Select a palette name from the pop-up menu and your new choice will be the default palette used.

STEPS: Creating a Custom Pattern for the Current Document

1. Choose Options ⇨ Edit Patterns. If the Accents windoid is not already showing, this will display it with the Patterns panel selected, as well as displaying the Pattern Editor dialog box (see Figure 6-15).

Edit the pattern in this box

Sample box

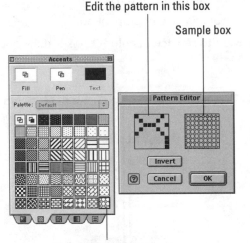

Selected pattern

Figure 6-15: The Patterns panel and Pattern Editor dialog box

2. Select any pattern you want to modify in the Patterns panel to have the Pattern Editor load it.

3. In the box on the left side of the Pattern Editor dialog box, click or drag to change the pattern. White spots that are clicked change to black, and black spots that are clicked change to white. To reverse the pattern (swapping whites for blacks and vice versa), click the Invert button.

4. Click the OK button to accept the new pattern, or click the Cancel button to revert to the previous pattern. The edited pattern appears in the panel in place of the pattern you double-clicked.

5. *Optional:* Repeat Steps 2 through 4 for any additional patterns you want to modify or replace.

Tip   You also can double-click any pattern in the Patterns panel to invoke the Pattern Editor with the chosen pattern loaded.

If you want to have this palette of patterns available for use in other documents, choose Save as from the Pattern panel's Palette pop-up menu, name the palette (AppleWorks automatically navigates to the Palettes folder within the AppleWorks Essentials folder), and click the Save button.

AppleWorks 6 includes a collection of wallpapers (formerly called Textures) in the Wallpaper panel in the Accents window (third from the left), which you can use to fill draw objects and selected areas in paint documents and frames. Each palette includes 20 colorful wallpapers you can use as-is or replace with others of your own design. Additional Wallpaper palettes can be loaded from or saved to disk using the Wallpaper panel's Palette pop-up menu.

STEPS: Creating a Custom Texture for the Current Document

1. Choose Options ➪ Edit Wallpapers. If the Accents windoid is not already showing, this will display it with the Wallpaper panel selected, as well as displaying the Wallpaper Editor dialog box (see Figure 6-16).

   or

   Double-click any wallpaper on the Wallpaper panel you want to replace. The Wallpaper Editor appears, set for the chosen design.

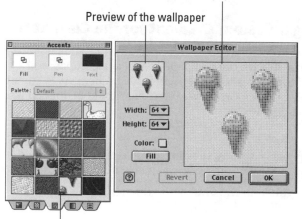

Figure 6-16: The Wallpaper panel and the Wallpaper Editor

2. Select a height and width for the wallpaper from the pop-up menus on the left side of the Wallpaper Editor. To choose an editing color, click the Color pop-up palette. To fill the entire wallpaper with the current color (to serve as a background, for example), click the Fill button.

3. In the box on the right side of the Wallpaper Editor, click or drag to change the current texture. As you edit, the changes are shown in the sample in the upper-left corner of the Wallpaper Editor dialog box.

4. Click the OK button to save the new wallpaper, click the Cancel button to ignore the changes, or click the Revert button to change the wallpaper back to what it was when you opened the Wallpaper Editor. The new wallpaper appears in the Wallpaper panel for the selected palette.

Tip

Although you can create new wallpapers by hand, you also can paste an existing wallpaper or graphic image into the Wallpaper Editor. Simply copy an image from AppleWorks, the Scrapbook, or another graphics program and then—with the Wallpaper Editor onscreen—choose Edit ⇨ Paste (or press ⌘+V).

Every gradient is a sweep from one color to another and can contain two to four colors. AppleWorks supports three types of sweeps: directional, circular, and shape burst. Every sweep has a focus (shown as a hollow circle or hollow square in the Focus section of the Gradient Editor dialog box). In a directional sweep, the focus is the position at which the final color appears. In a circular sweep, the focus is the point around which the gradient sweeps. A shape burst sweep is based on the shape of the rectangle around which the gradient sweeps, and the focus is the lower-right corner of the rectangle.

The following steps explain how to create your own gradients. When working in the Gradient Editor, you can immediately see the effects of your changes by watching the Sample box.

STEPS: Creating a Custom Gradient for the Current Document

1. Choose Options ⇨ Edit Gradients. If the Accents windoid is not already showing, this will display it with the Gradients panel selected, as well as displaying the Gradients Editor dialog box (see Figure 6-17). Click any gradient you want to modify or replace in the Gradients panel and it will be loaded into the Gradient Editor dialog box.

   or

   If the Gradients panel is already showing, double-click any gradient you want to replace. The Gradient Editor dialog box appears, set for the chosen gradient.

2. Choose a sweep type from the Sweep pop-up menu.

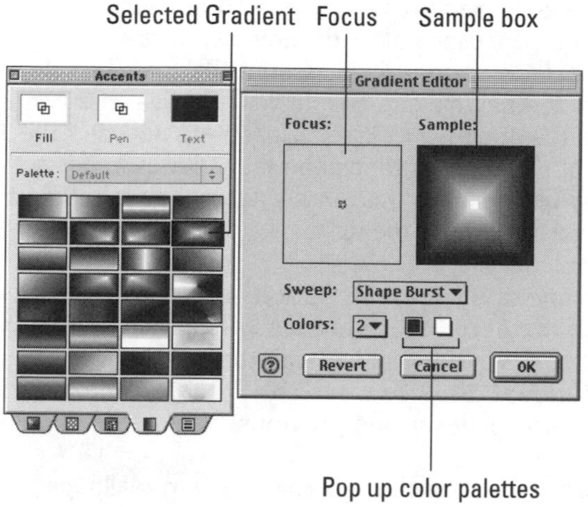

Selected Gradient   Focus   Sample box

Figure 6-17: The Gradient palette and the Gradient Editor

Pop up color palettes

3. Make the changes you want. The options are as follows:

- **Directional sweep.** You can set the number of colors by choosing a number from the Colors pop-up menu. Select the specific colors for the sweep from the pop-up color palettes. To change the focus, drag the hollow circle in the (unlabeled) Focus section of the Gradient Editor. You can set a new angle for the sweep by dragging the line or by typing an angle in the Angle text box.

- **Circular sweep.** You can set the number of colors by choosing a number from the Colors pop-up menu. Select the specific colors for the sweep from the pop-up color palettes. To change the focus, drag the hollow circle in the (unlabeled) Focus section of the Gradient Editor. You can set a new angle for the sweep by dragging the filled circle or by typing an angle in the Angle text box.

- **Shape burst sweep.** You can set the number of colors by choosing a number from the Colors pop-up menu. Select the individual colors for the sweep from the pop-up color palettes. To change the size of the shape burst focus, press the Option key and drag the black handle of the focus box in the Gradient Editor's Focus section. You can set the location of the focus by dragging the focus box to a new position.

4. Click the OK button to save the new gradient, the Cancel button to ignore the changes, or the Revert button to change the gradient back to its AppleWorks default.

Tip   As with custom color palettes, pattern, wallpaper, and gradient palettes also can be saved to disk and loaded for use in other documents. To save a custom pattern, wallpaper, or gradient palette, choose Save as from that panel's Palette pop-up menu. Type a name for the new palette (AppleWorks navigates automatically to the Palettes directory in the AppleWorks Essentials folder), and click the Save button. All saved palettes of the appropriate type in the Palettes folder are available through the Palette pop-up menus in the various Accents panels. Select one you want to load from the Palette pop-up menu.

Be aware that if you invoke an editor from the Options menu and the Accents window is not already showing, the Accents window also disappears when you exit from the editor. If you want to save the modified palette for use in other documents, you will need to choose Window ➪ Show Accents (⌘+K), select the appropriate panel, and then save the palette as described previously.

Tip   If you clicked the OK button to save a changed color, pattern, wallpaper, or gradient for use in this document (you haven't issued a Save as command to replace the palette) and you later decide you want the color, pattern, wallpaper, or gradient you replaced, save the current palette under a new name as described previously and then reload the original palette from disk using the Palette pop-up menu.

Adding pages to a draw document

By default, a draw document contains only a single page. Adding more pages can be useful (when you are creating a newsletter or brochure, for example). To add pages to a draw document, choose Format ➪ Document. The Document dialog box appears. Increase the number of pages across and/or pages down in the Size section of the dialog box. Click the OK button. The pages you specified are added to the document.

Down to business: Creating border designs

Whether you're getting ready for a presentation or just want to add some pizzazz to your document, a border frame is often a nice touch. For example, adding a border to a flyer can make the contents stand out. The following steps show you how to create a simple but attractive border that is composed of overlapping diamonds.

STEPS: Creating a Simple Border

1. Launch AppleWorks and create a new draw document.

2. Make sure Autogrid is enabled. (The command in the Options menu should read Turn Autogrid Off.) Having Autogrid enabled makes aligning the shapes easy.

3. Select the regular-polygon tool from the Tool panel. (It's shaped like a triangle.)

4. Choose Edit ⇨ Polygon Sides, type **4** in the dialog box that appears, and then click the OK button.

5. Select a fill color and/or pattern, wallpaper, or gradient from the relevant Accents windoid panel(s). You also can change the pen color and/or thickness to change the object's border.

6. Drag to create a small diamond shape and place the shape in the upper-left corner of the page.

7. With the shape still selected, choose Edit ⇨ Duplicate (or press ⌘+D).

8. Press the up-arrow key once. The second diamond overlaps the first one and is slightly offset to the right.

9. Press ⌘+D repeatedly to create additional diamonds for the top border. Each one should overlap the previous diamond in exactly the same way as the first duplicate did. Stop when the top border is the desired width.

10. Using the pointer, drag a selection rectangle around the row of diamonds.

11. Choose Arrange ⇨ Group (or press ⌘+G). The row of diamonds is now treated as a single object.

12. With the row still selected, choose Edit ⇨ Copy (or press ⌘+C).

13. Choose Edit ⇨ Paste (or press ⌘+V). A copy of the row is pasted over the original row.

14. Choose Rotate from the Arrange menu, type **90** in the dialog box that appears, and then click the OK button. A vertical column of diamonds appears.

15. Drag the column to the left side of the page and place it so that it overlaps with the left edge of the original row of diamonds.

16. With the column still selected, choose Copy and then Paste from the Edit menu. A copy of the column is pasted over the original column.

17. Drag the column to the right side of the page and place it so that it overlaps with the right edge of the original row of diamonds. If you press the Shift key as you drag, the column moves in a perfectly straight line.

18. Click to select the top row of diamonds and choose Copy and then Paste from the Edit menu. A copy of the row is pasted over the original row.

19. Drag the copy down until it overlaps with the bottom edges of the two columns. The resulting border should look like the one shown in Figure 6-18.

20. After the border is satisfactory, you can lock the rows and columns in place. Shift-click to select the four elements (or choose Select All from the Edit menu), and then choose Arrange ⇨ Lock (or press ⌘+H).

If you plan to use this border frequently, you can save it as an AppleWorks template rather than as a normal document. (For instructions on working with templates, see Chapter 1.)

Figure 6-18: The finished diamond border

Creating Master Pages for Your Documents

Although you can use headers and footers to make graphics and other items appear at the top and bottom of every page of a document, the process gets a bit sticky when you want an item to appear somewhere else on every page. To handle this situation, at least in draw documents, AppleWorks provides a feature called the *master page*.

Think of a master page as an extra layer or special page that appears onscreen (and is printed) behind every page of the document. A master page lends consistency to the background elements in a document without forcing you to paste and realign the objects on every new page. Master pages are commonly used to create backgrounds for AppleWorks slide shows (see Chapter 7), but are also useful for adding static information to letterhead templates and corporate forms. Objects you might want to place on a master page can include rules (solid lines that appear at the top of each page or that separate columns of text), page borders, a solid background or gradient, company logos, or presentation instructions (for example, "Press Tab to advance to next slide; press Shift+Tab to view previous slide").

You can create master pages only in draw documents. However, because you can place word processing, paint, and spreadsheet frames on draw documents, you should consider this a minor limitation, rather than a major inconvenience.

You can easily create master pages to add the same background elements to all pages in a document.

STEPS: Creating a Master Page

1. Open an existing draw document by pressing ⌘+O, or create a new one by clicking the Drawing button in the button bar or the Drawing thumbnail on your Starting Points Basics panel. (Alternatively, you can choose File ⇨ Open or File ⇨ New ⇨ Drawing.)

2. Choose Options ⇨ Edit Master Page. A blank master page is displayed, as shown in Figure 6-19. To remind you that you are editing a master page rather than working in the normal layer of the draw document, a checkmark appears next to the Edit Master Page command in the Options menu and the page number indicator at the bottom of the document window is replaced with the text "Master Page."

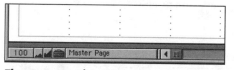

Figure 6-19: The Master Page indicator helps you to distinguish a master page from other pages of the document.

3. Add the master page elements to the page.

4. Choose Options ⇨ Edit Master Page. The checkmark next to the Edit Master Page command in the menu disappears, and the regular document is displayed.

5. If you are not in Page view, choose Window ⇨ Page View (or press Shift+⌘+P). You can view master page elements only when the document is in Page view.

You can edit master page elements, just as you can edit any other object, image, or text string that appears in a regular AppleWorks document. Simply choose Options ⇨ Edit Master Page and make whatever changes are necessary.

Quick Tips

The following quick tips tell you how to add a rotated rubber stamp to a master page and how to hide master page elements.

Adding a rotated rubber stamp to a master page

Rubber stamps, such as "Confidential," "Draft," or "Paid," are excellent objects to include on a master page. Text placed over a Confidential or Draft rubber stamp, for example, is still perfectly legible, but the stamp clearly shows that the document is not intended for general distribution.

To achieve a rubber stamp effect in versions of ClarisWorks prior to 4.0, you had to create the text in a paint document or frame, rotate the text, copy it, and then paste the text into the master page of the draw document. Free rotation was only available for paint images. Objects, such as text strings, could also be rotated, but only in 90-degree increments. AppleWorks 6 has powerful rotation commands. Objects of any sort, including text, can be directly rotated to any angle, not just in 90-degree increments as described earlier in this chapter.

All you have to do to create the rubber-stamp look is to place a text object (Text tool) on the master page, size it, rotate it, and position it using the methods previously described. Using the Outline style (Text ⇨ Style ⇨ Outline) is very effective for such stamps, as illustrated in Figure 6-20.

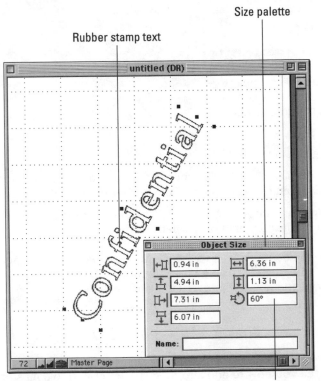

Figure 6-20: An example of rotated text on a master page

Obscuring elements on the master page

Occasionally, you may want to obscure some of the elements on the master page. For example, you may want all elements to show through on every page except on the document's first page. (Perhaps you intend to use the first page as a title page.) A simple way to hide a master page element without altering the master page itself is to cover the element with an opaque white square, which you place on the regular document page. The following instructions describe how to hide the Draft rubber stamp shown in Figure 6-21.

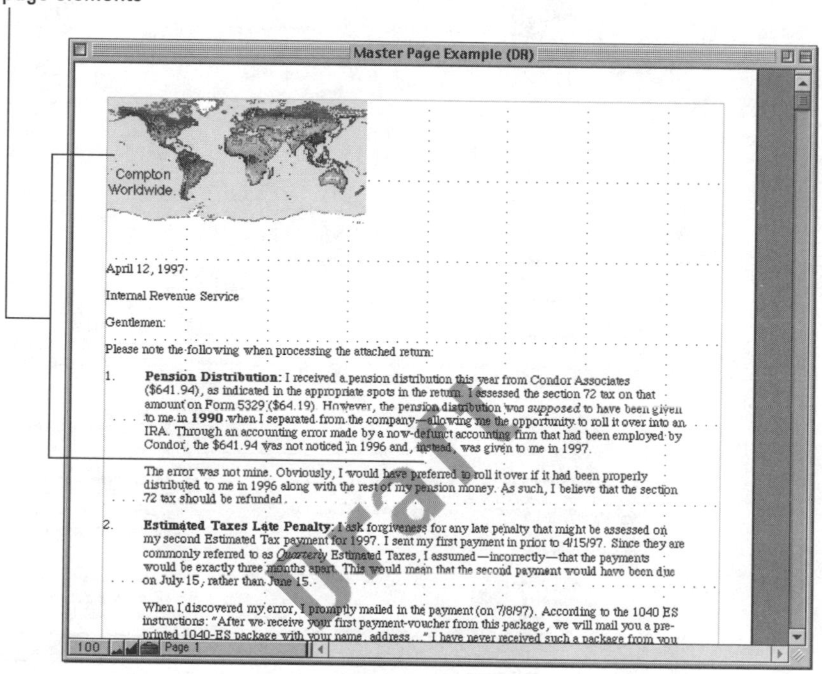

Master page elements

Figure 6-21: The original document with two master page elements: a logo and a Draft rubber stamp

STEPS: Hiding a Master Page Element

1. Open the draw document that contains the master page.

2. Pull down the Options menu and make sure Edit Master Page does not have a checkmark beside it. If it does, choose it again. (This action ensures that you are editing the regular document page, not the master page.)

3. If you cannot see the master page elements, choose Window ⇨ Page View (or press Shift+⌘+P).

4. Select the rectangle tool in the Tool panel.

5. Draw a rectangle that completely covers the master page element you want to hide.

6. With the rectangle still selected, set the fill and pen color to white, and set the fill and pen pattern to opaque. The document should look like the one shown in Figure 6-22.

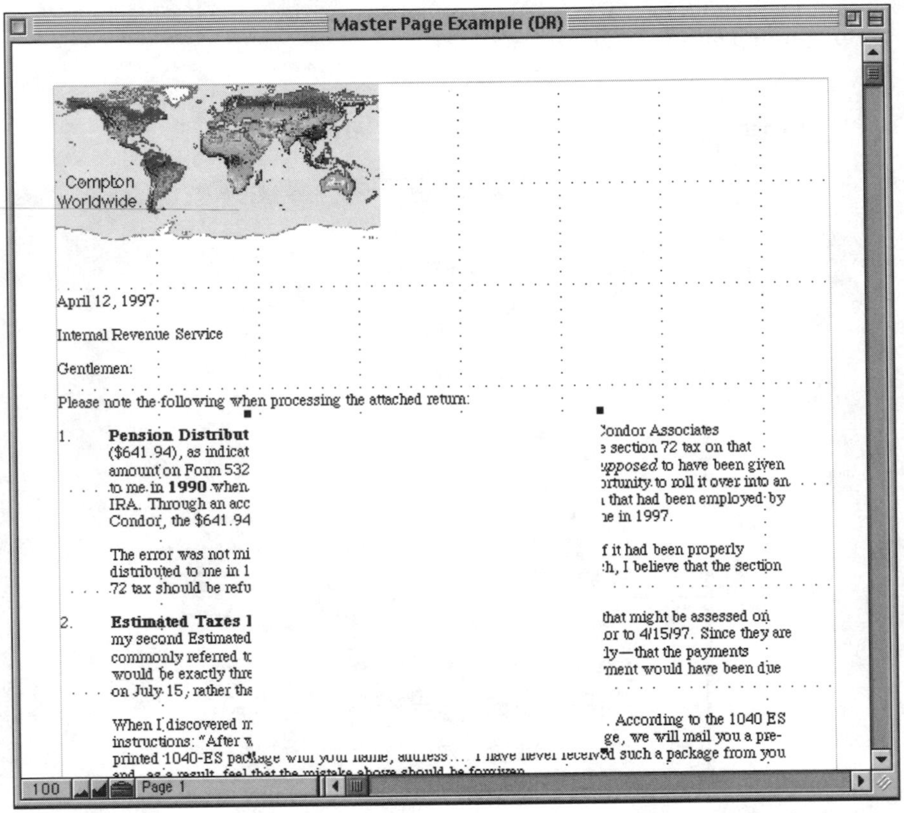

Figure 6-22: The opaque white rectangle obscures the master page Draft element.

Notice that, in addition to obscuring the master page Draft element, the white rectangle obscures much of the body text of the document. To correct this problem, you need to move the rectangle into the proper document layer.

7. Choose Move Backward from the Arrange menu or press Shift+⌘+– (minus sign). The rectangle moves into the layer between the master page and the body text.

Using the Master Page to Obscure Objects

In previous versions of AppleWorks you could move objects behind the master page layer. This is no longer possible with documents created in AppleWorks 6 — the master page layer is purely a background layer. However, in an effort to not "break" documents created in earlier versions, if you open a document with that layering effect, you can still move objects in front of or behind the master page elements.

The Paint Environment

The paint environment enables you to create and edit bitmapped images, which are graphics composed entirely of dots. Unlike draw objects, paint images can be edited at the dot level. In fact, only dots or groups of dots can be edited. The precise control this capability provides is what makes the paint environment so useful in creating complex illustrations.

Creating a new paint document or frame

Although you can create draw objects in almost any document type, you must either design paint images in a paint document or place them in a paint frame in another AppleWorks environment. To create a new paint document, choose File ➪ New ➪ Painting, or click the Painting icon in the Button Bar.

Note
If sufficient memory is not available, you might be notified that the document size will be reduced. For instructions on increasing the available memory (and, in turn, the size of your paint documents), see "Quick Tips" at the end of this chapter.

To create a paint frame in another AppleWorks environment, click the painter's palette tool in the Frames panel and drag to draw the paint frame.

Note
You also can drag the painter's palette tool to the layout surface and a default-sized paint frame (200 by 132 pixels) will be created.

Paint frames and paint documents can contain only bitmapped graphics. Although you can place draw objects and frames from other environments into a paint frame or document, the object or frame from the other environment loses its environmental identity the instant you deselect it — by clicking outside the frame, choosing another tool, or so on. At that moment, the object or frame is converted to a paint image, which you can edit only by using the paint tools. The same is also true for text you type or paste into a paint document or frame.

Tip   As with other frames, a paint frame is surrounded by a rectangular border. To make the border invisible (so the paint image will blend with the rest of the document), set the pen color to white, the line width to none, or set the pen pattern to transparent.

While you are working in a paint frame or in a paint document, the normally grayed-out paint tools are made available for use (see Figure 6-23).

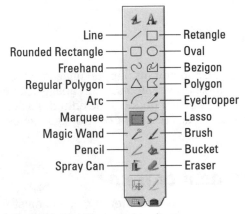

Figure 6-23: The paint tools

Note   The upper nine tools that, in ordinary circumstances, produce draw objects, are now paint tools. When you use them in a paint frame or a paint document, these tools create bitmapped graphics — not objects. For instructions on using these tools in a paint frame or paint document, see "Creating objects with the draw tools," earlier in this chapter. The information in that section concerning the Shift constraint also applies.

Many of the object modification commands are no longer available as menu commands when you are working in the paint environment. However, you can make the following dialog boxes appear:

✦ **Round Corners.** Double-click the rounded rectangle tool in the Tool panel.

✦ **Modify Arc.** Double-click the arc tool in the Tool panel.

✦ **Number of sides.** Double-click the regular polygon tool in the Tool panel.

Tip

You might also want to experiment by double-clicking other tools while working in a paint document or frame. Double-clicking the eraser erases the entire frame or paint document. Double-clicking the spray can presents a dialog box in which you can edit the spray pattern. Double-clicking the paint brush presents a dialog box in which you can select a brush size and shape. Double-clicking the lasso selects the entire frame or document less any white border. Double-clicking the pencil zooms the magnification level. Double-clicking the selection marquee selects the entire frame or paint document (holding down the ⌘ key while double-clicking the marquee gives the same result as double-clicking the lasso).

Paint modes

AppleWorks supports three paint modes:

✦ **Opaque.** Any color, pattern, wallpaper, or gradient placed on another image completely covers the image beneath it.

✦ **Transparent pattern.** Any pattern that contains white areas or dots enables the image beneath to show through. A gradient, wallpaper, or solid color placed over another image, however, is still treated as opaque (completely covering the image beneath it).

✦ **Tint.** A color, pattern, wallpaper, or gradient placed on another image results in a blending of the colors. Depending on the colors chosen, the overlap might not show the change. For best results, use colors with greater contrast.

Figure 6-24 shows examples of the three paint modes.

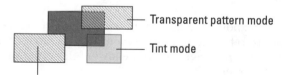

Transparent pattern mode

Tint mode

Opaque mode

Figure 6-24: The three paint modes

To set the paint mode, choose Options ➪ Paint Mode. The Painting Mode dialog box appears. Click the radio button for Opaque, Transparent pattern, or Tint, and then click the OK button.

Using the paint tools

When you create draw objects, you can set attributes before or after you create the object. When you work in the paint environment, on the other hand, you should generally select fill and pen attributes before you use each tool. Except for filling closed images, assigning attributes after you create an image can be very difficult.

> **Note**
> When you select a paint tool from the Tool panel, it automatically remains selected until you choose a different tool. Double-clicking the tool, as you do to keep one selected in the draw environment, generally has a different effect, as described previously.

Using the pencil

You use the pencil tool to create and edit single dots, make freehand drawings (much as you do with the freehand tool), and draw thin lines. When you first open a paint document or paint frame, the pencil is automatically selected.

Only the fill color setting affects the pencil. Other settings from the Accents window have no effect.

You can click to create single dots or click and drag to create lines. If you press the Shift key as you draw with the pencil, you can make straight vertical or horizontal lines.

When you click a blank or colored pixel on the screen with the pencil, a dot of the current fill color is produced (black, if a wallpaper or gradient is selected as the Fill). If you click a pixel that is the same color as the current fill color, on the other hand, the pixel changes to white.

Double-clicking the pencil tool icon zooms the document window to 800 percent, making it easy to do fine editing. To return to the 100-percent view, double-click the pencil tool again, or click the Zoom Percentage box in the lower-left corner of the document window and select 100 percent.

Using the brush

Use the brush tool to paint in the current Fill color and pattern. (You cannot use a gradient fill with the brush, but you can use a wallpaper.)

> **Note**
> If your Fill is set to a gradient, the last combination of color and pattern selected as a fill in this document (black and solid are the defaults) will be used.

To change to a different brush shape, double-click the brush icon in the Tool panel or choose Options ➪ Brush Shape. The Brush Shape dialog box appears.

To choose a different brush, select it and click the OK button. To create a new brush (by editing one of the existing brush shapes), select a brush shape and click the Edit button. The Brush Editor appears.

Alter the brush shape by clicking and dragging in the box. When you click a white spot, it becomes black. When you click a black spot, it becomes white. Click the OK button to accept the new brush shape (for this document only), and then click the OK button again to close the Brush Shape dialog box.

The Brush Shape dialog box now sports an Effects pop-up menu, which enables you to change the effect the brush has on existing pixels it touches. Normal simply paints over them, but you also can choose Blend, Lighter, Darker, or Tint.

 Tip You can cut brush patterns out of images by setting the fill color to white or the fill pattern to transparent before you use the brush. Be sure the brush effect is set to Normal.

Using the paint bucket

The paint bucket tool's sole function is to fill a closed area with a color, pattern, wallpaper, or gradient. The tip of the bucket (the tiny stream of paint pouring over its side) is the active area of the paint bucket cursor (see Figure 6-25). It shows where the paint will be applied.

 Figure 6-25: The paint bucket is poised to fill the pimento inside this olive.

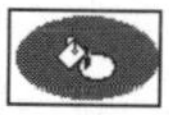

If the paint bucket is applied to an area that is currently filled with a pattern, wallpaper, or gradient, a solid color fill will seldom be successful. The procedure for refilling an area that contains a pattern or gradient is to select it and then choose Transform ➪ Fill. (If the area is filled with a solid color, on the other hand, you can use the paint bucket to fill the area with a color, pattern, wallpaper, or gradient.)

 Caution If the area you're attempting to fill is not completely closed, the fill color, pattern, wallpaper, or gradient might be applied to many unintended areas in the document or frame. Choose Edit ➪ Undo (⌘+Z) immediately to remove the fill. Before filling again, zoom the screen to locate and fill in the pixels needed to close the area. If you deliberately apply the paint bucket to a blank area in the background, on the other hand, you can quickly add a color, pattern, wallpaper, or gradient to the entire background for a picture or paint frame.

Using the spray can

The spray can tool works like an artist's airbrush. You can change both the dot size and the flow rate to achieve different effects.

To use the spray can, select a fill (color and pattern, wallpaper, or gradient), select the spray can in the Tool panel, and either click the mouse to spray or press the mouse button and drag. To spray in a straight vertical or horizontal line, press the Shift key as you click and drag.

STEPS: Changing the Spray Can Settings

1. Double-click the spray can icon in the Tool panel or choose Options ⇨ Edit Spray Can. The Edit Spray Can dialog box appears, as shown in Figure 6-26.

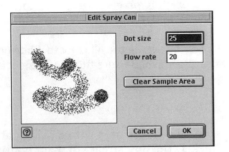

Figure 6-26: The Edit Spray Can dialog box

2. Specify new figures for Dot Size (1 to 72) and Flow Rate (1 to 100).

   Dot size is in pixels (an inch has 72 pixels). (Dot size doesn't really vary the size of the dots; it changes the size or spread of the dot pattern.)

   Flow rate governs how fast the paint flows. At the highest setting, you get splotches of color everywhere the spray pattern touches.

3. To test different combinations of dot size and flow rate with the current fill color (even if you have a fill wallpaper or gradient selected, you will get the last color selected for a fill), click and drag in the sample area of the dialog box. (If you want to test different combinations in a clean sample area, you can click the Clear Sample Area button at any time.)

4. Click the OK button when the settings are to your liking.

Editing paint images

As in most other graphics programs, you usually spend as much time editing an image as you do creating it. Editing tools include the eraser, the selection rectangle, the lasso, and the magic wand.

Using the eraser

You use the eraser tool to erase portions of a paint image. Click to erase the part of the image that is beneath the eraser. You can click and drag to erase larger portions of the image. If you press the Shift key as you erase, you can drag the eraser in a straight horizontal or vertical line. (The first move you make as you drag determines the direction—if you move at an angle, it will drag in whichever direction is closer between horizontal or vertical.)

Tip   You cannot resize the eraser. If it's too big to erase a small section of a painting, zoom the screen to a greater magnification.

Selecting images and portions of images

When you want to work with a portion of a picture—to cut, copy, or move it; change the fill; or add a special effect to it—you first have to select the specific portion of the picture you want to edit. With draw objects, this task is simple. You just click the particular object you're interested in. In a paint document or frame, on the other hand, everything is just dots. Three tools are available for selecting a portion of a picture:

✦ The selection rectangle tool (called a *marquee*) enables you to make rectangular selections. Click to position one corner of the marquee, and then drag. When you release the mouse button, the selection is defined by the area enclosed in the flashing rectangle. You also can use a selection rectangle in the following ways:

- Press ⌘ while you drag a marquee around an image to make the selection snap around the image, just as the lasso tool does (described later).

- Double-click the marquee icon in the Tool panel to select the entire paint document or frame.

- Press ⌘ while you double-click the selection rectangle icon to select only the images within the paint document or frame (ignoring blank spaces).

- Press Option while you drag a selection to make a copy of it. (For example, you can use this feature to take a picture of one car and change it into a traffic jam.)

Tip   The trick of holding down the Option key when you drag something in AppleWorks to create a duplicate is omnipresent in all graphic activities, whether you're using draw or paint tools—it will even let you duplicate a frame.

✦ The lasso tool enables you to make irregular selections in a paint document or frame. Click and then drag around the area you want to select. When you release the mouse button, the lasso snaps around the images you have selected, ignoring blank background areas.

You can double-click the lasso icon in the Tool panel to select only the images within the paint document or frame. You also can press the Option key while you drag a selection to make a copy of it.

✦ The magic wand tool enables you to make selections based on color. When you position the head of the magic wand over the desired color or pattern and click the mouse button, all adjacent pixels that are the same color or pattern are selected.

✦ When you are attempting to select a pattern, dragging the magic wand through a small area of the pattern might be easier than just clicking. As you drag, a freehand-style line is displayed. When you release the mouse button, the selection is made. This last technique is a handy way of creating cutouts against a solid or patterned background as shown in Figure 6-27.

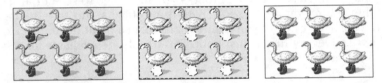

Figure 6-27: Create cutouts using the magic wand.

To deselect an image, click outside of the selection, click any tool icon, choose Edit ➪ Undo Select (or press ⌘+Z).

Moving, cutting, copying, or duplicating a selection

When you move the cursor over a selection you have made, the cursor changes to a pointer. If you click while the pointer is visible, you can drag the selection to a new location. If you press the Shift key as you drag, you drag straight horizontally or straight vertically.

You also can use the arrow keys to move the selection one pixel at a time. (If Autogrid is enabled, the selection moves one grid-point at a time.)

Commands in the Edit menu become available after you select an image or a portion of an image. You can cut (⌘+X) or copy (⌘+C) the image to the clipboard, clear the image, or duplicate it (⌘+D).

Applying special effects to a selection

Special effects in the Transform menu also become available after you make a selection. These effects include Slant, Stretch, and Add Perspective. Slant adds a vertical or horizontal slant to a selection. Stretch enables you to stretch an image in any direction. Add Perspective makes the image appear as if you are viewing it from an angle.

STEPS: Slanting, Stretching, or Adding Perspective to a Selection

1. Select a portion of the image by using one of the selection tools (selection rectangle, lasso, or magic wand).

2. Select Slant, Stretch, or Add Perspective from the Transform menu. Blank handles appear around the selection.

3. Drag a handle to achieve the desired effect.

4. Click away from the selection to remove the handles.

Figure 6-28 shows the effects of applying Slant, Stretch, and Add Perspective to an image.

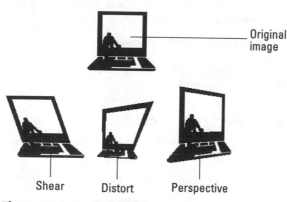

Figure 6-28: Special effects

> **Tip**
>
> You lose resolution when you modify an object by using these commands. Because you're (usually) in a 72-dpi mode and are in a bitmapped document, the pixels are modified during the transformation. Some pixels become larger, some smaller. This change is normal. If the result has too many jagged edges, clean up by zooming in and using the tools to smooth out the image. Another trick is to use the Blend option. This option makes the edges less noticeable.

Changing the size of a selection

Two commands in the Transform menu enable you to change the size of a selection: Resize and Scale By Percent. To change the size manually, use the Resize command. To change the size by specifying scaling proportions, use Scale By Percent.

STEPS: Using the Resize Command

1. Select a portion of the image by using one of the selection tools (the selection rectangle, lasso, or magic wand).

2. Choose Transform ➪ Resize. Blank handles appear around the selection, as shown in Figure 6-29.

Figure 6-29: The Resize command adds handles to the selection.

3. Drag a handle to change the size of the selection. When you release the mouse button, the selection is redrawn to the specified size.

4. Click away from the image to eliminate the Resize handles.

Note

If you press the Shift key as you drag a handle, the original proportions of the selection rectangle are maintained.

STEPS: Using the Scale By Percent Command

1. Select a portion of the image by using one of the selection tools (the selection rectangle, lasso, or magic wand).

2. Choose Transform ➪ Scale By Percent. The Scale By Percent dialog box appears, as shown in Figure 6-30.

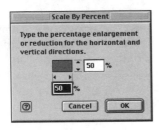

Figure 6-30: The Scale By Percent dialog box

3. Type percentages for enlargement (greater than 100 percent) or reduction (smaller than 100 percent). If you want to maintain proportions, enter the same percentage for both the horizontal and vertical dimensions. A 50 percent reduction is the default.

4. Click the OK button. The selection is resized.

Orientation transformations

The same commands available in the draw environment for changing an object's orientation are also available in the paint environment. To change the orientation of a selection, select a portion of the image and choose Flip Horizontally, Flip Vertically, Free Rotate, or Rotate. The first three commands — Flip Horizontally, Flip Vertically, and Free Rotate — work exactly the same way they do in the draw environment. (For additional information, see the description of these commands in "Flipping and rotating objects," earlier in this chapter.)

As with the Object Size command in the draw environment, the paint environment's Rotate command enables you to enter a rotation angle for a selection directly. To use the Rotate command, select a portion of the image by using one of the selection tools (the selection rectangle, lasso, or magic wand). Choose Transform ➪ Rotate. The Rotate dialog box appears. Enter a number (in degrees) for the counterclockwise rotation you desire. Click the OK button. The selection is rotated.

New Feature ClarisWorks 4.0 had a Rotate 90° command that was not available in AppleWorks 5. However, like General MacArthur returning to the Philippines, Rotate 90° has returned to AppleWorks 6.

Color transformations

At the bottom of the Transform menu are a number of useful color-related transformation commands. Here is what they do:

✦ **Fill.** This command duplicates the function of the paint bucket tool, enabling you to fill any selection with a color, pattern, wallpaper, or gradient. The difference is that the fill is applied only to the selected area, so it does not matter whether an image is closed or open; nor does it matter whether the selected area contains a solid color, a gradient, a wallpaper, or a patterned color.

✦ **Pick Up.** This command enables you to transfer the design and attributes of one image to another image. To use the command, select an image, drag it over another image, and choose Transform ➪ Pick Up.

Tip Creating patterned text is one interesting application of Pick Up. Type the text, select it by pressing ⌘ as you drag the selection rectangle tool around it, move it over an interesting pattern, and choose the Pick Up command. Figure 6-31 shows some text with a gradient pattern that was created in this manner.

✦ **Invert.** Use this command to make a negative image of a selection. Colors in the image are reversed, but not necessarily as you might expect them to be. An inverted grayscale gradient, for example, might show shades of yellow, green, and blue.

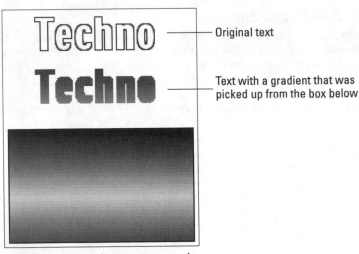

Figure 6-31: Gradient text created with the Pick Up command

✦ **Blend.** Use Blend to provide a smoother color transition between neighboring pixels by adding intermediate shades.

✦ **Tint.** Choose Tint to tint a selection with the current fill color.

✦ **Lighter and Darker.** Use these commands to add white or black to a selection, making it lighter or darker.

When you use any of the color transformation commands, make sure you select only the outline of an object and not part of the background, too. Each command applies to everything within the selection. To select only an object without the surrounding background, use the lasso or press ⌘ while you drag the selection rectangle.

Creating custom colors, patterns, textures, and gradients

As in the draw environment, you can replace colors, patterns, wallpapers, and gradients in the palettes with ones of your own choosing. Follow the instructions presented earlier in this chapter (in "Creating custom colors, patterns, wallpapers, and gradients" for the draw environment).

Other paint settings

Other menu commands that appear in the paint environment enable you to change the document size, the depth and resolution of the image, and the grid size (in conjunction with the Autogrid feature).

To change the size of a paint document, choose Format ➪ Document. The Document dialog box appears, as shown in Figure 6-32. In the Size section of the dialog box, type new numbers for pixels across and pixels down. As with points, an inch has 72 pixels. The maximum for either dimension is 2,000 pixels; the minimum is 36 pixels. Click the OK button to resize the document to the new dimensions.

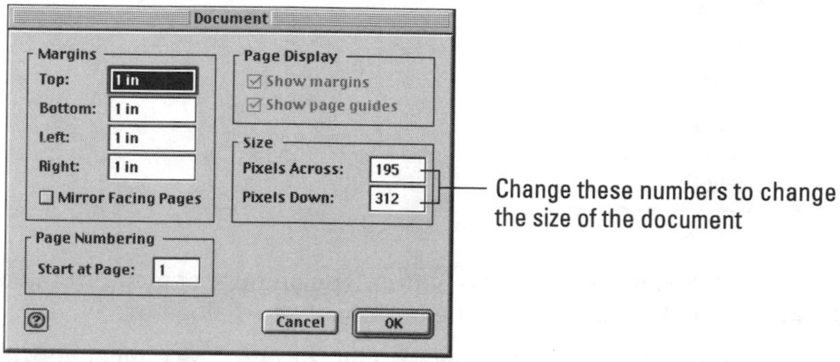

Figure 6-32: The Document dialog box

The resolution of a paint document is initially set to match the resolution of a typical Macintosh screen — 72 dots per inch (dpi). If you are printing on a high-resolution printer, you can change the resolution to match that of the printer.

As you increase the resolution, however, the document and its contents shrink accordingly. At 300-dpi, for example, a standard paint document reduces to about 1.5 to 2.25 inches. If you have enough free memory, you can increase the size of the document by following the preceding steps. You should note, however, that the higher the resolution and the larger the document size, the more memory is required. For this reason, many users will prefer to use the default 72-dpi setting for resolution.

Depth refers to the number of colors available for displaying the document. Depth is initially set to match the setting in the Monitors control panel.

STEPS: Changing the Depth and Resolution of a Paint Document or Frame

1. Choose Format ➪ Resolution & Depth from the Format menu. The Resolution and Depth dialog box appears, as shown in Figure 6-33.

2. Choose a resolution by clicking its radio button. Follow these guidelines:

   • Use 72 dpi for a document you intend to display only onscreen or print on a dot-matrix printer (if any of you still have such a printer). You also can use higher multiples of 72 (144 and 288) to maintain proportions when you print to an ImageWriter or equivalent printer.

- Use 300 dpi to match the resolution of many laser printers.
- Use 360 dpi to match the resolution of many ink-jet printers.

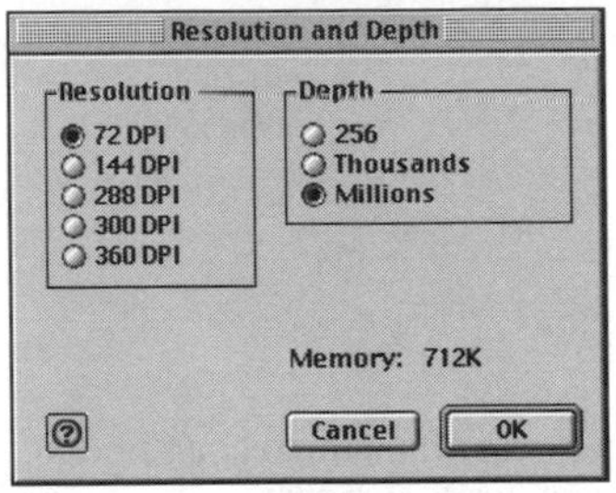

Figure 6-33: The Resolution and Depth dialog box

3. Choose a depth by clicking its radio button. The amount of memory the new Depth setting requires is shown at the bottom of the dialog box.

4. Click the OK button to accept the new settings, or click the Cancel button to ignore any changes.

If your paint frame is not active, select the frame and then choose Edit ➪ Frame Info. A similar dialog box appears, which enables you to set the resolution, depth, and the origin (starting point) for displaying the contents of the frame. Type in values (in pixels) for the horizontal and vertical coordinates. (See Chapter 14 for additional information.)

When importing a PICT file into a paint frame or document, AppleWorks automatically matches the resolution of the image and uses the document's original color table.

To change the grid size, choose Grid Size from the Options menu. The Painting Grid Size dialog box appears. Click the radio button for the desired grid size, and then click the OK button.

Tip

When the Autogrid option is enabled (in the Options menu), the grid size determines where you can place objects and how far they will move at each step when you drag or nudge them with an arrow key. The larger the setting for grid size, the farther apart the grid locations are. You can set the grid size to 2 pixels for fine control over image placement.

Note

If you want even more versatile screen-capture facilities, freeware, shareware, and commercial offerings are abundant. We used Snapz Pro 2 from Ambrosia Software (www.ambrosiasw.com) to create the figures in this book.

Screen Captures

If you're new to the Mac or haven't perused your MacOS Help files, you might not be aware that the Mac has a built-in screen-capture utility. By pressing the Shift+⌘+3, you instruct the Mac to capture (make a copy of) the current screen image. Commercial screen-capture utilities add other functions, such as the capability to capture a selected portion of the screen, capture pull-down menus, hide or display the cursor in the capture, and more.

If you press Shift+⌘+4, you can capture a selected area of the screen rather than the full screen, and if you press Shift+⌘+4 with the Caps Lock key down, you are presented with an "8-ball" cursor, which you can click in any window for a picture of just what it bounds.

Using the screen-capture utility and the tip for converting between paint and drawing described under Quick Tips, you can graphically illustrate how to perform various functions on your Mac.

Quick Tips

The following quick tips describe how to edit draw objects in the paint environment, change an edited paint image into a draw object, increase the memory available to AppleWorks, create and work with a second copy of a paint document, preview images before opening them, and insert graphics from the AppleWorks Clippings.

Editing draw objects in the paint environment

Occasionally, being able to edit draw objects at the dot level is useful. To perform this task, you simply copy the object, paste it into a paint document, edit, copy again, and then paste it back into the original document.

Although this procedure works, it has an unfortunate side effect: When you paste the image back into the original document, it is a paint frame—a bitmap. It is enclosed by a border, and you can no longer resize it the way you can resize an object. Here's a better method.

STEPS: Changing a Paint Image into a Draw Object

1. After you finish editing in the paint document, select and copy the image.
2. Pull down the Apple menu and choose the Scrapbook desk accessory.
3. Press ⌘+V. The image is pasted into the Scrapbook.

4. Press ⌘+X. The image is removed from the Scrapbook and copied to the clipboard as an object.

5. Open the target document (a draw or word processing document, for example) and choose Edit ➪ Paste (or press ⌘+V). The image is pasted into the document as an object.

Paint memory requirements

If you plan to work in the paint environment regularly — particularly with full-screen images — increasing the memory available to AppleWorks is a good idea. Otherwise, you'll frequently see the following message: "The document size has been reduced to fit available memory."

STEPS: Increasing the Memory Available to AppleWorks

1. Quit AppleWorks (if it is running), go to the desktop, and select the AppleWorks program icon.

2. Choose File ➪ Get Info ➪ Memory (or press ⌘+I and select Memory from the pop-up menu). The Info window for AppleWorks appears, as shown in Figure 6-34.

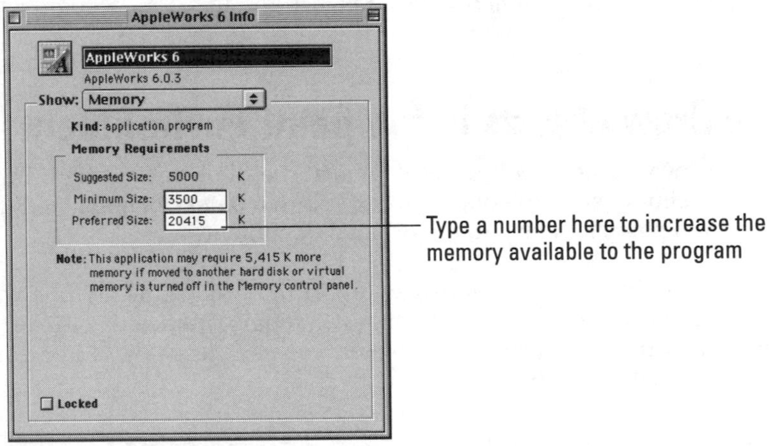

Type a number here to increase the memory available to the program

Figure 6-34: The AppleWorks Info window

The Info window enables you to change the program's memory allocation (the amount of memory the system will give you to run AppleWorks and work with AppleWorks documents).

3. Type a larger number in the Preferred Size text box.

4. Click the Info window's close box.

You can change the memory allocation as often as necessary. To track how much memory you're using in AppleWorks, go to the desktop and select ✿ ➪ About This Computer. A window appears that shows how much memory the system and any open programs (AppleWorks, for example) are currently using (see Figure 6-35).

Figure 6-35: The About This Computer window shows how much memory the system and any open programs are currently using.

You also can see the amount of memory that is still free for use by other programs, desk accessories, and so on. A bar for each program shows the total memory allocated to the program. The dark area of each bar represents memory currently in use. The light area is memory you can use to open additional documents or expand the size of current documents.

Painting in two views

When you edit a paint image at a high magnification, seeing a normal view of the image at the same time is sometimes helpful. To create a second copy of a paint document, choose Window ➪ New View. To help you see both copies at the same time, choose Tile Windows from the Window menu. The two copies are displayed together, one above the other. Set the magnification for one of the copies to a higher level (between 200 percent and 800 percent, for example) by clicking the Zoom Percentage box in the lower-left corner of the document.

Changes made in one copy of the document are simultaneously reflected in the other copy. However, scrolling is not synchronized between the two documents. You have to manually scroll the copies to make sure the same portions of the document are displayed in both copies.

If you were working in a paint frame rather than a paint document, you should choose Window ➪ Open Frame and then proceed as previously described.

Previewing documents

If you haven't disabled Apple's QuickTime extensions when you started your computing session (QuickTime 4 is automatically installed when you install AppleWorks 6), you can preview graphics files before you open them in Apple-Works 6. In the Open dialog box, AppleWorks can present a thumbnail image of any graphics file saved with a preview. If you have a large number of files, using the Preview feature can help you avoid opening the wrong document. (For information on creating previews, see Chapter 1.)

You also can automatically create previews of your AppleWorks graphics documents by setting Create Custom Icon in your General Preferences.

Inserting art from Clippings

AppleWorks 6 includes hundreds of clip-art images you can use in your own documents. These images are stored in collections on your hard disk or accessible from the Web via your Clippings windoid.

STEPS: Adding a Clipping to a Draw or Paint Document

1. Choose the category of interest from the tabs at the bottom of the Clippings windoid. The selected collection's thumbnails appear.

2. Scroll to the image you want to use.

3. To add the image to the current document, do one of the following:

    • Drag the name of the image onto the document.

    • Drag the thumbnail picture of the image onto the document.

    • Select the image or its name, and choose Edit ⇨ Copy (⌘+C). Click in your document, and then choose Edit ⇨ Paste.

The image is inserted into the document. When added to a draw document, the graphic is inserted as a draw object; when added to a paint document or frame, the graphic is a paint (bitmapped) image.

Caution   When adding a Clipping to a paint frame, be sure you are in paint mode. (When in paint mode, the paint tools are enabled in the Tool panel.) If you are not in paint mode, the chosen image is added as a free-floating draw object rather than as a paint graphic.

You also can add your own graphics to existing categories or create new categories. (To learn more about working with Clippings, see Chapter 13.)

Moving On Up

When — or if — your image-creation and editing needs expand, you can choose from dozens of commercial graphics programs. These programs can be classified roughly according to their capabilities:

✦ **Draw programs.** If objects are your thing, you might prefer a capable draw program, such as CorelDraw (www.corel.com).

✦ **PostScript drawing programs.** These programs are capable of creating extremely complex and detailed PostScript images — the natural choice of illustrators and designers. The most popular of these programs are Adobe Illustrator (www.adobe.com) and FreeHand (Macromedia) (www.macromedia.com). PostScript drawing programs tend to have a very steep learning curve, however. They're not for casual artists or users with simple graphics needs.

✦ **Image editors/high-end paint programs.** These programs extend paint capabilities by enabling you to create or edit 8-, 16-, 24-, or 32-bit color or grayscale images. If you need to edit scanned images or video captures, a program such as Adobe Photoshop (www.adobe.com) is a godsend.

✦ **QuickTime editors.** If you want to make your own QuickTime movies, you need software tools that make it possible. Adobe Premiere is a popular choice, as is Apple's iMovie (www.apple.com/imovie) or Final Cut Pro (www.apple.com/software) if you have a digital camcorder and a FireWire-equipped Mac.

✦ **Special-purpose graphics programs.** A variety of graphics niche programs are also available. Some specialize in 3D images (Specular Infini-D (specular.homepage.com), Strata 3D (strata.com), and Adobe Dimensions (www.adobe.com), for example; some enable you to switch freely between paint and PICT modes or combine them in the same document (Canvas, for example); and some imitate an artist's brush strokes (Fractal Design Painter [now from Corel, www.corel.com], for example).

Depending on your graphics needs, you might find that you require several programs — each for a different purpose. (You might also need more memory, or even a newer Mac or hardware add-ons.)

Summary

✦ AppleWorks includes a pair of fundamental graphics environments. You use the draw environment to create objects and the paint environment for bitmapped images.

✦ Draw objects are solid; you can edit them only as a whole. Paint images are composed of dots; you edit them at the dot level.

✦ The first step in editing a draw object is to select it. After you have made a selection, you can move, resize, or reshape the object, apply different fill and pen attributes to it, or choose editing commands. You also can select several objects at the same time.

✦ Elements you place on a master page automatically appear in the same position on every page of the draw document.

✦ Although you can create a master page only in a draw document, you can get around this limitation by placing word processing, paint, and spreadsheet frames on draw documents.

✦ You can edit master page elements as often as you like. However, you can only see master page elements when you are editing the master page or have chosen Page View from the Window menu.

✦ When you want to edit a paint image, three tools enable you to select a portion of a picture: the marquee, the lasso, and the magic wand. After you make a selection, you can move it, resize it, or alter its attributes.

✦ Unlike draw objects (which you can place in almost any environment), you can use paint images only in paint documents and paint frames.

✦ Although you can easily add to or change the attributes of a draw object at any time, setting paint attributes is much easier before you create each portion of an image than it is afterward.

✦ Paint documents can be memory hogs. You might have to increase the memory available to AppleWorks if you regularly work with large paint documents.

✦ AppleWorks 6 includes hundreds of pieces of clip art that you can insert into your documents.

✦   ✦   ✦

The Presentation Environment

Presentations aren't solely the province of conference speakers and marketing people. They're the most vocal customers for presentation software. If you've ever sat though slide shows that chronicles someone's vacation, you've seen a presentation. If you've sat in class and watched the teacher project transparencies onto a screen or the wall using an overhead projector, you've seen a presentation. The only thing that has changed is the amount of "theatre" that accompanies the presentation: transitions, embedded movies or background music/narration, and graphic decoration.

You don't need fancy software to create and display most presentations. All you need is a program with a slide show feature—the capability to present a series of text charts, graphs, and other images onscreen. AppleWorks has had such a feature for quite a while and you can use it from any environment (except the new Presentation environment), but it doesn't have many of the bells and whistles found in dedicated Presentation software, such as Microsoft PowerPoint. AppleWorks 6 provides a new, dedicated presentation environment designed to satisfy many of the feature requests Apple received.

The bulk of this chapter discusses the new Presentation environment—how you create and run a slide-show using it, but you'll also learn about the old Draw-based slide show capabilities for a couple of reasons. One, you might receive a slide show from an AppleWorks 5 or ClarisWorks user. Two, the old slide shows still provide a few capabilities that are not present in the new Prention environment, such as presenting a database report or a spreadsheet as a slide show, or producing overhead slides such as those we all saw in the classroom—at least those of us who went to school before personal computers became common in the classroom.

Presentation Fundamentals

When you create a Presentation document, you're presented with two windows: a document window and a Controls windoid. The document window is, for all intents and purposes, a size- and orientation-constrained drawing document window. The Controls windoid has four tabs; from left to right, they are Master (a star), Slides (a rectangular frame with an orange center), Organize (a file folder), and Show (a button with a right-pointing triangle), as shown in Figure 7-1.

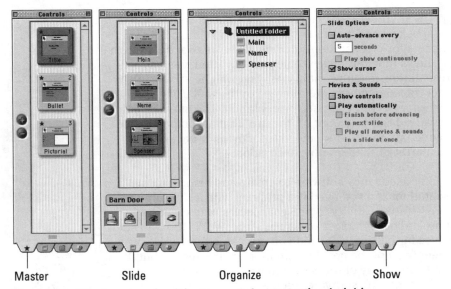

Master   Slide   Organize   Show

Figure 7-1: The four panels of the Presentation Controls windoid

> **Note**   Depending upon whether you look at the contextual menus, balloon help, or Apple-Works Help, you might find that the Organize panel is sometimes called the Groups panel.

Each slide in your presentation is 640 by 480 pixels in size, the 4:3 ratio that is so commonly found in multimedia and typical of the capability of a vast majority of computer displays.

Every slide in a slide show is based on a *master slide*, which is a sort of slide template. You can have one or more master slides. For example, you might have one for title slides, another for bullet lists, and yet another for multimedia-based slides.

When you create a new slide, you start with a copy of the master slide on which it is based, even if that slide is simply the blank default master slide that is automatically created for you when you choose File ➪ New ➪ Presentation.

You can group your slides into pseudo-folders. The order in which the slides appear in the folders reflects the order in which they'll appear in your slide show.

Slide shows can be controlled manually or run automatically. You also can control how multimedia (QuickTime movies and sounds) is presented.

Creating a Presentation

As with any other AppleWorks document, you can create a Presentation in one of two ways. You can start with a template file, or you can create one from scratch. We'll discuss both options.

Starting with a template

The home base for choosing a template is your Starting Points window's Templates panel. If your Starting Points window isn't showing, choose File ⇨ Show Starting Points (or press ⌘+1). Then, click the Templates tab to display the thumbnails of your various AppleWorks templates, both those that came with AppleWorks 6 and ones you've created or acquired elsewhere.

Initially, what you'll see is an alphabetical listing of your templates. Unfortunately, no indicator on a thumbnail tells you what kind of document it creates. You can, however, re-sort the thumbnails by document type: Control+click in the Templates panel to present the contextual menu and choose By Kind from the Sort submenu. Then, scroll down until you see a thumbnail with Presentation as part of its name.

Note At the time of this writing (version 6.0.4 is the latest), a slight bug exists in the sorting algorithm. As a result, one of the presentation templates — Family Slide Show — sorts to the very end of the list.

Find a presentation template on which you would like to base your presentation and click. The template you select appears on the screen, filled with placeholder text and graphics and named untitled (PR), or untitled (PR) followed by a number, as shown in Figure 7-2.

Tip AppleWorks provides only six Presentation templates in its Templates folder, but you should remember the Templates link on your Starting Points Web panel. Many more templates are available for download from the AppleWorks Web site.

Select some of the dummy text (such as Title, as shown in the figure) and either press the Clear, Delete, or Del keys to remove it, or start typing to replace the existing text. You'll repeat this action for each of the text blocks on the slide containing text you want to replace and again for each slide in the show.

Figure 7-2: A Presentation template gives you a starting point for your presentation.

Tip

On slides, it is quite common to use white text against a dark background. Unfortunately, if you set the text color to white, you won't see what you're typing, or what text is in the text block when it is active. Your best bet, if you want to use this visual effect, is to change the color before you edit, and then change it back when you're finished.

Now that you've made changes to the slide, it is time to add more slides to flesh out your presentation.

Click the Master tab and select the master slide that you want to use for your next slide. We'll discuss Master slides in more detail later in this chapter, when we discuss creating a presentation from scratch. What is important here is that when you first create a slide, you need to have a master slide selected on which you will base your next slide.

Note

Most Presentation templates provide multiple Master slides. Each Master slide is a template containing prepositioned graphic objects, text, and other frames.

Go back to the Slide panel and click the + button (near the center of the Slide panel's left side). AppleWorks creates a new slide and adds its thumbnail to the scrolling list on the Slide panel of the Controls windoid (see Figure 7-1, earlier in this chapter). Create as many slides as you need based on the selected master slide, clicking the + button for each slide you want to add, and continue to replace, add, or delete text and objects in the document window. Repeat these steps for other master slides on which you're going to base more slides until your presentation is complete.

Starting from scratch

Six templates don't comprise much of a selection when you're talking about presentations. It's also highly likely that none of the templates will match the design or color schemes your company or organization prefers. Most of the time, you'll be starting from scratch or, at least, starting from scratch occasionally and creating your own template(s) for use in subsequent presentations.

The first step is to create a new Presentation document, which is analogous to creating a new document in any other AppleWorks environment. You can choose File ⇨ New ⇨ Presentation, or you can click either the Presentation button in the Button Bar or the Presentation thumbnail on the Starting Points Basics panel. You'll then be presented with a blank, untitled document window (which looks suspiciously like a drawing window) and the Controls windoid showing the Slide tab (see Figure 7-2, earlier in this chapter).

Most presentations consist of groups of slides with a common design: the backgrounds are the same, the headings are in the same place, the logos and other graphics are identically positioned on each slide, and the expository text (or bullet lists) are positioned in the same manner. Some subtle differences exist, of course, and that is where master slides come into the picture. A typical corporate presentation might use three kinds of slides: title slides, bullet list slides, and chart slides. When you create three master slides — one for each type of slide you need in your presentation — you ensure that all your title slides will have the same look and layout, as will your bullet list and chart slides.

Creating a consistent background

Of course, you also might want all slides of all types to have certain elements in common. Perhaps the company logo should be in the upper-left corner and the word "Confidential" should be centered at the lower edge of every slide. You could create these basic elements on each of the master slides, but AppleWorks gives you a simpler method of creating global elements — the *background*. Choose Options ⇨ Edit Background to be presented with a drawing layer on which you can create the constant elements you want on every slide you create — the word Background will appear in the name box in the lower portion of your document window.

One of the most common elements on a background is a block of color that fills the slide. The easiest way to create this effect is using the following steps:

1. Draw a rectangle (if the Tools panel is not showing, either click the Toolbox icon in the lower portion of the document window, choose Window ⇨ Show Tools, or press Shift+⌘+T).

2. Set the line width for the Pen to None in the Accents windoid (choose Show ⇨ Accents, or press ⌘+K if the Accents windoid is not present).

3. Set the Fill for the rectangle to the color, pattern, wallpaper, or gradient you want to use in the Accents windoid.

Tip Unless the colors used are very muted or very consistent in intensity, gradients, wallpaper, and patterns can make your presentation difficult for an audience to follow.

4. In the Object Size windoid (choose Options ➪ Object Size if the windoid isn't showing), set the width to 640 pt, the height to 480 pt, the left and top offsets to 0, the bottom offset to 480 pt, and the right offset to 640 pt (see Figure 7-3).

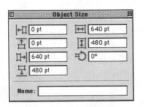

Figure 7-3: Filling the background is easy if you use the Object Size windoid.

Tip This is easier to accomplish if you set the Ruler units to Points, but you can type **640 pt**, for example, when the units are inches, and the Object Size windoid makes the conversion to 8.89 in for you.

Now, it is a simple matter to place any other static elements on your background using the Tool panel, File ➪ Insert, the Clippings windoid (see Chapter 13 for detailed coverage of the Clippings windoid), drag-and-drop, or copy and paste. An example of a background for a presentation about Boston Terriers is shown in Figure 7-4.

Figure 7-4: A consistent background for all slides in the presentation

Once you have established the static elements, choose Options ⇨ Edit Background again to clear the checkmark and return to editing your slides and master slides.

Caution Changes made to the Background will propagate to slides that already exist. Changes made to a master slide will not affect existing slides that were based upon that template; changes will only affect new slides that you create from that point forward.

Creating and editing master slides

Master slides are where you place those elements (or placeholders for them) that you want to have appear on each slide of a given type. For example, a title slide's master slide would typically include a text block for the section title, as well as a placeholder for the presenter or author name. It might also include a placeholder for a department or project logo. The master slide for a bullet list often includes a block of text telling to which section it belonged, in addition to a text block for the bullet list. Finally, a graphic master slide would have a block set aside into which the graphic would be placed, as well as a caption area that tells about the picture or chart being displayed. Continuing with the background we created earlier, Figures 7-5 through 7-7 show the document window for these three master slides and Figure 7-8 shows the Controls windoid.

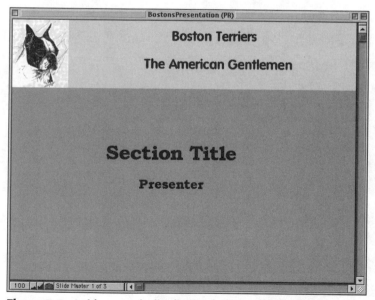

Figure 7-5: A title page, bullet list, and pictorial master slide with the Controls windoid

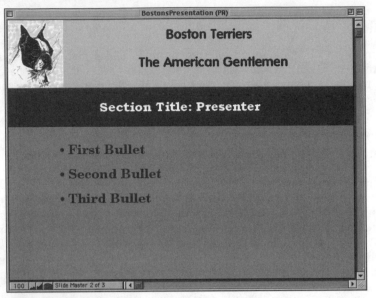

Figure 7-6: A bullet list

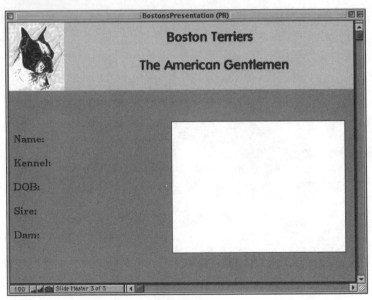

Figure 7-7: A pictorial master slide

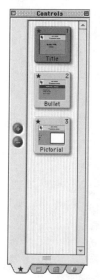

Figure 7-8: The Controls window

Each of your master slides has a type and ordering centered in the lower portion of its thumbnail on the Master panel. Unfortunately, even if you give them more meaningful names, the names are all the same — Slide Master — followed by the sequence number and the total number of master slides. To change the name of a master slide, click in the text portion of the slide (it doesn't have to be the selected master) so that it highlights the name, and then type a new name. Pressing the Enter or Return keys, or clicking elsewhere in the slide, will accept the change. Names that are longer than about eight characters will not display in their entirety unless they're selected.

> **Note** As with any of the tabbed windoids in AppleWorks, you can choose to hide the tabs using that windoid's contextual menu, and then use the contextual menu to switch between panels. Because you might not have the Master tab forward, telling you that you're on the Master panel, each master slide's thumbnail also bears the star tattoo in its upper-left corner. A sequential number also appears in the upper-right corner of the thumbnail to tell you how many thumbnails you are from the top of the list.

Creating your slides

Now that you have the master slide selected on which you want to base one or more slides, click the Slide tab or Control+click in the Controls windoid and choose Switch To ➪ Slide from the contextual menu. This is where you'll be doing the bulk of your work in the Presentations environment. It is at this stage that the Control windoid Slide panel will provide you with additional tools, as shown in Figure 7-9.

— Hidden Slide

— Don't Print icon

— Hide

Show

Resize handle

Don't Print

Print

Figure 7-9: The Slide Controls enable you to
create special effects and set slide preferences.

Note You cannot delete the only slide in a slide show.

Click the + button to create a slide that is an exact copy of the master slide you
chose earlier. Remember that the document window is a drawing layout. Anything
and everything that you can do in a drawing document (other than resizing the document), you can do here. (See Chapter 6 for a complete discussion of the drawing
environment.)

In addition to creating and modifying elements on your slide, the Slide panel provides some additional controls. You might want to present only a subset of your
slides to one audience. The two "eye" buttons near the lower edge of the windoid
let you hide a slide (the closed eye) or show a slide that is currently hidden (the

open eye). When you select a slide and click the Hide button, a set of lowered venetian blinds appears over the image in that slide's thumbnail. Click the Show button and the blinds disappear. In many presentations, a set of handouts containing copies of the slides are given to the audience. AppleWorks lets you designate slides as nonprinting if you want — just select them and click the Don't Print button each time. If you change your mind, select the slides and click the Print button for each.

Note Nonprinting slides have a small circle with a slash through it in the upper-left corner of the thumbnail.

Slides also can be brought onscreen with a special effect, such as sliding in from the side or opening from the center. These special effects are called *transitions,* and AppleWorks provides 26 transitions from which you can choose (in addition to None). You'll find these transitions in the pop-up menu between the thumbnails and the buttons.

Tip Be conservative when you use transitions. It is easy to go overboard and have them detract from your presentation.

A Nontransition Special Effect

One of the most common and useful special effects is usually called a *Bullet Build,* and it is one that you can include in your presentations without ever touching the Transitions pop-up menu.

When you show a slide having multiple bullet points, your audience has a tendency to read ahead or lose track of just where you are on a slide. You can, however, build to that multiple bullet slide one bullet point at a time. All you have to do is create as many copies of that particular slide as there are bullet points.

This is actually a pretty good use for a special purpose master slide. You could start with one having just the first bullet point. Then, add a point to the second slide, another point to the third slide, and so on, until you have as many slides as you have points. It is a lot easier, however, to create a master slide having all the points, and then simply delete the appropriate number of points on each generated slide, Deleting is a lot faster than typing, even if you copy from the previous slide, paste to the new slide, and then just type a single point.

Using this technique, your audience sees the point you're addressing at the bottom of the bullet list each time, so they won't get lost and they won't jump ahead of you.

While you don't need to use a transition for this effect, you can make the new point appear to unveil itself from left to right by using the Wipe Horizontal transition. The other items won't appear to change because the existing items are the same on both the outgoing and incoming slide.

If you're creating handout sets, you'll probably want to make the intermediate slides nonprinting.

If you want to permanently remove a slide from your presentation, you can do so by selecting it and clicking the – button (so long as it isn't the only slide). However, if you feel that you might want to add it back into the presentation at a later time, or that you would like to preserve it for reference purposes, you can click both the Hide and Don't Print buttons so that it will be out of your presentation but still available later.

Tip   You also can delete a slide (or master slide) by selecting its thumbnail and dragging it to the Trash icon on the desktop.

Although you could add a QuickTime movie (or sound) to a master slide, you'll usually find that you don't want that same movie or sound on multiple slides. For that reason, it is more customary to place the QuickTime objects on the actual slides. The settings for these multimedia objects are controlled through the Show panel and are discussed later in this chapter.

Using Notes View

Have you ever watched someone give a presentation and lose their place, or worse, drop the stack of index cards with their notes? AppleWorks can't prevent you from clumsiness with the notes, but it can help you ensure that your notes for each slide are on the printout for that slide. Where you can enable and disable Page View for other document types, you can enable or disable Notes View for presentations, as well. After all, what good is a page view on a document that is constrained to a fixed, one-page size? When you choose Notes View, your slides are displayed, centered, and reduced 50 percent across the upper portion of a standard letter-size page (landscape orientation). With this positioning, you can create callouts and annotations on both sides and below the slide body.

In addition to the speaker script notes you would add to such slides, you also can add reminders to yourself or the presenter, such as "Pause partway through this slide and scan the audience," or "This might be a good time to ask for questions."

To access Notes View, choose Window ➪ Notes View. When you want to print out your notes, you can be in either view. To exit Notes View, choose Window ➪ Notes View again to remove the checkmark. When you choose File ➪ Print (or click the Print button on your Button Bar), you will find a checkbox in your Print dialog box for Notes — click in it.

Note   In some Print dialog boxes (such as the LaserWriter 8 Print dialog box), you will have to switch to the AppleWorks 6 panel (choose it from the pop-up menu) to find this and other application-specific printing options.

Organizing your slides

Slides are presented in the order the (unhidden) slides appear on the Slides panel, and you can reorder them by dragging their thumbnails up or down the list. However, this can quickly become very tedious. The Organize panel (shown earlier in Figure 7-1) enables you to create pseudo-folders, or groups of slides, as well as to name them. Then, you can drag the folder up or down the list in the Organize panel to move groups of slides at one time. Similarly, you can open the folder and rearrange slides within the group. All changes to slide order that are made in the Organize panel are immediately reflected in the Slide panel.

Initially, AppleWorks presents you with one folder, with the original name of Untitled Folder (shown earlier in Figure 7-1), containing all the slides you've created to this point. As with master slides and slides, you create a new folder by clicking the + button. You can reveal what is inside a folder by clicking its disclosure triangle, just as you do in a Finder list view or a standard Open dialog box.

After you create the groups you want, drag the slides to the folder where you want them to be located. Then, drag the folders into the order you want them to appear.

Note You cannot simultaneously select multiple slides by Shift+clicking or ⌘+clicking them, and you also cannot nest one folder within another. This is where the analogy with the Finder and real folders falls apart. Apple listens to its customers, so perhaps the company will enhance that capability if enough requests are received for it.

Showing your presentation

When you reveal the Show panel, you're no longer working on or with the slides, you're working with your presentation. The Show panel is your control center for the show as a whole. The Show panel (shown earlier in Figure 7-1) is divided into two groups of settings, plus a Play button.

The first group of settings, Slide Options, is where you determine whether you're going to advance from one slide to the next by clicking the mouse or pressing a key, or whether your presentation will display a new slide (Auto-advance) at a fixed time interval (the default is 5 seconds). If you choose to Auto-advance, you also are given the option of having the presentation play continuously (this is usually referred to as looping or kiosk mode.) Table 7-1 details which keys control a presentation. The final option in this set is to determine whether your mouse cursor will be visible during the presentation. If you're standing out in front of an audience and someone else (or your computer) is advancing the presentation from one slide to the next, you'll probably want to hide the mouse cursor and use a laser pointer or similar device to point things out on the projection screen. On the other hand, if you're sitting at your computer giving the presentation, you might want to use the arrow pointer instead.

Table 7-1
Presentation Keyboard and Mouse Controls

Command	Key or Action
Show next slide	Mouse click, right-arrow key, down-arrow key, Page Down, Return, Tab, or spacebar
Show previous slide	Left-arrow key, up-arrow key, Page Up, Shift+Return, Shift+Tab, or Shift+spacebar
Show final slide	End
Show first slide	Home
Play a QuickTime movie	Click in the movie frame
Pause or resume a movie	⌘+click or Option-click in the movie frame
Halt a QuickTime movie	Click in the playing movie's frame
End the slide show	⌘+. (period), or the Q, Esc, or Clear keys

Beneath the Slide Options is your second group of settings: Movies & Sounds. These settings determine the appearance and behavior of any multimedia on your slide, as follows:

✦ **Show controls**: Every QuickTime element has a slide along the lower edge containing buttons to play, rewind, fast forward, control the volume, and so forth. If you choose not to select the Play Automatically checkbox, you might wonder how to make a movie play when the controls are hidden. The answer is to double-click the frame to start the movie playing. A second double-click stops the playback, and a single click will pause it. Finally, if you've chosen to hide the mouse pointer, Option+clicking anywhere onscreen will cause your multimedia to start playing.

✦ **Play automatically**: If you select the Play Automatically checkbox, your movies will start to play when the slide appears onscreen. Checking this checkbox also presents you with two more choices. "Finish before advancing to next slide" overrides any Auto-advance settings you've made (described previously) and will not advance to the next slide until the movie has played to completion — it has no effect on slides that are manually controlled. "Play all movies & sounds in a slide at once" does just as the name implies. This option is useful when you have a sound narration and a movie clip on the same slide, when you want to use some other voice-over technique, or when you want to emulate a television studio's bank of wall monitors, each displaying separate shows.

Movies and sounds, while reasonably compact on disk, can consume a lot of memory when decompressed for use. If you often use movies or sounds in your presentation, you really should increase the amount of RAM allocated to AppleWorks (see the Tips at the end of Chapter 6).

While most QuickTime objects are free-floating objects, occasions might arise where you want to place one object as an in-line object (see Chapter 3 for a discussion of in-line versus free-floating objects). When the QuickTime object is an in-line object, the tiny film *badge* (iconic marker) in the lower-left corner of the frame no longer activates the QuickTime control bar. Thus, you will either need to have all your movies and sounds automatically play, or you must double-click or option-click the object during the presentation.

Caution   AppleWorks doesn't save QuickTime movies or sounds as part of a Presentation document. Instead, to keep the size down, it keeps an internal alias to the files on your hard disk. Therefore, if you delete the multimedia files or copy the presentation to another machine without including the movies and sounds, your presentation won't play them and you'll be presented with a standard Open dialog box asking you to point out their location. We recommend that if you're going to include multimedia in your presentations, you should keep the presentation document and all the assorted multimedia files together in a folder that you can transfer intact.

You have a multiplicity of methods to start playing a slide show: the big Play button at the lower edge of the Show panel, the Play button in your Button Bar, control-clicking and choosing Slide Show from the contextual menu, or choosing Window ⇨ Slide Show. When you start your slide show, AppleWorks takes over the entire screen, changes your screen resolution to 640 by 480, and then displays the first slide. When your presentation ends, your screen resolution is set back to its original state. However, you might find that many windows in AppleWorks, other running applications, and possibly even icons on your desktop have been moved or resized to accommodate the temporary 640 by 480 resolution.

Tip   Totally undocumented by Apple, holding down the Option key while clicking the Play button (or using other methods of starting a presentation) will cause the screen resolution to remain as it was and have the slides scaled up to the screen's resolution. This can result in some blockiness in bitmap graphics, but it does avoid the side effects brought on by this temporary resolution change. It also can be used to advantage if you have some large graphics — reduce them in size, but increase the resolution (for example, scale a 640 by 480 digital photo to 320 by 240, but at 144 dpi) — when you use the Option+Play key combination, they will be scaled up appropriately, without the loss of clarity common to bitmap graphics that have been enlarged.

Slide Show Fundamentals

In previous versions of AppleWorks and ClarisWorks, you used the Draw environment to create presentations and the Window ⇨ Slide Show feature to display them, as discussed at the beginning of this chapter. Because those capabilities are still present, we're going to discuss them here.

Note   You can also use the Window ⇨ Slide Show feature to display database reports, spreadsheets, and word processing document pages as slides—a sort of Page Preview slide show.

Every slide show is based on a single AppleWorks document, and each page of the document is treated as a separate slide. Within the slide show document, you can do the following:

✦ Rearrange pages to display them in a different order

✦ Make pages opaque, transparent, or hidden

✦ Designate border fills and page placement within the context of the entire screen

✦ Select special effects for the presentation, such as fading out between slides and looping (for continuous, self-running demonstrations)

✦ Place QuickTime movies on slides

After you create a document, you can choose Window ⇨ Slide Show, set options, and then run the slide show. Creating an effective slide show tends to be an iterative process that consists of refining the slides, trying out different backgrounds, and experimenting with effects until you have the presentation you want. While this seems of dubious value for documents that were not created to be a slide show, the capability functions give you a limited Page Preview of your document.

Preparing for a Slide Show

Although you can take any document and instantly transform it into a serviceable slide show, a polished presentation requires that you spend some time examining different options and determining which options are best for the presentation. This section examines the slide show features and explains how each feature affects the presentation.

Setting the number of slides

Either implicitly or explicitly, you will have to somehow specify or limit the number of slides that will appear in your slide show.

Tip   Regardless of the environment you use, be sure that AppleWorks is set for Page View in the Window menu (or press Shift+⌘+P) so you can see where the page breaks occur. In addition, unless Page View is selected, the Display options in the Document dialog box are grayed out.

The instructions that follow explain how to establish the number of slides in different environments.

Draw documents

To set the number of slides for a draw document, choose Format ⇨ Document. The Document dialog box appears, shown in Figure 7-10. In the Size section of the dialog box, specify the number of pages across and pages down. (When presented as a slide show, draw pages are shown across and then down.)

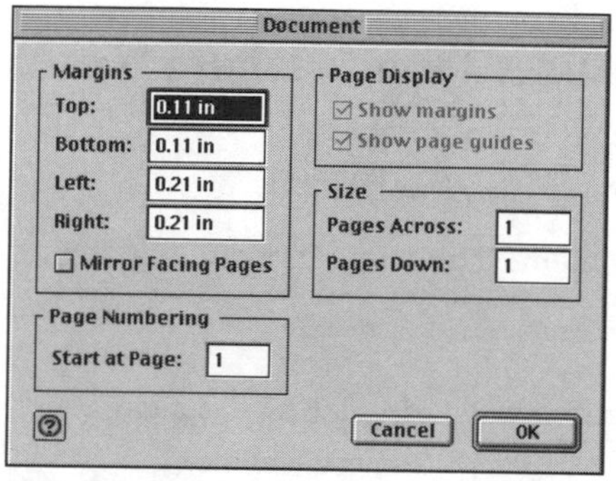

Figure 7-10: The Document dialog box for a draw document

Note

A draw document also can have a *master page*. You use a master page to display a logo or other static objects on each slide. A master page is to a draw document what a background is to a presentation.

Paint documents

To set the number of slides for a paint document, choose Document from the Format menu. The Document dialog box appears, as shown earlier in Figure 6-32. In the Size section of the dialog box, specify the number of pixels across and down. (An inch equals 72 pixels.) Unless the paint document is larger than a page, you will have only one slide.

Caution

Large paint documents use a lot of memory, so they are not well suited for slides.

Spreadsheet documents

To set the number of slides for a worksheet, you have two methods from which to choose.

You can choose Format ⇨ Document. The Document dialog box appears, as shown earlier in Figure 4-17. In the Size section of the dialog box, specify the number of columns across and rows down. Using the default column width and row height, a standard slide page is 7 columns wide and 50 rows high (or 9 columns wide and 37 rows high in landscape mode).

Alternatively, you can choose Options ⇨ Set Print Range to specify how much of your spreadsheet is to be included. Personally, this is the preferred method because your page breaks are shown in Page View and you don't have to do the calculations to find out what will fit if you have resized any rows or columns.

Database documents

Follow these steps to set the number of slides to be the same as the number of records for an AppleWorks database.

STEPS: Setting the Number of Slides for a Database Document

1. Create a layout that displays a single record per page.

2. Choose Layout ➪ Browse (Shift+⌘+B).

3. Choose Slide Show from the Window menu. The Slide Show dialog box appears, as shown in Figure 7-11.

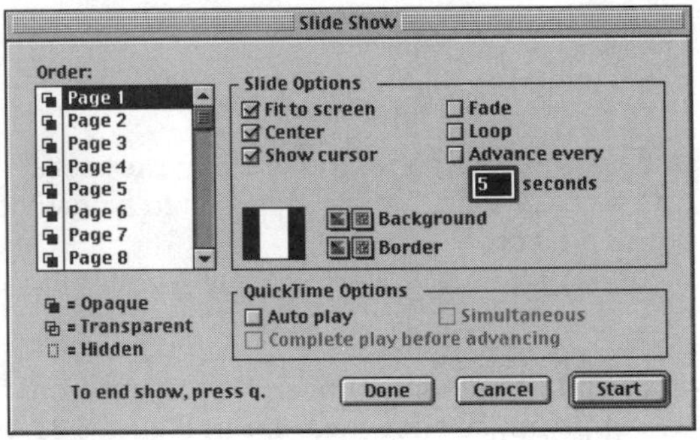

Figure 7-11: The Slide Show dialog box

4. Set options and click the Start button.

5. If more than one record appears on each slide, or if the record isn't properly positioned on the slide screen, choose the Document command from the Format menu. Change the margins and then repeat Steps 3 and 4 until only a single record is displayed on each slide. (As an alternative, you can change the record layout so it fills the screen by choosing Layout ➪ Layout (Shift+⌘+L) and dragging the body part downward.)

Note   If you don't set the number of slides as described, the page number references (shown earlier in Figure 7-8) won't make much sense as you won't have a way to reconcile how many records show per page or whether a record spans a page boundary. This is not to say that you have to set the number of slides to perform a database slide show, but it can be helpful. Remember that this functions as a Page Preview and your summary fields will show up on the slides, as will headers and footers.

When creating a database slide show, you can use the Layout ⇨ Find command (or press Shift+⌘+F) to choose the records you want to display as slides. If you want to display all records, choose Organize ⇨ Show All Records (or press Shift+⌘+A).

Changing the order of slides

The slide order is displayed in the left side of the Slide Show dialog box. To alter the order, you simply select a page with the mouse and then drag it to a new position in the Order list.

Setting layering options

Each slide can be opaque, transparent, or omitted (hidden) from the presentation. An opaque slide is solid and completely obscures any slides you have already shown. A transparent slide, on the other hand, lets the slide beneath it show through. You can place several transparent slides on top of one another to create special effects. One common use for a series of transparent slides is to present a text chart that adds one new bullet point per slide. This is analogous to the bullet build described earlier in this chapter.

To change a slide's layering in the Order list, click the icon to the left of the page number. As you click, the layering cycles through its three options: opaque, transparent, and hidden. Figure 7-12 shows examples of icons for pages that are opaque, transparent, and hidden.

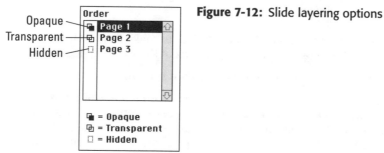

Figure 7-12: Slide layering options

If you are using a master page as a background for a draw document, it will show through on all slides, regardless of whether they are opaque or transparent. (See Chapter 17 for more information on master pages.)

Slide display options

You also can use the Slide Show dialog box to set slide display options.

STEPS: Setting Slide Display Options

1. Open the document you want to use for the presentation.

2. Choose Window ➪ Slide Show. The Slide Show dialog box appears (refer to Figure 7-11, shown earlier).

3. Set the Slide and QuickTime options you want to use in the slide show (as described in the "Slide options" and "QuickTime options," later in this chapter).

4. Click the Start button to see the slide show.

5. Press the Q, Clear, or Esc keys to exit the slide show (or press ⌘+. [period]).

6. Click the Done button to save the settings and return to the document, or click the Cancel button to ignore the new settings and revert to the previous settings.

You can repeat Steps 3 through 5 as many times as necessary. If you want to permanently record the slide show settings, save the document using the File ➪ Save or File ➪ Save As commands.

Options in the Order section of the Slide Show dialog box are covered earlier in this discussion. The next two sections describe how the Slide options and QuickTime options affect a slide show.

Slide options

The upper-right section of the Slide Show dialog box contains the Slide options that govern the display of the slides and the manner in which they are presented. Slide options include the following:

✦ **Fit to Screen.** This option resizes each slide to make it fit on the current screen. The slides maintain the proportions of the original document pages.

✦ **Center.** This option centers the slides on the screen.

✦ **Show Cursor.** With the Show Cursor checkbox enabled, the mouse pointer remains onscreen as a pointer throughout the presentation. This feature is useful if you want to point to objects or text during the presentation. Leave the Show Cursor checkbox cleared if the presentation is a self-running (looping) demonstration, or if you're going to be projecting it on a large screen and want to use a pointer device.

✦ **Fade.** When the Fade checkbox is checked, it causes the screen to fade out and then fade back in between each pair of slides.

✦ **Loop.** Check the Loop checkbox if you want the slide show to run continuously. After completing a cycle through the slides, the show starts over again from the beginning. Normally, you use the Loop function in conjunction with the Auto-advance feature (the Advance Every x Seconds option). You stop a looping presentation in the same manner you stop a normal presentation — by pressing the Q, Clear, or Esc keys (or pressing ⌘+. [period]).

✦ **Advance Every *x* Seconds.** When this option is checked, slides automatically advance at the rate set in the text-edit box. When it is unchecked, you have to advance pages manually by clicking the mouse or by pressing special keys (see "Running a Slide Show," later in this chapter). Note that even when the Auto-advance feature is set, you can still manually advance any slide.

✦ **Background.** Choose from these pop-up palettes to add a color or fill texture to the background of a slide. The background is used for the entire slide show. The default background is white.

✦ **Border.** Choose from these pop-up palettes to add a color or fill wallpaper to the border of a slide (the area around the outside edges of the slide page). The border is used for the entire slide show. The default border is black.

> **Tip**
>
> If a slide almost fills the screen, the border might be very thin. In this case, you might want to set the background and border to the same color.

QuickTime options

The QuickTime options are selectable only if the QuickTime extensions are active when your Mac starts up. You can set the following QuickTime options in the Slide Show dialog box:

✦ **Auto Play.** When this option is checked, a QuickTime movie automatically runs when the slide in which it is embedded appears onscreen.

✦ **Simultaneous.** If you have more than one QuickTime movie on a slide, checking this option enables them to play at the same time. When this option is unchecked, the movies play in sequence from back to front according to the draw layer in which they are embedded.

✦ **Complete Play Before Advancing.** This option forces the slide show to wait until the QuickTime movie has finished before moving to the next slide. It is only enabled when the Advance Every *x* Seconds checkbox is checked. Manual advancement of the slide show overrides this setting.

For more information about incorporating QuickTime movies into your AppleWorks documents, see Chapter 16.

> **Note**
>
> In ClarisWorks 3.0 and earlier versions, a QuickTime movie in a slide show always played from the point at which it was last stopped. You had to make sure the movie was set to its beginning before starting the presentation. In AppleWorks 6, however, a movie is automatically reset to its beginning whenever you display the slide in which it is embedded. Thus, whether you are presenting a slide show to a new audience or are simply returning to a slide that contains a QuickTime movie, the movie plays from the beginning. This rule has one exception: If you have been playing a movie manually — outside the slide show — or you've set the QuickTime options to play only a selection, the movie starts from the point at which you stopped it. You must manually reset the movie to its beginning before starting the slide show. Otherwise, it continues to start from the point at which it was manually stopped.

Running a slide show

To run a slide show, choose Window ➪ Slide Show, set options, and then click the Start button. You also can start a show without displaying the Slide Show dialog box by pressing the Option key while choosing Window ➪ Slide Show.

While a slide show is running, you can use the keyboard commands and mouse actions (shown earlier in Table 7-1) to control the presentation.

Quick Tips

The following quick tips tell you how to use Page Setup to make slides fit on the screen, how to create overlays and animate objects, how to create appealing bullet characters, and how to run a remote slide show.

Using Page Setup for correct slide display

In most cases, monitors are considerably wider than they are tall. If you find that portions of the slides are clipped at the edges, choose File ➪ Page Setup, and then set the document for landscape mode by clicking the sideways icon in the Page Setup dialog box. AppleWorks uses the Page Setup settings when displaying documents onscreen and when printing them.

Movement in presentations

By making several consecutive transparent slides, you can create overlays. One example is a bulleted list that adds a new bullet on each slide — enabling you to build on points as you move through the presentation.

Better bullets for text charts

Items in text charts are frequently preceded by a bullet character (•). Everyone recognizes the standard bullet (Option+8), and it's available for every font. Unfortunately, it's dull. If you have the Zapf Dingbats font, on the other hand, you have dozens of interesting characters to choose from. Table 7-2 lists some Zapf Dingbats characters you might prefer to use as bullets, adding visual appeal to your slides.

Tip   The Symbol font — available on every Mac — also has characters you can use as bullets. You also can paste a draw object (a circle with a gradient, for example) as an in-line graphic for a really unique and interesting bullet character.

	Table 7-2
	Zapf Dingbats Characters

Character	Keystroke
✓	3
✔	4
☛	Shift+8
☆	Shift+p
●	l
○	m
■	n
❑	o
❐	p
❒	q
❒	r
▲	s
◆	u
➠	Shift+Option+7
➢	Shift+Option+0
➣	Shift+Option+W

Running a remote slide show

AppleWorks 5 included an AppleScript called Remote Slide Show, which enabled you to use one computer on your network to remotely control an AppleWorks slide show running on another computer. This AppleScript will also work with AppleWorks 6, if you have it or can obtain it. (For information on using this AppleScript, read the "About the AppleScripts" document located in the AppleWorks Scripts folder for AppleWorks 5.)

Summary

Note that in the summary that follows, "presentation" implies a Presentation document, and "slide show" refers to the "old" capabilities.

✦ AppleWorks 6 includes a brand-new Presentation environment.

✦ AppleWorks 6 provides six Presentation templates, and more are available on the Apple Web site.

✦ You can create a consistent background to appear on all the slides in your presentation.

✦ You can create multiple master slides—templates for the slides in your presentation.

✦ You can name your master slides, and you also can name and group your slides.

✦ You have 26 transition effects to choose from for presentations, in addition to no transition effect.

✦ You can use Notes View to put speaker's notes and reminders on your presentation printouts.

✦ You can set slides to be nonprinting and can hide some to have them not appear in the presentation until you unhide them.

✦ You can use documents from any environment (except Presentation) as the basis for a slide show.

✦ You can use the slide show feature as a Page Preview, which is especially handy with database reports and large spreadsheet documents.

✦ In environments other than the word processing environment, you might want to use a special procedure to create a multipage document (if you want to include more than one slide in a presentation, for example).

✦ You can change the order in which slides are presented without affecting the contents of the underlying document. You also can specify which slides are shown as opaque, transparent, or hidden.

✦ If you base a slide show on a draw document, you can create a master page and use it to display static information on every slide (a company logo, for example).

✦ You use the Slide Show dialog box to set most options for the slide show, including the placement of the slides onscreen, background and border colors or wallpapers, special effects, and play settings for QuickTime movies.

✦   ✦   ✦

Integrating the AppleWorks Environments

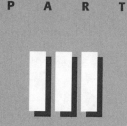

Generating a Mail Merge

A merge combines information from a database with a
word processing document. In the most common use
of a merge — a mail merge — you personalize form letters by
inserting names from a database into a word processing document. The merged letters read "Dear Mickey" or "Dear Mrs.
Samuels," rather than "Dear Friend" or "Dear Customer."

Every merge has two components: a database and a merge
form. The database contains the information you want to
insert into the merge form (names and addresses of friends,
sales commission figures, or descriptions of catalog items,
for example). The merge form is a text document, such as a
form letter. You insert placeholders in the merge form, and
each placeholder indicates the name of a database field (Last
Name, for example). During the merge, data from the fields of
each visible database record is inserted into the placeholders
in the merge form. One copy of the merge document is printed
for each visible (selected) database record.

> **Tip** Although a merge form is usually a word processing docu-
> ment, you can create it within a text frame in any Apple-
> Works environment, and even into a spreadsheet document
> or frame. For example, you can design a party invitation in a
> draw document and personalize it with information you
> place in a text frame.

Preparing to Merge

As stated previously, you need to establish a source database
containing the data to be merged, create a document containing placeholders for the data, and establish the relationship
between the document and the database. Within the document (merge form), you can apply any of the styling and formatting you wish.

Creating the merge database

You create a merge database as you do any other type of AppleWorks database—by defining fields and creating records. (Refer to Chapter 5 for detailed information on AppleWorks databases.)

You also can use the Address List Assistant to create an address database. If your Starting Points window is not showing, choose File ➪ Show Starting Points (or press ⌘+1), click the Assistants tab, and then click the Address List thumbnail. After answering the Assistant's questions, you'll be presented with a new address database. Save your new address database before continuing.

The elements of a merge form

As previously discussed, the merge form contains placeholders for data from database fields. Each placeholder contains the name of a database field, surrounded by special bracket symbols—<< (Option+\) and >> (Option+Shift+\) that are added automatically when you select field names from the Mail Merge windoid (see Figure 8-1, later in this chapter). To insert a field name and its surrounding brackets, you must select the field in the Mail Merge windoid (typing the name, including the brackets, will not work), as explained in the step-by-step instructions for creating a merge form, later in this chapter.

As with any other text in a word processing document or frame, you can apply different fonts, styles, colors, or other formatting options to the placeholders. You simply double-click to select the entire field name, including the brackets, and then apply formatting options.

You can use punctuation and spaces to separate merge fields from each other and from surrounding text. If the merge form contains two placeholders for the components of a name, as in <<First Name>><<Last Name>>, when the merge is performed, the result is the first name followed immediately by the last name (with no space in between), as in TomJohnson. To separate the two fields in the merge, add a space between the fields, as in <<First Name>> <<Last Name>>.

You also can combine merge fields with normal text. For example, you can embed a merge field in a sentence:

✦ Just imagine your surprise when our prize van pulls up to the doorstep of the <<Last Name>> household.

✦ Because your sales were so extraordinary this quarter, <<First Name>>, please find enclosed a commission check for <<Commission>> and a 15 percent bonus of <<Bonus Amt>>.

Creating a merge form

To create a merge form, you type the basic text for the letter or document (that is, all the text that will be identical for each letter or document). Then, using the Mail Merge windoid, insert field placeholders at the appropriate positions in the text body using the following steps:

STEPS: Inserting Fields into a Merge Form

1. Open the merge document or create a new one. (Remember that the merge form can be a word processing document, something other than a word processing document that contains a text frame, a spreadsheet document, or a spreadsheet frame.)

2. Choose File ➪ Mail Merge. A standard Open dialog box appears.

3. Choose a merge database and click the Open button. If the database is not already open, it now opens. The Mail Merge windoid appears, as shown in Figure 8-1.

Choose merge fields from the list

Insert selected field at text insertion point

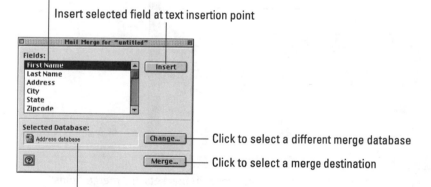

Click to select a different merge database

Click to select a merge destination

Currently selected merge database

Figure 8-1: The Mail Merge windoid

If you discover you've opened the wrong database for the merge, click the Change button in the Mail Merge windoid, and then choose another database from the standard Open dialog box that appears.

4. In the merge document, set the text insertion point where you want to insert the first field placeholder.

5. In the Field Names list box of the Mail Merge windoid, select the field you want to insert.

6. Click the Insert button to add the field name and its surrounding brackets at the current text insertion point.

7. Repeat Steps 4 through 6 for additional field placeholders you want to add to the merge form.

8. Save the merge document. Saving the merge form associates the merge database with it. The next time you open the merge form and choose the Mail Merge command, the associated database automatically opens.

Figure 8-2 shows a completed merge form.

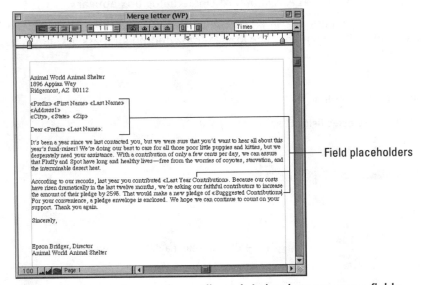

Figure 8-2: A typical merge form. All words in brackets are merge fields.

Performing a Merge

After the merge form is ready, the mechanics of performing the merge are straightforward.

STEPS: Performing a Merge

1. Open the merge database, if it is not already open.

2. To merge the entire database with the merge form, choose Organize ➪ Show All Records (or press Shift+⌘+A), and then go to Step 3.

or

To merge selected records with the merge form, choose Layout ⇨ Find (or press Shift+⌘+F). When the blank find request appears, specify criteria to find the record or records you want to print. Click the Visible radio button to search only the visible records, or click the All radio button to search the entire database. Click the Find button to execute the search.

3. *Optional:* If you want the merge documents to print in a specific order (alphabetically by last name or in Zip code order, for example), sort the records by choosing Organize ⇨ Sort Records (or press ⌘+J).

4. Open the merge document.

5. Choose File ⇨ Mail Merge. The Mail Merge for *file name* windoid appears.

6. Click the Merge button in the Mail Merge windoid. The Mail Merge Destination dialog box appears.

New Feature

In previous versions of ClarisWorks/AppleWorks, you could only print a merge. AppleWorks 6 adds two additional options — "Save in a new document" and "Save each final document on disk" — to "Send documents to printer." The "Save in a new document" option creates a new Untitled document onscreen, which is a single file containing all the generated documents, with a section break after each one. The "Save each final document on disk" option presents you with a standard Save As dialog box. When you click the Save button, AppleWorks creates a new folder with the name you specified and fills it with your merge documents. In addition, an alias to this newly created folder will be placed in your Starting Points folder, adding a new tab to your Starting Points window so that you can quickly access any of the merge documents.

7. Select your choice of output format, and the merge commences. One copy of the merge document is produced for each visible database record.

Tip

Before committing yourself to a massive print merge, examine a few records onscreen by clicking the "Save in a new document" radio button. You can click the Stop button in the progress dialog box partway through the process and peruse the output generated to that point. This procedure can save an enormous amount of paper if, for example, you have selected a wrong database field, forgotten to restrict the records to a particular subset, or incorrectly set the spacing between fields.

Down to Business: An Envelope Merge

After you understand the mechanics of a merge, the process becomes routine. Rather than step you through another typical mail merge, the following instructions explain how to perform a type of merge you might not have considered — an envelope merge. With a little experimentation, not only can you format and print envelopes from AppleWorks, but you also can use a merge to automate the process by grabbing the mailing addresses from a database (an essential technique for mass mailings).

Tip   If you just want to print a single envelope, you can use AppleWorks' Envelope or Address Envelope Assistant. (See Chapter 3 for details.)

Designing the merge form

This section explains how to create an envelope merge form as a document in the word processing environment. Figure 8-3 shows one such form that was designed for a center-feeding Apple LaserWriter II NTX. The graphic rulers are displayed, rather than the normal word processing ruler, to show the approximate placement of the mailing address and return address sections.

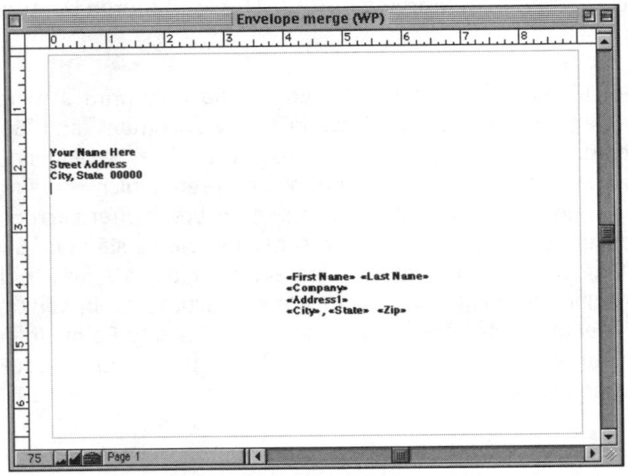

Figure 8-3: An envelope merge form

STEPS: Creating the Envelope Merge Form

1. Create a new word processing document by choosing File ➪ New ➪ Word Processing (or pressing ⌘+N).

2. Choose File ➪ Page Setup. The Page Setup dialog box appears.

3. Click the icon for landscape mode printing (the sideways icon). Then select the paper option that corresponds to a #10 business envelope — in LaserWriter 8 (version 8.7), choose Com10 Envelope Center Fed. Then click the OK button.

4. Choose Format ➪ Rulers ➪ Ruler Settings. The Ruler Settings dialog box appears.

5. Click the Graphics and Inches radio buttons, and then click the OK button. The graphics rulers appear at the top and left sides of the blank word processing document (as shown earlier in Figure 8-3). The outline of the document page should correspond to that of a #10 business envelope — 6.5 by 9 inches.

6. Type the return address in the position shown in Figure 8-3 or, if your envelopes are already imprinted with a return address, leave this part of the envelope blank.

   These instructions assume that you are using a center-feed printer. If the printer is a right- or left-feed printer, type the mailing address and return address at the upper or near the lower section of the form, respectively.

7. For the mailing address section, press the Return or Enter key several times until you reach the 3.5- to 4-inch mark on the vertical ruler.

8. To align the lines of the address, choose Format ➪ Tabs. The Tab dialog box appears (see Figure 8-4). Set a left tab at the 4-inch position by matching the settings shown in the figure, and then click the OK button. Press the Tab key once. The text insertion point is now correct for the first field of the mailing address.

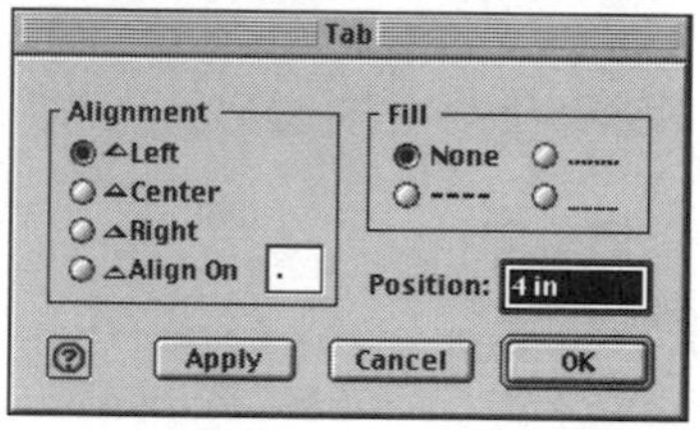

Figure 8-4: To create a left tab at the 4-inch mark, match these settings.

9. Choose File ➪ Open and select the database that contains the mailing addresses.

   (The remainder of this example uses the field names from Address List. If you are using your own database, substitute field names as appropriate.)

10. Select the envelope word processing document from the Window menu.

11. Choose File ➪ Mail Merge. A standard Open file dialog box appears. Choose your address database, and then click the Open button. If the database is not already open, it opens now. The Mail Merge windoid appears (refer to Figure 8-1, shown earlier in this chapter).

12. In the Mail Merge windoid, select the name of the first field you want to insert and click the Insert button. For this example, insert a First Name field.

13. Press the spacebar once to add a space after the field and insert the next field (in this case, Last Name).

14. Press the Return or Enter key to start a new line, followed by a tab to align the text with the line above it. Then insert the Address1 field.

15. Press the Return or Enter key to start another new line, followed by a tab to align the text with the line above it. Then insert the City field.

16. Type a comma and a space, and then insert the State field.

17. Type one or two spaces and insert the Zip field.

18. If you want to apply different fonts, sizes, or styles to the text, do so now.

19. Save the merge form as a normal AppleWorks document.

As mentioned in Step 6, if your envelopes have a return address printed on them, leave the return address section of the template blank. If you routinely use both kinds of envelopes — blank envelopes and envelopes with a preprinted return address — you can create two envelope merge forms.

Testing the merge form

Now comes the fun part — making sure the mailing and return addresses print correctly. Before even thinking of printing on an envelope, however, you should do a few test printouts on standard letter-sized paper by either merging to a new file or merging to files on disk, and then running your test with those documents. You do test printouts for a more important reason than to avoid wasting envelopes. If you insert an envelope into the printer and it prints outside the area of the envelope, it is printing onto the printer drum or platen rather than onto the envelope. You won't have that problem with letter paper.

Before printing, place a small pencil mark on the paper in the upper-right corner of the page. When you issue the Print command, you might see a message saying some of the printing might be clipped. Ignore it. When the printout appears, the pencil mark tells you the following:

✦ The side of the paper on which the printer prints (so you know whether to insert the envelopes right-side up or upside down)

✦ Which edge of the envelope to insert into the printer (left or right)

✦ Whether the printing is being clipped

Now check the positions of the mailing and return addresses on the test printout. (You might want to lay the printout over an envelope to see how well they match up.) If necessary, adjust the positions of the mailing and return addresses and do another test. When you hold the printout sideways (so you can read it), the printing should be centered from top to bottom on a center-feed printer, near the upper edge of the page on a right-feed printer, or near the lower edge of the page on a left-feed printer. When the alignment looks correct, repeat the test with an envelope. After you can correctly print an envelope, you can do the merge, as described in the next section. If this is a merge form you might wish to reuse, you should Save it at this point.

Envelope Feed Methods and Page Setup Dialog Boxes

Unfortunately, no one method for printing envelopes is universal to all printers. Some printers, such as the original ImageWriter, weren't designed to handle envelopes. You can use the instructions in this chapter with such printers, but we don't recommend doing so.

In general, laser and inkjet printers are best for printing envelopes. They have trays that ensure that the envelopes are correctly aligned and the envelope's paper path (the route the paper takes after you feed it into the printer) is straight. ImageWriters use a standard platen (roller bar) to feed paper. Although the platen is excellent for tractor-fed paper (paper with tiny holes on both sides) and reasonably good for letter paper, it's only so-so for envelopes. Envelopes tend to slide around too much and can easily jam.

The method for feeding envelopes varies considerably among Macintosh-compatible ink-jet and laser printers. Some printers, such as the LaserWriter II series, expect you to *center-feed* envelopes (center them on the manual feed tray or in an envelope tray) and insert them facing up with the left edge of the envelope forward. Other printers require that you feed envelopes from the left or right side of the feed tray. Some printers are designed so that you have to feed paper upside down.

If you aren't sure of the printer's envelope feeding requirements, check its manual. The envelope template shown in this chapter is designed for a center-feed printer. You need to adjust the placement of the text to make it work properly with a right- or left-feed printer.

To make things more complicated, every printer also has its own version of the Page Setup dialog box. Luckily, the dialog boxes contain options that make formatting a standard #10 business envelope simple. The figure shows the settings for LaserWriter printers. (Note the envelope paper choice, as well as the Landscape Orientation option.)

Performing the envelope merge

Because different people have different merge needs, this section contains instructions for two types of envelope merges: printing a single envelope and printing a series of envelopes.

STEPS: Printing a Single Envelope

1. Open the merge database.

2. Choose Layout ➪ Find (or press Shift+⌘+F). A blank find request appears.

3. Specify criteria to find the record you want to print. Click the Visible radio button to search only the visible records, or click the All radio button to search the entire database.

4. If more than one record is found, use the mouse to select the specific record you want to print. (To select a record, click anywhere in the record other than inside a field.) Then choose Organize ➪ Hide Unselected. All records other than the one you selected are hidden.

5. Open the envelope document.

6. Choose Mail Merge from the File menu. The Mail Merge windoid appears.

7. Click the Merge button. The Mail Merge Destination dialog box appears.

8. The Send Documents to Printer radio button should be selected; select it if not and click the Continue button. The Print dialog box appears.

9. Insert an envelope into the manual feed tray of the printer and click the Print button to print the envelope.

Occasionally, you might want to use the merge form to do a mass mailing — perhaps to send holiday greetings to all your friends or a business message to your clients or coworkers.

STEPS: Printing a Set of Envelopes

1. Open the merge database.

2. *Optional:* If you want to merge only a subset of records from the database, select the records you want to use. To select the records, use the Find command or the Match Records and Hide Unselected commands. (Remember, the merge prints an envelope for every visible database document, so you have to hide all the records you do not want to print.) For instructions on using the Find and Match Records commands, refer to Chapter 5.

3. *Optional:* If you want the envelopes to print in a specific order (alphabetically by last name or in Zip code order, for example), sort the records by choosing the Sort Records command from the Organize menu.

4. Open the envelope document.

5. Choose File ➪ Mail Merge. The Mail Merge for *file name* windoid appears.

6. Click the Merge button. The Print dialog box appears.

7. Insert an envelope into the manual feed tray or paper tray for the printer, turn the printer on, and then click the Print button to print the envelopes. As each envelope feeds into the printer, insert the next envelope. Continue until all the envelopes have been printed.

Tip

If you have an envelope tray for your printer, you can print 15 to 20 envelopes at a time without having to stand and watch the process.

Quick Tips

The following quick tips explain how to:

✦ Use a calculation field to perform a conditional merge

✦ Use a merge to address a form letter when you don't know the names of all of the customers

✦ Insert one of two different amounts in a merge

✦ Use a spreadsheet frame as a merge form

✦ Update merge forms created in older versions of the program so they work with AppleWorks 6

Conditional merges

If you're searching for the conditional merge capabilities many of the popular standalone word processing programs offer, you can stop looking—AppleWorks doesn't have them. An example of a conditional merge is: "If database field *X* contains information that matches these criteria, do this; otherwise, do something else."

Although AppleWorks isn't equipped for sophisticated conditional merges, you can jury-rig basic conditional tests by creating calculation fields that use the IF database function. The following examples illustrate this application. (Refer to Appendix B for more information on database functions.)

Example 1

You have a customer database that contains a title, first name, last name, and address for each customer. Now you want to mail a form letter to everyone telling them about your annual fall sale. Unfortunately, through sloppy record keeping, you didn't always record the customers' names. How do you address the letters? Use the following steps.

STEPS: Addressing a Form Letter When You Don't Know Some Customers' Names

1. In the address database, choose Layout ➪ Define Fields (or press Shift+⌘+D). The Define Fields dialog box appears.

2. Define a new calculation field called "Name Present?" using this formula:

```
IF('Last Name'="","Customer",'Prefix'&" "&'Last Name')
```

The formula checks to see whether the Last Name field is blank. If it is, the word "Customer" is entered in the Name Present? field. If the Last Name field is not blank, the prefix (Mr., Dr., and so on), a blank space, and the last name are combined and copied into the Name Present? field (Ms. Smith, for example).

The field names in the formula are those from the Address List database created with the AppleWorks Assistant. If you are using a different database, substitute the names of your fields for Last Name and Prefix.

3. In the Format result as pop-up menu, choose Text.

4. Use the following line as the salutation line of the form letter:

Dear <<Name Present?>>:

When the merge is performed, the Name Present? placeholder is individually evaluated for each record included in the merge. If a last name has been recorded for a given customer, it is combined with a prefix, producing "Dear Mrs. Johnson," for example. If no last name is found for a record, the line becomes "Dear Customer."

As this example illustrates, you can use any properly defined field in a database as a placeholder in a merge form. The field does not need to be visible in the layout. You also can nest the IF statements to use the First Name field if the prefix is also missing, for example.

Example 2

You've volunteered as a fundraiser for a local nonprofit organization. The amount each patron contributed last year is recorded in an AppleWorks database. You've decided that to request increased contributions this year you will ask patrons who gave $50 or more last year to consider increasing their donation by 25 percent. If they gave less than $50, you will ask them for the same amount. How can you accomplish this task? Use the following steps:

STEPS: Inserting One of Two Different Amounts in a Merge

1. In the address database, choose Layout ➪ Define Fields (or press Shift+⌘+D). The Define Fields dialog box appears.

2. Define a new calculation field called Suggested Contribution. Use the following formula for the field:

```
IF('Last Year Contribution'>=50,'Last Year
Contribution'*1.25,'Last Year Contribution')
```

The formula checks the amount in the field named Last Year Contribution. If it is greater than $50, the amount is multiplied by 1.25 to increase the amount by 25 percent. Otherwise, the Last Year Contribution field is copied directly into the Suggested Contribution field.

3. In the Format result as pop-up menu, choose Number.

4. In the form letter, insert the Suggested Contribution field in the line of text where you suggest a donation amount, as shown in the following example:

```
Based on your generous contribution last year, we suggest a
donation of <<Suggested Contribution>>.
```

You do not need to place the calculation field in a database layout. As long as you have properly defined a field, you can use it in the database as a placeholder in a merge form, even if it is not visible in a layout.

Using a spreadsheet frame as a merge form

At the beginning of this chapter, we mentioned that a spreadsheet or spreadsheet frame also can serve as a merge form. You might ask, "Why would you want to use a spreadsheet in this manner?" We thought for a long time and came up with an instance where this might be useful: for filling in spreadsheet tables.

As an example, suppose you've designed a letter you want to send to all members of your company's sales force. In the word processing document, you can embed a spreadsheet table that shows each salesperson's quarterly or monthly sales and commissions earned. Because the information is merged into a spreadsheet frame rather than a text frame or document, you also can use the power of the spreadsheet to create formulas that further manipulate the merged data. Formulas could calculate each person's total annual sales or average monthly sales, for example.

Updating old merge forms for AppleWorks 6

In versions of ClarisWorks prior to 4.0, there were two ways to insert fields into a merge form:

✦ Choosing field names from the Mail Merge windoid

✦ Typing the brackets and field names directly into the merge form

Starting with ClarisWorks 4 (and continuing with all versions of AppleWorks), however, you must select all fields from the Mail Merge windoid — typed fields and brackets are not recognized as merge fields.

If you have merge forms created in earlier versions of ClarisWorks, you can update them so they will work with AppleWorks 6 by replacing each field with one listed in the Mail Merge for *file name* windoid. To do this, select the field in the merge form (including its surrounding brackets), choose a field name in the Field Names list of the Mail Merge windoid, and click the Insert button.

Tip

Not sure which fields are old, or which fields have already been updated or replaced? On the merge form, double-click anywhere in a field name. If it has been updated, the entire field — including the surrounding brackets — will be selected. If the field was inserted or typed in a previous version of ClarisWorks, only a portion of the field name will be selected (one word of a multiword field name, or the field name but not its surrounding brackets, for example). The important point to remember is that, starting with ClarisWorks 4, AppleWorks treats an inserted field name as a single entity, starting with the left bracket and ending with the right bracket.

Summary

✦ A merge requires two components: a database and a merge form (a word processing document, text frame, spreadsheet document, or spreadsheet frame). Information from the database fields is inserted into field placeholders in the merge document.

✦ Every merge field name is surrounded by special brackets (<<>>). The brackets are added automatically when you select the field names from the Mail Merge windoid.

✦ Punctuation and spaces can separate merge fields from each other, as well as from surrounding text. You also can apply formatting, such as different fonts and styles, to the merge fields.

✦ AppleWorks 6 adds the capability to output your merge to a folder of individual documents on disk or a single document where each generated form is in its own section.

✦ In a merge, every visible database record produces its own merge document. You can restrict the number of records by using the Find or Match Records commands. You also can arrange the records in a particular order by using the Sort Records command.

✦ Merge forms designed in versions of ClarisWorks prior to 4.0 must be updated before you can use them with AppleWorks 6. Field names must be reinserted by choosing them from the Mail Merge windoid.

✦   ✦   ✦

Adding Tables and Charts to Reports

Only high-end word processing programs include a special feature for laying out tables. When you use a word processor without such a feature, your only recourse is to set a series of tabs and use them to format a table.

Although you can use tabs to create tables in the AppleWorks word processor, you have two better ways to make a table, depending on how you want to use it. The first method, the new Tables feature in AppleWorks 6 (discussed in Chapter 3), lets you create relatively freeform tables, where each cell is its own word processing frame. The other method is to use a spreadsheet frame. This method enables you to reap the benefits of working in an environment where you can manipulate numbers and generate charts, as well as manipulate text, but that also places limits on the formatting of the table and on the cell contents. (For information on the spreadsheet environment's features and functions, refer to Chapter 4.)

This chapter explains how to add a spreadsheet table or chart to a word processing document. Because of the tight integration of AppleWorks environments, however, you can apply the techniques described in this chapter in the other environments as well — in presentation or draw documents, for example.

Spreadsheet Tables

Although you can design a spreadsheet table in the spreadsheet environment, creating a spreadsheet frame in a word processing document is simpler. This method also enables you to tell whether the table is the correct size for the document.

STEPS: Creating a Spreadsheet Table

1. Open an existing word processing document or create a new one by choosing the appropriate command from the File menu (Open or New ➪ Spreadsheet), clicking the Word Processing button in the Button Bar, clicking the Word Processing thumbnail in Starting Points Basics panel, or clicking any appropriate word processing template in the Templates panel.

2. If the Tools windoid isn't visible, click the Show/Hide Tools control at the lower edge of the document window.

3. Select the spreadsheet tool (the grid with numbers on it in the Frames panel).

Tip

You can control-click in the document window and choose Frame Tools ➪ Spreadsheet from the contextual menu to replace Steps 2 and 3, thus not having to use the screen space for the Tools windoid.

4. To create the table, click where you want the upper-left corner to start and then drag down and to the right. When you release the mouse button, a new spreadsheet frame appears, as shown in Figure 9-1.

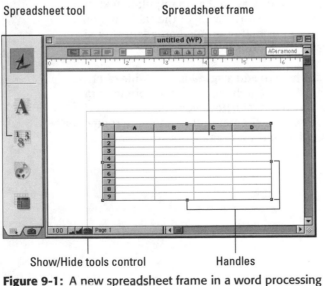

Spreadsheet tool   Spreadsheet frame

Show/Hide tools control   Handles

Figure 9-1: A new spreadsheet frame in a word processing document

Tip

Alternatively, you can drag the spreadsheet tool from the Frames panel into your document to create a default spreadsheet frame — two columns and eight rows will be visible.

Don't be overly concerned about the initial appearance or dimensions of the table. You can change its size, the number of columns and rows, column widths, and row heights as needed. You also can hide the grid lines, as well as the column and row headings.

Entering data

To add text and data into the spreadsheet table, click the table once to select it and then click any cell in the table. The selected cell has a dark border around it. You can now enter data in that cell or anywhere else in the spreadsheet, as shown in Figure 9-2, by typing in the Entry bar.

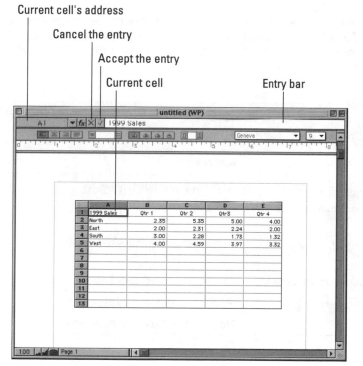

Figure 9-2: Entering data in a cell

As you type an entry for a cell, text or numbers appear in the entry bar, which is shown in Figure 9-2. (Note that as you work in the spreadsheet frame, the word processing ruler is still visible but not active.) To accept the entry, do any of the following:

✦ Click the checkmark (which is the Accept button).

✦ Press the Enter or Return key.

✦ Press an arrow key (or an Option+arrow key).

✦ Press the Tab or Shift+Tab keys.

To cancel a cell entry, click the X button in the entry bar.

Note In AppleWorks 6, the functions of the arrow and Option-arrow keys are defined in Spreadsheet Preferences (see Chapter 10). To accept a cell entry or move to another cell, you can use either the unmodified arrow keys or the Option+arrow keys — depending on how you set these preferences.

Clicking the checkmark or pressing Enter accepts the entry but leaves the cursor in the current cell. The other options (Return, arrow key or Option+arrow key, Tab, and Shift+Tab) accept the entry as well, but they move the cursor to a new cell, as described in Table 9-1.

Table 9-1	
Cell Navigation	
Key	*Movement*
Return	To the cell immediately below
Right arrow (or Option+right arrow) or Tab	To the cell immediately to the right
Left arrow (or Option+left arrow) or Shift+Tab	To the cell immediately to the left
Down arrow (or Option+down arrow)	To the cell immediately below
Up arrow (or Option+up arrow)	To the cell immediately above
Enter	No movement (can be changed in Preferences)

Note In AppleWorks 6 you also can set the behavior of the Enter key in your Spreadsheet Preferences (see Chapter 10).

You also can use the keys in Table 9-1 for pure cursor movements. If you are not entering data, pressing these keys simply moves the cursor in the direction stated.

You can move directly to any cell by clicking it with the mouse. In many cases, this method is the quickest way to get to any cell in the table that is not adjacent to the current cell.

Note

You also can choose the Go to Cell command from the Options menu (or press ⌘+G) and specify the coordinates of the desired cell (A7, for example) in the dialog box that appears. Because most tables are rather small, however, clicking a cell to select it is usually quicker.

For fast data entry in contiguous cells, you can select a cell range by Shift+clicking. The current cell (which is white) is in the upper-left corner of the selected range, as shown in Figure 9-3. If you press Return after you enter the data for each cell, the current cell automatically shifts on a column-by-column basis, as shown in the table at the top of the figure. If you press Enter or Tab as you complete each cell entry, the current cell automatically shifts on a row-by-row basis, as shown in the table at the bottom of the figure.

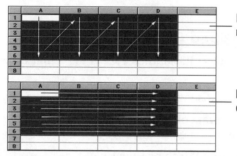

Press Return after each entry to move the cursor in this pattern

Press Enter or Tab to move the cursor in this pattern

Figure 9-3: Entering data into a selection of cells

Changing the appearance of the table

By using the mouse and menu commands, you can make any of the following changes to the appearance of the table:

✦ Change the number of columns or rows displayed

✦ Change row heights and column widths

✦ Make text wrap within selected cells

✦ Add shading to selected cells

✦ Display or hide the cell gridlines, column letters, and row numbers

✦ Adding or changing cell borders

Changing the number of displayed columns or rows

Although a spreadsheet frame is simply a window into a larger worksheet, you can increase or reduce the number of visible columns and rows. To change the number of displayed columns or rows, click the spreadsheet table once to select it. Then, click one of the table's handles and drag. When you release the mouse button, the table reforms and displays only the columns and rows you have indicated.

Note Many finished tables look better if you hide the column and row headings (as described later in this chapter). If hiding the headings leaves an extra blank row at the lower edge or a blank column on the right side of the table, you might need to resize the table again.

Changing row heights and column widths

AppleWorks enables you to include varying sizes of text in a worksheet. You can adjust the heights and widths of individual rows and columns to accommodate large headings (formatted as 24-point text, for example) or long text strings that spill over into adjacent cells.

STEPS: Changing Row Heights and Column Widths

1. Click the spreadsheet table once to select it. Handles appear at its four corners, and the cursor changes to a pointer.

2. Click any cell in the column or row whose width or height you want to change.

   To change the width or height of several columns or rows simultaneously, Shift+click to select a series of contiguous columns or rows.

3. From the Format menu, choose Column Width or Row Height, as appropriate. The Column Width or Row Height dialog box appears. Figure 9-4 shows the Column Width dialog box.

Click to reset the column width to the default (72 pts or one inch)

Enter a width

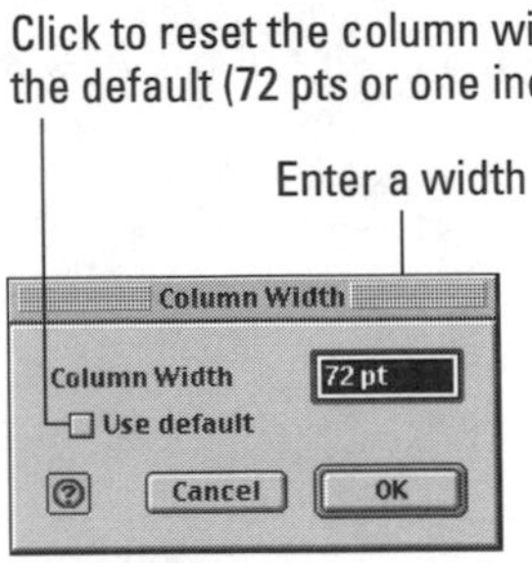

Figure 9-4: The Column Width dialog box

New Feature
Both the Column Width and Row Height dialog boxes are accessible from contextual menu choices in AppleWorks 6.

4. Specify a new number for the width or height.

   Height and width numbers are shown in points rather than in characters. Points are often used for measuring type. (An inch contains 72 points.)

5. Click the OK button. The new column width or row height is put into effect. If multiple rows or columns were selected, they will all have the same height or width, respectively.

Tip
Although the default unit of measurement for specifying row heights and column widths is points, you can use other units by typing the appropriate abbreviation after the numeric portion of the entry in the text box. You can use inches (in), millimeters (mm), centimeters (cm), points (pt), or picas (pc).

Manually changing column widths or row heights by using the mouse—as described in the following steps—is sometimes easier.

STEPS: Changing Row Heights and Column Widths Manually

1. Click the spreadsheet table once to select it. Handles appear at the four corners, and the cursor changes to a pointer. Click again, inside it, to be in the spreadsheet environment.

2. Move the pointer into the heading area for the column or row whose width or height you want to change. As the cursor moves over the right edge of the column or the bottom edge of the row, a two-headed pointer appears.

   To change the width or height of several columns or rows simultaneously, Shift+click to select a series of contiguous columns or rows.

3. While pressing the mouse button, drag to change the column width or row height.

4. When the width or height is correct, release the mouse button.

AppleWorks 6 provides a third way to adjust rows and columns that you'll find handy. Using the following technique, you can automatically resize rows or columns so they are the minimum height or width necessary to accommodate the largest cell in the range:

✦ To autosize a row, move the pointer into the row headings area of the worksheet (on the far left) and double-click the bottom of the row you want to resize. The row height adjusts to fit the tallest text in the row. You also can click the Autosize Row button on the Button Bar to adjust the width of the selected rows.

✦ To autosize a column, move the pointer into the column headings area of the worksheet (at the upper edge) and double-click the right side of the column you want to resize. The column width adjusts to fit the longest text string in the column. You also can click the Autosize Column button on the Button Bar to adjust the width of the column(s) selected.

This technique also can be used to simultaneously autosize a series of rows or columns. Select the rows or columns, and then double-click the bottom of any of the selected rows or the right side of any of the selected columns. AppleWorks determines the minimum height or width necessary to accommodate the largest or longest text in the selected range. All selected rows or columns are resized to match that height or width.

New Feature   AppleWorks 6 adds two menu commands to the Format menu: Autosize Rows and Autosize Columns.

Setting text wrap for a cell

When a text string is too long to fit in a cell, it spills into adjacent empty cells. (The direction in which it spills depends on the original cell's Alignment setting.) To keep the entire string in its original cell, you can either widen the column (as described previously) or format the text to wrap within the cell.

To make text wrap within selected cells (if the spreadsheet frame is not active), click the spreadsheet table twice to make the spreadsheet environment active. Select the cell or cells to which you want to apply the Wrap format. Then, choose Format ➪ Alignment ➪ Wrap. If the text no longer fits in the cell (some of it might be clipped at the bottom of the cell), you can change the row height by using any of the methods described earlier.

Note   Wrap is a higher precedence of formatting attribute to autosizing. When a cell has wrapping enabled, autosizing the row height or column width will adjust those dimensions based on the wrapped height and width.

Shading cells

To highlight important data or simply to dress up your worksheet, AppleWorks 6 enables you to apply shading to individual cells. Begin by selecting the cells to which you want to apply the shading. Then, select a fill color and pattern from the Accents windoid. (If the Accents windoid isn't visible, choose Window ➪ Show Accents or press ⌘+K.) The color and pattern are applied to the selected cells.

Note   You cannot apply fill gradients or wallpapers to cells, nor can you apply a pen pattern or line width. Although you can select these options, AppleWorks ignores them. If you try to set a pen color, you will not see any effect until and unless you add a border to the cells.

Applying styles

The AppleWorks 6 stylesheet contains several predefined spreadsheet styles you might find helpful in creating attractive tables. To see the stylesheet, choose Format ➪ Show Styles or press ⌘+W.

To apply an SS-table style to a worksheet frame, click to select the worksheet frame or the specific range you want to format. Then choose any of the predefined styles in the stylesheet. Figure 9-5 shows a table formatted with the 3D Table 2 style. (See Chapter 15 for more information on using stylesheets.)

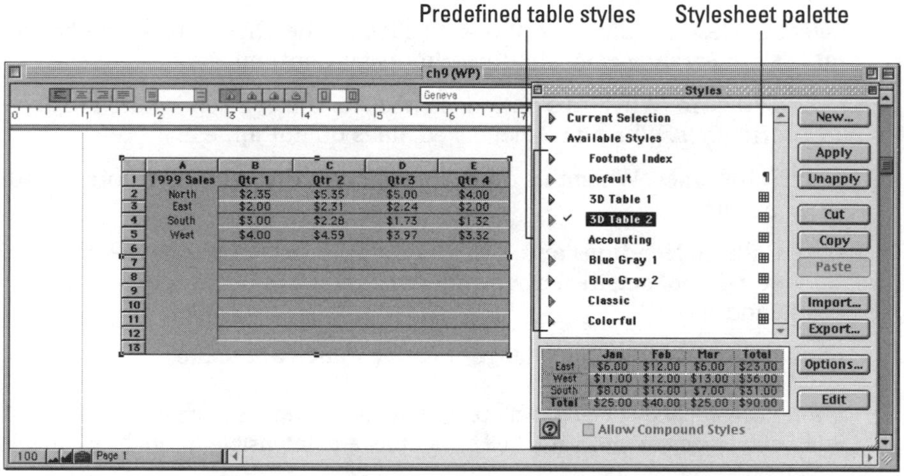

Figure 9-5: A table formatted using one of AppleWorks's predefined styles

Setting display options

By setting options in the Display dialog box, you can change the onscreen and printed look of any worksheet or table.

STEPS: Displaying or Hiding the Cell Gridlines, Column Letters, and Row Numbers

1. Click the spreadsheet table once to select it. Handles appear at the four corners, and the cursor changes to a pointer.

2. Click in any cell of the spreadsheet. The spreadsheet menus appear in the menu bar.

3. Choose Options ➪ Display. The Display dialog box appears, as shown in Figure 9-6.

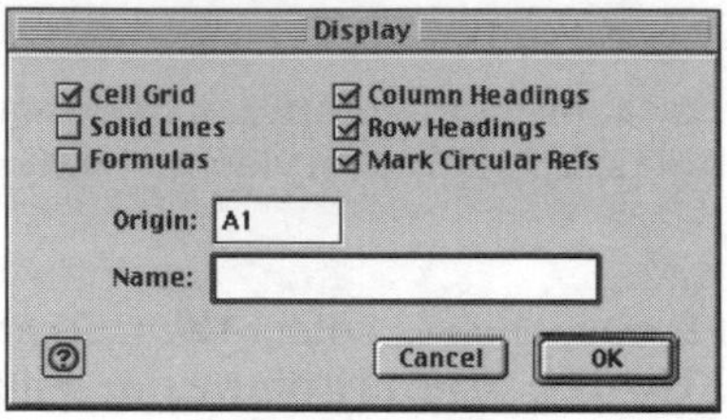

Figure 9-6: The Display dialog box

You also can open the Display dialog box by selecting the spreadsheet frame and choosing Edit ➪ Frame Info.

4. Select or deselect display options by clicking the checkboxes. To change the table's appearance, consider these important options:

- **Cell Grid.** When this option is checked, the cell separators are dotted grid lines. When it is unchecked, lines do not appear.

- **Solid Lines.** When this option is checked, the cell separators are solid grid lines.

- **Column Headings and Row Headings.** If these options are unchecked, you do not see the letters and numbers normally used to label columns and rows.

5. Click the OK button. The changes in appearance are made.

Note If you have applied shading to all cells in the table, the display settings for Cell Grid and Solid Lines are irrelevant. Cell separators are not visible through cell shading.

Positioning the table

After you finish entering data and formatting the table, you might want to change the table's position on the page. Up to this point, the spreadsheet frame has been just another object floating on the document page. You can leave it that way and, optionally, specify a text wrap for it (remember, it's an object — just like a draw graphic), or you can move it into the text as an in-line graphic. Because AppleWorks treats in-line graphics as text, you can apply paragraph formatting commands to center the table on the page and separate it from the surrounding paragraphs. Figures 9-7 and 9-8 show the two table treatments.

To treat a spreadsheet table as an object, click the spreadsheet table once to select it. Drag the table to its new position, and then choose Options ➪ Text Wrap from the Options menu. The Text Wrap dialog box appears. Click the Regular or Irregular icon and then click the OK button. Nearby text wraps around the table. Continue to drag the spreadsheet until the text wraps exactly as you want. You can fine-tune the position of the table by pressing the arrow keys. You can specify a distance (in points) between the object and the surrounding text by typing a number in the Gutter text box in the Text Wrap dialog box.

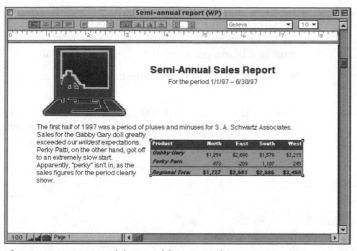

Figure 9-7: A spreadsheet table as an object

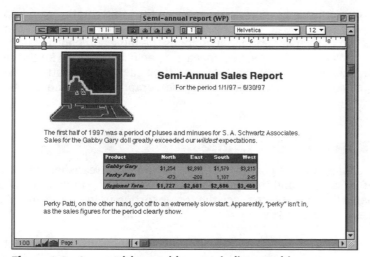

Figure 9-8: A spreadsheet table as an in-line graphic

STEPS: Treating a Spreadsheet Table as an In-line Graphic

1. Click the spreadsheet table once to select it. Handles appear at the corners.

2. Choose Edit ⇨ Cut (or press ⌘+X). The worksheet is removed, and a copy of it is placed on the clipboard.

3. Click the text tool (the capital A) in the Tools panel and move the text insertion point to where you want to place the table. (Because formatting is much simpler when the table is in a paragraph by itself, you might want to press the Return or Enter key to create a blank paragraph to receive the table.)

4. Choose Edit ➪ Paste (or press ⌘+V). The table is inserted at the text insertion point.

5. *Optional:* If you want to center the table on its line, place the text insertion point at the beginning or end of the paragraph that contains the table and then click the Centered Alignment control in the ruler bar (see Figure 9-9).

Centered Alignment control

Figure 9-9: Use the Centered Alignment control to center the table.

6. *Optional:* If you want to add some space between the table and the paragraphs that lie immediately above and below it, place the text insertion point at the beginning or end of the paragraph that contains the table and choose Format ➪ Paragraph. The Paragraph dialog box appears. Specify new figures for Space Before and Space After (1 li, for example), and then click the OK button. The table is now separated from the surrounding paragraphs by the amount of space you entered.

Deleting a spreadsheet frame

At some point, you might decide you don't need a particular spreadsheet table after all. To delete a table, select it and then press the Delete key. If the table is an in-line graphic rather than a floating object, place the text insertion point at the end of the table and then press the Delete key.

If you want to use the table on a different page or in a different document, select the table and then press ⌘+X or choose Edit ➪ Cut. You can then use the Paste command to move the table to its new location.

You also can drag the table to another open AppleWorks document or another location within the same document — taking advantage of AppleWorks 6's support for drag-and-drop.

Adding or changing cell borders

When you prepare a spreadsheet frame to illustrate part of a report, you will usually want to call special attention to some cell or cell range. AppleWorks enables you to put *borders* (lines) on any side of a cell or combination of cells. You can even place an outline around a range of cells. To add a border, you can click any of the border buttons in your Button Bar (Outline Border, Right Border, Top Border, Bottom Border, and Left Border), or summon the Borders dialog box (see Figure 9-10) by either choosing Format ➪ Borders or choosing Borders from the spreadsheet frame's contextual menu. The borders reflect the Pen color choices made in Accents.

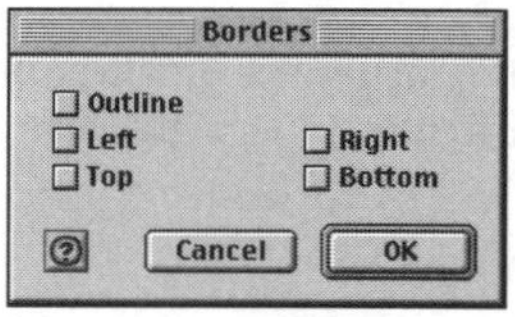

Figure 9-10: The Borders dialog box lets you put frames around a cell or cells.

Note

Outline adds the outline around the outside of a range of cells. If you want every cell in the range to be individually outlined, you need to add left, right, top, and bottom borders from the Borders dialog box.

Spreadsheet Charts

You also can place spreadsheet charts in word processing reports. The easiest way to create a chart is to do so in a spreadsheet document (rather than in a spreadsheet frame in the word processing document).

STEPS: Adding a Chart to a Word Processing Document

1. Open an existing spreadsheet or create a new one by choosing Open or New from the File menu.

2. Select the cell range from which the chart will be created.

3. Choose Options ➪ Make Chart. The Chart Options dialog box appears, as shown in Figure 9-11. (See Chapter 4 for details on creating and modifying charts.)

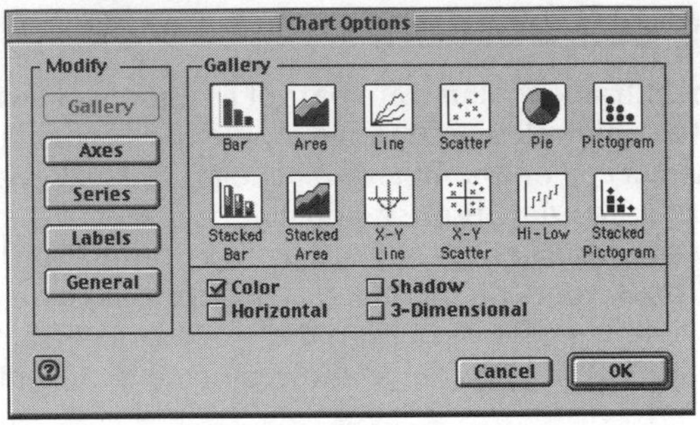

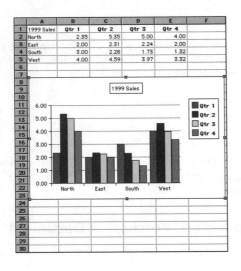

Figure 9-11: To design a chart, select options from the Chart Options dialog box.

4. Select a chart style and click the OK button. The chart appears on the current document page and is automatically selected, as shown in Figure 9-12 (note the handles).

Figure 9-12: A new chart created in the spreadsheet environment simply floats on the page.

5. Choose Edit ⇨ Copy (or press ⌘+C). A copy of the chart is placed on the clipboard.

6. Switch to the word processing document by selecting its name from the list at the bottom of the Window menu. (If it isn't already open, choose File ⇨ Open.)

7. Choose Edit ⇨ Paste (or press ⌘+V). The chart appears in the word processing document.

You can change the chart's position and size — as well as treat it as an object or an in-line graphic — by following the directions given earlier for spreadsheet tables. And as stated previously, you can move the chart using drag-and-drop (rather than cut-and-paste), if you prefer.

Note   Any chart pasted into a document in this manner is a static entity. If you later change the chart's worksheet, the pasted chart will not reflect the changes. If you want to keep a live link between the chart and the data that generated it, you will need to have both in the frame.

Quick Tips

As you design the table, keep in mind that you are working in a spreadsheet that just happens to be embedded in a word processing document. All the power of the spreadsheet environment can be brought to bear on the table. Not only can you enter calculations and formulas, you also can choose from additional formatting options, such as the following:

✦ Choosing different fonts, styles, sizes, and colors for the text in selected cells

✦ Changing the alignment of text and numbers within cells

✦ Applying special formats for displaying numbers and dates

✦ Sorting cells

✦ Embellishing the table with graphics

As an example, Figure 9-13 shows a fully dressed spreadsheet table with multiple font styles, sizes, and alignments; cell shading; selective cell borders; and graphics embellishments (an oval around a number, an arrow, and a callout that contains text). (Refer to the instructions in Chapter 4 for help in formatting spreadsheet tables.)

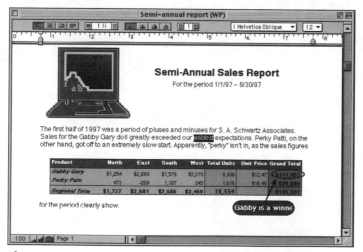

Figure 9-13: An example of a formatted spreadsheet table

Summary

✦ Using a spreadsheet frame for a table in a word processing environment enables you to reap the benefits of working in an environment where you can manipulate numbers as well as format text.

✦ Some of the changes you can make to spreadsheet tables include modifying row heights and column widths (to properly display text), changing the table's size, adding text wrap for some cells, applying cell shading, and hiding row and column headings.

✦ You can change column widths and row heights manually, or you can change them by entering numbers in a dialog box. Manually changing them is often the most accurate method.

✦ As with spreadsheet tables, charts can also be used to dress up a text-based report or memo.

✦ You can position tables and charts as floating objects (with text wrap) or as in-line graphics (which are subject to regular paragraph formatting commands). Both approaches work well.

Mastering AppleWorks

CHAPTER 10

Setting Preferences

✦ ✦ ✦ ✦

In This Chapter

Default and document-specific preferences

General preferences

File preferences

Text preferences

Graphics preferences

Spreadsheet preferences

✦ ✦ ✦ ✦

By setting preferences, you can customize AppleWorks to fit the way you work. To view or change your current preferences settings, choose Edit ➪ Preferences ➪ General. The Preferences dialog box appears (see Figure 10-1). In the upper part of the Preferences dialog box is a Topic pull-down menu listing the different parts of AppleWorks you can customize. The areas for which you can set preferences in AppleWorks 6 are General, Files, Text, Graphics, and Spreadsheet.

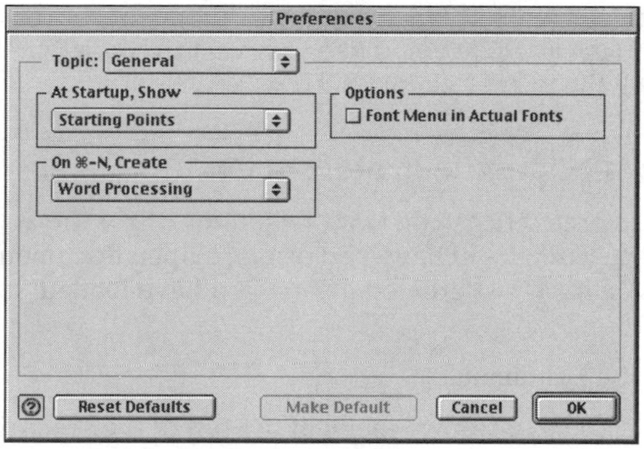

Figure 10-1: The Preferences dialog box (General preferences displayed)

Default and Document-Specific Preferences

AppleWorks gives you the capability to create a group of default preferences that will be automatically used for all new documents (of that type) in the current and future sessions. Additionally, you can set document-specific preferences that apply to the currently active (front most) document and that are saved with that document.

STEPS: Setting New Default Preferences

1. Choose Edit ⇨ Preferences ⇨ General.

2. Choose a category from the Topic pull-down menu in the upper portion of the Preferences dialog box to select the type of preference settings you want to modify.

3. Change the settings in the dialog box as desired.

4. Repeat Steps 2 and 3 for any other preferences you want to change.

5. Click the Make Default button.

The new preferences become the default settings for all new documents you create in this and future sessions. If you ever decide you'd like to revert to AppleWorks 6's original preference settings, click the Reset Defaults button.

STEPS: Setting Document-Specific Preferences

1. Select the document whose preferences you want to set, making it the active document (bringing it to the front if you have two or more open documents). You can use a document you have just created or one you have loaded from disk.

2. Choose Preferences from the Edit menu.

3. Choose a category from the Topic pull-down menu at the top of the Preferences dialog box to select the type of preference settings you want to modify.

4. Change the settings in the dialog box as desired.

5. Repeat Steps 3 and 4 for any other preferences you want to change.

6. Click the OK button.

The new settings apply only to the current document. Other new documents you create in the session will still use the default settings, unless you also set preferences for them. Because preference settings are saved with each document, the next time you run AppleWorks and open the document, the preferences will be intact.

Note   Preferences are also stored with files you save as template documents.

General Preferences

You use General preferences to customize a few of the basic options in AppleWorks (shown earlier in Figure 10-1), such as what document type is created with the ⌘+N keyboard shortcut and how the Font menu is displayed. You also can use General preferences to set the startup action for AppleWorks.

Note   Although you normally use the Make Default and OK buttons to modify the AppleWorks default and document-specific preferences settings, the OK button has a different function when you use it in conjunction with General preferences. Clicking the OK button puts the changed settings into effect for the entire session (until you quit the program), rather than just for the current document. For example, if you clear the Font Menu in Actual Fonts checkbox and click the OK button, the Font menu will be displayed with Font names in the System font during the session. In the next AppleWorks session, however, you'll find that the Font Menu in Actual Fonts setting is selected again. To set new General preferences as permanent defaults, click the Make Default button.

General preferences settings include the following:

✦ **At Startup, Show.** Determines what you see first each time you launch AppleWorks. The default choice is to display the Starting Points windoid. Alternatively, you can have the program display the Open dialog box (to open an existing document) or no dialog box or window at all. If you normally begin each session by opening an existing document, you can choose Open Dialog Box from the pop-up menu. If your initial action varies from one session to the next, you are better off leaving it set for Starting Points, enabling you to use its various panels at startup, or choosing Nothing if you like an uncluttered screen.

✦ **Font Menu in Actual Fonts.** Shows font names in their respective typefaces in the Font submenu of the Format or Text menu, the Font pop-up menu on the text ruler (version 6.0.3 or later), and Font pop-up menus in dialog boxes.

Tip   The option to display the "Font Menu in Actual Fonts" can be very slow on some machines. If you already know what your fonts look like, if you find the varied fonts make the menu hard to read, or you find that the Font menu displays or scrolls very slowly, you might want to disable this option.

✦ **On ⌘+N, Create.** This preference determines which document type will be created with the ⌘+N shortcut. The default is Word Processing, on the assumption that this is the most frequently created document type; however, if you most frequently create a different document type, you should choose that type from the pop-up menu.

Files Preferences

The Files preferences settings apply both to opening and saving documents. They also control AppleWorks 6's new Auto-Save settings and the settings for the Recent Items submenu of the File menu. This panel is shown in Figure 10-2.

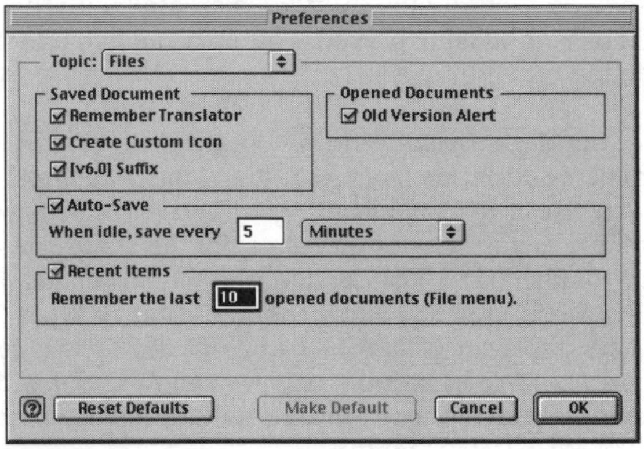

Figure 10-2: Files preferences

The Preferences settings for Files are as follows:

✦ **Remember Translator.** Click this checkbox to assist you in saving translated documents in their native formats. With this option chosen, each time you edit a translated document and then save it, the File Format pop-up menu is automatically set for the program in which the translated document was created (Microsoft Word, for example). Of course, you can still select AppleWorks or any other supported file type as the File Format format.

> **Note** This is how this preference is documented, but its behavior has been inconsistent. You would do well to check the File Format pop-up to make sure it hasn't reset itself to AppleWorks (even for imported documents), especially for graphics documents translated from QuickTime or documents that are opened by dragging their icons onto the AppleWorks icon.

✦ **Create Custom Icon** has AppleWorks create an icon for saved (graphic) documents that are miniaturized images of the document's first page rather than using the standard AppleWorks document icons.

✦ **[v6.0] Suffix.** Appends this suffix to the name of any file you open that was created with an earlier version of AppleWorks or ClarisWorks. Because adding the suffix changes the file name, this option protects the original file from being accidentally overwritten.

✦ **Old Version Alert.** Displays a warning message whenever you open a file created with an earlier version of the program.

✦ **Auto-Save.** Determines whether backup copies of your open documents will be made for recovery purposes in case of a crash or freeze. If this box is checked, you can set the frequency with which the backups are made using the "When idle, save every *n* minutes" setting. You type a number in the minutes text box, and then choose Seconds, Minutes, or Hours from the pop-up menu (the default is every 5 minutes).

✦ **Recent Items.** Determines whether there will be a Recent Items tab on your Starting Points windoid and whether the File ➪ Open Recent submenu will be available. This preference is checked by default, and 10 is listed as the default number of documents. The Recent Items panel, on the other hand, is not constrained to this number of files — you are well-advised to cull it frequently. A very large folder of these aliases in your Starting Points folder can significantly impact the program's performance.

New Feature

Auto-Save and Recent Items are both new features.

Text Preferences

Text preferences apply to any text you type in an AppleWorks document, regardless of the environment you're in. Some of the options on this panel might not seem like "Text" items to you, but this is where AppleWorks' designers decided they belong. Figure 10-3 shows the Text preferences options.

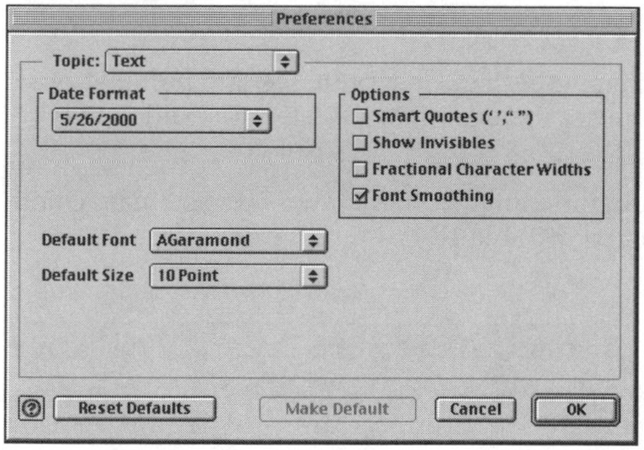

Figure 10-3: Text preferences

Text preferences options include the following:

✦ **Date Format.** The format you select is used each time you insert the current date into a document by choosing Edit ➪ Insert Date.

The order in which the three fields appear and the separator used will be based on the settings in the Date & Time control panel.

✦ **Smart Quotes (' '," ").** With Smart Quotes enabled, AppleWorks automatically translates your presses of the ' or " keys into curly quotes (' or ' and " or "), as shown in Figure 10-4. Smart Quotes are intelligently applied. In most cases, the program can correctly determine when a right- or left-facing quotation mark is appropriate.

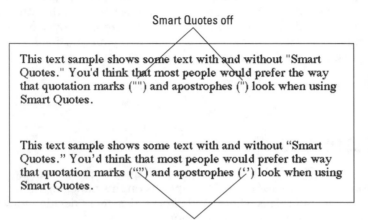

Figure 10-4: Examples of Smart Quotes settings

Curly quotes are preferred in modern correspondence and publications. Correct uses for straight quotes include displaying feet (') and inches (") in measurements.

To manually insert curly quotation mark characters—when Smart Quotes is disabled—use the keys listed in Table 10-1.

Table 10-1
Curly Quote Keys

Character	Key
"	Option+[
"	Shift+Option+[
'	Option+]
'	Shift+Option+]

✦ **Show Invisibles.** When this option is checked, you can see characters that are normally invisible, such as tabs, spaces, and end-of-paragraph markers (see Figure 10-5). Enabling this option after you finish a report or letter makes clean-up editing simpler. For example, it enables you to find extra spaces between words. You also can toggle this option off and on in the Button Bar.

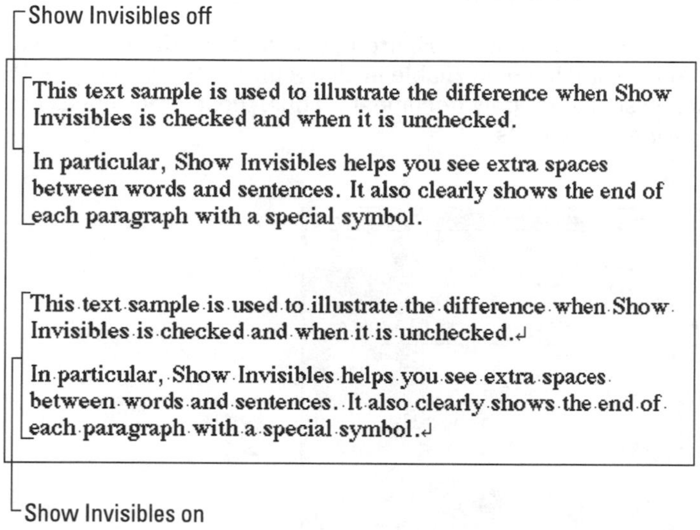

Show Invisibles off

> This text sample is used to illustrate the difference when Show Invisibles is checked and when it is unchecked.
>
> In particular, Show Invisibles helps you see extra spaces between words and sentences. It also clearly shows the end of each paragraph with a special symbol.

> This·text·sample·is·used·to·illustrate·the·difference·when·Show· Invisibles·is·checked·and·when·it·is·unchecked.↵
>
> In·particular,·Show·Invisibles·helps·you·see·extra·spaces· between·words·and·sentences.·It·also·clearly·shows·the·end·of· each·paragraph·with·a·special·symbol.↵

Show Invisibles on

Figure 10-5: Examples of the Show Invisibles settings

✦ **Fractional Character Widths.** Choose this option to tighten spacing between characters (when printing to a laser printer, for example). Do not check this option if you are printing to an ImageWriter printer — unless you also have the ATM control panel from Adobe Systems installed.

✦ **Font Smoothing.** Clicking this checkbox antialiases (draws fonts using shades of gray and black) fonts larger than 12 points. This option overrides the "Smooth all fonts on screen" setting under the Fonts tab of your Appearance control panel.

✦ **Default Font.** Select a starting font to be used for all new documents and text frames. All fonts currently installed on your computer are listed in the pop-up menu.

✦ **Default Size.** Select a default font size to be used in new documents and text frames. For bitmap fonts, installed sizes will be in outline style in the pop-up menu.

 New Feature

Default Size is a new feature.

Note In ClarisWorks 3.0 and earlier, the Text preferences settings also included settings for footnotes. Those settings are now document-specific rather than preferences. To set footnote options, choose Document from the Format menu.

Graphics Preferences

The Graphics preferences shown in Figure 10-6 affect both draw and paint graphics. Remember that draw tools are available in all document types and that Presentation documents are, essentially, Draw documents. Thus, these preferences apply in all environments for draw objects.

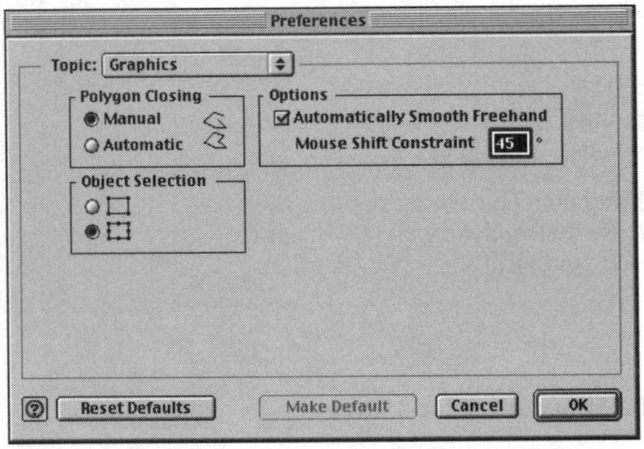

Figure 10-6: Graphics preferences

The Preferences settings for Graphics are as follows:

✦ **Polygon Closing.** Polygon closing can be Manual or Automatic. When you choose the Automatic setting, you don't have to complete the final side of a draw or paint figure. You simply double-click the last point of the polygon. In Manual mode, if you want a closed polygon, you have to finish the figure by clicking its starting point. (If most of your polygons will be closed, selecting Automatic can save considerable time compared to manually clicking an object's starting point.)

Note The Polygon Closing preference setting also affects bezigons.

✦ **Object Selection.** This is only pertinent to draw objects, not paint. When you select draw objects with the pointer, they can be displayed with four or eight handles. Note that the extra handles do not provide additional object manipulation capabilities.

Note   Be aware that in AppleWorks 5, the default was four handles and that AppleWorks 6 provides eight handles by default.

✦ **Automatically Smooth Freehand.** When this option is enabled, shapes that are drawn freehand are automatically transformed into relatively smooth curves.

✦ **Mouse Shift Constraint.** You use this setting to specify an angular constraint for drawing with the mouse while the Shift key is pressed. The default setting enables you to draw in increments of 45 degrees, as shown in Figure 10-7.

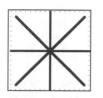

Figure 10-7: Lines drawn with a mouse Shift constraint of 45 degrees

Spreadsheet Preferences

The Spreadsheet preferences (see Figure 10-8) enable you to customize the way the arrow keys and Enter key are used when you are working in a spreadsheet document or frame and determine how to handle externally referenced spreadsheets.

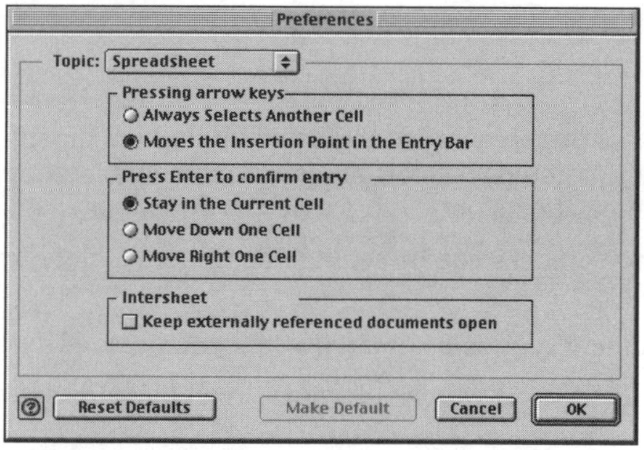

Figure 10-8: Spreadsheet preferences

Depending on which "Pressing arrow keys" setting you select, pressing an arrow key does one of the following:

✦ **Always Selects Another Cell.** Selects the cell to the immediate right, left, above, or below the current cell when you press the right-, left-, up-, or down-arrow keys, respectively.

    ✦ **Moves the Insertion Point in the Entry Bar.** Used only for typing and editing data. This is the default setting

Regardless of which setting you choose, you can achieve the opposite function by pressing the Option key in combination with an arrow key. Thus, if you elect to use the arrow keys for cell selection, you can still move to the right or left when you add or edit data by pressing the Option+right-arrow or Option+left-arrow keys, respectively.

The "Press Enter to confirm entry" setting enables you to set the action that occurs when you complete a cell entry by pressing the Enter key. If you've used other spreadsheet programs, you might prefer to use the default setting: Stay in the Current Cell. Other options enable the Enter key to duplicate the function of the Return key (Move Down One Cell) or the Tab key (Move Right One Cell).

New Feature
The only setting under Intersheet is "Keep externally referenced documents open." AppleWorks 6 adds the capability for one spreadsheet to reference cells and ranges in another spreadsheet (see Chapter 4). When this box is checked, externally referenced spreadsheets will be kept open for faster access when recalculating formulas.

Remember that like some of the other preferences we've discussed, you can set Spreadsheet preferences either for a single document or globally. Most users prefer to choose one way of doing things and then click the Make Default button to set preferences for all future AppleWorks worksheets.

Summary

    ✦ AppleWorks has two kinds of preferences settings: default and document-specific. Changing a default preference affects all new documents. Setting a document-specific preference affects only that particular document.

    ✦ Program areas for which preferences can be set include General, Files, Text, Graphics, and Spreadsheet.

    ✦ You can set a default document type to be created when you press ⌘+N.

    ✦ Auto-Save lets you set the interval at which your autosaved backups are created.

    ✦ Curly quotes, which are automatic with the Smart Quotes text preferences option, help create more professional-looking documents.

    ✦ The Show Invisibles text setting is useful when you perform a clean-up edit on documents.

    ✦ The Spreadsheet preferences specify the actions that occur when you press arrow keys or the Enter key during data entry and editing and whether to keep externally referenced spreadsheets open.

✦   ✦   ✦

Using Starting Points

In earlier versions of AppleWorks and ClarisWorks, new and infrequent users found it difficult to navigate through the process of modally creating new documents, using AppleWorks Assistants, and using Templates (then called *stationery*). In AppleWorks 6, all of these capabilities — and more — have been consolidated into an easy-to-use, nonmodal floating window called Starting Points. By default, five panels are populated in the Starting Points windoid, and you can use a sixth to create your own panels: Basic, Assistants, Templates, Recent Items, Web, and +.

Basic Panel: Creating New, Blank Documents

When you want to create a new document from scratch, this is the easiest and most versatile place to turn. While you can create a new document for any of the environments from the File ⇨ New submenu or from the Button Bar, these only give you the current environmental default document (see the "Using Templates to Set New Environment Defaults" section later in this chapter). The Basic panel will also include thumbnails for the original AppleWorks default documents, in case you don't want to use your customized default document this time. See Figure 11-1 for an example of the Basic panel with a customized Spreadsheet default document.

Click the thumbnail you want and a new, default document will open.

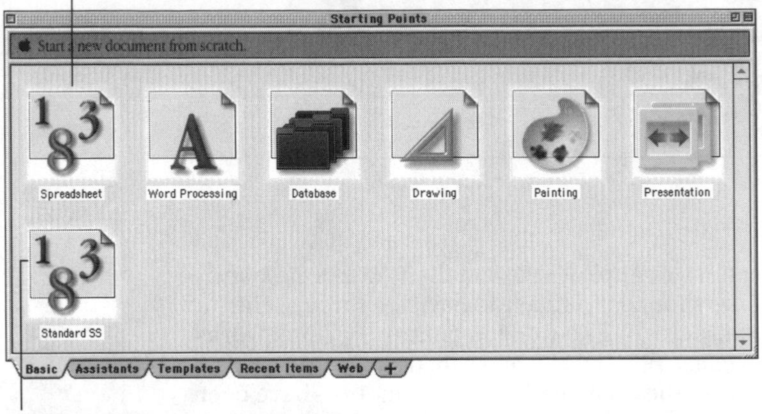

A customized default spreadsheet

The AppleWorks default spreadsheet

Figure 11-1: The Basic panel

Assistants Panel: Help with Creating Documents

You've already encountered a couple of AppleWorks Assistants: Insert Citation (Chapter 3) and New Label Layout (Chapter 5). AppleWorks 6 also includes six Assistants to facilitate the creation of various complex and/or common documents as shown in Figure 11-2.

AppleWorks and ClarisWorks 5 included some additional Assistants that have been either eliminated as unnecessary in AppleWorks 6 or replaced by Templates, described as follows:

✦ **Address List.** Creates a personal, business, or student name and address database.

✦ **Business Cards.** Designs a business card for business or personal use in a variety of styles.

✦ **Calendar.** Creates a single- or multiple-month calendar. Each month is a separate AppleWorks drawing document with each calendar being a table.

✦ **Certificate.** Creates decorative certificates, awards, and diplomas.

✦ **Envelope.** Creates a word processing document formatted as an envelope (with an addressee and a return address) based on the page size you specify in the final step's Page Setup dialog box.

✦ **Home Finance.** Creates worksheets that help you compute the answers to common financial questions.

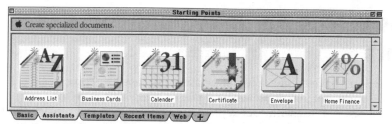

Figure 11-2: The Assistants panel

Templates Panel: Creating New Documents Based on a Template

When you have a document you work with frequently, but which you usually need to modify slightly, the best way to save it is as a template rather than as a normal AppleWorks file. It can include static text and graphics, as well as placeholders for other text elements you intend to change each time you use the document. A letterhead is an example of a document that would make a good template file. In the template, you can include your return address, a standard salutation, and a closing. Then, when you want to write a new letter, you just open the template, enter the addressee's name and address, and fill in the body of the text.

AppleWorks 6 comes with 36 templates, and many more are available on the Internet (see the Web panel discussion, later in this chapter). Figure 11-3 shows the Templates panel and some of the available templates.

Figure 11-3: The Templates panel

Templates Versus Normal AppleWorks Documents

Of course, you don't have to save a template as a template file. You can save it as a normal AppleWorks document. However, if you accidentally issue the Save command while you are working with such a pseudo-template, you will replace the template with a filled-in copy of the letterhead, fax, or whatever type of document you are working on. Bye-bye template.

Saving as a template document protects you from this kind of mistake. When you open an AppleWorks template file, you're opening a copy of the file, rather than the original. In fact, AppleWorks treats the document that appears onscreen just as it treats a file you create with the New command. It even names the file Untitled to remind you it's not the original.

> **Tip**   In the Finder, if you choose File ➪ Get Info ➪ General for a template file (or press ⌘+I, or choose Get Info ➪ General from the contextual menu), you'll see that the Stationery file checkbox in the lower-left corner is checked. You can change whether a file is a template with this checkbox.

Creating Templates

You can easily create a template from any AppleWorks file. To save a document as a template, choose File ➪ Save As. The standard Save As dialog box appears (see Figure 11-4). Click the Template radio button. Type a name for the document, and save the template (when you click the Template radio button, AppleWorks will automatically navigate to the Templates folder inside Starting Points).

If you don't want this template to appear in your Starting Points Templates panel, save it elsewhere.

Any AppleWorks template you save or move into the Starting Points:Templates folder is available in the Templates panel of Starting Points.

> **Tip**   In versions of ClarisWorks prior to 4.0, the ClarisWorks Stationery folder was located inside the Claris folder, which was within the System Folder of the startup hard disk, or within the program's application folder. If you have stationery documents created with ClarisWorks 4 that you would like to use with AppleWorks 6, simply copy or move the files into the Templates folder (located in the AppleWorks 6 Starting Points folder).

Of course, as with any other documents, you can save templates anywhere you choose. If you save them in a different location, they still function as templates, but you have to load them by using the File ⇨ Open command or double-click them in the Finder, rather than accessing them through the Templates panel.

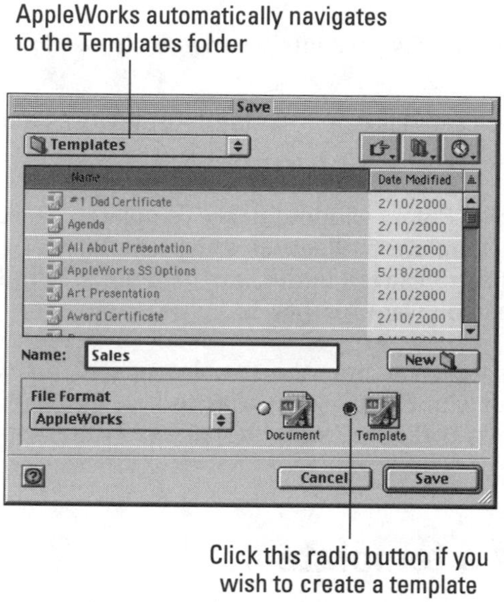

AppleWorks automatically navigates
to the Templates folder

Figure 11-4: Any document can be saved as a normal AppleWorks file or a Template.

Click this radio button if you
wish to create a template

> **Note** AppleWorks enables you to set preferences (such as the date format) that you can save with the current document. When you open the document, its preference settings override the normal AppleWorks preferences. If you set preferences for a document and then save it as a template, this rule still applies. Each time you open a copy of the template, any preferences you have set for the document take precedence over the AppleWorks preferences. (For additional information on preferences, see Chapter 10.)

Special considerations when saving templates

When you save an AppleWorks 6 document as a template, it is presented in the Templates panel with a thumbnail representation of its appearance — actually just the appearance of the document's first page. You can save with a distinctive graphic as a placeholder on the first page to make your template's image easy to recognize.

> **Note** In previous versions of AppleWorks and ClarisWorks, the Document Summary information (now called Properties) was accessible when you were curious about a template. Unfortunately, this capability is lacking in AppleWorks 6, rendering the Properties dialog box nearly useless.

Opening a template

You can open a stationery document in precisely the same way that you open any other document:

✦ Select it from the file list that AppleWorks presents when you choose File ➪ Open (or press ⌘+O).

✦ Double-click the document icon on the desktop to launch AppleWorks and open the document simultaneously.

In addition to these methods, the Starting Points windoid has a Templates panel where you can see your AppleWorks 6 templates collection. If the template is one that came with AppleWorks 6 or one that you saved in the Starting Points:Templates folder, you can click its thumbnail when you want to open it.

Tip   If you want to have your template accessible from the Templates panel, but you don't want to store it in that folder, you can place an alias to it in the Starting Points:Templates folder. (AppleWorks 5 did not recognize aliases in the Apple-Works Stationery folder.)

Making a new version of a template

After you open a copy of a template, you can edit the document and then save it with a new name, or you can simply close the file without saving it if you don't need a copy on disk. If, on the other hand, you've modified the template with the intent of making a new, improved template, you can save the new file over the old one by typing the original template file name and clicking the Template radio button in the Save As dialog box. Click the Replace button when the program asks whether you want to replace the original file.

Tip   If you aren't using the Starting Points:Templates folder for your templates, be sure to save the revised template in the same folder as the original. Otherwise, you could end up with multiple versions of the same file.

Using Templates to Set New Environment Defaults

Although the Edit ➪ Preferences command enables you to set a handful of default options for several environments (see Chapter 10), you can add many more settings as defaults so they will automatically be in effect whenever you create a new document. To add settings as defaults, simply create a document that contains the new default settings and then save it as a specially named template in the Starting Points:Templates folder. Apple refers to these special documents as default stationery documents.

To save documents as default stationery documents, you need to name the files as shown in Table 11-1.

Table 11-1 Default Stationery File-Naming Conventions	
Environment	*Name of Default Stationery Document*
Word Processing	AppleWorks WP Options
Drawing	AppleWorks DR Options
Painting	AppleWorks PT Options
Spreadsheet	AppleWorks SS Options
Database	AppleWorks DB Options
Presentations	AppleWorks PR Options

For example, so that the word processing environment will open new documents with specific defaults, create a blank template, set the starting font to Times, define four frequently used text styles, and add the styles to the stylesheet for the document. Now, every new word processing document you create defaults to the Times font, and the four text styles are always available.

You can create your own default stationery documents with the options you prefer. Note, however, that you can have only one default stationery document for each environment. If you want to change an existing default stationery document, you need to save the new one over the old one — in other words, replace it.

STEPS: Creating an Environment Default Stationery Document

1. Choose the environment of your choice from the Edit ➪ New submenu.

2. Set options for the document (and, if you want to, set preferences by using the Edit ➪ Preferences command).

3. Choose File ➪ Save As. The normal Save dialog box appears.

4. Click the Template radio button. The AppleWorks 6:Starting Points:Templates folder is automatically selected for you.

5. Name the file according to the conventions listed in Table 11-1 (presented earlier in this chapter), and then click the Save button.

After you save a default stationery document, AppleWorks adds it to the list of environments in the Basic panel. The default stationery document you save replaces the original AppleWorks default document as the one that will be automatically used for that environment. The original default document is retained as the "Standard" document for the environment.

For example, if you create an AppleWorks WP Options file, it will be shown in the Basic panel as Word Processing. If, at any time, you'd like to use the original AppleWorks default for the environment, click Standard Word Processing.

Tip   If you already have some default stationery files you designed for ClarisWorks 4 or AppleWorks 5, you can use them with AppleWorks 6 if you like. Just copy or move the files into the Templates folder inside the AppleWorks 6 folder's Starting Points folder.

Recent Items: Opening Recently Used Documents

Clicking the Recent Items tab reveals thumbnails of documents you have opened in the past. This is a new capability in AppleWorks 6. While only the last 10 (or the number you specify in your Preferences — see Chapter 10) are accessible from the File ⇨ Recent Items submenu, this panel will be a history of the files you've worked with, even if the file no longer exists (you'll get an "Unexpected Error: #120" message or "The file "filename" can't be opened because it has been deleted" message if you click such a thumbnail).

Tip   Every time you open a file in AppleWorks, an alias to it is placed in your Starting Points folder's Recent Items folder. You should periodically clean this folder out to remove deadwood (files you no longer need or that no longer exist) and improve AppleWorks' performance.

Web Panel: Retrieving Documents from the Internet

AppleWorks 6 significantly enhanced its integration with the Internet, and the Web panel is one of the places where that is evident. In AppleWorks 5, you could click a link in a document, or you could select text and click the Open URL button to launch your Web browser or e-mail program, but you can now actually connect to Web servers and open AppleWorks documents that are located there. This little feat is accomplished from the Web panel, which comes presupplied with two links: an AppleWorks Newsletter thumbnail and a Templates thumbnail pointing to more templates in a variety of categories available from Apple's Web site. You can add more links to this panel using the following steps.

Steps for Adding a Document Link to the Web Panel

1. Type the URL for the AppleWorks document in any drag-and-drop-aware application (such as AppleWorks).

2. Select the URL and drag it to the desktop to create a Web Page Location file (a special kind of clipping file).

3. Drag that Web Page Location file onto the Web panel of your Starting Points windoid. Alternatively, you could just drag the icon into your Starting Points folder's Web folder.

 Tip   Depending on your Internet connection type and speed, you might need to choose Reload Starting Point from the contextual menu that appears when you Control-click the thumbnail so it will function.

There will be further discussion about placing AppleWorks documents on the Web in Chapter 19.

+: Adding Your Own Starting Points Tabs

If the presupplied panels are not enough for you, AppleWorks 6 lets you create more tabs. As one example, you might want to create separate tabs for business, organizational, and personal finance documents that require frequent updating or access.

When you click the + tab, you are presented with the Add Tab dialog box (see Figure 11-5). If you select My Computer in the pop-up menu, the panel becomes a focal point for various documents on your hard drive. However, if you select the Internet-based location from the pop-up menu, you can use the tab as a way to reach graphic documents on other computers on the Internet or your corporate intranet (assuming your computer is set up for TCP/IP access to the Internet or intranet).

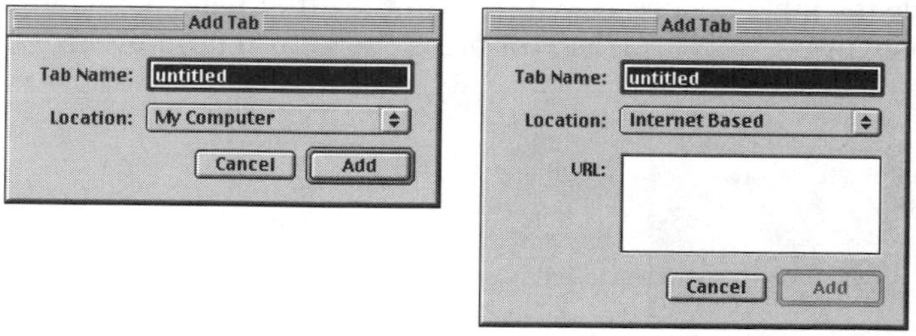

Figure 11-5: The Add Tab dialog box for local documents (left) and Internet-based documents (right)

To populate your new tab (assuming you chose My Computer), just drag the icons for the AppleWorks files onto the panel and AppleWorks will add a thumbnail for each file. If you chose Internet-based document, you provided a URL. Assuming that your Internet connection is active, you should see thumbnails for any graphics documents at that location (see Figure 11-6).

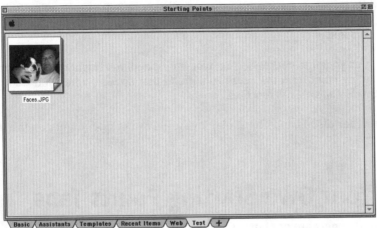

Figure 11-6: An example of an Internet-based tab

Deleting Tabs

AppleWorks 6 won't let you delete any of the default tabs (except Recent Items, and you do that by clearing the Recent Items checkbox in your preferences setting — see Chapter 10); however, you can delete tabs that you created, either temporarily or permanently. To delete an added tab, you must use the contextual menu. Control-click either the tab or the panel that the tab reveals, and then choose Delete Tab from the contextual menu. You'll be presented with a caution alert (see Figure 11-7) asking whether you want to Cancel, Disable Tab, or Move to Trash (the default button). If you only want to hide the tab, choose Disable Tab. On the other hand, if you want to get rid of it for good, press Move to Trash (or press the Return or Enter keys).

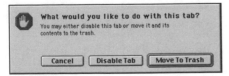

Figure 11-7: Choose how you want to delete the tab.

Customizing Starting Points

As with the other tabbed, floating windows in AppleWorks, you might make various customizations to its appearance and behavior. You can hide or show the tabs, move the tabs to either side of the windoid (rather than viewing them on the lower edge of the panels), and select from either large, medium, or small thumbnails (personally, we think of them as huge, large, and normal). If the panel is one you've added, you can select which banner and background are displayed.

All of the customizations listed are accessed from the Starting Points contextual menu. If you want to hide the tabs, select Hide Tabs; if you want to move the tabs to one side or the other, choose the side you want from the Reposition Tabs submenu; and, if you want to modify the appearance (background, banner, and thumbnail size), choose Starting Points Settings to bring up the Starting Points Settings dialog box.

The various banners and backgrounds are kept in folders named Banners and Backgrounds, respectively, in the Starting Points folder. These files are JPEG files and were created by Adobe Photoshop. You can open them in AppleWorks, if you like, and customize them or create additional variations. Banners are 1,200 pixels long and 22 pixels high. Backgrounds are 48 by 48 pixels in size. Figure 11-8 shows a custom background and banner on a new tab.

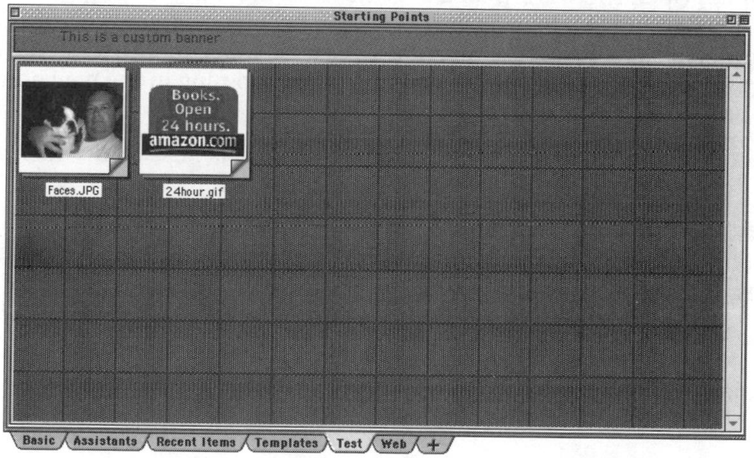

Figure 11-8: An added tab with a custom banner and background

Quick Tips

Any file you intend to reuse can be a template. Keep in mind, however, that if you never intend to alter the base document, saving it as a template is pointless. For example, if you have a letter you always send without changes, you can save it as a normal AppleWorks file and simply reprint it as often as you like.

Here are some ideas for templates:

✦ **Fax form or cover sheet.** Remove everything but the static information (the logo, return address, and phone number, as well as the reserved areas for the date, subject, number of pages, recipient's name, and fax number) from your normal fax form or cover sheet (which is probably a word processing or draw document). Then use the Edit ➪ Insert Date ➪ Auto-updating to insert the send date, so that each time you open a copy of the template, the current date is automatically filled in.

✦ **Letterhead.** If you have a laser or inkjet printer, you often can save money by printing your own letterhead, and you'll never need to worry about having to order a new supply from the print shop.

✦ **Weekly, monthly, quarterly, or annual worksheets.** Many worksheets are reusable. (You can keep your personal financial records in several of them, for example.) Open the worksheet and remove all the data, making sure to leave cells that contain labels or formulas intact. Then save the worksheet with a new name as a template. Whenever the new week, month, quarter, or year begins, you can open a copy of the template and plug in the new numbers. You can use the same tactic for record-keeping database templates.

✦ **Business forms.** Templates are perfect for standard business forms such as invoices, statements, petty cash vouchers, and so forth.

✦ **Contracts.** Most legal documents — wills, leases, work-for-hire agreements, and so on — consist largely of standard (boilerplate) language. By saving them as templates, you can dramatically reduce writing time on subsequent documents.

✦ **Presentations.** If you have standard presentation formats you use (backgrounds, boilerplate text, and so on), you can save time by saving the various master slides and the backgrounds in templates.

Summary

✦ Save files as templates when you want to use them as stationery.

✦ When you open a template, it is opened as a new untitled document — protecting the original from unintentional modifications.

✦ When you launch AppleWorks to create a new file, you can select any template in the Templates folder by clicking the Templates tab on the Starting Points windoid.

✦ You can set defaults for any environment by designing an AppleWorks default stationery document and following a special convention for naming the document when you save it in the Templates folder.

✦ AppleWorks includes Assistants that walk you through common business and home computing tasks.

✦ AppleWorks maintains a history of the files you've opened in the Recent Items panel.

✦ You can access AppleWorks documents and templates through the Starting Points Web panel.

✦ You can add panels to and otherwise customize the Starting Points windoid.

✦   ✦   ✦

Using the Button Bar

In ClarisWorks 4, you could open the Shortcuts palette — a tiny floating window covered with buttons — and click buttons to execute common commands, such as printing the current document or changing the style of selected text to italic. In ClarisWorks 5 and AppleWorks 5, the Shortcuts palette disappeared. In its place were Button Bars — customizable rows and columns of buttons that perform commands similar to the buttons in the former Shortcuts palette, but with a great deal more power. Now, with AppleWorks 6, you have one scrollable Button Bar that consists of one row or one column of large, colorful buttons that change with your environment, just as menus do.

In addition to buttons, the Button Bar can contain any or all of the following items (see Figure 12-1):

◆ Pop-up button menus that enable you to set attributes for selected text (font, size, style, and color)

◆ The Styles pop-up menu button

◆ ToolTips that provide a brief description of each button when the mouse pointer rests above it, just like Balloon Help

◆ A contextual menu enabling you to customize the Button Bar or delete buttons

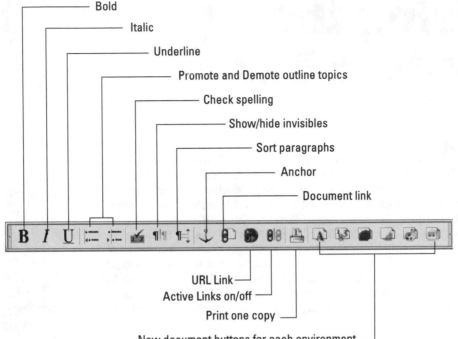

Figure 12-1: The default Button Bar for a word processing document

The buttons on the Button Bar automatically change to match the environment of the document or frame in which you are working. Spreadsheet-related buttons are presented only when you are working with a spreadsheet document or frame, for example.

AppleWorks provides more than 200 predefined buttons you can add to the Button Bar. You also can add custom buttons for executing macros you've created (see Chapter 17 for further discussion of Macros).

New Feature AppleWorks 6 adds the ability to execute AppleScripts you've installed in addition to opening documents, launching applications, or connecting to a URL.

Other customization options include the following:

✦ Choosing a location for the Button Bar (top, bottom, left, right, or free-floating) and resizing the bar

✦ Changing the arrangement of buttons on the Button Bar

✦ Adding a dividing line after a button to group buttons

✦ Removing unwanted buttons from Button Bars

To get you started, AppleWorks provides a standard Button Bar configuration for each environment, as well as a "no document open" button set. You can design your own custom Button Bar configuration with only the commands you need, as well as share buttons you have defined with friends and colleagues.

Setting Button Bar Options

Control-click the Button Bar and choose Customize Button Bar from the contextual menu, or choose Edit ➪ Preferences ➪ Button Bar to set options for the Button Bar, create and edit buttons, and customize the Button Bar. When you choose Customize Button Bar, the dialog box in Figure 12-2 appears. The left section lists the buttons available for each environment, as well as those you have created; the Description section displays the name of the button selected on the left and a brief description of what it does, as well as providing you with the option of placing a dividing line after it in the Button Bar; and the Options section enables you to specify the button (and thus the Button Bar) size (Button style) and whether the descriptive text will be displayed in a ToolTip when the mouse pointer rests over a button.

To specify a default screen position for displaying the Button Bar, grab it along an edge (the mouse pointer changes to a hand when it is over the edge and becomes a fist when you hold down the mouse button) and drag the Button Bar where you want it. When the fist mouse pointer is not within the Button Bar's height of a screen edge, the Button Bar will be a floating window. It can be collapsed, expanded, resized, and closed, as well as freely moved to any convenient location. When you are within the appropriate distance of a screen edge, the Button Bar will "dock" to that edge as a horizontal window (upper or lower edge of the screen) or a vertical window (left or right edge of the screen).

You also can specify whether information will appear whenever the mouse pointer rests over a button. Click the Show Tooltips checkbox if you want explanatory text to appear in balloon-style descriptions.

Note Help information displayed in the Button Bar balloons is identical to that displayed by Balloon Help. There is little point in selecting both forms of help.

The Button Bar displays only one row or column of buttons. The number of buttons shown is restricted by the size of your monitor and the length and height of the Button Bar, itself. To display additional buttons, click the small scroll arrows at either end of the Button Bar.

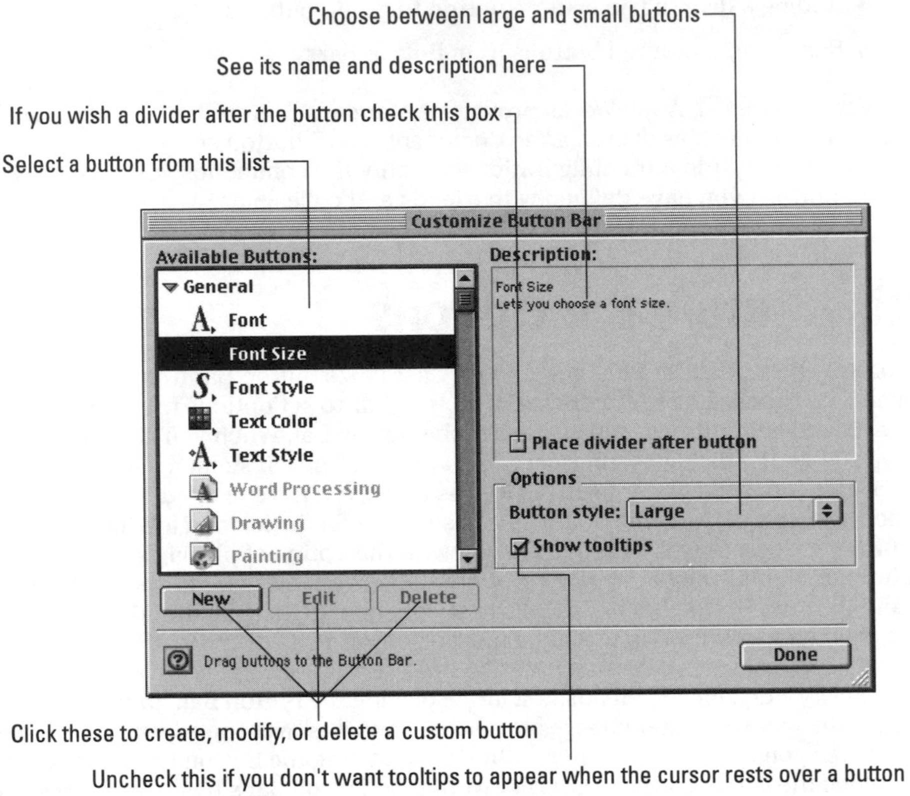

Choose between large and small buttons ─────────

See its name and description here ─────────

If you wish a divider after the button check this box ─┐

Select a button from this list ─────────

Customize Button Bar

Available Buttons:

▽ **General**

A, **Font**

   Font Size

S, **Font Style**

   Text Color

⁺A, **Text Style**

   Word Processing

   Drawing

   Painting

Description:

Font Size
Lets you choose a font size.

☐ **Place divider after button**

Options

Button style: │ Large   │ ⬍ │

☑ **Show tooltips**

[New] [Edit] [Delete]

⊘ Drag buttons to the Button Bar.   [**Done**]

Click these to create, modify, or delete a custom button

Uncheck this if you don't want tooltips to appear when the cursor rests over a button

Figure 12-2: The Customize Button Bar dialog box

Manually setting the Button Bar's appearance

To change the shape of a free-floating Button Bar, click and drag in the Grow box to change the length and height of the Button Bar. When a horizontal Button Bar is less than four buttons wide, it will reshape to a vertical bar. To change a button's position in the Button Bar, click and drag the button to a new location; a dark line will show the position where it will be inserted.

Hiding and showing the Button Bar

If the Button Bar is not onscreen, you can make it appear by choosing Window ⇨ Show Button Bar (Shift+⌘+X).

To hide the Button Bar from view, take any of the following actions:

✦ Choose Window ➪ Hide Button Bar.

✦ Press Shift+⌘+X.

✦ If the Button Bar is free floating, click the Close box in the upper-left corner of the bar.

Like other AppleWorks windoids, such as the Accents or Clippings windoids, the free-floating Button Bar has a Control box in its upper-right corner called the Collapse/Expand box (see Figure 12-3). If you click the Collapse/Expand box when the Button Bar is displayed, the bar shrinks to show only its title (similar to the way the Window-Shade box works in OS 8 and OS 9). If you click the box a second time, the bar expands to its normal size. The free-floating Button Bar also has a Grow box in the lower-right corner. Click and drag the Grow box to resize the Button Bar.

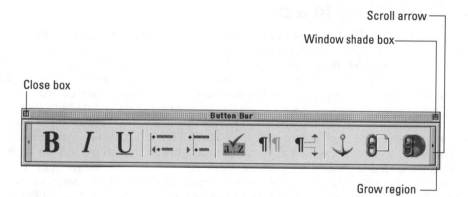

Figure 12-3: The Button Bar as a free-floating palette

Executing Buttons

Buttons in the Button Bar work just like buttons in other Macintosh programs. If the Button Bar is not visible, choose Window ➪ Show Button Bar (Shift+⌘+X). Position the mouse pointer in your document, select the item to be modified or perform whatever action is necessary — if any — to set up the conditions for the button, and then click the button. For example, if a button is designed to act on a graphic object, you must first select an object.

Note If you don't see a button you expect to see in the Button Bar, verify that you have an object or frame of the appropriate environment selected in your document. Like the menu bar, the Button Bar display is dependent upon the active Apple-Works environment.

Customizing the Button Bar

Although the default Button Bar offers a nice selection of commands, the fact that you can customize the bar in so many ways adds appreciably to its power. If you don't like the commands a given bar includes, you can remove them and, option-ally, replace them with commands that are more useful to you. You can even add buttons that execute macros you've created, open documents, launch applications, connect to URLs, or execute AppleScripts.

Adding buttons to a bar

The default Button Bar contains the buttons that Apple thinks are most useful in the various AppleWorks environments, as well as a collection of general buttons that Apple believes are useful from any environment. However, you can choose from many other predefined icons to add to the bar. These buttons are divided into eight groups. The General group contains buttons that can be active in any environment. One group exists for each of the six AppleWorks environments and its buttons appear only on the Button Bar when that environment is active (either in a frame or a document). A final group, User Buttons, is used for those buttons you create or define (if you haven't created any user buttons, this group will not appear in the list). As explained in Chapter 17, you can create AppleWorks macros (sequences of steps and commands), create buttons for them, and then add the macros to the Button Bar, just as you can add buttons to execute AppleScripts, launch applictions, open documents, or access URLs. (Designing your own buttons is described in "Creating and Editing User Buttons," later in this chapter.)

Tip Even if you believe the default Button Bar could stand some modification, you'll still want to check out the other predefined buttons. Just choose Customize Button Bar from the contextual menu (or choose Edit ⇨ Preferences ⇨ Button Bar), and select the button about which you're curious from the scrolling list (click the disclosure triangle to show the buttons available for each environment—the General group is expanded by default). Each button is accompanied by a descrip-tion in the Description area to the right of the buttons. Click a few buttons to see what you're missing.

STEPS: Adding Buttons to a Button Bar

1. Choose Customize Button Bar from the contextual menu or choose Edit ⇨ Preferences ⇨ Button Bar. The Customize Button Bar dialog box appears (see Figure 12-2, earlier in this chapter).

2. Click a category from the Available Buttons scrolling list.

3. Click any button to select it. A brief description of the selected button's function appears in the Description box.

4. To add the button to the Button Bar, double-click it to add it to the end of the group, or drag it to the Button Bar.

5. Repeat Steps 2 through 4 for additional buttons you want to add to the Button Bar.

6. Click the Done button to dismiss the dialog box.

Removing buttons from a bar

There's nothing sacred about the set of buttons AppleWorks initially includes in the predefined Button Bars. For example, many of the buttons correspond to menu commands that have Command-key equivalents. Similarly, some buttons you previously added might no longer be necessary. By eliminating some of these buttons, you can keep the Button Bar at a manageable size.

Note

Removing a macro-based button from a Button Bar does not delete the button; it simply removes the button from that Button Bar. It can still exist in or be added to other Button Bars. To delete the button and its associated macro, choose the File ⇨ Macros ⇨ Edit Macros (as explained in Chapter 17).

To remove a button from the Button Bar, Control-click the button and choose Remove Button from the contextual menu that appears.

Rearranging buttons

Another way you can customize a Button Bar is by changing the order in which the icons are displayed. For example, if you frequently use a few buttons, you can group them together to make them easily accessible.

To move a button to another position on the bar, click and drag the button. When the button is where you'd like it to be, release the mouse button.

Creating and Editing User Buttons

In ClarisWorks 4, new buttons were defined and their icons created as part of the macro recording process. In AppleWorks 5, button icons were designed separately from the macro recording process by choosing the New Button command from the pop-up menu at the end of the Button Bar. New functions could also be assigned to buttons, such as launching a program, opening a document in AppleWorks or another program, opening a URL, or running an AppleScript. These capabilities are also available in AppleWorks 6, but are accessed from the New button in the Customize Button Bar dialog box.

STEPS: Creating a New Button

1. Click the New button in the Customize Button Bar dialog box. The New Button dialog box appears (see Figure 12-4).

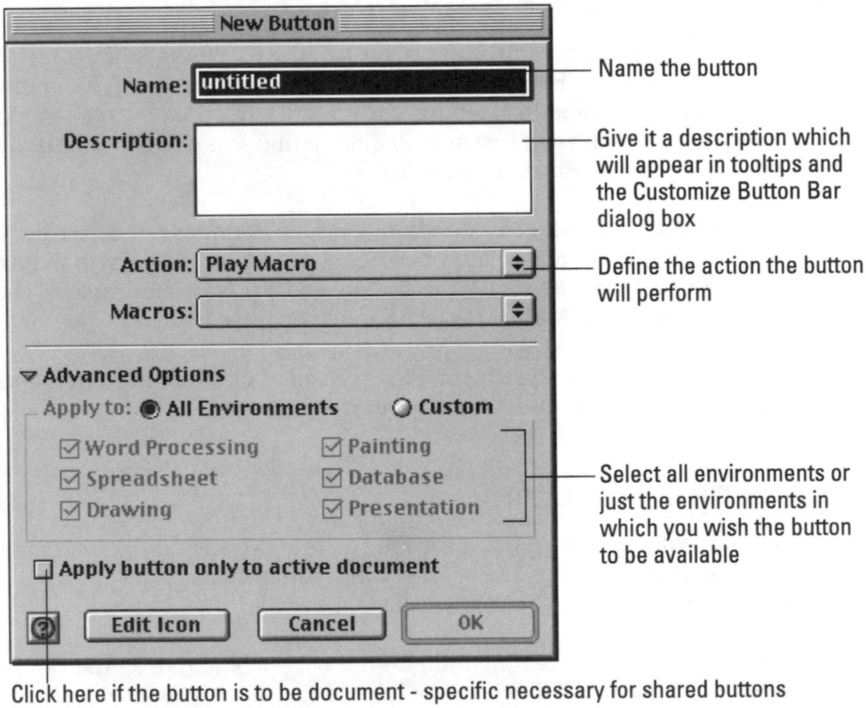

Figure 12-4, dialog box with callouts:

— Name the button

— Give it a description which will appear in tooltips and the Customize Button Bar dialog box

— Define the action the button will perform

— Select all environments or just the environments in which you wish the button to be available

Click here if the button is to be document - specific necessary for shared buttons

Figure 12-4: The New Button dialog box with and without an open document

2. Type a name for the button in the Name text box.

3. Type a description for the button in the Description text box.

   Text typed in the Description text box is displayed in the button's ToolTip when the mouse pointer rests over the button. If no description is provided, the button's name is displayed in the ToolTip.

   Note

   Although the Description text box looks like it will wrap text and autoscroll, the text entered displays on one line rather than wrapping and scrolls left and right only.

4. Choose an action for the button from the Action pop-up menu. Complete the action specification by selecting a macro to play, a URL to open, a document to open, an application to run, or an AppleScript to execute.

5. If you want the button to be available only in selected environments, click the Advanced Options disclosure triangle, select either the All Environments or the Custom checkbox, and then specify the environments in which you want the button to be available.

   The "Apply button only to active document" checkbox will not be present if you do not have a document open (see Figure 12-4, shown earlier).

6. To create or edit an icon for the button, click the Edit Icon button. The Edit Button Icon dialog box appears (see Figure 12-5).

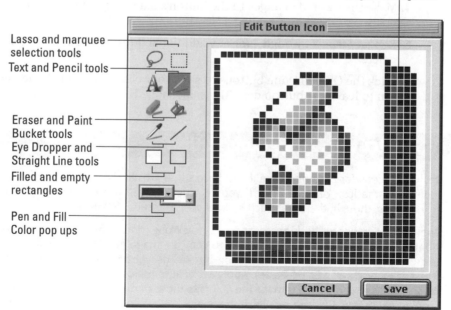

Design/working area

Lasso and marquee selection tools

Text and Pencil tools

Eraser and Paint Bucket tools

Eye Dropper and Straight Line tools

Filled and empty rectangles

Pen and Fill Color pop ups

Edit Button Icon

Cancel   Save

Figure 12-5: The Edit Button Icon dialog box

7. Create the icon by selecting tools and colors from the paint tools and palettes, and then drawing in the icon area. When you are done, click the Save button.

Note

When the button's action is set to launch a program, the program's file icon is automatically used as the button icon. When opening a document is the button action, the program's document icon is used as the button icon. When executing an AppleScript, the script's icon will be used. Like user-created icons, you are free to modify these icons as you want.

8. Click the OK button to save your changes.

Although you cannot change the definitions or icons for Apple-provided buttons, you can freely modify custom buttons that you have created. The following steps explain how to modify user-created buttons.

STEPS: Modifying a Custom Button

1. Choose Customize Button Bar from the contextual menu or Edit ⇨ Preferences ⇨ Button Bar to display the Customize Button Bar dialog box.

2. Choose a button to modify from the User Buttons group in the lower portion of the Available Buttons list.

3. Click the Edit button to change the selected button.

   (If you want to permanently remove the button, click the Delete button.)

4. Make the desired changes to the button's name, definition, or icon, as previously described in "Creating a New Button."

5. Repeat Steps 2 through 4 for any additional buttons you want to alter or delete.

6. Click the OK and Done buttons to save your changes, or click the Cancel button to leave the button definitions unchanged.

A Shortcut for Designing Buttons

Designing icons for buttons is fine if you have some artistic skills and can work within the confines of the icon drawing area. If you consider yourself the reigning king or queen of ugly buttons, though, there's a much simpler way to create attractive ones.

Open your Scrapbook desk accessory, an AppleWorks draw document, or a paint document, and then use the Copy command to copy an image you like (press ⌘+C or choose Edit ⇨ Copy). From the Edit Button dialog box (as described previously), paste the image (press ⌘+V or choose Edit ⇨ Paste). AppleWorks automatically reduces the image so that it fits on a button, and it then remaps the colors to those of the standard button color palette. Simple images give the best results. If the image is smaller than the button size, you might want to clear the drawing area first to avoid overlap with the existing image.

Sharing Buttons with Others

If you want to share buttons with another AppleWorks 6 user, click the checkbox for "Apply button only to active document" when you create the button and then give your cohort a copy of the file. For all buttons to function correctly on the other's computer, the following restrictions must be noted:

✦ If the button plays a macro, the macro must be saved as part of the document rather than as a general AppleWorks macro (see Chapter 17).

✦ If the button plays an AppleScript, you must provide the AppleScript to the user.

✦ If the button opens a document, provide the document to the user. The appropriate application also must be installed.

✦ If the button launches a particular program, the user must have that program installed on his or her computer.

✦ If the button launches the user's browser or displays a Web page, the user must have a default browser set in their Internet Preferences (or Internet Config if you are running MacOS 8.x).

Tip

For those buttons that open specific documents, execute AppleScripts, or launch programs on your hard drive or your network, your buttons probably won't work on your friend's Mac. Your friend can fix this problem, however, by selecting such a button (in the Customize Button Bar dialog box), clicking the Edit button, and then clicking the Choose button to reassign the button to a different file — or even to the same file in a different location.

Special considerations when sharing macro buttons

One point about sharing macro buttons — which is far from obvious to most users — is that buttons refer only to global and not document-specific, macros. To share the macro, you must make it document-specific. Because of this, it is necessary for the person with whom your share a macro-button combination to change the macro to global once they have it on their computer.

Summary

✦ AppleWorks includes several predefined buttons you can use to quickly execute common commands.

✦ The default Button Bar automatically changes to reflect the environment or frame in which you're working.

✦ You can show or hide the Button Bar, change its orientation between horizontal and vertical, and move it wherever you like. If the Button Bar is free floating, you also can collapse, expand, and resize it.

✦ You can add and remove buttons from any Button Bar. You can click and drag a button to a new location on the Button Bar.

✦ In addition to using dozens of predefined buttons, you can create your own macros, design custom icons for them, and add them to Button Bars. You also can create buttons that launch programs, open documents, open your Web browser to a given page on the World Wide Web, open your e-mail program to create a new message to a specific recipient, or run an AppleScript.

✦ If you want to share your custom buttons with other users, click the "Apply button only to active document" checkbox and then save the file. The custom button is automatically saved as part of your AppleWorks document.

✦   ✦   ✦

Working with Clippings

ClarisWorks 3.0 included an impressive collection of clip art for embellishing your documents. ClarisWorks 4.0 also included clip art, but made it easier to use because the clip art was in libraries — collections organized around a theme. ClarisWorks and AppleWorks 5.0 expanded your choices further by providing many new clip-art libraries. Using any image from a ReadyArt library was as simple as dragging the image of choice into your document or frame. Now, AppleWorks 6 goes a step further, replacing the libraries with collections of files and changing the paradigm to match that of the rest of the product. You are provided another huge collection of clip art, and you receive access from the Apple Web site to even more high-quality clip art through the new Clippings windoid and its search function.

Note You should note that most of the Web-based clip art is in EPS or JPEG format. EPS format is another indication that AppleWorks is MacOS X-ready, because PostScript is the underlying graphics model for MacOS X.

Clippings also can be used to hold things other than draw and paint images. You can, for example, store boiler-plate text, URLs, QuickTime movies, and frames of any type. Thus, in addition to using the provided clip art, you can add your own material to the Apple collections or create new collections.

When you open Clippings (choose File ➪ Show Clippings or press ⌘+2), you see the by now familiar floating window with tabs. Like other AppleWorks windoids, Clippings has a title bar, a close box, and a shrink/expand box, as shown in Figure 13-1.

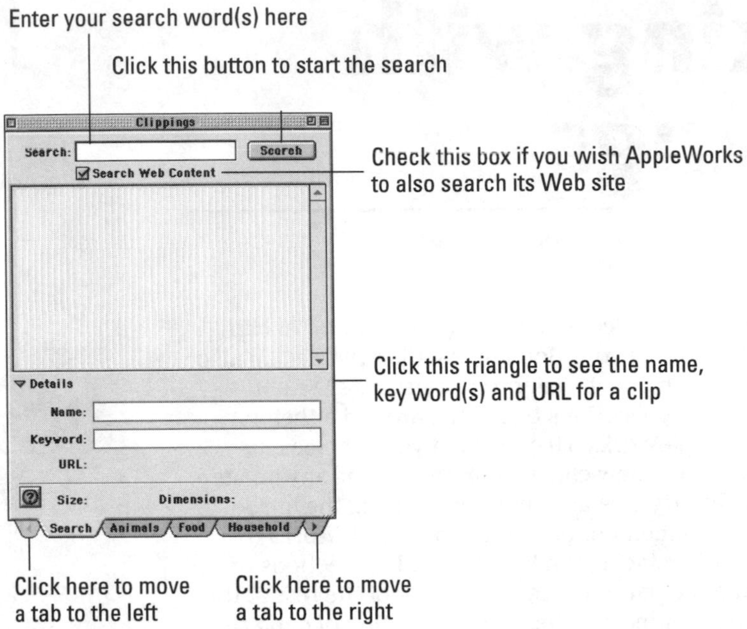
Enter your search word(s) here
Click this button to start the search
Clippings
Search:
Search
Search Web Content
Check this box if you wish AppleWorks to also search its Web site
Click this triangle to see the name, key word(s) and URL for a clip
Details
Name:
Keyword:
URL:
Size:
Dimensions:
Search
Animals
Food
Household
Click here to move a tab to the left
Click here to move a tab to the right

Figure 13-1: The Clippings windoid

Using Clippings

The Clippings windoid (we'll refer to it as *Clippings*—capitalized—for the rest of the discussion) is your repository for objects and other items—clip art, boilerplate text, Internet location files, frames—which you want to save for use in other documents. Clippings is also where you can see what is on the clipboard and search the AppleWorks Web site for more clip art.

To use a clipping in one of your documents, locate it in Clippings and drag it into your document. To save a selection as a clipping, drag the selection to the Clippings panel or tab where you want it saved.

Tip

Although this tip will work with all tabbed windoids in AppleWorks, it is most useful with Clippings, because Clippings has so many tabs that you frequently have to scroll with the arrow tabs on either end. If you ⌘+click a windoid, it will show a green interior border (you also can achieve this effect by Option+tabbing to cycle through the open windoids until you have the one you want). When the colored border is showing, ⌘+right arrow and ⌘+left arrow will cycle to the right and to the left between the tabs, respectively.

How It All Works

You will find a folder named Clippings within your AppleWorks 6 folder. Within that folder are other folders containing documents. Each of those documents is a clipping, and each of the folders (except the folder named Cache, which is a repository of material retrieved when you search the AppleWorks Web site for clippings) is a tab on your Clippings windoid. They are not, however, the only tabs. You will find three others: Search, Clipboard, and +. The Search tab is discussed in detail later in this chapter (see Searching Clippings), and the + tab is covered under Creating Your Own Tabs. These three tabs are the meat of Clippings, so much so that the first time you open Clippings during a session, you are presented with the Search tab. Thereafter, AppleWorks will remember the last tab displayed during the session and redisplay it when you reopen Clippings.

The Clipboard tab is AppleWorks' answer to the Finder's Edit ⇨ Show Clipboard command, except that it also recognizes AppleWorks objects and frames, displaying them appropriately. Unlike other Clippings panels, you cannot drag items to or from the Clipboard panel.

The remaining Clippings tabs are organizational conveniences, presenting you with a display of thumbnails for the clippings that fall into each category.

Creating Your Own Tabs

Although you might be satisfied with using the AppleWorks Clippings as is — by simply dragging the provided clip art into your documents — you might also want to create your own collections to store logos, scanned signatures, spreadsheet formulas, and important text.

To create a new tab, click the + tab on Clippings and type a name for your new tab, as shown in Figure 13-2. If you want to have a tab reflect all the graphics (IMG references) on a Web page, choose Internet Based from the Location pop-up menu and provide the Web page's full URL. When My Computer (the default) is chosen from the Location pop-up menu, AppleWorks will create a folder within your Clippings folder by the given name.

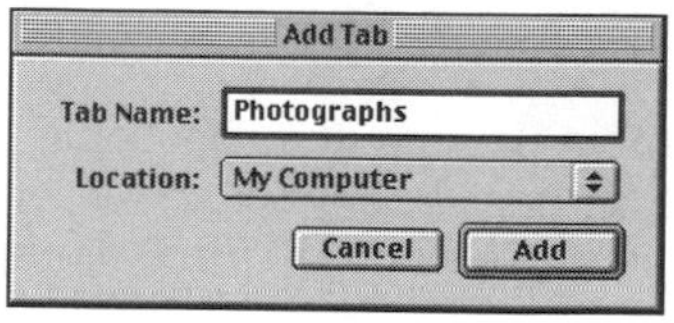

Figure 13-2: Add a tab to house your Clippings.

Note When a clipping is Web-based, its thumbnail will have a ribbon and bow across the upper-left corner. Additionally, the contextual menu for such a clipping will also sport an additional choice: Reload Clipping.

Adding items to your tab is simplicity itself. You drag the object or file icon to your new panel and (possibly after a short wait), a thumbnail will appear. For graphic objects and frames in an open AppleWorks document, you also can Control-click and choose Add to Clippings from the contextual menu, and select the panel you want from the submenu that appears — thus, Clippings doesn't even have to be open for you to add an object to Clippings.

Tip When you drag a file icon onto a Clipping panel, AppleWorks saves an alias to that file in the panel's folder. Similarly, if you have a folder of clip art that you want to add all at once, you can create an alias of that folder (drag down while the Option and ⌘ keys are pressed) inside the Clippings folder. Clippings takes longer to display the thumbnails for aliases than it does actual objects, but using this method enables you to keep your clip art separate from that provided by AppleWorks.

Using AppleWorks 5 Libraries with Clippings

For those who are upgrading from AppleWorks 5 to AppleWorks 6, one of the first things you'll notice about Clippings is that not nearly as many groups exist in Clippings as there were ReadyArt libraries in AppleWorks 5. Additionally, you might have created new libraries in AppleWorks 5 that you would like to be able to use in AppleWorks 6. You have not been left high and dry — ReadyArt libraries can be used in Clippings in a couple of ways.

✦ You can drag the ReadyArt library (or an alias to it) to the top level of the Clippings folder and a tab will appear in Clippings giving you access to the contents of the library (see Figure 13-3).

Note When you see these tabs in Clippings, you'll notice a small padlock icon in front of the tab's name to indicate that you cannot add objects to or delete objects from this panel, even though the Delete Object contextual menu item is enabled. Further, you cannot drag objects from a locked tab to another tab, even with the Option key held down, to create a copy.

✦ You can save the items in a ReadyArt library into a document using Apple-Works 5. Open that document in AppleWorks 6, choose Edit ➪ Select All (or press ⌘+A), and then drag the objects to a tab (or use the contextual menu as described earlier).

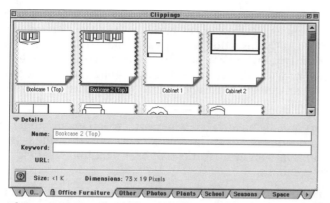

Figure 13-3: ReadyArt libraries from AppleWorks 5 appear as locked tabs in Clippings.

Of course, you can create variations on these themes, as well. For example, you could place the ReadyArt library at the top level of the Clippings folder, create a new document in AppleWorks 6, and then drag the objects onto that document from the locked panel. Then, add them back to Clippings on another tab. The unfortunate side effect of using the second method (or this variation) is that you lose the object names and have to manually add them back.

Note
One would think that named objects (you can name objects in the Object Size windoid) would keep their names when you add them to Clippings, but they don't.

Inserting Clippings into Documents

To add a clipping to a document, drag the object from Clippings into the document, and then release the mouse button.

Depending on the type of document or frame into which the object is being inserted, it will either appear as a floating object or an in-line object (see "Adding Graphics to Word Processing Documents" in Chapter 3).

✦ **Draw and Presentation documents:** All objects are inserted as floating objects unless you are in a text frame or a table cell. You can specify the approximate position to which the object will be placed by clicking the object with the pointer tool before you drag it to the document.

✦ **Paint documents or frames:** Objects — regardless of whether they are graphics or text — are inserted as bitmapped graphics. They are surrounded by a selection rectangle, enabling you to move or delete the graphic.

✦ **Word processing documents, frames, or table cells:** If a text-insertion point is currently set in the document, frame, or cell and you drag the clipping to it, a graphic object is added at the insertion point as an in-line object. If the insertion point is not currently set when you add the clipping, a graphic object is added as a floating object. You also can insert text clippings into word processing documents by dragging them, as described later in this chapter in "Text as Clippings."

✦ **Databases:** Clippings can only be inserted when you are in Layout mode. All objects are placed as floating objects. The sole exception to this rule is that you can insert clippings into an AppleWorks database's multimedia field when you are in Browse mode.

✦ **Spreadsheet documents or frames:** All graphics and text strings are added as objects that float on the spreadsheet.

Tip

As you're dragging an object into a document, you might notice it's either the wrong object or the wrong document. To cancel a drag in progress, move the hand mouse pointer back over the original Clippings panel and release the mouse button.

Editing Clippings Panels

The contents or appearance of an unlocked Clippings panel can be altered in several ways. Many of these alterations are most conveniently accessed via the contextual menu. You can:

✦ Add items to or remove items from a panel

✦ View the contents of a panel sorted in different orders

✦ Move or copy items from one panel to another

Adding items to a panel

The way in which an item is added to a library depends on whether the item is currently selected in a ClarisWorks document or has been copied (using the Copy command) from another program.

STEPS: Adding a ClarisWorks Object or Selection to a Library

1. Display the Clippings panel to which you want to add the item.

2. In the AppleWorks document or frame, select the object, text, frame, paint selection, or database data.

3. Drag the item onto the panel.

    or

Control-click the object and select the panel to which you want it added from the contextual menu's Add to Clippings submenu.

4. The material is added as a new item named Clipping x, where x is the number of the next unnamed object on that Clippings panel.

Tip　You also can use drag-and-drop to transfer items into Clippings from drag-and-drop-enabled programs, such as the Scrapbook desk accessory. Similarly, you can drag text or picture clippings from the desktop into a library, so long as AppleWorks is the active (frontmost) program. When AppleWorks is not the active program, Clippings — like all the windoids — is hidden.

There's a simple procedure for moving or copying an object in one panel into another panel. For the sake of convenience, you might want your company logo to appear in several panels, for example. Just select the object in any panel, and then drag or Option+drag it onto any other tab to move or copy it. Note that the object's original name is also transferred to the receiving panel.

Adding other types of items to Clippings

Because the supplied AppleWorks Clippings contain only clip art or photographic images, many users assume this is all a Clipping can be. As the preceding discussion attests, however, this assumption is incorrect. Clippings also can store text, movies, sounds, and frames. However, you should bear in mind some special considerations when adding and using such material as library items.

Database records as Clippings

In general, database fields cannot be selected and then added to Clippings, nor can you insert data into a database by dragging it from Clippings.

Note　AppleWorks's multimedia fields are an exception to these rules, however. The contents of multimedia fields can be added to Clippings, and such fields also can receive images from Clippings.

You can select an entire record and add it to Clippings. The fields will be tab-delimited when the Clipping is subsequently used in a text frame or word processing document.

Text as Clippings

As mentioned earlier in this chapter, it's easy to add text to Clippings. If the text is in an AppleWorks document, just select the text and drag it to a Clippings tab. If the text is from a non-AppleWorks document, select it, use the program's Copy command to copy it to the clipboard, switch to AppleWorks, paste it, and then drag it to the Clippings tab you want.

Inserting text from Clippings into word processing documents and frames is also simple. Position the text insertion point at the spot in the word processing document where you want to add the text, select the text in Clippings and drag it to the insertion point. The text is added at the insertion point.

To insert a text Clipping into a draw document (or the draw layer), presentation, spreadsheet, paint document, or paint frame, drag the text into position. Text inserted into a paint document or frame becomes a bitmapped graphic. Text inserted into a spreadsheet, draw, or presentation document is treated as a new text frame (unless you drag the text into a word processing frame inside the draw document).

Removing items from Clippings

You have two ways to remove a clipping from Clippings:

✦ **Delete.** To remove an item without transferring a copy of it to the clipboard, Control-click the item in Clippings and choose Delete Clipping from the contextual menu.

✦ **Cut.** To remove an item and simultaneously transfer a copy of it to the clipboard, select the item in Clippings and choose Edit ➪ Cut (or press ⌘+X).

The Cut command is useful for removing an item you also intend to paste somewhere else—into an AppleWorks document or a document in another program, for example. Much of the time, however, you only really care that the item is removed from Clippings. In those cases, you can use either command (if you don't care about what's on the Clipboard).

Renaming Clippings

When you add a new item to Clippings, AppleWorks assigns a generic name to the item of the form Clipping x. Because Clipping 12 isn't a very descriptive name—it's like naming a document Untitled 7—you can use Clippings' Details text boxes to assign a better name, as well as to assign search keywords. You must click out of the Name or Keyword text box or press Tab, Return, or Enter for the assignment to be accepted.

To rename a clipping, select the object in Clippings. If the lower portion of Clippings is not exposed, click the disclosure triangle beside Details. Delete the text in the Name text box and type a new name. The new name appears in the panel above. If you want to add search keywords to help you find the clipping at a later date using the Search tab, add them (delimited by spaces, commas, or tabs) in the Keywords text box.

Sorting Clippings

By default, clippings are displayed in alphabetical order. Renaming items will change that order. If you prefer items listed by their date, size, or kind, choose the appropriate criteria from the Clippings contextual menu's Sort submenu. If you later add new objects to the library and want the list to be alphabetical, you must choose By Name.

Selecting Clippings Settings

As with other AppleWorks windoids, you can set various options and preferences specific to the windoid. While this is a useful capability in most of the windoids, it is particularly important in Clippings. Control-click Clippings to display its contextual menu and choose Clippings Settings, as shown in Figure 13-4. These settings enable you to do the following:

✦ Require whole word matches or partial matches (the default) when comparing the search string against names and keywords.

✦ Set the size of the disk cache. This cache is where AppleWorks stores the temporary files retrieved when doing a search of the AppleWorks Web site. You also can opt to empty the cache at any time in this dialog box, freeing up some disk space and forcing AppleWorks to download again rather than working from its cached copy.

✦ Determine the size of the thumbnails displayed — small (about 48 by 48), medium (about 64 by 64), or large (about 96 by 96).

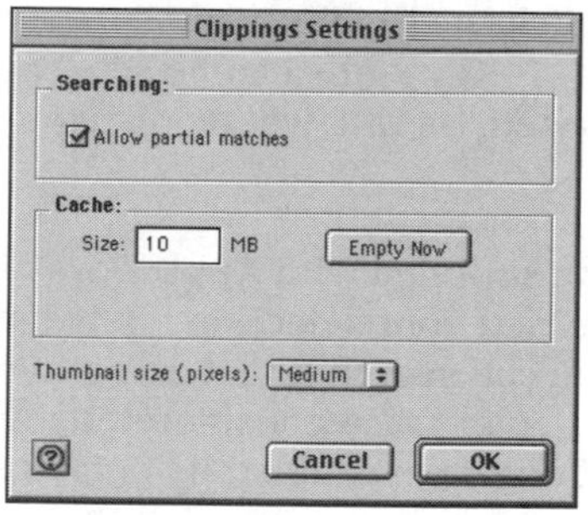

Figure 13-4: Set your Clippings preferences here.

Note   The reason we say "about" for the thumbnail size is because a border exists around the thumbnail that is a zigzag pattern and a turned-up lower-right corner. Consequently, thumbnails are not of constant width or height. We also haven't gotten a response to the question why "(pixels)" follows thumbnail size, because none of the choices offered in the pop-up menu has numeric dimensions.

Searching Clippings

Clippings has one other command—Search—which Apple believes is so important that each time you launch AppleWorks, you will be presented with it when you first choose File ➪ Show Clippings.

Finding Clippings

As shown earlier in Figure 13-1, the Search tab presents you with a text box into which you type a word or phrase. When you click the Search button, AppleWorks will commence a search of all your clippings for a match in either the name or the keywords for each item.

The Clippings accompanying AppleWorks 6 have all been assigned descriptive names, and most have been assigned one or more keywords. Clippings you find with an Internet search (discussed later) are also named, but are far less likely to have keywords attached. When you drag your own Clippings onto a panel, they will not have a keyword assigned, but if they are a named object or a file, they will retain their object name or the file name; otherwise, they will be named *Clipping n*, where n is a number.

To name a Clipping and assign search keywords, click the Details disclosure triangle to display the text boxes shown earlier in Figure 13-1. Keywords can be separated by spaces, commas, or tabs. If a Clipping is Web-based, its URL will be displayed below the Keywords text box.

As we mentioned earlier, the collection of clippings supplied with AppleWorks 6 is fairly large. Apple, however, has significantly increased your selection if you have an Internet connection. From the Search panel, you can search a vast and growing repository of clip art on the AppleWorks Web site. This is also considered by Apple to be of such major importance that Search Web Content is enabled by default (see Figure 13-1, earlier in this chapter).

If you clear the Search Web Content checkbox, AppleWorks will search just your Clippings folder (and the aliases you might have put in it) for full or partial matches (depending on your setting as described previously) in both the Name and Keyword fields.

When the Search Web Content checkbox is checked, AppleWorks will follow that up with a search of the AppleWorks Web site and its Clippings by downloading a compressed database of the available thumbnails (see Figure 13-5), decompressing that in your cache and searching for matches, and then downloading the thumbnails for the matches (see Figure 13-6). If you want to use one or more of those Web-based Clippings in your document, just drag the thumbnail to the document and AppleWorks will download the full image(s) from the Web site.

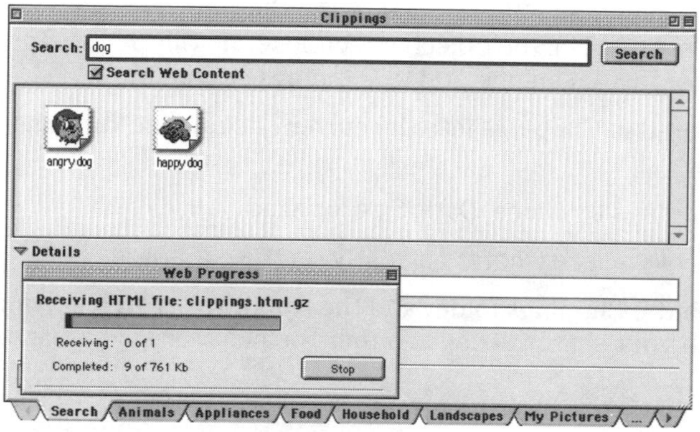

Figure 13-5: This is what you'll see as AppleWorks downloads its Clippings database from the Web site.

Figure 13-6: Now, AppleWorks downloads the thumbnails for which it found a match.

Note As with any other Internet activity within AppleWorks, you have to have an active Internet connection in place at the time you make the Search request.

When you drag a Web-based thumbnail to another tab, AppleWorks will redownload the images from the Web site. This is true not only of clippings found through the Search, but also any other Web-based images on other panels. Thus, if you drag a large number of Web-based thumbnails, you will have a lot of progress windows (similar to the one shown earlier in Figure 13-6) stacked on the left side of your screen.

Summary

✦ AppleWorks 6 includes an assortment of clip art. You also can create your own Clippings collections.

✦ AppleWorks 5 Libraries might be used as locked Clippings collections in AppleWorks 6 by copying them to the top level of the Clippings folder.

✦ To store a ClarisWorks object or text string in Clippings, select the object in the AppleWorks document and either drag it to the Clippings tab where you want to store it or Control-click the object and choose the Clippings panel you want from the contextual menus Add to Clippings submenu.

✦ To insert an item stored in Clippings into the current document, drag the item onto the document.

✦ You can sort the clippings by Name, Date, Size, or Kind.

✦ The Clipboard tab lets you see what is currently on the clipboard.

✦ You can Search both the Clippings folder and the AppleWorks Web site for clippings that match your search string in either the name or keywords fields.

✦   ✦   ✦

Working with Frames

Frames are what puts the integration into AppleWorks. You can create a document in one environment and embed other environments in the document by adding frames. For example, in a word processing document, you can embed paint frames containing illustrations, tables, and spreadsheet frames that contain data tables and charts (see Figure 14-1).

Of the six environments, only the spreadsheet, word processing, and paint environments can be frames; however, tables are treated as frames in almost every respect — you add them from the Frames panel in the Tools windoid, and they have their own set of tools on the Tools panel. When you work in a frame, it acts like a regular document created in its original environment — the same menu commands and tools are available.

Unfortunately, the types of documents that enable you to use frames, the methods with which you create frames, the modes in which you can access the frames, and so forth, are not consistent across the six AppleWorks environments. The next section lists the most important frame exceptions and "gotchas."

Paint frame   Spreadsheet frame

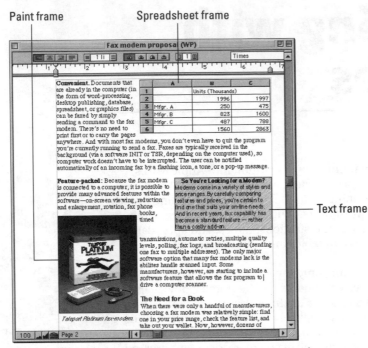

Figure 14-1: Frames embedded in a word processing document

Frame Exceptions

You should be aware of the following rules and exceptions when creating and working with frames. Many are obvious and are based on common sense (for example, no presentation frames exist, nor are frames allowed in paint documents). Others are simply Apple design decisions.

Read the rules once and then go about your normal AppleWorks business. If you don't remember whether a certain frame procedure works in a particular environment, just try it. Refer to this section only when you have problems. If you try to memorize any rules other than the most critical ones, you'll needlessly confuse yourself.

No presentation or database frames allowed

Presentation documents can contain frames, but you cannot embed a presentation frame in any other type of document.

Although you can embed frames within database documents (in Layout view only), you cannot create database frames in other kinds of documents.

Draw objects, not frames

No draw frames exist. Draw objects are always drawn directly onto a document or within a frame. Draw objects can be added to the word processing, spreadsheet, database, presentation, and draw environments.

Same-environment frames

You can place word processing frames into word processing documents and spreadsheet frames into spreadsheet documents. To do so, press the Option key while you draw the frame.

Adding frames to database documents

Frames can be placed and edited in database documents, but only when you're in Layout view.

Adding frames to paint documents

The moment you stop working in a frame that has been placed in a paint document, the contents of the frame become a regular paint image. In other words, you can no longer edit or manipulate the frame contents with its original environment tools — you can only use paint tools.

You cannot add draw objects to paint documents or frames, but draw documents can contain paint frames.

Creating text frames

You do not have to draw an outline to place a text frame in a document (as you do with spreadsheet and paint frames). You can simply click to position the cursor and then begin typing.

Opening frames

You can open spreadsheet or paint frames to display them separately in a full-sized window (Window ⇨ Open Frame), but you cannot open text frames in this manner.

You cannot open spreadsheet frames that are embedded in paint documents (because once they are placed in a paint document, all frames become bitmapped graphics).

Linking frames

You cannot link a pair of existing frames. You cannot link frames from different environments. You cannot link frames in a paint document.

See "Linking Frames," later in this chapter, for more information on linking.

Creating Frames

To create a table, or to create a spreadsheet, paint, or text frame within a document, select the appropriate tool from the Tools windoid's Frames panel (see Figure 14-2) and click to position one corner of the frame. Then, while pressing the mouse button, drag to complete the frame. Alternatively, you can drag the tool to the document to get a default-sized frame (or you can Control-click and choose the type of frame you want from the contextual menu's Frame Tools submenu), and then click and drag. After you release the mouse button, the frame appears. Figure 14-3 shows the creation of a spreadsheet frame within a word processing document.

Figure 14-2: To create a frame, first select one of these tools from the Tool panel.

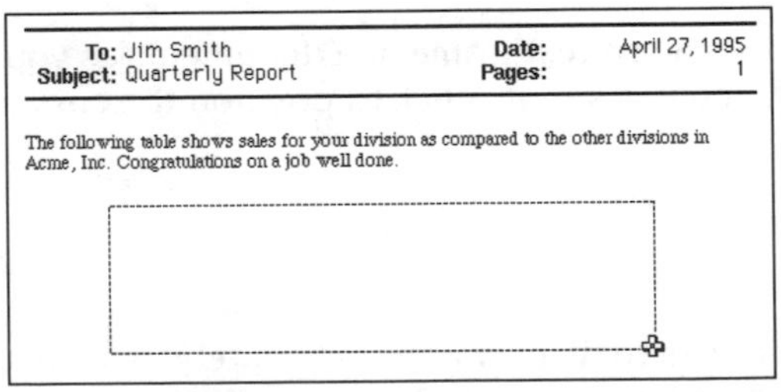

Figure 14-3: Drag the pointer to create a frame.

If Autogrid (from the Options menu) is selected, the frame aligns with the grid. (When Autogrid is selected, the menu command reads Turn Autogrid Off; when it is deselected, the menu command reads Turn Autogrid On.)

> **Tip** If frame links have not been set for the frame, a text frame will shrink to fit the text it contains. Additionally, text wrap will not work. To retain a full word processing frame (as you drew it), enable frame links (choose Options ➪ Frame Links, or press ⌘+L).

When you are creating frames, keep the following points in mind:

✦ Although no such thing as a draw frame exists, you can place a draw object into word processing, spreadsheet, draw, presentation, or database documents (in Layout mode only) by choosing a draw tool and then drawing.

✦ Spreadsheets and word processing documents can contain frames of their own type; that is, a spreadsheet can contain spreadsheet frames and a word processing document can contain text frames. To create such a frame, start by selecting the text or spreadsheet tool, as appropriate. While pressing the Option key, click the mouse button and drag to create the frame. Figure 14-4 shows a text frame in a word processing document.

✦ You can select the text tool and drag to create a text frame, but you don't have to go to that trouble. As long as you're not in a text environment, you can click once to create a small text frame and immediately begin typing. You can later resize the frame as required (see "Resizing and Positioning Frames," later in this chapter).

Text frame

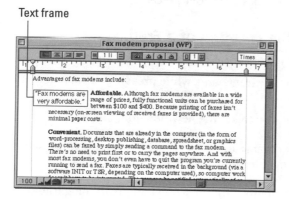

Figure 14-4: A text frame in a word processing document

Working in Frames

To work inside a frame, double-click it. The first click selects the frame; the second click moves you into the frame's environment and changes the pointer, tools, and menus to those of the new environment.

To stop working in a frame and return to the document's main environment, double-click anywhere outside the frame. If you happen to click within another frame (rather than in the main environment), the clicked frame is selected.

Resizing and Positioning Frames

After you place a frame in a document, you can treat its bounding rectangle just as you treat any other object: You can reposition it, color it, thicken or thin it, or use the handles to resize it.

STEPS: Changing the Size of a Frame

1. Click the frame once to select it. Handles appear at the corners of the frame.

2. Select any handle, press the mouse button, and drag to change the size of the frame.

   A frame pasted into a word processing paragraph as an in-line object has only a single handle (in the lower-right corner). To resize such a frame, drag the handle.

3. Release the mouse button to set the new size. Note that this procedure changes only the size of the frame, not the size of the image or data within the frame.

Tip   If you want to make precise changes to the size of a frame, you can use the Object Size windoid to type in new dimensions (choose Options ⇨ Object Size), or you can use the Arrange ⇨ Scale By Percent command to increase or decrease the horizontal and vertical dimensions by specific percentages.

STEPS: Changing the Location of a Frame

1. Click the frame once to select it. Handles appear at its corners.

2. Click anywhere inside the frame and, while pressing the mouse button, drag the frame to its new location.

3. Release the mouse button to set the new position.

Note   You also can move the frame using the Object Size windoid by specifying the frame's displacement from the upper and left edges of the page.

Keep in mind the following points about resizing and positioning frames:

✦ Although you can change the size of a text frame, the moment you leave the frame, it is adjusted to the smallest height that can still contain the text. Only the new width is retained. (Note, however, that if Frame Links is enabled, the height is retained.)

✦ You can drag spreadsheet frames to any size, but when you release the mouse button, the frame resizes itself to show only complete rows and columns.

✦ After you place a frame in a paint document, it ceases to be a frame — it becomes a paint image. The entire contents — both text and objects — are changed to patterns of dots. Text can no longer be edited and objects are no longer layered front-to-back. To move the contents of a former frame, select its contents with the marquee tool and drag it to a different location. To change the size of the contents of a former frame, select it with the marquee tool and choose the Resize command from the Transform menu.

Opening and Closing Frames

Because spreadsheet and paint frames are simply windows on what might be much larger documents, you can open these frames in separate document windows. Changes you make while the frame is open are automatically reflected in the frame in the containing document.

Note
When you resize either a paint or spreadsheet frame by making it smaller, the rest of the image or cells don't disappear. They're simply outside the frame window — temporarily out of sight.

To open a spreadsheet or paint frame, click the frame once to select it, and then choose Window ⇨ Open Frame. If a spreadsheet frame was selected, a full-screen copy of the frame opens in a new document window. If a paint frame was selected, a same-size copy of the frame opens in a new document window.

Tip
You also can open a spreadsheet or paint frame by selecting the frame and then pressing the Option key while double-clicking the frame.

To close an opened frame, click the close box in the upper-left corner of the window. The frame disappears, and you return to your original document.

Changing the Display of Spreadsheet and Paint Frames

You can, of course, open a frame to see and set its dimensions, but that seems awkward. To make this process easier, AppleWorks has a Frame Info command you can use with spreadsheet or paint frames:

✦ When you use Frame Info with a spreadsheet frame, you can decide whether the cell grid, row headings, and column headings should be visible or hidden and whether data or formulas are displayed. You also can set a different origin (the upper-left corner of the worksheet frame) to display.

✦ When you use Frame Info with a paint frame, you can set different resolution and depth values for the frame's contents, as well as specify a different origin.

STEPS: Modifying a Spreadsheet or Paint Frame

1. Select the frame. Handles appear around the border of the frame.

2. Choose Edit ➪ Frame Info. One of two dialog boxes appears, depending on whether a spreadsheet or paint frame is currently selected (see Figure 14-5).

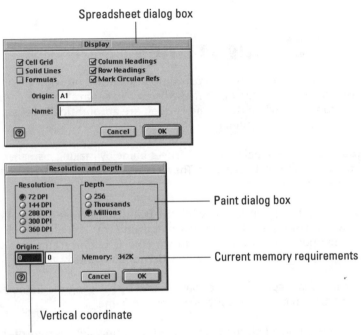

Spreadsheet dialog box

Paint dialog box

Current memory requirements

Vertical coordinate

Horizontal coordinate

Figure 14-5: Dialog boxes for modifying spreadsheet and paint frames

3. If a spreadsheet frame is selected, set options by clicking checkboxes. To set a different cell origin (the cell that appears in the upper-left corner of the frame), type the new cell coordinates (B14, for example) in the Origin text box.

    or

    If a paint frame is selected, you can set different resolution (the number of dots per inch) and depth (number of colors/data bits) values for the images in the frame. As you click different radio buttons, the amount of memory required is shown.

If desired, specify a different origin for displaying the paint image within its frame. The two Origin text boxes are used to set the horizontal and vertical coordinates (in pixels). An inch contains 72 pixels. For example, to specify starting coordinates of 1 inch to the right and 1.5 inches down, you type **72** and **108**, respectively.

4. Click the OK button to accept the changes.

When importing a PICT file into a paint frame or document, AppleWorks automatically matches the resolution of the image and uses the document's original color table.

Caution Changing the color depth of a paint frame can alter the colors in the painting. Such a change cannot be reversed with the Undo command. Thus, it's a good idea to save a copy of the document before changing the color depth.

Linking Frames

Although you can easily create multicolumn text in the word processor, Apple-Works provides a more flexible method for creating complex layouts. You can link text frames to one another, in much the same way as you can in desktop publishing programs. A document can contain a series of linked text frames that are placed wherever you like. When text exceeds the available space in one text frame, it automatically flows into the next linked frame (as shown in Figure 14-6). If the linked frames do not have enough room to contain the total text, an overflow indicator (a small box with an *x* in it) appears in the lower-right corner of the final frame. A document also can contain combinations of linked and unlinked frames.

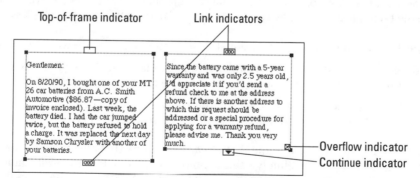

Figure 14-6: Linked text frames with indicator symbols

STEPS: Creating Linked Text Frames

1. Select the pointer tool in the Tools windoid.

2. Choose Options ➪ Frame Links (or press ⌘+L).

3. Select the text tool from the Tools windoid (either panel) and draw a text frame. (If the Tools windoid isn't visible, choose Window ➪ Show Tools or press Shift+⌘+T.)

4. Click outside the text frame. An empty text frame with top-of-frame and continue indicators appears, as shown in Figure 14-7.

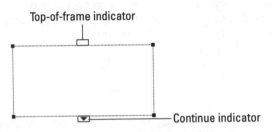

Top-of-frame indicator

Continue indicator

Figure 14-7: An empty linked text frame

5. Click the continue indicator (the black triangle at the lower edge of the frame) and draw a box for the next text frame.

> **Note**   Draw documents can have multiple pages, and you can link frames across pages (linking an article that starts on Page 1 to a continuation on Page 5, for example). To add pages to a draw document, first choose Format ➪ Document. In the Size section of the dialog box that appears, indicate the number of pages you want. To see the breaks between pages, choose Window ➪ Page View (or press Shift+⌘+P).

6. Repeat Steps 4 and 5 for any additional continuation frames you want to create.

7. Add text to the first frame by typing, pasting, or inserting. When the frame fills, additional text automatically flows into the other frames linked to it.

8. If additional frames are required, click the continue indicator of the last linked frame and draw another frame. Repeat this step as necessary.

You also can start with a single frame that already contains text and then link new text frames to the first frame. Simply use the pointer tool to select the first frame, choose Frame Links from the Options menu, and then go to Step 5 in the preceding instructions.

Note

You can insert a linked frame in the middle of several links — not just at the end. Simply use the pointer tool to click the link indicator on any linked frame, and then draw the new frame.

You also can create linked spreadsheet frames and linked paint frames. Unlike linked text frames, any linked spreadsheet or paint frame is merely a window into the complete spreadsheet or paint document. The purpose of creating linked spreadsheet or paint frames is to provide multiple views into the same document. You can, for example, show some pertinent raw data from a worksheet in one frame and display summary figures or a chart from the same worksheet in another frame.

To create linked spreadsheet or paint frames, start by using the pointer tool to select the frame. Choose Options ⇨ Frame Links (or press ⌘+L). Click the continue indicator at the lower edge of the frame and draw a box for the continuation frame. Repeat this process for any additional continuation frames you want to create.

Why Use Linked Frames?

In a word, freedom. Unlike in a word processing document — even a multicolumn one — you can place linked text frames anywhere you like. You also can have some text frames that are linked and other text frames that stand alone. By using linked text frames, you can create layouts that are as complex as layouts designed with some desktop publishing programs. The following figure shows a simple newsletter layout in a draw document that incorporates linked text frames, standalone text frames, and draw objects.

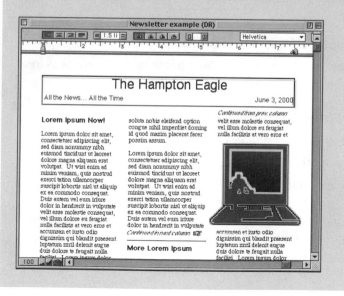

Tip   You can open a spreadsheet to full-screen size for editing or open a second view of a paint frame. You also can change the origin used to display any spreadsheet or paint frame. For details, refer to "Opening and Closing Frames" and "Changing the Display of Spreadsheet and Paint Frames," earlier in this chapter.

Quick Tips

The following quick tips give some examples of things you can do to frames and provide instructions for creating spreadsheet charts (within a frame or as free-floating objects).

Frames are objects

If it isn't apparent from the preceding discussion, we'll tell you now: Other than in the paint environment, all frames are objects. Anything you can do to an object, you can do to a frame. Examples include the following:

✦ Changing the pen color, line width, and pattern for the border (or making the border transparent)

✦ Adding a background color, pattern, or wallpaper

✦ Resizing the frame

✦ Placing one frame over another and sending frames forward or backward

Using spreadsheet charts in frames

You can embed spreadsheet charts in a spreadsheet frame or create them as free-floating objects.

STEPS: Making a Free-Floating Chart

1. Enter the spreadsheet frame by double-clicking a cell.

2. Select the data you want to use for the chart.

3. Choose Options ⇨ Make Chart (or press ⌘+M). The Chart Options dialog box appears.

4. Select a chart type and your chart options, and then click the OK button. The chart appears, separate from the worksheet.

STEPS: Making a Chart Within a Spreadsheet Frame

1. Enter the spreadsheet frame by double-clicking a cell.

2. Choose Window ➪ Open Frame. The worksheet expands to a full-screen view.

3. Select the data you want to use for the chart.

4. Choose Options ➪ Make Chart (or press ⌘+M). The Chart Options dialog box appears.

5. Select a chart type and set your options, and then click the OK button. The chart appears, embedded as an object in the worksheet.

6. Click the close box in the spreadsheet window to return to the original document.

Other objects — such as paint frames, text frames, and draw graphics — also can be embedded in a worksheet. The objects can be created or pasted while you're in the Open Frame view, or you can create them by drawing with the appropriate tool (the text tool, spreadsheet tool, paint tool, the table tool, or any of the draw tools).

Summary

✦ Any AppleWorks document other than a paint document can contain frames from other environments.

✦ When you work in a frame, the menu commands, Button Bar, and tools change to match the environment of the frame. When you leave the frame, they change back to match the base document's environment.

✦ Frames are objects, and you can resize or move them. You can apply any attribute to a frame that you can apply to an object.

✦ Spreadsheet and paint frames are simply windows into larger documents, and you can expand them to full-screen size.

✦ You can link text, spreadsheet, and paint frames to other frames. When you link text frames, text can automatically flow from one frame to another. Linking spreadsheet or paint frames enables you to display multiple views of the same underlying spreadsheet or paint document.

✦ ✦ ✦

Using Styles

AppleWorks's stylesheet feature enables you to create your own reusable text, paragraph, outline, table, and worksheet table styles and apply them to any text, tables, or worksheet areas you like. You also can design styles for objects — making it a snap to apply the same line settings, pen and fill colors, patterns, and gradients to objects. (You no longer have to guess what shade of blue you chose for text or a cell border, for example.)

By using styles instead of manually formatting text and objects, you can ensure that the appearance of elements will be consistent not only in the current document, but across an entire set of documents, as well.

In addition to reusability, the real power of styles becomes apparent when you change a style that's already in use in a document. For example, if you have a paragraph style called Main Head that is defined as centered, 18-point, Times, bold, italic text and then change the definition so that it is left-aligned, 14-point, Helvetica, and bold, all headings to which that style has been applied are immediately reformatted to match the new definition!

To see the Styles windoid, choose Format ➪ Show Styles or press Shift+⌘+W. To hide Styles, click its close box, choose Format ➪ Hide Styles, or press Shift+⌘+W. Styles is shown in Figure 15-1.

Sample callout

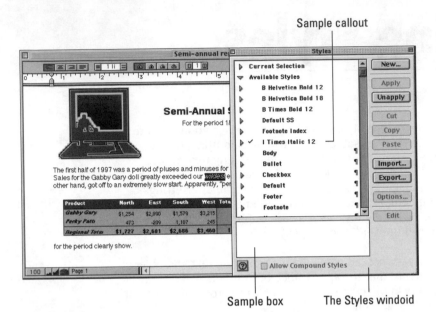

Sample box   The Styles windoid

Figure 15-1: Styles can be selected from the Styles windoid or the Text Styles pop-up menu.

Note The same styles also can be selected from the Button Bar's optional Text Styles pop-up menu button. If the Button Bar is hidden, you can display it by choosing Window ⇨ Show Button Bar (or pressing Shift+⌘+X).

You also can show or hide Styles by clicking the optional Styles button in the Button Bar (see Figure 15-2).

Figure 15-2: The Styles button

About the Stylesheet

Each document has its own stylesheet. When you save a document, you are simultaneously saving the current state of the stylesheet. Any changes you have made to the stylesheet — whether you have edited any of the standard styles, deleted some styles, or created your own styles — are stored with the document. When you change from one document to another, the stylesheet changes to display the styles of the document having the focus. Similarly, when you switch to a different environment within the same document, the classes of styles presented also change. SS-Table styles are shown only when a spreadsheet document or frame is currently selected, for example.

Five classes of styles exist. Each class corresponds to a particular type of Apple-Works element to which it can be applied:

✦ **Basic.** Basic styles are for formatting text selections (applying font, size, style, and color options) and objects, such as draw graphics, spreadsheet cells, and database fields.

✦ **Paragraph.** Paragraph styles are applied to entire paragraphs and include indents, tabs, alignment, line spacing, and before and after spacing values. Paragraph styles also can include text formatting commands (setting a font, size, style, and color for the text in the paragraph, for example).

✦ **Outline.** Outline styles are used to apply outline formats to paragraphs.

✦ **Table.** Table styles are used to apply cell shading and borders, as well as to apply basic styles to cells, cell ranges, or an entire table.

✦ **SS-Table.** Table styles enable you to apply cell shading, borders, and other formatting options to selected worksheet ranges or an entire worksheet.

To make it simple to identify the different classes of styles in the stylesheet, each has a distinctive icon that appears to the right of the style name, as shown in Table 15-1.

Table 15-1 **Style Icons**	
Icon	*Type of Style*
No icon (blank)	Basic style
¶	Paragraph style
▤	Outline style
▦	Table style
▦	SS-Table style

Applying Styles

To apply a style, select the text, paragraph, outline topic, or object to which you want to apply the style, and then select a style from Styles by selecting its name (as shown earlier in Figure 15-1) and clicking the Apply button (or double-clicking the style). Alternatively, you can choose the same styles from the Text Styles pop-up button in the Button Bar. If nothing is selected in the document when you choose a style from Styles or the Text Styles button, it is applied to the next text you type or object you create.

Caution   It is important for you to be aware that a paragraph style selected as described will be immediately applied to the paragraph in which the text cursor resides because AppleWorks considers that a paragraph is selected for these purposes if the cursor is blinking anywhere within it.

When working in a paint document or frame, you cannot apply basic styles to selected portions of a painting. Instead, any basic style chosen from the stylesheet or Text Styles pop-up button is applied to the next text you type or image you paint.

In ClarisWorks 4.0, styles could only be applied individually to selected text, objects, cells, and so on. If you applied one style from the stylesheet and then applied another, the second style replaced the initial style. Starting with ClarisWorks 5, on the other hand, you could combine styles. To allow multiple styles to be applied to selected text and objects in the current document, click the Allow Compound Styles button in Styles. With the Allow Compound Styles checkbox enabled, you might apply a basic style that sets the font and size to 24-point Times, for example, and then apply another basic style that adds italic.

Removing Applied Styles

Styles that have been applied to text, a paragraph, an object, a spreadsheet range, and so on can be removed with the Styles Unapply button.

Unapply is like an Undo button with an extremely long memory. You can use Unapply to remove any applied style whenever you like — even after hours of editing. As long as the original formatting was added by choosing options from Styles or the Text Styles button, the formatting can be removed with Unapply.

The following points explain how to remove the four classes of styles:

✦ **Removing a basic style from some text.** Reselect the text in the word processing document or frame, spreadsheet cell, or database field. A checkmark appears beside the name of the basic style that was previously applied to the text. Click the Unapply button.

✦ **Removing a basic style from an object (a draw graphic or a database field in Layout or List mode).** Reselect the object. A checkmark appears beside the name of the basic style that was previously applied to the object. Click the Unapply button.

✦ **Removing a paragraph or outline style from a paragraph.** Reselect the paragraph or outline topic. (It is not necessary to select an entire paragraph. As long as the text insertion point is somewhere within the paragraph, it is considered selected.) A checkmark appears beside the name of the paragraph style that was previously applied to the paragraph. Click the Unapply button.

Tip

You also can use the Unapply button on a series of contiguous paragraphs, as long as they were all formatted with the same paragraph style. If you select two or more paragraphs that were assigned different paragraph styles, the Unapply button is grayed out.

✦ **Removing a table style from a table or an SS-Table style from a worksheet.** Reselect the entire range of the table that was previously formatted with a table style. Click the Unapply button.

You can also use other procedures to remove applied styles:

✦ Reselect the style in Styles with which the text, object, or cell was previously formatted by double-clicking it. Doing so removes the selected style.

✦ To remove manually applied text styles, choose the same commands again from the Text ⇨ Style submenu or choose Text ⇨ Style ⇨ Plain Text (⌘+T).

Creating Styles

The process of creating a new style always includes the same series of initial steps, regardless of the type of style being created and whether compound styles are being allowed.

STEPS: Creating a New Style

1. Click the New button in Styles. The New Style dialog box appears, as shown in Figure 15-3.

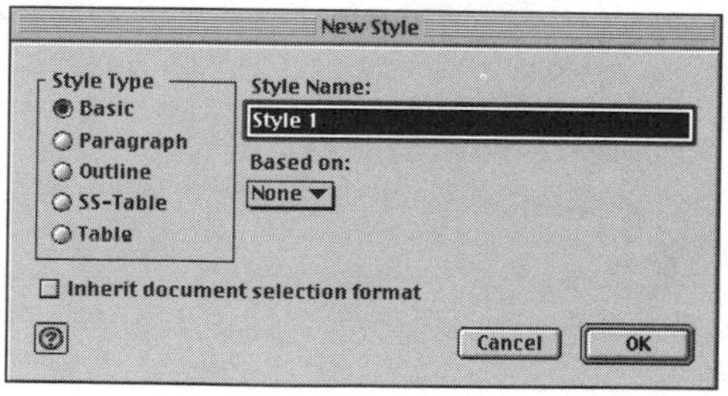

Figure 15-3: The New Style dialog box

2. Select a class of styles by clicking one of the Style Type radio buttons.

3. Decide whether the style should be based on an existing style. If so, select the style's name from the Based on pop-up menu. Choose None if you do not want to base the new style on an existing style.

4. Decide whether the new style should inherit format settings from the currently selected text, paragraph, cell, or object. To inherit settings, click the Inherit document selection format checkbox.

5. Type a name for the style in the Style Name text box, and then click the OK button. The new style's name is added to Styles.

This ends the first step of the style definition process. However, the definition might be incomplete, particularly if you chose not to base the style on an existing style or on a currently selected item (text, a paragraph, an object, and so on). The pointer changes to the stylesheet edit pointer (a hollow S) while it is over the document window.

The current properties for the style (the formatting options that make up the style definition) appear in the style's Properties list, and a sample is displayed in the box below the list, as shown in Figure 15-4. You can modify the properties by choosing formatting commands from the normal AppleWorks menus (such as the Text submenus), from the Button Bar, from the ruler bar (if you're working in a word processing document or frame and dealing with a paragraph style), and from the Accents windoid. When you are finished making changes, click the Done button.

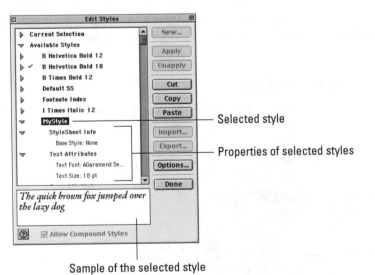

Figure 15-4: The Edit Style dialog box

The Scope of Styles

Style definitions are not universal. Each new style is only available in the document in which the style was created. If you create a new document or open another document, you'll see the styles you've defined have disappeared from Styles. They only return when you switch back to the document in which the styles were defined. If you want a given set of styles to be available for all new documents in an environment (word processing, for example), you should create a default template document that contains the new styles (see Chapter 11 for a discussion of template documents). You also can export a set of styles that you might want to reuse in other documents and then import them into the documents where you want to use them (see "Transferring Styles," later in this chapter).

Editing Styles

As mentioned earlier, editing is often a necessary part of the initial style definition process. On the other hand, editing styles that are already in use also might be necessary. By changing a paragraph style you previously defined for hanging indents, body text, or headings, for example, you can instantly change the formatting of those paragraphs throughout your document. Editing options for styles include renaming the style, changing the style on which the current style is based, and changing the style's properties.

Note When you edit styles, it is often helpful to see the cumulative effects of your edits. A sample of the selected style is displayed in the lower-left corner of Styles.

You can rename a style or change the style on which a style is based. Select the style's name in Styles and click the Options button. The Modify Style dialog box appears, as shown in Figure 15-5. Type a new name for the style and choose a different style on which to base the style from the Based on pop-up menu. Click the OK button to accept the changes.

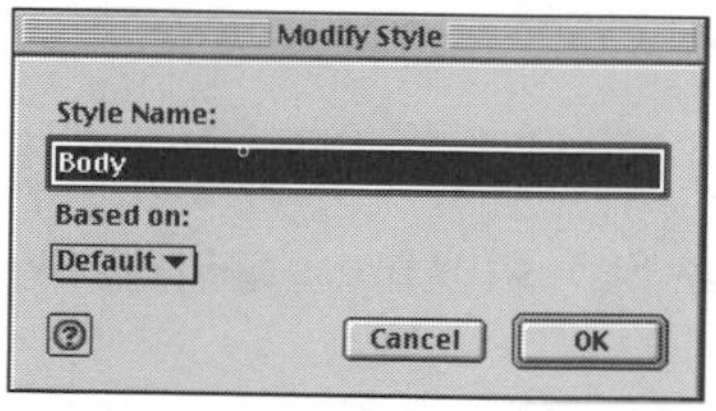

Figure 15-5: The Modify Style dialog box

Modifying style properties

Styles consist of properties (formatting options). To change a style, you change the properties of that style. After clicking the Edit button in the stylesheet and selecting a style to edit, you can use any of the following procedures to modify the properties of the style:

✦ Choose new properties from AppleWorks menus, the ruler bar, the Button Bar, and the Accents windoid. As you select them, the new properties are added to the style definition or replace components of the definition.

✦ Remove properties by selecting them in the Properties section of the style definition and then pressing the Delete key or clicking the Cut button in Styles. If you press the Delete key, you will be alerted that the action in not undoable and asked whether to proceed.

✦ Transfer properties from one style to another. Select a property in the Properties section of the stylesheet and click the Copy button. Select the style you want to modify, click in its Properties description, and then click the Paste button.

Tip   You can simultaneously copy and paste several properties, if you like. Before copying the properties, Shift+click to select several contiguous properties or ⌘+click to select noncontiguous properties.

When you are through editing styles, click the Done button. The new style definitions are immediately available for use.

Caution   No Cancel button exists in Styles when styles are being edited, nor can changes you make while editing a style be corrected with an Undo command. If you don't like the effects of your editing, you must either redo the editing, close the document without saving the changes, or use the Revert command to restore the document to its state as of the last save.

If certain styles become unnecessary (or you just want to eliminate the clutter in a crowded stylesheet), you can delete selected styles. If the style is currently in use somewhere in the document, however, you will not be allowed to remove it.

STEPS: Deleting a Style

1. If Styles is not visible, choose Format ⇨ Show Styles (or press Shift+⌘+W).

2. Select the style you want to delete.

3. Click the Cut button or press the Delete key. If you press the Delete key, you will be warned that the action is not undoable and asked whether to proceed.

   Cut places a copy of the style definition on the clipboard, enabling you to paste the style definition back into this or another stylesheet for another document. Pressing the Delete key simply deletes the style definition without placing a copy of it on the clipboard.

Transferring Styles

Because styles are document-specific (refer to the "The Scope of Styles" sidebar earlier in this chapter), you have to have at least one way of moving styles around. If you've defined a style you'd like to reuse in another document (or in many other documents), you can do any of the following:

✦ Save the document as a template. (Each copy of the file you open will contain the new styles you have defined.) See Chapter 11 for help creating templates.

✦ Save the document as a default template for an environment, such as word processing. (Every new document created in that environment will share the same initial stylesheet.) See Chapter 11 for help creating default templates.

✦ Copy the styles from the original document's stylesheet and paste them into the stylesheets of the other documents (described in the following steps).

✦ Use the stylesheet's Import and Export buttons (described later in this section).

STEPS: Transferring a Style to Another Document via Cut-and-Paste

1. If Styles is not visible, choose Format ➪ Show Styles (or press Shift+⌘+W).

2. Click the name of the style you want to transfer. A checkmark appears, indicating this is now the selected style.

3. Click the Copy Button.

4. Open or change to the AppleWorks document that is to receive the style.

5. Click the Paste button. The new style is added to the document's stylesheet. Repeat Steps 2 through 5 for any additional styles you want to copy.

Note

The stylesheet maintains its own equivalent of the Mac's clipboard. Any style that is copied or cut (with the Copy or Cut button) remains available for pasting — in as many documents as you like — until you replace the clipboard's contents by clicking the Copy or Cut buttons again.

Styles' Export button enables you to save a selected set of styles to a disk file. Then, by using the Import button in another document's stylesheet and choosing the style file, you can quickly merge those styles with the current styles of the document. The Export/Import procedure is the best means by which you move many styles between documents, as well as the primary method with which you can share your styles with other users.

STEPS: Exporting Styles

1. Open the document whose styles you want to export.

2. If Styles is not visible, choose Format ⇨ Show Styles (or press Shift+⌘+W).

3. Click the Export button. The Select Styles to Export dialog box appears, as shown in Figure 15-6.

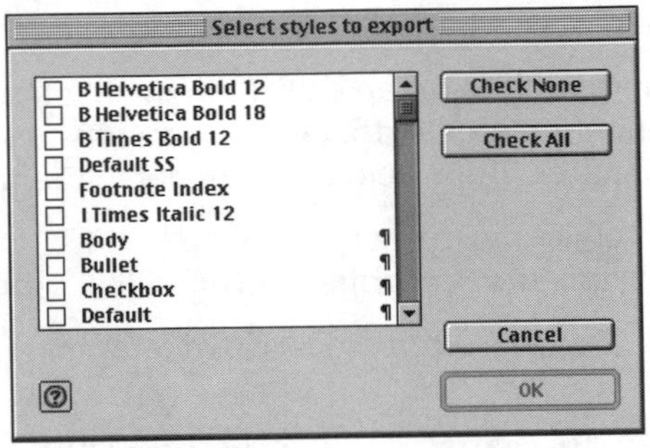

Figure 15-6: The Select Styles to Export dialog box

4. Click the names of the styles you want to export. You can use the Check All or Check None buttons to speed the style selection process.

5. In the standard Open dialog box that appears, type in a file name for the exported styles and navigate to the folder where you'd like to save them. (We recommend that you create an AppleWorks Styles folder within your AppleWorks folder.)

6. Click the Save button. The styles file is created.

STEPS: Importing Styles

1. Open the AppleWorks document into which you want to import the styles.

2. If Styles is not visible, choose Format ⇨ Show Styles (or press Shift+⌘+W).

3. Click the Import button. A standard Open dialog box appears. Navigate to the folder where you have the saved styles.

4. Choose the name of one of the style files, or navigate to a different drive and folder and choose another file. The Select Styles to Import dialog box appears, as shown in Figure 15-7.

5. Click the names of the styles you want to import. You can use the Check All or Check None buttons to speed the style selection process.

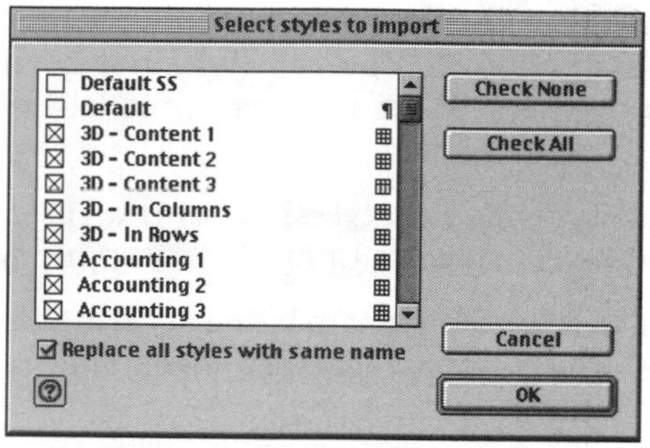

Figure 15-7: The Select Styles to Import dialog box

6. If you check the "Replace all styles with same name" checkbox, imported styles with names that match those of existing styles in the document automatically replace those styles.

 If you clear the checkmark, AppleWorks asks you how to handle each duplicate style name. You can either replace the old style with the imported style, or rename the imported style.

7. Click the OK button to import the selected styles. The imported styles appear in the document's stylesheet and can now be used.

Caution

Be careful when importing styles with names that duplicate those in the current stylesheet. If you check the Replace all styles with same name checkbox, and both stylesheets have a style named Body, for example, any text in the document that is already formatted as Body instantly changes to match the imported style's definition. Of course, in many cases, this is exactly what you want (for example, you might want to make the document's formatting consistent with a company-wide stylesheet).

Summary

✦ By using styles instead of manually formatting text, paragraphs, tables, worksheet cells, and objects, you can improve consistency in your documents. You also can save considerable time.

✦ Styles are document-specific; that is, they are only available in the document in which they were created. Saving a document also saves the styles that have been defined for that document.

✦ Five classes of styles exist: basic (for selected text and objects), paragraph, outline, table, and SS-Table (spreadsheet tables).

✦ You can choose styles from the stylesheet or from the (optional) Text Styles pop-up button in the Button Bar. If Allow Compound Styles has been chosen in Styles, you can apply multiple styles to text, objects, spreadsheet cells, and so on.

✦ Any style that has been applied by using the stylesheet or the Text Styles pop-up button can be removed by clicking the Unapply button in Styles.

✦ When you create a style, it can be based on any existing style in the current document; on the currently selected text, paragraph, object, and so forth; or it can be designed from scratch.

✦ When modifying a style, you can add new or replacement properties by choosing AppleWorks menu commands, clicking icons in the ruler bar (for paragraph styles), or choosing settings from the Accents windoid.

✦ Styles can be moved between documents by using copy-and-paste routines or by using the Export and Import buttons.

✦   ✦   ✦

Adding QuickTime Movies to Documents

QuickTime is an Apple-provided system extension that enables you to add movie clips, music, and sounds to Macintosh documents. You can insert QuickTime clips into most AppleWorks documents (and documents of other programs that support QuickTime), just as you now add static images such as logos. Anyone else who has the QuickTime extension and the program in which you created the document can play the movie.

If you are successfully running AppleWorks 6, you already have the necessary hardware and system software to use QuickTime. (AppleWorks 6 has more stringent hardware and system software requirements than QuickTime.)

If you have yet to install AppleWorks 6, you can determine which version of system software you're using by returning to the desktop, pulling down the Apple menu, and choosing About This Computer. The window that appears shows the system software version, along with the total memory installed in the Macintosh (see Figure 16-1).

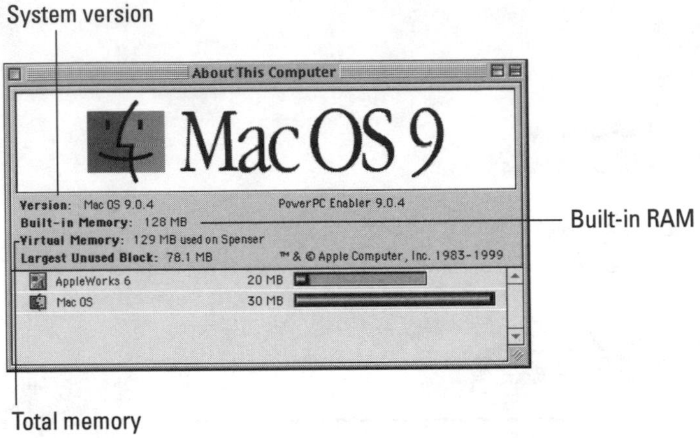

System version

Built-in RAM

Total memory

Figure 16-1: The system software version and the total installed memory are shown in the About This Computer window.

Obtaining and Installing QuickTime

You can obtain QuickTime in a number of ways. QuickTime is included when you buy a new Macintosh or purchase a system software update, and it is also included with AppleWorks 6 and automatically installed when you choose Easy Install. You also can download it from Apple's Web site. The current version of QuickTime (at this writing) is 4.1.2 — although new versions are released on a regular basis (and new updates are frequently made available).

Updaters for QuickTime can be downloaded from www.apple.com/quicktime and operate just like an Installer.

Inserting a QuickTime Movie into a Document

QuickTime uses the word "movie" to describe one of its files — whether or not it contains a video component. You can incorporate QuickTime movies in an AppleWorks document in several ways:

✦ Open them by choosing File ➪ Open (⌘+O) and choosing Drawing from the Document Type pop-up menu, and then choose either Movie [QT] or All Available from the File Format pop-up menu in the Open dialog box.

✦ Insert them into a word processing, spreadsheet, draw, or database document by choosing File ➪ Insert and choose either Movie [QT] or All Available from the File Format pop-up menu.

✦ Copy and paste them into a word processing, spreadsheet, draw, or database document by selecting the movie in the Scrapbook or another program, and then choose Edit ➪ Copy (⌘+C) and Edit ➪ Paste (⌘+V). You also can use drag-and-drop to move QuickTime movies between applications and documents.

As with other AppleWorks objects, you can add QuickTime movies as in-line graphics or as objects (refer to Chapter 3 for a discussion of in-line graphics and objects). In-line graphics become part of the paragraph into which you paste them, enabling you to format them with standard paragraph commands. To add a movie as an in-line graphic, set the text-insertion point within a word processing paragraph before choosing the Insert or Paste command.

Objects, on the other hand, are free-floating, and you can move them anywhere on the page. You also can specify a text wrap style if you place the object in a word processing document or frame (if it is a frame, Frame Links must be enabled, as described in Chapter 14, "Working with Frames"). To add a movie as a floating object, select the pointer tool from the Tools windoid before choosing the Insert or Paste command.

Note   A QuickTime movie you add to a paint document or frame appears as a static picture—you cannot play it.

Playing Movies

You can play a movie that is an object by double-clicking it or by using the special pop-up movie control bar. The only way to play movies that are in-line graphics is to double-click them or press the ⌘+right-arrow keys. (They have no control bar.)

Figure 16-2 shows a word processing document with a QuickTime movie. The control badge (the film strip icon) identifies the graphic as a QuickTime movie.

Using the double-click method

Double-clicking a movie causes it to automatically play with any options that are set for the movie. Normally, the movie plays from beginning to end with the default volume setting for audio that accompanies the clip. You can pause or stop the playback by clicking once anywhere on the screen. Double-click again to resume play from the point at which you halted the movie.

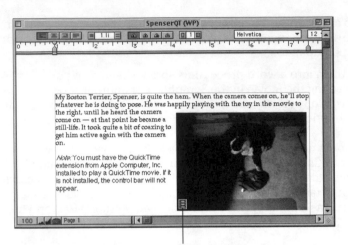

Click to display the controller

Figure 16-2: A document that includes a QuickTime movie

Using the movie control bar

For movies that are objects, clicking the film strip icon exposes a movie control bar at the lower edge of the movie, as shown in Figure 16-3.

— Step Forward

Step Backward

Forward/Reverse Slider

Play/Stop

Volume

Figure 16-3: The movie control bar

The control bar contains the following buttons:

✦ **Volume control.** Click this button to expose a slider control for playback volume. Move the slider higher for louder volume and lower for less volume.

✦ **Play/Stop button.** When the movie is not playing, this button appears as a right-facing triangle. Click it once to begin playing the movie. When the movie begins to play, the button changes to a Stop button with a pair of vertical lines on it. Click the Stop button to stop or pause the movie.

✦ **Forward/Reverse slider.** You can use the mouse pointer to drag this slider forward or backward in the movie to any point you want. As you drag the slider, the movie plays (without sound) either forward or backward until you release the mouse button.

✦ **Step Backward and Step Forward buttons.** The last two buttons enable you to step backward or forward through the movie one frame at a time — again, without audio.

Tip

You also can move the slider forward and backward by pressing the left-and right-arrow keys. Pressing ⌘+left arrow causes it to play in a backward direction, and ⌘+right arrow causes it to play in a forward direction.

Changing the Size of a Movie Frame

Movie frames are usually in a 4:3 size ratio, such as 160 by 120, 320 by 240, or 640 by 480, just like most monitors and TV sets. AppleWorks enables you to change the size of any movie frame, regardless of whether the movie is an in-line graphic or an object.

STEPS: Resizing a Movie

1. Click the movie once to select it. If the movie is an in-line graphic, a single handle appears at the lower-right corner of the movie frame. If it is an object, handles appear at all corners of the movie frame.

2. Select a handle with the mouse and then drag to resize the movie frame. (To maintain the original proportions of the frame, press the Shift key as you drag diagonally.)

3. Release the mouse button when the frame is the desired shape and size.

Note

You also can use Options ➪ Object Size to change the width and height of the QuickTime movie. The lower-left corner is the fixed point when you modify the size in this manner.

In addition to using the mouse pointer, you also can control playback directly from the keyboard. Table 16-1 shows some of the keyboard shortcuts.

Table 16-1	
Keyboard Shortcuts for Playback Control	
Key	***Effect***
Return, spacebar, or ⌘+right-arrow key	Start/Stop playback
Period (.) or ⌘+. (period)	Stop playback
Up-arrow key	Increase volume
Down-arrow key	Decrease volume
Right-arrow key	Step forward a frame at a time (hold the key down to step forward quickly)
Left-arrow key	Step backward a frame at a time (hold the key down to step backward quickly)
⌘+left-arrow key	Play movie backward

Setting Playback Options

You can set a variety of playback options for a movie you have added to an AppleWorks document as an object. (On the other hand, you can only play, pause, and restart in-line movies.) To see the different options, select the movie (the handles should appear) and choose Edit ➪ Movie Info. The Movie Info dialog box shown in Figure 16-4 appears.

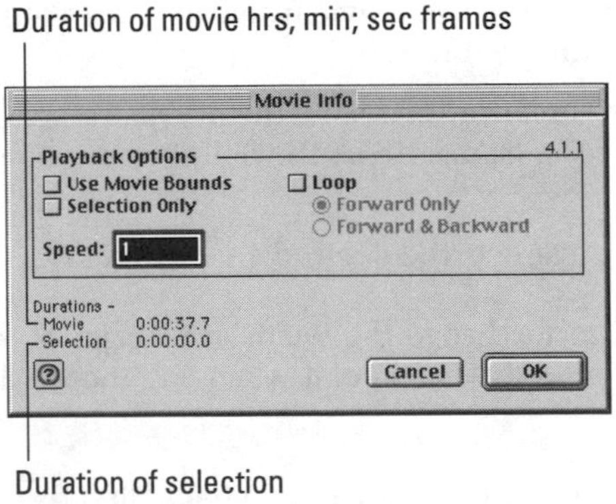

Duration of movie hrs; min; sec frames

Duration of selection

Figure 16-4: The Movie Info dialog box

Playback options in the Movie Info dialog box include the following:

✦ **Use Movie Bounds.** If you have changed the size of the movie window, clicking this checkbox restores the movie frame to its original size. If you have not resized the movie, this option is grayed out (unselectable).

✦ **Selection Only.** If you have selected only a portion of the movie, checking this option restricts playback to the selection, rather than to the entire movie. (See "Working with Movie Selections," later in this chapter.)

✦ **Speed.** By typing a number in the Speed text box, you can change the playback speed, as well as make the movie play backward. The default setting is 1. Table 16-2 shows how different settings affect playback.

Tip

You also can change the playback speed by pressing the Control key while you click either the Step Forward or Step Backward button on the control bar. A slider appears, which you can use to select a new playback speed. The center of the slider represents the normal speed setting. Moving the slider to the left of center sets backward playback speed, and moving it to the right of center sets forward playback speed.

✦ **Loop.** When this option is checked, the movie plays in a continuous loop. The radio button you click (Forward Only or Forward & Backward) determines the direction of playback. When Loop is set for a clip, you click once to halt the playback.

Table 16-2			
Effects of Different Speed Settings			
Direction	*Slower Speed*	*Normal*	*Faster Speed*
Play forward	Decimal between 0 and 1	1	Positive integer larger than 1
Play backward	Decimal between 0 and −1	−1	Negative integer smaller than −1

After setting options, click the OK button to put them into effect, or click the Cancel button if you change your mind.

Working with Movie Selections

As the discussion on setting playback options states, you also can work with selections (or portions) of any movie that is an object. This capability enables you to do some rudimentary movie editing, such as cutting and pasting selections into the same or another QuickTime movie.

Note   Most editing operations require that you upgrade to QuickTime Pro. This is accomplished by ordering a Registration number from Apple (under $30). Visit the upgrade page at www.apple.com/quicktime to order.

STEPS: Making a Selection Within a Movie

1. Use the Step Backward and Step Forward buttons or the Forward/Reverse slider in the movie control bar to find the starting frame of the selection.

2. Press the Shift key while you use the Step Backward and Step Forward buttons, the Forward/Reverse slider, or the left- and right-arrow keys to move to the end of the intended selection. The selected portion of the clip is shown as a dark area on the Play bar (see Figure 16-5).

— Movie selection

Play bar

Figure 16-5: The Play bar shows what portion of the movie is selected.

3. Release the Shift key and the mouse button when the selection is correct.

You can extend a selection or reduce its size in the same way you extend or reduce a text selection in a word processing document. Simply press the Shift key while dragging to the left or right. To clear a selection quickly, click the control bar once.

After you make a selection, you can perform either of the following tasks:

✦ Copy the selection by pressing ⌘+C.

✦ Delete the selection by pressing ⌘+X, or by pressing the Delete, Del, or Clear key.

After you copy (⌘+C) or cut (⌘+X) a selection from a movie, the selection is transferred to the clipboard where it is available for pasting. You can paste the selection into a different position in the same movie or into a different movie.

STEPS: Pasting a Movie Selection

1. Click the control badge (the film strip icon) on the destination movie to expose the control bar.

2. Use the Step Backward and Step Forward buttons or the Forward/Reverse slider to move to the position in the movie where you want to make the insertion.

3. Press ⌘+V. The selection is pasted into the movie.

Quick Tips

The following quick tips tell you how to store QuickTime movies in the Scrapbook, how to find missing movies, how to share QuickTime movies with other users, and how to eliminate choppiness when you play movies.

Using the Scrapbook to store movies

If you have the Scrapbook desk accessory installed, you can use it to store and play movies. Like movies pasted into documents, however, the movie does not actually reside in the Scrapbook. Instead, the Scrapbook maintains a pointer to the movie's actual location on disk.

STEPS: Inserting a Movie into the Scrapbook

1. Open the movie in any application that can read it. (You can insert it into an AppleWorks document, for example.)

2. Select the movie (its handles appear), and then choose Edit ➪ Copy (or press ⌘+C).

3. Choose ➪ Scrapbook. The Scrapbook opens.

4. Using the scroll bar at the lower edge of the Scrapbook window, move to the position in the Scrapbook where you want to insert the movie.

5. Choose Edit ➪ Paste (or press ⌘+V). The movie appears in the Scrapbook, as shown in Figure 16-6.

Figure 16-6: A movie in the Scrapbook
(MacOS 9.0.4)

Locating missing movies

When you attempt to display a movie file that is embedded in a document or on a page in the Scrapbook, QuickTime immediately searches for the disk on which the movie file is stored. If the original disk is not mounted on the desktop, the program asks you to insert it. Insert the requested disk. If the disk isn't available, click the Cancel button.

If you click the Cancel button, QuickTime automatically searches all mounted disks for a copy of the missing movie file. If it finds the movie file, it makes a record of the file's location and uses that file for all future requests. If it doesn't find the file, you get one last chance to find it, as shown in Figure 16-7.

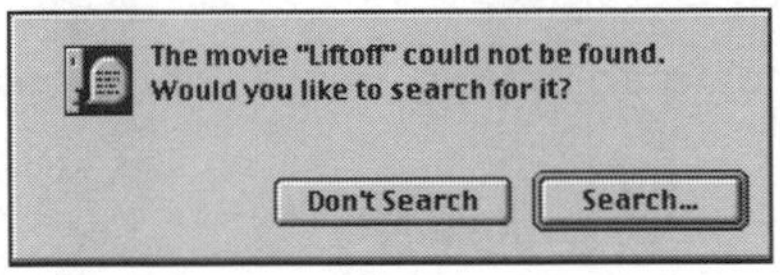

Figure 16-7: Last chance to find
the movie file

If you click the Don't Search button in the new dialog box, the movie is automatically changed to a static picture. If you think you can still find it (you have it on a different disk that is not currently mounted, for example), click the Search button. The Open dialog box shown in Figure 16-8 appears.

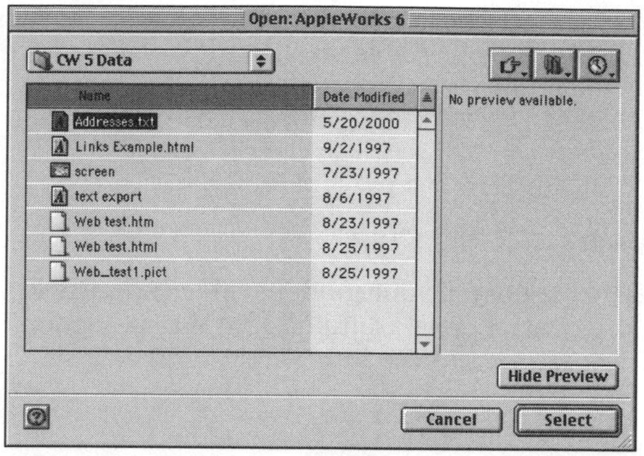

Figure 16-8: Insert the disk that contains the movie file, or manually search for the file here.

Sharing QuickTime movies with others

Again, because QuickTime movies aren't actually stored in the documents in which they're embedded, if you give someone an AppleWorks document or another type of document that contains a QuickTime movie, you need to give them a copy of the movie, too.

The first time the other person attempts to view the movie, a dialog box appears explaining that the original disk cannot be found and that it should be inserted. Clicking the Search button forces QuickTime to search for the file, and it will locate the file if your friend or colleague has copied the movie to a hard disk or has the document distribution disk inserted in a drive.

Improving QuickTime playback

If you want to play a movie with minimal choppiness, you can improve playback by storing the movie on the fastest disk drive you own, connected to the fastest bus interface on your computer. CD-ROM and floppy drives, for example, are extremely slow. ZIP disks and optical disks are faster. A hard disk is better still. A USB connection is slower than an IDE, SCSI, or FireWire connection.

If you intend to use QuickTime movies in a presentation and have the memory to spare, consider copying the movie to a RAM disk. A RAM disk is a temporary disk that is created from your Mac's memory. Because files and programs that are run from a RAM disk are accessed almost instantaneously (unlike a hard disk, a RAM disk has no moving parts), movie playback from a RAM disk is exceptional.

Note
Depending on the amount of RAM installed in your Mac and the size of the movie file(s), using a RAM disk might not be a workable solution. (If you don't have at least 8MB of free RAM, for example, a RAM disk for use with QuickTime isn't practical.) Any memory that is allocated for a RAM disk is not available for programs or desk accessories.

STEPS: Creating and Using a RAM Disk

1. Choose ✦ Control Panels ✦ Memory. If your model of Mac supports it, the lower portion of the Memory control panel contains a RAM Disk section (see Figure 16-9).

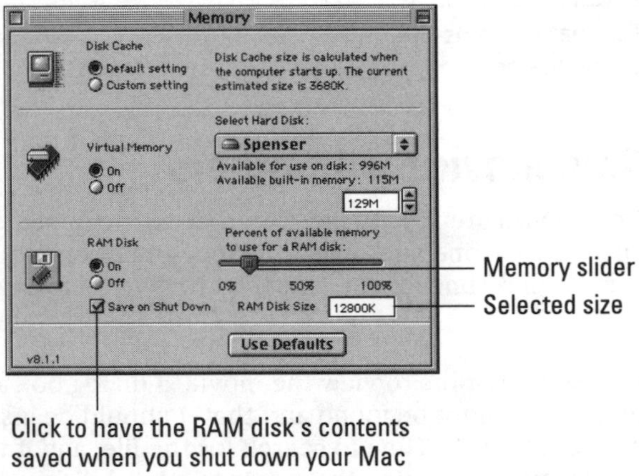

Click to have the RAM disk's contents
saved when you shut down your Mac

Figure 16-9: The MacOS 9 Memory control panel

2. Click the On radio button in the RAM Disk section and move the slider left or right to adjust the size of the RAM disk. (Try setting it to the total size of the AppleWorks document plus the movie file.)

3. Click the Memory control panel's close box to save the changes.

4. Restart the Macintosh. A RAM disk appears on the right side of the desktop.

5. Copy the AppleWorks document and movie files to the RAM disk.

6. Make a backup copy of the movie file on a floppy disk or removable hard disk, and then delete the original.

7. Double-click the AppleWorks document on the RAM disk to launch AppleWorks and load the document.

8. Because the QuickTime movie is no longer in its original location, a dialog box might appear to inform you of that fact. If the dialog box appears, click the Search button. QuickTime will locate the file on the RAM disk and use that copy to play the movie.

Later, to regain the memory that has been allocated to the RAM disk, open the Memory control panel again, click the Off button in the RAM Disk section, close the control panel, and restart your Mac.

Moving On Up

AppleWorks wasn't designed for heavy-duty QuickTime editing. Also, you can only use it to play movies that have been provided to you. If you want more control over the content of movies, want to add your own sound track, or want to make your own movies, you need to invest in some additional hardware and software.

If you want to capture video from an external source, such as a TV, videotape, or video camera, you need a way to change the video signals into a form that's compatible with the Macintosh. In most cases, you can use a video capture board or desktop video camera, such as the Connectix QuickCam, to accomplish this. You also can use the Apple Video Player software to control a TV Tuner Card or a VCR that is connected to the Mac's video input ports (if it has AV ports). Finally, if you have a FireWire-equipped iMac DV or other PowerMac and a digital camcorder, you can use Apple's free iMovie software to download from the camcorder using a FireWire connection and do quite a bit more editing than AppleWorks will allow. If you only want improved editing capabilities, you might want to invest in a video editing program such as Adobe Premiere or Apple's Final Cut Pro.

Summary

✦ You can add QuickTime movies to most AppleWorks documents. However, the word processing, draw, presentation, spreadsheet, and database environments are preferable for movie clips.

✦ As with static graphic images, you can paste or insert movies into documents as objects or as in-line graphics. If you want access to the movie control bar, however, you have to add the movies as objects.

✦ Movies you add as objects contain a pop-up movie control bar with which you can vary the playback direction and speed and do minor editing of the movie. You can only play, pause, and restart movies that are in-line graphics.

✦ You can change the size of any movie embedded in an AppleWorks document by dragging a handle on the movie frame.

✦ In the Movie Info dialog box, you can change playback settings for movies that are objects.

✦ In addition to working with the entire movie, you can select a portion of the movie (for selective playback or editing).

✦   ✦   ✦

Creating and Playing Macros

Although the AppleWorks macro recorder doesn't have many of the capabilities that standalone macro utilities have (such as repeating a macro, linking to other macros, and branching to different parts of a macro based on certain conditions), it does provide an easy way to perform many repetitive, well-defined tasks in AppleWorks.

The macro recorder works like a tape recorder. It simply watches the actions you perform when you click the mouse button (such as making choices in dialog boxes and choosing commands from menus) and keeps track of the characters you type. It does not record mouse movements, however. You cannot, for example, use the recorder to capture figures you create with the freehand drawing tool.

Caution Making choices in dialog boxes, clicking in windows, and menu choices are recorded by position, not by what the control is. Thus, if a different window is in front, or a different menu bar is showing, playing the macro back could well perform a different action than you intended.

To make it easy to execute some of your macros, you can assign keyboard shortcuts to them or add them to the AppleWorks 6 Button Bar (making them available at the click of a button). For help adding macros to Button Bars, see Chapter 12.

Recording a Macro

Although you can receive macros from other users as described in Chapter 12 ("Sharing Buttons with Others"), you will probably wish to create macros of your own at some point. AppleWorks makes recording a macro easy.

STEPS: Recording a Macro

1. To start the macro recorder, choose File ➪ Macros ➪ Record Macro (or press Shift+⌘+J). The Record Macro dialog box shown in Figure 17-1 appears.

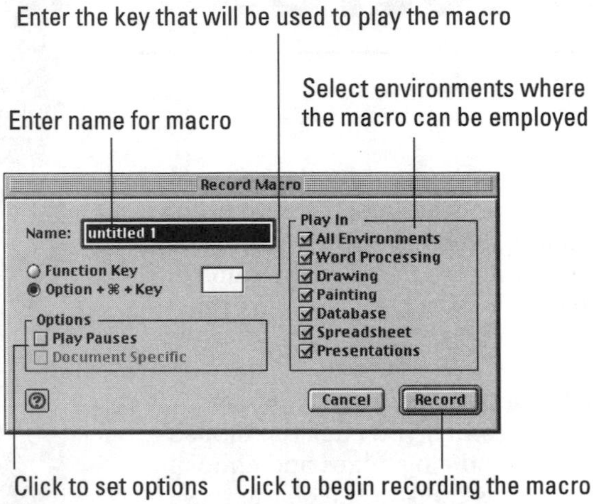

Enter the key that will be used to play the macro

Select environments where the macro can be employed

Enter name for macro

Click to set options   Click to begin recording the macro

Figure 17-1: The Record Macro dialog box

2. Name the macro and, optionally, specify a function key or Option+⌘ key combination that can be used to invoke the macro.

   The Function Key radio button is grayed out (unselectable) if your keyboard doesn't have function keys.

3. Set options for the macro as follows:

   • Choose Play Pauses if you want the macro to record the amount of time it takes you to perform each step. Otherwise, the macro plays back at the fastest possible speed. This option is particularly useful when you're using AppleWorks for step-by-step demonstrations or slide shows.

   • Choose Document Specific if you want the macro to be available only in this particular document, rather than in any AppleWorks document of the appropriate type. If no document is open when you record the macro, this choice is disabled.

4. Choose the desired Play In environments on the right side of the Record Macro dialog box. By default, AppleWorks automatically chooses the environment you are currently using, or everything if no document is open. Check all environments in which you want to be able to use the macro.

5. To begin recording the macro, click the Record button. You return to Apple-Works. To remind you that you are recording, a flashing cassette replaces the apple at the top of the Apple menu. (If you decide not to record the macro, click the Cancel button in the dialog box.)

6. Perform the steps you want the macro to repeat.

7. To end the macro, choose File ➪ Macros ➪ Stop Recording (or press Shift+⌘+J).

Playing a Macro

An unused macro does nothing but waste space. Using a macro is generally called *playing*, *running*, or *executing* the macro. Depending on the options you chose when you created the macro, you can run the macro in the following ways:

✦ Press the Option+⌘ key combination or the function key you assigned to the macro.

✦ Choose File ➪ Macros ➪ Play Macro. When the Play Macro dialog box appears (see Figure 17-2), choose the name of the macro and click Play.

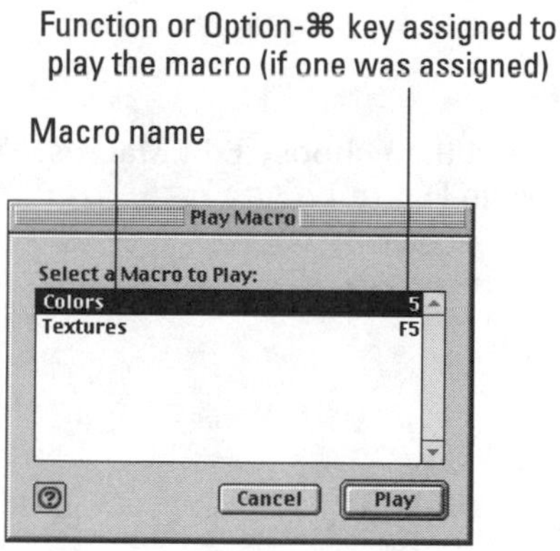

Function or Option-⌘ key assigned to
play the macro (if one was assigned)

Macro name

Figure 17-2: The Play Macro dialog box

✦ Click a button in the Button Bar that you created for the macro. (By following the instructions in Chapter 12, you can create custom icons for your favorite macros and add them to any Button Bar so they are readily accessible.)

Note   Remember to set up the conditions that are needed for the macro before you execute it. For example, if you need to select some text before you can use a word
processing macro, the macro will not work properly if you have not selected the
text. If the macro does not execute when you press its keyboard shortcut or click
its button in the Button Bar, or if it is not on the list in the Play Macro dialog box,
you are in the wrong environment, a window (such as Accents) that you need to
click in is not open, or you clicked the Document Specific checkbox when you
designed the macro and that particular document is not the active one.

Editing Macro Options

You cannot edit the steps of a macro. If you are dissatisfied with any step or need to
make a change such as adding a step, you have to re-record the macro.

On the other hand, if you want to change some of the options for a macro, you can
alter as many of them as you like at any time. You can even create or edit a Button
Bar icon if you like.

Note   You cannot use the same name or key combination for two macros. If you want to
reuse either component, you must delete the original macro first, as described in
"Deleting a Macro," later in this chapter.

STEPS: Editing Macro Options

1. Choose Macros from the File menu, and then choose Edit Macros. The Edit
   Macros dialog box appears, as shown in Figure 17-3.

Select a macro to edit from this list

```
┌─────────────────────────────────────┐
│            Edit Macros               │
│                                      │
│  Defined Macros:                     │
│  ┌──────────────────┐  ┌──────────┐  │
│  │ Colors      5 ▲  │  │  Delete  │  │
│  │ Textures    F5   │  └──────────┘  │
│  │                  │  ┌──────────┐  │
│  │                  │  │ Modify...│  │
│  │                  │  └──────────┘  │
│  │                  │                │
│  │                  │                │
│  │                  │  ┌──────────┐  │
│  │             ▼    │  │  Cancel  │  │
│  └──────────────────┘  └──────────┘  │
│  ⊚                     ┌──────────┐  │
│                        │    OK    │  │
│                        └──────────┘  │
└─────────────────────────────────────┘
```

Figure 17-3: The Edit Macros dialog box

2. Select the macro you want to edit from the scrolling list, and then click the
   Modify button.

3. Change whatever options you like, and then click the OK button.

4. Repeat Steps 2 and 3 for other macros you want to change.

5. To record the changes and return to AppleWorks, click the OK button. Or, to ignore all changes and leave your macros unaltered, click the Cancel button.

Deleting a Macro

If you no longer need a particular macro, you can remove it from the document in which it was saved or from AppleWorks (depending on whether you chose the Document Specific option). You also can delete a macro if you made a mistake in it or if it doesn't play back correctly. (Remember that you can't reuse a macro name or key combination unless you first delete the old macro.)

To delete a macro, choose File ⇨ Macros ⇨ Edit Macros. The Edit Macros dialog box appears, as shown earlier in Figure 17-3. Select the macro you want to remove and click the Delete button. If you want to delete other macros, you can do so now. To complete the deletions, click the OK button. If you change your mind and decide to leave the macro list unaltered, click the Cancel button.

Designing Automatic Macros

AppleWorks provides a special type of macro capability: automatic macros. You can create automatic macros that play whenever:

✦ AppleWorks is launched

✦ A new document is created in a particular environment (a new spreadsheet, for example)

✦ Any document from a selected environment is opened (a word processing file, for example)

To create an automatic macro, in the Record Macro dialog box (see Figure 17-1, shown earlier in this chapter), type one of the special names shown in Table 17-1 (spelling, capitalization, and hyphenation must be exact). Set options and select the appropriate Play In environment (or deselect all environments). Finally, record the macro steps (as described in "Recording a Macro," earlier in this chapter).

As you can see in the table, an automatic macro executes when one of three actions occurs: AppleWorks launches, a particular document type is opened, or a particular document type is created. You can have only one AppleWorks macro for each of the macro names listed earlier in Table 17-1.

Table 17-1
Automatic Macro Names and Definitions

Macro Name	Executes When . . .
Auto-Startup	AppleWorks is launched
Auto-Open WP	A word processing document is opened
Auto-Open DR	A draw document is opened
Auto-Open PT	A paint document is opened
Auto-Open SS	A spreadsheet document is opened
Auto-Open DB	A database document is opened
Auto-Open PR	A presentation document is opened
Auto-New WP	A new word processing document is created
Auto-New DR	A new draw document is created
Auto-New PT	A new paint document is created
Auto-New SS	A new spreadsheet document is created
Auto-New DB	A new database document is created
Auto-New CM	A new presentation document is created

If you want to delete an automatic macro, choose File ➪ Macros ➪ Edit Macros, select the macro from the scrolling list, and then click the Delete button.

The Auto-Open macro

Although the Auto-Open macros normally run whenever you open any document in the chosen environment, you can restrict an Auto-Open macro to a particular document by clicking the Document Specific checkbox when you define the macro. By linking the Auto-Open DB macro to one particular database file, for example, you can automatically sort that database and display the last record each time the file is opened. If any other database is opened, the macro will not play. If you use the Auto-Open DB macro in this manner, however, you cannot also create a similar macro for any other database, nor can you design a macro that will run when any database is opened. Remember that only one macro can be defined for each macro name.

Automatic macros versus templates

You can easily create templates or choose certain preference settings to accomplish many of the tasks that environment-specific automatic macros perform. For example, you can use a template or default stationery document (see Chapter 11 for more information about templates and stationery)—rather than an Auto-New WP macro—to set a particular font, display the current date, and include a Memo heading. To be truly useful, automatic macros should accomplish tasks that templates and preferences cannot perform. For example, you can use an automatic macro to customize an environment by hiding or showing rulers, setting a zoom level, choosing a given tool in the Tools windoid, or switching to a specific database layout.

Getting Down to Business: Creating a Small Caps Macro

Although AppleWorks has many of the text formatting options other word processing programs offer, it does not provide a small caps feature. (A phrase or text string formatted with small caps is completely capitalized, but the letters that are normally not capitalized are slightly smaller than the surrounding text.) However, by typing text in all capital letters and choosing a smaller point size, you can create the effect of small caps in AppleWorks.

STEPS: Manually Creating Small Caps

1. Type the text in all caps. Alternatively, you can add the Make Uppercase button to the Button Bar, select the text, and then click the button to change the text's case (see Figure 17-4).

 Figure 17-4: The Make Uppercase button

2. Select the part of the text you normally would have typed in lowercase letters. Ignore letters you normally capitalize (the first letter in a proper noun or the first letter of the word at the beginning of a sentence, for example).

3. In the Text ⇨ Size submenu, choose the next smaller point size. As an alternative, you can click the (optional) Decrease Font Size button in the Button Bar a few times to change the font size.

Now that you know how to generate small caps, you can design a macro that will perform the small caps conversion for you.

STEPS: Creating the Small Caps Macro

1. Create a new word processing document or open an existing document.

2. Add the Make Uppercase button to the Button Bar as follows:

    • If the Button Bar is currently hidden, choose Window ⇨ Show Button Bar (or press Shift+⌘+X).

    • Choose Edit ⇨ Preferences ⇨ Button Bar (or Control-click the Button Bar and choose Customize Button Bar from the contextual menu).

    • Click the disclosure triangle beside Word Processing in the Available Buttons list, double-click the Make Uppercase button's icon (refer to Figure 17-4), or drag the button into position on the Button Bar.

3. Type a single word (macros, for example).

4. Position the cursor so that it is directly in front of the "m" in macros.

5. To start the macro recorder, choose File ⇨ Macros ⇨ Record Macro (or press Shift+⌘+J).

6. Name the macro (Small Caps, for example) and set other options for it, such as the Option+⌘ key combination or Function key you'll use to invoke the macro.

    Because you'll want to be able to use the macro in other word processing documents, be sure that you do not check the Document Specific checkbox.

7. Click the Record button to begin recording the steps of the macro.

8. Press Shift+Option+right arrow. The entire word (macros) is selected.

9. Click the Make Uppercase button in the Button Bar. The word is changed entirely to uppercase (capital letters). Letters already in uppercase are unchanged.

10. Click the Decrease Font Size button in the Button Bar twice (shown in Figure 17-5). The point size of the word is reduced by two points.

 Figure 17-5: The Decrease Font Size button

11. To complete the process, choose File ⇨ Macros ⇨ Stop Recording (or press Shift+⌘+J). The macro is saved in the document or in AppleWorks (if you checked Document Specific when you named the macro).

STEPS: Playing the Small Caps Macro

1. Position the cursor immediately in front of the first letter of the word you want to change to small caps.

2. Press the ⌘+Option keystroke or function key you assigned to the macro.

   or

   If you didn't assign a special keystroke to the macro, choose File ➪ Macros ➪ Play Macro, and then choose the macro from the list that appears.

   The macro automatically converts any word to an all caps version of the word, two points smaller than the surrounding text.

The manner in which you have constructed this small caps macro has several advantages:

✦ Because the macro works on selected text, you can use it to convert an entire word (by positioning the insertion point just before the first letter of the word) or everything except the first letter of the word (by positioning the insertion point just after the first letter of the word).

   Any word that is composed entirely of lowercase letters should be completely converted. If a word begins with a normal capital letter, on the other hand, the macro should be applied to everything but the first letter of the word.

✦ Clicking the Make Uppercase button relieves you from typing the original text in uppercase or making the selection from the Text ➪ Style submenu.

New Feature

In AppleWorks 5 (or ClarisWorks) you had to use a button or shortcut to convert text to all uppercase or lowercase. AppleWorks 6 added UPPERCASE and lowercase to the Style submenu.

✦ Clicking the Decrease Font Size button is a more flexible approach than selecting a specific font size from the Text ➪ Size submenu.

   The macro always reduces the size by two points, regardless of whether the original text size was 10, 12, or 14 points, for example.

   If you had simply instructed the macro to set the selected text size to 10 points, the macro would not have worked with 10-point or smaller text, and it would have looked ridiculous when applied to large text, such as 24-point or bigger. (Admittedly, though, a 2-point reduction applied to a large text size will probably not have the intended visual effect.)

Quick Tips

The following quick tips discuss one-time macros, ideas for macros, how to avoid keystroke conflicts, and transferring macros to other users.

Sometimes once is enough

Most people normally think of using macros when they have a task they will need to repeat, perhaps frequently. Sometimes, however, you have a task that might never come up again, but you need to perform it 25 times in the current document (changing every occurrence of "Ace Auto Parts" to Helvetica italic, for example).

Just because you won't use a particular macro again after today doesn't mean you shouldn't make the macro. Create the macro and make it specific to the document in which you use it, or just delete it when you're done.

Macro ideas

Having trouble coming up with reasons to create macros? Here are a few suggestions that might start those neurons firing:

✦ **Create keyboard shortcuts for menu commands that don't have shortcuts.** In the word processor, for example, you can create a macro that inserts the current date, one that pops up the Paragraph dialog box from the Format menu, and another that chooses a particular font and applies it to the currently selected text.

✦ **Try to think in terms of many steps.** You'll get the greatest gains in productivity by automating complex, multistep procedures. For example, you can create a macro that chooses a specific database layout, performs a Find to select only specific records, performs a sort on the fields necessary, and then generates and prints your report.

✦ **Think about AppleWorks activities you routinely perform.** Not every macro needs to have a grandiose purpose. If you use a macro regularly for even small tasks, you will save a considerable amount of time.

Note Remember that you also can create separate custom buttons for macros so you don't have to memorize any additional commands.

Avoiding keystroke conflicts

You can assign AppleWorks macros to function keys or to Option+⌘ key combinations. Because AppleWorks uses neither of these approaches for invoking its menu commands and keyboard shortcuts, the particular key combinations you choose should be of little consequence, right? Well, maybe.

Many desk accessories and control panels have key combinations you can use to pop them up or to make them perform particular functions. This can cause conflicts with your AppleWorks macros. The usual symptom of a conflict is the AppleWorks macro does not function and is overridden by the desk accessory or control panel (or vice versa). The solution is to choose another key combination for the AppleWorks macro or choose another key combination for the desk accessory or control panel, if you can.

Another problem arises if you choose the digits 1 or 2 as the key. AppleWorks will ignore the Option key when you press it with the ⌘ key and then type a number. Thus you will get Starting Points and Clippings, respectively, rather than the macro you wanted to execute.

Transferring macros to other users

You can share macros with friends and colleagues. You simply save the macros in a document file, rather than in AppleWorks itself. All your friend has to do is open the file and change each macro from a document-specific macro to an AppleWorks macro.

STEPS: Transferring Macros

1. Create a new document (choose an environment from the File ⇨ New submenu) and record the macros.

2. When saving the macros, click the Document Specific checkbox.

3. Save the document and give a copy of it to the other user.

4. The other user launches AppleWorks and opens the document in which you saved the macros.

5. The user chooses File ⇨ Macros ⇨ Edit Macros. The Edit Macros dialog box appears (see Figure 17-3, earlier in this chapter).

6. The user selects a macro to add to AppleWorks and clicks the Modify button.

7. The user removes the checkmark from the Document Specific checkbox by clicking once in the checkbox, changes other options (such as the key combination used to invoke the macro) as desired, and then clicks the OK button.

   To add other macros to AppleWorks, the user repeats Steps 6 and 7.

8. The user clicks the OK button to save the changes.

Moving On Up

The AppleWorks macros are fine for simple tasks, but you might want to investigate one of the more powerful commercial macro programs for your more complex tasks. In addition to working with AppleWorks, these macro programs also work in other programs and with the Finder.

QuicKeys (CE Software, www.cesoft.com) is a general-purpose macro utility intended for the "typical" Macintosh user. The program provides a recorder function you can use to record most macros, as well as the capability to edit macros without re-recording them.

Finally, AppleWorks has an extensive AppleScript dictionary. Teaching AppleScript is a subject for a book of its own, but Apple has extensive online documentation at www.apple.com/applescript. T&B Consulting provides quite a collection of scripting information specific to AppleWorks at www.tandb.com.au/appleworks as well as supplying sample scripts with your copy of AppleWorks 6 that might be accessed from your Scripts menu (the scroll icon on your menu bar)—and the documentation for them.

Summary

✦ Macros enable you to automate AppleWorks tasks and perform them by clicking a button or pressing an Option+⌘ key combination or function key.

✦ Every macro can be a general AppleWorks macro (available in any new document of a correct type) or document-specific (available only when a particular document is active).

✦ You can assign a macro to a Button Bar and display a custom icon on the macro's button.

✦ Although you cannot edit the steps of a macro, you can edit the options for a macro.

✦ You can delete macros when you no longer need them.

✦ You can create automatic macros that automatically run when you launch AppleWorks, open a particular document type, or create a new file in a specific environment.

✦ You can share macros with another user by creating several macros in the same document and making them document-specific. The recipient then opens the file and changes the macros to general AppleWorks macros.

✦   ✦   ✦

AppleWorks 6 and the Internet

Bookmarks, Document Links, and URL Links

One of the most interesting and useful features intro-
duced in ClarisWorks 5 was *links*. After embedding links
in an AppleWorks document, you could click the link to jump
to a particular location in the same document, open another
AppleWorks document, or launch a browser to view a Web
page on the Internet. In AppleWorks 6, the interface has been
updated, simplified, and made even more useful.

You can define three kinds of links: anchors (formerly called
bookmarks), document links, and URL links. Anchors are used
to mark places you want to be able to quickly access in a document. Document links are clickable links in a document that
display an anchor in the current document, open a different
AppleWorks document, or go to an anchor in another Apple-
Works document. URL links are links in a document that —
when clicked — instruct AppleWorks to open a connection
to the Internet, launch your default Web browser (Internet
Explorer, Netscape Navigator, or iCab, for example), and display a specific page on the World Wide Web. URL links also
can instruct your Mac to launch its default e-mail program or
connect to a file download site on the Internet. URL links can
be embedded in a normal AppleWorks document or in a Web
page you've designed in AppleWorks (see Chapter 19).

To help you create and manage links, AppleWorks 6 provides
Links, yet another floating window (see Figure 18-1).

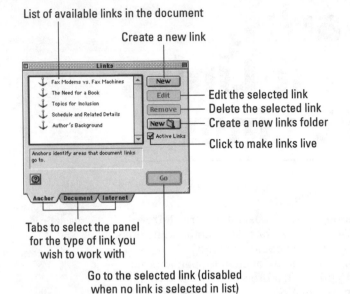

List of available links in the document

Create a new link

Edit the selected link
Delete the selected link
Create a new links folder
Click to make links live

Tabs to select the panel
for the type of link you
wish to work with

Go to the selected link (disabled
when no link is selected in list)

Figure 18-1: The Links windoid

You can use Links to create new links, jump to any defined link, and edit or delete links. To display (or close) Links, choose Format ➪ Show (or Hide) Links Window (or press Shift+⌘+M). Additionally, you can reorder the links in a Links panel's list by dragging them.

New Feature

In AppleWorks 6, you also can organize groups of links into *folders*. These are really pseudo-folders, bookkeeping conveniences that do not create new folders on any disk.

General Information About Links

As you've seen earlier in this chapter, AppleWorks has three basic link categories, but regardless of the types of links you are creating or modifying, you should understand the following basic rules and procedures.

When creating and saving links, you should remember that:

✦ Links are created by selecting text, objects, frames, or spreadsheet cells to define the link, choosing the link type tab in Links, and then clicking the New button on that panel.

✦ Regardless of whether you are creating, editing, or managing links, you can only work with one link type at a time. Click the tab for the link type you want from the bottom of Links.

✦ If you use the links-related buttons in the Button Bar (Anchor, Document Link, URL Link, and Links On/Off), you can create links by clicking buttons, rather than by selecting panels in Links.

✦ A given anchor can be associated with multiple document links. If you are creating a series of related Web pages, you might place a Home icon on each page, which displays the main Web page when clicked, for example.

✦ Links are always document-specific. When you create links of any type, they are automatically saved as part of the document.

When viewing and testing links:

✦ Text links are shown by default as blue underlined text (unless you edit the link styles). The appearance of other types of links (objects, frames, images, and spreadsheet cells) is unchanged.

✦ If the live links feature is enabled, you can test document and URL links by clicking them. When the mouse pointer moves over a text link, it changes to a pointing hand to show that a link is present. To activate a nontext document link or URL link (or to check if the item is a link), you often must click it two or three times. The number of clicks depends on the mode you are currently in and whether the link is an object, frame, or an item or selection within a frame.

✦ It's often helpful to disable live links when editing link items.

✦ The live links feature is document-specific. It must be enabled or disabled for each document.

✦ You can no longer specify the order in which links are listed in Links. They are always sorted alphabetically by name.

When moving and deleting links:

✦ If an item that defines a link is deleted, the associated link is automatically removed from Links, as well.

✦ When an item that defines a link is moved within the current document (using cut-and-paste or drag-and-drop), the link continues to work normally.

✦ Links also can be moved between AppleWorks documents using cut-and-paste or drag-and-drop routines. URL links and anchors moved in this fashion will function correctly. Document links, on the other hand, are a special case. If a document link and its anchor were originally in the same document, the destination of the document link is treated as undefined; you must create or choose a new anchor with which to associate the document link. On the other hand, if the object of the document link was another AppleWorks document or a specific bookmark in another document, the document link functions properly in the new document.

Anchors

Anchors are special, nonclickable placeholders in an AppleWorks document. You can attach an anchor to almost any item in an AppleWorks document, such as a text string, paint image or selection, draw object, frame, spreadsheet cell, or a cell range. You cannot, however, choose a table cell or cell range as an anchor. You can instantly go to a given anchor by double-clicking its name in Links, clicking its name, and then clicking the Go button in Links, or by clicking a document link that has been associated with that anchor (in the current document or a different AppleWorks document).

Although anchors are often associated with document links, they don't have to be. Such standalone anchors, however, can only be reached by double-clicking their names in Links or by selecting their name in Links and clicking the Go button.

Creating anchors

Whether you just want to mark important positions in a document so you can immediately find them, or you intend to create clickable document links that transfer the reader to a particular section in this or another AppleWorks document, you must create the necessary anchors.

STEPS: Creating a New Anchor

1. If Links isn't open, choose Format ➪ Show Links Window (or press Shift+⌘+M).

2. In the AppleWorks document, select the text string, object, image, frame, or spreadsheet cells that will serve as the anchor.

3. Click the Links Anchor tab.

4. On the Anchor panel, click the New button (the upper-right button). The New Anchor dialog box appears, as shown in Figure 18-2. Alternatively, you can click the Anchor button in the Button Bar to summon the New Anchor dialog box.

Figure 18-2: The Anchor button and the New Anchor dialog box

5. Type a name to identify the anchor. (If a text string is currently selected in the AppleWorks document, the selected text will automatically be proposed as the anchor's name.)

6. Click the OK button to create the anchor.

Note Anchors are attached to a particular text, object, image, frame, or so forth — not to a location in the document (Page 12, for example). If you delete or cut the anchor item, the anchor ceases to exist and its name is automatically removed from Links. If you move the anchor item to a new location in the document — either by dragging or using cut-and-paste — the anchor moves to the new location, too.

Editing anchors

Existing anchors can be deleted, renamed, and moved to or from folders. To delete an anchor, select its name in Links and click the Remove button.

Caution When you elect to delete an anchor (or any other type of link), the command is carried out immediately and cannot be undone.

To rename an anchor, select the anchor's name Links and click the Edit button. The Edit Anchor dialog box — identical to the New Anchor dialog box (except for the name) — appears. To change the anchor's name, edit or replace the text in the Name text box. Click the OK button to save your changes. We discuss creating and using anchor folders next.

Organizing anchors

AppleWorks helps you organize anchors in two ways:

First, you can specify the order in which they are listed in Links by dragging them into a different order.

Second, if the document contains many anchors, or you simply want to impart additional order on them (perhaps breaking them up according to key document sections), you can create folders in which to store the anchors. Anchor folders serve the same function as the folders on your hard disk in which you organize files and programs. If you like, you can even create folders nested within other folders.

STEPS: Creating a New Anchor Folder

1. Select the Anchor panel by clicking the Links Anchor tab.

2. Click the New Folder button. The New Folder dialog box appears (see Figure 18-3).

Figure 18-3: The New Folder dialog box

3. Type a name for the folder in the Name box.

4. Click the OK button to create the folder, or click Cancel if you change your mind.

Now, you can drag anchors to the new folder or even drag the folder onto another folder to nest them.

Document Links

Every document link is associated with an anchor in the current document, with another AppleWorks document, or with a specific anchor in another AppleWorks document. When you click a document link, AppleWorks automatically displays "the associated anchor or AppleWorks document. For example, you can use document links to create a live table of contents. When the user clicks an entry, the associated chapter document will open or AppleWorks will scroll the current document to the appropriate heading. You also can embed document links in Web pages you've created in AppleWorks, enabling the user to navigate to particular sections of the document by just clicking. Such document links are automatically converted to appropriate HTML instructions when you save the page as an HTML document (that is, a Web page).

STEPS: Creating a Document Link

1. If Links isn't open, choose Format ➪ Show Links Window (or press Shift+⌘+M).

2. In the AppleWorks document, select the text string, object, image, frame, or spreadsheet cells that will serve as the document link.

3. Select the Document panel in Links.

4. Click the New button. The New Document Link dialog box appears, as shown in Figure 18-4.

Tip
> You can click the Document Link button in the Button Bar to bypass Steps 1 through 4; however, you will not see the new link in the list unless Links is open and displaying the Document panel.

5. Type a name to identify the document link. (If a text string is currently selected in the AppleWorks document, the string will automatically be proposed as the document link's name.)

Tells what document you're linking to

Name the link

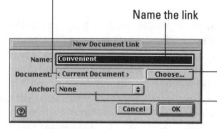

Click to get Open dialog to choose
a new destination document

Select the anchor within the destination
document from this pop up menu

Document Link button

Figure 18-4: The Document Link button and the New Document Link dialog box

6. To associate the document with an anchor in the current document, choose one from the Anchor pop-up menu.

   or

   To cause the document link to open a specific AppleWorks document to its first page, click Choose, navigate to and select the desired AppleWorks file.

   or

   To cause the document link to open a specific AppleWorks document to a particular anchor, click the Choose button, and then select the desired AppleWorks file. Then, choose an anchor from the Anchor pop-up menu.

7. Click the OK button to create the document link.

To test a document link, enable live links by clicking the Active Links checkbox in Links, choosing Format ➪ Turn Active Links On, or by clicking the Links On/Off button in the Button Bar (if the button is displayed). Then click the document link. (Note that you can go directly to any document link in the current document by selecting its name in the Links palette and clicking the Go button. This command selects the link without executing it.)

To modify a document link, select the link in Links and click the Edit button. The Edit Document Link dialog box appears, which looks just like the New Document Link dialog box. You can change the link's name, associated anchor, and the destination document to display. Click the OK button to save the changes.

Document links can be deleted by highlighting the link in Links and clicking the Remove button. Note that when you delete a Document link, the command is carried out immediately and cannot be undone.

URL Links

When you click a URL link, your Web browser opens and displays a particular page from the World Wide Web, addresses an e-mail message to a specific recipient, or performs some similar action. (See "Creating non-HTTP URL links" at the end of this chapter for additional information.) When you click a URL link, a Web browser opens if you've set up your MacOS Internet Preferences to establish a default Web browser, which is usually done automatically the first time you start your Mac after installing a new MacOS release or taking a new Mac out of the box. The document in which the URL link is embedded can be an ordinary AppleWorks document (an interoffice memo that has related information stored on the Internet or the company's intranet, for example), or it can be a Web page that was created in AppleWorks (as explained in Chapter 19) or another program.

Note   For URL links to function properly, several conditions must be met. The user must have a way to connect to the Internet or a corporate intranet (typically over a modem, network, or dedicated line), a Web browser must be installed and designated as the default browser in Internet control panel or Internet Config, and the URL address must be correct. (For more information about connecting to the Internet, see Chapter 19.)

STEPS: Creating a New URL Link

1. If Links isn't open, choose Format ➪ Show Links Window (or press Shift+⌘+M).

2. In the AppleWorks document, select the text string, object, image, frame, or spreadsheet cells that will serve as the URL link.

3. Display the Internet panel in Links.

4. Click the New button. The New URL Link dialog box appears, as shown in Figure 18-5.

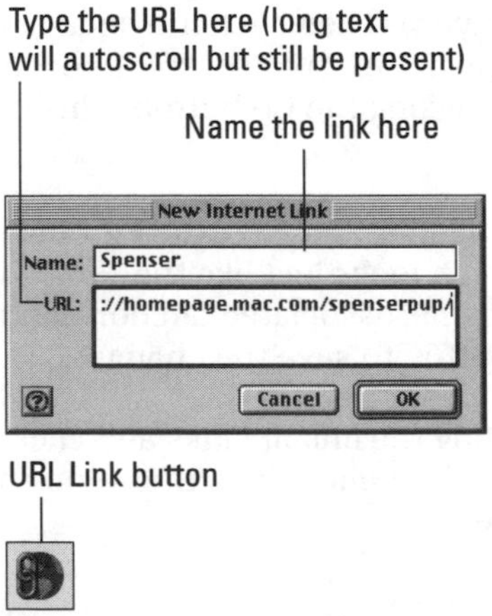

Type the URL here (long text
will autoscroll but still be present)

Name the link here

Figure 18-5: The New URL Link dialog box

URL Link button

Tip   You can click the URL Link button in the Button Bar to bypass Steps 1 through 4; however, you will not see the new link in the list unless Links is open and displaying the Internet panel.

5. Type a name to identify the URL link. (If a text string is currently selected in the AppleWorks document, the string will automatically be proposed as the URL link's name.)

6. Type a complete Web page address, mailto command, ftp command, newsgroup name, or newsgroup message ID in the URL text box. (See "Creating non-HTTP URL links" at the end of this chapter for help typing URLs.)

Note   Although the text box into which you type the Web page address looks like it will wrap, it merely autoscrolls to the left and right.

7. Click the OK button to create the URL link.

Although a hypertext URL link can be the Web page's address (such as `http://www.abbott.com`), it can just as easily be any text string (such as "Click here to visit my home page").

Tip   It's easy to mistype a URL; many Web page addresses are long and complex. To avoid mistyping the URL, open your Web browser, go to the desired Web page, copy the URL from the browser's Address box, and then paste it into the New URL dialog box.

To test a URL link, enable links by clicking the Active Links checkbox in Links, by choosing Format ➪ Turn Active Links On, or by clicking the Links On/Off button in the Button Bar (if the button is displayed). Then click the URL link. (Note that you can go directly to any URL link in the current document by selecting its name in the Links palette and clicking the Go button. This command selects the link without executing it.)

To modify a URL link, select the link in Links and click the Edit button. The Edit URL Link dialog box appears and displays the current name and URL for the chosen link. You can change the link's name, destination address, or both. Click the OK button to save the changes.

URL links can be deleted by highlighting the link in Links and clicking the Remove button. Note that when deleting a URL link, the command is carried out immediately and cannot be undone.

Quick Tips

The following quick tips show how to create links using the Button Bar rather than Links, how to use links to create Help files for complex AppleWorks documents, and how to launch your browser to view a Web URL represented by a text string in an AppleWorks document.

Using the Button Bar to create links

While it is simple to designate new links by clicking the New button in Links, it's also the slow way. If you want to quickly create new links, consider using the three links buttons and the Links On/Off button. These buttons are all available in the standard Button Bar.

Creating Help links

If you have ever wanted to create Help files for some of your more complex documents, you can now use a document link for this purpose. Figure 18-6 shows one such paired document and Help file.

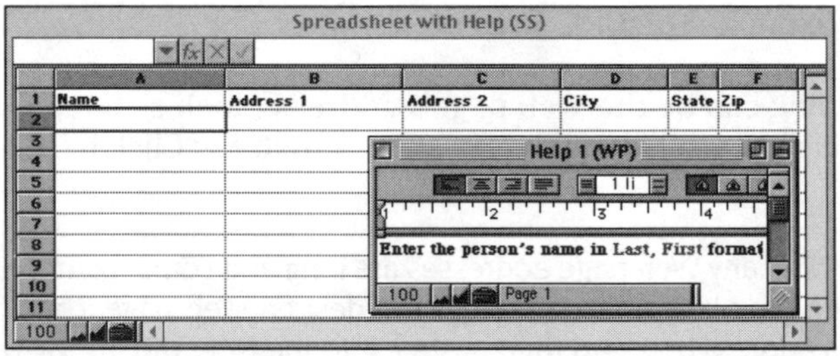

Figure 18-6: All cells in Column A are a document link to a Help file. To view the associated Help document, the user only has to click a cell in the column. Displaying the Help file can be avoided by using the cursor keys for between-cell movements or by turning off active links.

Treating a text selection as a URL

When the Open URL button (see Figure 18-7) has been added to the current Button Bar, AppleWorks can treat a selected text string as a URL, launch your browser, and attempt to display the URL's page from the World Wide Web. You can create a spreadsheet or database of technical support, shareware, or financial news URLs, for instance. To view a Web page, select the text for the URL in the AppleWorks document, and then click the Open URL button.

 Figure 18-7: The Open URL button

Creating non-HTTP URL links

While URL links are most commonly used to display particular Web pages, you also can create URL links with any of the functions shown in Table 18-1.

Table 18-1
URL Links

URL Prefix	Function(s)	Example(s)
http://	Display a Web page or a particular location on a page; download a file to user's computer	http://www.Korinna.com/index.html (display a Web page); http://www.kemco.com/update.sit.hqx (download a compressed file encoded in BinHex format)
ftp://	Enable user to download a file from an ftp (file transfer protocol) server	ftp://ftp.smartsoft.com/pub/avatar.hqx
mailto:	Launch user's e-mail program and create a message for a specific e-mail address	mailto:mjones@aol.com
news:	Display a given message from a newsgroup or a list of all messages in a newsgroup	news:340BF126.2208@acenet.com (specific message ID); news:comp.sys.mac.databases (list of all messages from a newsgroup)

Summary

✦ To provide improved connectivity within and between documents, Apple-Works 6 supports three kinds of links: anchors (a marked location in a document), document links (a link to an anchor in the same or a different document or to another document), and URL links (links to pages on the World Wide Web, newsgroup messages, downloadable files, and so on). Links are created and managed in the Links windoid.

✦ Many items in AppleWorks documents can be designated as links — including text strings, paint images or selections, draw objects, frames, and spreadsheet cells.

✦ The Button Bar contains buttons you can click to quickly create new links. The buttons duplicate commands found in the Links windoid.

✦ With active links enabled, you can test document and URL links by clicking them.

✦ When clicked, a document link can bring you to a selected anchor in the current document, open another AppleWorks document to its first page, or open another AppleWorks document to a particular anchor.

✦ A document link or URL link also can be executed by double-clicking the link name in the Links windoid.

✦ You can locate a link by selecting its name in the Links windoid and clicking the Go button in Links.

✦　　✦　　✦

Creating Web Pages for the Internet

The World Wide Web—a network of computers providing information and resources on the Internet—grew out of a hypertext project started at CERN, the European Laboratory for Particle Physics. As a resource for finding information and services ranging from ancient Mayan archeological digs to pizza deliveries, the World Wide Web (WWW)—or Web, for short—has become a centerpiece of the information super-highway. To access information on the Web, you use a hyper-text-based browser application that leads you to the desired documents and then displays that information on your computer screen.

At the heart of the Web is a platform-independent page descrip-tion language called HyperText Markup Language (HTML). Based on the Standard Generalized Markup Language (SGML), HTML is used to prepare documents (referred to as Web pages) for the Web that contain embedded formatting codes. Different codes (commonly referred to as tags) are used to designate titles, headings, text formatting, and hypertext links. Figure 19-1 shows a typical Web page.

To access the WWW and display Web pages on your computer, you must have access to the Internet—either through an infor-mation service (such as CompuServe, Prodigy, or America Online), from an Internet service provider, or through a direct connection (such as your school, corporation, or organization). You must also have an application called a Web browser, such as Netscape Navigator, Netscape Communicator, Internet Explorer, or iCab. A Web browser interprets the HTML code, displaying it as formatted text and graphics.

The HTML code

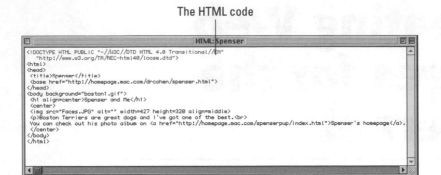

The Web page the code produces (when viewed in a Web browser)

Figure 19-1: The HTML code at the top produces the Web page at the bottom.

If you're not content to just look at other people's Web pages, you can use Apple-Works's HTML translator to design your own Web pages in the word processor. With AppleWorks's capability to launch your preferred browser, you can quickly see how your page will look when viewed on the Internet by others.

Note If you previously used the WWW [HTML] stationery document to design Web pages with ClarisWorks 4 or the HTML file format translator in ClarisWorks and Apple-Works 5, this chapter is essential reading. The procedures and features for creating Web pages in AppleWorks 6 have dramatically changed.

What Is HTML?

If you can remember the early days of personal computing (way back in the late 1970s) and the first word processing programs, you're already familiar with the way HTML works. Back then, if you wanted to print some selected text in bold or italic, you had to embed control codes in the document—one to enable boldface (at the beginning of the text string) and a second to disable boldface (at the end of the text string).

HTML works in much the same way. Most tags work in pairs; the first tag enables the feature and a second copy of the tag that is preceded by a slash (/) disables the feature. For instance, to mark a level-one heading, the text is surrounded by a pair of tags like this:

```
<H1>HTML for Fun and Profit</H1>
```

Note HTML defines *headings* in six *levels*, H1 through H6. A level-one head is the most important and is, by default, shown in the largest font size. Each successive heading level is in a decreasing font size. If you think of an HTML page as a book, then a level-one head might correspond to a part, a level-two head to a chapter, a level-three head to a section, and so forth.

When a browser sees this tagged text, it interprets the tags and then formats the text according to the conventions set for the browser—typically, a level-one head is displayed in a large, bold font.

Note Little standardization exists among Web browsers. Unlike PostScript (a device-independent printing language that provides the same results on a wide variety of printers), conventions set in the user's browser application determine the way HTML text is displayed. Thus, while a particular head might appear as 24-point Times in one browser, it might appear in a smaller font size in all capital letters when viewed with a different browser.

Using the AppleWorks HTML Translator

When you use AppleWorks 6 to design Web pages, the program simultaneously functions as a word processor and a crude browser. There's no need to apply HTML tags as you did in ClarisWorks 4, and you don't have to apply HTML-specific styles to things as you did in ClarisWorks and AppleWorks 5. Instead of manually typing tags or choosing them from an HTML stylesheet, you simply format the page as you would any other AppleWorks document. Using the Links windoid, you can add hyperlinks to the documents, which can be used to navigate within the page or to a different page or site on the World Wide Web.

Instead of displaying the tags as part of the text (as most text editors, word processors, and HTML editors do), AppleWorks presents the document as an approximation of what it might look like in a browser. As a result, you don't see the tags at all, unless you later open the document as a text file rather than as an AppleWorks file. When you save the document as an HTML file, AppleWorks does the necessary conversions for you — adding HTML tags as necessary and changing all images on the page to PNG (Portable Network Graphics) or JPEG (Joint Photographic Experts Group) files.

Note

In previous versions, GIF (Graphics Interchange Format) was used rather than PNG; however, the licensing fees imposed by Unisys for the usage of their patented Lempel-Ziv-Welch (LZW) compression technology in GIF has caused Apple and others to deemphasize GIF files in favor of the open PNG standard. You can still open GIF files with AppleWorks because the decompressor is not subject to the license fee, but AppleWorks will not create them. If you want to use GIF files, we would recommend a shareware utility such as GraphicConverter (www.lemkesoft.de).

Prerequisites and caveats

Consider the following information when deciding whether to use AppleWorks to create HTML documents:

✦ You should know how to use the AppleWorks word processing environment, as well as the Button Bar, Styles windoid, and Styles pop-up button in the Button Bar. (For more information on these topics, refer to Chapters 3, 12, and 15, respectively.)

✦ You should have Internet access (through an information service, Internet service provider, or direct network connection) and a Web browser, as discussed earlier in this chapter. Although you can create and view your Web pages exclusively in AppleWorks, you create HTML documents to prepare pages that will be displayed on the World Wide Web and viewed by others in their browsers.

✦ Although knowing HTML is not essential, a basic understanding of HTML is helpful — particularly if you want to tweak the HTML files generated by or HTML preferences used by AppleWorks or understand the techniques used by others to create their Web pages. Similarly, you also need to consider HTML style. The correct use of HTML only ensures that your document will display properly, not that it will be attractive or make efficient use of space, for example. If you are new to HTML, see "Quick Tips" at the end of this chapter for useful reference material concerning HTML definitions, coding practices, and style.

✦ You should understand that AppleWorks's HTML support is relatively basic, albeit improved over that present in earlier versions. Although you can certainly use AppleWorks to create attractive Web pages (complete with graphics and hyperlinks to other pages), you will find it difficult to design the eye-popping pages like those you've seen in magazines or on corporate Web sites — unless you're willing to work in text mode and enter and modify the necessary HTML tags by hand, adding JavaScript for some of the other special effects. A better approach is to use one of the many Web page design programs or editors, such as FileMaker Home Page, Adobe GoLive, BBEdit, or Dreamweaver.

✦ AppleWorks 6 adds the capability of sharing AppleWorks documents with other AppleWorks users over the Web without the necessity of using a browser. While this feature is quite useful if you know that your audience is composed solely of AppleWorks users, it does limit your document's reach.

New Feature   Sharing AppleWorks documents with other AppleWorks users over the Web without having to use a browser is a new feature.

Configuring AppleWorks to work with a Web browser

Although you can do all your work in AppleWorks 6, you should have an installed Web browser (or two or three) so you can see your creations as they will look to others viewing them on the Web. By clicking the Open Document in Browser button on the Button Bar, you can instruct AppleWorks to convert the current document to HTML format and then display it in your chosen browser. Because creating Web pages is an iterative process, this is the best way to design pages in AppleWorks 6.

STEPS: Specifying a Web Browser to Use with AppleWorks

1. If the Button Bar is currently hidden, choose Window ➪ Show Button Bar (or press Shift+⌘+X).

2. If you have not already added the Configure Internet button (shown in Figure 19-2) to the Button Bar, do so now — it's in the General group of buttons.

  Figure 19-2: The Configure Internet button

3. Click the Configure Internet button. Your Internet control panel (Internet Config — a program used to configure a Mac for using the Internet — if you're still using MacOS 8.1) launches, as shown in Figure 19-3.

4. If you don't see a tab named *Advanced*, choose Edit ➪ User Mode and select Advanced from the dialog box that appears.

5. Select the Advanced tab in the Internet control panel window.

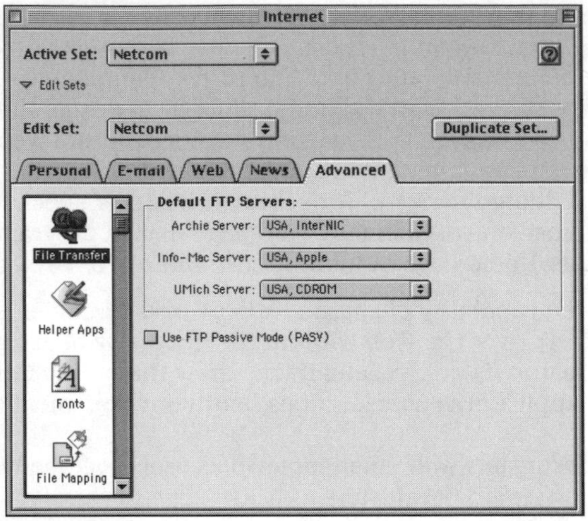

Figure 19-3: Configure your Macintosh for the Internet by setting options on the various tabs in the Internet control panel (MacOS 8.5 or later).

6. Select Helper Apps from the scrolling list on the left. The "Helper Application Assignments" list appears in the panel.

7. Scroll down and locate the HTTP item, and then click the Change button. The Edit Helper Application dialog box appears. Click the Select button.

8. In the Open dialog box that appears, locate and select your Web browser (such as Internet Explorer or Netscape Communicator), and click the Select button. The Open button's name changes to Select when a file is selected in the list.

9. To save your changes, click the OK button, choose File ➪ Save Settings, and exit Internet control panel by choosing File ➪ Quit.

> **Note** When you choose a browser in the Internet control panel, that browser becomes the default browser for all Internet-related programs — not just AppleWorks. If you have another browser installed on your Macintosh that you occasionally want to use, you can still launch it by double-clicking its icon in the Finder.

Creating Web pages

AppleWorks 5 included a dozen Web Page Template stationery documents to help you design Web pages. In AppleWorks 6, no such templates are included, although you can still use the stationery from AppleWorks or ClarisWorks 5, if you like. We suggest you create pages from scratch using ordinary word processing documents. Regardless of the approach you use, AppleWorks attempts to match your paragraph formatting, text formatting, and graphic placement as closely as possible — within the limits of the HTML translator — when converting the document to HTML.

If the Button Bar is currently hidden, choose Window ⇨ Show Button Bar (or press Shift+⌘+X). If you have not already done so, add the Internet buttons to the Button Bar as described in Chapter 12. The Internet buttons that are not standard on the Button Bar are shown in Figure 19-4. Create a new word processing document, either from scratch or using one of the templates.

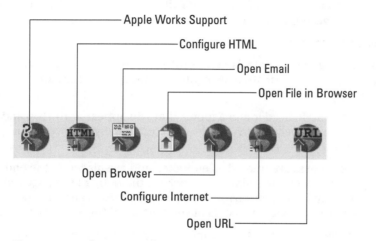

Figure 19-4: The Internet buttons

Now that you have a word processing document onscreen and have displayed the Internet buttons, you are ready to begin creating the contents for your Web page.

As you type, you can press the Return key to end a paragraph or press the Shift-Return keys to create a line break. Most browsers display paragraphs by adding white space after each paragraph. A break, on the other hand, simply starts a new line without adding white space after it. You also can make text boldface or italic by selecting it and then choosing the appropriate option from the Text ⇨ Style submenu, or by clicking the Bold or Italic button on the Button Bar.

Considerations when creating pages

When creating your pages, be aware of the following suggestions and limitations that affect the way pages are translated:

✦ Do not bother using multiple fonts when formatting text. The fonts displayed will be based on the settings made in the viewer's browser for serif, sans serif, and monospaced fonts. On the other hand, you can vary the size, style, and color of text, and AppleWorks will attempt to match it.

✦ You should avoid formatting text with the underline style. Underlined text in a Web page normally indicates a hypertext link and might confuse people who are viewing the page.

> **Note** The Outline, Shadow, Condense, and Extend styles are converted to plain text. Similarly, Double Underline is converted to a single underline. Both Superior and Superscript are converted to superscript, and both Inferior and Subscript are converted to subscript. These mappings are in the advanced HTML Export settings described under "Configuring HTML Import and Export," later in this chapter.

✦ Do not use tabs to format text. When the HTML file is generated by the translator, tabs are converted into single spaces.

✦ Soft hyphens are ignored.

✦ You can use the alignment controls on the ruler bar to set left-, right-, or center-aligned text. Text formatted as justified is interpreted the same as left-aligned text.

✦ You can specify a single header and a footer that will appear at the top and bottom of the page, respectively. A header is automatically followed by a horizontal rule and a footer is preceded by one.

✦ Footnotes and endnotes are treated as endnotes and are placed at the end of the Web page. Footnote or endnote numbers in the body of the page are shown as superscript numbers surrounded by parentheses, and they become clickable links to their respective notes at the bottom of the Web page.

✦ Do not use the Insert Page Number command to generate page numbers. Such page numbers are displayed as the number (#) sign.

✦ To create bulleted lists, format the items using the Diamond, Bullet, or Checklist outline styles.

✦ To create numbered lists, format the items using the Harvard, Legal, or Number outline styles.

✦ In ClarisWorks 4, rules were inserted by clicking a button on the Shortcuts palette. This button no longer exists in AppleWorks 6. To add a horizontal rule to a page (useful for breaking a page into sections), position the cursor and choose Insert Page Break or Insert Section Break from the Format menu. (AppleWorks ignores automatic page breaks and column breaks when creating HTML files.)

✦ To create tables in Web pages, use a table or a spreadsheet frame. The table will be aligned with the left or right margin, depending on its position in the original document.

✦ Pages can include in-line and floating graphics and frames. An in-line graphic or frame appears in its original position. A floating object or frame is placed at the left or right margin, depending on its location in the original document. All graphics are automatically converted to PNG or JPEG files, depending on the option chosen in the HTML Preferences (Basic) dialog box. (See "Adding graphics and a page background," later in this chapter.)

✦ Floating text frames are ignored.

Working with links

A hyperlink is a text string or graphic that, when clicked, typically displays another Web page or scrolls to a different position in the current page. AppleWorks 6 supports three types of links: Anchors, Document Links, and URL (Uniform Resource Locator) Links, as described in Chapter 18. Anchors are placeholders in the document; an anchor is the object of a document link. When a document link is clicked, the browser scrolls to display the anchor in the same Web page associated with that document link. A URL link is used to link to a different Web page — either within the current Web site or a completely different site. (For information about other types of URL links you can embed in Web pages, see "Creating non-HTTP URL links" in Chapter 18.)

Note

Anchors and document links can be attached to text strings, objects, graphics, paint frames, or spreadsheet frames.

Links can be created by clicking Internet buttons on the Button Bar, or by using the Links windoid (choose Format ➪ Show Links Window or press Shift+⌘+M). Because the Button Bar approach is extremely simple, it's described here. For information about using the Links windoid, refer to Chapter 18.

Creating document links and anchors

To let the user easily navigate within a given Web page, you only need to pair a document link (a clickable text string or graphic) with an anchor (another text string or graphic or a frame or table cell/cell range) in the same Web page. When the user clicks the document link, the browser automatically scrolls to display the specified anchor. You can pair document links with anchors to implement a live table of contents, or to create clickable buttons at the bottom of each Web page to carry the user forward or backward one page, for example.

STEPS: Creating a Paired Document Link and Anchor

1. Select the text string or graphic that will serve as the bookmark (the position in the Web page that will be displayed when the associated document link is clicked).

2. Click the Anchor button (see Figure 19-5) in the Button Bar. The New Anchor dialog box appears.

 Figure 19-5: The Anchor button (left) and Document Link button (right)

3. Name the anchor and click the OK button.

4. Select the text string or graphic that will serve as the clickable document link.

5. Click the Document Link button (just shown in Figure 19-5) in the Button Bar. The New Document Link dialog box appears (see Figure 19-6).

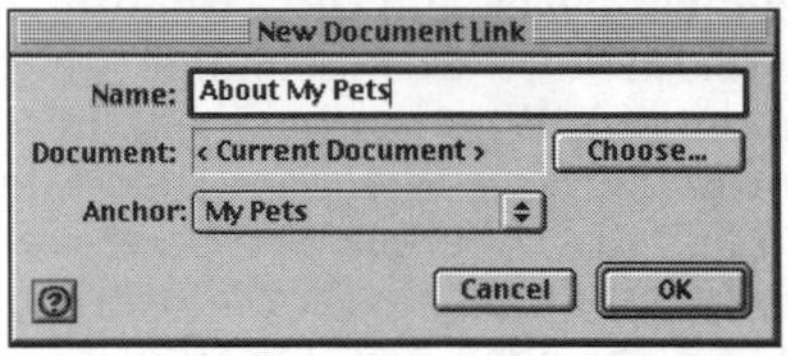

Figure 19-6: The New Document Link dialog box

6. Name the document link, choose an anchor to associate with the link from the Anchor pop-up menu, and then click the OK button.

If AppleWorks's Active Links feature is enabled (the default), you can test document links within the AppleWorks document. (Otherwise, links can only be tested in a Web browser.) To enable or disable active links, click the Links On/Off button in the Button Bar (see Figure 19-7). Repeatedly clicking this button switches active links on and off. (You also can enable or disable live links in the Links windoid or by choosing Format ➪ Turn Active Links On/Off.)

Figure 19-7: The Links On/Off button

Creating URL links

When clicked, a URL link carries the user to a different page on your or another person's Web site, according to the address or URL you specify when you create the link. A URL link is clickable and can be a text string, graphic, object, text frame, paint frame, spreadsheet frame, spreadsheet cells or range, or a selection in a paint image. Some examples of URLs are:

✦ www.apple.com/appleworks — This URL points to Apple Computer's AppleWorks home page on the World Wide Web.

✦ www.aladdinsys.com — This URL points to Aladdin Systems' home page. The company produces StuffIt and a number of other products that are extremely helpful when transmitting data across the Internet.

✦ www.macworld.com/buyers/hotdeals — This URL points to a particular page within *Macworld's* Web site.

> **Note**   URL links also can be used to download a file from an FTP (file transfer protocol) site, open the user's e-mail program to send a message, or to display a message from a newsgroup. (For information about these types of URL links, see "Creating non-HTTP URL links" in Chapter 18.)

STEPS: Creating a URL Link

1. Select the text string, object, graphic, or other item that will serve as the URL link (the location in the Web page that the user will click).

2. Click the URL Link button (see Figure 19-8) in the Internet Button Bar. The New URL Link dialog box appears (see Figure 19-9).

Figure 19-8: The URL Link button

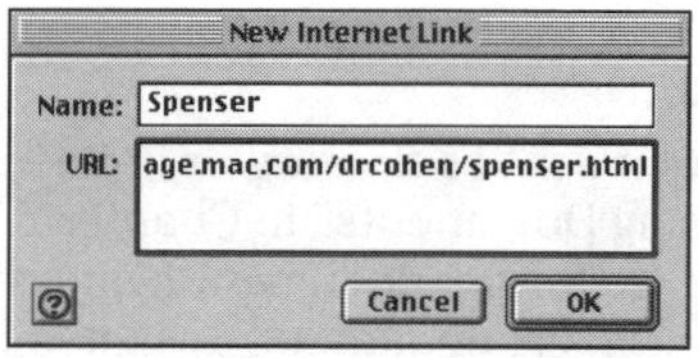

Figure 19-9: The New URL Link dialog box

3. Type a name for the URL link in the Name text box.

   The link's name is simply an identifier to enable you to distinguish one link from another. The specific name chosen is entirely up to you.

4. Type the destination address of the link in the URL text box and click the OK button. The link is added to the Links windoid's Internet panel for the current document.

> **Note**
>
> For some reason (our belief is that it is a bug), AppleWorks 6 doesn't wrap the text within the URL text box. Instead, it autoscrolls left and right as you edit the URL. For this reason, part of your URL will be scrolled out of view, as shown earlier in Figure 19-9 (unless your URL is very short).

If active links are currently enabled for the document, you can test the link by clicking it. Your Mac will attempt to connect to the Internet (if you are not already connected), your browser launches, and an attempt is made to find the Web page specified by the link's URL.

Users normally see text links as underlined text (such as Current Catalog or Résumé of Robert Jones), frequently in another color (blue is typically the default). Objects such as buttons or pictures are also frequently used to indicate URL links. Modern browsers typically have one or more ways of showing that a graphic is actually a link, rather than just another picture. In Internet Explorer, for example, when the user moves the mouse pointer over any URL link, the link address is shown in the browser's status bar and the mouse pointer changes to a hand pointer.

Note   By default, text URL links are formatted as blue underlined text in most browsers. In AppleWorks 5, you had to edit the styles for anchors (called bookmarks in that version), document links, and URL links if you wanted to alter their appearance. In AppleWorks 6, you also can create styles for these entities; however, many attributes could be overridden by the viewer's Web browser.

Modifying links

To change or delete anchors, document links, or URL links, open the Links windoid for the document (choose Format ⇨ Show Links Window or press Shift+⌘+M). Select the tab for the type of link you want to modify. Select the appropriate link from the displayed list, and then click the Edit or Remove button, as appropriate.

Adding graphics and a page background

Graphics can be added to your Web page document as floating or in-line images. (Refer to "Adding Graphics to Word Processing Documents" in Chapter 3.) The images can be pasted or dragged onto the page from a document in another graphics program, imported by choosing the File ⇨ Insert command, designed in Apple-Works, or added from Clippings (refer to Chapter 13).

New Feature   GIF, PNG, and JPEG images are the only types of viewable graphics that can be embedded in Web pages. AppleWorks 6 now supports both the PNG and JPEG formats. When you save a Web page as an HTML file, AppleWorks automatically converts all embedded images to the PNG or JPEG format, as specified in the Configure HTML dialog box when Export Preferences (Basic) is chosen from the pop-up menu (see Figure 19-10). The following steps explain how to set a preferred export format for embedded images and how to select a background color or graphic for Web pages.

Set a background color or image

> **Configure HTML**
>
> Topic: [Export Preferences (Basic) ▼]
>
> ┌ Document Background ─────────────
> │ **Choose a background for your HTML document**
> │ Color: [None ▼]
> │ [Set Background Image...] [Remove Background Image]
> │ Image:
> └──────────────────────────────────
>
> ┌ Images ──────────────────────────
> │ **Specify the format for exported AppleWorks images**
> │ Image Export Format: [JPEG ▼]
> └──────────────────────────────────
>
> ⓘ   [Restore All HTML Defaults] [Cancel] [OK]

Select an output image format

Figure 19-10: Set graphic-handling options and specify a background color or image for Web pages in the Configure HTML dialog box's Export Preferences section.

STEPS: Setting Basic Export Preferences

1. If the Button Bar is currently hidden, choose Window ➪ Show Button Bar (or press Shift+⌘+X).

2. If you haven't added the Internet buttons to the Button Bar as recommended previously, do so now.

3. Click the Configure HTML button, as shown in Figure 19-11. The HTML Configuration dialog box appears (as shown earlier in Figure 19-10).

 Figure 19-11: The Configure HTML button

4. To specify a background color to appear behind the Web page, choose it from the pop-up Color menu.

 Tip

Other than None, you have only eight choices in this pop-up menu for a background color. You can, however, edit the generated HTML to use different colors if you know the RGB (red-green-blue) codes for the desired color. One way to do this is to double-click the color you want to use in Accents and look at the values in the RGB Picker. Unfortunately, this gives you your values as percentages, and you'll need to do a little math (multiply the percentage by 255, and then convert the result to hexidecimal). An easier way is to use a tool such as GraphicConverter, Photoshop, or other similar tools to do the conversion.

5. To choose a background image to appear behind the Web page, click the Set Background Image button and select a graphic file from the Open dialog box that appears. (If you do not want a background image for the current Web page and one is currently set, click the Remove Background Image button.)

 Note

Although you can specify both a background image and a color, it is more common to choose only one or the other. A background image will tile to fill the window if it is smaller than the window. See Figure 19-1, earlier in this chapter, for an example.

6. Select an export format for converting embedded graphics from the Image Export Format pop-up menu.

7. To accept the new settings, click the OK button.

Note

The options you choose in the Configure HTML dialog box affect all future Web pages you design in AppleWorks — not just the current page. If you want to use a different background image or color for a new page, you must change the settings in the Configure HTML dialog box.

Configuring HTML Import and Export

If you don't want to have the Configure HTML button on the Button Bar, you also can reach this dialog box by choosing Edit ⇨ Preferences ⇨ HTML Import/Export. The Configure HTML dialog box has four presentations based on your choice from the Topic pop-up menu — "HTML Export (Basic)," as described previously, is just one. You also can choose "HTML Export (Advanced)," "HTML Import (Advanced)," and "Escape Codes (Advanced)," as shown in Figure 19-12.

In general, it is inadvisable to modify the advanced settings; however, some minor modifications are fairly common and reasonable. In both the advanced export and import panels, you see a list of AppleWorks Attributes and HTML Start Tags and End Tags. You cannot add recognized AppleWorks Attributes to the list, but you can modify the HTML to which they correspond. For example, if you don't want the extra lines in your HTML document, you can eliminate the NEWLINE characters around the Table Row or Table Cell (Open/CloseTableCol) tags when exporting. Similarly, you might want to have Centering export with the same tags (<CENTER> and </CENTER>) that it imports — this is especially true if your document centers a number of graphics. The Escape Codes exist because certain characters (such as <, &, >) are co-opted by HTML and you need a way to display in your text without confusing the Web browser. Similarly, ASCII is only fully standardized on the first 128 characters (0-127) and accented characters, as well as other characters (fonts placed in the upper [high ASCII] 128 character positions vary from platform to platform). This necessitates a series of escape codes to map the ASCII characters to codes that will be platform-independent. You will probably not touch this table.

> **Note**
>
> You should be aware that HTML tags are not case-sensitive, but the Codes are (for example, ñ denotes a lowercase character, but Ñ denotes an uppercase character). Additionally, you should make sure that the names you use in your URL links match in case, because many Web servers (in particular, those on Unix platforms) are case-sensitive when dealing with file names.

Viewing the Web page in a browser

Although AppleWorks can show you an approximation of what your Web page will look like in a Web browser, you must view the page through a real Web browser, such as Netscape Communicator, iCab, or Internet Explorer, to see what it will really look like. If you click the Open File in Browser button on the Button Bar (see Figure 19-13), an HTML file is automatically created from the current AppleWorks document and displayed in your designated browser (see Figure 19-14).

> **Tip**
>
> You also can manually load any saved HTML file by choosing the browser's Open, Open File, or Open Local command. As you make changes to the HTML document in AppleWorks, you can view the modifications in your browser by clicking the Open File in Browser button. (Click the browser's Reload or Refresh button to make sure you are viewing the most recently saved copy of the HTML document.)

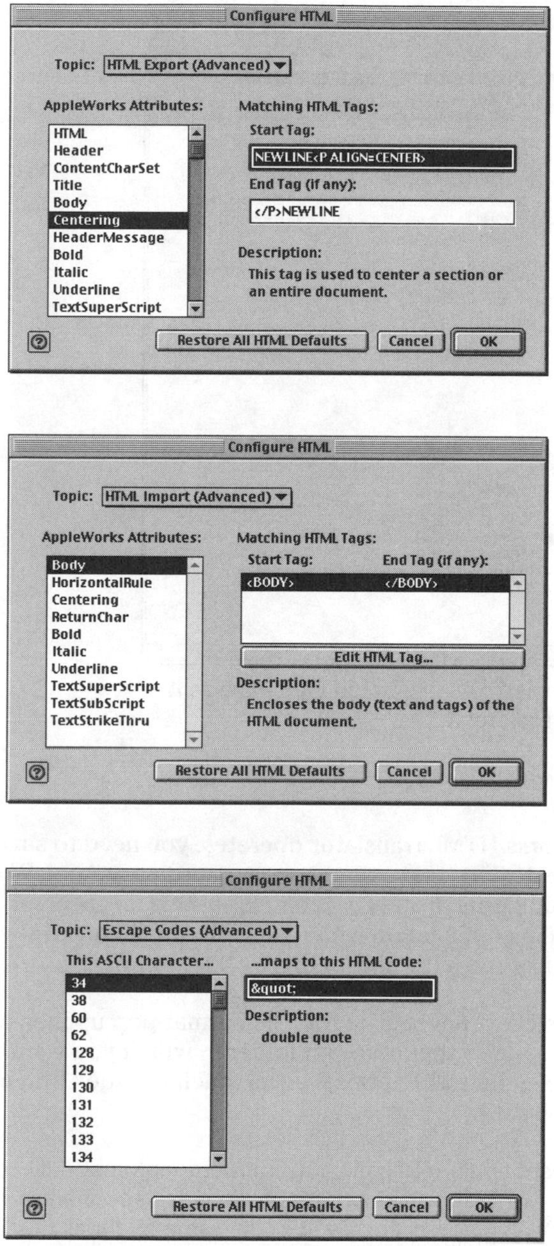

Figure 19-12: Your advanced Configure HTML options

Figure 19-13: Click this button to convert the current document to HTML format and display it in your browser.

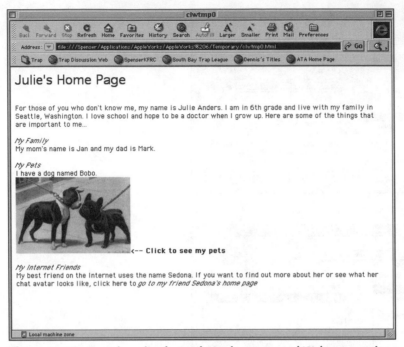

Figure 19-14: Here is a simple AppleWorks-generated Web page as it appears when viewed in Internet Explorer 4.5.

Saving an HTML document

Because of the way the AppleWorks HTML translator operates, you need to save two files for every Web page you create. First, save the page as an ordinary AppleWorks document. You will make any additional, necessary changes in this file. Second, you must use the Save As command in combination with the HTML translator to save the page in HTML format. You will post the latter file on the World Wide Web.

To create the HTML file, choose File ➪ Save As. In the File Format pop-up menu, select HTML as the format. Navigate to the drive and folder in which you want to save the file, type a file name ending with .htm or .html (such as Index.htm or Index.html), and click the Save button.

Tip   When you save the document as an HTML file, the translator automatically converts all graphics in the file to either PNG or JPEG format (as specified in the Configure HTML dialog box). All graphics are saved in the same folder as the one specified for the HTML file. Because it is easier to maintain a Web page if you keep all necessary files together, you might want to create a separate folder for your Web page and its graphics.

When you are ready to post your Web pages for others to view, contact your Internet provider or information service for instructions concerning uploading the page elements to their Web server.

Opening an existing HTML document

If you later need to make changes to a Web page you created in AppleWorks, you should open and edit the original AppleWorks document, rather than the exported HTML file. This will enable you to continue working with the Web page as a normal document — shielding you from the embedded HTML codes. AppleWorks also can open and convert HTML code created outside of AppleWorks so you can work with it as you do a normal AppleWorks file.

Note   The HTML Import capabilities are even more constrained than the Export capabilities. For example, although you can export tables and spreadsheet frames to create HTML tables, the HTML Import translator will not recognize tables on import and you will lose the formatting.

On the other hand, you might sometimes prefer to work directly with the actual HTML code. The following steps explain how to open existing HTML documents as AppleWorks documents and as HTML documents.

Note   HTML documents you retrieve from the Web almost certainly will be littered with HTML tags that are not supported by the AppleWorks translator. They will appear in the file as embedded tags and formatting codes.

STEPS: Opening an HTML File in AppleWorks

1. In AppleWorks, choose File ➪ Open, and then navigate to the drive and then folder that contains the HTML document you want to open.

2. To open an AppleWorks document you created, simply select the original document — not the converted HTML file — from the file list and click the Open button.

   or

   To open a foreign HTML file as an AppleWorks document (similar to what appears when designing pages in AppleWorks), choose HTML from the File Format pop-up menu, select the HTML file you want to open, and click the Open button. AppleWorks attempts to convert the file to AppleWorks format prior to opening it.

   or

   To work directly with the embedded HTML code in an AppleWorks-created or foreign HTML file, select the HTML file, and click the Open button. This will bring it in as plain text with all the embedded codes.

Summary of File Procedures

Even if you have some HTML experience or have already read the reading material suggested at the end of this chapter, if you keep the following points and procedures in mind you'll have a much easier time using AppleWorks to create and edit Web pages.

✦ You create HTML files from a normal AppleWorks word processing document. AppleWorks makes the necessary conversions when you save the document as an HTML file.

✦ **Saving an HTML document:** Choose File ➪ Save As, choose HTML from the File Format pop-up menu, add .htm or .html to the end of the file name, and click the Save button. The document is converted to HTML format. If you think you might need to make further modifications to the document, save it as a normal AppleWorks document, too (after removing the .htm or .html extension).

✦ **Opening an HTML file:** If you want to make changes to an AppleWorks-generated Web page, open the original AppleWorks document — not the HTML file. To convert non-AppleWorks HTML files so they can be worked with in AppleWorks, choose HTML as the file format in the Open dialog box. (The only reason to use the normal Open procedure is if you want to view the actual HTML tags in the file rather than the formatted text.) To use the Internet-related buttons when working with the document, add the Internet buttons to the Button Bar.

Quick Tips

The following quick tips offer methods for gaining a better understanding of HTML, as well as ways to work more productively and efficiently with HTML.

Learn from others

Perhaps the fastest way to learn about HTML conventions and how to create pages that have class is by examining other people's Web pages. Most browsers have a Save, Save Page, Save Source, Source, or View Source command that enables you to examine and save the HTML code of any page you're currently viewing. Grab some good examples from the Web in this manner and check out the tags they used by opening the document in AppleWorks.

More powerful HTML editors

If you want to move beyond the tags supported by the AppleWorks HTML translator, you might want to check out one of the many Web page layout programs, such as FileMaker Home Page, Dreamweaver (Macromedia), and GoLive (Adobe Systems). Many advanced designers might prefer to work in a text or an HTML editor, such as BBEdit (Bare Bones Software).

Help with HTML

If your appetite for HTML has been whetted, several excellent sources of in-depth HTML information are available — in print and on the Web itself. Several titles from IDG Books Worldwide explain how to work with HTML:

✦ *Creating Cool HTML 4 Web Pages, 2nd Edition* by Dave Taylor

✦ *HTML & Web Publishing Secrets* by Jim Heid

✦ *HTML 4 For Dummies, 3rd Edition* by Ed Tittel and Stephen Nelson James

✦ *HTML Master Reference* by Heather Williamson

✦ *Teach Yourself HTML Visually* by Ruth Maran

In addition, some useful documents you can find on the Web include the following:

✦ **A Beginner's Guide to HTML:**

www.ncsa.uiuc.edu/General/Internet/WWW/HTMLPrimer.html

✦ **HTML Quick Reference:**

www.cc.ukans.edu/~acs/docs/other/HTML_quick.shtml

✦ **HTML 4.0 Tags:**

http://stars.com/Authoring/HTML/4/Tags

✦ **HTML 4.01 Specification (the definitive standards document):**

www.w3.org/TR/html4

Note

Unlike books, the content of Web sites changes constantly. Occasionally, the particular site that contains an item of interest — like these documents about HTML — also changes. (Don't blame us if they've moved.)

Summary

✦ AppleWorks 5 included a dozen Web Page Templates you could use to design a simple Web page. These did not ship with AppleWorks 6; however, they can still be used. As an alternative, you can create Web pages from scratch in an AppleWorks word processing document.

✦ AppleWorks 6 provides a translator that enables you to create, edit, and save documents in HTML format — the language used to display pages on the World Wide Web. The translator attempts to match the formatting you have applied to the document as closely as possible, although it is deficient in many of the more advanced HTML areas.

✦ The Internet Button Bar buttons enable you to configure AppleWorks (and the rest of your applications) for use with a Web browser, set conversion preferences, add document and URL links to the page, and display the current document in the browser as a finished Web page.

✦ All graphics in a document are automatically changed to Web-compatible PNG or JPEG files when you save a document as an HTML file.

✦ You can modify the HTML that AppleWorks will produce by making changes to the Advanced settings in the Configure HTML dialog box.

✦   ✦   ✦

Keyboard Shortcuts

Tables A-1 through A-16 list AppleWorks keyboard short-cuts that will increase your productivity and make you feel at ease if you're not used to using a mouse, or you don't like taking your hands away from the keyboard.

Table A-1
General Menu Commands (Available in Most Environments)

Command	Key Sequence	Menu
Bold	⌘+B	Text ⇨ Style or Format ⇨ Style
Center	⌘+\	Format ⇨ Alignment or Alignment pop-up menu in the Paragraph dialog box
Check Document Spelling	⌘+= (equal sign)	Edit ⇨ Writing Tools
Check Selection Spelling	Shift+⌘+Y	Edit ⇨ Writing Tools
Clear	Clear	Edit
Close	⌘+W	File
Copy	⌘+C, F3	Edit
Cut	⌘+X, F2	Edit
Find/Change	⌘+F	Edit ⇨ Find/Change
Find Again	⌘+E	Edit ⇨ Find/Change
Find Selection	Shift+⌘+E	Edit ⇨ Find/Change
Frame Links	⌘+L	Options
Help Contents	⌘+?, Help	Help
Italic	⌘+I	Text ⇨ Style or Format ⇨ Style
Justify	Shift+⌘+\	Format ⇨ Alignment
Larger	Shift+⌘+>	Text ⇨ Size or Format ⇨ Size
Left	⌘+[	Format ⇨ Alignment
New (default environment)	⌘+N	File
Open	⌘+O	File
Other	Shift+⌘+O	Text ⇨ Size or Format ⇨ Size
Page View (Notes View when in Presentation)	Shift+⌘+P	Window
Paste	⌘+V, F4	Edit
Plain Text	⌘+T	Text ⇨ Style or Format ⇨ Style
Print	⌘+P	File
Quit	⌘+Q	File
Record Macro/Stop Recording	Shift+⌘+J	File ⇨ Macros

Command	Key Sequence	Menu
Right	⌘+]	Format ⇨ Alignment
Save	⌘+S	File
Save As	Shift+⌘+S	File
Select All	⌘+A	Edit
Show/Hide Accents	⌘+K	Window
Show/Hide Clippings	⌘+2	File
Show/Hide Button Bar	Shift+⌘+X	Window
Show/Hide Links Window	Shift+⌘+M	Format
Show/Hide Rulers	Shift+⌘+U	Format ⇨ Rulers
Show/Hide Starting Points	⌘+1	File
Show/Hide Styles	Shift+⌘+W	Format
Show/Hide Tools	Shift+⌘+T	Window
Smaller	Shift+⌘+<	Text ⇨ Size or Format ⇨ Size
Thesaurus	Shift+⌘+Z	Edit ⇨ Writing Tools
Underline	⌘+U	Text ⇨ Style or Format ⇨ Style
Undo/Redo	⌘+Z, F1	Edit

Table A-2
General Navigation Commands

Command	Key Sequence
Go to beginning of document	Home or ⌘+up arrow
Go to end of document	End or ⌘+down arrow
Next tab in selected floating window	⌘+right arrow
Previous tab in selected floating window	⌘+left arrow
Scroll down one screen	Page Down
Scroll up one screen	Page Up
Select next floating window	Option+Tab

Table A-3
Other General Commands

Command	Key Sequence
Cancel printing and most dialog boxes	⌘+. (period)
Delete character to left of cursor	Delete
Delete character to right of cursor	Del
Discretionary hyphen	⌘+- (hyphen)
End slide show	q, ⌘+. (period), Esc
First slide	Home
Last slide	End
Next slide	Right arrow, down arrow, Page Down, Return, Tab, spacebar
Previous slide	Left arrow, up arrow, Page Up, Shift+Return, Shift+Tab, Shift+spacebar

Table A-4
Database Menu Commands

Command	Key Sequence	Menu
Browse	Shift+⌘+B	Layout
Define Fields	Shift+⌘+D	Layout
Duplicate Record	⌘+D	Edit
Find	Shift+⌘+F	Layout
Go To Record	⌘+G	Organize
Hide Selected	⌘+(	Organize
Hide Unselected	⌘+)	Organize
Layout	Shift+⌘+L	Layout
List	Shift+⌘+I	Layout
Match Records	⌘+M	Organize
New Record	⌘+R	Edit
Show All Records	Shift+⌘+A	Organize
Sort Records	⌘+J	Organize

Table A-5
Database Navigation Commands

Command	Key Sequence
Move to beginning of field	Up arrow or ⌘+left arrow
Move to end of field	Down arrow or ⌘+right arrow
Move to next field	Tab
Move to previous field	Shift+Tab
Move to next record (same field)	⌘+Return or ⌘+down arrow
Move to previous record (same field)	Shift+⌘+Return or ⌘+up arrow

Table A-6
Other Database Commands

Command	Key Sequence
Deselect records	Return
Insert a tab in a text field	Control+Tab
Paste current date, time, or record number	⌘+- (hyphen)*

* You must be in a field of the correct type (that is, a date, time, or number field).

Table A-7
Draw and Presentation Menu Commands

Command	Key Sequence	Menu
Align Objects	Shift+⌘+K	Arrange
Align to Grid	Shift+⌘+L	Arrange
Duplicate	⌘+D	Edit
Free Rotate	Shift+⌘+R	Arrange
Group	⌘+G	Arrange
Lock	⌘+H	Arrange
Move Backward	Shift+⌘+- (hyphen)	Arrange
Move Forward	Shift+⌘++ (plus sign)	Arrange
Reshape	⌘+R	Arrange

Continued

Table A-7 *(continued)*

Command	Key Sequence	Menu
Smooth	⌘+(	Edit
Turn Autogrid On/Off	⌘+Y	Options
Ungroup	Shift+⌘+G	Arrange
Unlock	Shift+⌘+H	Arrange
Unsmooth	⌘+)	Edit

Many of the commands for the Arrange and Options menus in Tables A-7 and A-8 also are available to you when creating or modifying database layouts (in Layout mode).

Table A-8
Other Draw and Presentation Commands

Command	Key Sequence
Complete open or closed polygon or bezigon	Return
Move selected image one pixel or gridpoint	Any arrow key
Select eyedropper tool	Tab

Table A-9
Paint Menu Commands

Command	Key Sequence	Menu
Duplicate	⌘+D	Edit
Free Rotate	Shift+⌘+R	Transform
Turn Autogrid On/Off	⌘+Y	Options

Table A-10
Other Paint Commands

Command	Key Sequence
Complete open or closed polygon or bezigon	Return
Move selected image one pixel or gridpoint	Any arrow key
Select eyedropper tool	Tab

Table A-11
Spreadsheet Menu Commands

Command	Key Sequence	Menu
Apply Format	Shift+⌘+V	Edit
Calculate Now	Shift+⌘+= (equal sign)	Calculate
Copy Format	Shift+⌘+C	Edit
Delete Cells	Shift+⌘+K	Format
Fill Down	⌘+D	Calculate
Fill Right	⌘+R	Calculate
Go to Cell	⌘+G	Options
Insert Cells	Shift+⌘+I	Format
Lock Cells	⌘+H	Options
Make Chart	⌘+M	Options
Number	Shift+⌘+N	Format
Sort	⌘+J	Calculate
Unlock Cells	Shift+⌘+H	Options

Table A-12
Spreadsheet Navigation Commands

Command	Key Sequence
Move one cell down	Return, down arrow (or Option+down arrow)*
Move one cell up	Shift+Return, up arrow (or Option+up arrow)*
Move one cell right	Tab, right arrow (or Option+right arrow)*
Move one cell left	Shift+Tab, left arrow (or Option+left arrow)*
Move one character right (in entry bar)	Option+right arrow (or right arrow)*
Move one character left (in entry bar)	Option+left arrow (or left arrow)*
Stay in current cell	Return*

* Whether you use an arrow key or an Option+arrow combination — and what the Return key does — depends on spreadsheet preferences settings.

You also can use each of the commands in Table A-12 to complete a cell entry. The functions of these keys are determined by the settings in Spreadsheet Preferences.

Table A-13
Other Spreadsheet Commands

Command	Key Sequence
Cancel entry	Esc
Clear cell contents and format	Clear
Delete character to left (in entry bar)	Delete
Delete character to right (in entry bar)	Del

Table A-14
Word Processing Menu Commands

Command	Key Sequence	Menu
Apply Ruler	Shift+⌘+V	Format ⇨ Rulers
Copy Ruler	Shift+⌘+C	Format ⇨ Rulers
Insert Column Break	Return	Format
Insert Blank Footnote	Shift+⌘+F	Format
Insert Page Break	Shift+Return	Format
Insert Section Break	Option+Return	Format
Move Above	Control+up arrow	Outline
Move Below	Control+down arrow	Outline
Move Left with Subtopics	Shift+⌘+L/Control+left arrow	Outline
Move Right with Subtopics	Shift+⌘+R/Control+right arrow	Outline
New Topic Left	⌘+L	Outline ⇨ Move Left
New Topic Right	⌘+R	Outline ⇨ Move Right
Subscript	Shift+⌘+- (hyphen)	Text ⇨ Style
Superscript	Shift+⌘++ (plus sign)	Text ⇨ Style

Table A-15
Word Processing Navigation Commands

Command	Key Sequence
Move up one line	Up arrow
Move down one line	Down arrow
Move left one character	Left arrow
Move right one character	Right arrow
Move to beginning of document	⌘+up arrow
Move to end of document	⌘+down arrow
Move to beginning of line	⌘+left arrow
Move to end of line	⌘+right arrow
Move to beginning of paragraph	Option+up arrow
Move to end of paragraph	Option+down arrow
Move to beginning of word	Option+left arrow
Move to end of word	Option+right arrow

Table A-16
Other Word Processing Commands

Command	Key Sequence
Accept footnote entry and return to main body of document	Return
New outline topic at same level	⌘+Return
New outline topic with same format as previous topic	Return
Select outline topic and its subtopics	Shift+Control+spacebar
Select text from insertion point to beginning of document	Shift+⌘+up arrow
Select text from insertion point to end of document	Shift+⌘+down arrow
Select text from insertion point to beginning of paragraph	Shift+Option+up arrow
Select text from insertion point to end of paragraph	Shift+Option+down arrow
Show/Hide invisible characters	⌘+; (semicolon)

Shortcuts for Dialog Box Buttons

With the exception of the default button in dialog boxes (a button surrounded by a double line that you can select by pressing the Enter or Return key), you normally have to use the mouse to click buttons. But some people are lazy. Dragging the mouse to the correct position just so you can click a button sometimes seems like more work than it's worth. Recognizing this fact, AppleWorks has built keyboard shortcuts into its dialog boxes so that you can click buttons from the keyboard.

To click a dialog box button using the keyboard, press the ⌘ key while the dialog box is onscreen. Any button that has a ⌘ key equivalent will change to display the proper keystrokes inside the button (see Figure A-1).

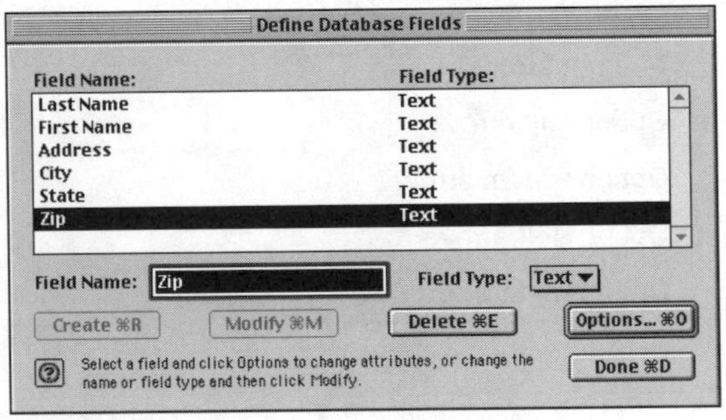

Figure A-1: In the Define Database Fields dialog box, for example, the Create, Modify, Delete, Options, and Done buttons have Command-key equivalents.

◆   ◆   ◆

Spreadsheet and Database Function Definitions

Appendix B is a complete reference to the spreadsheet and database functions of AppleWorks 6. The functions are listed alphabetically. Each section includes the format for the function (that is, how it is entered in a worksheet or database formula, along with the types of arguments required), a description of how the function works, and one or more examples for the spreadsheet and database environments.

Note

Some functions are available in the spreadsheet environment only; they cannot be used in a database. These functions are listed with the following text: "This is a spreadsheet-only function." Note also that some functions have optional arguments. Such arguments are surrounded by bracket symbols ({}).

ABS (Absolute Value)

Format: ABS (number)

ABS is used to calculate the absolute value of a worksheet cell address, a number, or a database field, ignoring the result's sign. The result is either a positive number or zero. ABS is used when you are interested in the magnitude of a number or a difference, irrespective of the sign. Note that the absolute value of an empty cell or field returns a value of zero (0).

Spreadsheet examples: The formula =ABS(-17.35) returns 17.35; =ABS(18-A3) returns 5, where cell A3 evaluates as either 13 or 23; =ABS(C7) returns 18.5, where cell C7 evaluates as either 18.5 or –18.5; =ABS(B4) returns 0, where cell B4 contains the number zero, evaluates as zero (as in the formula =5-5), or is blank.

Database examples: The formula ABS('GRADE 1'-'Grade 2') can be used to evaluate the difference between two Grade fields. The result, however, shows only the magnitude of the difference between the two grades; that is, it is a measure of change, not the direction of the change (whether the grade improved or became worse).

ACOS (Arc Cosine)

Format: ACOS (number)

ACOS calculates the arc cosine (inverse of a cosine), returning an angle in radians ranging from 0 to π. Taking the cosine of the result produces the argument to the function.

The argument to ACOS must be a number ranging from –1.0 to 1.0 or an operation that yields a value within that range.

Note If a blank cell or blank field is used as an argument, ACOS treats the blank as though it contains a zero.

Spreadsheet examples: =ACOS(3/4) returns 0.7227 radians; =ACOS(0) returns 1.5708; =ACOS(1) returns 0; =ACOS(-2/3) returns 2.3005 radians; =ACOS(-1) returns 3.14159 or [1].

Database examples: ACOS('Field 1') returns the arc cosine of the field.

ALERT

Format: ALERT (message {, type})

ALERT displays a dialog box with a message of your choosing (message). If the optional type argument (discussed later) is omitted, the alert box includes only an OK button that the user must click to dismiss the alert. When the alert is triggered, the contents of the ALERT message are entered into the current cell.

Tip By including an optional Type number, you can specify the buttons that appear in the alert box, as shown in the following table. Depending on the button clicked, either a 0 or 1 is returned in the current cell. You can then create other formulas that take different actions based on the returned value.

Type Number	Buttons	Default Choice	Values Returned
1	OK; Cancel	OK	OK = 1; Cancel = 0
2	Yes; No	Yes	Yes = 1; No = 0
3	OK; Cancel	Cancel	OK = 1; Cancel =0

Because a text message is part of an ALERT, this function might be preferred to that of BEEP, which only plays the current system sound. This is a spreadsheet-only function.

Spreadsheet examples: =IF(C12<0,ALERT("Accept a score less than zero?",2),"") asks how you want to handle a negative number that was entered in cell C12. The 2 at the end of the formula instructs AppleWorks to present Yes and No buttons in the alert box. An alternate formula =IF(C12<0,ALERT("This score is less than zero"),"") simply notifies you that a negative number was entered in the same cell, and returns only the alert message.

AND

Format: AND (logical1, logical2, . . .)

AND enables you to evaluate one or more arguments or conditions, and returns TRUE if all arguments or conditions are true; otherwise, it returns FALSE. A zero value is false, any other number is true.

Spreadsheet examples: The formula =AND(A1>50000,B1<35) could be used to identify individuals with salaries of more than $50,000 who are less than 35 years old. =AND(D3) returns true if D3 contains any number other than zero.

Database examples: To determine if a customer is eligible for a special discount, you could use a formula such as AND('Product Total'>250,'MemberTime'>3). This equation yields a 1 (TRUE) only if the current order is for more than $250 of goods and the individual has been a member of the club or service for more than three years.

ASIN (Arc Sine)

Format: ASIN (number)

The ASIN function is used to calculate the inverse of a sine (the arc sine). The result is an angle in radians in the range $-\pi/2$ to $\pi/2$. The argument to ASIN must be a sine value (a number ranging from −1.0 to 1.0) or a simple operation that yields a sine.

Spreadsheet examples: =ASIN(1) returns 1.570796; =ASIN(-1) returns –1.570796; =ASIN(0) returns 0; =ASIN(0.75) returns 0.848062.

ATAN (Arc Tangent)
Format: ATAN (number)

The ATAN function calculates the inverse of a tangent (the arc tangent). The result is an angle in radians in the range –π/2 to π/2.

Spreadsheet example: The formula =ATAN(1) returns 0.7854.

ATAN2 (Arc Tangent 2)
Format: ATAN2 (*x* number, *y* number)

The ATAN2 function calculates the angle in radians between the positive X axis and a line that starts at the origin (coordinates 0, 0) and passes through the specified X and Y coordinates. The result is an angle in radians, in the range –π to π (or –3.14159 to 3.14159).

Spreadsheet examples: The formula =DEGREES(ATAN2(5,5)) returns 45, indicating that a straight diagonal line (passing through coordinate 0,0 and 5,5) is a 45-degree angle.

AVERAGE
Format: AVERAGE (number1, number2, . . .)

AVERAGE calculates the arithmetic mean of a set of numbers expressed as numbers, cell references, a range, or field names. The formula for an AVERAGE is the sum of the values divided by the number of values in the set.

Spreadsheet examples: =AVERAGE(7,12,5) returns 8 (that is, 24/3); =AVERAGE(A1...A5) returns 10, where cells A1, A2, A3, A4, and A5 contain 12, 4, 8, 16, and 10, respectively (that is, 50/5).

Database example: You could use AVERAGE('SCORE 1','SCORE 2') to determine the average of the two scores for each record.

BASETONUM
Format: BASETONUM (text, base)

BASETONUM examines a text string and interprets it as a number in the specified base (ranging from 1 to 36). The text string must be less than 256 characters long.

Spreadsheet example: The formula =BASETONUM(10110,2) returns 22; that is, the base 2 number 10110 is 22.

> **Note**
>
> An anomaly exists in AppleWorks' handling of BASETONUM in that it accepts digits outside the range of the numeric base. For example, in a base 6 number, all digits should be from 0 to 5; however, BASETONUM will accept a "6" as a valid digit. This bug only applies to digits that are the same as the base.

BEEP

Format: BEEP ()

BEEP plays the alert sound that is currently set in the Sound (or Monitors & Sound) control panel. You can use BEEP to notify you of an unusual or important situation, such as a data entry error.

Spreadsheet example: =IF(C12<0,BEEP(),IF(C12>4,BEEP(),"")) could be used to notify you of a numeric grade in cell C12 that was out of range; that is, less than 0 or greater than 4.

Database example: IF('Due Date'< NOW( ),BEEP(),"Due in "&'Due Date'-TRUNC(NOW()))&" days.") could be used to let you know when a project is overdue. If the due date for a record has passed ('Due Date'< NOW()), a beep is sounded. If the due date still lies ahead, on the other hand, a message is displayed in the field, as in "Due in 10 days."

CHAR (Character)

Format: CHAR (number)

The CHAR function returns the ASCII (American Standard Code for Information Interchange) character that corresponds to the number in the specified cell or database field. If the number contains a fractional part, the fraction is discarded when the number is evaluated.

Note that ASCII codes can range from 0 through 255. Numbers outside of that range return an error. Also, depending on the font selected, not all codes have an associated character, and codes less than 32 are control characters. In general, codes from 32 to 127 correspond to the normal typewriter letters, numbers, and symbols, while codes above 127 correspond to the foreign language characters and special symbols. Non-Roman fonts (such as Zapf Dingbats) might display decidedly different characters from Roman fonts (such as Times). In addition, codes in the range 128 to 255 will generally vary from one platform to another (Mac and Windows).

Spreadsheet examples: =CHAR(68) returns a D; =CHAR(154) returns an ö.

Database example: CHAR('ITEMNO')

CHOOSE

Format: CHOOSE (index, value1, value2, . . .)

The CHOOSE function is used to select a value from an array of values. The value of the index argument (a number or numeric expression) determines which value in the array is chosen. The values in the array can contain text or numeric expressions. If index is less than one or greater than the number of values, an error is returned.

Spreadsheet examples: The formula =CHOOSE(2,15,"Apple",7,"Medium",15) returns Apple; the formula=CHOOSE(B6,"Sunday","Monday","Tuesday", "Wednesday", "Thursday","Friday","Saturday") returns a day of the week, assuming that cell B6 contains an index value from 1 to 7; and the formula =CHOOSE(4, B1, B2, B3, B4, B5) returns the contents of cell B4.

CODE (ASCII Code)

Format: CODE (text)

CODE returns the ASCII code (American Standard Code for Information Interchange) of the first character in the text string of a selected cell or field.

Spreadsheet examples: =CODE("a") returns 97; =CODE("Schwartz") returns 83, which corresponds to the code for a capital S; the formula =IF(OR(CODE(A1)<65, CODE(A1)>90),"Not a capital letter","Okay") could be used to check if a cell's text begins with a capital letter. Any character outside of the range A–Z results in the message: Not a capital letter.

Database example: A similar formula to the preceding error-checking formula can be used to check that each last name begins with a capital letter, as in IF(OR(CODE('Last Name')<65,CODE('Last Name')>90),"Error in Last Name","OK").

COLUMN

Format: COLUMN ({cell})

Returns the number of the column referenced by cell or the column in which the current cell is contained. This is a spreadsheet-only function.

Spreadsheet examples: =COLUMN(C12) returns 3, because Column C is the third column; =COLUMN() returns the column in which the formula is located.

Tip
If you want to number a group of columns beginning with Column A quickly, type the formula **=COLUMN()** in Column A, highlight that cell as well as the appropriate cells to the right, and then choose Calculate ⇨ Fill Right (or press ⌘+R).

CONCAT (Concatenation)

Format: CONCAT (text1, text2, . . .)

CONCAT is used to join text strings, producing a single text string as a result.

Spreadsheet examples: =CONCAT(A1," ",B1) returns Steve Schwartz when A1 contains "Steve" and B1 contains "Schwartz." Note that text strings also can be concatenated with the & symbol, as in =A1 & " " & B1.

Database examples: CONCAT can be used to create a new field that combines First Name and Last Name fields into a single Name field, as in CONCAT('First Name'," ",'Last Name'). To generate a sentence in a merge form, you could use CONCAT in the following manner: CONCAT("Your commission is $",'Commission',".").

COS (Cosine)
Format: COS (number)

COS calculates the cosine of a number, where the number is an angle in radians.

Spreadsheet example: =COS(1) returns 0.5403.

COUNT
Format: COUNT (value1, value2, . . .)

Count is used to display the number of values (numbers, text, cell or range references, or formulas) in a list. Empty worksheet cells or database fields are not counted.

Spreadsheet examples: The formula =COUNT(B1, B2*3, 5) returns 2 or 3, depending on whether cell B1 is blank. Note that even if B2 is blank, the formula B2*3 still adds one to the count.

One typical use of COUNT is to determine the number of nonempty cells in a range, such as =COUNT(C1..C10). To display the number of blank cells, the previous formula could be changed to read =10-(COUNT(C1..C10)).

Database example: Suppose you want to calculate an average of four numeric fields, but some of the fields might be empty. If you use the AVERAGE function, the results would be erroneous because AVERAGE treats the missing fields as though they each contain zero (0) and then divides by four. To calculate a true average, you can use the COUNT function, as follows:

    ('q1'+'q2'+'q3'+'q4')/COUNT('q1','q2','q3','q4')

COUNT2
Format: COUNT2 (search value, value1, value2, . . .)

Use COUNT2 to show the number of values in a list that match the specified search value. The values can be numbers, text, cells, or fields.

Note that when COUNT2 is used in a database formula, a separate value is returned for each record. COUNT2 does not summarize a search across all records. Note, too, that COUNT2 does not count instances in which the search value is embedded in a text string or sentence. For example, in a database, COUNT2("Macintosh", 'Comments') only counts instances in which the Comments field contains only the word Macintosh.

Spreadsheet examples: The formula =COUNT2(4,3,7,4,-1) yields 1, because only a single instance of the search value (that is, 4) occurs in the list. The formula =COUNT2(0,A1..A20) returns the number of cells in the range that contain 0. In an address book worksheet, the formula =COUNT2("CA",G2..G400) could be used to count the number of cells in the range for which CA was entered as the state (assuming that Column G was used to enter state information).

Database example: COUNT2(100,'Score1','Score2','Score3') counts the number of times 100 was achieved as a score in the three fields.

DATE
Format: DATE (year, month, day)

Use the DATE function to convert a date to a serial number that represents the number of days since January 1, 1904.

Spreadsheet examples: =DATE(1995,9,21) yields 33501. If you have spread the components of a date across cells A1 through C1 in month, day, year order, the formula =DATE(C1,A1,B1) could be used to combine them.

Database examples: If a date has been entered as three separate components, each in its own field, you could use the following formula to combine it into a single field: DATETOTEXT(DATE('Ship Year','Ship Month','Ship Day')) The DATE portion of the formula creates a serial number from the three date components; the DATE-TOTEXT function changes the serial number into a normal date, such as 9/21/95.

DATETOTEXT
Format: DATETOTEXT (serial number {, format number})

The DATETOTEXT function changes a serial number (the number of days that have passed since January 1, 1904) to a normal date in a particular format. Format options are as follows:

> 0 = 10/15/95 (the default format)
>
> 1 = Oct 15, 1995
>
> 2 = October 15, 1995
>
> 3 = Sun, Oct 15, 1995
>
> 4 = Sunday, October 15, 1995

Note The separator used — and the order of the month, day, and year — is determined by the Date & Time control panel settings.

Spreadsheet examples: =DATETOTEXT(33525,1) yields Oct 15, 1995; =DATETOTEXT(33525) yields 10/15/95, the default date format; =DATETOTEXT (A7,1) yields Nov 5, 1995 when cell A7 contains a date or serial number that represents 11/5/95.

The latter example illustrates a way to convert one date format to another — just change the format number in the formula. Of course, you could also use the spreadsheet's Format Number command to select a different date format.

DAY

Format: DAY (serial number)

For any serial number, DAY returns the day of the month.

Spreadsheet examples: =DAY(33525) yields 15, because the serial number 33525 represents October 15, 1995.

Tip You also can use the DAY function to extract the day number from a formatted date. The formula =DAY(A9) yields 7 when A9 contains a date, regardless of how it is formatted (for example, 12/7/00 or Wed, Jun 7, 2000).

Database example: DAY('DATE')

DAYNAME

Format: DAYNAME (number)

DAYNAME converts a number from 1 to 7 into the appropriate day name, as follows:

Number	Day Name
1	Sunday
2	Monday
3	Tuesday
4	Wednesday
5	Thursday
6	Friday
7	Saturday

Note that the argument to the DAYNAME function must always be, or evaluate to, a number from 1 to 7. Anything else, such as a complete date or a serial number, will result in an error.

Spreadsheet examples: =DAYNAME(5) yields Thursday.

> **Tip**
>
> One use for the DAYNAME function is for a worksheet heading listing the days of the week. To create them as column headings, type the formula **=DAYNAME(COLUMN())** into Column A, and then use the Fill Right command (⌘+R) to add the formula to the cells in Columns B through G. To create day name row headings, type the formula **=DAYNAME(ROW())** into Row 1, and then use the Fill Down command (⌘+D) to add the formula to the cells in Rows 2 through 7. You can achieve the same result using the Fill Special command.

DAYOFYEAR

Format: DAYOFYEAR (serial number)

DAYOFYEAR extracts the day of the year from a serial number. Note that this function also works on formatted dates.

Spreadsheet examples: =DAYOFYEAR(33525) yields 288, where 33525 is the serial number for October 15, 1995; =DAYOFYEAR(33247) yields 10, where 33247 is the serial number for January 10, 1995.

Database example: DAYOFYEAR('DATE')

DEGREES

Format: DEGREES (radians number)

The DEGREES function converts radians to the corresponding number of degrees.

Spreadsheet examples: =DEGREES(1.58) returns 90.5273; =DEGREES(1) returns 57.29578; =DEGREES(-3) returns –171.8873; =DEGREES(PI()) returns 180; =DEGREES(-(PI())) returns –180.

ERROR

Format: ERROR ()

The ERROR function returns #ERROR! It has no arguments.

Spreadsheet examples: The formula =IF(C2>2,ERROR(),"OK") returns #ERROR! if the value in cell C2 is greater than 2; otherwise, it returns OK. If you only want the erroneous condition to return a text string, the formula could be changed to read =IF(C2>2,ERROR(),"").

Database example: You can use the ERROR() function to report the result of a test on a field, as in IF('Hours'<0,ERROR(),"OK!").

EXACT

Format: EXACT (text1, text2)

EXACT compares two text strings, and returns TRUE when the two strings are identical — including case. Otherwise, it returns FALSE.

Spreadsheet examples: =EXACT(A1,A2) returns true only when the contents of cells A1 and A2 are identical. The formula =EXACT("Minnesota",B5) returns FALSE if cell B5 contains anything other than the string Minnesota. If B5 held MINNESOTA, the formula would still return FALSE, because the case of the two strings is different.

Database example: EXACT('Last Name','First Name') returns 1 (True) when the contents of the Last Name field matches that of the First Name field; otherwise, it returns 0 (False).

EXP (Exponent)

Format: EXP (number)

EXP calculates *e* (Euler's number) to the power of the argument.

Spreadsheet examples: =EXP(1) yields 2.718281; =EXP(2) yields 7.389 (or e^2).

FACT (Factorial)

Format: FACT (number)

FACT calculates the factorial of any positive whole number. Factorials of negative numbers or fractional numbers produce errors. Note also that the factorials of 0 and 1 are both 1 and that the largest argument that will not produce an error is 171.

Spreadsheet examples: =FACT(3) returns 6 (or 3*2*1); =FACT(4) returns 24 (or 4*3*2*1); =FACT(B7) returns 120 when cell B7 contains, or evaluates as, 5.

FIND

Format: FIND (find-text, in-text {, start-offset})

The FIND function searches the text specified in in-text and attempts to locate an occurrence of the search string (find-text). It returns the position of the first instance that it finds, if any. (0 is returned if the find-text is not found.)

Optionally, you can specify a character starting position by adding the start-offset; that is, the number of characters from the beginning of the text string. Each search is case-sensitive and blanks are counted.

Spreadsheet examples: The formula =FIND("Beth","Where is Beth?") returns 10; =FIND("BETH","Where is Beth?") returns 0 because the case of the find-text does not match that of the text within the string that was searched.

Adding a start-offset, such as =FIND("Beth","Where is Beth?",5) makes the formula begin its search with the fifth character in in-text. The result is still 10, because Beth is found starting at the tenth character of in-text. On the other hand, if a start-offset of 11 was used, Beth would not be found and a result of 0 (zero) would be presented.

FRAC (Fraction)

Format: FRAC (number)

The FRAC function calculates the fractional part of a real number. The result is always a positive number.

Spreadsheet examples: The formula =FRAC(17.237) returns 0.237, the part of the number to the right of the decimal point; the formula =FRAC(-123.7) returns 0.7; and the formula =FRAC(10) returns 0 (zero).

Database example: FRAC('Hours') returns the fractional portion of the number in the Hours field.

FV (Future Value)

Format: FV (rate, nper, pmt {, pv} {, type})

FV calculates the future value of an investment, given a particular interest rate per period (rate) and number of periods (nper). Specifying the present value of the investment (pv) and the payment type (type) are optional. The default type is 0, indicating that the payment is made at the end of the first period. A type of 1 means that the payment is made at the beginning of each period.

The rate can be entered as a percentage (9.5%) or a decimal (.095). Payment amounts and the present value should be entered as negative numbers, because they represent money paid out.

Spreadsheet examples: The formula =FV(10%,10,-500) returns $7968.71, the future value of an annual investment of $500 for 10 years at an annual interest rate of 10 percent. Because the type was not indicated, it is assumed that each yearly investment is made on the last day of the year. On the other hand, if the annual investment was made on the first day of each year, as shown in the revised formula =FV(10%,10,-500,0,1), the result is $8765.58 — a gain of almost $800. To calculate the future value of an initial investment of $10,000 with annual additions of $1,000 at an interest rate of 5.5 percent over a five-year period (with each addition made at the beginning of the year), you would use this formula:

```
=FV(5.5%,5,-1000,-10000,1)
```

returning an answer of $18,957.65.

Note If the interest is compounded more frequently than the investments are made, you should enter the APR (annualized percentage rate) rather than the purported rate.

HLOOKUP (Horizontal Lookup)

Format: HLOOKUP (lookup value, compare range, offset {, method})

HLOOKUP checks the top row of the compare range for the lookup value. If the search condition is met, the row number of the found cell is increased by the amount of the offset and the function returns the contents of the new cell. If the search condition is not met, an error is returned.

Specifying a method is optional. When the values in the first row are arranged in increasing order, use a method of 1 to find the largest value that is less than or equal to the lookup value. When the values in the first row are arranged in decreasing order, use a method of –1 to find the smallest value that is greater than or equal to the lookup value. Use a method of 0 to accept only an exact match. This is a spreadsheet-only function.

Spreadsheet example: In the grading spreadsheet shown in Figure B-1, the formula =HLOOKUP(A5,A1..F2,1,1) in cell B5 examines the numeric score that has been entered in cell A5 and then returns the letter grade to be assigned. The compare range (A1..F2) contains the possible scores in the top row (the row that the function searches), and the corresponding letter grades are listed in the second row. Note that the scores in Row 1 represent the minimum score required to achieve a particular grade.

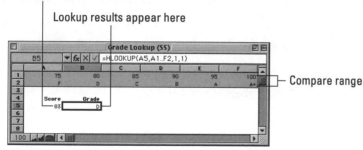

Figure B-1: A grading worksheet that uses the HLOOKUP function

HOUR

Format: HOUR (serial number)

The Macintosh represents the current date and time as a single serial number, such as 35221.346644, for June 6, 2000 at 8:19 a.m. The date portion of the number is to the left of the decimal; the time is to the right of the decimal. The HOUR function extracts the hour from the time portion of a serial number (the numbers to the right of the decimal point). The return value is a whole number ranging from 0 to 23.

Spreadsheet examples: The formula =HOUR(33370.80478) returns 19 (for 7:00 p.m.); =HOUR(33370.402) returns 9 (for 9:00 a.m.).

Tip   To calculate the current hour, you can use the formula =HOUR(NOW()).

Database example: HOUR('TIME')

IF

Format: IF (logical, true value, false value)

Use IF to perform a conditional test. If the test condition is fulfilled, the true value is displayed or performed. If the test condition is not fulfilled, the false value is displayed or performed.

Spreadsheet examples: The formula =IF(A10=1053,"You're rich! You chose today's number!","Too bad. Try again.") could be used to check cell A10 for the winning number for today's lottery. If the number found is 1053, the first message (the true value) is displayed. If any other number is found, the second message (the false value) is displayed.

The formula =IF(B7,2,4) displays 2 if B7 contains any value at all, but shows 4 if the cell is blank.

Database example: IF('Result'>0,"Positive trend","Negative trend or no change").

INDEX

Format: INDEX (range, row, column)

The INDEX function is used to reference the contents of a cell that is x number of rows and y number of columns away from the first cell in the range. The referenced cell must be within the specified range. This is a spreadsheet-only function.

Spreadsheet examples: =INDEX(A55..C63,7,2) returns the contents of cell B61, seven cells down in the range and in the second column of the range.

Note Because the first argument to the Index function is a range, you also can use a named range. For example, a column might contain the names of the months of the year for which you have created a named range called Months. The formula =INDEX(Months,5,1) would return Might.

INT (Integer)

Format: INT (number)

The INT function returns the largest integer (whole number) less than or equal to the value of the argument number. For any positive number, INT simply returns the integer portion of that number (the same as the TRUNC function). For negative numbers, the next lowest whole number is returned.

Spreadsheet examples: =INT(4.53) returns 4; =INT(-2.33) returns –3; =INT(0.321) returns 0; =INT(-0.321) returns –1.

Database example: INT('Item 1'+'Item 2').

IRR (Internal Rate of Return)

Format: IRR (range {, guess})

IRR is an approximate interest rate returned on an investment consisting of a series of payments (negative values) and income (positive values). If an optional initial guess for the internal rate of return is not entered, a default rate of 10 percent is used. If a result is not obtained (for example, the calculation doesn't converge to a single value) within 20 iterations, the function returns a #NUM! error.

The range contains future cash flow amounts in the order that they are paid out or received. The first amount is the amount of the initial investment and is entered as a negative number. This is a spreadsheet-only function.

Spreadsheet example: When formatted as a percent, the formula =IRR(B1..B5) returns 6.65% when B1..B5 contains –10000, 2000, 2500, 2500, 5000.

ISBLANK

Format: ISBLANK (value)

The ISBLANK function enables you to distinguish between blank cells or fields and those that contain an entry. If the cell is empty, ISBLANK returns TRUE. If the cell contains text or a number, ISBLANK returns FALSE. When ISBLANK is used in a ClarisWorks database, the return values are 1 and 0 rather than TRUE and FALSE, respectively.

Spreadsheet examples: =ISBLANK(5.45), =ISBLANK(0), and =ISBLANK("IDG") return FALSE. The formula =ISBLANK(B6) returns TRUE only if cell B6 is empty; otherwise, it returns FALSE.

Database example: =ISBLANK('Last Name') returns 1 if the contents of the Last Name field is empty; otherwise, it returns 0 (zero).

ISERROR

Format: ISERROR (value {, error type})

The ISERROR function is used to check for errors in expressions. Optionally, ISERROR can check for a specific type of error, rather than errors of any type. ISERROR returns TRUE or FALSE in a worksheet, and 1 or 0 in a database.

Error types that can optionally be included are as follows:

Error Type	Explanation
#ARG!	Incorrect number of arguments, argument value, or argument type
#DATE!	Invalid date
#DIV/0!	Divide by zero
#ERROR!	General error
#N/A!	Not available
#NUM!	Incorrect number or numeric overflow/underflow
#REF!	Reference to incorrect cell
#TIME!	Invalid time
#USER!	User-defined error
#VALUE!	Invalid value

Spreadsheet examples: The formula =ISERROR(F5) examines the contents of cell F5 and returns FALSE (if no error exists in cell F5) or TRUE (if an error does exist in cell F5). The formula =ISERROR(F5,#DIV/0!) examines cell F5 and returns TRUE if it contains a divide by zero error. If it contains no error or an error of another type, it returns FALSE.

Database example: The formula ISERROR('Division Result',#DIV/0!) checks the field called Division Result and displays a 1 (TRUE) if a divide by zero error is detected. Other errors or no error result in a returned value of 0 (FALSE).

ISLOGICAL

Format: ISLOGICAL (value)

The ISLOGICAL function determines whether the argument contains a Boolean expression; that is, one that can be evaluated as either TRUE or FALSE. If so, ISLOGICAL returns TRUE; otherwise, it returns FALSE.

Spreadsheet examples: The formula =ISLOGICAL(1.5>4) returns TRUE because the argument is a Boolean expression. As this example shows, it doesn't matter whether the expression is true or false; only that it is a Boolean expression. The formula =ISLOGICAL(C1) checks to see if cell C1 contains a Boolean expression.

ISNA (Is Not Available)

Format: ISNA (value)

ISNA checks for the presence of the #N/A! (Not Available) error. If that specific error is found, TRUE is returned. If no error (or an error of another type) is found, FALSE is returned. Because the MATCH, LOOKUP, VLOOKUP, and HLOOKUP functions might return an #N/A! error, ISNA can be used to check the results of formulas that include these functions. This is a spreadsheet-only function.

Spreadsheet examples: The formula =ISNA("Happy!") returns FALSE, because "Happy!" is a text expression and not the #N/A! error. The formula =ISNA(C3) returns TRUE only if cell C3 contains the #N/A! error. The formula =ISNA(NA()) returns TRUE because NA() is the Not Available error.

ISNUMBER

Format: ISNUMBER (value)

The ISNUMBER function enables you to check the contents of a cell or database field for the presence of a number. If the cell contains a number, ISNUMBER returns TRUE. If the cell contains text or is blank, FALSE is returned.

When ISNUMBER is used in an AppleWorks database, the return values are 1 and 0 (rather than TRUE and FALSE, respectively). Note, however, that ISNUMBER is seldom used in AppleWorks databases because:

✦ Number fields can only contain numbers, so there's no reason to check them further.

✦ A number found in a Text field is treated as text, so ISNUMBER always returns 0 (false).

✦ When importing data, text in Number fields is ignored (so there's no reason to use ISNUMBER to check for import errors).

On the other hand, ISNUMBER can be used to check for blank Number fields, much as the ISBLANK function is used. For blank fields, ISNUMBER returns 0 (false), while ISBLANK returns 1 (true).

Spreadsheet examples: The formula =ISNUMBER(17.235) returns TRUE; =ISNUMBER("Apple") returns FALSE; =ISNUMBER(D5) returns TRUE if cell D5 contains a number or a formula that results in a number, or returns FALSE if the cell contains text or is empty.

Database example: ISNUMBER('Amount') returns 0 (false) if the Amount number field is empty; otherwise, it returns 1 (true).

ISTEXT

Format: ISTEXT (value)

The ISTEXT function is used to determine whether an expression is text, or a cell reference, function, or number that evaluates as text. ISTEXT always returns either TRUE or FALSE.

Note

Applying the ISTEXT function to cells that contain dates or times can give confusing results. If a date or time is entered directly (as 1/12/96 or 4:43, for example), it is a number; ISTEXT returns FALSE. However, if a date or time is entered as text (="1/12/95"), ISTEXT returns TRUE. Finally, if a slash- or dash-delimited date is entered with a century (as in 12/14/1996), it is treated as text by ISTEXT and returns TRUE.

Spreadsheet examples: The formula =ISTEXT(D2) returns TRUE if the cell contains text, or a cell reference, function, or number that evaluates as text;=ISTEXT(Snakes) and =ISTEXT("24 Sapperstein Way") both return TRUE; =ISTEXT(147) and =ISTEXT(PI()) both return FALSE. The complex formula =ISTEXT(123/5 &" is the answer") returns TRUE. Although the formula contains numeric data, the result of the calculation is text (that is, "24.6 is the answer").

LEFT

Format: LEFT (text, number of characters)

The LEFT function returns a text string that contains the number of characters specified, counting from the leftmost character in the target text string. Note that if the target text string contains fewer characters than the number specified in the LEFT function, those characters that are present are returned. Also, the LEFT function can be applied to numbers, but the returned value is text.

Spreadsheet examples: =LEFT("123 Williams Avenue",3) returns 123;=LEFT ("Samuel Smith",3) returns Sam; =LEFT(47259,4) returns 4725; =LEFT (Apple,12) returns Apple, because fewer than 12 characters exist in the string.

Database example: LEFT('ID',5) returns the leftmost five characters of the contents of the ID field.

If you have a worksheet or database that contains nine-digit Zip codes, you can convert them to five-digit codes by using the LEFT function, as follows:

✦ **In a worksheet:** =LEFT(C1,5)

✦ **In a database:** LEFT('ZIP Code',5)

Similarly, if you have a worksheet or database that holds phone numbers that are formatted as 303-772-0054, you can extract the area code with the following formulas:

✦ **In a worksheet:** =LEFT(F1,3)

✦ **In a database:** LEFT('Phone Number',3)

LEN (Length)
Format: LEN (text)

LEN counts the number of characters in a text string. Spaces, numbers, and special characters also count toward the total.

Spreadsheet examples: =LEN(A1) returns 16, where A1 contains the string "Washington, D.C." The formula =IF(LEN(A1)>5,BEEP(),) checks the length of the text string in cell A1, and beeps if it contains more than five characters. Otherwise, it does nothing.

Database examples: The formula LEN('Last Name') returns the number of characters in the Last Name field.

LN (Natural Log)
Format: LN (number)

LN calculates the natural logarithm (log base e) of a positive number.

Spreadsheet example: The formula =LN(5) returns 1.6094.

LOG
Format: LOG (number {, base})

The LOG function calculates the logarithm of a positive number to a base. If no base is specified, it is assumed to be base 10.

Spreadsheet examples: The formula =LOG(5) returns 0.69897; =LOG(5,2) returns 2.3219.

LOG10 (Log to Base 10)

Format: LOG10 (number)

LOG10 calculates the logarithm of a positive number to base 10.

Spreadsheet examples: The formula =LOG10(1000) returns 3; =LOG10(10000) returns 4.

LOOKUP

Format: LOOKUP (lookup value, compare range, result range {, method})

The LOOKUP function searches for the lookup value row-by-row within the compare range and then returns the value of the corresponding cell in the result range. It is assumed that the values in the compare range are organized in ascending order — going from left to right and top to bottom. If they are arranged in descending order, type in **–1** for the optional method.

When the search is conducted, ClarisWorks seeks the largest number that is less than or equal to the lookup value. If no cell satisfies the search criteria, an error is returned. This is a spreadsheet-only function.

Spreadsheet example: Figure B-2 contains a worksheet that can be used to calculate the amount of postage required for a specific weight of letter. The exact weight is entered in cell A2; the lookup weights and corresponding postage amounts are listed in C2..C11 and D2..D11. The LOOKUP formula presents the answer in cell B2, using the formula:

```
=LOOKUP(IF(TRUNC(A2)=A2,A2,A2+1), C2..C11,D2..D11)
```

Enter a lookup value here (cell A2)

Results appear here (cell B2)

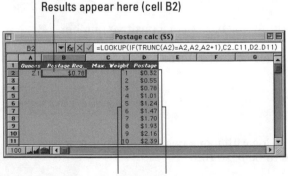

Compare range   Result range

Figure B-2: This small worksheet uses the LOOKUP function to determine the correct postage for a letter of a particular weight.

The IF function checks the contents of cell A2. If the value in A2 is equal to the truncated value of the same number (for example, A2 contains a whole number), A2 is used as the lookup value. If A2 contains a fractional portion, an additional ounce (1) is added to it, so A2 +1 is used as the lookup value. (The post office requires that all fractional weights be increased to the next full ounce).

The formula then compares the lookup value to the values in Column C of the worksheet and locates the largest weight value that is less than or equal to the lookup value. It then returns the appropriate postage amount from Column D.

LOWER

Format: LOWER (text)

The LOWER function converts uppercase letters in text to lowercase letters.

Spreadsheet examples: =LOWER("FuNnY") returns funny; =LOWER("Bob lives in DC.") returns bob lives in dc.

Database example: The formula LOWER('Comments') converts the entire contents of a Comments field to lowercase letters.

MACRO

Format for macros and buttons: MACRO (name {,type})

Format for AppleScripts: MACRO (name {,type} {, subroutine} {, . . .})

Use the MACRO function to execute a named macro, click a button on the Button Bar, or run an AppleScript. The macro name must be enclosed in quotation marks, spelled correctly, and have the proper capitalization. Refer to AppleWorks Help for additional details.

Spreadsheet example: The formula =IF(A1,MACRO("Chart"),0) checks cell A1 for the presence of any nonzero number and, if it finds one, the macro named Chart is played.

MATCH

Format: MATCH (lookup value, compare range {, type})

The MATCH function checks a specified range for a matching value and, if it finds one, reports the element number (the position) of that cell within the range. The compare range can contain text or numeric expressions. It is assumed that the values in the compare range are arranged in ascending or descending order, moving from left to right and top to bottom of the range. Optionally, you can enter **1** for the type to indicate an ascending range, **–1** to indicate a descending range, or **0** for an exact match (range order is unimportant). This is a spreadsheet-only function.

Spreadsheet example: In Figure B-3, the compare range (C1..D7) contains the numbers from 1 to 14 and is shown in light gray. The formula =MATCH(5,C1..D7,1) in cell A1 instructs AppleWorks to locate the first 5 in the compare range and specifies that the array is arranged in ascending order. The equation reports a match position at the fifth cell in the range (5).

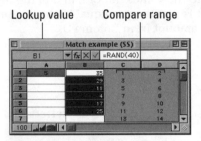

Figure B-3: An example of the MATCH function

MAX (Maximum)

Format: MAX (number1, number2, . . .)

The MAX function returns the largest number in a list of values. This function is often used to identify the largest number in a worksheet column or row. Note that blank cells are ignored when calculating the MAX value for a worksheet range.

Spreadsheet examples: The formula =MAX(17,23,4,19,-111) returns 23; =MAX(5,3,6.27) returns 6.27; =MAX(C2..C25) returns the largest number in the range from cell C2 to C25.

Database example: The formula MAX('Sale 1','Sale 2','Sale 3') identifies the largest of the three sales for each record.

MERGEFIELD

Format: MERGEFIELD (text)

As explained in Chapter 8, a worksheet also can be used as a merge form. Use the MERGEFIELD function to create merge fields in a worksheet. This is a spreadsheet-only function.

Spreadsheet example: The formula =MERGEFIELD("First Name") results in <<First Name>> being entered in the cell. When a merge is performed with this worksheet, data from the First Name field will replace the <<First Name>> placeholder.

MID (Middle)

Format: MID (text, start position, number of characters)

MID examines a target text string and returns a string of a specific number of characters, based on the starting position indicated in the formula. Note that when counting character positions, a blank is also considered a character, as are all letters, numbers, and punctuation marks.

Spreadsheet example: `=MID("Steven Alan Schwartz",8,2)` returns Al, because the starting position is the eighth character and the desired string is two characters long.

Database example: Assuming that you have a database with a phone number field and every number is formatted as ###-###-####, the formula `MID('Phone',5,3)` could be used to extract the phone number's exchange.

MIN (Minimum)

Format: MIN (number1, number2, . . .)

The MIN function returns the smallest number in a list of values. The MIN function is often used to identify the smallest number in a worksheet column or row. Note that blank cells are ignored when calculating the MIN for a worksheet range.

Spreadsheet examples: The formula `=MIN(17,23,4,19,-5)` returns –5; `=MIN(5,3,6.27)` returns 3; `=MIN(C2..C25)` returns the smallest number in the range from cell C2 to C25.

Database example: The formula `MIN('Sale 1','Sale 2','Sale 3')` identifies the smallest of the three sales for each record.

MINUTE

Format: MINUTE (serial number)

The MINUTE function calculates the minutes for a serial time or date number. Note that in a serial date, the numbers to the right of the decimal represent the time.

Spreadsheet examples: `=MINUTE(33374.41288)` and `=MINUTE(0.41288)` both return 54, because the time represented is 9:54 a.m.

MIRR (Modified Internal Rate of Return)

Format: MIRR (safe, risk, values, . . .)

The MIRR function calculates the modified internal rate of return of a series of cash flows, given particular safe and risk investment rates. Safe is the rate returned by the investment that finances the negative cash flows; risk is the rate at which positive cash flows can be reinvested; and the values are the future cash flows. Ranges also can be specified for the values.

Spreadsheet example: The formula =MIRR(5%,15%,C12..C16) returns 18.65% when cells C12..C16 contain the values –5000, 2000, 4000, –2000, and 5000.

MOD (Modulo)

Format: MOD (number, divisor number)

The MOD function returns the remainder when one number is divided by another. The sign of the result matches that of the dividend.

Spreadsheet examples: The formula =MOD(5,2) returns 1; =MOD(-5,2) returns –1; and =MOD(5,-2) returns 1. The formula =MOD(5.75,3) returns 2.75. The formula =MOD(16,2) returns 0 because there is no remainder; that is, 2 divides evenly into 16.

MONTH

Format: MONTH (serial number)

The MONTH function converts a date serial number into the number of the corresponding month (1 through 12). MONTH also can be used to extract the month from a numeric date referenced in another cell.

Tip   To calculate the current month, use the formula =MONTH(NOW()).

Spreadsheet examples: The formula =MONTH(23140) returns 5, because this is the serial number for Might 10, 1967; =MONTH(B5) returns 4 when cell B5 contains 4-15-85 or April 15, 1985, for example.

Database example: The formula MONTH('Start Date') can be used to extract the month number from a date in the Start Date field.

MONTHNAME

Format: MONTHNAME (number)

The MONTHNAME calculates the text name of a month. Acceptable arguments are the numbers from 1 to 12. Real numbers and numbers that are out of range (less than 1 or greater than 12) return errors.

Spreadsheet examples: The formula =MONTHNAME(5) returns Might; =MONTHNAME(12) returns December; =MONTHNAME(B10) returns January, when B10 contains 1 or evaluates as 1.

Database example: The formula MONTHNAME(MONTH('Start Date')) extracts the name of the month from the date in the Start Date field.

Note The nested MONTH function is required in order to reduce the date in Start Date to a month number ranging from 1 to 12 that MONTHNAME can act upon.

NA (Not Available)

Format: NA ()

The NA() function takes no arguments and returns the error value #N/A!

> **Spreadsheet examples:** An IF formula can use the NA() function to force an error for one condition, such as `=IF(ISBLANK(E1),NA(),"Okay")`. In this instance, if cell E1 is blank, it generates the #N/A! error.

NOT

Format: NOT (logical)

NOT returns the opposite result of a logical expression, in the form TRUE or FALSE. The argument must evaluate as a Boolean expression.

Spreadsheet examples: The formula `=NOT(C1)` returns TRUE only if C1 evaluates as 0; in all other cases, the formula returns FALSE. The formula `=NOT(C1>D1)` returns TRUE if C1 is less than or equal to D1; otherwise, it returns FALSE.

 Tip You can use a formula in the form `=NOT(ISBLANK(D4))` to test for the presence of any value in a cell. If cell D4 contains anything (text, a number, or a formula), the formula returns TRUE; if D4 is empty, it returns FALSE.

NOW

Format: NOW ()

The NOW function returns the current date and time (according to the Macintosh clock), expressed as a serial number (representing the number of days since January 1, 1904). NOW takes no arguments and is written as NOW(). You can update a `=NOW()` formula to the current date and time by choosing Calculate ➪ Calculate Now (Shift+⌘+=).

 Note The result of NOW() is shown by default as a serial number. In most cases, however, you'll probably want to show it as a date. NOW() can be displayed in any of several date formats, such as 5/12/95 or Might 12, 1995, for example, by assigning a date format to the cell or field.

To set a date format in a worksheet, highlight the cell and choose Format ➪ Number. To display NOW() as a date in a database field, specify Date as the result type for the calculation. Then choose a date format by changing to Layout mode (Shift+⌘+L), selecting the field, and then choosing Options ➪ Field Format.

Note that you also can express =NOW( ) as a time rather than a date by setting a time format for the cell or Time as the result type for the database field. The desired time format can be set as discussed previously for setting a date format.

Spreadsheet example: The formula =NOW() could return 33369.876875, 5/12/95, Might 12, 1995, or Friday, Might 12, 1995, depending on how the field was formatted. Note that the fraction in the serial number represents the fractional portion of the day at the moment NOW() was calculated (that is, the number of seconds that have elapsed since midnight divided by the number of seconds in a day—86400).

Database example: NOW()

NPER (Number of Periods)
Format: NPER (rate, pmt, pv {, fv} {, type})

NPER is used to calculate the number of periods required for an investment involving constant cash flows. Rate is the interest rate per period; pmt is the payment to be made each period; pv is the present value of the investment; fv is the future value of the investment after the last payment is made (fv is optional—if not included, it is assumed to be 0); and type represents the payment scheme (type is optional—if included, enter **0** if payments are due at the end of each period or **1** if payments are due at the beginning of each period; 0 is the default).

Spreadsheet example: The formula =NPER(8.75%/12,-250,10000) returns 47.46 as the number of periods (payments) required to pay off a $10,000 loan at an annual rate of 8.75 percent, assuming that each payment is $250.

NPV (Net Present Value)
Format: NPV (interest rate, payment1, payment2, . . .)

Use NPV to calculate the net present value of an investment based on a series of future payments or income, assuming a fixed interest rate. Payments can be replaced with a range, rather than listing the individual values within the formula.

Spreadsheet example: The formula =NPV (8%, -10000, 0, 12000, 12000, 12000) returns $17,254.08, and represents an initial investment of $10,000 with annual income of $0, $12,000, $12,000, and $12,000.

NUMTOBASE
Format: NUMTOBASE (number, base {, minimum digits})

The NUMTOBASE function converts a number (base 10) to another base and returns a string representing the converted number. Base can be any number ranging from 1 to 36. Minimum digits is optional and represents the minimum number of digits that will be returned in the result. If the result requires fewer digits, leading zeroes will be added to the result.

> **Note** A base of 1 is really only useful for returning a string of ones whose length is the same as the number. For example, =NUMTOBASE(12,1) returns a string of 12 ones.

Spreadsheet example: The formula =NUMTOBASE(200,2) converts the number 200 to base 2, returning 11001000.

NUMTOTEXT

Format: NUMTOTEXT (number)

NUMTOTEXT changes a number into a text string.

Spreadsheet example: To retain leading zeroes in a set of imported numeric Zip codes (for example, 07146), you can change the contents of the cells from numbers to text. (Numbers cannot have leading zeroes.) To add a leading zero to any four-digit codes that are found, you could use this formula:

```
=IF(LEN(D11)<5,"0" & NUMTOTEXT(D11),NUMTOTEXT(D11))
```

This formula examines the contents of a cell (D11, in this instance), and checks to see if it contains fewer than five characters. If fewer than five characters exist, it creates a new Zip code by converting the numeric Zip code to a text string and appending a zero to the string (as in 04331). If the Zip code already contains at least five characters, it also is converted to a text string but passed through unchanged (as in 34412 or 12203-3802).

OR

Format: OR (logical1, logical2, . . .)

The OR function tests the logical arguments specified and returns TRUE if any argument is true; otherwise, it returns FALSE.

Spreadsheet example: The formula =OR(A1, B1, C1) returns TRUE if any of cells A1, B1, or C1 evaluates as true.

Database example: The formula OR('QTR 1','QTR 2') returns 1 (True) if either of the fields QTR 1 or QTR 2 contains a value.

PI

Format: PI ( )

PI produces the value of π (that is, 3.141592653 . . .). Note that PI has no arguments.

Spreadsheet example: Use =PI()*(A9^2) to calculate the area of a circle, where cell A9 contains the radius.

Database example: PI()*('RADIUS'^2).

PMT (Payment)
Format: PMT (rate, nper, pv {, fv} {, type})

The PMT function is used to calculate payments given a specific interest rate, number of periods, present value, future value, and type of payment. The last two arguments are optional. The future value (fv) represents the value of the investment or cash value remaining after the final payment. The default value is 0. Type determines whether payments are due at the beginning (1) or end (0) of each period; 0 is the default.

Spreadsheet example: To calculate monthly payments on a car loan, you could enter **=PMT(8.75%/12,36,19000,-9000,1)**. This indicates an annual percentage rate of 8.75 percent, a three-year loan (36 months), a cost (pv) of $19,000, a future value of –$9,000 (the down payment), and that payments are made at the beginning of each period.

PRODUCT
Format: PRODUCT (number1, number2, . . .)

Product calculates the product of the numbers in the argument list; that is, it multiplies them together.

Spreadsheet examples: The formula =PRODUCT(1.5, 4.5) returns 6.75; =PRODUCT(A1..A3) multiplies the contents of cell A1 times cell A2 times cell A3 (or A1*A2*A3).

Database example: PRODUCT('HEIGHT','WIDTH')

PROPER
Format: PROPER (text)

Use the PROPER function to capitalize the first letter of every word in a cell or field.

> **Note** Be aware that this will also capitalize articles (a, an, the) and prepositions, which are not normally capitalized in titles.

Spreadsheet example: =PROPER("Spenser's great adventure") returns Spenser's Great Adventure.

Database example: PROPER('Book Title').

PV (Present Value)
Format: PV (rate, nper, pmt, {, fv} {, type})

PV calculates the present value of an investment; that is, the amount of money you'd have to invest now — in addition to making fixed payments at specific periods getting a fixed interest rate — in order to have fv dollars at the end. Type is optional; the default of 0 means that payments/investments are made at the end of each period; 1 indicates that payments/investments are made at the beginning of each period.

Spreadsheet example: The formula =PV(8%,36,-250,10000) indicates that to have $10,000 after three years (36 payments) of investing $250 per month at 8 percent annual return, an initial investment of $2,303.05 is required.

RADIANS

Format: RADIANS (degrees number)

Use RADIANS to convert a number of degrees to radians (standard units for trigonometric functions).

Spreadsheet examples: The formula =RADIANS(45) returns 0.785; =RADIANS(120) returns 2.094.

RAND (Random)

Format: RAND ({number})

Use the RAND function to generate random numbers. If no argument is given, as in RAND(), the returned value is a fraction between 0 and 1. If an argument is given, an integer is returned between 1 and the argument.

Negative arguments are also allowed. For the formula =RAND(-20), an integer ranging from –20 to 1 is returned.

Tip

Because the RAND function gives a different answer each time it is calculated, you can instantly generate a new set of random numbers by choosing Calculate ⇨ Calculate Now (or pressing Shift+⌘+=). If you're a lottery fan, for example, you can use the RAND function to generate number choices. For example, if your lottery is based on the numbers ranging from 1 to 40 and you must choose six numbers, type the formula **=RAND(40)** in a cell, select the cell and the five beneath it, and then choose Fill Down from the Calculate menu (or press ⌘+D). Each time you press Shift+⌘+=, a new set of six random numbers appears. (Note, however, that you might get some duplicate numbers in a set. They are random, after all.)

Spreadsheet examples: =RAND( ) can return any fraction between 0 and 1, such as 0.49774; =RAND(10) returns a whole number from 1 to 10, such as 7; the range and type of random number returned for =RAND(B2) depends on the contents of cell B2.

RATE

Format: RATE (fv, pv, term)

The RATE function is used to determine the interest rate needed for a present value to grow to a given future value over a particular term, where fv is the future value of the investment; pv is the present value of the investment; and term is the number of payments.

Spreadsheet example: The formula =RATE(10000,6000,5) returns 10.76%. It means that if you currently have $6,000 to invest and need it to be worth $10,000 in five years, you must find an investment paying an annual yield of 10.76 percent to reach your goal.

REPLACE

Format: REPLACE (old text, start position, number of characters, new text)

The REPLACE function is used to replace one text string with another string, starting from the indicated start position and continuing for number of characters.

Spreadsheet example: The formula =REPLACE(D32,8,4,"Yahoo!") takes the text string in cell D32, counts eight characters into the string, removes four characters (characters 8–11), and inserts the string Yahoo! at that position. Assuming that cell D32 contained Steven Alan Schwartz, the cell with the preceding formula would contain Steven Yahoo! Schwartz.

REPT (Repeat)

Format: REPT (text, number of times)

The REPT function repeats a given text string the specified number of times.

Spreadsheet examples: The formula =REPT("Hello! ",5) returns Hello! Hello! Hello! Hello! Hello!; =REPT("•",10) returns ••••••••••.

RIGHT

Format: RIGHT (text, number of characters)

The RIGHT function returns a text string that contains the number of characters specified, counting from the last character in the target text string. Note that if the target text string contains fewer characters than the number specified in the RIGHT function, those characters that are present are returned. Note, too, that the RIGHT function can be applied to numbers, but the returned value is text.

Spreadsheet examples: =RIGHT("123 Williams Avenue",6) returns Avenue; =RIGHT("Samuel Smith",5) returns Smith; =RIGHT(47259,4) returns 7259; =RIGHT("Apple",12) returns Apple, because fewer than 12 characters exist in the string.

Database example: You could create a customer identification number by taking the final four digits of his/her phone number or Social Security number, as in RIGHT('Phone',4) or RIGHT('Soc. Sec. #',4).

ROUND

Format: ROUND (number, number of digits)

Use ROUND to specify the number of digits from the decimal point to which a number should be rounded. Note that the number of digits can be positive (to the right of the decimal) or negative (to the left of the decimal).

Spreadsheet examples: =ROUND(A3,2) rounds the contents of cell A3 to two decimal places. If A3 contains 14.33632, the result is 14.34; if A3 contains 14.333, the result is 14.33. The formula =ROUND(4235,-3) produces a result of 4000, while =ROUND(4512,-3) produces a result of 5000.

Database example: ROUND('Grand Total',0) could be used to round a total figure to a whole dollar amount.

ROW

Format: ROW ({cell})

Returns the number of the row referenced by cell or the row in which the current cell is contained (when no argument is included). This is a spreadsheet-only function.

Spreadsheet examples: =ROW(C12) returns 12, because cell C12 is in the 12th row; =ROW() returns the row in which this formula is located.

Tip

If you want to number a group of rows beginning with Row 1 quickly, type the formula **=ROW()** in Row 1, highlight that cell as well as the appropriate cells below, and then choose Calculate ⇨ Fill Down (or press ⌘+D).

SECOND

Format: SECOND (serial number)

The SECOND function calculates the seconds for a given serial number. It also can return the number of seconds from a normal time.

Spreadsheet examples: The formula =SECOND(NOW()) returns the number of seconds for the current time (press Shift+⌘+= and watch the seconds change); =SECOND(D7) returns 27 when cell D7 contains 1:43:27; =SECOND(0.5003) returns 26.

Database example: SECOND('End Time'-'Start Time').

SIGN

Format: SIGN (number)

SIGN returns the sign of a numeric value. It displays 1 for a positive number, –1 for a negative number, and 0 for zero (or for a blank cell or field).

Spreadsheet examples: =SIGN(-423.75) yields –1; =SIGN(12) yields 1; =SIGN(0) yields 0; =SIGN(A2-3) yields 0, when the contents of cell A2 evaluate as 3. A formula such as the following can use the SIGN function to test cell contents:

```
=IF(SIGN(B5),"OK","Empty or zero")
```

If the sign of the cell is nonzero (either 1 or –1), OK is returned. If the cell is blank or evaluates as zero, Empty or zero is returned.

SIN (Sine)

Format: SIN (number)

The SIN function calculates the sine of a number, where that number is an angle in radians.

Spreadsheet examples: =SIN(RADIANS(15)) yields 0.25881; =SIN(RADIANS(90)) yields 1.0.

SQRT (Square Root)

Format: SQRT (number)

SQRT calculates the square root of a number. Note that square roots can only be calculated for nonnegative numbers.

Spreadsheet examples: =SQRT(2); =SQRT(5.73); =SQRT(A1); =SQRT(A1+(B7/5))

Database example: SQRT('LENGTH').

STDEV (Standard Deviation)

Format: STDEV (number1, number2, . . .)

The standard deviation is a measure of how values are spread around the mean (average). The larger the standard deviation, the greater the spread. The STDEV function calculates the standard deviation of a population from the list of sample arguments provided. (Note that the standard deviation is simply the square root of the variance, another statistical measure of spread; see VAR.)

The formula used to calculate the standard deviation is:

$$\sqrt{\sum_{i=1}^{N} \frac{(X_i - \overline{X})^2}{N-1}}$$

Spreadsheet examples: The formula =STDEV(12,3,15,7.2,8) returns 4.616; =STDEV(125,100,110,115) returns 10.408.

SUM

Format: SUM (number1, number2, . . .)

SUM adds the numbers in the argument list. The arguments can be numbers, cell references, or database field names. The SUM function is particularly useful for totaling worksheet columns or rows.

Spreadsheet examples: =SUM(A1..A4) adds the contents of cells A1, A2, A3, and A4; =SUM(A1,B5,17.4) adds the contents of cells A1 and B5, and then adds 17.4 to the total; =SUM(B1..B3,5.7,C5) totals the contents of the cells in the range B1..B3, and then adds 5.7 plus the contents of cell C5.

Database examples: SUM('Product Total',5,'Product Total'*.06) could be used to add a fixed shipping charge of $5 and a sales tax of 6 percent to a customer's order total. This same formula also could be created without using the SUM function, as in 'Product Total'+5+('Product Total'*.06).

TAN (Tangent)

Format: TAN (number)

The TAN function calculates the tangent of a number, where the argument is an angle in radians.

Spreadsheet example: The formula =TAN(RADIANS(0)) returns 0.

TEXTTODATE

Format: TEXTTODATE (date text)

The TEXTTODATE function is used to convert a date in text form to a date serial number. The date text can be in any acceptable date format.

Although TEXTTODATE normally expects quoted date text as the argument, it also works with cell references that contain date text. The following date styles are treated as text by AppleWorks and can be used with the TEXTTODATE function:

✦ Any date entered as a formula, such as ="3/5/95," ="5/25/1915," ="7/19/45," or ="Mar 4, 1943"

✦ Any slash- or dash-delimited date that includes the century as part of the year, such as 3/4/1927 and 4-5-1996

✦ Any date with a one- or two-digit year ranging from 00 to 09, such as 5/12/06, 12/18/02, and April 4, 02 (representing dates from the year 2000 through 2009)

Spreadsheet examples: The formula =TEXTTODATE("12/5/96") returns 33942; =TEXTTODATE("Jan 5, 1960") returns 20458; =TEXTTODATE(C1) returns 33942, when C1 contains an acceptable date such as 12/5/1996, ="12/5/96," ="12/5/1996," or ="Dec 5, 1996."

TEXTTONUM
Format: TEXTTONUM (text)

TEXTTONUM converts a text string to its numeric equivalent. Nonnumeric characters are ignored when converting the string to a number. (Note that when applied to a number rather than a text string, TEXTTONUM passes the number through unaltered.)

Spreadsheet examples: The formula =TEXTTONUM("$12,453.47") returns 12453.47; =TEXTTONUM("123 Apple Way, Apt. 4") returns 1234 (the numeric digits are extracted and combined); =TEXTTONUM("(602) 555-1295") returns 6025551295; =TEXTTONUM(B2) returns 477401122, when B2 contains the Social Security number 477-40-1122; =TEXTTONUM(45.67) returns 45.67 (numbers are passed through unaltered).

TEXTTOTIME
Format: TEXTTOTIME (time text)

The TEXTTOTIME function converts a time text string into a time serial number. The text time is expressed in hours, minutes, and seconds order. The seconds and an AM/PM suffix are optional.

Spreadsheet examples: The formula =TEXTTOTIME("1:15 PM") returns 0.5521; =TEXTTOTIME("1:15") returns 0.0521 (times without at AM/PM suffix are assumed to be in 24-hour format); =TEXTTOTIME("10:20:23 PM") returns 0.9308.

TIME

Format: TIME (hour, minute, second)

The TIME function converts a time (based on a 24-hour clock) into a serial number between 0 and 1, representing the fractional portion of the day from midnight.

Note that all arguments must be present; those that are not normally needed are represented by zeroes. For example, 7:00 a.m. would be shown as =TIME(7,0,0); that is, 7 hours, 0 minutes, 0 seconds.

Spreadsheet examples: The formula =TIME(7,45,30) returns 0.3233 (for 7:45:30 a.m.); =TIME(17,30,0) returns 0.7292 (for 5:30 p.m.); =TIME(12,0,0) returns 0.5 (for noon).

Database example: TIME('Hours','Minutes','Seconds') returns a fraction based on the contents of three fields named Hours, Minutes, and Seconds.

TIMETOTEXT

Format: TIMETOTEXT (serial number {, format number})

Use TIMETOTEXT to convert a time serial number to text. (Note that the time portion of a serial number is found to the right of the decimal point. This function also works with a complete serial number, and simply ignores the digits to the left of the decimal point.)

Add an optional format number if you want to specify a format for the time text. If a format number is not entered, AppleWorks uses format 0. If you mistakenly enter a format number that is out of range (such as –3 or 4), AppleWorks also treats it as though you requested format 0.

Format Number	Format Applied
0	Hours:Minutes AM/PM (12-hour clock)
1	Hours:Minutes:Seconds AM/PM (12-hour clock)
2	Hours:Minutes (24-hour clock)
3	Hours:Minutes:Seconds (24-hour clock)

Spreadsheet examples: The formulas =TIMETOTEXT(33373.6009375) and =TIMETOTEXT(0.6009375) both return 2:25 PM. Because a format number was not entered, format 0 is used. The formula =TIMETOTEXT(0.653,0) returns 3:40 PM; =TIMETOTEXT(0.653,1) returns 3:40:19 PM; =TIMETOTEXT(0.653,2) returns 15:40; and =TIMETOTEXT(0.653,2) returns 15:40:19.

Applying the TIMETOTEXT function to a serial number has the same effect as selecting a time formatting option from the Number command in the Format menu. To display the current time, use the formula =TIMETOTEXT(NOW()).

TRIM

Format: TRIM (text)

The TRIM function removes extra spaces from text strings. Each group of spaces is reduced to a single space. TRIM can be very useful in cleaning up text.

Spreadsheet examples: =TRIM("Woodsbridge, MD 30919") returns Woodsbridge, MD 30919.

Database examples: TRIM('Comments') can be used to remove extraneous spaces in a text field named Comments.

TRUNC (Truncate)

Format: TRUNC (number)

TRUNC discards the decimal portion of the argument number, returning only the whole number that remains.

Spreadsheet examples: =TRUNC(12.365) returns 12; =TRUNC(0.12) returns 0; =TRUNC(-5.67) returns –5.

Database example: Assuming that Total Hours is a calculation field that sums the number of hours worked, the formula TRUNC('Total Hours') returns the number of hours worked during the period, ignoring any fractional part of an hour.

TYPE

Format: TYPE (value)

The TYPE function evaluates the contents of the argument and determines its data type. Possible return values are as follows:

Data Type	*Returned Value*
Blank	1
Logical	2
Number	3
Text	4

Spreadsheet examples: The formula =TYPE(C7) returns 1 if cell C7 is empty; =TYPE(FALSE) and =TYPE(ISBLANK(D3)) both return 2; =TYPE(0.56) and =TYPE(-147) both return 3; =TYPE(Kenneth) and =TYPE("Empire State") both return 4.

UPPER

Format: UPPER (text)

UPPER converts lowercase text to uppercase text. Nontext characters, such as numbers and punctuation marks, are passed through unaltered.

Spreadsheet examples: =UPPER("Steve") returns STEVE; =UPPER("January 5, 1996") returns JANUARY 5, 1996.

Database example: In a field intended for state abbreviations, UPPER('State') could be used to change all entries to uppercase, such as MN, AZ, and NY.

VAR (Variance)

Format: VAR (number1, number2, . . .)

Variance is a statistical formula reflecting the distribution of values in a data set. The VAR function calculates the population variance from the sample that you provide as arguments. Arguments can include numbers, cell references, or ranges. The square root of the variance is the standard deviation (see STDEV).

The formula used to calculate variance is:

$$\sum_{i=1}^{N} \frac{(X_i - \overline{X})^2}{N - 1}$$

Spreadsheet examples: The formula =VAR(12,3,15,7.2,8) returns 21.308; =VAR(125,100,110,115) returns 108.333.

VLOOKUP (Vertical Lookup)

Format: VLOOKUP (lookup value, compare range, offset {, method})

A vertical lookup (VLOOKUP) conducts a lookup based on columns. It searches the leftmost column of the compare range for the specified lookup value. If the lookup condition is met, the column number of the found cell is offset by the amount specified in the offset and the function returns the contents of that cell. An error is returned if the search condition is not satisfied.

Method is optional. Type in **1** to locate the largest value that is less than or equal to the lookup value; type in **–1** to find the smallest value that is greater than or equal to the lookup value; or type in **0** to return only an exact method. If no method is specified, a match of 1 is used. This is a spreadsheet-only function.

Spreadsheet example: The worksheet shown in Figure B-4 uses VLOOKUP to choose the proper postage for any weight entered in cell A2. The formula in B2 (where the result is returned) is:

```
=VLOOKUP(IF(TRUNC(A2)=A2,A2,A2+1), C2..D11,1,1)
```

Enter a lookup value here (cell A2)

Result appears here (cell B2)

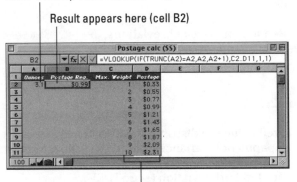

Compare range

Figure B-4: A VLOOKUP example

The IF function checks the contents of cell A2. If the value in A2 is equal to the truncated value of the same number (for example, A2 contains a whole number), A2 is used as the lookup value. If A2 contains a fractional portion, an additional ounce (1) is added to it, so A2 +1 is used as the lookup value. (The post office requires that all fractional weights be increased to the next full ounce).

The formula then compares the lookup value to the values in Column C of the worksheet and locates the largest weight value that is less than or equal to the lookup value (as specified by the method entry of 1). It then uses the offset value (the first 1) to return the postage amount from Column D.

WEEKDAY

Format: WEEKDAY (serial number)

The WEEKDAY function extracts the day of the week from any serial number (the number of days since January 1, 1904). WEEKDAY returns a value from 1 to 7, representing the days from Sunday (1) to Saturday (7).

Note The WEEKDAY function also can be used to return the day of the week from a date in month/day/year format, such as =WEEKDAY(C1), where C1 contains 3/18/96.

Spreadsheet example: The formula =WEEKDAY(33369) returns 6, because 33369 is the serial number for Might 12, 1995 (a Friday).

Database examples: The formula DAYNAME(WEEKDAY('Important Date')) returns the name of the day of the week that corresponds with the date entered in the Important Date field. (If the DAYNAME section of this formula is removed, the number of the day of the week is returned rather than the day's name.)

WEEKOFYEAR

Format: WEEKOFYEAR (serial number)

The WEEKOFYEAR function calculates the week of the year from a serial number (the number of days since January 1, 1904).

 Tip The WEEKOFYEAR function also can be used to extract the week of the year from a date in month/day/year format, such as =WEEKOFYEAR(C1), where C1 contains 3/18/96, for example.

Spreadsheet example: The formula =WEEKOFYEAR(20776) returns 47. (The serial number 20776 represents November 18, 1960, and November 18th fell within the 47th week of the year.)

Note AppleWorks calculation for WEEKOFYEAR always has January 1 in week 1, regardless of the day of week. This might not agree with the week of year calculations used by some calendars, where the day of the week on which January 1 falls has an impact on the week numbering.

YEAR

Format: YEAR (serial number)

The YEAR function calculates the year from a serial number (the number of days since January 1, 1904).

The YEAR function also can be used to extract the year from a date in month/day/year format, such as =YEAR(C1), where C1 contains 3/18/96, for example.

Spreadsheet example: The formula =YEAR(20776) returns 1960. (20776 is the serial number for November 18, 1960.)

✦   ✦   ✦

Index

Continued

Continued

my2cents.idgbooks.com

Register This Book — And Win!

Visit **http://my2cents.idgbooks.com** to register this book and we'll automatically enter you in our fantastic monthly prize giveaway. It's also your opportunity to give us feedback: let us know what you thought of this book and how you would like to see other topics covered.

Discover IDG Books Online!

The IDG Books Online Web site is your online resource for tackling technology — at home and at the office. Frequently updated, the IDG Books Online Web site features exclusive software, insider information, online books, and live events!

10 Productive & Career-Enhancing Things You Can Do at www.idgbooks.com

- Nab source code for your own programming projects.

- Download software.

- Read Web exclusives: special articles and book excerpts by IDG Books Worldwide authors.

- Take advantage of resources to help you advance your career as a Novell or Microsoft professional.

- Buy IDG Books Worldwide titles or find a convenient bookstore that carries them.

- Register your book and win a prize.

- Chat live online with authors.

- Sign up for regular e-mail updates about our latest books.

- Suggest a book you'd like to read or write.

- Give us your 2¢ about our books and about our Web site.

You say you're not on the Web yet? It's easy to get started with IDG Books' *Discover the Internet,* available at local retailers everywhere.